Handbook of Twentieth-Century Literatures of India

Edited by
NALINI NATARAJAN

Emmanuel S. Nelson, Advisory Editor

GREENWOOD PRESS
Westport, Connecticut • London

Library of Congress Cataloging-in-Publication Data

Handbook of twentieth-century literatures of India / edited by Nalini Natarajan.
p. cm.
Includes bibliographical references and index.
ISBN 0–313–28778–3 (alk. paper)
1. Indic literature—20th century—History and criticism—Handbooks, manuals, etc. 2. Indic literature—20th century—History and criticism. 3. Indic literature (English)—20th century—History and criticism—Handbooks, manuals, etc. 4. India—Intellectual life—20th century. I. Natarajan, Nalini.
PK5416.H27 1996
891'.1—dc20 95–20938

British Library Cataloguing in Publication Data is available.

Library of Congress Catalog Card Number: 95–20938
ISBN: 0–313–28778–3

First published in 1996

Greenwood Press, 88 Post Road West, Westport, CT 06881
An imprint of Greenwood Publishing Group, Inc.

Printed in the United States of America

The paper used in this book complies with the Permanent Paper Standard issued by the National Information Standards Organization (Z39.48–1984).

10 9 8 7 6 5 4 3 2

for my parents

Contents

Acknowledgments ix

Introduction: Regional Literatures of India—Paradigms and Contexts 1
Nalini Natarajan

1. Twentieth-Century Assamese Literature 21
Mahasveta Barua

2. Twentieth-Century Bengali Literature 45
Sudipto Chatterjee and Hasan Ferdous

3. Twentieth-Century Indian Literature in English 84
Alpana Sharma Knippling

4. Twentieth-Century Gujarati Literature 100
Sarala Jag Mohan

5. Twentieth-Century Hindi Literature 134
Nandi Bhatia

6. Twentieth-Century Kannada Literature 160
Ramachandra Deva

7. Twentieth-Century Malayalam Literature 180
Thomas Palakeel

8. Twentieth-Century Marathi Literature 207
Shripad D. Deo

9. Twentieth-Century Panjabi Literature 249
Atamjit Singh

10. Twentieth-Century Tamil Literature 289
P. S. Sri

11. Twentieth-Century Telugu Literature 306
G. K. Subbarayudu and C. Vijayasree

12. Twentieth-Century Urdu Literature 329
Omar Qureshi

13. Dalit Literature in Marathi 363
Veena Deo

14. Parsi Literature in English 382
C. Vijayasree

15. Sanskrit Poetics 398
Arasu Balan

16. Perspectives on Bengali Film and Literature 410
Mitali Pati and Suranjan Ganguly

Selected General Critical Bibliography 423

Index 425

About the Contributors 439

Acknowledgments

First and foremost, I wish to thank the contributors for their hard work and cooperation throughout this project. I thank Emmanuel Nelson and the editors at Greenwood Publishing Group for their interest when I first proposed the project and for their cooperation along the way. The Department of English and the College of Humanities, University of Puerto Rico, Rio Piedras, helped with release time to firm up some aspects of the book. My gratitude to them and to other colleagues in the English Department. I thank Bruce Hathaway and my research assistant, Maritza Stanchich, for help with computer work related to the book. Thanks also to Purnima and Vinod Vyasulu and Svati Joshi for help in locating contributors. Finally, for their moral support, I thank my family and friends, especially my husband John Parrotta.

Introduction: Regional Literatures of India—Paradigms and Contexts

NALINI NATARAJAN

SCOPE OF THE BOOK

The chapters in this reference book have the general aim of introducing the reader to post–1900 literary works from India. This is done through surveying each of the major literatures from the many regions. The survey chapters and their attached bibliographies are intended to serve as introductory tools to scholars seeking an overview of broad trends in the literatures. The book's value is its focus on the regional literatures, that is, literatures written in languages *other* than English. "Postcolonial" works from India in English are generally well known in the metropolis, but little is known to the general reader of writing in Malayalam or Telugu, Panjabi or Gujarati.[1]

Very recently, certain sectors of regional Indian literatures have begun to be constituted as fields of progressive critical interest in the metropolis. Gayatri Spivak's translations of Bengali author Mahasweta Devi's work, *Imaginary Maps* (1995), Kalpana Bardhan's *Of Women, Outcasts, Peasants and Rebels* (1990), and Susie Tharu and K. Lalitha's *Women Writing in India* (1992) are recent examples. On the critical side, Aijaz Ahmad's essay in his book *In Theory* (1992) outlines the conceptual problems associated with the study of regional literatures in current metropolitan and Indian academic contexts.

This book hopes to initiate the discussion of *more* of the regional literatures under a common platform. Often, literatures are known metonymically by famous works of antiquity (such as *Silappatikaram* in Tamil). The import of Tharu and Lalitha's "gynocritical" work, for instance, cannot be fully grasped unless one can place it within the larger archive of works by men *and* women, as also the "singularity" of Mahasweta Devi's work within the Bengali tradition (Spivak 1996, 162). Given India's enormous linguistic diversity, it is virtually impossible to ensure that *all* literary traditions are included. This volume, therefore, does not claim to be comprehensive, but it does cover nearly all major literary traditions of India, including English. In addition, we have included chapters on two subcultures, Dalit and Parsi.[2]

Surveys are undertakings connected to the notion of literary history. Literary history was formerly discredited on grounds of what Sisir Kumar Das, noted historian of Indian literature, has called, "an exaggerated faith in the autonomy of literary work" at the expense of historical connections between "literary activity and other human activities in the world" (Das 1991, 12). In this book, the survey chapters list authors and works in the century within an appropriate framework, which is cognizant of the changing sociohistorical, literary-productive conditions of modern India. The contributors' interdisciplinary affiliations underline the connection of the literary text with other discourses—periodical literature and belles lettres (Jag Mohan/Gujarati; Barua/Assamese), politics (Ferdous/East Bengali; Deo/Dalit; Qureshi/Urdu), sociology (Deo/Marathi), performance and popular reading (Sri/Tamil).

There are problems, however, in surveying a regional literature in a colonial language, English. Tharu and Lalitha, notwithstanding their own use of English translation, concede that the very act of representing a local culture through the medium of a more dominant one can result in reduction and homogenization (Tharu and Lalitha 1993, xx). Besides, like translation, the survey could facilitate appropriation of regional cultures by dominant ones in conditions of "asymmetry and inequality of relations between peoples, races, languages" (Niranjana 1992, 1; see also Spivak 1993, 182).

We attempt to contextualize this problem in the use of English by drawing attention in a later section to the important possibilities for English within the Indian academy. But we wish to stress that this book is an invitation to deeper knowledge of the regional languages, not a substitute for such knowledge. Our aim is to provide not packaged information, but a stepping-stone. In order not to privilege the English reader (which can mean the Indian, as well as the Western, reader), we therefore have kept the translation of titles to a discretionary minimum, retaining them only to ensure the understanding of the context of the particular sentence. As titles are usually cataloged in their original form, this should pose no problem to the reader who wishes to pursue a reference. We have used a user-friendly method of transliteration, rather than an elaborate Indological system (see Tharu and Lalitha 1993, xxiii). In general, this is how the titles would be encountered in critical/popular contexts within India. In some cases, contributors have provided phonetic specificities where they deemed them necessary (Chatterjee and Ferdous/Bengali).

ORGANIZATION

The survey chapters follow methods of organization appropriate to their subject, given the specificities of each region's literary history. Each chapter offers a brief introductory section to the literature concerned. The body of the chapter is divided on the basis of sociohistorical events (e.g., preindependence, postindependence, the partition of the subcontinent) or literary form/genre (e.g., novel/poetry). In some cases, the literature is presented within broad descriptive or analytic trends. All methods were effective as organizing principles, allowing for mention of major authors and works. The bibliography posed special problems for authors, as no uniform standard for bibliographic information is easily available in India. For example, conventional documentation in libraries in India does not often include publishers' names. Contributors used standard and nonstandard sources, private collections, and, in some cases, trips to publishing houses in India. Publishing companies have sporadic histories, and many texts were out of print and hard to trace. The bibliographies were thus put together from various sources, including various catalogs within the metropolis.

CONTEXTS AND PARADIGMS

It will be obvious that the chapters represent a variety of ideological approaches to literature. While some chapters use "traditional" terminology, others reflect the recent changes in the humanities. The publications of the Sahitya Academy (the coordinating body for Indian literatures) reflect the long institutional history of humanist scholarship in India. While it is important for "progressive" cultural criticism to resist, in Fred Pfeil's terms, "the tyranny of enforced signification" (Pfeil 1988, 387), caution is required, as Gayatri Spivak warns in the context of feminism, in applying First World terminology such as "gendering" to Third World contexts (Spivak 1993, 188). While we are in the process of negotiating this impasse, contextualizing of *any* approach is urgently necessary. In the rest of this introduction, I suggest some points of entry for the nonspecialist reader who wishes to contextualize some of the approaches underpinning the surveys.

First, this chapter wishes to discuss the emergence of *printed* (as distinct from oral and written literatures, both of which have a much longer tradition in India) regional literatures as "constructed" rather than "transcendent." This "construction" took place within the colonial idea of the "vernacular" or through nationalist, regional-chauvinist, and other ideologies. Colonial discourse analysis has sensitized us to imposed languages (such as English), ignoring the processes of construction that go on within indigenous languages.[3] The effect of this binary relation to English may be a tendency to read regional literature in a "transcendent" way, as if it were "always there," instead of produced as a result of a certain nexus of cultural, economic, political, and other factors. The task of this introduction is to indicate some of the paradigms or constructs—materialist, generic, disciplinary, hermeneutic—that may serve as entry points. An ideological construct in this context is adapting Greg Bailey's very useful formulation, an intellectual paradigm that establishes meaning in a mass of cultural data (Bailey 1989, 86). There is obviously some violation involved in the process, where the heterogeneity of culture may be made to "fit" into ideologically imposed paradigms. The paradigms may reflect the variety of historical and cultural ideologies that underpin contemporary literary-cultural production in India—reformist (liberal-humanist), *swarajist*/nationalist, secular/revivalist, progressive. They may represent "borrowed" literary genre or mode—such as romanticism or realism—within which experience is sought to be represented. They may also reflect the academic and marketplace factors underlying "Indian" literature.

Literary Discourse

However, current theoretical concern with the sociality, historicity, and materiality of literature (and the concomitant concern with the fictiveness of sociology and history) could ignore the specific nature of *literary discourse,* its power, and its seductions. Without idealizing literature, it is necessary to read it at the confluence of several layers of interpretation—aesthetic/poetic, material, sociohistorical, and philosophical. Exclusive focus on any one of these at the expense of the others cannot, in my view, engage with the complexity of literature's effects.[4] Indian regional literatures could, for instance, reinforce prevalent constructions (and reflect current perceptions) of national identity, redefinitions of femaleness, and so on, in response to different historical moments. But literary forms such as the domestic novel, introduced into India from Western Europe, *allow* a treatment of emerging subjectivities such as those of women. At the same time, their very popularity at a certain time indicates the arrival of a moment when such subjectivities are politically useful (e.g., to buttress social reform movements). Victorian melodrama (Mrs. Henry Wood's *East Lynne,* for instance, which was wildly popular in late colonial India) could be read as interacting with inherited myths of Sita to produce a certain narrative of Hindu womanhood in works such as Tripathi's *Saraswatichandra* (Gujarati 1909). Such novels suggest the use of melodrama in representing the long-suffering Hindu woman as a Sita figure. Like Sita, the woman suffers rejection by the husband. But the rejected woman has a moral authority that is read, even today, as representative of Hinduism's resilience. It is significant that the husbands represent Western-style modernization (represented by a preference for alcohol). The novels of R. K. Narayan (English) and Kalki (Tamil), for instance, depict literary instances of such women.

Literary works may also be silent about aspects of public and private life in ways that are profoundly material and social[5] but also literary. The literary form of the polite novel allowed little scope for the kind of social protest associated with the progressive writers' manifesto after the 1930s, but the popularity of these kinds of novels (and of English polite literature, such as Austen) reflected the sociopolitical agendas of the time. Last, attention to the process of reading, which can yield the way literary works may deconstruct their perceived meanings, becomes essential to understanding the place of the literary in Indian culture. The power and seductions of literature, its ability to mask as well as further ideology, and the space it gives to multiple and ambivalent reading positions and practices have a particular specificity in the modern Indian context. In order to suggest what a reading public may mean in the regional Indian context, I deal in the next two sections with factors of market production and pedagogy, the market and the classroom being two important sites for the dissemination of printed literature.

Regional Publishing

Literature is both a marketable commodity and a pedagogical unit. In the regional Indian case, both aspects bear a vexed relation to colonial presence, which played a definite role in the construction of the "vernacular." Questions such as who does the publishing, and who are the readers and the writers establish the materiality of literary production. What role did interregional hierarchies play in establishing genres that were to be imitated? What were the roles of translations, from English or from one language to another, in forming literary traditions?

Regional literary history was inextricably tied to the history of vernacular language standardization, with literary language representing the elite, standardized form (on language, Cohn 1985, 276–329; Padikkal 1993, 220–41). The "modernization" and systematization of the vernaculars took place under the colonial aegis (Padikkal 1993, 225). Modern, regional, Indian-published literature occupied a double space—furthering the aims, first, of the colonizers and, then, of the nationalists. From the eighteenth century through the nineteenth and early twentieth centuries, it helped in the consolidation of Christian and colonial influence. This was done through Bible translation into the "vernaculars" as well as through the publicizing of colonial legal and administrative edicts.[6] This colonially "constructed" aspect of literature is emphasized in many of the survey chapters.

But literature was also crucial in the nationalist-patriotic cultural resistance to British rule. The beginnings of the nationalist movement gave literature a new purpose, the forging of regional/national print-communities. But, as Aijaz Ahmad has noted, this process was significantly different from such formation of print-communities in early modern Europe (Ahmad 1992, 255). In India, regional print-communities nested into larger anticolonial pan-Indian movements, leading, for instance, to Tamil poet Bharati's translation into far-off Gujarati. A certain multilingual exchange was thus built into this process. Shivarama Padikkal points out how "language-centred regionalism" and a nationalism that "transcend[ed] linguistic divisions" emerged as complementary notions (Padikkal 1993, 226).

Among the countercolonial activities of the vernacular presses was the construction of a Hindu reading public—through tracts ranging from *ayurveda* to astrology. Colonial and earlier European publishing in the regional languages, such as Assamese, Bengali, and Tamil, had concentrated on religious instruction in Christianity (see *SAE* 1987, 3340–59). In turn, Hindu nationalists used the print-community for the spread of religion, often in a "modernized" form but also reinforcing traditional beliefs. For instance, the Hindu astrological almanac (*panchangam*) was one of the early documents with a wide circulation (*SAE* 1987, 3343).

But regional publishing also had a very local aspect. One notes the crucial role of local philanthropists, the involvement of family members (such as M. N. Tripathi, who published his brother Govardhanram Tripathi's work) or self-publishing (Vishwanath Satyanarayana in Telugu or Subramania Bharati in Tamil). Locality supersedes religious affiliation, as can be seen in the interesting hybridity in the early stages of publishing history, where, within Gujarat, Parsi philanthropists published Hindu literature (*SAE* 1987, 3340–59). Certain presses gained prominence in certain regions, causing some specialization of publication. Thus, Navjivan published Gandhi's works, Malayala Manorama gained prominence in Kerala, and so on. The local element of publishing continues to this day and can have negative, as well as positive, effects. For instance, a recent center-page article in the *Times of India* claimed that the vernacular presses are often used to whip up local, communal sentiments (Kumar 1994).

Published literature emphasized religious and domestic themes, often in the context of defining the parameters of national identity. (Sumit Sarkar [1983, 83–86] cites Dinabandhu Mitra's study of indigo exploitation, *Nil Darpan* [1860], as one of the few socially committed novels in the midst of a plethora of patriotic literatures.) The rise of regional literatures intersects with the rise of high Hindu culture as national culture in late colonial India. At the same time, the regional specificities of each middle class as distinct from European models of middle-class formation need to be acknowledged.[7] For instance, the role of Urdu in similarly constructing Muslim identity in the prepartition period is discussed by Qureshi in the survey chapter on Urdu literature.

Another factor to be considered in the connection of the material to the literary is the phenomenon of hierarchy *within* Indian languages. Certain languages/regional cultures (e.g., Bengali, due, ironically, to a longer history of the colonial presence) acquired a sense of superiority. In the case of Assamese, for instance, the large Bengali-speaking bureaucratic cadres influenced the marginalization of Assamese. Certain factors in Assamese history, such as the Ahom cultural influence, were written out by a metonymic identification of Assamese with "a few words of Sanskrit" (Barua/Assamese survey). Also, Bengali translations brought many English literary works to regional languages (Singh/Panjabi). Similarly, the survey chapter on Hindi shows how the demarcation of Urdu and Hindi as literary/cultural areas was deeply political. The movement for Hindi domination made it difficult to find publishers for Urdu material. In the chapter on Hindi literature, Nandi Bhatia outlines this process. The famous Hindi writer Premchand wrote in Urdu until 1915, after which he switched to Hindi in an effort to find publishers. In the case of Tamil literature, the classic Tamil past took on an anti-Brahman cast (Sarkar 1983, 85).

Moreover, the borders of the linguistic areas were drawn in the process of regional cultural construction, and these areas were subject to the same processes of cultural hegemonization accorded imperially to English. These vernaculars selected upper-caste Hindu society and courtly Muslim traditions as representative. Shivarama Padikkal points out the construction of a systematized, grammarized, elite vernacular, which marginalized dialectical variations and mediated modernity in ways that favored the languages of the modern educated classes (Padikkal 1993, 225). Print-capitalism favored print transmissions and the classes that patronized these over other popular modes of cultural transmission (see Ahmad 1992, 255). Also marginalized were the borders between regions, where multilinguality in various languages was common. The construction of vernaculars erased the polyglot nature of much culture under the unifying effects of print-capitalism (see Sisir Kumar Das, 1–19; Ahmad 1992, 248).

In the contemporary scene, one material factor affecting regional writing must surely be the power of the media. Playwright-turned-film-director/actor Girish Karnad confesses to casting novellas into film scripts even as he reads them, and he, indeed, has been crucial in the entry of regional literatures into the film world (Karnad 1979, 7). At the same time, regional films have been crucial in popularizing regional literatures, and prominent writers like Kalki were closely connected to emerging Tamil cinema.

Regional Literature in the Indian Academic Scene

What questions may be asked of the disciplinary field within which regional languages are situated in India?[8] Earlier, I raised the question of the mediating role of English. First and foremost, regional language departments suffer from the postcolonial phenomenon of a "defensive" position (see following extract by Das) with respect to English departments. Sisir Kumar Das's broad vision in his introductory essay "Muses in Isolation" to the volume *Comparative Literature: Theory and Practice* clarifies the conflicts within the academic discipline in India. He argues for the continuing use of English in India, but in a new form (for the role of English thus far in postcolonial India, see Sunder Rajan [1992] and Joshi [1991]). For instance, English can play a role in arresting the move from patriotism to chauvinism in many regional Indian departments:

> Most modern literatures were included in the university curriculum during the stormy days of our national movement. . . . But soon patriotism degenerated into chauvinism-linguistic identities became more pronounced than other aspects of our identities and literary study preferred a vicious vernacular obscurantism to an enlightened cosmopolitanism. Critical rigour and breadth became the first casualties in the wake of linguistic patriotism and the departments of modern Indian literatures became its worst victims. On top of that, the sneering attitude of the scholars of English literature towards Indian literatures, which is a lingering vestige of Macaulayan arrogance, makes the scholars of modern Indian literatures unnecessarily defensive. (Das 1989, 13–14)

English literary study, he concludes, if it is not to remain an instrument of alienation in India, must concern itself with the regional literatures, in a spirit of cooperation rather than appropriation. It is time, indeed, to break the disciplinary binarism between English and the regional languages. An important aspect of this move is the acceptance of literary expression in English as also intrinsic to modern Indian cultural experience. In this context, the struggle for acceptance to include Indian literature in English as an "authentically" Indian expression is interesting (Knippling/Indian literature in English). The younger poets are especially interested in questioning the binarism between English and the regional languages, using English, in Sudeep Sen's words, without "the . . . traces of the use of archaic forms of British English" (Sen 1993, 45). Here we must emphasize the use of English not as an imperial language but in the service of a "complete and final decolonization" (Gonzalez 1990, 30), in common with African, Antillean, and other colonized peoples.

The disciplinary construction of regional Indian literature as embattled by a still-colonial educational system and reactionary cultural politics explains the desire among scholars to establish "Indian" literature as a concept free from regional chauvinisms (see Ahmad, Joshi, Das). Comparative literature specialists within the Indian academy advance the argument for treating "Indian" literature as a unity in several ways. Uma Shankar Joshi (1988) points, for instance, to medieval India of the Bhakti period for commonalities (though in different languages) embodying "the Indian Spirit." He also calls for a theorizing of premodern Indian poetics. Subramania Bharati, the Tamil poet, called this commonality one "thinking" (*chintanai*). Joshi argues in this essay that it is necessary to appreciate the commonality before the individual aesthetic quality of any work may be grasped. For Joshi, "Indianness" is then intrinsic to aesthetic quality. Similarly, the call to comparatism urges a view of modernity on a national, rather than on a regional, basis: "[T]he literary community in India can attain some sense of identity only as a result of taking to the work of translation on a huge scale" (Joshi 1988, 9). The lack of a productive cultural interaction between languages is what Ahmad refers to when he says that we cannot yet speak of "Indian literature" as a field. The attempt to mark "Indian" or "national" from "chauvinist-regional" needs to be noted, in the light of Western distrust of "nation." In the Indian case, literary "nationalism" is an attempt to contain regional chauvinisms.

In his illuminating study of nineteenth-century Indian literature, Das (1991) notes the many indigenous literary traditions that have been assimilated into the more modern forms of narrative, poetry, and drama.[9] These influences could be pan-Indian or regional. Thus, *khandakavyas* (miniature epics) or *lilas* (based on the tales of Lord Krishna and other mythological stories) recur in more than one tradition, while *ghazals* (Urdu), *atta kathas* (Malayalam), *kummi* (a Tamil popular poetic genre), *buranji* (Assamese prose chronicle), *bakhar* (Marathi prose), and *kissa* (Panjabi) were specific forms. These areas offer the most fertile challenge to original research. Many of the survey chapters refer to classical

(Sanskritic or Perso-Arabic), as well as popular, traditions discernible in twentieth-century writings. Notable in this regard are the survey chapters in Telugu (C. Vijayasree and G. K. Subbarayudu) and Gujarati (Jag Mohan). But with the intervention of English literature, the modern European literary forms supply important models within which writers organize literary representation, and scholars seek to understand regional Indian literatures.

Western Literary Genre

If the "Indianness" of regional literatures is a paradigm favored by comparatists, the English literary influence on Indian literature is unmistakable, for the history and influence of the discourse of English literature and Western humanism cannot be easily written out of literary history. In a society where the material network of printing and publishing was only barely in place, the English book, be it the Bible or the complete works of Wordsworth, occupied a hallowed place. It was inevitable that writers write against those influences. As U. R. Anantha Murthy points out, the notion of the reading public in India has been so shaped by the history of English literature that the sensibilities and "cultural and literary expectations" of the reading public construct the literary historiography of modern Indian literatures (Anantha Murthy, quoted in Sunder Rajan 1992, 17). Within the Indian university, the study of Indian literature has been deeply influenced by the pedagogic methods of English literary studies; "the corpus is divided by period or genre, each exemplified by its representative half-dozen canonical texts" (Sunder Rajan 1992, 7). The survey chapters thus use genre (novel/poetry/drama; realism/romanticism) as a way of organizing the material, while defining the specificity of each region's use of it.

Genre works as both a historical and literary category. Genres such as romanticism and realism signify the ideological and cultural penetration of English literary forms on the modern Indian consciousness, but, at the same time, they resonate ideologically with movements such as *swaraj* (self-rule), reform, or social protest. Another significant factor here is the "telescoping" and "belatedness" of English literary influence on Indian literatures. That is, there is a time lag between literary movements in Europe and their period of influence in India. The late nineteenth century marked the phase of translations from English, the 1920s saw the influence of Romanticism, and Modernism and the progressives came together in the 1940s (Trivedi 1991, 198).

Genre was traditionally seen as a pact between writer and reader within which meanings operate, but, more recently, genre has been seen as a cognitive structure operating on sociohistorical formations (Bhatnagar 1986, 172).[10] Because modern literary genres are interlinked with Western cultural history, much indigenous cultural material escapes the constraints of Western genre. Also, English can only partly translate the regional or folk cultural idiom. The realistic novel's interest in individualism and notions of personal growth does not help represent particularly community-oriented notions of individuation. The psychological novel's use of Western distinctions such as primary and secondary processes cannot adequately convey the intervention of the Hindu symbolic in psychic life (see Seshadri-Crooks 1994, 206). Post-Freudian categories like repression need rethinking in contexts where withdrawal and abstinence are connected to processes of psychosocialization (Kurtz 1993). Repression in U. R. Anantha Murthy's *Samskara* is connected to the specificities of southern Brahman psychosexuality, even while its mode is the novel. Notions of genre and canon, while ambiguously useful, can be neither jettisoned as modes of understanding cultural data nor granted omnipotent explanatory power. Thus, readers are urged to problematize genre even as they read.

Literary Genre: Romanticism

Many of the survey chapters refer to the literary mode of Romanticism. The context of the surveys will make clear that regional Romanticisms must be distinguished from Western Romanticism. First, there was a significant time lag between the former's heyday in Europe and its influence in India (Chayavadi in Hindi, Asan/Vallathol in Malayalam, Jonaki era in Assamese, and so on were influential in the early decades of the twentieth century). Ideologically, too, distinctions need to be made. Aijaz Ahmad points out the association between European Romanticism's "obscurantist tendencies" and high Brahmanism in Orientalist constructions of India in the late eighteenth and early nineteenth centuries (Ahmad 1992, 259). The Romantic writers in the regional languages often attack Brahmanism (see Palakeel/Malayalam) or other local elitisms. In Hindi, Chayavad was a reaction to the prosaic matter-of-factness of the earlier mode, *khadiboli.* Chayavad's emotionalism lent itself to patriotic compositions. In Assamese, "Jonaki" writing's lyrical descriptions of the Assamese landscape may be connected to Assam's specific material relation to industrialization and, at the same time, may be seen as a vehicle for reform and nationalism. Romantic poetry in Tamil also broke with earlier convention but used it to affirm nationalism. If English Romantic literature was instrumental in constructing civic colonial subjects, its indigenous variants were unseating traditional caste and linguistic orthodoxies, while proclaiming a new "middle-class" ideology—anticolonial nationalism. One could say that the impulse to characterize all these specific attempts to revolt against literary forebears has been understood under the umbrella of "Romanticism," but they are really distinct. In order to make this process clear, authors have retained in the survey both the umbrella (Western) term and its local manifestation.

Romanticism in India, moreover, has a special context in its specific application by Gandhi. The "Romantic critique of industrialism" in Carlyle and Ruskin was taken over and extended by Gandhi (Sarkar 1983, 180). Its anti-industrial thrust, which supported Gandhi's critique of colonialism, influences many writers, from Gujarat (Betai, Umashankar Joshi) to Tamilnadu (Subramania Bharati) to Assam (Jonaki writers). In this sense, Romanticism is not merely a literary attitude but is connected to a popular program for both national autonomy and social uplift.

It is thus fruitful to see, in Shivaram Padikkal's terms, the role of Indian history in the trajectory of Western genre as it unfolds in the Indian context: "[T]he reception of a literary form is . . . a complex historical transaction rather than the decision of an individual author" (Padikkal 1993, 222). It could be argued that nineteenth- and early twentieth-century social reform was structurally connected to literary realism just as Gandhian anti-industrialism expressed an Indian version of Romanticism. As activist sections of the middle classes relinquished liberal positions for more socially conscious positions in the wake of widespread peasant and communal unrest, liberal realism gave way to more progressive realisms. The manifesto of the progressive writers' association, formed all over India during the 1930s, outlines this commitment.

Genre: Realism

Realism in the twentieth-century Indian context is connected with the formation of reading publics attempting to construct identity in anticolonial struggles and nation-building. This attempt combined liberal-reformist ideology with an affirmation of an "Indian" cultural specificity, which, however, tended to be middle-class and Hindu. The realist novel's focus on growth (*bildung*) and individual freedom/choice is transformed in the Indian context with the economic conditions of uneven capitalism. The contradictory forces that are held in uneven balance are economic, political, social. Economically, we have the coexistence of premodern modes of production with, in Kalpana Bardhan's terms, "the adaptive dexterity" of capitalist exploitation (quoted in Spivak 1990, 117). Repressive postcolonial state apparatuses coexist with liberal humanist ideologies, which continue to dominate areas of public life, the academic scene for instance. Official secularism coexists with the persistence and reconstituting of mythological symbolics (as in "new" goddesses like Jai Santoshi Ma or the furor over god Rama's birthplace). Modernizing forces such as women's education and employment go along with reactionary practices like dowry or sati. These dual realities produce a multiplicity of subject positions that the realist novel can represent. As Kalpana Bardhan has said, literary realism can reveal the "nuances" of the relation between dominant/dominated in a complex way (Bardhan 1990, 3).

Satendra Singh, in a somewhat homogenizing but useful schema, notes that realist novels in the regional languages deal with themes that can be called "pan-Indian"—landlord–tenant relationship, economic exploitation of the peasant/bonded laborer, untouchability, natural calamities and urban capitalism and their intrusion into rural life, Gandhian and revolutionary preindependence political themes, postcolonial themes such as politics and corruption, partition themes, lives of fishing communities, tribal communities (Singh 1989, 209–11). In the representation of the struggles of the lower classes, we also need to distinguish, as Bardhan notes, between a middle-class realism that sentimentalized poverty and a more progressive realism in writers such as Bengali Mahasweta Devi. Regional crises such as famine (Bengal), peasant and popular uprisings (Tebhaga, Telengana), drought (Tamil Nadu), student and tribal uprisings, and partition constitute traumatic events represented in fiction from many regions, as these survey chapters show. The survey chapters indicate the many themes taken up by the twentieth-century realist novels (Palakeel/Malayalam; Sri/Tamil; Singh/Panjabi; Bhatia/Hindi). In the chapter on Dalit writing, Veena Deo deals with problems of realist representation for hitherto excluded groups. Dalit writing becomes significant, for it is an attempt at self-representation of groups that were always considered outside representation.

One of the important dimensions of regional realisms becomes closely connected with the emergence of women within new constructions of domesticity. The typical nineteenth-century regional novel depicting women, in Meenakshi Mukherjee's analysis, had represented a "conflict between the restrictive social norms and half-articulated yearnings to achieve selfhood" (Mukherjee 1988, 99). In general, its scope was insular and local, mediating a colonial form—realism—with local issues such as child-widowhood in Maharashtra or courtesanship in Lucknow. Novels of the national movement give women a larger arena for action. In Tamil novelist Kalki's *Thyagabhoomi,* (1939–40), for instance, woman's situation is seen within both the local regional space of Madras (set in the context of the Congress's campaign for prohibition) and the larger national space. See, for an example of this movement between local/family space and larger national space, several stories in Tharu and Lalitha's collection. The temporary solutions posed by the nationalist era and its attendant euphoria may be read in the happy endings of some early twentieth-century plots: in *Thyagabhoomi,* for instance, the nationalist movement supplies a (false) resolution to gender conflict. On one hand, the work uncompromisingly attacks male dominance. The abused wife leaves her husband and earns some autonomy as a leading social figure; yet, at the end, the couple come together in the prison van, imprisoned as nationalists. Realism in the twentieth century would, among other things, cover greater interregional mobility of both men and women, bringing with it new perceptions of the city and consequent alienations.

Interregional mobility also meant a large reading public for diasporic publications. The pulp periodical magazine—like *Kalki, Ananda Vikatan,* and *Kumudam* in Tamil—or organizations like the Tamil Sangam sought to bring regional arts to diasporic populations and catered to the large clerical and professional sectors living outside their regions of origin. In the main, realist narrative also supplied usable raw material for popular film. From Tagore, to Kalki, to Mahasweta Devi (the award-winning film *Rudali*), realism both humanist and progressive has contributed to the consolidation of print- and film communities.

Film could participate in the insertion of Western-style subjectivities through its propagation of viewing practices[11] connected to the emergence of the subject in Europe and America. At the same time, the deployment of "Indian" images on screen fulfilled an important ambition of Swarajist filmmakers such as Dadasaheb Phalke (Dhareshwar 1993, 8). Film continues to be a medium that can manipulate subjectivities. The chapter on Bengali film and literature (Pati and Ganguly) compares literature to film in the Bengali context and concludes that most popular films reduce the original novel's subversive potential.

Aesthetics and Ideology

The interplay of aesthetics and ideology—which supply critical paradigms in the study of culture and literature—is crucial in considering regional literatures. Aesthetics in India has an old tradition, generally upholding the cultural status quo (see Sanskrit poetics/Balan). In recent times, as has already been said, much literary production is often constructed, then analyzed, within the aesthetics of liberal humanism, which dominated both reform and nationalism. The emphasis on individual freedoms, rather than radical social transformation, on lyricism and romantic aesthetics over the socioeconomic coordinates of literary production, remains a prominent concern in the study of regional literatures. In his book *Indian Literature: Personal Encounters,* prominent poet Umashankar Joshi, winner of the prestigious Gnanpith Award, discusses both the appeal and the dangers of Western-style aestheticism. On one hand, lyric genres such as the ode, elegy, monologue, and sonnet enabled the singing of ''personal love'' in a rigidly stratified society (Joshi 1988, 5). On the other hand, the artist's self-absorption could alienate him or her from the common people who spoke his or her language (Joshi 1988, 7).

The persistence of idealist aesthetic criteria in regional literary evaluations merits attention. Many literary critics of literature in the regional languages use emotive hyperbole in describing the aesthetic experience of a particular work or tradition. Poo Vannan's recent history of Tamil literature, which is a source for the chapter on Tamil literature, is an example (Sri/Tamil). To contextualize this obviously idealist/romantic aesthetic, I suggest that the aesthetic may be seen as another terrain of contestation between Western and colonial/postcolonial ways of reading.[12]

Classical, idealist aestheticism can, as Terry Eagleton has said, disengage art from its material referents, severing ''the bond between use and pleasure, necessity and desire . . . in a privileged disconnection from material determinacy'' (Eagleton 1990, 205). Umashankar Joshi's critique quoted earlier makes the same point, although from a depoliticized angle. But unraveling the appeal of aestheticism in India (in literature, music, and art) can hardly be divorced from colonial procedures in hierarchizing languages and cultures and in the Indian cultural response to such hierarchies (Chatterjee 1994), for the binarisms of colonial and postcolonial society divided experience along official/practical/intellectual spheres dominated by English and the emotive/personal/familial spheres denoted by the mother tongue.[13] In the current pedagogic system in India, knowledge of one's mother tongue, especially in its emotive aspect, is relegated to an intimate realm, before "clear memory began," as Gayatri Spivak describes Bengali songs "sung day after day in family chorus" (Spivak, quoting her unpublished essay, 1993, 180).

Earlier, a connection between linguistic processes and literary activity was stressed. "Standard" vernaculars helped in establishing elite regional literatures. It may thus be useful to consider the question of literary aesthetics, with caution, against a psychoanalytic-linguistic model.[14] Again, the aim is not to stress the universality of Western psycholinguistic models but to connect them to an implicit monolingualism, making them inapplicable in a multilingual (and colonized) society. The Western model equating language with the father and the prelingual with the mother is complicated in a multilingual consciousness, where the "mother tongue," though it also marks the accession to a symbolic realm, is most often not the language of power. It contends not only with the colonial language English but with other languages in various degrees of dominance. But the role of the mother tongue in the first perception of the phenomenal and moral world gives it a place in one's memory of imaginary plenitude, which protects it from later ideological scrutiny. At the same time, the "mother" tongue, like the psychoanalytic omnipotent/threatening mother, is also ambivalently rejected (by some sections of the middle class) in the pursuit of English and more dominant tongues.

When the linguistic model is applied to literary activity, complications emerge. I find useful here Peter Brooks's recent distinction between poetics—"as certain imaginative modes, conventions and rules"—and aesthetics—"in the limited sense of the discrimination of the beautiful and significant in art" (Brooks 1994, 511). If poetics can reflect the norms of inherited or imposed culture (in psychic terms, the Lacanian Law of the Father), a multilingual's aesthetic attachment to the cultural productions in the mother tongue, the first language of infancy—as a more emotive activity, constitutive of textual pleasure—might stand for an in-between stage, an "other" semiotic phase *between imaginary and symbolic.* This notion is similar to Kristeva's sense of a "female semiotic."

But the association of the mother tongue with this "other" semiotic phase, "before clear memory began" (to borrow Spivak's phrase) is but illusory, as the mother tongue is itself, at a different historical moment, the upholder of a patriarchal, feudal-casteist, or courtly tradition. As a Tamil speaker, my own oral appreciation of the lyricism of the Tirukkurals (aphoristic couplets from Tamil classical tradition) connects with a certain balance in the lifestyles of rural Thanjavur, remembered from early childhood. However, adult semantic scrutiny reveals its construction within Brahmanic/Puranic linguistic and social ideologies of caste and gender. Because Tamil has always been placed within a position of pre-Sanskritic and "Dravidian" alterity, its own literary implication within the cultural hegemony of Brahmanization can easily be missed. Also, much publication of Tamil literature took place within the linguistic politics of colonial "divide and rule" and was used to further its constructions of race.

For Urdu speakers, the emotive force of the *ghazal* may similarly obscure its courtly origins (on the debate over the poetics and politics of the *ghazal,* see Qureshi/Urdu).

I am arguing, thus, for attention to the aesthetics of literary creation in the Indian languages from a perspective apart from the idealist/materialist binarism and the Western psychoanalytic model. Applying this binarism to a colonized multilingual consciousness ignores the different semiotic space occupied by the lyrical, sensuous, or aesthetic (in literary language as in other spheres) played in the formation of Indian multilingual cultural subjectivity.

Philosophical Constructs in Reading Regional Literatures

The need to understand cultural hermeneutics in India, not only in a functional relation to the colonial encounter but as articulating provocatively between this encounter and diverse indigenous histories, has a philosophical dimension. Within what indigenous philosophical constructs may we read regional literature? Such a quest might release us from dependence on what is essentially a Western, post-Enlightenment archive. One Indian writer who has relentlessly pursued such options is Girish Karnad. In a recent play *Taladanda,* Girish Karnad fictionalizes an historical twelfth-century poet-community in Kalyan, which he labels "founders of Kannada literature," whose "philosophy and devotion" fired social reform (Karnad 1992, 75–76). These "Sharanas" decided to challenge the caste system with the marriage of a Brahmin girl to an untouchable. In the holocaust that followed (in Karnad's own summary), the couple's parents were blinded, the Sharanas were slaughtered, and the movement went underground for several centuries and emerged, ironically, as the caste-ridden Lingayats. Karnad's own rendition of this narrative draws parallels between the event and contemporary slaughter in India in the name of religion and caste. It presents a very culturally specific problematic for those cultural analysts of India who attempt to make connections between a usable past and contemporary realities. This problematic is summarized by Karnad later in the piece—that between *sanatana* (fundamentalist-dogmatic tradition) and *bhakti* (radical-liberal). Both of these predate the epistemic interference of European colonialism but take new forms as a result of imperially constructed communalisms and casteisms (see Pandey 1992).

The narrative illustrates the hybridities, conflicts, and transitional orthodoxies of the past that defeat attempts to recover a pristine history advocated by the proponents of Hindutva, and the connection of literature to violence underlines its potentially radical role. Karnad's always creative use of history and fiction and their interpenetration is a salutary attempt to reinterpret cultural motifs deriving from both Hindu and Muslim traditions (Dharwadker 1995, 43–58).

Along with *sanatana-bhakti, pravritti-nivritti* (renunciation-worldliness) is considered another philosophical paradigm within which to place "Indian" cultural production. This latter is Louis Dumont's formulation ("ascetic versus man in the world'') and has dominated Indian studies (see Bailey 1989, 86). Such paradigms construct a certain Indian culture as an object of study even as they may illuminate aspects of it. Folk epistemologies or those of minority religious communities are clearly omitted in this foregrounding of ''Hindu'' philosophy, itself deeply imbued within Orientalist categorizations.

However, studies that debunk the old models carry their own traps. Vijay Mishra's characterizing of Indian society as decentered at the level of deep structure, while usefully challenging the Dumontian model, nevertheless represents Indian culture in terms recognizable to a deconstructivist readership (Bailey 1989; Mishra 1987, 83–88). As I said at the start of this chapter, the terms, concepts, modes, or genres heretofore discussed are less absolute concepts but signifiers; that is, in Greg Bailey's terms, they ''organize cultural data'' and assign it meaning. In doing so, they are still responsive to the intellectual forces dominated by the West. Any detailed study, literary-textual or sociohistorical, of regional literatures attempts to traverse a veritable minefield in extricating ''indigenous'' from ''metropolitan'' and in seeking more representative and democratic indigenisms.

At the same time, juxtaposing formulations of Hindu subjectivity with Iqbal's concept of *khudi* (self-hood Qureshi/Urdu) or Bhai Vir Singh's concept of the ''ideal Sikh'' or Dalit explorations of subjectivity may help to bring all of these, in Gayatri Spivak's terms, to ''crisis,'' helping unravel their ideological underpinnings in the ''national'' culture they inhabit (Spivak 1990, 73). We hope the basic information on the regional literatures in this book is a stepping-stone to such a comparative inquiry.

NOTES

I thank Barbara Southard for a supportive, close reading of this chapter.

1. Depending on which source one quotes, the number of languages may be 16, 22, or 1,600 (Trivedi 1991, 182).

2. Contributors were invited through the usual academic methods of advertisements in the Modern Language Association (MLA) and at Sahitya Academy Conferences in India and through announcements sent to area studies departments in the United States, as well as at other international conferences. An interdisciplinary approach to literature was encouraged. Hence, contributors are from the fields of language area studies, translation, English and creative writing, political science, philosophy, film, and sociology. The contributors are active multilinguals, reading widely in their native language and also, in some cases, writing or translating creatively in it. Given the role of English in the formation of India's elites, especially in the postindependence generation, such multilinguality is the exception, rather than the rule, in the academic context of the big cities.

3. Aijaz Ahmad notes that the construing of English as an ''imposition'' is ''inaccurate,'' given the acceptance of English by prominently multilingual reformists as well as nationalists (Ahmad 1992, 268).

4. For a recent essay that argues for a return to poetics, see Peter Brooks 1994, 509–24.

5. See, for an example of this kind of silence, Nancy Armstrong's *Desire and Domestic Fiction* (New York: Oxford University Press, 1987), 162.

6. The Sahitya Academy's *Encyclopaedia of Indian literatures A to Z,* edited by Amaresh Datta, gives a detailed history of publishing in the various Indian languages. Hereafter referred to as *SAE.*

7. Materialist analyses attempt to create a sense of modern Indian literary production as paralleling literary modernity in the West or reading it entirely within mode-of-production narratives. In such models, the rise of the novel in India denotes a Western-style rising middle class. In an account of the rise of the Hindi novel, with special reference to a late nineteenth-century novel, *Parikshaguru,* A. S. Kalsi points out the specificities of the north Indian middle class, which calls for different models to understand its relation to literary production. As Kalsi puts it, "The Western educated intelligentsia that filled the professions was the product of bureaucratic decision rather than economic change and can best be perceived as a social group rather than an economic group" (Kalsi 1992, 763–90).

8. The academic study of literatures in the Indian languages varies greatly within India and in the metropolis. In the metropolis, it is largely determined by the ideologies of area studies, whereby metropolitan universities "divided up" the world for academic and pedagogic scrutiny. Excellent scholarly work in anthropology, literary study in the regional languages, and translation has come out of these area studies programs, but the very concept of area studies (i.e., one linguistic area distinct from another) complicates, even precludes, their study within a mutually illuminating, common platform. It is significant that the flexibility to move beyond literary borders has come out of English departments. Using literary feminism as an organizing category, Susie Tharu and K. Lalitha have brought regional languages into a platform for discussion. Increasingly, translations and other studies have emerged from bilingual English teachers (in India, the Katha series in Delhi is an example). We must be aware here of a replaying of the colonial scenario, with the English academic mediating the role of the bilingual informant; however, the aim here is less to "take over" the field but to delineate a new, more culturally dynamic role for English in the spirit of Sisir Kumar Das's comment, quoted in the chapter.

9. The subject of traditional and folk literary continuity and regional commonalities is profoundly interesting. For a stimulating account, see Das 1991, Vol. 8, 50–80.

10. Here, Ahmad's very provocative formulation on the "genealogy" and "sociology" of genre is useful: "The genre often serves as the very horizon which defines the general semantic field, the presumptions of belief systems. . . . For instance . . . the name of 'Kabir' can simply become a collective signature for certain kinds of utterances" (Ahmad 1992, 251–52).

11. The conventions of realism operate in cinema as well as fiction, constructing subjects akin to the middle-class European subject. Susie Tharu points out, in the reading of a film narrative based on the Marathi novel *Umbartha,* that the viewing process in that film suggests boredom as a possible motivation of female activism. The resolution of disorder in the plot works as "domesticating device," inscribing the woman into middle-class ideology. See Tharu 1986, 864–67.

12. I thank Sandhya Shetty for her helpful feedback on a first draft of this section. I intend this section to be merely suggestive, as the subject requires much more detail than can be offered here.

13. It is noteworthy that some recent poststructuralist criticism duplicates similar di-

visions, reading Western-derived rational-intellectual value systems as cognitively more formative than "other" more indigenous modes of existence, such as tastes in cooking and popular literature (Radhakrishnan 1994, 305–40). One could argue that these less intellectual activities are no less real and no less constitutive of subjectivity. It all depends on what one assigns cognitive power to.

14. Christine van Boheemen (1987) points out, quoting from Winnicott's studies, that in Freud, rhythm and verbal play sublimate the anxiety of separation from the mother: "Language is patterned as ritual play *poetry almost* . . . the patterning of sound and meaning alleviates the self-alienation caused by self-alienation from the mother. It cleverly turns language—the mark of detachment—into its own object" (18; emphasis added). On art and the pleasure and reality principles, see Freud 1966, 376. On the colonial implication of Freud's theory of art and sublimation, as also the need to reexamine Western psychoanalysis in the Indian context, see Seshadri-Crooks 1994, 203–4, 175–218, respectively.

WORKS CITED

Ahmad, Aijaz. "Indian Literature—Notes towards a Definition of a Category." In *Theory: Classes, Nations, Literatures.* London: Verso, 1992.

Bailey, Greg. "On the Deconstruction of Culture in Indian Literature: A Tentative Response to Vijay Mishra's Article." *South Asia* 12:1 (1989): 85–102.

Bardhan, Kalpana. "Introduction." *Of Women, Outcastes, Peasants and Rebels.* Berkeley: University of California Press, 1990.

Bhatnagar, Rashmi. "Gender and Genre: A Reading of Tagore's *Nashtanir* and R. K. Narayan's *The Dark Room.*" *Woman/Image/Text.* Trianka: Delhi, 1986.

van Boheemen, Christine. *The Novel as Family Romance: Language, Gender and Authority from Fielding to Joyce.* Ithaca: Cornell University Press, 1987.

Brooks, Peter. "Aesthetics and Ideology: What Happened to Poetics?" *Critical Inquiry* 20 (Spring 1994): 509–24.

Chatterjee, Partha. *The Nation and Its Fragments: Colonial and Postcolonial Histories.* Princeton, NJ: Princeton University Press, 1994.

Cohn, Bernard. "The Command of Language and the Language of Command." *Subaltern Studies.* Vol. 4. Delhi: Oxford University Press, 1985.

Das, Sisir Kumar. "Muses in Isolation." *Comparative Literature: Theory and Practice.* Calcutta: Allied, 1989.

———. *A History of Indian Literature, 1800–1910.* Vol. 8. Delhi: Sahitya Akademi, 1991.

Datta, Amaresh. *Sahitya Akademi Encyclopaedia A to Z.* Delhi: Sahitya Akademi, 1987.

Dev, Amiya, and Sisir Kumar Das. *Comparative Literature: Theory and Practice.* Calcutta: Allied, 1989.

Devi, G. N. *After Amnesia: Tradition and Change in Indian Literary Criticism.* Bombay: Orient Longmans, 1992.

Dhareshwar, Vivek, Tejaswini Niranjana, and P. Sudhir. *Interrogating Modernity.* Calcutta: Seagull Press, 1993.

Dharwadker, Aparna. "Historical Facts and Postcolonial Representation: Reading Girish Karnad's *Tughlaq.*" *Publications of the Modern Language Association* 110:1 (January 1995): 43–58.

Eagleton, Terry. *The Ideology of the Aesthetic.* Oxford: Basil Blackwell, 1990.
Freud, Sigmund. *Introductory Lectures on Psychoanalysis.* New York: Norton, 1966.
George, K. M. *Modern Indian Literature: An Anthology: Surveys and Poems.* Delhi: Sahitya Akademi, 1992.
Gonzalez, José Luis. *Puerto Rico: The Four-Storeyed Country.* Translated by Gerald Guinness. Maplewood, NJ: Waterfront Press, 1990.
Joshi, Svati. *Rethinking English.* Delhi: Trianka, 1992.
Joshi, Umashankar. *Indian Literature: Personal Encounters.* Calcutta: Papyrus, 1988.
Kalsi, A. S. "Pariksaguru (1882): The First Hindi Novel and the Hindu Elite." *Modern Asian Studies* 26:4 (1992): 763–90.
Karnad, Girish. "Introduction." *The Woods* (Kaadu) by Shrikrishna Alanahally. Delhi: Orient Paperbacks, 1979.
———. "Where Is the Tradition?" *Frontline* (September 25, 1992): 74.
Kumar, Krishna. "Perils of Literacy: Awakening Can Be Harmful." *Times of India,* October 8, 1994.
Kurtz, Stanley. *All the Mothers Are One—Hindu India and the Cultural Reshaping of Psychoanalysis.* Princeton, NJ: Princeton University Press, 1993.
Mishra, Vijay. "David Shulman and the Laughter of South Indian Kings and Clowns." *South Asia* 10 (1987): 83–88.
Mukherjee, Meenakshi. *Realism and Reality: The Novel and Society in India.* Delhi: Oxford University Press, 1988.
Niranjana, Tejaswini. *Siting Translation.* Berkeley: University of California Press, 1992.
Padikkal, Shivarama. "Inventing Modernity: The Emergence of the Novel in India." *Interrogating Modernity.* Calcutta: Seagull Press, 1993.
Pandey, Gyanendra. *The Construction of Communalism in Colonial North India.* Delhi: Oxford University Press, 1992.
Pfeil, Fred. "Postmodernism as a 'Structure of Feeling.' " *Marxism and the Interpretation of Culture.* Urbana: University of Illinois Press, 1988, 381–403.
Radhakrishnan, R. "Postmodernism and the Rest of the World." *Organization* 1:2 (1994): 305–40.
Sarkar, Sumit. *Modern India 1885–1947.* Madras: Macmillan, 1983.
Sen, Sudeep. "Modern Indian Poetry: The New Generation." *Poetry Review* 83:1 (Spring 1993): 43–55.
Seshadri-Crooks, Kalpana. "The Primitive as Analyst: Post-colonial Feminism's Access to Psychoanalysis." *Cultural Critique* (Fall 1994): 175–218.
Singh, Satendra. "Towards a Concept of the Indian Novel: A Thematic Construct." *Comparative Literature: Theory and Practice.* Calcutta: Allied, 1989.
Spivak, Gayatri. "The Post-Colonial Critic." In *The Post-Colonial Critic: Interviews, Strategies, Dialogues,* edited by Sara Harasym. New York: Routledge, 1990b.
———. "Woman in Difference: Mahasweta Devi's 'Douloti the Bountiful.' " *Cultural Critique* (Winter 1990a): 105–28.
———. "The Politics of Translation." *Outside in the Teaching Machine.* New York: Routledge, 1993.
———. "More on Power/Knowledge." In *The Spivak Reader*, edited by Donna Landry and Gerald Maclean, 141–74. New York and London: Routledge, 1996.
Sunder Rajan, Rajeshwari. The Lie of the Land: English Literary Studies in India. Delhi: Oxford University Press, 1992.
Tharu, Susie. "Third World Women's Cinema: Notes on Narrative, Reflections on Opacity." *Economic and Political Weekly* 21:20 (May 17, 1986): 864–67.

Tharu, Susie, and K. Lalitha. *Women Writing in India.* 2 vols. Delhi: Oxford University Press, 1993.

Trivedi, Harish. ''Reading English, Writing Hindi: English Literature and Indian Creative Writing.'' In *Rethinking English,* edited by Svati Joshi. Delhi: Trianka, 1991.

1

Twentieth-Century Assamese Literature

MAHASVETA BARUA

INTRODUCTION

Assamese literature's advent into the twentieth century was fittingly called the Jonaki age. The period took its name from the Assamese periodical *Jonaki,* first published February 9, 1889, by Chandra Kumar Agarwala. The periodical defined Assamese literature's coming into its own after nearly half a century of linguistic colonialism. *Jonaki* marked a coming of age, just as another periodical, *Orunodoi,* first published in 1846, marked the rebirth of Assamese literature. To understand the development of Assamese literature in the modern era, it is essential to realize the importance of these two periodicals. Since the British annexation of Assam in 1826, Assamese literature's progress has been one of discontinuity and dissonance. *Orunodoi,* literally, ''sunrise,'' rose out of a period when Assamese was disallowed as the language of Assam. A brief survey of the events leading up to the publication of *Orunodoi* shows us that geography has as much to do with the development of this literature as history does.

Assam's position in the northeast corner of India, joined to the rest of the country by a narrow bottleneck, had always protected it from the foreign rules that had been established in most parts of India, first by the Muslim invaders and then by the British. However, Assam had seen a large influx from the east; and for the 600 years prior to British annexation, Assam was ruled by Ahom rulers, descendants of an exiled prince from Thailand. The Ahoms adopted the language of their subjects, and Assamese culture during the six centuries of their reign developed through assimilation rather than domination. In 1826, the Treaty of Yandaboo between the East India Company and Burmese invaders placed Assam in British hands. Assamese literature before this period largely comprised devotional literature inspired by the neo-Vaishnavite movement of the late fifteenth–early sixteenth centuries, Assamese versions and translations of sacred texts and the epics, and the *buranjis,* or chronicles kept by the Ahom rulers.

Though there was a large body of oral and folk genres, popular published literature was nonexistent. If Assam's location had protected it from external rule via its western borders, this same location had also been responsible for keeping Assamese literature marginalized and slow to receive newer ideas and perspectives.

In 1826, when the British first came to Assam, they brought with them the administrative infrastructure from their then-capital at Calcutta in West Bengal. It is believed that relying on the words of Bengali clerks, the British government came to the conclusion that Assamese was simply a dialect of Bengali. According to Dimbeswar Neog:

> It is a fact that when about this time the East India Company took the administration of Assam, a large number of Bengalees for their living came to this province as clerks and they were totally ignorant of the language of the soil. They happened to catch a word or two of Sanskrit origin from the lips of the people and, failing to make neither head nor tail of the rest of their vocabulary, chose to call it at random a patois of Bengali and advised the rulers, who were then equally innocent of the language, to replace it by [sic] the Bengali language. It was the matter of a minute as it was the question of whims; and the mischief was done. (Neog 1982, 340)

Whether the decision was, in fact, so whimsical can be questioned; administrative expedience had probably more to do with the decision than mere whim. Whatever the cause, the result was that Bengali was declared the language of education and administration in 1838 and remained so till 1873. Ironically, the revival of the language through proof of literature was a process that involved another group of foreigners—American missionaries. Missionaries of the American Baptist Mission Foreign Society in Burma entered Assam to spread their Christian message and turned to Assamese as the language through which to propagate their message. In doing so, they became involved in the promotion of Assamese literature and language. The most notable among the missionaries were Rev. Miles Bronson, who brought out the first Assamese dictionary in 1867; Rev. Nathan Brown, who published an Assamese grammar in 1848; and Rev. Oliver T. Cutter, who edited the first Assamese journal, *Orunodoi.* Through *Orunodoi* and through letters, petitions, and scholarly works, the missionaries sought to establish Assamese as the official language of Assam. Though these particular men did not live to see their goal achieved, their efforts were responsible for reviving the language, and, as Maheswar Neog says in his introduction to *The Orunodoi,* "for culturing the language along modern lines, endowing it with a grammar, a dictionary and a large mass of writings in modern prose" (Neog 1983, 56). Additionally, the Christian influence, rather than threatening Hindu culture, liberalized Assamese culture and helped modernize the language.

In reviewing Assamese literature till the mid-twentieth century, it becomes apparent that writings of a certain period can be categorized by ideology and style. However, unlike most Western literatures, where common ideas and approaches are identified through our review of various individual publications such as treatises, novels, poetic volumes, and plays that generally appeared separately, early Assamese literature, regardless of genre, was generally published through a single forum—the journal. Thus, these journals defined the literary periods, and, for this reason, Assamese literature is usually divided into ages or eras when the works appearing in the premier journals were most influential. Additionally, in reviewing early Assamese literature, we find the contributions of female writers to be almost nonexistent. This is not because women did not write at all; however, in the traditional, patriarchal society of nineteenth-century India, it was considered anomalous for a woman to write and publish, and, when she did so, it was not considered part of mainstream literature. Nevertheless, a number of women wrote and published in various genres. These women are discussed as a group following the discussion of nineteenth-century Assamese literature, because their approaches and publishing practices were not similar to those of the men who were their contemporaries. Twentieth-century women writers, however, are often considered among the best writers of their period and must therefore be considered alongside their male counterparts.

THE *ORUNODOI* ERA

The Mid-Nineteenth Century

The early issues of *Orunodoi* carried this descriptive statement: "A monthly Paper, devoted to Religion, Science, and General Intelligence." The periodical was true to its wide-ranging intent, as the first issue published in January 1846 reveals. It contained a review of events, national and international, of the previous year (a regular feature thereafter); an article entitled "Dharamor Katha," subtitled "Religious Intelligence," dealing with numerous converts to Christianity; and articles on the evils of opium and the tombs of the Ahom kings. In later years, it included brief critical essays on literature and Assamese culture, folktales, and short, original poems. Though religion was an important focus of the journal, *Orunodoi* was never an organ for aggressive Baptist propaganda. Maheswar Neog accurately points out: "That the *Orunodoi* was devoted to 'Science and General Intelligence' is especially to be emphasized, as its pages went a long way to extend the intellectual horizons of the readers. The columns brought various news from all corners of the globe. . . . The news of great events in India and in foreign countries were brought to the door of the Assamese even as they took place" (Neog 1983, 66). Neog goes on to say that as much as this news reshaped the Assamese mind, it also glorified colonialism as beneficial (66). Nevertheless, it brought to Assam a greater awareness of the world beyond and provided a forum for early Assamese writers of the nineteenth century. Among these was a trio who defined Assamese literature of the mid-nineteenth century: Anandaram Dhekiyal Phookan, Hemchandra Barua, and Gunabhiram Barua.

Assamese literature during this period and the Jonaki era must be discussed through the contributions of particular writers, rather than the development of genres. Literary genres such as poetry and drama had to be reestablished, and those such as the novel and short story had to be introduced before genre-specific traditions could be generated. Furthermore, lacking a continuous tradition, Assamese literature had to take a big leap to adopt modern trends. One particular trend that this era established was the use of the colloquial in prose, as opposed to the rhythmic speech patterns established by devotional literature. These three nineteenth-century writers established the foundations upon which the Jonaki era writers would thrive.

Anandaram Dhekiyal Phookan (1829–59) was not only an early contributor to *Orunodoi* but an active participant with the Baptist missionaries to remove the Bengali language from Assam. He was in a particularly advantageous position, as he was an officer of the provincial administration and rose to the post of junior assistant to the commissioner. His essay ''A Few Remarks on the Assamese Language'' (1855), published anonymously as ''A Native,'' contains an account and analysis of 62 religious poetical works and 40 dramatic works. The culling of such a list was particularly significant as evidence of a literary tradition in Assam and validated the claims that Assamese was a language rather than a dialect, as had been supposed. If Dhekiyal Phookan brought Assamese literature to the attention of the world at large, he also brought information about the world to Assamese readers. His unfinished series *Asamiya Lorar Mitra* (Assamese Boy's Companion, 1849) was written as handbooks containing information on various subjects such as history, geography, and science. Besides his use of modern prose, he attempted to write translingual Assamese–English dictionaries, which were left unfinished but parts of which appeared in *Orunodoi.* The simple, clear, efficient prose that modern Assamese literature adopted is best exemplified by Dhekiyal Phookan's essay ''Englandor Vivaran'' (*Orunodoi* 2:4 [April 1847]). In it, he addresses the readers, the Assamese people, directly as he calls to them to emulate the civilization and progress that were England's. However, the message is a call not to mimic English ways but rather to improve one's own country. The picture that he paints of the possible future, of an Assam rich in industry and learning and free of communal and racial bigotry, shows him to be rather a visionary.

Where Dhekiyal Phookan could not complete the task of writing a dictionary, Hemchandra Barua's (1835–96) most important work was his *Hemkosh* (Golden Treasury), an Anglo–Assamese dictionary published posthumously in 1900. Barua's contribution was linguistic as well as literary. Barua's articles in *Orunodoi,* his dictionaries, and his grammatical texts all sought to replace the simplified Assamese used by the missionaries with a version closer to Sanskrit patterns of speech and to strengthen the use of Assamese by native speakers. Among these were *Asamiya Vyakaran* (1873), *Asamiya Lorar Vyakaran* (1892), and *Pathsalia Abhidan* (1892). His literature, too, reveals a concern for social reform. His novel *Bahire Rongsong Bhitore Kowan Bhaturi* (1876) refers to the idiom

"Empty vessels make most sound" and criticizes social customs and religious hypocrisy through the supposedly respectable characters. In his life, too, he protested against restrictions on widow remarriage. He protested the double standard by refusing to remarry, though widowed at an early age. An article in *Orunodoi* (9:4 [April 1856]) entitled "Anek Bia Kora Ajugut" (It Is Wrong to Marry Many), attributed to a "Shri Sonar Chanda," was obviously by him. His drama *Kaniyar Kirtan* (or *The Gospel of an Opiumeater*) (1861) highlights the effects of opium. In later years, Hemchandra Barua edited an Anglo–Assamese weekly paper, *Assam News,* which ensured the influence of his linguistic practices on following generations. In his personality and his place in the literature of his time, Hemchandra Barua is quite often likened to Samuel Johnson. However, it must be pointed out that, though Johnson's dictionary was a prodigious work by a single individual, it did not reshape his native language, English. Hemchandra Barua's dictionary did reshape Assamese.

Like Hemchandra Barua, Gunabhiram Barua (1837–94) was an ardent social reformer whose work reveals his reformist zeal. His *Ram-Navami* (1858), the first modern Assamese play, focuses on widow remarriage through the character of Navami, a young widow in love with a young man, Ramachandra. The discovery of this love leads to religious ostracism; however, the religious leader later recounts a dream that he had advocating remarriage, and the play ends with Navami's remarriage. Despite this happy ending, the ostracism is not removed. The play thus advocates widow remarriage while criticizing the practice of ostracism. In keeping with his beliefs, Gunabhiram Barua married a widow, Bishnupriya, after his first wife's death. Gunabhiram Barua was also the first Assamese biographer with his *Anandaram Dhekiyal Phookanar Jivan Sarit* (1880). His humorous work *Kathin Shabdar Rahasya Byakhya* (published posthumously in 1912) contains wonderfully comic interpretation of words. Gunabhiram Barua's other contribution was to the literary essay. *Asom Bandhu* (Friend of Assam), a journal that he edited from 1885 to 1886, carried numerous essays by him and other early essayists. His prose is extremely modern in that it rejects declamation and opts for naturalness and directness. The simplicity, strength, and clarity of his prose style in such articles as "Saumar Bhraman" and "Alikhit Buranji," which appeared in *Jonaki,* were carried over to the next generation of prose writers.

THE JONAKI ERA

Turn of the Century

The Jonaki era is also known as the age of Romanticism in Assamese literature. Though by 1889 the Romantic age had long faded in English literature, the Romantic ideal appealed, and was most applicable, to writers of an emergent literature. The term "Romantic" itself is used by Assamese writers and critics and implies the same approach to literature as it does in English literature. It would not be correct to say that writers of this era imitated Wordsworth, Shelley, or Keats; rather, they were strongly influenced by the Romantic sensibilities of these English poets. It is fitting that Assamese writers of this period would look to the Romantics rather than their contemporary Victorians. Assam was still untouched by industrialization and urbanization, the natural landscape held much scope for literary exploration, and the literary climate was full of promise and possibilities. The literature of this period utilized the lyric and ballad forms; it focused on man and his relation to beauty, nature, and the arts. In his introduction to *Kuri Satikar Asamiya Kabita* (Twentieth-Century Assamese Poetry), the poet Nilamoni Phookan aptly sums up romantic poetry as a movement away from theocentrism to anthropocentrism. The central theme changed from devotion to God to devotion to the world, its beauties, man as a reflection of the supernatural, and man's pursuit of joy and beauty (Phookan 1977, 1). However, this was still a literature of the early twentieth century and could not be totally divorced from modernity. The acceleration of the independence movement and the social and cultural reformation movements in Bengal and other parts of the country influenced it and made it also a literature that examined social and nationalist issues. During this period the Asom Sahitya Sabha (Assam Literary Association) was formed in 1917. The Sahitya Sabha facilitated the exchange of ideas, popularized Assamese literature, art, and culture, and provided a forum for literary debate and discussion through its conventions, journals, and publications. It continues to be the primary literary association for the state even today.

Their predecessors had given them their voice, and writers of this era used it to express a wide range of issues through a variety of forms. *Jonaki* was an early and important vehicle for this expression. First published on February 9, 1889, by Chandrakumar Agarwala (1867–1938), it was the journal of the Asamiya Bhashar Unnati Sadhini Sabha (Society for the Development of the Assamese Language), a society that included later *Jonaki* editors Lakshminath Bezbarua (1868–1938) and Hemchandra Goswami (1872–1928). This trio dominated the literature of this period.

Poetry

Chandrakumar Agarwala's poems, published first in *Jonaki* and collected later in *Pratima* (Image, 1913) and *Bin Boragi* (The Wandering Bard, 1923), best exemplify the Romantic ideal of the poetry of this age. His poem "Niyor" (The Dewdrop) looks at a single drop of dew and, in describing it, evokes an intense longing to discover its origins and the meaning of its beauty. The small drop of dew speaks volumes to the poet, who imagines it to be a pearl dropped from the ornaments of a girl dancing amid the flowers at night or perhaps her tear shed at the sight of sunrise. Poems like this display a Keatsian gaze at an object of beauty. Agarwala's poems like "Manav Bandana" (Worship of Humanity) and "Bin Boragi" glorify man as a reflection of the Supreme Being and are reminiscent of the search for the sublime in eighteenth- and nineteenth-century

English literature. This search for the sublime and the beautiful is found in a long line of poets following Chandrakumar Agarwala. In his contemporary Hemchandra Goswami's sonnet "Priyatamar Sithi" (My Beloved's Letter), the first Assamese sonnet, an examination of poetry and nature is woven into the description of the letter itself. Lakshminath Bezbarua brought a simplicity to the Romantic tradition through poems such as "Basanta" (Spring) and his "Bin Boragi." But beyond that, Bezbarua revived Assam's existing folk-song tradition through his ballads and pastorals. In his poems, too, we find a patriotic idealism and optimism about Assam past and present and its potential. His "O Mor Aponar Desh" (My Dearest Country) displays an intense pride in his place of birth and has become the state's anthem.

Whereas these poets used the simple rhyme schemes and meter typical of the lyric, other Romantic poets used blank verse, too. Padmanath Gohain Barua's (1871–1946) poems in his *Juroni* (1900) utilize the blank verse form of the much earlier classical *kavyas* (or verses). Notable among the early twentieth-century poets who first published in *Jonaki* were Raghunath Choudhari (1879–1968), who was also known as *bihogi-kabi,* or bird-poet, for his numerous poems with birds as the central character in nature and whose first collection of poems, *Sadori,* was published in 1910; Bholanath Das (1858–1929), whose poetic contribution preceded *Jonaki;* and Anandachandra Agarwala (1874–1939), who translated numerous English and American poems and whose collection of original poems, *Jilikoni* (Glittering), was published in 1920.

The influence of the Jonaki era's Romanticism was far-reaching and is still felt today. In poetry especially, even as the conditions of the modern world forced poets to turn to realism and naturalism and adopt a cynical attitude toward man and society, the romantic vision continued to manifest itself in the works of numerous poets who had grown up in the first two decades of the twentieth century. Though Romantic poetry was written well into the 1950s and 1960s, this poetry was also contemporaneous in that it included the concerns of a newly independent country. Among the poets of this continuing stream of Romanticism were Ambikagiri Raichoudhuri (1885–1967), whose first collected poems were *Tumi* (You, 1915) and who brought a revolutionary ideal to all his works; Jatindranath Duara (1892–1968), whose translation of Omar Khayyam's *Rubaiyat* was a brilliant example of this genre; Parvati Prasad Baruva (1904–64), who, from his first poetic drama *Lakhimi* (1931) and through his poems and songs, expressed the eternal search for the sublime through contemplation of simple things in nature; and Jyotiprasad Agarwala (1903–51), whose poetry was but part of a prolific body of works that enriched Assamese literature immeasurably.

Prose

Where Chandrakumar Agarwala was a pioneer in poetry, Lakshminath Bezbarua was the high priest of Assamese prose and is still considered to be so. Bezbarua's prose works are remarkable for their modern style and vision, qualities found in his novels, short stories, and essays. His first novel, *Padum-Konwori* (The Lotus Queen, 1905), appearing originally in installments in *Jonaki,* was structured around a historical event. But his *Kripabor Baruar Kakotor Topola* (Kripabor Barua's Bundle of Papers, 1904; originally serialized in *Jonaki*) established his reputation. This and the later *Kripabor Baruar Obhotoni* (1909) are farcical and satirical collections that touch on Assamese politics and society. Bezbarua had the Dickensian ability to combine serious social commentary within humorous depictions. His *Nomal, Pasani,* and *Sikarpati Nikarpati* are all in a similar farcical vein. However, his prose contributions extended beyond this. His *Junuka* (Anklets, 1910), *Burhi Air Sadhu* (Grandmother's Tales, 1911), and *Kokadeuta Aru Natilora* (Grandfather and Grandson, 1912) are collections of traditional Assamese folktales that revived and popularized this age-old oral genre for adults as well as children. Among Bezbarua's original short story collections are *Surabhi* (1909), *Sadhu Kathar Kuki* (1912), and *Jonbiri* (1913). *Baheen* (Flute), the journal Bezbarua edited from 1909 to 1929, became a vehicle for his essays on literature and language. Though the sheer volume and skill of Bezbarua's prose tend to overshadow the works of other prose writers, other writers did produce a body of novels, histories, and critical studies during this period.

Benudhar Rajkhowa's (1872–1956) *Lakhimi Tirota* (The Auspicious Wife) is notable in that it is a dialogue depicting a good or ideal wife. His other prose writings include essays such as *Bihu* on the practice of this Assamese festival, English essays such as *Short Accounts of Assam* (1915), and *Historical Sketches of Assam* (1917), among others. Surya Kumar Bhuyan (1894–1964), known primarily as a historian, established the art of the biography with his *Anandaram Barua* (1920). Rajanikanta Bordoloi (1867–1939) produced an impressive four-volume saga of the final days of the Ahom dynasty and of the Burmese invasion and misrule in *Manomati* (1900), *Rangili* (1925), *Nirmal Bhakat* (1928), and *Rohdoi Ligiri* (1930). These novels are all the more significant since the horror of the Burmese invasion was still fresh in the collective minds and imaginations of the Assamese. Though Bordoloi wrote other historical novels and is often likened to Sir Walter Scott, his romantic novel *Miri Jiyori* (1895) remains one of the most enduring romances in Assamese literature.

Drama

The dramatic works of this period had more literary, than theatrical, value. Much of the drama of this period was read rather than performed, and the following generation would put this drama on stage or at least borrow from their themes to do so. The first dramatic work of this period was Lakshminath Bezbarua's *Litikai* (The Pages, or Lackeys), a farce serialized in 12 parts from the first issue of *Jonaki.* His other dramas were historical ones such as *Chakradhwaj Singha* and *Joymati Kunwari,* both taking up Ahom royalty as their primary characters. It was Benudhar Rajkhowa who was a more prolific playwright and whose plays contain strong satirical and often farcical characteristics. His plays, such as *Kali Yuga* (written in collaboration with another noteworthy litterateur, Durga Prasad Majindar Barua), *Tini Ghaini* (Three Wives), *Asikshit Ghaini* (The Uneducated Wife), and *Sorar Sristi* (The Thief's Invention), depict various aspects of Assamese society of his day. With these plays, too, performance was not the primary concern. It is remarkable that, though early-modern Assamese literature, with a few exceptions, does not yield great dramas, Assamese society has always been a theatergoing one. Drama developed in Assam contemporaneously with English drama in the fifteenth century. As with the English church performances, mysteries, and morality plays, the neo-Vaishnavite movement established religious drama and, with it, a classical dance form, the *satriya* (of the *satras* or monasteries). But Assamese drama did not develop in the manner of English drama, and the classical, devotional, and historical strains were still strong into the twentieth century. Modern Assamese drama was established in the 1940s by Jyotiprasad Agarwala and continues to flourish. But even today, perhaps fittingly, successful dramatists are defined by performances at large, rather than by publications. Masses of people flock to the touring theater companies that move through the Assamese countryside and towns performing popular plays that are not to be found in published form. The establishment of All India Radio in 1948 saw the rise of another form of nonliterary drama.

In establishing eras for literature, we realize that such categorizations are ultimately artificial ones. The Jonaki age is considered to have lasted till the 1930s, and the decade of the 1940s is considered separately and specifically as the decade that gave birth to modern Assamese literature. Nevertheless, the careers of numerous writers spanned the 1930s, 1940s, and beyond. More important, certain writers transcend categorization and cannot be made to fit into either category. They defined the transitional phase from Romanticism to Modernity. Banikanta Kakati (1894–1952) was one such writer whose scholarship and leadership shaped modern Assamese literature. Kakati used his education in English literature and language and his wide knowledge of Assamese literature and history to establish in Assam a body of reliable research tools. His *Assamese: Its Formation and Development* (1941) is still considered the definitive work on the language. His *Purani Asamiya Sahitya* (1940) and *Life and Teachings of Shankardeva, Vishnuite Myths and Legends* (1952), among others, provide a core of scholarly research for the study of Assamese culture. Though earlier writers had written on some of these subjects, their works were generally incomplete in scope. Kakati, whose career was as an educator in Assam's major college and university, saw the lack of available, reliable information for the study of Assamese and made it his goal to correct the situation. That Assamese literature today has a body of scholarly apparatus is entirely due to Kakati's early efforts. Another such figure was Jyotiprasad Agarwala. His educational background included a term of study in England and Germany. The exposure to broader Indian and Western ideas led him to the genre that has become so significant in modern culture—cinema. Agarwala wrote, produced, directed, and provided music for the first Assamese movie, *Joymati,* in 1935, followed by *Indramalati* in 1936. *Joymati* took its subject from Lakshminath Bezbarua's *Joymati Konwari.* It was a historical tale of Joymati's refusal to reveal the whereabouts of her husband, Gadadhar Singha, to those who wished to usurp the throne by eliminating legitimate heirs. Joymati remained stoic in the face of cruel punishment and torture; though she ultimately dies, she embodied resistance to injustice. Though the tale was historic, it was particularly relevant in an India entering the last phase of its resistance to British rule. Agarwala's films, like his plays, which will be discussed later, were socially significant dramas. Agarwala's poetic vision, too, was popularized through his body of songs, now termed Jyoti-Sangeet, and their accessibility was ensured for generations of readers and nonreaders alike. Jyotiprasad Agarwala defined an important aspect of Assamese literature—its function in popular culture. Intellectual that he was, he realized that literature and culture could not exist through intellectuals alone. Revolutionary that he was, he realized that ideas must also be felt and heard to be accepted. Another personality who left an indelible impression on Assamese literature and culture was Bishnu Rabha. Rabha represented indigenous Assam; his was a robust voice and vision that sprang from his tribal culture, a culture that existed and flourished in Assam much before the spread of a predominantly Hindu culture. Like Jyotiprasad Agarwala, Rabha wrote prose, poetry, and drama. His legacy remains in a large body of songs popular even today. Unfortunately, many of his works perished before they could be collected and published and thereby preserved.

Early Women Writers

So far this discussion of Assamese literature has shown it to be a literature of men; and indeed, male hegemony of education and letters was present here as it was in literature the world over. However, despite adverse circumstances, lack of opportunity, and even lack of proper education, Assamese women have made considerable and consistent contributions to literature down the ages. Some of the early women who contributed to Assamese literature had the advantage of being born into literary, progressive families that allowed them to receive educations superior to those of other women. One member of Anandaram Dhekiyal Phookan's family who made a mark on her own was his daughter Padmavati Devi Phookanani (1853–1927). Her *Sudharmar Upakhyan* (Sudharma's Tale, 1884) can be considered the second novel by an Assamese writer, male or female. The novel relates the travels and trials of Sudharma, her husband, and their friends amid settings reminiscent of early classical tales. She was a poet and critic and even wrote a children's book, *Hitosadhika.* She wrote a number of articles that display her feminism in journals of her time, such as *Baheen* and *Jonaki.* Most notable were her ideas on the conditions of women. She was widowed at 32, and her article in *Baheen,* "Bidhoba," speaks of the harsh life of the widow in Indian society. She comments on the general condition of women in an article she sent to the Sahitya Sabha (the Assamese Literary Association) called "Samajot Tirutar Sthan" (Women's Place in Society). Gunabhiram Baruah's daughter Swarnalata Baruah (1871–1932), too, contributed articles to *Assam Bandhu Bijuli,* and she wrote *Aahi Tiruta* while quite young. Unfortunately, her family life proved too difficult and tragic for her to be able to continue writing. In the early twentieth century, three women who became known on their own strength were Dharmeswari Devi Baruani, Jamuneswari Khatoniyar, and Nalinibala Devi. Kabya Bharati Dharmeswari Devi Baruani (1892–1960) rose above immense physical and mental difficulties to become known as a poet. Soon after her marriage to Durganath Barua, Dharmeswari Devi was struck by a debilitating illness that left her an invalid. Poetry and the love and support of her husband, which she expressed in her poetry, sustained her, but she was soon widowed. From a life such as this and a body that was gradually losing its abilities, she made her poetic voice heard in her works: *Phulor Sorai* (1929), *Pranor Parash* (1952), and *Ashrudhan Aru Jivantari* (1963), all of which were influenced by Romanticism. Though she takes her imagery from nature, her poetry reveals a strong devotion to the Creator. In 1956, she received the title "Kabyabharati" from the Assam Sahitya Sabha. Whereas Dharmeswari Devi lived a long life of much suffering, Jamuneswari Khatoniyar (1899–1924) accomplished what she did in a life that ended at age 25. Educated privately, since a public school education was not allowed young girls of the time, Jamuneswari passed her middle school examination with her private education, soon after which she sought to remedy the inequality in education by opening, and teaching in, a primary school for girls. The school, Mudoigaon Girls' School, still remains as a testimony to her reformatory zeal. In 1920, she married the poet Bhairab Chandra Khatoniyar and died four short years later. But in those four years she created a forum for the expression and exchange of ideas by establishing Juroni Sabha, a religious and literary gathering at her house each evening. She left one volume of collected poems, *Arun* (1919), and published poems in *Baheen.*

Nalinibala Devi (1898–1977) is probably the best-known female poet of her era. She wrote her first poem, "Pita," when she was 10 years old. Though widowed at a very early age in an era that considered widowhood the end of a constructive life, Nalinibala rose above this misfortune and began her life as a prolific poet and writer. Her poetic works include *Sandhiyar Sur* (1928), *Saponar Sur* (1943), *Parashmoni* (1954), *Alakananda* (1967), and *Jagriti* (1962), among others. She was awarded the Sahitya Akademi in 1968 for *Alakananda.* Her prose works include her father Nabin Chandra Bordoloi's life, *Smritir Tirtha* (1948), her autobiography, *Eri Aha Dinbur,* and her collected articles, *Shanti Path.* Numerous other works are still to be found unpublished, in manuscript form. Nalinibala Devi was one of the major poets of the Jonaki era who brought her feminine, Romantic vision well into the mid-twentieth century. Her position in the Assamese poetic canon was acknowledged even in her lifetime, as evidenced by her presidency of the Assam Sahitya Sabha in 1954. Nalinibala Devi's works cover the range of any major writer, and she placed Assamese women firmly in the history of Assamese literature and language. Thereafter, the products of women writers, though underrated and understudied, have come to be considered within mainstream literature.

THE JAYANTI ERA

A Decade of Transition

The decade of the 1940s is considered the Jayanti era, taking its name from the quarterly *Jayanti,* first published on January 2, 1938, with Raghunath Chaudhari as editor during its first year. It became a monthly from its fourth year and in its decade and a half of existence experienced numerous changes in publisher and editor. From its seventh year onward, *Jayanti* saw the establishment of a new form of literature. If *Jonaki* took literature from the devotional to the Romantic, *Jayanti* moved it to the realistic. Starting with Ambikagiri Raichoudhuri and Jyotiprasad Agarwala, literature turned away from nostalgia regarding the past to immediate concerns. The focus was now on patriotism, social causes, and protest of injustice. In *Jayanti*'s sixth year, Anandeswar Sharma's article "Aajir Ei Sandhikhyanat" warned against taking refuge in the past while ignoring the injustices of the present. He pointed to the examples of Russia and China and the role of writers there in bringing about social change. Indeed, Assamese writers did try to follow these examples, as much of the writing of, and beyond, this period is politically motivated, too. Though the Romantic influence is still displayed well beyond *Jayanti,* it would be safe to say that Assamese literature lost its innocence in the 1940s. Many contemporary writers are products of the Jayanti age.

Jayanti was not the only journal to follow *Jonaki* and *Baheen;* among other important journals were *Abahon, Surabhi,* and *Ramdhenu.* Even in the 1940s, Assamese literature was dependent on journals. There are two reasons for this. First, there has never been a strong print culture or publishing industry in Assam that could issue independent works from manuscript. The publishing concerns that did exist generally took up a writer's works based on a well-established reputation, and reputations could be established only through journals. In fact, writers often issued their own works through small print shops. Second, World War II reached Assam in 1939 and brought inflation and shortage of goods, including paper. This shortage affected journals, too; certainly, mass publication of single works was not possible. The same conditions of deprivation and instability that the war brought influenced literary ideas. The 1940s brought another change to all of India: independence and the establishment of a democratic state. Such upheavals, both the negative and the positive one, meant that writers could not carry on with earlier perceptions of society and the world. Modern Assamese writers display the angst of modern writers everywhere.

Poetry

The poetry published in *Jayanti* reveals a sharp shift away from the optimism of the earlier period. Writers challenged the established norms and complacency of a society based on caste and class distinctions. Their poetry reflects a disillusionment and cynicism that stemmed from the knowledge that a free, modern India did not imply freedom and equality. Progress, technological and industrial, was felt to be dubious if it ignored the concerns of a large part of society. Amulya Barua (1922–46) was the foremost poet of this generation. His "Andharor Hahakar" (The Tumult of Darkness) is a brilliant antiromantic poem. It evokes the traditional Romantic image of an autumnal, moonlit night to have it reveal horror, death, and decay. His "Beisya" (The Prostitute) is a controversial poem that points contemptuously to the upper echelons of society who are united with the prostitute in a single act that they publicly scorn but privately practice. Where the prostitute's behavior arises out of dire need, the behavior of the men is shown to be self-indulgent and thus more contemptible. In a similar vein, in Keshav Mahanta's (1926) "Suror Koiphiyot" (The Thief's Justification), which appeared in the first issue of *Jayanti*'s important seventh year, the protagonist, a thief, points at social conditions as being responsible for the path he must take. In the second issue of that year, Amulya Barua's "Biplobi" (Revolutionary) explains the modern revolutionary vision, a vision that was not oppositional but sought ideological reforms through knowledge and tolerance. It was a bitter irony that the ignorance, bigotry, and social divisiveness that Amulya Barua spoke out against were the cause of his death in the communal riots in Calcutta during partition. In the same issue of *Jayanti,* Hem Barua's "Guwahati—1944" described the state of the nation as one crowded with wartime difficulties and political and ideological struggles.

The language of this poetry was immediate, accessible, forceful. Its tone was questioning, probing, revealing. Among the notable poets of this period were Prasannalal Choudhuri, Shashikanta Gogoi, Bhaba Prasad Rajkhowa, Said Abdul Malik, Narayan Bezbarua, Mahesh Deb Goswami, Maheswar Neog, and Deva Kanta Barua, some of whom are still writing. It would be inaccurate to call all these poets antiromantic, as many of them still leaned toward the earlier Romantics. But poetry in general showed the influence of English poets such as Yeats, Pound, and Elliot, and this modern poetry was the dominant one.

Prose

Prose fiction of this period was weaker than its poetry. We notice the publication of more short stories than novels. Novelists who would emerge in contemporary literature were starting their careers as short story writers. Said Abdul Malik's (1919) collection of short stories, *Parashmoni,* was published in 1946. The short story "Parashmoni" was a simple yet relevant story of love, friendship, and misunderstanding; but Malik's direct language and expressions made this story of human relationships appealing. It established Malik as one of contemporary Assam's most popular writers. On the other hand, Birendra Kumar Bhattacharya's (1924) short stories focused on social, rather than interpersonal, subjects. His short story "Jetiya Sihonte Noporhe," which appeared in the April issue of *Abahon,* examines, through its characters' search, Marxist philosophy as a means of social change. His "Agyat Japani Sainik," which appeared in *Jayanti*'s seventh year, focuses on the war. His "Sei Ekhon Jogotor Katha," too, describes the conditions generated by war and, through these descriptions, comments on communal divisiveness.

The Assamese novel of this period was still the traditional, plot-driven novel. But its subjects and plots were no longer those of the traditional romances. Modernity implied a harder look at life, and novelists examined contemporary social and political changes closely. Birinchi Kumar Barua (1908–64), who also wrote under the pseudonym Bina Barua, was a novelist whose works *Jivanor Batot* (On the Journey of Life, 1944) and *Seuji Pator Kahini* (A Story of Green Leaves, 1958) depict the gradual disappearance of a rural, natural lifestyle due to the spread of industry and commerce. The heroine of *Jivanor Batot,* Togor, embodies rural simplicity, while the hero Kamalakanta represents urbane, so-called progressive society. Kamalakanta's deception and exploitation of Togor's innocence through a pretended marriage upturn her hitherto safe, protected life. The allusions to the nation's upheaval are very clear in this tale. As Bina Barua, he also wrote novels that looked at the romantic relations between college students, which, too, were indicative of the changes taking place in Assamese society. Another novelist to write college romances was Roma Das (1909–81). Other notable novelists of this period were Kaliram Medhi (1878–1954) and Bhabananda Datta (1918–59). But the novelist whose work demonstrates modernity in its style and structure as well as subject is Prafulla Dutta Goswami (1919). His novels include *Shesh Kot* (Where Does It End?, 1948) and *Kesa Pator Kapani* (The Trembling of New Leaves, 1952) and show the influence of Joseph Conrad, Virginia Woolf, and James Joyce. Though his novels cannot be termed stream-of-consciousness in structure, the emphasis is on internal thought rather than external action. The story of *Kesa Pator Kapani* unfolds through its hero's dilemma at having to reject his parents' way of life in choosing his own. The hero Utpal is not a vehement rebel, simply a modern man having to make modern choices. His uncertainty symbolizes modern insecurity. Dutta Goswami's novels are part of contemporary literature; but his works were the earliest to have taken this vital step toward modern structure and language in the Assamese novel.

Drama

The drama of this period can be divided into three categories: the mythological, the historical, and the social. The structure of drama saw a major change in that it moved away from the rigidity of the classical five-act form. This flexibility allowed the later introduction of the one-act play. A major player in development of drama was radio. The ability to perform and broadcast a play without any visuals or costumes on radio shows freed drama from mere stage effects. The message and dialogue became important and thus more efficient. The influence of Shaw and Ibsen's message-oriented drama can be seen in the social drama of this period.

Historical dramas took up Assamese figures of recent history as their subjects, especially figures who symbolized resistance to British rule. The Nagaon Natya Samiti's *Piyoli Phookan* (1948), Prabin Phookan's (1912–85) *Lachit Borphookan* (1946) and *Maniram Dewan* (1948), and Surendranath Saikia's *Kushal Konwar* (1949) dramatized the historical and personal events surrounding these well-known personalities of Assam's history. Surendranath Saikia also wrote a number of mythological plays, such as *Karna* (1947) and *Lakshman* (1949). But such plays were fewer in number. It was the social drama that gained popularity and importance, and Jyotiprasad Agarwala was the dramatist who popularized this drama. In his *Lobhita* (1942), though the play is set within two political events, World War II and the 1942 independence movement, the social message is most relevant. Its heroine, Lobhita's, reaction to events around her, her courage and determination amid intense struggles, her ultimate sacrifice characterize a pride and patriotism that allowed this young Assamese woman to face modern problems unafraid. Agarwala's message was that young Assamese men and women be able to encounter the complexities of the modern world with self-confidence and pride in their heritage and reject earlier tendencies to marginalize themselves. His *Karengor Ligiri* (The Palace Maid, 1936), too, dramatizes the dehumanizing effects of traditional class structures. Among his other plays are the symbolic dramas *Nimati Kanya, Rupalim,* and *Sonit-Kunwori.* They are all notable for experimenting not only with form but with technique, including the incorporation of songs and music in what can be termed poetic dramas. Other social dramas of this period are Satya Prasad Barua's (1919) *Sakoi-Sokuwat* (1940), Susibrata Raichoudhuri's *Kon Bate* (1948), and Dandiram Kalita's *Porasit* (1946). We do find a number of comedies written during this period, but the comic vision was not predominant in the 1940s.

POSTINDEPENDENCE LITERATURE

1950s to the Present

Assamese literature today cannot be characterized as having a single, common vision or belonging to a particular school. The ready availability of newly published works from around the world, the advent of technology and mass media, and the easy access to travel and study across the world all influenced writers in various ways. Ideologically, it reflects a post-Freudian, post-Marxist, postmodern world. Furthermore, recent political upheavals in the country and the state, the breakdown of public morals, and economic progress continue to affect present-day writers. Literature today includes a wide range of poetry, novels, short stories, dramas, and subgenres such as folklore, science fiction, children's literature, biographies, and translations. Thus, a short survey cannot do real justice to, nor encompass, a continuing literature.

Poetry

Modern poetry reveals personal reflections and focus on the immediate and shifting trends of modern life, often within urban settings. The poetry that evokes natural, Romantic imagery, too, brings to these images a modern perspective. Modern poetry takes many forms; some poets still use traditional lyric forms and rhymes, whereas others use blank and free verse in ordinary, rather than poetic, language. Some of these trends had been displayed in the poetry of the 1940s. Though contemporary poetry displays a cynicism and dismay at modern conditions, it is not as vehement as the poetry of the 1940s, nor does it contain that revolutionary zeal. Modern poetry is both symbolic and realistic.

Navakanta Barua's poetic works, *He Aranya, He Mahanagar* (1951), *Eti Duti Egharoti Tora* (1958), *Samrat* (1962), *Ravan* (1963), *Monor Khobor* (Songs, 1963), and *Mor Aru Prithivir* (1973), all reveal a symbolic, often surrealistic, often dramatic approach to his depiction of the gradual destruction of modern society. He began his writing in the 1940s, and his poetic vision, expressed through a career that has spanned six decades, has established him as one of the leading poets of Assam. Though his approach is modern, his imagery combines the Romantic as well. His subjects include the natural landscape of Assam, especially its rivers, and he falls back on traditional folk songs and folk dances, as well as the colloquial, for his meter. His recent works, such as *Ratnakar aru Ananya Kabi* (1986) and *Ekhon Swasa Mukhare* (1990), reveal that, though the poet is faced with, and must accept, present-day reality, there are a continued lingering of, a longing for, the idealism and simplicity of the past.

One of the poets who define contemporary Assamese poetry is Nilamoni Phookan (1933). From his first collection of poems, *Surya Henu Nami Ahe Ei Nadiyedi* (1963), Phookan expresses the loneliness and isolation of modern man in a society that seems to have lost its moorings. Though his poems contemplate society, his poetry embraces the Assamese landscape and takes its themes from the natural and historical. His other works are *Nirjanatar Shabda* (1965), *Kabita* (1978), and *Golapi Jamur Lagna* (1985). In these, too, Phookan reflects on a wide range of universal issues such as love, life, and death. His style is at once expressionistic and symbolic; his language combines the sound of folk literature with the meter of European literature. A contemporary of Nilamoni Phookan, Nirmalprabha Bordoloi (1933) is not only a remarkable female poet but one of the best-known Assamese poets writing today. Bordoloi's poetry is self-expressive and contemplative. Her reflections span man and nature alike. Her imagery is symbolic as well as evocative of the past. In many of her works, she has focused on social issues and redefined mythical heroines such as Draupadi,

Gandhari, and Sita. Her works include *Bon Phoringor Rong* (1967), *Dinor Pasot Din* (1977) and *Antaranga* (1978). The extremely lyrical quality of her poetry has made them easy to adapt to song. Another important modern poet who has kept alive the strain of lyricism in poetry is Hiren Bhattacharya (1932). Bhattacharya's poetry utilizes the power of words to universalize even the most personal experiences; it is at once intimate and revelatory. Bhattacharya is one of the most influential of modern Assamese poets. His works include *Sugandhi Pokhila* (1981) and *Soisor Pothar Manuh* (1991). Another notable modern poet is Ajit Barua (1928), who began his career in the 1940s. In early poems, such as "Tikha" and "Haturi," which appeared in journals, he focuses on social reform and expression of freedom. His later works, such as *Kisuman Padya aru Gaan* (1982) and *Brahmaputra Ityadi Padya* (1989), are more expressionistic and symbolic. One young poet who effectively represents the contemporary trend in Assamese poetry is Samir Tanti (1956), whose works include *Yudha bumir Kabita* (1985) and *Shokakol Upatyaka* (1990). His poetic vision reflects on Third World conditions as present in Assam/India today, and in these reflections he shares much with poets from Third World countries the world over. Harsh realities often make these poets revolutionary and leftist in their views; but this is a leftism that is not necessarily aligned to any one political ideology. Among other noteworthy Assamese poets writing today are Bhaben Barua (1941), in whose work *Sonali Jahaj* (1977) we find a contemplation of the seasons and imaginative play on words; Hiren Datta (1939), whose works include *Somadhirir Sowarani aru Ananya Kabita* (1981); and Harekrishna Deka (1943).

It would be remiss to end this section on poetry without mentioning Bhupen Hazarika. Hazarika has achieved national fame as a lyricist rather than a poet; nevertheless, since lyricism has been a definitive quality of Assamese poetry throughout its history, the poetic value of Hazarika's works cannot be ignored. Bhupen Hazarika's songs and poetry have covered a wide range of subjects, from the intensely personal to the extremely political. In his works, he has used the traditional hymn, the native folk song, and his original music to interpret national and international concerns, and, by using them, he has popularized old forms. Though he is a popular public figure and a performing artist, his contribution to literature has been acknowledged through his appointment to the presidency of the Assam Sahitya Sabha in 1993. That same year, Hazarika won India's prestigious Dadasaheb Phalke Award for cinematic contributions, establishing his role in yet another genre—cinema.

Prose

Contemporary Assamese literature displays a strong tradition of novel and short story writing. Most writers today have produced works in both genres. Contemporary prose fiction is extremely conscious of its social function and political responsibility and takes as its subjects events surrounding the last stages of the independence struggle and the shifting social and economic conditions of modern India. Two writers who started writing and established reputations quite early are Said Abdul Malik and Birendra Kumar Bhattacharya. As with his earlier short stories, Malik's novels concentrate on the relationships between men and women, on ordinary events that touch and change the lives of ordinary people, and on the universal relevance such relationships and events have. Some of these novels are *Adharsheela* (1966), *Rajanigandhar Sokulu* (1972), and *Dr. Arunabhar Asampurna Jivani* (1975). Certain of his novels, such as *Prasin aru Kankaal* (1968) and *Sonali Sutare Bondha* (1972), look at unnatural manifestations of love and intense passion. However, his novels are not restricted to romance alone. Two novels that examine social conditions are *Surujmukhir Sapna* (1960) and *Oghori Atmar Kahini* (1969). *Surujmukhir Sapna* is primarily about the life of a Muslim village by the river. Through his descriptions of a simple rural people, their joys, sorrows, and hopes, Malik brings the village to life. *Oghori Atmar Kahini,* on the other hand, is placed in an urban setting and looks at middle-class life and problems associated with it. Malik's prose writings include two well-known biographies: Jyotiprasad Agarwala's life, *Rupotirtha Jatri* (Vol. 1, 1963; Vol. 2, 1965), and the Assamese Vaishnav saint and reformer Sankardev's life, *Dhanya Nara Tonu Bhala* (1987). Among Malik's many works are *Rothor Sokori Ghure* (1950), *Bonjui* (1956), *Sobighar* (1958), *Matir Saki* (1959), and *Anya Akash, Anya Tora* (1962). Birendra Kumar Bhattacharya's novels, too, display the same political concerns that his short stories exhibited. In technique, his novels are more experimental and modern than Malik's. His first novel, *Rajpothe Ringiyai* (1955), employs stream-of-consciousness narrative to some extent. The novel moves over the course of one day in the life of the protagonist, an important day for India—August 15, 1947, independence day. We see the limitedness of independence through the hero's eyes and ultimately the false claims of independence as the day ends with the hero's being attacked by the police. His second novel, *Iyaruingom* (1960), is set in the Naga hills of the independence era and narrates the divisions that arise out of ideological differences. One group within Naga society believes in Subhash Chandra Bose's message of active, armed resistance to the British in India with the help of the Japanese army; the other group has faith in Gandhi's nonviolent methods. This division echoes that apparent in the rest of India. In the end, though the first group is victorious and attempts to form an independent state in the Naga hills, it is clear that the larger nationalistic forces will ultimately take over. Bhattacharya's novels consistently question and reveal the false assumptions on which society's definitions of freedom, nationalism, faith, and religion are based. His *Mritunjoy* (1970), which again is set in preindependent India during the Quit India movement of 1942, focuses on a Vaisnavite and a Gandhian who must turn to violence. His *Pratipod* (1970) uses the workers' strike of 1940 in the British-owned Assam Oil Company at Digboi as its subject and the unity displayed by the workers and the ultimate political intervention as its theme. Two recent novels that again turn to democracy and nationalism are *Munisunir Pohor* (1979) and *Kalor Humunia* (1982). Bhattacharya's novels, such as *Sataghni* (1968) and *Kobor aru Phool* (1972), examine the effects of war on humanity. Other novels, such as *Nastachandra* (1968), *Sinaki Shuti* (1971), and *Daini* (1976), are studies of the human condition.

Another contemporary novelist whose novels examine various forms and whose subjects are often political in the manner of Bhattacharya is Homen Borgohain (1931). His first novel, *Suwala* (1963), is narrated in the first person and is the account of the life of its heroine, a simple village girl who comes to town in hopes of finding a better life and whom social and economic conditions push toward prostitution. Borgohain's second novel, *Tantrik* (1967), is an ideological novel that examines the values of mysticism as opposed to naturalism or existentialism, where plot is secondary. In both novels, we see the influence of Western philosophical schools. Borgohain's *Antaraag* (1986), however, is a novel that shows the relevance and applicability of these ideas to modern-day India. Borgohain's political novels include *Kushilav* (1970) and *Timir Tortha* (1975), both of which expose the corruption and decay of Indian politics both local and national. His extremely popular novels such as *Halodhiya Soaiye Baudhan Khai* (1973), *Pitaputra* (1975), and *Matsyagandha* (1987) take on more social concerns and depict the continuing social inequities and injustices. Navakanta Barua's novels, too, examine social conditions, but more in the manner of Malik than Bhattacharya. His two best-known novels are set in Nagaon district of Assam and have almost a historical quality. *Kapili Pariya Sadhu* (1926) is set around the river Kapili, and the riverbank takes on a life of its own through Barua's poetic descriptions. But his second novel, *Kokadeutar Had* (1954), established the poet as a novelist. The novel is the saga of two well-placed families in late eighteenth-century Nagaon. Their story of bitter rivalry, deceit, and violence is told through a present-day narrator, a grandmother reflecting on her family's past as she tells the tale to future generations. Through the rivalry of the two families and their manipulation of the lower classes, the novel touches on the continuing exploitation of one class by another. Barua usually takes figments of history and folklore and builds his novels around them. Two other such novels are *Garama Kunwori* (1979) and *Manuh Ataibor Dwip* (1981).

Among notable modern novelists we find women writers such as Nirupama Borgohain (b. 1932), Nilima Dutta (1925), and Mamoni Raisom Goswami (b. 1943). Nirupama Borgohain's first novel, *Sei Nadi Niravadhi* (1963), is yet another modern novel whose setting is a riverbank. The story of life in the region is told through the life and love of the female protagonist, whose life is inextricably intertwined with the river itself. Another novel centered around a heroine is *Dinor Pisot Dinot* (1968). Where these novels are female-oriented, Borgohain's *Anya Jivan* (1986) and *Champavati* (1990) can be termed feminist novels. *Anya Jivan* is probably the first Assamese feminist novel, in that it examines the opposition women face in determining themselves as individuals in a patriarchal society. Though the novel is set in an interior village, its society is but a representation of society at large. As a socially concerned novelist, Nirupama Borgohain does not simply examine feminist issues. Her *Iparor Ghor Siparor Ghor* (1979) describes the breakdown of rural society due to postindependent economic problems and the further problems that face rural migrants in urban settings. This novel and others, like *Dinor Pisot Din* and *Bhabishyat Ronga Surya* (1980), realistically depict social and economic degeneration in free India. Among Borgohain's better-known works are *Antah Shrota* (1969), *Hridoy Eta Nirjon Dwip* (1970), *Samanya Asamanya* (1971), and *Cactus Phool* (1976). Nilima Dutta's novels generally take up ordinary life and realistic concerns. But her most recent novel, *Dhumuhar Pisot* (1992), looks at the student-led political agitation in Assam of the 1980s, the formation of a government by former students, and the effects of the movement in general and is a timely examination of a historical movement that continues to affect Assam today. Mamoni Raisom Goswami's novels, too, concern themselves with recent events and often take a socialistic approach. The subject of her *Sinabor Sot* (1972) is the exploitation of its laborers by a bridge construction company; through this subject, she exposes the inhuman treatment of one class by another, based on socioeconomic differences, that has become an acceptable aspect of life in India. *Ahiron* (1976) and *Mamore Dhora Tarowal* (1980), too, are similar to this first novel in their empathy for the underclass. In *Nilakanthi Braj* (1976), Goswami contrasts the abstraction of spiritual beauty with the reality of physical squalor. The young widowed heroine encounters overwhelming poverty and dire need, inhumanity and debased behavior in Mathura, one of the holiest shrines of Hinduism and a place that should have embodied the high ideals of the religion itself. Her *Dontal Hatir Uiye Khowa Howda* (1988), set in an Assamese *satra,* or monastery, also exposes religious hypocrisy.

We see a variety of novels, traditional and experimental, romantic and realistic, being produced by novelists today. Lakshminandan Borah (b. 1931), notable as a short story writer, focuses on ordinary life, especially rural life, in his novels, which include *Ganga Silonir Pakhi* (1965), *Nishar Purobi* (1962), and *Matit Meghor Sanh* (1970). Borah's more socially and politically conscious novels are *Patal Bhairbi* (1965), *Uttar Purush* (1970), and *Dohon Dulori* (1971). Jogesh Das (1927) looks back at World War II and the conditions it created in India in his most notable novel, *Dawor Aru Nai* (1955). Many of Das's novels show the restrictive nature of our society, especially concerning women. Two of these are *Jonakir Jui* (1959) and *Nirupai, Nirupai* (1963). Debendranath Acharya (1937–81), in his novels *Kalpurush* (1967), *Anya Jog Anya Purush* (1971), and *Jangam* (published 1982), was the first to write in the surrealistic mode. His novels take and explore particular events in Assam's past imaginatively, rather than historically. Assam's large aboriginal tribal society has always been a presence in its literature and folklore, though somewhat an overlooked one. But Karbi writer Rong Bong Terang's novel *Rongmilir Hanhi* (1981) brought Karbi society to mainstream literature. A novelist who experiments with form and subject in novels such as *Madhupur* (1971), *Tarangini* (1971), *Godhuli*

(1981), and *Anusandhan* (1987) is Shilabhadra (Revatimohan Dutta Choudhuri [1924]). Short story writer and playwright Bhabendranath Saikia's (1932) novel *Antarip* (1986) is extraordinarily progressive in its feminist statement, as it entertains the idea of feminine subversion in the 1930s. Other contemporary novelists and short story writers include Chandra Prasad Saikia (1927), Medini Choudhuri (1929), Arunachali writer Lummer Dai (1940), Troilokyanath Goswami (1906–88), Sneha Devi, Hiren Gohain, and Govindaprasad Sharma, to name just a few.

Drama

Modern Assamese drama, too, displays social analysis and structural experimentation. However, the publication history of drama is still not as strong as that of poetry and prose. Most dramas appear in journals or remain unpublished, though performed. The influence of drama of the Western world is very apparent. The prominent influence regarding drama's message has been that of Ibsen, Chekov, and Shaw; and regarding drama's form it has been Beckett, Ionesco, and Brecht, among others. In fact, translations of Western plays are an important aspect of modern Assamese drama. Apart from translations of Shakespearean drama, we find a number of translations of Ibsen's plays. These include Suresh Goswami's *Runumi* (1946, from Ibsen's *The Vikings of Helgeland*), Padma Borkakoti's *Putola Ghor* (1959, from *A Doll's House*), Satyaprasad Barua's *Banahansi* (1962, from *The Wild Duck*), and Mahendra Borah's *Bhoot* (1965, from *Ghosts*).

One important form that has developed in present-day Assamese drama is the one-act play. The formation of the Asom Natya Sanmilan (Assam Dramatic Society) in 1959 and its regular one-act play competition have helped in the development of this form. Some notable one-act plays are Durgeswar Borthakur's *Nirodesh;* Satyaprasad Barua's *Anarkali, Kunaal-Kanchan, Ranadil, Saswati,* and *Bhaswati;* Prabin Phookan's *Tritaranga;* Bhabendranath Saikia's *Putola-Nas;* Tafajjul Ali's *Nepati Kenekoi Thako;* and Bhupen Hazarika's *Era Bator Sur.* The subjects of this drama range from the historical to the contemporaneous.

The influence of the absurd and the symbolic play is not as widespread in Assam, though we find a few notable examples. Arun Sharma's *Shri Nibaron Bhattacharya* (1967) and *Ahar* and Basanta Saikia's *Manoh* and *Asur* are absurd in the manner of Ionesco and Beckett. But the better-known plays of this generation combine elements of modern drama the world over to propagate socially relevant messages, a characteristic of contemporary Assamese poetry and prose, too. Himendrakumar Borthakur's *Bagh* (The Tiger, 1971) dramatizes political manipulation of the naive, trusting rural population and general political corruption. Satyaprasad Barua's *Nayika Natyakar* (1976) and *Mrinal Mahi* (1977) are both plays that show the psychological ramifications of social problems.

A significant number of modern plays also revive traditional folk and classical forms. As with the rest of India, Assam, too, has seen a revival of ancient genres such as *bhavna* and *yatra,* a revival that has allowed these forms to be applied to modern subjects. Mitradev Mahanta's *Prassanna Pandav* (1956), Jugal Das's *Bayonor Khel* (1982), Anandamohan Bhagavati's *Jatugriha,* Satish Bhattacharya's *Maharaja,* and Munin Bhuyan's *Hati aru Phandi* are some such dramas.

Twentieth-century Assamese literature has come quite a ways from its tentative beginnings. The study of this literature itself has become well established; numerous schools of thought and critical approaches are apparent in the writings of literary scholars today. There can no longer be any question about Assamese being a major language with its own literature; that part of the battle has been won. It is also true that, since the Jayanti era, the works of major Assamese novelists and poets have been regularly translated into Hindi and other languages, thus ensuring a wider readership. However, as a literature of a border region of India, it is still marginalized and often plays second fiddle to Bengali literature. Assamese literature is a product of Assamese society, and Assamese society has specific qualities that separate and distinguish it from its western neighbors. Assam has generally been freer of caste oppression, untouchability, and communalism than other parts of India. Its history, till the sociopolitical movement of the 1980s, has never included religious persecution or divisiveness. Its women have never been debased by a dowry system, and female infanticide is rare. Its literature reflects these liberal aspects and, as such, can take its place among major Indian literatures. The task still remains for turn-of-the-twentieth-century writers to popularize this literature by seeking wider publication and taking the Assamese voice confidently to the rest of the world.

WORKS CITED

Neog, Dimbeswar. *New Light on History of Asamiya Literature: (From the Earliest until Recent Times) including an Account of Its Antecedents.* Guwahati, Assam: Suwani Prakash, 1982. (First published 1962.)

Neog, Maheswar, ed. *Orunodoi 1846–1854, Vols. 1–10.* Guwahati, Assam: Assam Prakashan Parishad, 1983.

Phookan, Nilamoni, ed. *Kuri Satikar Asamiya Kabita.* Guwahati, Assam: Assam Prakashan Parishad, 1977.

SELECTED PRIMARY BIBLIOGRAPHY

Acharya, Debendranath. *Kalpurush.* Duliajan, Assam: Banti Prakashan, 1976.

Agarwala, Jyotiprasad. *Rasanavali.* Guwahati: Assam Prakashan Parishad, 1981.

Barua, Amulya. "Kukur." *Jayanti* 6:12 (1944).

Barua, Atul Chandra. *Rasanavali.* Guwahati: Barua Prakashan, 1993.

Barua, Gunabhiram. *Ananda Ram Dhekiyal Phukanar Jivan Charitra.* Guwahati: Assam Prakashan Parishad, 1971.

Barua, Hem. "Guwahati: 1944." *Adhunik Asamiya Kavita.* Edited by Jatindranath Sharma. Jorhat: Friends, 1946.

Barua, Navakanta. *Mor Aru Prithivir.* Guwahati: Asom Book Depot, 1973.

———. *Kokadeutar Haad.* Guwahati: Friend's Book Agency, 1975.

———. *Ekhon Swasa Mukhare.* Guwahati: Lawyer's Book Stall, 1990.

Baruva, Parvati Prasad. *Rasanavali.* Guwahati: Assam Sahitya Sabha, 1981.

Bezbaruah, Lakshminath. *Grathavali,* Vol. 1. Guwahati: Sahitya Prakash, 1968.

———. *Granthavali,* Vol. 2. Guwahati: Sahitya Prakash, 1970.

———. *Mor Jivan Sowaran.* Guwahati: Assam Sahitya Sabha, 1970.

Bhattacharya, Birendra Kumar. *Mritunjoy.* Guwahati: Sahitya Prakash, 1970.

———. *Iyaruingam.* Guwahati: Lawyer's Book Stall, 1979.

Bhattacharya, Hiren. *Soisor Potharor Manuh.* Guwahati: Student's Stores, 1991.

Bora, Lakshminandan. *Uttar Purush.* Tinsukia, Assam: Mitra Agency, 1970.

———. *Patal Bharavi.* Guwahati: Sahitya Prakash, 1986.

———. *Jakeri Nahike Upam.* Guwahati: Sahitya Prakash, 1993.

Bora, Mahim. *Bahu Bhuji Tribhuj.* Guwahati: Bharati Prakash, 1967.

Bordoloi, Nirmalprabha. *Sahitya aru Sanskriti.* Guwahati: Deka, 1987.

———. *Devi.* 2d ed. Guwahati: Sahitya Prakash, 1989.

Bordoloi, Rajanikanta. *Monomati.* Guwahati: Sahitya Prakash, 1991. (Reprint.)

Borgohain, Homen. *Saudar Putake Nao Meli Jai.* Guwahati: Student's Stores, 1987.

Borgohain, Nirupama. *Mar Prati Morom aru Ashrudhar, Tinikanya.* Guwahati: Asom Book Depot, 1978.

———. *Iparor Ghor, Shiparor Ghor.* Calcutta: Bhabani Publishing Concern, 1979.

———. *Anya Jivan.* Dibrugarh, Assam: Students Emporium, 1990.

Borkakoti, Hari. *Swanirbachita Kavita.* Guwahati: AMII Group, 1994.

Borkakoti, Padma. *Abandhana.* Guwahati: Guwahati Book Stall, 1979.

Das, Jogesh. *Tribeni.* Guwahati: Lawyer's Book Stall, 1963.

———. *Sanh Jui Khedi.* Guwahati: Jnanpith Book Agency, 1964.

Deka, Harekrishna. *Aan Ejon.* Guwahati: Barua Agency, 1986.

Devi, Nalinibala. "Tarun Pragati." *Surabhi* 2:4 (August 1946).

Devi, Sneha. *Sneha Devir Shrestha Galpa.* Guwahati: Bani Prakash, 1981.

———. *Sneha Devir Ekuki Galpa.* Guwahati: Bani Prakash, 1982.

Hazarika, Bhupen. *Gitavali.* Guwahati: Bani Mandir, 1993.

Kakati, Banikanta. *Assamese, Its Formation and Development.* 2d ed. Guwahati: Lawyer's Book Stall, 1962.

Malik, Said Abdul. *Dhanya Naratanu Bhal.* Guwahati: Student's Stores, 1987.

———. *Parashmoni.* Guwahati: Lawyer's Book Stall, 1994. (First published in 1946.)

Mishra, Govinda. *ShiMadBhagavat Gita.* Edited by Munindra Narayan Dutta Barua. Guwahati: Jana Jagrity Prakashan, 1983.

Neog, Maheswar, ed. *Bhagavati Prasad Baruva: Writings of and on Him.* Jorhat: Assam Sahitya Sabha, 1983.

———. *Banikanta Rasanavali.* Guwahati: Assam Prakashan Parishad, 1991.

Phookan, Lakshminath. *Bapukan.* Guwahati: Bani Prakash, 1987.

Phukan, Anandaram Dhekiyal. *A Few Remarks on the Assamese Language.* Sibsagar: Assam, 1855. (An Assamese translation by Maheswar Neog, Jorhat, Assam: Assam Sahitya Sabha, 1958).

Raisom Goswami, Mamoni. *Nilkanthi Braj.* Guwahati: Lawyer's Book Stall, 1976.

———. *Ishwari, Jakhmi Jatri, aru Ananya.* Guwahati: Jyoti Prakashan, 1991.

Saikia, Bhabendranath. *Sendur.* Guwahati: Lawyer's Book Stall, 1988.
Saikia, Chandra Prabha. ''Daibagya Duhita.'' In *Lekhikar Galpa,* edited by Preeti Barua. Guwahati: Lekhika Santha, 1989.
Saikia, Chandra Prasad. *Mandakranta.* Guwahati: Udayan, 1960.
Sharma, Benudhar. *Congressor Kansuali Rodot.* Guwahati: Asom Jyoti, 1959.
———. *Dunori.* Guwahati: Asom Jyoti, 1963.
———. *Dakhinpat Satra.* Guwahati: Asom Jyoti, 1966.
Tanti, Samir. *Yudhabhumir Kavita.* Guwahati: Sahitya Prakash, 1985.
———. *Shokakul Upatyaka.* Guwahati: Sahitya Prakash, 1990.

REFERENCES

Barua, Birinchi Kumar. *History of Assamese Literature.* New Delhi, 1964.
Barua, Hem. *Adhunik Sahitya.* Guwahati, Assam: Lawyer's Book Stall, 1991. (First published by Sankardev Library, Guwahati, 1950.)
Borgohain, Homen, ed. *Asamiya Sahitya Buranji, Sastha Khanda,* Vol. 6. Guwahati, Assam: Anundoram Borooah Bhasha-Kala-Sanskriti Santha, 1993.
Borthakur, Sheela, ed. *Lekhikar Jivani.* Tezpur, Assam: Sodou Asom Lekhika Samaroh Samiti, 1987.
Gogoi, Lila, ed. *Adhunik Asamiya Sahityar Parisay.* Dibrugarh, Assam, 1990.
Gohain, Hiren. *Asamiya Jatiya Jivanat Mahapurushia Parampara.* Guwahati: Lawyer's Book Stall, 1990.
Phookan, Nilamoni, ed. *Kuri Satikar Asamiya Kabita.* Guwahati, Assam: Assam Prakashan Parishad, 1977.
Mahanta, Pona. *Western Influence on Modern Assamese Drama.* New Delhi, 1985.
Neog, Dimbeswar. *New Light on History of Asamiya Literature: (From the Earliest until Recent Times) including an Account of Its Antecedents.* Guwahati, Assam: Suwani Prakash, 1982 (First published 1962.)
Neog, Maheswar. *Assamese Drama and Theater.* New Delhi, 1965.
———. *Asamiya Sahityar Ruprekha.* Guwahati, Assam, 1970.
———, ed. *Orunodoi 1846–1854, Vols. 1–9.* Guwahati, Assam: Assam Prakashan Parishad, 1983.
Sharma, Anjali. *Among the Luminaries in Assam.* New Delhi: Mittal, 1990.
Sharma, Satyendranath. *Asamiya Upanyas Gatidhara.* Guwahati, Assam: Bani Prakash, 1976.
———. *Asamiya Sahityar Samikhyatmak Itibritta.* 4th ed. Guwahati, 1989.

2

Twentieth-Century Bengali Literature

SUDIPTO CHATTERJEE AND HASAN FERDOUS

LITERATURE OF PREINDEPENDENCE BENGAL (1900–1947) AND WEST BENGAL (1947–PRESENT)

In the nineteenth century, Bengali (Beng. Bāṅglā) literature was enriched by the fruits of the Bengal (Beng. Bāṅglā or Baṅga) Renaissance,[1] which led to the birth of several new genres and modes of literary expression. The novel, short story, epic poetry, journalese prose, and Western-style drama all matured independently in the nineteenth century in the hands of various talented writers who became both pioneers and, some of them, first masters of those genres.[2] By the close of the century, however, a conservative smugness set in. The British colonial policy of divide and rule had successfully segregated the Hindu and Muslim communities among the Bengali, which, in turn, led to the rise of religious orthodoxy and dogmatism, especially on the Hindu side of the population. Reactionary journals like the *Baṅgabāsī,* led by people like J̄ogendracandra Basu (Ang. Bose) and Indranāth Bandyopādhyāya (Ang. Banerjee/ji [1849–1911]), were vociferous in their expressions of Hindu orthodoxy and efforts at enforcing a Hindu hegemony over all aspects of Bengali culture. Among the few who resisted this regressive, reactionary trend was Rabīndranāth Tagore (Beng. Thākur [1860–1941]), who had started writing regularly from the last quarter of the nineteenth century. Independent, progressive thinking and accommodating the free circulation of a multiplicity of opinions and ideas were cardinal elements in Rabīndranāth's ideology. He gave vent to it in his editorial journey with, first, the *Hitabādī* (established April 1891) and, subsequently, *Sādhanā* (established November 1891). While in the former he experimented with the short story genre, in the latter he performed the role of the inspirational editorial manager who brought together several other talented writers.

Rabīndranāth Tagore (1900–1913)

Rabīndranāth's figure dominated over at least the first half of the twentieth century. He stood like an enormous edifice whose shadow cast itself on all and sundry. It is not an exaggeration to say that there is hardly an aspect of Bengali literature (nay, culture!) that is truly free of Rabīndranāth's influence. Any consideration of Bengali literature in the twentieth century, thus, must necessarily begin with the contribution of Rabīndranāth Tagore. Post-Tagore Bengali literature, as well, worked with the "anxiety" of Tagorean influence. In trying to do justice to both Tagore's preeminence and the writers who were his contemporaries, the first part of this chapter (the Tagore period) has subheadings that mark either (1) phases in Tagore's career or (2) all other genres/movements and time frames. This shall, we hope, allow the reader to observe the growth and development of Bengali literature in the present century as a whole but without undermining the role Tagore played in shaping it.

Rabīndranāth Tagore was born in an affluent and culturally progressive family, and, although he had little formal education, his literary talents flourished at a very early age. His literary ideals were formed under the peerage of his elder siblings, almost all of whom were artistically inclined, and his illustrious philosopher-cum-religious-reformer father, Debendranāth. His early work in the last quarter of the nineteenth century is characterized by a certain exotic aura plugged right into the English Romantic tradition and a simultaneous Orientalist rediscovery of his own cultural heritage. Toward the end of the century, however, Tagore began to emerge as a more mature artist. His maturity was reflected most prominently in his firm rejection of religious orthodoxy, which had risen at the expense of secularism. He was writing poetry, prose, and drama—all concurrently—expressing in no uncertain terms his humanist view of civilization through all the literary genres over which he had command. His most important works from the last 15 years of the nineteenth century are the three books of poems *Kaṛi o Komal* (Sharps and Flats, 1887), *Mānasī* (The Heart's Desire, 1890), and *Sonār Tarī* (The Golden Boat, 1893); the play *Bisarjan* (Sacrifice, 1890); and a crop of short stories—covering a huge range of subjects—between 1891 and 1903.

By the turn of the century, Rabīndranāth had recognized the joys of colloquial speech and set about to consciously incorporate it into his writings. This was an important change of direction for Bengali literature, which had hitherto favored a stilted, formal mode of writing over the language of everyday speech. Rabīndranāth's journey to the earthy roots of his language was complemented at an ideological level by a rising patriotic consciousness. This new political awareness is exemplified in his epic collection of narrative poems, *Kathā o Kāhinī* (1900), and a collection of poems he put out the year after, *Naibedya.* In October 1905, the British administration, led by Lord Curzon, divided the province of Bengal into a western Hindu part and an eastern Muslim part. This was a direct result of the avowed divide-and-rule policy of the British government, geared toward nullifying the united momentum of the nationalist movement in Bengal. Almost immediately, the entire Bengali population burst into furious agitation. Rabīndranāth took an active part in the antipartition movement (although he was to withdraw from it later, disappointed with its increasingly Hindu chauvinistic character), and during this period he wrote his best patriotic poetry. But he was already ahead, with his work as an educator, of the political agendas pressed into action by the political parties. He established a school in Śantiniketan in 1901 and worked simultaneously on several other projects for the spread of education and elimination of blind orthodoxy.

In 1907, he started serializing a new novel—*Gorā* (The Fair One)—in *Prabāsī,* a renowned Bengali magazine. The antiorthodoxy and secular theme is proposed urgently in the very kernel of the plot; the hero is a young man, Gorā, who is the adopted son of Hindu parents and who is an orthodox Hindu himself without realizing that he was born of Catholic Irish parents. The novel is about Gorā's realization of the ineffectuality of orthodoxy and the liberation that can be obtained from a secularist view of the world. The novel was completed and published as a book in 1910. The ineffectuality of orthodoxy of any kind was a major theme with Rabīndranāth in this period. He explored the same issue, but in more general terms, in his next work, *Acalāyatan* (Unmovable, 1911), a play in which he ruthlessly criticized the repercussions of conservative social repression.

At around the same time, Rabīndranāth was also composing poetry of a very different kind. In 1910, he published a collection of poems that is better known to the English-reading world as *Gitanjali: Song Offerings.* The Bengali version of the same book, *Gītāñjalī,* is not the same as its English counterpart, which is a loose translation of the original poems along with some others interpolated from *Naibedya* (mentioned earlier) and *Kheyā* (another book of poems). The eight years that followed the failed partition of Bengal (1905) saw Rabīndranāth in the role of the dramatist in *Rājā* (The King, 1910) and *Ḍākghar* (The Post Office, 1912). In 1913, Rabīndranāth was awarded the Nobel Prize in literature, which secured his fame at an international level and effectively silenced his local critics, making him a national celebrity. Rabīndranāth's plays, however, were not particularly well received during his own lifetime, even after the Nobel Prize. They did not receive much more than some amateur attention.

Drama (1900–1926)

By the first decade of the twentieth century, a professional theater industry was flourishing in Calcutta (Beng. Kolkātā), and many plays were being written. Among the playwrights whose works filled the theaters during this period, the leading name was that of Girish Chandra Ghosh (Beng. Giriś Candra Ghoṣ [1844–1911]), who towered over the contemporary theatrical scene. He was not only one of the pioneering producers for the professional Bengali theater but also one of its greatest director-actor-regisseurs, an innovative designer, a lyricist-composer, and undoubtedly its first great playwright. His plays were imbued with a sense of deep social commitment that expressed itself both directly as well as metaphorically. In a career spanning over four decades, Girish wrote more than 40 plays—historical, mythological, social—and innumerable essays on theater and social issues. Besides his numerous contributions to Bengali theater, Girish gave Bengali poetic drama the gift of a resonant meter, commonly known as the "Gairiś" (the Bengali adjectival form of Girish) prosodic measure. He started his career with adaptations of already famous narrative and epic poems of the nineteenth century but soon achieved enough mastery over the dramatic form to write original plays. Writing copiously during the last quarter of the nineteenth century and the first decade of the twentieth, Girish Ghosh gave Bengali literature its first volume of masterful drama that reflected the Bengali taste for theater. The last decade of his life, also the first decade of the twentieth century, was probably one of the most prolific periods of Girish's career. During this period, he wrote two of his most dramaturgically accurate historical plays on the early days of British rule in Bengal—the serial plays *Sirāj-Ud-Daulā* (1905) and *Mir-Qāsim* (1906). In 1905, he also wrote the second of his 2 most celebrated social plays, *Balidān* (The Sacrifice). In 1907, he wrote *Chatrapati Śivājī*, a biographical play on the Mārāṭha king who daunted the mighty Mughals.

Among the other major playwrights writing at the turn of the century was Girish's friend and colleague Amṛtalāl Basu (1853–1929), also an actor-producer, whose forte was comedy and social satire. Among his notable achievements after 1900 are a Bengali adaptation of Molière's *The Miser* in 1900, as *Kṛpaṇer Dhan* (The Miser's Wealth), *Ādarśa Bandhu* (The Ideal Friend, 1900), and *Nabajauban* (Early Youth, 1914). Another contemporary of Girish was Dwijendralāl Rāy (1863–1913), who gave to Bengali theater some of its best patriotic plays. Rāy was also a great composer and lyricist, whose songs continue to be sung and released on albums. Two of his best plays are *Śājāhān* (1910), on the last days of the second to last Mughal emperor, who died in captivity, and *Candragupta* (1911), set in ancient India. The other notable playwright at this time was Kṣirodprasād Bidyābiṇod (1863–1927), who will be remembered for his highly popular Bengali version of *Alibābā* (1897), from the *one thousand and one Arabian Nights,* and his historical and mythological plays, which include *Baṅger Pratāpāditya* (1903) and *Naranārāyaṇ* (1926).

Prose (1900–1931)

On the prose front, a number of writers were producing thought-provoking work. Among them were Rāmendrasundar Tribedī (1864–1919), a professor of science, who was one of the most revered essayists of his time, considered second to none but Rabīndranāth. His extensive range of scholarship—from science, to religion, to philosophy, to linguistics—set him apart from his contemporaries. His major works include *Prakṛti* (Nature, 1896), *Jijñāsā* (Query,

1903), *Karmakathā* (Talks on Karma, 1913), and *Śabdakathā* (Talks on the Word, 1917). Akṣaykumār Maitreya (1861–1930) was a lawyer who doubled as a historian and contributed to *Sādhanā,* the journal Rabīndranāth edited (see earlier). His important works include *Sirājuddaulā* (1897), *Mirkāsim* (1904), and *Phiriṅgi Baṇik* (The European Merchants, 1922). The most important prose writer, after Rabīndranāth, during this period, however, was Prabhāt Kumār Mukhopādhyāya (Ang. Mukherjee/Mukerji [1873–1932]). He, too, was a lawyer who doubled as a writer. Under Rabīndranāth's encouragement, Mukhopādhyāya produced some of the best short stories the Bengali language has known. They are characterized by an acute sense of observation and an uncanny sense of humor. Among his major works are *Nabakathā* (New Tales, 1900), *Galpāñjali* (Story Offerings, 1913), and *Jāmātā Bābāji* (Dear Son-in-Law, 1931). Prabhāt Kumār Mukhopādhyāya also wrote some novels, *Ratnadīp* (The Jeweled Lamp, 1915) being the best known.

The second decade of the twentieth century was marked by the rise of perhaps the most loved novelist in Bengali literature, Śaratcandra Caṭṭopādhyāya (Ang. Chatterjee/ji [1876–1938]), who had started writing in 1903 but was not noticed until 1913, when he started writing regularly for periodicals like the *Jamunā, Sāhitya,* and *Bhāratbarṣa.* Drawing from his own experience, which was rich and varied, Śaratcandra wrote from the layperson's point of view, with no literary pretensions; and although he wrote in the formal Bengali (*sādhū-bhāṣā*), his prose was pedestrian and addressed his readers directly. As a result, his writing stands out, not so much for literary polish but for its genuine warmth of understanding and poignant realism. The persistent theme underlying almost all his novels is a deep and sincere sympathy for women and their inhuman exploitation in a patriarchal society. Consequently, we meet several female characters in Śaratcandra's novels who have shaken off social bondage, choosing the hazardous life of the outcast instead. Through his writing, Śaratcandra was responding to the rising consciousness of women's rights in his own society and forwarding the cause by participating in creating a base of public opinion in favor of suffering Bengali women. Śaratcandra's zeal for advancing women's rights was nothing short of the social thinker and political activist.

Although Śaratcandra's fame rests primarily on his novels, he also wrote short stories. Two of his best-known short stories are *Maheś* and *Abhāgīr Swarga.* Śaratcandra's works continue to be read even today by the Bengali reading public with the same enthusiasm with which they were first received. Prolific as he was, his best novels include *Debdās* (written 1901, published 1917), *Bindur Chele* (Bindu's Son, 1913), *Rāmer Sumati* (Ram's Return to Sanity, 1914), *Pariṇīta* (The Married Girl, 1914), *Birāj Bau* (Mrs. Birāj, 1914), *Pallī Samāj* (The Village Commune, 1916), *Śrikānta* (4 volumes, 1917, 1918, 1927, 1933), *Swāmī* (The Husband, 1918), *Gṛhadāha* (Burning the Home, 1919), *Denā-Pāonā* (Debts and Demands, 1923), and *Pather Dābī* (The Demand of the Road, 1926). The last mentioned was very different from the rest of Śaratcandra's corpus since its content was directly political, as a result of which it was proscribed by the British administration soon after publication. Almost all of Śaratcandra's novels have been staged, made into movies and television series, and translated into almost all Indian languages. However, his overt emotionalism, which spilled very often into the area of sentimentalism, has prevented Śaratcandra Caṭṭopādhyāya's works from winning sustained popularity in the West. In fact, some literary scholars have proposed, albeit arguably, that the innately Bengali character of his writing has prevented Śaratcandra's works from being successfully translated into English and other European languages.

Writing in Śaratcandra's footsteps were several novelists, among whom was Nirupamā Debī (1883–1951), a noted woman novelist, whose collection of short stories *Āleyā* (Will O' the Wisp, 1917) and more than a dozen novels secured her a place in the upper ranks of Bengali novelists. The very first novel she wrote, *Annapūrṇār Mandir* (Annapūrṇā's Temple, 1913), remains her best-known work. Her other important work, *Śyāmalī* (1919), about the awakening of a mentally challenged girl, was later turned into a stage play that received wide commercial success. The other woman novelist who cut ripples of controversy at around the same time was Śailabālā Ghoṣjāyā (1894–1973), who, like Nirupamā, was also doubling as a short story writer and novelist. She was a daring writer and braved subjects like interreligious relationships. Her first novel, *Śekh Āndu* (serialized 1915–17), was about the love between an educated Hindu girl and the Muslim chauffeur of her father. Śailabālā went on to publish several collections of short stories and some 24 novels.

Journals (1900–1919)

Literary journals have always held an important place in Bengali literature, not only by allowing writers to make their first appearances but also by providing the site for major debates and identifying new trends. We have already mentioned nineteenth-century journals that continued to serve as cultural forums for the Bengali literati—*Baṅgabāsī, Hitabādī,* and *Sādhanā.* In 1914, yet another journal, *Sabujpatra* (Green Leaf), came out under the stewardship of Pramatha Caudhurī (Ang. Chaudhuri/Choudhury), a lawyer who taught in the Law Department of the University of Calcutta and who had married a niece of Rabīndranāth. This journal, too, was initiated by Rabīndranāth. Caudhurī's incisive prose—lucid and thought-provoking—and the editorial choices he made strongly promoted the argument for the adoption of colloquial Bengali as the standard of writing as well. Pramatha Caudhurī wrote under the pseudonym of Bīrbal, the legendary courtier of the Mughal emperor Akbar, who was famous for his subversive wit and biting sarcasm. His important prose collections include *Bīrbaler Hālkhātā* (Bīrbal's Accounts, 1917) and *Cār-iyāri-kathā* (Tales of Four Friends, 1916).

Another major journal in the second decade of the twentieth century was the revitalized *Bhāratī,* which had been taken over by a younger group of writers. The most important prose writer to emerge from the pages of the new *Bhāratī* was Rabīndranāth's nephew, Abanindranāth Tagore (1871–1951). But Abanindranāth was more a peer for the *Bhāratī* group (he was the father-in-law of its editor, Matilāl Gaṇgopādhyāya [Ang. Ganguly]) than a product. He is better known as one of the pioneers of modern Indian art. His greatest contribution to Bengali literature lies in the large number of yarns he spun (and illustrated) for children, in ever so popular books like *Bhutpatrīr Deśe* (The Land of Ghosts and Goblins, 1915) and *Khātāñcir Khātā* (An Accountant's Journal, 1916). *Kṣīrer Putul,* his famous fairy-tale novella for children, continues to remain one of the best stories ever written for the young in the Bengali language. Abanindranāth also wrote some scholarly monographs and articles on women's folk rites in Bengal and their art, most notably *Bāṅglār Brata* (Folk Ritual Rhymes of Bengal, 1919).

The literary scene at this time was not confined to the Hindu Bengali community alone. There was a considerable amount of literary activity in the Calcutta-based Bengali Muslim community as well. The work of the Mohammedan Literary Society deserves to be mentioned, in this context, among the organizations that contributed to the literary fashions of this period. Also noteworthy were the contributions of publisher/editors like S. Wājed Āli and the journals *Mihir* and *Mohāmmadī.*

Poetry (1900–1927)

A major writer who emerged from the pages of *Bhāratī* was Satyendranāth Datta (Ang. Dutta/Dutt [1882–1922]). Datta's work in the second decade of the twentieth century presents a foil to the kind of poetry Rabīndranāth was producing at this time; Datta was more interested in experimenting with versification and prosody. Starting with *Benu O Bīṇā* (The Flute and the Lute) in 1906, where the influence of predecessors is clear, he produced more mature work in *Phuler Phasal* (The Crop of Flowers, 1911) and *Abhra-Ābir* (Mica and Vermilion Dust, 1916). The latter work is characterized by brave metrical experiments, unparalleled in Bengali poetry. Datta's metrical accomplishments opened up the formal possibilities of Bengali poetry, and he is fondly remembered as its "Metrical Wizard."

In general, the turn of the century was not a very productive time for Bengali poets. But among the few who wrote good poetry was Priyambadā Debī (1871–1935), whose work stands out prominently. Sukumār Sen, the literary historian, in writing about her, said, "Priyambadā's poems are redolent with the soft fragrance of a woman's heart; the tone is quiet, tender and subdued." (Sen 330). Writing mainly for the revived *Baṅgadarśan* (Viewing Bengal, edited by Srīṣ candra Majumdār), a late nineteenth-century literary journal, she also published collections of her poems, namely, *Renu* (1900), *Patralekhā* (1910), and *Aṇśu* (1927). Two other poets who need to be mentioned here as followers of Tagore are Rajanīkanta Sen (1865–1919) and Atulprasād Sen (1871–1938). However, since they were both primarily songwriters, as opposed to poets, it is predominantly in the shape of songs that their creations have endured in Bengali culture. Their songs continue to be performed and recorded by leading Bengali vocalists for commercial consumption.

Tagore (1913–41)

However, throughout this early period of the twentieth century, Rabīndranāth Tagore continued to dominate the Bengali literary scene. The Nobel Prize in 1913 had asserted his fame in the West as a mystical poet from the East, and Rabīndranāth himself fanned this rather partial view of his literary accomplishments for some time by continuing to write in that mystical-lyrical-religious fashion till 1914. The two works that reflected this continuing preoccupation with a spiritual view of the world were *Gītimālya* (Song Garland, 1914) and *Gītālī* (Songs, 1914); even the titles of the collections bear testimony to Rabīndranāth's continued allegiance to the *Gitanjali* frame of mind. In 1916, Rabīndranāth changed gears with *Balākā* (Swans), in which he used the traditional Bengali *payār* meter to express very different themes. In *Balākā,* Rabīndranāth replied to the youthful response the Indian nationalist movement had generated by welcoming the "new," which also called for the smashing of the old and the degenerate. He changed mode once again with the publication of his next volume of poems, *Palātakā* (Fugitive, 1918), which was intended to communicate at a more social level, voicing the frustrations of the oppressed.

Palātakā signaled Rabīndranāth's return to the humanist frame of mind. The short stories that he produced during this period, too, reflected this renewed engagement with social conditions and the plight of the downtrodden, especially women. His most important short story of this period is *Strīr Patra* (The Letter of a Wife, 1914). The story revolves around Mṛṇāl, a young housewife, who leaves her family and husband to protest the oppressive social system that had forced her sister, who was married to a lunatic, to take her own life.

At around the same time, in 1916, Rabīndranāth's novel *Caturaṅga* (The Quartet) was serialized in *Sabujpatra* (see earlier). The novel comprises four ostensibly disconnected episodes from the lives of four persons who control the destiny of the heroine. Immediately following *Caturaṅga* was *Ghare Bāire* (The Home and the World, 1915–16), also serialized in *Sabujpatra. Ghare Bāire* was written as a two-pronged ideological battleground where nationalist politics, on one hand, meets gender politics, on the other. In this work, Rabīndranāth goes back to the early days of the Indian nationalist movement, when all British goods were asked to be boycotted, notwithstanding the harm it wrought on local traders. One such nationalist demagogue, Sandīp, comes to visit his landowner friend, Nikhileś, for refuge. Nikhileś is a true liberal but does not believe in Sandīp's brand of nationalism, which he finds to be mere lip-service. He is, however, a strong believer in women's liberation and, going against the age-old Hindu custom, considers his wife Bimalā an individual on her own right and indoctrinates her with the same ideas. Sandīp, in order to fill both his lust and coffers, seduces Bimalā out of wedlock. Nikhileś, with full awareness of Bimalā's extramarital affair, continues to honor her freedom of choice. Finally, Sandīp's betrayal surfaces for both Bimalā and Nikhileś, who is killed while trying to rescue his villagers from the hands of the ultranationalists. This novel became highly controversial and enraged a number of nationalists. Artistically, too, it did not receive the acclaim that generally greeted Rabīndranāth's work. E. M. Forster allegedly called the novel "a boarding-house flirtation that masks itself in mystic and patriotic talk" (Zbavitel 1976, 266). The novel was made into a film by Satyajit Rāy (1985), which, too, received lukewarm praise. *Ghare Bāire* continues to baffle readers; one is not quite sure of its political intent. What is sure, however, is that Rabīndranāth, in 1916, was steadily drifting away from the mainstream of the nationalist campaign, moving toward an internationalist view of the human race.

In the same year, he started his travels to Japan and America, delivering lectures on nationalism and the evils of imperialism. But his emphasis continued to remain on the social ills of India, not its political movement that was fermenting to shake off the yoke of colonial bondage. Rabīndranāth was more interested in awakening the nation's "mind" than in a feverish brand of shortsighted nationalism. Although he did protest the 1919 Amritsar massacre by writing to the viceroy and declining the knighthood bestowed upon him by the British monarch, his eyes were set more on realizing his ideal of global sympathy and understanding, recognizing the common bonds between human beings from all over the world, "the spiritual unity of mankind" (Zbavitel 1976, 267). In May 1922, he officially founded the Vishwabharati (Beng. Biśwabhāratī) University at Śāntiniketan. The word "Vishwabharati/Biśwabhāratī" literally means "the world of/in India," Rabindranāth's vision.

In 1930, Rabīndranāth visited Soviet Russia and responded immediately with the epistolary collection *Rāśiār Ciṭhi* (Letters from Russia), where he openly recorded his positive impressions of the socialist system, comparing it with the colonial system of British India. The English translation of the book was promptly proscribed by the British government. Rabīndranāth's trip to Russia gave him a parameter to judge the sociopolitical conditions of his own country. It came as a confirmation of the ideas he had explored a few years earlier in his full-length poetic play, *Raktakarabī* (Red Oleanders, 1924), of the fall of authoritarian monarchies and the freedom march of the working class. In 1932, he rewrote a one-act play he had written in 1923 into a full-length play, *Kāler Jātrā,* where he once again identified the oppressed as the immediate saviors of civilization.

His subsequent political essays and speeches, too, from this point on, began to ring with a decidedly firmer anti-British, pro-socialist tone. In *Pariśeṣ,* too, Rabīndranāth took a stance in favor of the suffering millions, and the poems in this collection played the proverbial "still, sad music of humanity." Especially noteworthy in this collection is the narrative poem *Bāṁśī* (The Flute), where Rabīndranāth plays with a deceptive meter that reads like prose, despite its unorthodox but measured prosodic scheme. *Bāṁśī* is about a young Calcutta clerk who is even poorer than the lizard scaling his tenement walls. This singular poem, more than anything else, stands as the cornerstone of the modernist movement in Bengali poetry. The modernist element in Rabīndranāth's poetry revealed itself further in his next collection, *Punaśca* (Postscript, 1932), especially so in the "prose poem" *Sādhārāṇ Meye* (Ordinary Girl), where the female narrator in a letter to the novelist Śaratcandra Caṭṭopādhyāya (see earlier) implores him to write about an ordinary girl who "does not know French or German,/but who knows how to weep" (Zbavitel 1976, 270).

After *Punaśca,* Rabīndranāth revisited the world of novels for the last time with *Dui Bon* (Two Sisters, 1932), *Mālañca* (The Flower Garden, 1933), and *Cār Adhyāy* (Four Chapters, 1934). Of the three, the last brought Rabīndranāth back to the theme of the nationalist movement—this time, the terrorist movement—where he placed his protagonists, two lovers, both of whom are freedom fighters, amid the unavoidable contradictions inherent in any form of violent politics, the choices and sacrifices that have to be made. In 1935, Rabīndranāth published *Śeṣ Saptak* (The Last Sextet) and *Bīthikā* (The Flower Alley), both containing poems that took stock of the poet's life thus far—74 years. In the same year, Rabīndranāth published yet another collection of poems, this time in "free verse," entitled *Patrapūṭ* (Armful of Leaves), where he mixed his continuing look at his own life and creativity with a reflection on history and humanity. In 1937, Rabīndranāth fell seriously ill, but that did not stop him from working. He was back on the road by January 1938, when he published *Prāntik* (On the Borderline), where, as the title suggests, he was expressing his desire of drinking life to the lees. But in the last two poems of the collection, Rabīndranāth protested fascism. In the same year, he put out a second edition of *Patrapūṭ* with two additional poems, one of which, *Āphrikā* (Africa), was a direct invective against Western and fascist exploitation of the Dark Continent. Rabīndranāth was elected the president of the Indian Committee of the League against Fascism, also in 1937. In 1938 came *Seṁjuti* (Evening Lamp), Rabīndranāth's next collection of poems, where he was, yet again, thumbing self-critically through the pages of a very long and rich life. At this time, he also became an active prose writer, moving back and forth among essays, speeches, and publishable epistles. But the poetic productions continued unhindered through thick and thin. In 1940 came *Nabajātak* (The Newborn), which anticipated the next generation, the nameless "newborn," whom Rabīndranāth was inviting to take over. He put some other minor poems written between 1938 and 1940 in a separate collection entitled *Sānāi* (Shehnai). The year 1940 was also significant because of Rabīndranāth's final formal experiments with the short story genre in the three pieces of *Tin Saṅgī* (Three Companions). In the same year, he also wrote an autobiographical account of his childhood for his younger readers, *Chelebelā* (Boyhood). Rabīndranāth fell ill again in September 1940, but in early 1941 he was publishing his next collection of poems, *Rogaśayyāy* (In Illness), followed by a second one within a couple of months,

Arogya (Reconvalescence). In May 1941, the entire Indian nation observed Rabīndranāth Tagore's 80th birthday, and he himself celebrated the occasion with two more books, *Janmadine* (Birthday) and *Galpasalpa* (Chitchat). On August 7, 1941, Rabīndranāth breathed his last. He had, in *Janmadine*, etched his final messages for the world, although the posthumously published collection *Śeṣ Lekhā* (Last Writings) actually carried his few last poems. He left his epitaph in one of the poems of *Janmadine*, where he called himself "a poet of the world" and invited the new poet "who is near to the soil" to be the "kinsman" of the voiceless who would "find glory in your glory."

The Kallol Generation (1923–47)

Rabīndranāth's new poets, the bearers of his mantle, were, indeed, singing for the downtrodden, and some of them had already been writing during his lifetime. The decade between the two world wars especially saw in Bengali literature the rise of an awareness of trends in world literature, coupled with a committed sociopolitical consciousness among writers in the wake of the first surge of the noncooperation movement and the disillusionment that came after World War I. Perhaps the most important writer during this decade was Kāzi Nazrul Islām (see later). Nazrul, although politically committed, was not a scholar-writer who responded to the literary fashions of the Western "modernist" schools. But a host of other writers, most of them belonging to the same generation, did respond to Western "modernism" and started expressing themselves through several journals, engaging in healthy debates on the state of Bengali literature.

Journals

A journal culture had developed from the nineteenth century in Bengali literary circles, some examples of which we have seen. They always played a major role in Bengali literature when it came to deciding which way the literature was heading. When *Kallol* (Stormy Current), the literary journal, was founded in 1923 by Gokulcandra Nāg (1895–1925) and Dineshrañjan Dās (1888–1941), Bengali literature was a crossroads of conflict where the "traditionalist" camp, consisting of older writers, faced the "progressive" pro-modernist younger writers. The young and unknown writers of *Kallol*, by their unorthodox literary means and products, raked the ire of the conservative/traditionalist camp led by Aśok Caṭṭopādhyāya and Sajanīkanta Dās (1900–62), who replied with their own journal, *Śaṇibārer Ciṭhi* (The Saturday Post), founded in 1924. A virulent debate ensued between the "progressive" and "traditional" camps, and soon other journals were founded to bolster the Kallol camp, namely, *Kālī O Kalam* (Pen and Ink, 1927), edited by Premendra Mitra, Muralidhar Basu, and Śailajānanada Mukhopādhyāya from Calcutta, and Nareś-candra Sengupta and Buddhadeb Basu's *Pragati* (Progress, 1928) from Dhākā. The debate got so rough that Rabīndranāth, the only person respected by both camps, was forcibly pulled into its vortex: which way should Bengali literature go? In March 1927, Rabīndranāth presided over two meetings between the warring camps. He proposed a compromise, but not to the satisfaction of the "progressive" camp. More intellectual repartee followed in the literary journals until, finally, Rabīndranāth silenced all by his formally innovative novel *Śeṣer Kabitā* (1928) and the timely creation of *gadya kabitā* (free prosaic verse, a close approximation of vers libre), which culminated in the collection entitled *Pariśeṣ* (The End, 1932).

The influence of the Kallol generation had led to the birth of three more journals that were destined to have a major impact on Bengali poetry: Sudhindranāth Datta's *Paricay* (Acquaintance, 1931), *Purbāśā* (Hope of the East), edited by Sañjay Bhaṭṭācārya (Ang. Bhattacharya), and Buddhadeb Basu's *Kabitā* (Poetry, 1935).

Poetry

Jatīndranāth Sengupta (1887–1958) and Mohitlāl Majumdār (1882–1952) were two important poets who consciously tried to be different from Tagore. Amiya Cakrabartī (1901–86) developed under the wings of Rabīndranāth as his secretary, and traces of Tagorean poetry can be seen in his first collection, *Khaśṛā* (Rough Draft, 1938). But Cakrabartī eventually developed his own voice, which was heard in his later books—*Pārāpār* (Crossovers, 1953) and *Pālābadal* (Change of Time, 1955). Samar Sen (1916–86) was one of the leading figures in the new poetry movement in the Kallol generation (see earlier) who, however, gave up writing poetry altogether but greatly contributed to the development of non-Tagorean Bengali poetry. His two most important collections are *Kayekṭi Kabitā* (A Few Poems, 1937) and *Tin-puruṣ* (Three Generations, 1944). Sudhindranāth Datta (1901–60), also the editor of *Paricay,* was close to Rabīndranāth in personal life, although his poetry was radically and consciously different from that of the maestro. It was deeply personal, but rich with linguistic inventions and neologisms in its effort to be free of clichés and hackneyed poetic norms. Datta was not prolific and published only a few, though important, books. His best works include *Arkesṭrā* (Orchestra, 1935), *Uttarphālgunī* (The Northerlies, 1940), and *Saṅbarta* (Cataclysmic Clouds, 1953). Buddhadeb Basu (1908–74) was not only the editor of *Kabitā,* but also a noted poet himself who ventured out into the world of prose, drama, and scholarship with equal aplomb. His best poetical works include *Kaṅkābatī* (1937) and *Damayantī* (1943). Among his plays the best known is *Tapaswī O Taraṅginī* (The Hermit and Taraṅginī, 1967). He also penned numerous short stories, novels, and scholarly essays on a variety of literary matters. Among the other Kallol generation writers, Premendra Mitra (1904–88), who was coeditor of *Kālī-O-Kalam* (see earlier), was a literateur of considerable versatility and also worked in the broadcast and film world. His poetry, however, was relatively free of the complexities that marked his modernist compatriots. Among his verse collections are *Prathamā* (The First, 1932), *Samrāṭ* (The Emperor, 1940), and *Sāgar Theke Pherā* (Return from the Sea, 1956).

The most prominent member of the Kallol generation, however, was the poet Jibanānanda Dāś (1899–1954). Though not recognized very much in his own lifetime, Jibanānanda Dāś has come to be regarded as probably the most important Bengali poet since Rabīndranāth. Starting tentatively with *Jharā Pālak* (Cast-off Feathers, 1928), he soon severed his ties with traditional Bengali prosody and began to play with different, highly original modes of poetic expression. His experimentations with metaphors—drawn out of the natural world and interwoven with shreds and dregs ripped out of his own unconscious and reconfigured in an incredible maze of images—conjure a rare, mystifying beauty that holds the reader in thrall. Jibanānanda's yearning for a better world lurked wistfully, but surely, behind the ghastly images he portrayed in his phantasmagoric rendition of the contemporary; it is the same wish for better tidings that enlivened his impressionistic pen sketches of Bengal's natural splendors, which he adored with almost pantheistic passion. Jibanānanda Dāś was a reclusive man and did not publish much, but what he did allow to appear in print comes down to us as, undoubtedly, some of the finest verses ever composed in Indian, if not world, literature. After *Jharā Pālak,* Jibanānanda published only four more collections of poetry: *Dhūsar Pāṇḍulipi* (The Faded Manuscript, 1936), *Baṇalatā Sen* (1942), *Mahāpṛthibī* (The Great Earth, 1944), and *Sātṭi Tārār Timir* (The Darkness of the Seven Stars, 1948). He died untimely in a road accident, at the early age of 55, and Bengali literature lost one of its most original poets.

Probably the most important poet in the period immediately following Jibanānanda Dāś is Biṣṇu De (Ang. Dey [1909–82]), although both are of the same generation. A professor of English by profession, De freely incorporated his study of Western literature into the mosaic of his poetry. Although a Marxist, his poetry stayed away from the slogan-based, party-line kind of propagandist writing. Heavily inspired by Pound, Yeats, Eliot, and the Greeks, the sophistication of Biṣṇu De's poetry rested mainly on complex imagery and references to obscure worlds and lost civilizations. Among his several volumes of poetry are *Ūrbasī O Arṭemis* (Urbasi and Artemis, 1933), *Smṛti Sattā Bhabiṣyat* (Remembrance, Self, Future, 1963), and *Saṅgbād Mūlata Kābya* (News Is Essentially Poetry, 1969). His major prose work is a collection of essays on literature, *Sāhityer Bhabiṣyat* (The Future of Literature, 1952). Most of the poets of the Kallol generation lived on to pursue their careers well into the 1960s and some into the 1970s.

Prose

Not all writers from the Kallol generation were poets. Premendra Mitra, whose poetic works we have discussed, is better known in the Bengali literary circuit as a short story writer, as the creator of the inimitable Ghaṇādā—the Bengali Münchhausen—whose imaginary flights of fancy continue to fascinate both the young and the young-at-heart. Among his notable novels and short story collections are *Pañcaśar* (Five Arrows, 1929) and *Kuyāśā* (Mist, 1938). His short story "Janaika Kāpuruṣer Kāhinī" was made into a short film by Satyajit Rāy. "Telenāpotā Ābiṣkār," another of Mitra's acclaimed short stories, was turned into a successful Hindi feature film, *Khanḍhar,* by Mrinal Sen. Manīṣ Ghaṭak (1902–79), who wrote under the pseudonym of Jubanāśva (Young Horse), was another important member of the Kallol generation, although he did not write much. He is best known for his collection of short stories—*Paṭ aldāngār Pāṁcālī* (The Ballads of Paṭaldāṅgā)—which has been identified by scholars as an emblematic document of the literary trend of the age. Maṇīndra Rāy (1919) is another major poet of the 1940s. His major work is the collection *Mohinī Āṛāl* (The Bewitching Veil, 1967).

Prose (1929–Present)

We need to return to an earlier period to trace the development of Bengali prose after Śaratcandra Caṭṭopādhyāya. The most important fiction writer in Bengali literature after Śaratcandra was Bibhūtibhūṣaṇ Bandyopādhyāya (1899–1950), who, in a short life span, produced some of the most remarkable Bengali novels. His works evince more psychological depth than can be seen in Śaratcandra's writings. Bibhūtibhūṣaṇ will be best remembered for his Apu novels, *Pather Pāṁcāli* (Song of the Road, 1929) and its sequel, *Aparajita* (Undefeated, 1932), a fictionalized version of the author's own life. *Pather Pāṁcāli,* especially, paints a poignant picture of rural life and the journey of a poor Brahman (Ang. Brahmin) family through the eyes of a child protagonist. The two novels were turned into the famous Apu-trilogy films by Satyajit Rāy in the 1960s. Among his other works are *Āraṇyak* (The Wild, 1938), *Ādarśa Hindu Hoṭel* (The Ideal Hindu Hotel, 1940), and *Anubartan* (Recycle, 1942). He also wrote books for children and numerous short stories.

Two of Bibhūtibhūṣaṇ's lesser contemporaries were Acintyakumār Sengupta (1903–76) and Śailajānanda Mukhopādhyāya (1900–1976). Although Sengupta was very prolific and popular, he did not always succeed artistically. His best works include *Bede* (The Gypsy, 1928) and *Prācīr O Prāntar* (The Wall and the Distance, 1932). He is well known for a host of short stories that he wrote over a protracted writing career. Mukhopādhyāya's fame rests mainly on his sympathetic depiction of the life of the coal miners in his home district of Burdwan (Beng. Bardhamān), whom he had observed very closely from childhood. His treatment is often realistic, and the stories tragic. His best-remembered works include two short story collections, *Kaylākuṭhī* (The Coal Miner's Office, 1930) and *Din-Majur* (Day Laborer, 1932), and the novels *Jhoṛo Hāoā* (Stormy Wind, 1923) and *Ṣolo-Ānā* (Sixteen Annas, 1925).

Among the fiction writers who wrote their best works during the political transition period of India from British rule to independence (1947) are Sañjay Bhaṭṭācārya (1909–69), who wrote in the style of the "novel of ideas," and Jagadīś Gupta (1886–1957). Gupta is also regarded by some historians as a member of the Kallol group. He is also the precursor of one of the most prominent novelists of this period, Māṇik Bandyopādhyāya (1910–56). Bandyopādhyāya was an active political worker from East Bengal, and his work is imbued with impressions of the natural surroundings and the people of that region. Nature and human beings are shown to face each other as both adversaries and allies in his famous and mysterious novel *Padmā Nadīr Mājhi* (The Boatman of the River Padmā, 1936, English in 1948). Māṇik will also be remembered for his *Putulnācer Itikathā* (The Story of the Puppet Dance, 1936), also on the subject of nature's unfair clashes with human beings, who are themselves deeply entrenched in the inescapable complexities of their own psychophysical desires. Māṇik Bandyopādhyāya also wrote several short stories, among which are *Prāgaitihāsik* (Prehistoric, 1937) and *Āj-Kāl-Parśur Galpa* (Stories of Today, Tomorrow and the Day After, 1946). A brilliant film version of *Padmā Nadīr Mājhi* was made by Gautam Ghosh (Beng. Ghoṣ) in 1992.

A contemporary of Māṇik Bandyopādhyāya was Tārāśaṅkar Bandyopādhyāya (no relation), who hailed from Bīrbhūm, a district in West Bengal, and also used the familiar locale of his home as a setting for his stories. Like most Bengali fiction writers, Tārāśaṅkar wrote short stories as well as novels. His novels are marked with a remarkable clarity of expression, a keen sense of drama, and a heartfelt sympathy for rural folk. The last explains why the best of his stories and novels are set in village surroundings. His noted novels are *Dhātrī Debatā* (The Nursing Deity, 1939), *Kālindī* (1940), *Gaṇadebatā* (Dieux Populi, 1942), and *Hāṁsuli Bāṁker Upakathā* (The Legend of the Hāṁsuli Bend, 1947). Almost all of his novels have been turned into commercially successful films. His short story ''Jalsāghar'' (The Music Room, 1937), a touching tale of the last days of an impoverished aristocrat, was turned into an acclaimed film by Satyajit Rāy.

Nārāyaṇ Gaṅgopādhyāya (1918–70) was another noted fiction writer who emerged at around the same time as Tārāśaṇkar and Māṇik Bandyopādhyāya. Although he, too, started with rural life as his primary material, very soon he was dealing with life in metropolitan Calcutta. Two of his important novels, out of dozens, are *Upanibeś* (The Colony, 1943) and *Megher Upar Prāsād* (Castles upon Clouds, 1963). He also wrote several short stories and one-act plays for adults and children. Another major writer from this period is Narendranāth Mitra (1916–75), whose works include *Bini Sutor Mālā* (1962) and *Anāgata* (1972), a collection of short stories.

Rajśekhar Basu (1880–1960), mainly a philologist and a major translator of ancient literary masterpieces of India, is better known among Bengali readers as Paraśurām, a pseudonym he used for his creative writing that was predominantly satirical. One of his well-known stories, *Mahāpuruṣ,* about an amateur sleuth who uncovers a holy man's fraud, was made into a short film by Satyajit Rāy. Among his major translation works are the *Rāmāyana* and the *Mahābhārata,* along with Kālidāsa's famous Saṅskṛt poem ''Meghadūta'' into Bengali prose.

Śibrām Cakrabartī (1909–80) was one of the most popular humorists Bengali literature has known, along with Syed Mujtabā Āli (1904–74). The most dearly remembered humorist in Bengali literature, however, is Sukumār Rāy (1887–1923), who is the progenitor of the nonsense-rhyme genre in Bengali. His famous book of nonsense poems, *Ābol-Tābol* (Gibber-Gabber, 1923), continues to be one of the first books read to a Bengali child. Sukumār Rāy also wrote several other humorous tales and plays and was the editor of *Sandeś,* a magazine for children founded by his father, Upendra Kiśor Rāycaudhurī (1863–1915). Sukumār Rāy was the father of Satyajit Rāy, the filmmaker, whose literary works are discussed later.

Bengali prose literature has always boasted a high output in prose productions of all standards throughout the twentieth century. The legacy of Rabīndranāth, Śaratcandra, Bibhūtibhūṣaṇ, and Māṇik Bandyopādhyāya has been carried forward bravely by forthcoming generations. Among the writers who have carried the Bengali prose tradition forward, besides those discussed earlier, there are many whose works cannot be discussed here for lack of space, but we can mention a few and some of their notable works. Among the older writers, predominantly novelists and short story writers, who continue to write or have passed away only recently are Annadāśakar Rāy (1904), Jarāsandha (1904), Jājābar (1909), Satīnāth Bhāduṛi (1906–65) (*Jāgarī* [The Vigil, 1965] and *Digbhrānta* [Lost, 1966]), Kamal Kumār Majumdār (1915–79) (*Antarjalī Jātrā* [The Final Passage, 1962] and *Nim Annapūrṇā* [1965]), Bibhūtibhūṣaṇ Mukhopādhyāya (1896–1987), Prabodhkumār Sānyāl (1907–83), Subodh Ghoṣ (1909–80), Balāicāṁd Mukhopādhyāya (1899–1979), who wrote under the pen name of Baṇaphul, Manoj Basu (1901–79) (*Bhūli Nāi* [Haven't Forgotten, 1943] and *Jaljaṅgal* [Rivers and Forests, 1951]), Gopāl Hāldār (1902–93), Śaradindu Bandyopādhyāya (1899–1970), who is best known for his detective and semihistorical novels, Bimal Mitra (1912) (*Sāheb Bibi Golām* [King, Queen and Jester, 1953]), Śaktipada Rājguru, and Aśutoṣ Mukhopādhyāya (1920). Two other major novelists from this period are Dhūrjaṭiprasād Mukhopādhyāy (1894–1961) and Adwaita Mallabarman. Of the two, Mallabarman died prematurely but will be remembered for his singular work *Titās Ekṭi Nadīr Nām* (Titās Is the Name of a River, 1962), brilliantly filmed in the early 1970s by Ṛtwik Ghaṭak.

One writer who has to be set apart from this group in Samareś Basu (1923–89), generally referred to as the successor of Māṇik Bandyopādhyāya. Basu, also hailing from the leftist bloc of Bengali prose writers, has written prolifically, moving freely between rural and urban milieus, his subject the oppressed lower and middle classes. The tautness of his prose, its unforgiving realism, dramatic plots, and boldness in portraying sexual relationships have made Basu one of the foremost fiction writers in Bengali literature. His major works include *Gaṅgā* (1957), *Bibar* (The Chasm, 1966), *Bi ṭi Roḍer Dhāre* (On the Side of the B. T. Road, 1953), *Joārbhāṁṭā* (Ebb and Tide, 1960), *Prajāpati* (The Butterfly, 1967), *Pāṛ* (The Crossing, 1978), and *Dekhi Nāi Phire* (Haven't Turned to Look Back, 1988). Basu also wrote under the pen name of Kālkūṭ, producing semi-mythological novels like *Amṛta Kumbher Sandhāne* (In Search of the Nectar of Immortality, 1971) and *Śāmba* (1978), the latter being a fictive biography of the son of Kṛṣṅa. He was also a prolific master of the short story genre. A number of his short stories and novels have been turned into films and plays.

Among the older contemporary prose writers who started in the 1960s and are still writing, the most noteworthy figures are Sunīl Gaṅgopādhyāya (1934) and Śaṅkar (Maṇiśaṅkar Bandyopādhyāya (1933). Gaṅgopādhyāya, who also doubles as a poet, continues to write prolifically and is one of the most popular writers of today. His novels are set predominantly in urban, middle-class environs. He also writes under the pseudonym of Nīlalohit (Blue-Blooded). His major works include *Araṇyer Dinrātri* (Days and Nights of the Forest, 1966), *Pratidwandī* (The Adversary, 1970), *Arjun* (1978), and *Sei Samay* (Those Times, 1980). Of these four, the first two were made into films by Satyajit Rāy. Śaṅkar commands the same popularity that Gangopādhyāya does, if not more, and has also written novels that continue to be best-sellers. His best-known works are *Cauraṅgī* (196?), *Nibeditā Risārc Lyāboraṭāri* (Nibeditā Research Laboratory, 1966), *Sīmābaddha* (Ltd., 1971), *Jana Araṇya* (The Human Jungle, 1977), and *Marubhūmi* (The Desert, 1978, sequel to the preceding). *Sīmābaddha* and *Jana Araṇya* were made into feature films by Satyajit Rāy. Satyajit Rāy (1922–92) himself was an accomplished prose writer. Although he always called himself a filmmaker first, the lucid simplicity of his prose, the clarity of his thought, his characterization, and his adept incorporation of filmic details have earned him a spot among the best prose writers in Bengali. His greatest creation is the character of Pheludā, the detective, and his endearing cohorts Topśe and Jaṭāyu. He will also be remembered for his original screenplays and science fiction (especially the diaries of Professor Śaṅku)—both of which are relatively underexplored genres in Bengali literature—and *Sandeś* (see earlier), the childrens' magazine he edited after his father and grandfather. The authors previously listed are known primarily for their association with leading commercial publishing houses. Sunīl Gaṅgopādhyāya, for example, is known for his longtime professional association with the Ānanda Bazār Patrika Group (of whom he is an employee), which, as one of the largest newspaper and magazine publishing houses in India, with its numerous newspapers, periodicals (English, Bengali, and Hindi), and a subsidiary book publishing concern, has come to dominate the Bengali book market at a commercial level. Besides Gaṅgopādhyāya, the group has, over the years, also employed many other prominent writers in editorial positions for its numerous publications. Writers who have worked or continue to work for Ānanda Bazār include poets Nirendranāth Cakrabartī (see later), Śakti Caṭṭopādhyāya (see later), Śyāmal Kānti Dās, and Jay Goswāmī (see later) and prose writers like Santoṣ Kumār Ghoṣ, Ramāpada Caudhurī (1922), Śīrṣendu Mukhopādhyāya (1936) (*Ghūṇpokā* [The Woodworm]), Sunīl Basu, Sañjīb Caṭṭopādhyāya (*Śwetpātharer Ṭebil* [The Marble Table]), Gour Kiśor Ghoṣ, and Śekhar Basu. Many other authors have enjoyed commercial success through publishing with the Ānanda Bazār Group. Popular authors like

Satyajit Rāy and Samareś Majumdār (*Dour* [The Run], *Kālbelā* [Latter Day], *Uttarādhikār* [Inheritance]), for example, mostly appeared first in Ānanda Bazār periodicals, or special issues thereof, before appearing as books from Ānanda Publishers. However, the Bengali intellectual world has come to regard the role of this publishing group more as an agent of commercializing hegemony than an outfit that has genuinely contributed to the advancement of Bengali literature, in general. Many important writers continue to survive outside the Ānanda Bazār ambit.

Other major prose writers, writing both for Ānanda and otherwise, include Amiyabhūṣaṇ Majumdār, Bimal Kar, Jyotirīndra Nandī, Sandīpan Caṭṭopādhyāya, Debeś Rāy (*Jajāti* [1963] and *Tistāpārer Bṛttānta* [Tales from the Banks of the Tistā, 1990]), Dīpendranath Bandyopādhyāya, Nanī Bhaumik, Guṇamay Mānnā, Śyāmal Gaṅgopādhyāya (*Śāhājādā Dārāśuko,* Vols. 1 and 2, 1991), Nimāi Bhaṭṭācārya, Mati Nandī, Baren Gaṅgopādhyāya, Saiyad Mustāfā Sirāj, Asīm Rāy, Bāṇī Basu, Atīn Bandyopādhyāya, and Ābul Bāśār, among many others. Other writers who have written or continue to write in an antiestablishment vein are Subimal Mitra, Udayan Ghoṣ, Jyotsnāmay Ghoṣ, Malay Rāy Caudhurī, Utpalkumār Basu, Sabyasācī Sen, Swapnamay Cakrabartī, Jayanta Joādār, and others.

Among the women prose writers who have made a major contribution to the genre are Āśāpūrṇā Debī (1909), Mahāśwetā Debī (1926), Maitreyī Debī (1914–88), and Līlā Majumdār (1908). Āśāpūrṇā Debī is known for her remarkably perceptive and intimate study of the role of the woman in a patriarchal, middle-class milieu, best represented in her semiautobiographical trilogy—*Pratham Pratisruti* (The First Promise), *Sūbarṇalatā,* and *Bakul-Kathā* (Bakul's Story). Daughter of the Kallol generation writer Manīś Ghaṭak (see earlier), Mahāśwetā Debī has contributed to Bengali prose writing with her extensive work on the subaltern aboriginal peoples of Bengal and adjacent Bihār. Her noteworthy works in this area are *Araṇyer Adhikār* (The Rights of the Forest, 1978) and *Coṭṭi Muṇḍā Ebaṅg Tār Tīr* (Coṭṭi Muṇḍā and His Arrows, 1981). She has also written extensively on the urban situation, best represented by *Hājār Curāśir Mā* (Mother of 1084, 1986), which was also made into a play, and short stories like "Stanydāyinī" (Breast-Giver, 1977) and "Rudāli" (Weepers, 1980). Maitreyī Debī is best known for her semiautobiographical novel *Na Haṇyate* (It Does Not Die, 1975) and her illuminating reminiscences on Tagore. Līlā Majumdār has written extensively for children and is currently the editor of *Sandeś* (see earlier), one of the oldest magazines for children in West Bengal. Among other major women prose writers are Pratibhā Basu, from the older generation, and Nabanitā Deb-Sen, who is also a poet (see later), from the younger.

Poetry (1950–Present)

Contemporary Bengali poetry, too, like its prose counterpart, spreads itself over the older post-Kallol group of writers and a new crop of younger poets.

Among the older generation are Subhaṣ Mukhopādhyāya (1919), the erstwhile champion of Marxist politics among Bengali poets, who continues to write and inspire younger poets. His important collections are *Padātik* (Foot Soldier, 1940), *Jata Dūrei Jāi* (As Far As I Wander, 1962), *Kāl Madhumās* (It's Spring Tomorrow, 1966), and *Ei Bhāi* (Hey Brother, 1970). Aruṇ Mitra (1909) is the other senior poet who is still writing. His major books include *Prantarekhā* (The Borderline, 1943), *Mañcer Bāire* (Off-Stage, 1970), and *Śudhu Rāter Śabda Nay* (Not Just the Sound of the Night, 1978). Other poets of the same generation who must be mentioned are Magalācaraṇ Caṭṭopādhyāya (1920), Birendra Caṭ ṭopādhyāya (1919–87), Nareś Guha (1921), Jagannāth Cakrabartī (1924–89), Rām Basu (1925), Sukānta Bhaṭṭācārya (1926–47), the talented poet who died very young, and, Binay Majumdār (*Phire Eso, Cākā* [Come Back, Cākā], 1962).

Śaṇkha Ghoṣ (1932) rose to prominence as a poet from the late 1960s, although he was writing since the mid-1950s. Today, he is regarded as one of the greatest poets to be writing in the Bengali language and continues to exert an abiding influence on the younger generation of poets. His undisguised antiauthoritarian stance and the distilled, laconic quality of his poetry, its economy of utterance, have made him one of the most respected poets in contemporary Bengali literature. Ghoṣ's important collections are *Dinguli Rātguli* (Days and Nights, 1956), *Mūrkha Baṛo, Sāmājik Nay* (A Fool He Is, Not Social, 1974), *Tumi To Teman Gaurī Nao* (You Are Not the Gaurī I Thought You Were, 1978), *Pāṁjare Dāṁṛer Śabda* (Sound of Oars in the Ribs, 1980), and *Mukh Ḍheke Jāy Bijñāpane* (Advertisements Cover the Face, 1984). Śaṅkha Ghoṣ has also written essays and books on aesthetics and literature and is a revered scholar on Rabīndranāth, besides being an acclaimed translator of poems and plays.

His adventurous experiments with language, style, and complexity of images have made Śakti Caṭṭopādhyāya (1934) one of the foremost Bengali poets to have emerged in the post-Jibanānanda era. His major books include *Dharmeo Ācho Jirāpheo Āche* (In Religion, in Giraffes Too, 1972), *Hemanter Araṇye Āmi Postmyān* (Postman in the Autumnal Forest, 1977), *Mānuṣ Baṛa Kāṁdche* (Mankind Is Weeping Too Much, 1978), and *Jete Pāri Kintu Kena Jābo?* (I Can Go, But Why Should I?, 1982). The other senior poet we need to mention, before moving to the younger generation, is Nīrendranāth Cakrabartī (1924), whose major works are collected in *Andhakār Bārānda* (The Dark Veranda, 1954), *Kolkātār Jīśu* (The Christ of Calcutta, 1970), and *Ulaṅga Rājā* (The Emperor's Clothes, 1971). Cakrabartī has also been the editor of *Ānandamelā*, a leading magazine for children. Sunīl Gaṅgopādhyāya, whose contributions as a prose writer we have discussed earlier, is also a major poet. His important poetic works include *Bandī Jege Ācho?* (Prisoner, Are You Awake?, 1969), *Haṭhāt Nīrār Janye* (Suddenly for Nīrā, 1978), and *Sonār Mukuṭ Theke* (From the Golden Crown, 1982). Special mention needs to be made here of their biweekly cultural journal, *Deś* (published by the Ānanda Bāzār Group), which has been a major outlet for poets and prose writers in Bengal ever since it was founded in the 1930s.

Among the important writers who started their careers in the late 1960s or 1970s and continue to write are Alokrañjan Dāśgupta (1933), Tārāpada Rāy (1936), Amitābha Dāśgupta (1935), Praṇabendu Dāśgupta (1937), Śamsul Haq, Kabirul Islām, Pūrnendu Patrī (also a leading artist and filmmaker), Samarendra Sengupta, Sunīl Basu, Saratkumār Mukhopādhyāya, Buddhadeb Dāśgupta (also a leading filmmaker), Aśis Sānyāl, Siddheśwar Sen (1926), Ratneśwar Hājrā, Maṇibhūṣaṇ Bhaṭṭacārya, Partha Pratim Kāñjilāl, and Bhāskar Cakrabartī. Among the leading women poets from the same generation are Kabitā Sinha (1931), Sādhanā Mukhopādhyāya, Bijayā Mukhopādhyāya, Debārati Mitra, Ketakī Kuśārī-Dyson (1940), and Nabanītā Deb-Sen (1938). Kuśārī-Dyson and Deb-Sen (see earlier) are also prose writers and scholars of renown. Ketakī Kuśārī-Dyson is the most recent translator of Tagore's poetry into English (*I Won't Let You Go,* 1992).

Among the younger poets who are currently writing in West Bengal, the first name that demands attention is that of Jay Goswāmī (1954), whose daring and commanding play with words and brave infusion of colloquial Calcutta street jargon into poetry have already earned him a revered place in Bengali poetry. His poems are vibrant with unusual metaphysical imagery that is adeptly colluded with a masterful manipulation of prosodic possibilities. Among his major works to date are *Pratnajīb* (Archaic Organism, 1978), *Unmāder Pāṭhakram* (Syllabi for the Deranged, 1986), *Bhūtum Bhagabān* (Bhūtum, the God, 1988), and *Ghumiecho Jhāupātā?* (Asleep Are You, Fern Leaf?, 1989). Besides Goswāmī, two other poets who have been using a postmodernist diction in Bengali poetry are Añjan Sen and Amitābha Gupta. Among the other younger poets to reckon with are Jaideb Basu, Mṛdul Dāśgupta, Pārtha Pratīm Kañjilāl, Mahuā Caudhurī, Bhāskar Cakrabartī, and Soumya Dāśgupta. Several of the previously mentioned new-generation poets of West Bengal have consciously chosen not to publish their works with the Ānanda Bāzār Group publications (see earlier), which they feel have monopolized the literary scene and try to regulate the direction of Bengali literature according to vested political interests. Instead, these poets have gone to the numerous little magazines published in and around Calcutta, the leading ones among which are *Anuśṭup, Prama, Paricay, Jijñāsā, Kourab,* and *Kabitīrtha.* These magazines are also the main outlet for nonfictional prose writing in Bengali before their appearance in the book form.

Drama (1940–Present)

Drama in West Bengal has always lacked the fertility enjoyed by its counterparts in prose and poetry. After the late nineteenth- and early twentieth-century outburst of activity (see earlier), dramatic writing in Bengal petered out into a sorry state of mediocrity until it was revived during the 1940s at the behest of the Indian People's Theatre Association (IPTA—the cultural wing of the Communist Party of India), which encouraged several playwrights like Bijan Bhaṭṭācārya (1907–77) and Tulsī Lāhiṛī (1897–1959) to write new plays in the realistic mode that depicted the lives of the downtrodden and inaugurated what would eventually become the New Drama movement. Bhaṭṭācārya wrote *Jabānbandī* (The Statement) and *Nabānna* (New Harvest) in 1944, both of which had considerable impact on the Bengali theatergoers. Lāhiṛī wrote *Pathik* (Traveler, 1949) and *Cheṁṛā Tār* (The Broken String, 1950). In the wake of IPTA's work, in the late 1950s and early 1960s, several theater groups were born and launched, what is now identified as the Group Theatre movement, which, in its turn, took the New Drama movement to different pastures and updated Bengali theater with what was happening in the West. New Drama, however, did not produce as many original playwrights, since it was mainly interested in bringing the best of Western theater—Ibsen, Chekhov, Pirandello, Brecht, Wesker, Miller, and others—to the Bengali audience than creating its own. But the playwrights who copiously adapted foreign plays also wrote some significant original plays. For example, Śambhu Mitra (1915), who adapted Ibsen and translated Sophocles for the first time in Bengali, wrote *Ṭerodyāktil* (Pterodactyl) and *Cāṁdbaṇiker Pālā* (Cāṁdbaṇik's Play); Ajiteś Bandyopādhyāya (1933–83), who specialized in adapting Chekhov and Brecht, wrote *Saodāgarer Naukā* (The Merchant's Boat); and Cittarañjan Ghoṣ, who translated Annouilh (1928), wrote *Nidhubābu* and *Dāo Phire Se Araṇya.* The one person who prolifically wrote original plays in Bengali was Utpal Dutt (1929–93). In an amazing display of versatility as producer-director-actor-writer, Dutt (Beng. Datta) wrote more than 30 original plays in Bengali on subjects ranging from the Sepoy mutiny of 1857 to the Germany of World War II. Some of his celebrated plays include *Angār* (Coal, 1959), *Kallol* (The Sound of Waves, 1968), *Ṭiner Taloār* (The Tin Sword, 1973), *Duhswapner Nagarī* (Nightmare City, 1974), and *Barricade* (1975). Two important playwrights came into prominence in the 1970s—Manoj Mitra (1937) and Mohit Caṭṭopādhyāya (1935). Some of Mitra's major plays are *Cāk Bhāṅga Madhu* (The Stolen Honey, 1972), *Narak Guljār* (Heaven out of Hell, 1976), *Sājāno Bāgān* (The Well-Nursed Garden, 1977), and *Rājdarśan* (To See the King, 1982). Mohit Caṭṭopādhyāya will be best remembered for his play *Rājrakta* (Royal Blood, 1971) and *Socrātes* (1986).

While Utpal Dutt, Mitra, and others were writing largely realistic plays intended for the proscenium stage (Dutt had, earlier, tried his hand at *jātrā,* the nonproscenium folk theater form), the Bengali alternative avant-garde theater was fed by Bādal Sircar (Beng. Sarkār), who started with the proscenium stage but rejected it in favor of the arena form that he identified as the "third theater." *Ebaṅg Indrajit* (And Indrajit, 1962), *Bāki Itihās* (The Remaining History, 1967), *Kabī Kāhinī* (The Poet's Story, 1968), *Sārā Rāttir* (All Night, 1969), *Ballabhpurer Rūpkathā* (The Fairy Tale of Ballabhpur, 1970), and *Pāglā Ghoṛā* (The Crazy Horse, 1971) are best known among Bādal Sircar's plays for the proscenium stage, while *Triṅgśa Śatābdī* (Thirtieth Century, 1975), *Michil* (Procession), and *Bhomā* (1976) are his best-known arena "third theater" plays. Among the lesser playwrights whose careers have spanned the 1950s through the 1970s are Manmatha Rāy, Bidhāyak Bhaṭṭacārya, Kiraṇ Maitra, Dhanañjay Bairāgī,

Saileś Guha Niogī, Jyotu Bandyopādhyāya, and others. In the present generation, the major playwrights are Candan Sen, Debāśis Majumdār, Samīr Dāśgupta, and Indrāśis Lāhiṛī, who, it is our hope, will bring better health to the poverty-stricken corpus of Bengali drama in West Bengal.

LITERATURE OF EAST PAKISTAN (1947–72) AND BANGLADESH (1972–PRESENT)

While the geopolitical division of Bengal may now seem clear and well defined, its division as regards its language and literature is far from so. With the exception of differences in dialects, which may prove quite formidable at places, Bengali (or Bāṅglā) remains the dominant language spoken on both sides of Bengal. Despite the widening political rift between Bangladesh and its neighboring India, the people of Bengal on both sides of the political divide continue to share a common culture. They both consider themselves to be parts of the same literary traditions.

The Legacy of Communal Politics

Thus, if a ''Bangladeshi literature'' as a distinct trend is to be identified, it would largely mean the literature of the Bengali Muslims, as opposed to the literature in West Bengal, which has consisted predominantly of works by Hindu writers. In the aftermath of India's division in 1947 into two independent states based primarily on religious differences, the majority of the Bengali Muslims found East Pakistan, later, Bangladesh, to be their home. Though, in general terms, literature of the Bengali Muslims, whether of East or West Bengal, remains an integral part of the overall body of Bengali literature, a complex set of sociocultural and political factors and turn of events have lent it a distinct character.

Before India was colonized by the British, it had been under Muslim rule for several centuries. In Bengal, as in the other parts of the subcontinent, the language and literature received generous support and encouragement from its Muslim rulers, who often came from outside India and did not speak Bengali. In the years between the fifteenth and seventeenth centuries, Bengali literature quickly prospered, with both Hindus and Muslims equally benefiting from it. The situation was reversed in the eighteenth century, when the British, after inflicting a punishing defeat on the Nawāb of Bengal in 1757, seized control over Bengal. The Muslims, who felt humiliated and betrayed, refused to learn English and virtually withdrew from the nation's political, economic, and cultural mainstream. The void was quickly filled by the Hindus and other religious groups. Calcutta, now promoted to the status of capital of British India, became the hub of a new, urban Bengali culture and literature, the core of which was formed by an emerging Hindu middle class. Much of East Bengal, still very much rural and economically dependent, remained shrouded in a dark veil of ignorance.

At the turn of the twentieth century, however, the political reality in East Bengal began to change gradually. The Muslims started to emerge from their shell, seeking to reestablish themselves both politically and economically. After years of rejection, they finally began to learn English. But the Hindus were already far ahead in their quest for government jobs and investment opportunities. As they began entering the job market, the Muslims found the Hindus to be their prime rivals. At this time, the British decided to divide Bengal into East and West. Though administrative convenience was the argument advanced by the British in support of the division, its underlying reason was to further exploit the growing rivalry between Hindu and Muslim communities and use it to prolong British rule in India. Not surprisingly, though the majority of the Hindus opposed the partition of Bengal, the mood in East Bengal was decidedly opposite. While they did not call for Bengal's partition, the emerging Muslim middle class clearly favored it, believing this to be beneficial both economically and politically. The partition, which took place in 1905 in the face of strong Hindu resistance and protest by several all-India Muslim leaders, ignited a surge of nationalist revival in East Bengal. Within a year, the All-India Muslim League was formed in Dhākā as the first national political organization of the Indian Muslims. The stage was thus set for a course of confrontation between India's two major religious communities, the Hindus and Muslims.

The next 40 years of India's history were characterized by unprecedented violence and bloodbath. The rivalry between the Hindus and Muslims, with a history of suspicion and hatred sewn over several centuries, eventually resulted in the partition of India in 1947. East Bengal, now East Pakistan, became part of an independent, largely Muslim Pakistan. West Bengal, with its Hindu majority, remained a part of India as a separate state. East Bengal, which had become East Pakistan, now came to lend voice to the Muslim part of Bengal's population. Even before partition, East Bengal has always been known for its rich and vibrant folk culture. With the growth of urban centers, oral and folk traditions gradually found their influence limited to the rural environ. There is, however, no denying that some of Bengal's best-known writers, including the Nobel laureate Rabīndranāth Tagore, were deeply touched by the vigor and freshness of folk traditions (especially the music of the rustic poet Lālan Phakir) and their search for a deeper meaning of life.

Kāzi Nazrul Islām—A Secular Voice Misunderstood

But the first writer who discovered the mind of a modern Bengali Muslim was Kāzi Nazrul Islām (1899–1978). Though he was born in West Bengal and married a Hindu woman, Nazrul easily rose to become the mouthpiece of the Bengali Muslims at the turn of the twentieth century.[3] (Later, after Bangladesh became independent, he was to be honored as National Poet.) Nazrul was deeply secular and committed to socialist ideals, yet his emergence as the preeminent "Muslim" poet was caused largely by two factors: first, neither the Hindus nor the Muslims could ignore his poetic genius; and, second, Nazrul fashioned a new, modern language and literature for Bengali Muslims, rescuing them from the medieval religiocentric literature that continued to prevail in the Bengali Muslim circuit. He gave the Bengali Muslims a cause for pride, a new sense of identity. Nazrul was also the voice of a rebellious Bengal. No Bengali writer before him, Hindu or Muslim, had so forcefully articulated the desire for freedom and called for resistance against British colonialism. Bengalis fondly endowed him with the honorific title "Rebel Poet." Religious, yet politically progressive, secular, yet imbued with Islamic values, Nazrul was also able to gain recognition as the first major Bengali poet and writer not totally influenced by the genius of Tagore. Nazrul wrote copiously and has more than 50 publications to his credit in a literary career that spanned only 23 years, as he was struck with cerebral paralysis in 1943 and spent the last 40 or so years of his life in total inactivity. His most memorable works are the two poetic collections *Agnibīṇā* (The Fiery Lute, 1922) and *Biṣer Bāṁśi* (The Poison Flute, 1924), besides many other poems and songs that were published in various journals. Nazrul also composed more than 3,000 songs, setting most of them himself to music with brave melodic experiments. In the literary context, however, he will be remembered as the "Rebel Poet" and for his emotionally charged protest poetry.

While the "Rebel Poet" gave the Bengali Muslims a presence in the sphere of poetry, they remained largely unrepresented in fiction. There were no significant Muslim writers, with rare exceptions, like Mīr Maśārraf Hosen (1848–1911), who became best known for *Biṣādsīndhu* (a passionate novel about the death of Prophet Muhammad's grandsons in the Battle of Kārbālā) and the play *Jamidār-darpaṇ,* which he had written in 1873, and Begam Rokeyā Hosen (see later). Hindu writers, Rabīndranāth included, seemed neither interested nor concerned enough with the life of Bengali Muslims. Acutely aware of this vacuum, the *Muslim Yubasamāj* of Dhākā once urged Saratchandra Chatterjee, best known for his sentimental portrayal of the Hindu middle class, to devote some of his energies to focusing on the Bengali Muslims.

Among Nazrul's contemporaries who followed the path he had lighted was Begum Sufiā Kāmāl (see later). Also noteworthy were the poets Ābdul Kādir (1906–84), whose major works include *Dilruba* (Beloved, 1933) and *Uttar Basanta* (Northern Spring, 1967), and Ābul Hossain (1921), the author of *Nababasanta* (The New Spring, 1942). However, contrary to intentions of Nazrul and all who followed in his footsteps, Nazrul's religious writings soon found a strong following among a section of Bengali Muslim writers who considered his call for freedom a summons to join hands in the battle for revival of old Islāmic glories. It is not difficult to understand this narrow interpretation of Nazrul's message when viewed in the backdrop of the mounting tension between the Hindus and Muslims in India in the 1930s and 1940s. As a matter of fact, a growing number of Bengali Muslim writers began to express their commitment to an "Islamic Renaissance" and firmly supported the idea of creating Pakistan as a separate homeland for the Muslims of India. Notable writers such as Golām Mostāfā (1897–1964), Ābul Mansur Āhmed (1898–1979), and Ābul Kalām Śāmsuddin (1897–1978) held the view that creation of Pakistan would greatly facilitate the growth of art and literature for Bengali Muslims.

East Pakistan: Search for New Cultural Identity (1947–71)

After India's partition in 1947, the political scenario changed, but the questions of religion and political identity continued to stir writers and intellectuals in East Pakistan. Within years of Pakistan's creation, new voices were heard on the literary scene challenging the very concept of Pakistan, the basis of which was identification of the Muslims and the Hindus as two separate nations. Instead, they stressed the commonness, in terms of both history and culture, of all the Bengalis, whether Hindu or Muslim. The best exponents of this trend were Muhammad Śahīdullāh (1885–1969), Kāzi Ābdul Odud, Ābul Hosen, Motāhār Hosen, and Ābul Fazal (1903–83).

Ābul Mansur Āhmed's opinion, in his *Pāk Bāṅglār Kālcār* (The Culture of Pakistani Bengal, 1962), was that the literature created by Bidyāsāgar, Baṅkimcandra (leading literary figures in the nineteenth century), and Rabīndranāth could not belong to the Muslims of East Pakistan, because they did not belong to the Muslims of Bengal. The same argument was later advanced by Syed Ali Āhsān (1922), who claimed that the literature of East Pakistan was different from that of West Bengal. Golām Mostāfā (1897–1964), outdoing them both, advocated that everything "un-Islāmic" should be discarded and proposed to edit out all such references in Nazrul's writings.

Mohammed Śahīdullāh, perhaps the best-known Bengali Muslim linguist, rejected the view that the cultural identity of the Bengalis could be divided. "It is true that we are either Muslims or Hindus, but it is far more true that we are all Bengalis," he wrote in 1948. Despite obvious government patronage for the fashioning of a pro-Islamic cultural identity, a new political movement grew in East Pakistan, at the heart of which lay the demand for the recognition of Bengali as its official language. On February 21, 1952, several students and youths were killed in Dhākā by the police while demanding recognition of Bengali as the state language. Their death and the political turmoil that followed set the stage for a Bengali nationalist movement in East Pakistan. The Bengalis of East Pakistan, no longer confident in their union with West Pakistan purely on religious affinity of the two peoples, began demanding greater political rights for themselves. Language and culture became the two powerful beacons uniting them in their quest for a national identity. Two decades later, this would mature into a liberation war and lead to the emergence of Bangladesh.

The events of February 1952 left a deep imprint on the cultural and political psyche of the Bengali people in East Pakistan. Even those who had so steadfastly claimed their cultural identity to be separate from that of the Hindus of West Bengal began to play a new tune. For example, Ābul Mansur Āhmed, who had,

20 years before, spoken against the integration of the literatures of the Bengali Hindus and Muslims, wrote in 1962 that the people of both Bengals were tied together by a common language. "Our literary traditions are common. Poets and writers like Rabīndranāth, Śaratcandra, Nazrul Islām and Satyendranāth Datta inspire all Bengalis."

Later, in the second half of the 1960s, when nationalistic aspirations of the Bengalis of East Pakistan gained new recognition from a burgeoning political movement, leading intellectuals defined their political and cultural identity independent of religion without any problems. The Bengalis, whether Hindu or Muslim, whether they lived in East Bengal or in the West, were all united by a common culture and a set of common traditions, they argued. In a definitive statement of this new inclusive conviction, Munier Caudhurī (1925–71), the playwright-linguist, wrote in 1968: "The Bengali language and its literature are more than a thousand years old. Any literature written in this language is an inalienable part of our cultural identity." Badruddin Umar (1931), a political scientist who later chronicled the language movement and its political impact, also argued that there could not be any contradiction between being a Bengali and a Muslim at the same time.

The first phase of the Bengali Muslim's quest for self-identity virtually ended in 1971, when the state of Bangladesh was created after a nine-month-long liberation war fought against Pakistan. The bloody war, waged by the militarily better equipped Pakistan army against Bengali nationalists led by the Awami League of Śekh Mujibur Rāhmān, practically buried the idea of religion-based nationhood. What may seem ironical is the fact that the contradictions that appeared to have ended with the birth of a new nation resurfaced within years after the emergence of Bangladesh. Śekh Mujibur Rāhmān, considered by many the father of the nation, was assassinated in 1975, and political power was grabbed by a military dictatorship closely aligned with conservative forces that, in the past, strongly opposed any separation from Pakistan or the ideology that lay beneath its creation.

The changing of the guards at the political level signaled the beginning of a renewed struggle, this time within the country itself. The attempt to reinfuse religion as a political driving force generated strong opposition from the country's intellectual mainstream. Writers, using literature as their weapon, turned into activists and converted issues like resistance to communal politics, greater rights for women, and the right to dissent into the new leitmotifs of a resurgent cultural battle. The contradictions and conflicts that lay at the heart of political and ideological transformations in Bangladesh—first following India's partition and then, 25 years later, following the creation of an independent country—led to the development of a literature new in both its form and content.

It is impossible not to note that, despite the apparent success of the neoconservative forces at the political level, the most popular and best-known writers in East Pakistan, later, in Bangladesh, have always been on the side of progress and liberalism. Faced with new social and political realities, many who once considered religion a necessary element in national identity reversed their positions. Ābul Fazal (1903–83), who had, in 1947, written *Quāid-E-Āzam,* a play eulogizing Pakistan's founder, Mohammad Ali Jinnāh, wrote in 1957 a novel, *Rāṅgā Prabhāt* (The Red Dawn). Its story woven around the love of a Muslim boy and a Hindu girl, the novel celebrated the unity of Bengalis irrespective of their religious affiliations. Though weak as a work of art, this novel is often considered a significant turning point in Ābul Fazal's own position on questions of religion and society.

In 1953, on the first anniversary of the language movement, Hāsān Hāfizur Rāhmān (1932–83) compiled and edited a collection of essays, poems, and short stories. Simply called *Ekuśe Februārī* (February 21), the collection contained promises of a new literature, independent of cultural conservatism and opposed to communal divisiveness. Śaokat Osmān (1917), one of the foremost prose writers of Bangladesh, was a direct product of this new consciousness, better known as "Ekuśer Cetanā," the "consciousness of the 21st [February]." Osmān's deep-felt humanism and social concern continue to inform the prose writers of today. His major works include *Jananī* (The Mother, 1958), *Krītadāser Hāsi* (The Slave's Laughter, 1962), *Rājā Upākhyān* (The Tale of the King, 1971), and *Dui Sainik* (Two Soldiers, 1973). The most important work of this period, also a product of changing political and social perceptions, was Syed Wāliullāh's (1922–71) remarkable first novel, *Lāl Śālu* (Red Fabric, 1948). While portraying the darkness that cast a boding shadow over rural Bengal, still steeped in superstition and religious traditionalism, the book served as a rude awakening to the tragic reality of the time. It was also a testament of resistance against the forces that had controlled rural Bengali society for centuries, unopposed, unquestioned. Wāliullāh also wrote *Cāṁder Amābasyā* (The Moon's Umbra, 1967) and *Kāṁdo Nadī Kāṁdo* (Weep, River, Weep, 1969). But *Lāl Śālu* remains his most enduring work.

Lāl Śālu was significant in its own time for another reason. Though Bangladesh is largely rural, the novel was one of the very few powerful depictions of sociopolitical reality and power relationships in villages. Later in the 1960s, writers who were ideologically aware of the need for changes would shift their focus to the villages. Notable novels written during this period were *Sūrỳa Dighal Bāṛi* (The Enchanted House, 1955) by Ābu Iśāq (1926), *Sāreṅg Bau* (The Sareṅg's Wife, 1962) and *Saṅgsaptak* (The Saṅgsaptak Battalion, 1965) by Śahidullāh Kāysār (1931–71), and *Hajār Bachar Dhare* (For a Thousand Years, 1964) by Zahir Raihān (1933–71).

Attempts to rediscover the village were also made in poetry, but success was even more limited there. Jasimuddīn (1903–76), best known for his lyrical ballads on beauty and life in rural Bengal, had set a powerful example of this rediscovery of the basic fabric of rural life in Bengal in his numerous collections of poems, which include *Rākhālī* (Pastoral, 1929), *Raṅgilā Nāyer Mājhi* (Sailor of the Colorful Boat, 1933), and *Padmā Pār* (Banks of the Padmā, 1949), with balladic pieces like *Naksī-kāṁthār Māṭh* (Field of the Embroidered Quilt, 1929) and *Sakinā* (1960). He also wrote memorable lyric poems compiled in collections like *Bālucar* (Sandbanks, 1930) and *Māṭir Kānnā* (The Earth's Cry, 1951). He also wrote plays based on tales drawn out of the rich storytelling tradition of Bengal. However, no significant poet emerged to follow in Jasimuddīn's footsteps. Later, in the 1960s and 1970s, Āl Māhmud (1936) would return to villages, trying to build a subliminal bridge between the village he had left behind and the city he chose to adopt. Among the poets following Jasimuddīn who distinguished themselves but wrote a very different kind of poetry were Āhsān Habib (1917–85), the author of *Rātri Śeṣ* (Edge of the Night, 1947) and *Chāyā Hariṇ* (The Shadow Deer, 1962); Sikāndār Ābu Jāfar (1919–75), who wrote *Prasanna Prahar* (Pleased Time, 1965), *Bairī Bṛṣṭite* (In Contending Rain, 1965), and *Bāṅglā Chāṛo* (Quit Bengal, 1971); Sānāul Haq (1924–93), the author of *Sambhabā Ananyā* (Pregnant Par Excellence, 1962) and *Prabāse Jakhan* (When in Exile, 1981); Ābdul Gaṇi Hājārī (1921–76), who wrote *Sūryer Sṁiṛi* (The Sun's Ladder, 1965), and Māzhārul Islām (1928), who authored *Bicchinna Pratilipi* (The Torn Transcript, 1970), among others. Other authors are Śamsuddin Ābul Kālām (1926), Ābu Jāfar Śamsuddin (1911), Ābu Ruśd (1919), and Mirzā Ābdul Hāi.

As Bangladesh moved into the last quarter of the century, large cities became home for millions and the center of all civil activities, and writers scrambled to express their interpretations of the emerging experiences. Among the fiction writers, most notable for their attempts, if not for their successes, were Syed Śamsul Haq (1935), who wrote *Ek Mahilār Chabi* (The Portrait of a Woman, 1959), *Rakta Golāp* (The Crimson Rose, 1964) and *Bṛṣṭi* (Rain, 1989); Raśīd Karim (1934), author of *Uttampuruṣ* (First Person, 1961), *Prasanna Pāṣāṇ* (The Happy Stone, 1963), *Ekāler Rūpakathā* (Today's Fable, 1980), and *Āmār Jata Glāni* (All My Shame); Jyotiprakaś Datta (1939), who wrote *Bahenā Subātās* (The Pleasant Breeze Doesn't Blow, 1967) and *Sītāṅgśu, Tot Samasta Kathā* (All Your Stories, Sītāṅgśu, 1969); Śaokat Ali (1935); Raśīd Hāidār (1941); Hāsān Āzizul Haq (see later); Māhmudul Haq (1940); and Ākhthāruzzāmān Ilyās (see later). Some of them, like Syed Śamsul Haq, Hāsān Āzizul Haq, Ilyās, and Jyotiprakaś Datta, were hailed as brave, new experimenters with language and style. They were also among the first to explore areas beyond the personal and social and connect them with emerging political patterns.

The pains that followed the reversal of political gains also found powerful expression in the stories and novelettes of Hāsān Azizul Haq (1939). Heralded as a master storyteller following the publication of *Ātmaja O Ekti Karabī Gāch* (The One Born of Me and a Karabī Tree, 1967), Haq rose to become one of the finest short story writers of his time. Like his predecessor Syed Wāliullāh, Hāsān's immediate concern is the village and its seemingly unchanging flow of life, its sociopolitical power structure that is ever so hostile to the poor and the disfranchised. His short stories in *Jīban Ghose Āgun* (Fire Rubbed Out of Life, 1973), *Nāmhīn Gotrahīṇ* (Nameless without Lineage, 1975), and *Pātāle Hāspātāle* (In Hell and Hospital, 1981) are documentations of the deepening crisis, moral rejection, and growing resistance of a whole new generation of people. Yes, resistance, but Hāsān Aziz seems to concede that those living at the fringe of society, at the lowest rung of the social totem pole, are increasingly at a loss, incapable of swimming back.

This fall and ruination were captured equally powerfully, albeit in the context of the big cities, by Ākhthāruzzāmān Ilyās (1943). Three of his best-known books, *Anyaghare Anyaswar* (Other Voices in Other Rooms, 1976), *Khoāṛi* (1982), and *Dudhbhāte Utpāt* (Strife in Milk and Rice, 1985), were published in the postliberation years. Most of his stories in these collections capture the day-to-day reality of the decaying life in downtown Dhākā, the capital. Here, in this big metropolis, people had once dared to dream, but, burdened by poverty, these dreams are all but lost. Now, the primary concern of all is not lofty moral values or elevated social consciousness. Food is what they need most. Sheer survival is their primary preoccupation. No one has better captured the meaning of this cruel reality in current Bangladesh. His ambitious novel *Cilekoṭhār Sepāi* (The Soldier of the Attic, 1988), written in the backdrop of the civil uprising of 1969, is also one of the most successful political novels in recent years. Other notable writers to have emerged in this period are Hasnāt Ābdul Hāi, Selinā Hosen (see later), Rāhāt Khān (1939), Rijiyā Rahmān (1939), Sucarit Caudhurī (1930), Ābubākar Siddiq (1934), and Āhmad Chafā (1943).

Poetry

In the new poetry that emerged in the newly formed Bangladesh, most notable was the success of the poets who wrote about their city experiences. Once tremendously influenced by such modernist writers of the 1940s and 1950s from the "other" Bengal as Biṣñu De, Buddhadeb Basu, and Jibanānanda Dāś (see earlier), Bangladeshi poets gradually discovered their own voice and claimed respect for their strength and originality. As political realities changed rapidly, and cultural distance between the two Bengals widened, poets in Bangladesh became chroniclers of the new times and new concerns and established their own distinctive styles. Almost all of Bangladesh's notable poets live in cities, mostly preoccupied with their own concerns in coping with the anxieties and alienation of the fast-rising metropolis.

Śāmsur Rāhmān, with more than 50 volumes of poetry to his credit, is perhaps the most popular and famous poet in Bangladesh. At the outset of his poetic journey, he was a romantic submerged in his own alienation from both his immediate environment and the larger society. But, as Bangladesh changed, so did Śāmsur Rāhmān. In the 1970s and later in the 1980s and 1990s, he became perhaps the most eloquent voice among Bangladesh's poets and linked the personal with the general and made social and political questions the focus of his constant concern. Rāhmān's poetry symbolized the hopes and agonies of the struggle for liberation. He also encapsulated the anger and concern of a people left incredulous at the loss of a newborn dream and unsure how the course could be reversed. His major works include *Pratham Gān, Dwitīya Mṛtyur Āge* (The First Song, Before the Second Death), *Āmi Anāhārī* (I Am Unfed), *Āmār Kono Tāṛā Nei* (I Am in No Rush), *Roudra Karoṭite* (In the Sun-Drenched Skull, 1963), *Nija Bāsbhūme* (In My Own Homeland, 1970), *Bandī Śibir Theke* (From the Prison Camp, 1972), *Duhsamayer Mukhomukhi* (Face to Face with Bad Times, 1973), *Ek Dharaner Ahaṅgkār* (Pride of Sorts, 1975), *Bāṅglādeś Swapna Dekhe* (Bāṅglādeś Dreams, 1977), *Udbhaṭ Ūṭer Piṭhe Caleche Swadeś* (My Country Rides an Absurd Camel, 1982), and *Khanḍita Gourab* (Broken Pride, 1992).

Though often shadowed by Śāmsur Rāhmān's poetic presence, several of his contemporaries gained prominence for their eloquence and distinctive style. Nourished in the romantic liberalism emanating from "Ekuśe" February, these poets helped create the moral fabric that, in the later years, gave poetry its unique place in the social psyche of Bangladesh. Among them are Hāsān Hāfizur Rāhmān (1932–83), who has authored collections like *Ārta Śabdābalī* (Scared Words, 1968) and *Āmār Bhetare Bāgh* (The Tiger within Me, 1983); Śahīd Kādri (1942), who has written *Uttarādhikār* (Inheritance, 1969), *Tomāke Abhibādan Priyatamā* (Salutations to You, Beloved, 1974), and *Kothāo Kono Krandan Nei* (There's No Weeping Anywhere, 1978); Ābu Jāfar Obāydullāh (1934), whose works include *Kamaler Cokh* (The Eye of the Lotus, 1974) and *Āmi Kiṅgbadantir Kathā Balchi* (I Am Talking about Legend, 1981); Āl Māhmud (1936), a major poet with landmark collections like *Sonālī Kābin* (1973), *Kāler Kalas* (Time's Pitcher, 1976), and *Māyābī Pardā Dule Oṭho* (Flutter, Magical Veil, 1976); Syed Śamsul Haq (see earlier), who has also published collections of poems like *Baiśākhe Racita Paṅgktimālā* (Lines Written in April 1969), *Pratidhwanitān* (Echoed Chorus, 1973), and *Parāner Gahīn Bhitar* (In the Depth of the Heart, 1981); and Mahādeb Sāhā (1944), who has written *Ei Gṛha Ei Sannyās* (This Home, This Hermitry, 1972), *Mānab Esechi Kāje* (Man I Have Come to Work, 1974), *Dhulo Māṭir Mānuṣ* (Earthen Man, 1983), and *Ekā Haye Jāi* (I Become Alone, 1993).

The romantic traditions of the 1950s–1960s received a jolt in the late 1960s and following the birth of Bangladesh in 1971, when a whole generation of new poets burst into the poetic scenario. Often indistinguishable in their collective anguish and anger, despite their obvious narcissism and pronounced individualism, these poets often found inspiration from the West, including the poets of the "Beat Generation." Included in this group are Rafiq Āzād (1943), whose major works include *Asambhaber Pāye* (At the Feet of the Impossible, 1973) and *Hāturir Nīce Jīban* (Life under a Hammer, 1984); Nirmalendu Gün (1948), one of the best poets writing out of Bangladesh today, who wrote *Premaṅgśur Rakta Cāi* (Wanted, Premāṅgśu's Blood, 1970), *Nā Premik Nā Biplabī* (Neither Lover Nor Revolutionary, 1972), and *Kabitā, Amimāṅgsīta Ramanī* (Poetry, the Undecided Woman, 1973); Ābul Hāsān (1947–75), who is best known for his *Rājā Āse Rājā Jāy* (Kings Come and Kings Go, 1973); and Ābdul Mānnān Syed (1943), who wrote *Jyotsnā Roudrer Cikitsā* (Moonlight, Treatment for the

Sun, 1982). Mention must be made here of poets like Mohāmmad Rafik (1943), Farhād Mājhār (1946), Sikdār Āminul Haq (1942), Humāyun Ājād (1947), Hābībullāh Sirājī (1948), Muhāmmad Nurul Hudā (1949), and Āltāf Hosen (1947).

Younger poets of Bangladesh, though heirs to the poetic traditions set by Śāmsur Rāhmān and others, are often better understood in the context of the continuously changing political scenario of Bangladesh. These poets, among them Sānāul Haq Khān (1947), Khondakār Āśrāf Hosen (1950), Rudra Mohāmmad Śahīdullāh (1956–92), Śihāb Sarkār (1952), Hāsān Hāfiz (1955), Kāmāl Caudhurī (1957), Mohan Rāyhān, and Samudra Gupta have mostly distinguished themselves for their recordings of the political turns and twists and their ability to link them with the accompanying social and political upheavals. As a matter of fact, poets and poetry have always been major players in the political scenarios acted out in contemporary Bangladesh. The language movement had already planted a powerful seed. In subsequent years, many major political events had their beginning in the month of February, a month associated with the images of protest and resistance, images reshaped and repainted by poets over and over again to suit new and emerging political needs. In the 1980s, poets were in the lead of a unified social movement to resist the military rule. So powerful and plainly visible was their influence that the head of the military government unabashedly courted the poets, himself trying his hand at writing poetry. One obvious consequence of all these events was that politics became the heartbeat of Bengali poetry. The most representative poets of the 1980s are Farid Stalin, Sājjād Māsud Khān, and Subrata Augustine Gomez, among others.

Poetry in Bangladesh has not sold itself out totally to the literary supermarket and, in the view of many, is still vibrant, still fresh. There is obviously a historical reason for this, but no less important is the general intellectual framework of the Bengali mind. Instead of rigorous scientific scrutiny of the historical moment, poetry has given them the romantic distance to ruminate about it in metaphysical terms, both as an escape from reality and as a form of passive resistance.

Drama

Politics has also been a driving force behind the growth of drama as a powerful literary genre. In the 1970s and mostly in the 1980s, drama was consciously—and perhaps concertedly—used as a tool to regenerate support for the failing spirit of the liberation war. Successfully employing theater as a medium, Syed Śāmsul Haq (see earlier) produced such powerful plays as *Pāer Āoāj Pāoā Jāy* (Hear the Footfall), *Nuraldiner Sarajīban* (The Complete Life of Nuraldin), and *Gaṇanāyak* (The People's Hero) to transmit the message of popular resistance and show their linkages with people's aspirations for greater freedom both in a historical context and also in contemporary Bangladesh. Two other dramatists who have also won admiration for their innovations and skills are Selim Āl Dīn (1948) and Ābdullāh Āl Māmun (1943).

Nonfictional Prose

In recent years, as forces opposed to the ideals of liberation war strengthened their political position, and fundamentalism gained new ground, writers and intellectuals have refocused themselves to unite positive social forces. In their resistance to new challenges from fundamentalists and communal forces, the need to identify the traditional roots of the Bengali was felt with new urgency. In this new phase of resistance, prose writers have come for the first time to the forefront, both to define the nature of the political and historical identity of the Bengalis as well as to rally popular support for resistance against fundamentalism. Ānisuzzamān (1937), Badruddin Umar (1931), Serājul Islām Caudhurī (1936), Sālāhuddin Āhmed (1924), and Āhmed Śarīf (1921), all of them better known as academicians and intellectuals, have emerged as principal voices of the new times. Mention must be made also of Ābul Kaśem (1920), Śamsuzzāmān Khān (1937), Hāyāt Māmud (1939), Saiyad Akrām Hosen (1944), Muntāsīr Māmun (1951), Jatīn Sarkār, and Fajlul Haq.

While contemporary literature in Bangladesh is reflective of the current political realities and social changes, it is yet to produce a significant number of fiction writers capable of dispassionately examining the times they live in. The liberation war, which is often compared to a struggle of epic proportions, still remains incomplete. Other forces, social and economic, seem to be working against the growth of a healthy culture in Bangladesh. Though predominantly an agricultural economy, its villages still tied to medieval feudalism, the country has leaped into twentieth-century consumerism with a vengeance. The disparity between life in the villages and life in the city has greatly widened, and poverty has become endemic in the countryside. The standard of education has faltered, nourishment of the intellect has taken a back seat, and television has taken over as the principal medium of communication. The genre of literature that seems to be thriving in today's Bangladesh is that of cheap, sentimental, short novels, the typical supermarket pulp fiction. The commercial success some writers have met with, however, is truly astounding and gives proof of increasing literacy among the masses, if not anything else. Among the writers who have to be commended for their commercial achievements are Humāyun Āhmed (1948), the prolific novelist best known for *Nandita Narake* (In Blissful Hell), Māhmudul Haq (see earlier), and Imdādul Haq Milan (1955). Among the younger writers emerging now are Bipradās Baṛuā (1942), Mañju Sarkār (1954), Mainul Āhsān Sāber (1958), Suśānta Majumdār, Biplab Dās, and Nasrin Jāhān.

Little Magazines—Filling a Void

Bangladesh has a very low literacy rate, a small middle-class base, and no significant institutional literary publication. Growing through contradictory and sometimes hostile ideological environments, mainstream literature in Bangladesh has often had to rely on the friendly embrace of literary periodicals and journals.

Samakāl and *Parikramā,* published from Dhākā, and *Pūrbamegh,* from Rājśāhi, nurtured the liberal ideals of the post-''Ekuśe'' years, giving the emerging writers an effective forum for voicing their hopes and channeling their anger. In the 1960s, *Swākkhar* and *Kanthaswar* were the two most popular periodicals, both products of the changed sociopolitical realities. New and ''angry'' writers, making their first contacts with the new trends in the West, quickly found in them a reliable ally. These and other noninstitutional literary journals mostly bore the characteristics of ''little magazine,'' so called for their habitual departure from tradition, irregularity of publication, and their ''collective'' nature. Filling a void, they helped capture—and often define—the new moods and literary/cultural trends, but they rarely lived long. In fact, the limited breadth of the middle-class intelligentsia, weak economic base, and the overwhelming influence of the government in the economy generally worked against the healthy growth of creative and independent literary journals. For new writers, little magazines were often the only refuge.

The growth of little magazines was further helped by the observance of ''Ekuśe'' February, an annual ritual that gave the Bangladeshis an opportunity to renew their cultural unity. Each year, at the time of the ''Ekuśe,'' dozens of commemorative little magazines are published all around the country, giving the new writers their first opportunity to get printed. ''Ekuśe'' celebrations have also helped set the tradition of *bai melā*—book fairs. In Bangladesh, the greatest number of literary books is published in the months of January and February and sold at the ''Ekuśe'' book fairs. What has also supplemented the flow of a vibrant literary life in Bangladesh are the ''literary pages''—weekly literary sections of major vernacular daily newspapers. Most major writers often first publish their new works in these ''pages.'' Since publishing is not a lucrative business in Bangladesh, and royalties are rather novelties, writers often rely on honoraria they receive from these newspapers to supplement their income.

Women Writers of Bangladesh

The first Muslim woman writer to earn a name for herself on either side of Bengal was Rokeyā Sākhāwāt Hosen (1880–1932). Though she grew up under very adverse conditions—in a strictly segregated society with limited educational opportunities and life under veil—and published at a time when she was practically the lone practitioner of the art, Rokeyā earned respect from female, as well as male, readers for her creativity and fierce ''feminism.'' Her novels *Matichur* (Jewel-Dust, 1904) and *Sultāner Swapna* (The Sultan's Dream, 1912) and *Abarodh-Basinī* (Woman Imprisoned), a collection of short essays, were noted for their bold portrayal of the Bengali Muslim woman's life in early twentieth century.

Though several Muslim women were known to have published books and written for literary journals in the 1930s and 1940s, very few emerged as writers of any importance in the years after India's partition. Sufiā Kāmāl (1911) is the lone poetess of these years, whose soft lyrics captured ''feminine moods'' but also provided a vital link between past and emerging present. She excelled in portraying tender emotions—love and nature. Her *Sāṁjher Māyā* (Twilight Magic) appeared as early as 1938. She continued to write after independence and published collections like *Māyā Kājal* (The Magic Collyrium, 1951) and *Man O Jīban* (Mind and Life, 1960). As a peaceful, quiet voice that did not seem threatening to the male members of society, Sufiā Kāmāl—in her poems, essays, and political statements and particularly through cultural activism—articulated and, perhaps, even defined a new role for the urban Bengali Muslim in the 1960s and 1970s. None, other than Sufiā Kāmāl, among women writers between 1952 and 1971, seemed to have been touched by the changing political realities of the country. Fiction was the most popular medium chosen by them, but practically none of them were notable for either their craft or an understanding of the challenges facing women. This perhaps was a reflection of the non-presence of women in sociopolitical spheres. It was also reflective of a lack of strong tradition of female participation in the literary scene.

Selinā Hosen (1947) was the first significant woman writer to emerge in the 1970s and continued through the next years as a powerful chronicler of life in rural Bengal. A strong sense of history, close links with life beyond the city, and a clear faith in the essential goodness of life have earned her a remarkable readership in Bangladesh. Among her better-known novels are *Hāngar Nadī Greneḍ* (Sharks, Rivers, Grenades, 1976), *Magnacaitanye Śis* (Whistling High, 1979), *Caṁd Bene* (Caṁd, the Merchant, 1984), and *Ṭānāpoṛen* (Warp and Woof, 1994).

Unlike Selinā, who refuses to be limited to ''feminist'' themes alone, Taslimā Nāsrin (1962) has remained, almost from the very onset of her career, an angry, rebellious, ''feminist'' voice. A poet of considerable talent and later a novelist with a penchant toward stirring up controversies, she rose to prominence following the publication of her polemical writings, *Nirbācita Kalām* (Selected Columns, 1992). In numerous essays featured in this book, Taslimā flagrantly displays her contempt for conventional notions of marriage, frankly discusses female sexuality, both as right as well as denial, and rejects religion for restricting women's freedom. If these columns seemed ''irritable'' and merely bruised male egocentrism, her novel *Lajjā* (Shame, 1993) pitted her against the conservative theocracy and those aligned with them in the government. In this and in a subsequent book—*Pherā* (The Return, 1994)—Taslimā explores the growing communal discrimination in Bangladesh, practiced at all levels (often tacitly endorsed by the government) by the country's Muslim majority toward the Hindu minority. *Lajjā* was banned by the government for allegedly trying to incite religious disharmony. Later, her strong antitheocracy articles drew fanatical responses from the country's religious Right, who proclaimed a ''death sentence'' against Taslimā. In 1994, after spending some time in hiding, Taslimā chose to go into exile in Europe.

Pūrabī Basu (1949), also a feminist writer with a critical view of religious fundamentalism in Bangladesh, has traversed a less controversial path but achieved a different kind of acclaim for her short stories. Like Taslimā, Pūrabī has sought to portray the marginalization of women from within a conscious, committed, and feminist context. In three collections of short stories—*Pūrabī Basur Galpa,* (Pūrabī Basu's Stories, 1989), *Ājanma Parabāsī* (Exiled Forever, 1992), and *Se Nahi, Nahi* (That's Not Me, Not Me, 1995)—Pūrabī has explored male–female relationships, often examining the woman's subordination to tradition and culture in an urban setting. Written with a measured economy, often veiled in sophisticated symbolism, Pūrabī's stories, along with her growing number of nonfictional essays, have invited her growing number of readers to go beyond the superficial niceties of familial relationships and reinterpret them from a woman's perspective.

Bangladesh is still a new country. It is an heir to ancient and rich cultural traditions. Faced with inner contradictions and fiercely competing social forces, these traditions and cultural trends are still in the process of being defined fully, giving the masses the strength to strive for unity and reasons for hope. The literature created as a result of the changing social realities is sure to find its own distinctive seat in the culturally undivided map of Bengali literature, charting newer frontiers.

A NOTE ON BENGALI PRONUNCIATION

The Bengali language, as it is spoken, presents a major problem when it comes to spelling the words, since the way Bengali words are pronounced often has very little to do with the system of spelling, which is predominantly Sanskṛt-based. Several sounds in the Sanskṛt language are not pronounced in Bengali but are faithfully rendered, nevertheless, in the written form. This causes a great deal of confusion, especially when one has to transliterate Bengali words into the Roman script. The choice for the transliterator, for better or for worse, is either (1) to represent the Bengali pronunciation exactly without caring for the spelling or (2) to follow the way the words are spelled, with full respect for the Sanskṛt norm. Neither of the two choices is entirely satisfactory. The problem is accentuated further with the non-Sanskṛt words that abound in the Bengali language: how do you account for them? Keeping these rather perplexing and controversial issues in mind, we finally decided to strike a mean by maintaining the Sanskṛt mode of transliteration but, for the sake of balance, also supplementing it with the following glossary, which sketchily explains how spoken Bengali differs from what its Sanskṛt-based spelling suggests. With names of persons, especially Hindu names, we have used either a transliterated version based on the Bengali spelling or, in a few cases, the Anglicized versions the persons themselves used in public life that have become very common through usage (e.g., "Tagore" instead of "Ṭhākur"). Most of the Muslim names have been spelled with their Arabic or Persian pronunciations in mind, with some exceptions where the names are better known in their Bengali forms, for example, "Rāhmān" instead of "Rehmān" or "Ākhthār" instead of "Akhthar."

Vowels

A/a	generally pronounced like the word *awe* but occasionally also pronounced as "o" (there is no fixed rule)
Ā/ā	like "a" in father
I/i	like "i" in spin
Ī/ī	like "ee" in keen
U/u	like "oo" in good
Ū/ū	like "oo" in food
Ŗ/ŗ	a quickly pronounced syllable like "r" in Rick

Consonants

ṅ	like "n" in gong or bonk
Ñ/ñ	like "n" in inch or engine
ṇ	difference between this and the regular "n" in Bengali is only "seen" in the spelling, not heard
Ṭ/ṭ	upper-palatal "T" (hard) like in Tat, unlike the regular dental "T" (soft)
ḍ/ḍ	upper-palatal "D" (hard) like in Dad, unlike the regular dental "D" (soft)
Ś/ś	like "sh" in should
ṣ/ṣ	similar to "Ś/ś" but pronounced with slightly more air pressure, e.g., shhoot, instead of shoot
ṛ	a mixture of "Ḍ/ḍ" and the regular "r"
ṁ	a nasal accent like the French "en" in rendezvous
J̄/j̄	difference between this and the regular "j" in Bengali is only "seen" in the spelling; it is a Sanskŗt form of "y" that is used only in the Bengali script but never pronounced

NOTES

1. Under the impact of colonialism, Bengal in the nineteenth century witnessed a cultural "resurgence" that has been, not without argument, identified by many as the "Bengal Renaissance." This period, in addition to its numerous social changes, was marked by an enormous amount of literary output as a result of the democratization of the print medium.

2. The two most notable figures in Bengali literature in the nineteenth century are Baṅkimcandra Caṭṭopādhyāya (1838–94), in the case of the novel and Bengali prose in general, and Michael Madhusūdan Datta (1824–73), for Bengali epic poetry and Western-style drama.

3. In order to trace and identify the trends of Bengali literature in (East Pakistan and) Bangladesh, it is imperative to look at the originative points of the literature of the Bengali Muslim in the early twentieth century, which allows us to consider the works

of Nazrul in this latter section of the chapter instead of the earlier part where it would have been, perhaps, chronologically more appropriate.

SELECTED PRIMARY BIBLIOGRAPHY

Āhmed, Humāyun. *In Blissful Hell.* Translated by Mohammad Nurul Huda. Dhaka: Somoi Prokashon, 1993.

Bandyopādhyāya, Bibhūtibhūṣaṇ (Bibhutibhushan Banerjee/Bandyopadhyay). *A Strange Attachment and Other Stories.* Translated by Phyllis Granoff. New York: Mosaic Press, 1984.

Bandyopādhyāya, Māṅik (Manik Banerjee/Bandyopadhyay). *Boatman of the Padmā.* Translated by Hirendranath Mukherjee. New Delhi: National Book Trust, 1987.

———. *Serā Māṇik.* Edited by Śikha Ghoṣ. Kolkātā: Mitra O Ghoṣ Pābliśārs, 1993.

Bandyopādhyāya, Tārāśaṅkar (Tarashankar Banerjee/Bandyopadhyay). *Kālindī.* Translated by Leila L. Javitch. New Delhi: Munshiram Manoharlal, 1978.

———. *Serā Tārāśaṅkar.* Edited by Sarit Bandyopādhyāya. Kolkātā: Mitra O Ghoṣ Pābliśārs, 1993.

Basu, Buddhadeb (Buddhadev Bose). *Racanā Saṅgraha.* Edited by Subīr Rāycaudhurī and Amiya Deb. Kolkātā: Granthālaya, 1975.

———. *Three Mahabharata Verse Plays.* Translated by Kaṅak Kānti Rāy. Calcutta: Writers Workshop, 1992.

Basu, Samareś (Samaresh Bose/Basu). *Āmi Tomāderi Lok.* Kolkātā: Jagaddhātrī Pābliśars, 1986.

Cakrabartī, Nirendranāth (Nirendranath Chakrabarti). *Nirendranāth Cakrabartīr Śreṣṭha Kabitā.* Kolkātā: De'j Pābliśiṅg, 1981.

Caṭṭopādhyāya, Śakti (Shakti Chatterjee/Chattopadhyaya). *Padyasamagra.* Vols. 1, 2. Kolkātā: Ānanda Pābliśārs, 1989.

Caṭṭopādhyāya, Śaratcandra (Saratchandra Chatterjee/Chattopadhyay). *The Golden Book of Saratchandra.* Edited by Satyabrata Ray. Calcutta: All Bengal Sarat Centenary Committee, 1977.

———. *Saratbabu's Srikanto.* Translated by K. C. Sen. Bombay: Jaico Publishing House, 1987.

———. *The Homecoming: Translation of Palli Samaj.* Translated by Prasenjit Mukherjee. Calcutta: Rupa, 1989.

———. *The Right of Way: Translation of Pather Dabi.* Translated by Prasenjit Mukherjee. Calcutta: Rupa, 1993a.

———. *Śarat Racanāsaṅgraha.* Kolkātā: Ānanda Pābliśars, 1993b.

Dāś, Jibanānanda. *Jibanānanda Daśer Kabyagrantha.* Vols. 1, 2. Kolkātā: Bengal Pābliśārs Prāibheṭ Limiṭeḍ, 1985.

———. *The Beauteous Bengal.* Translated by A. K. Basu Majumdar. Delhi: Mittal Publications, 1987.

Datta, Jyotiprakaś (Jyoiprakash Dutta). *Durbīnita Kāl.* Dhākā: Samabāy Prakāśnī, 1987.

Debi, Āśāpūrṇā (Ashapurna Devi). *Snakebite and the Distant Widow: Two Novels.* Translated by Anima Bose. New Delhi: Prachi, 1983.

Debi, Mahāswetā (Mahasveta Devi). *Aranyer Adhikār.* Kolkātā: Karuṇā Prakaśaṇi, 1987.

———. *Bashai Tudu.* Translated by Samik Banerjee and Gayatri Chakravorty Spivak. Calcutta: Thema, 1990.

———. *Imaginary Maps.* Translated by Gayatri Chakravorty Spivak. New York: Routledge, 1995.

Debi, Maitreyī (Maitreyee Devi). *It Does Not Die: A Romance.* (Translated by Author [?]). Calcutta: Writers Workshop, 1976.

Gaṇgopādhyāya, Sunīl (Sunil Ganguly/Gangopadhyay). *Arjun.* Translated by Chitrita Banerjee-Abdullah. New York: Viking Penguin, 1987.

———. *Sunīl Gaṅgopādhyāyer Śreṣṭha Kabitā.* Kolkātā: De'j Pābliśiṅg, 1989.

———. *For you, Neera.* Translated by Surabhi Banerjee. New Delhi: Rupa, 1993.

Ghoṣ, Śaṅkha (Sankha Ghosh). *Kabitāsaṅgraha.* Kolkātā: De'j Pābliśārs, 1987.

———. *Emperor Babur's Prayer and Other Poems.* Translated by Kalyan Roy. New Delhi: Sahitya Akademi, 1992.

Goswāmī, Jay (Joy Goswami). *Kābyasamagra.* Kolkātā: Ānanda Pābliśārs, 1989.

———. *Bhūtum Bhagabān.* Kolkātā: Ānanda Pābliśārs, 1990.

Gun, Nirmalendu. *Nirbācitā.* Dhākā: Jātīya Sāhitya Prakāśanī, 1992.

Haq, Hāsān Āzizul (Hasan Azizul Huq). *Selected Stories.* Translated by Ali Anwar. Dhaka: Bangla Academy, 1985.

———. *Āmrā Apekṣā Karchi.* Dhākā: Muktadhārā, 1989.

Haq, Syed Śāmsul (Syed Shamsul Huq). *Deep within the Heart.* Translated by Sonia Khan. Dhaka: Sabyasachi, 1984.

———. *Nāṭya-Saṇgraha.* Dhākā: Pallab Prakāśanī, 1990.

Ilyās, Ākhthāuzzāmān (Akhtharuzzaman Ilyas). *Cilekoṭhār Sepāi.* Dhākā: Iunibhārsiṭi Pres Limiṭeḍ, 1988.

Māhmud, Āl (Al Mahmud). *Selected Poems.* Translated by Kabir Chowdhury. Dhaka: Bangla Academy, 1987.

Mitra, Premendra. *Adventures of Ghanada.* Translated by Lila Majumdar. New Delhi: National Book Trust, 1982.

Mukhopādhyāya, Subhāṣ. *Subhāṣ Mukhopādhyāyer Śreṣṭha Kabitā.* Kolkātā: De'j Pābliśiṅg, 1982.

Nasrin, Taslimā (Taslima Nasreen). *Light Up at Midnight: Selected Poems.* Translated by Carolyne Wright, Fazlul Alam, Mohammad Nurul Huda, and Farida Sarkar. Dhaka: Biddyaprakash, 1992.

———. *Lajjā.* Dhaka: Pārl Pāblikeśāns, 1993.

———. *Lajja/Shame.* Translated by Chitrita Banerjee. New York: Viking Penguin, 1994.

Nazrul Islām, Kāzī (Kazi Nazrul Islam). *The Fiery Lyre of Nazrul Islam.* Translated by Abdul Hakim. Dhaka: Bangla Academy, 1974.

———. *Kazi Nazrul Islam: A New Anthology.* Edited by Rafiqul Islam. Dhaka: Bangla Academy, 1990.

———. *The Morning Shanai: Twenty Poems of Kazi Nazrul Islam.* Translated by Kabir Chowdhury. Dhaka: Nazrul Institute, 1991.

———. *Janani.* Translated by Osman Jamal. Oxford: Heinemann, 1993.

Osmān, Śaokat (Shaokat Osman). *Selected Stories.* Translated by Osman Jamal. Dhaka: Bangla Academy, 1985.

Rāhmān, Śāmsur (Shamsur Rahman). *Śāmsur Rāhmāner Śreṣṭha Kabitā.* Kolkātā: De'j Pābliśiṅg, 1985.

———. *Selected Poems of Shamsur Rahman.* Translated by Kaiser Haq. Dhaka: BRAC Prokashona, 1985.

Rāy, Satyajit (Satyajit Ray). *The Adventures of Feluda.* Translated by Chitrita Banerji. New York: Penguin Books, 1988.

———. *The Incredible Adventures of Professor Shanku.* Translated by Surabhi Banerjee. New York: Penguin Books, 1994.

Rāy, Sukumar. *The Select Nonsense of Sukumar Ray.* Translated by Sukanta Chaudhuri. New York: Oxford University Press, 1987.

Sarkār, Bādal (Badal Sircar). *Three Plays: Procession, Bhoma, Stale News.* Translated by Samik Banerjee and Suchanda Sarkar. Calcutta: Seagull Books, 1983.

Ṭhākur, Rabīndranāth (Rabindranath Tagore). *Rabīndra Racanābalī.* Śantiniketan: Biśwabhāratī, 1960.

———. *Collected Poems and Plays of Rabindranath Tagore.* New York: Macmillan, 1964.

———. *Gitanjali: Song Offerings.* New York: Collier Books, 1971.

———. *Gora.* Delhi: Macmillan, 1980.

———. *Selected Poems.* Translated by William Radice. New York: Viking Penguin, 1985.

———. *I Won't Let You Go: Selected Poems.* Translated by Ketaki Kushari-Dyson. New Delhi: UBSPD, 1992.

———. *Selected Short Stories of Rabindranath Tagore.* Translated by Krishna Dutta and Mary Lago. Caclutta: Rupa, 1992.

REFERENCES

Bāṅglā Ekāḍemī (Bangla Academy). *Bāṅglādeśer Lekhak Pariciti.* Dhākā: Bāṅglā Ekādemī, 1984.

Bhaṭṭācārya, Pareścandra. *Samagra Bāṅglā Sāhityer Paricay.* Kolkātā: Jaydurgā Librerī, 1988.

Hāldār, Śibaprasād. *Ādhunik Bāṅblā Sāhityer Paricay.* Kolkātā: Di Buk Eksceñj, 1967.

Mukherji, Jagomohon. *Bengali Literature in English: A Bibliography.* Calcutta: M. C. Sarkar, 1970.

Quader, Abedin, ed. *An Anthology of Modern Literature from Bangladesh.* Dhaka: Saptapadi Publications, 1985.

Sen, Sukumar. *The History of Bengali Literature.* New Delhi: Sahitya Akademi, 1965.

———. *Bāṅglār Sāhitya-Itihās.* Natun Dillī: Sāhitya Ākādemi, 1980.

Zbavitel, Dusan. *Bengali Literature.* Wiesbaden: O. Harrassowitz, 1976.

3

Twentieth-Century Indian Literature in English

ALPANA SHARMA KNIPPLING

INTRODUCTION: THE EVOLUTION OF INDIAN LITERATURE IN ENGLISH

Not surprisingly, Indian literature in English evolved alongside the consolidation of British imperialism in India. There is a variety of opinion about the first definitive Indian text in English, although critics agree that Indian literature in English dates back to at least the early nineteenth century. Its beginnings receive their impetus from three sources: the British government's educational reforms, the work of missionaries, and the reception of English language and literature by upper-class Indians. First, there are the educational reforms called for by both the 1813 Charter Act and the 1835 English Education Act of William Bentinck. In an effort to redress some of the avaricious, hence compromising, practices of the East India Company servants, the English Parliament approved the Charter Act, which made England responsible for the educational improvement of the natives. The subsequent English Education Act, prompted by Thomas Babington Macaulay's (in)famous minute on Indian education, made English the medium of Indian education and English literature a disciplinary subject in Indian educational institutions.

In her study of the history of English in colonial India, Gauri Viswanathan usefully points out that even before Bentinck's 1835 English Education Act, instruction in English certainly existed in Indian colleges (Viswanathan 1989, 45). In the early 1800s, English was taught side by side with Oriental studies, its teaching marked by the sort of classical approach taken to Latin and Greek in British colleges. However, with the withdrawal of funds to Oriental studies, the secular character of such instruction was to give way to an increasingly Christian inflection. Hence, what makes the act so decisive is not the introduction of English in Indian colleges but, rather, the new charge, religious and moral, that English was allowed to bear in the classroom. Missionary activity, a second aspect contributing to the genesis of Indian literature in English, profited directly from this shift in emphasis. The 1813 Charter Act had opened India to the missionaries, but it posed no serious threat to the Orientalists; with the passing of the 1835 English Education Act, Orientalism received its most severe blow, and, most satisfyingly to the missionaries, English emerged as the sole bearer of morality and normativeness.

But neither these educational reforms nor the ensuing missionary activity in Christian schools alone could have ensured the hegemony of English in India. There needed to be a vested concern on the part of upwardly mobile Indians to receive the benefits of English, for without this Indian reception of English, the language simply would not have held the sort of sway that it did. Hence, the third impetus to the beginnings of Indian writing in English would have to engage this reception. The postcolonial critic Gayatri Chakravorty Spivak theorizes such a reception as a kind of "negotiation with the structures of violence" (Spivak 1990, 101). This would imply a space in which imperialism did not work its power absolutely or uniformly upon Indians for the exclusive benefit of the British. Rather, given the violence that imperialism wrought as it disrupted Indian history, it makes sense to elaborate how aspects of British power were appropriated and rearranged by Indians. An example of such a "negotiation" or appropriation is the subject of Homi K. Bhabha's essay "Signs Taken for Wonders," in which Bhabha looks at the reception of the English Book (i.e., the Bible) by a group of Indian natives (Bhabha 1985). Upon the Indian catechist Anund Messeh's introduction of the Bible to them, the Indians fail to recognize, automatically, the authority of this text, thereby producing an ambivalent, "hybrid" space that may productively resist colonial power.

All of this is to suggest that the reception of English in India, or the third impetus to early Indian writing in English, needs to be understood as radical and history-changing, yet subject to ambivalence, negotiation, and subversive appropriation on the part of Indians themselves. Thus, we have to acknowledge a nascent space in which British and Indian social codes and value systems began to intersect and mutually determine one another in nineteenth-century India; but, having done so, we also have to leave room for a reception of English that was necessarily reinventive and improvisational, not merely imitative.

EARLY WRITING IN ENGLISH: "NEGOTIATING WITH THE STRUCTURES OF VIOLENCE"

The first literary texts in English emerge from Bengal. Raja Rammohun Roy (1774–1833), the progressive advocate of English civilization and culture, wrote numerous essays and treatises, which were collected in a complete volume in 1906. But it seems that poetry was the genre that first took flight in the Indian imagination, the best-known nineteenth-century poets being Henry Derozio (1809–31), Michael Madhusudan Dutt (1827–73), Toru Dutt (1856–77), her cousin Romesh Chunder Dutt (1848–1909), and Manmohun Ghose (?–1924).

To a greater or lesser degree, all these poets were influenced by the idealistic strain of romanticism, their poetry alternately recording lyrical and Christian sentiments. (David McCutchion points out that the first volume of poetry in English came out even before these poets made their mark, citing *Shair and Other Poems* [1830] by Kasiprasad Ghose [McCutchion 1969].) By the turn of the century and into the early twentieth century, three more poets were to join their ranks, outdoing them with a far greater success and fame. These were Rabindranath Tagore (1861–1941), Sri Aurobindo Ghose (1872–1950), and Sarojini Naidu (1879–1949).

Tagore, by and large a lyrical poet, was brought to the attention of the West by his 1912 English translation of his Bengali poems; entitled *Gitanjali (Song-Offering),* the volume secured him international recognition. Some critics argue that W. B. Yeats's celebratory interpretation of Tagore's poetry as purely mystical has misled readers and obscured Tagore's actual innovation in *Gitanjali:* the use of prose poetry instead of strict meter and rhyme (see, e.g., Williams 1977, 26–28). Though he went on to translate more of his poetry, Macmillan publishing the *Collected Poems and Plays* in 1936, Tagore is still best known for his first collection of poems and the creation of his experimental school, Santiniketan, in Bolpur. Unlike Tagore, Sri Aurobindo wrote originally in English, more justly deserving the title of mystic and visionary with such well-known works as *Savitri* (1936) and *The Life Divine* (1939–40). Initially, Sri Aurobindo embarked on a career in the Indian civil service with a degree in the classics from King's College, Cambridge. The years of Anglicization came to an end when he rediscovered Indian religion and philosophy; after a period of nationalist activity, he established an ashram in Pondicherry, where he began to write his epic-style philosophical works and acquire a large religious following. Like Sri Aurobindo, Sarojini Naidu went to King's College in England, returning eventually to India on the advice of Edmund Gosse, who found her early poems "too English" (Williams 1977, 33). Her three volumes of poetry, *The Golden Threshold* (1905), *The Bird of Time* (1912), and *The Broken Wing* (1917), earned her much fame and popularity in England; at home, she became a well-known public figure.

What seems most remarkable about these early poets is that most of them saw no contradiction between their Indian and Anglicized identifications. Henry Derozio, for instance, was a fervent nationalist; yet, his love of the romantics found him riding an Arab horse through the streets of Calcutta. Similarly, Toru Dutt went to Indian myth and legend for her themes in *Ancient Ballads and Legends of Hindustan,* freshly reinterpreting some of these; yet, she remained attached to France and French literature, even writing a novel in French and translating French poems into English. Macaulay's "Indians in blood and colour, but English in taste, in opinions, in morals, and in intellect" (Macaulay 1952, 719–30), these early writers were mediators between East and West. But, "negotiating with the structures of violence," they did not merely reproduce the axioms of imperialism and mindlessly imitate Western literature. Perhaps an exception to this seemingly noncontradictory, almost arbitrary comingling of Indian and Anglo-European influences, both cultural and literary, may lie in Manmohan Ghose, who remained acutely alienated from Indians and supported British imperialism right through World War I.

THE STATUS OF THE ENGLISH LANGUAGE IN INDIAN LITERATURE IN ENGLISH: INDO-ANGLIANS VERSUS REGIONALISTS

In contrast to poetry, Indian novels in English did not come fully to light until organized movements of civil disobedience against British imperialism had begun, and Indian nationalism had become the rallying cry of the day. This may be why, to this day, novel writing in English bears the brunt of criticism by writers in regional languages, who maintain that writing in English is a disloyal, Anglophilic activity. This damaging charge is hardly surprising or unexpected. The history of English in India is such that the language cannot be read outside its determining ideological and political functions. If, on one hand, English worked to secure a common medium of communication across the diverse states of India, it also, on the other hand, achieved a bitter splintering among Indians. There are, for instance, regional writers who have opposed the very use of English as an artistic medium. According to them, the use of English is traitorous; it has, both literally and figuratively, ''sold'' an exoticized India to the West and alienated the writer in English from his or her ''native'' country. Using the term ''Indo-Anglian'' to describe themselves, writers and literary critics in English have frequently resorted to a defensive tone, insisting on their nationalistic and patriotic identifications even as they write in the master language of English.[1]

Interestingly, both parties have cast their arguments in the terms of nationalism: regional writers claim that they are more thoroughly nationalistic than Indo-Anglian writers, while Indo-Anglian writers argue that their access to nationalism is as unmediated as the regionalists'. Further, many Indo-Anglian writers and literary critics see their use of English as itself participating in a nationalistic effort to Indianize English. The classic example of such an Indianizing effort would have to be Raja Rao's *Kanthapura.* In the well-known Author's Foreword to the novel, Rao professes the nature of his experimental nativization of English with a certain ambivalence, insisting that the English language is a part of Indians' ''intellectual make-up'' but not of their ''emotional make-up''; in this way, English is and isn't an ''alien language'' (Rao 1938, vii). Locating himself at the tenuous juncture where English and Indian influences conjoin and conflict (''We cannot write like the English. . . . We cannot write only as Indians''), he undertakes a project that is both modernist and nationalist: *Kanthapura* relates, in the speech of a pious old Brahmin woman's ''native'' cadence and rhythm, the story of a small village's growing involvement in Gandhi's Quit-India campaign against the British.

But the project initiated by Rao in 1938 was to become more and more embattled and beleagured by the postcolonial 1960s. During the 1960s, such Indo-Anglian writers as P. Lal, teacher at St. Xavier's College, Calcutta, and early leader of the Calcutta-based group of writers called the Writers' Workshop, was rehearsing heated and impassioned debates with regional writers (see McCutchion 1969, 20–22). Since that time, debates between the two opposed positions have become part and parcel of the history of literary production in English.

Briefly summarized, the regionalist position maintains that writers can be "true" to India only if they write in languages other than English; the Indo-Anglian position maintains that writers can be "true" to India in spite of the language they use and, sometimes, because of the language they use (as in the case of Indianizing English). Because both groups have articulated their positions in terms of truth—truthfulness, authenticity, "true" nationalism, even "true" patriotism—they have polarized debate over the singular question, Which group is "true" to India? It is less interesting to range ourselves either on one side of this debate over English or on the other. To do so means to devalue the history attached equally to both sides. In fact, both sides have had to elaborate their relation to English, one through vehement denial, the other through creative incorporation. Also, as I have tried to show, Indian writing in English has opened up a space that is not purely imitative of English in an empty kind of way but, instead, subject to productive innovation and reinvention.

Given the historical "impurity" of both sides, it seems more instructive to study the process by which both the Indo-Anglian and the regionalist sides equally and convincingly articulate certain "truths" about Indian national identity. We must keep in mind, however, that these "truths" are contestatory discursive effects; they are not true in and of themselves. Michel Foucault's genealogical work shows that the subject of "truth" is not something that lies outside, or transcends, discourse. It is, instead, an effect of discourse, which in itself is neither true nor false: "Truth is a thing of this world: it is produced only by virtue of multiple forms of constraint. And it induces regular effects of power. Each society has its own regime of truth, its 'general politics' of truth: that is, the types of discourse which it accepts and makes function as true (Foucault 1980, 131)." In a country that historically has both accepted and tenuously managed regional and cultural differences, what is at stake for the Indo-Anglian and regionalist production of "truth" is nothing less than the whole subject of Indian nationalism.

INDIAN LITERATURE IN ENGLISH FROM 1935 TO 1970

While poetry took precedence over novels, novel writing did go on in the nineteenth century. Pyaricharan Mitra's *Alaler Gharer* (The Spoilt Child, 1858) seems to be the first Indian novel. The first Indian novel in English, however, may be Bankim Chandra Chatterjee's *Rajmohun's Wife* (1864); ironically, this was also to be his last novel, for after its appearance, Chatterjee wrote in Bengali for his remaining writing career. To this novel may be added Sorabji's *Love and Life behind the Purdah* (1901) and S. B. Banerjea's *Tales of Bengal* (1910). But in the turbulent 1920s, 1930s, and 1940s Indian novel writing in English became a viable industry.

The decades of the 1920s, 1930s, and 1940s witnessed cataclysmic changes, as discourses of nationalism and colonialism collided, even as India was thrust into modern conditions of living and thinking. These years produced three Indian novelists, often referred to as the three ''greats'' of Indian literature in English: Mulk Raj Anand (1905), R. K. Narayan (1906), and Raja Rao (1909). At the crossroads where discourses of colonialism, nationalism, and modernity intersected and began to mutually inform one another, Anand, Narayan, and Rao tackled the issues of the time in strikingly different ways: Anand through the social idealist's vision of Marx; Narayan through the comic-satirist's recording of everyday life in the fictitious town, Malgudi; and Rao through the Brahmin philosopher's caste-inflected ruminations on Indian culture.

Anand is best known for the novels *Untouchable* (1935), *Coolie* (1936), and *Two Leaves and a Bud* (1937); the trilogy *The Village* (1939), *Across the Black Waters* (1940), and *The Sword and the Sickle* (1942); and *The Private Life of an Indian Prince* (1953). What characterizes most of these novels is the repeated depiction of a beleagured, working-class protagonist, whose oppression marks the oppression of rural India by the twin systems of empire and capital. In *Untouchable,* for instance, Anand depicts a day in the life of a sweeper and latrine cleaner, Bakha, in whose tortured and split consciousness Anand shows the debilitating effects of the Hindu caste system. In doing so, he also puts the colonial language of English and all of its elite associations at the service of an ideological necessity to speak for those who cannot speak for themselves. This literary attempt at subaltern representation may be productively read in relation to the current historiographical project of the Subaltern Studies historians, who are engaged in recuperating the marginalized perspectives of the subaltern classes through Indian colonial and neocolonial history.

Narayan's oeuvre is enormous, but most worthy of note are *Swami and Friends* (1935), *The English Teacher* (1945), *The Financial Expert* (1952), *Waiting for the Mahatma* (1955), *The Guide* (1958), *The Man Eater of Malgudi* (1962), *My Days: Memoirs* (1974), and *The Painter of Signs* (1976); most recently, Narayan has published *A Storyteller's World* (1989, 1990) and *The World of Nagaraj* (1990). Perhaps to a larger extent than Anand, Narayan established the global stakes for Indian literature in English. With the ingenious invention of a fictitious small town, Malgudi—where all his novels are set—Narayan was able to convey the cultural nuances of India itself to both Indians and Western readers. His international popularity is readily evident in the many reprints of his novels by the University of Chicago Press and Penguin in the 1980s and 1990s. But, unlike Anand, Narayan does not revise English itself for a new political purpose. His prose is lucid yet predictable in pattern, its chief characteristic being an understated, modest, tongue-in-cheek irony, which works excellently at deflecting any ultimate seriousness of theme and purpose that we may attribute to his text.[2]

Like Anand, Raja Rao deliberately set out to rewrite English for Indian ends. However, Rao's first novel, *Kanthapura* (1938), which marks a fascinating experiment to Indianize the English language, was later disavowed by Rao when he found his guru, Shri Atmananda, and his faith in the Sanskritic philosophy of Vedanta. His next novel, *The Serpent and the Rope* (1960), explores his religious faith, as does *The Cat and Shakespeare* (1965). Rao's *Comrade Kirillov* (1976) shows his interest in Marxism, but it was conceived in the early 1950s, before Rao came to believe that Vedantism transcended Marxism. As a writer who has ''rediscovered'' his Vedantic origins, Rao has exchanged one brand of nationalism—anticolonialism in the British Raj—for another—pro-Hinduism in postindependence India. His writing seems to have begun the move from the public, communal scene inclusive of all castes and class, to the introspective, private musings of a Brahminical life.

Anand and Rao have traveled extensively abroad; but all three writers demonstrate a comfortable ease with English. In the postcolonial period, such an ease ceases to be unusual or unexpected. Instead, it bears the mark of an everyday sort of casualness, almost obscuring the fact that systematic access to English is still limited to the upper and middle classes. Indian diasporic literature in the Anglo-United States, the most Western(ized) example of Indian literature in English, perhaps bears out this point most convincingly. But Anand, Narayan, and Rao secured the future of Indian writing in English by turning writing in English into a solidified material project that had assumed international proportions by the 1940s. In the process of producing and participating in this project, they also show the discontinuous historical trajectory in which competing and contradictory discourses of colonialism, nationalism, and modernity collide.

Literature of this period must, however, also include the novels of Bhabani Bhattacharya, G. V. Desani, and Sudhindra Nath Ghose. Of these, one must especially note G. V. Desani, whose satiric comedy *All about H. Hatterr* (1948) broke new ground in its subversive treatment of British–Indian relations and the English language. In the period of decolonization that followed Indian independence, a new set of novelists emerged, the leading ones quickly identifying themselves as Anita Desai, Manohar Malgonkar, Kamala Markandaya, Balachandra Rajan, Nayantara Sahgal, and Khushwant Singh. Inheritors of India's postindependence history, these authors seem quite aware of writing in the wake of the literary successes of Anand, Narayan, and Rao. Singh and Malgonkar chose among their early subjects the communal violence unleashed by the horrific specter of independence and partition, the former in *Train to Pakistan* (1956) and the latter in *Distant Drum* (1960) and *A Bend in the Ganges* (1964).

In dramatic contrast, Desai, Markandaya, and Rajan articulated an interest in the psychosocial space in which their characters struggled toward a privatized and individualistic self-awareness informed by essentially Western (but now seen as fairly universal) ideals. In particular, the early fiction of Desai (1937)—*Cry the Peacock* (1963) and *Voices in the City* (1965)—depicts intensely privatized lives of middle-class women and men, as does the fiction of Markandaya (1924). In the novels, *Nectar in a Sieve* (1954), *Some Inner Fury* (1955), *A Silence of Desire* (1960), *Possession* (1963), *A Handful of Rice* (1966), and *The Coffer Dams* (1969), Markandaya weaves the lives of women, often of subaltern classes, into the sociopolitical backdrop of rural India. Both Desai and Markandaya have diasporic identifications, Desai teaching creative writing for one semester at Mount Holyoke College and spending the remainder of her time in India and Markandaya, living in England since 1948. Both women also have European affiliations, the former with half-German parentage and the latter with an English husband. This bicultural background may be understood as productive of some tension, as these writers locate their domicile elsewhere, yet continue to use India as their primary setting. (While Ruth Prawer Jhabvala is regarded by some critics as an Indo-Anglian writer, her own admission that she is "not [Indian], and less so every year" and her recent relocation to the United States prevent discussion of her writing in these pages.[3])

The impingement of discourses of nationalism, colonialism, and modernity on the literature produced by Indian novelists in this period shows a script that was making a transition from the public to the private in an increasingly global way. If Anand, Narayan, and Rao were preternaturally aware of the public arena in which their fiction would participate, Desai and Markandaya seem interested in staging the private world of individualism for a global audience. What is evident in the fiction of the 1950s, 1960s, and 1970s seems to be paralleled in the poetry. In this period, Indian poetry in English attempted to break away from the sentimentality commonly associated with Tagore, Aurobindo, and Naidu. In keeping with the new, modernist poetics sought by T. S. Eliot and Ezra Pound abroad, Indian poets in English similarly strove for a symbolic yet realistic style. Leading poets of the 1950s and 1960s include Kamala Das, Nissim Ezekiel, P. Lal, Dom Moraes, and A. K. Ramanujan. Of these, Kamala Das deserves special mention; her poetic innovation consisted in creating a bold and passionate medium in which to explore the range of female anxiety and sexuality. These poets were joined, in the late 1960s and early 1970s, by Dilip Chitre, Arun Kolatkar, Jayanta Mahapatra, Arvind Krishna Mehrotra, and Pritish Nandy, among others. Their poetry demonstrates a vivid grasp of world literature, not limited to Eliot and Pound but extending, instead, to French experimental poetry from Rimbaud to dadaism and surrealism; as well, Chitre, Kolatkar, and Ramanujan are interested in incorporating regional influences (King 1992, 5).

One key participant in this process of globalization has been the Western critic of Indian literature in English. If "truth" of Indian national identity is what preoccupies Indian writers and critics, one may ask what the stakes are for all those Western critics who have played such a key role in the history of the production of Indian literature in English. As far back as 1882, when Edmund Gosse's critical introduction to Toru Dutt's *Ancient Ballads and Legends* established Toru Dutt as a leading lyrical poet, the mediating role of the Anglo-American critic emerged. This mediation's power cannot be underestimated, as the careers of many indigenous Indian writers in English have depended on the work of patronage, promotion, and representation by Western critics. The following are just a few examples of Western mediation: Edmund Gosse's "discovery" of Toru and Aru Dutt's English translation of French poems, "a shabby little book. . . . A hopeless volume it seemed with its queer type," which, when Gosse read it, elicited his great "rapture" (see Narasimhaiah 1987, 24); Gosse's acquaintance, in London and Cambridge, with Sarojini Naidu, whom he urged to go home for "some revelations of the heart of India" (Williams 1977, 33); E. M. Forster's introduction to Mulk Raj Anand's *Untouchable,* which had been turned down by 19 publishers before Wishart Books agreed to publish it, provided Forster wrote the introduction; and Graham Greene's rave review of the young Narayan's first work, *Swami and Friends,* which helped put Narayan on the global map.

As facilitators or participants in the global circuit of literary production and reception, Western critics have taken sides in the debate between Indo-Anglians and regionalists, and, thanks to the covering over of their own ideological stakes in the debate, they have given it a strange and different twist. In dramatic contrast to the Indo-Anglian writers and critics who have repeatedly expressed their stakes and insisted on issues to do with truth, self-representation, authenticity, and Indian national identity, such Western critics as David McCutchion and William Walsh have not found it necessary to account for their own vested interest in Indian literature in English. Nor, significantly, do they discuss their own ideological and geopolitical positioning, as Western, vis-à-vis their analyses of Indian texts in English. Seemingly disinterested and neutral bystanders, these readers, in fact, reveal their cultural biases in numerous ways, as when they customarily situate Anglo-American literature as normative, thus (out)casting Indian literature in English in the dubious light either of an embarrassing aberration or of a poor imitation. In both cases, the literature seems to emerge as second-best. Indeed, Walsh's essay, "Sweet Mangoes and Malt Vinegar: The Novels of R. K. Narayan," published in a collection of critical essays edited by K. K. Sharma, seems to imply that Narayan achieved literary greatness, not because of, but *in spite of,* being Indian (Walsh 1977, 121–40).[4]

INDIAN LITERATURE IN ENGLISH AT THE BRINK OF THE TWENTY-FIRST CENTURY

In *The Indo-English Novel: The Impact of the West in a Developing Country,* Klaus Steinvorth argues that Indian literature in English is written primarily for Western readers. He demonstrates this thesis on the basis of such evidence as the detailed explanation of Indian cultural and sociohistorical heteroglossia in many of the texts: why would an Indian writer need to include such obvious and, hence, redundant explanations of Indian customs to Indian readers? Steinvorth also calls attention to all those book jackets that bear photographs of sari-clad women writers and wonders what these exoticized representations do to the market sales of the books in the West. In the current period, Steinvorth's 1975 critique of Indian literature in English reminds us that visual textual signifiers—reproductions of Mughal-style paintings of princesses, handmaidens, and elephants on book covers, for instance—are in the service of global commodity production and circulation. In the case of Indian literature in English, such visual textual signifiers may serve only to reproduce, for readers, the kinds of Orientalizing gestures that Edward Said criticized in *Orientalism.* In other words, the literature stands to be appropriated as an exoticized Other that consolidates the neoimperialist self of the Anglo-United States. In some senses, since its inception in British colonialism in the mid-nineteenth century, the literature has always run the risk of appropriation as an exoticized Other. However, with the insertion of modernity, the difference that the twentieth century brings is, first, a kind of solidification of a project of writing that has begun to render national boundaries irrelevant. Such is the determining function of multinational publishing corporations that national boundaries almost cease to matter.

Related to this is the second different twist that the (late) twentieth century has performed: it is becoming more difficult to make critical distinctions between indigenous Indian writers and writers of the Indian diaspora. Although this point may be argued, surely it is symptomatic that Viney Kirpal's 1990 collection of critical essays, *The New Indian Novel in English: A Study of the 1980s,* published in India by Allied Publishers, makes no distinction between indigenous and diasporic writers. Indeed, its express aim is to show that, in "the New Indian novel, the world itself is regarded as one big home. . . . The awareness of the world as a larger place is in" (Kirpal 1990, xxii).[5] When a critical distinction is made, it falls between the "Old Masters" (Narayan and Anand) and subsequent generations, while the indigenous novels of Upmanyu Chatterjee, Shashi Deshpande, Namita Gokhale, Arun Joshi, Chaman Nahal, Ranga Rao, Nayantara Sahgal, and Pratap Sharma are treated alongside those of the diasporic writers Anita Desai, Amitav Ghosh, Kamala Markandaya, Salman Rushdie, and Vikram Seth (Rushdie securing the attention of no less than 6 of the 27 essays).

A similar global awareness is at work in current English-language poetry. According to Arvind Krishna Mehrotra, poet and editor of *Twelve Modern Indian Poets,* no significant distinction obtains between the indigenous poetry of Dilip Chitre, Keki N. Daruwalla, Eunice de Souza, Nissim Ezekiel, Adil Jussawalla, Arun Kolatkar, Jayanta Mahapatra, and Manohar Shetty and the diasporic poetry of Agha Shahid Ali, Dom Moraes—who, Mehrotra points out, has lived in Bombay for the past decade—A. K. Ramanujan, and Vikram Seth. In fact, it proves difficult even to typify writers of the second group as diasporic: they continue to work on Indian material and, according to Mehrotra, all, excepting Moraes, Seth, and the early Jussawalla, incorporate their "native" regional tongues into English. In the introduction to his critical study, *Modern Indian Poetry in English,* Bruce King similarly argues that the poetry demonstrates a global awareness, with many poets indebted to North and South American and early Indian regional verse (see King 1992, 1–10).

All of this goes to show that the yielding of national boundaries to the uncanny spaces of the diaspora does not lead us to presume the irrelevance of the nation. On the contrary, the diaspora recasts nationalism, or, as Arjun Appadurai puts it, "the nationalist genie, never perfectly contained in the bottle of the territorial state, is now itself diasporic," (Appadurai 1993, 411–29). But one area that still draws meaningful distinctions between indigenous and diasporic agendas in literature is that of women's writing. Indeed, one significant gain in the entry of Indian literature in English in the public and global realms has been the possibility of a space opened up to women's writing in India. Such feminist publishers as Kali for Women have brought out significant anthologies of stories by Indian women, both originally in English and translated into English from the regional languages: for example, *In Other Words: New Writing by Indian Women* and *The Slate of Life: An Anthology of Stories by Indian Women.* In addition, Kali for Women has brought out collections of critical essays on issues to do with feminism, colonialism, and nationalism: Kumari Jayawardena's *Feminism and Nationalism in the Third World* and Kumkum Sangari and Sudesh Vaid's edited volume, *Recasting Women: Essays in Colonial History.* Most worthy of mention is the groundbreaking, comprehensive collection of writing by women, *Women Writing in India: 600 B.C. to the Present,* two volumes, edited by Susie Tharu and K. Lalita. With the single exception of the New York City-based writer and teacher Meena Alexander (whose short story is featured in *The Slate of Life*), all the writers represented in these anthologies are, or, in their lifetime, were, residents of India. In fact, Tharu and Lalita pointedly exclude diasporic women writers like Anita Desai, Meena Alexander, and Suniti Namjoshi from their *Volume Two: The Twentieth Century.* In their general introduction, they also very carefully separate their feminist agenda from that of Anglo-U.S. feminists, reading the scene of Indian women's writing against and through issues to do with literacy, class, and caste.

NOTE ON DRAMA

Both H. M. Williams and M. K. Naik have asserted that Indian drama in English has never reached a point of competition with novels and poetry. This failure of the development of Indian drama has been attributed to the fact that English is not always a comfortable language in which to converse on an Indian stage. Even though Tagore and Sri Aurobindo showed considerable interest in producing dramas, their difficulty in conveying poetry through the medium of the stage proved a drawback. Similarly, as Williams points out, Desani's play *Hali* was praised as poetry rather than drama by T. S. Eliot (Williams 1977,

122). Other dramatists worthy of mention are Asif Currimbhoy, Santha Rama Rau, and Partap Sharma. Among these, Currimbhoy is distinguished by his ability to incorporate Indian dance and folk traditions. For discussion of Indian drama in English, readers are referred to the critical studies of K. R. Srinivasa Iyengar, Naik, and Williams.[6]

NOTES

1. For the most exhaustive articulation in defense of Indian writing in English, see Narasimhaiah 1987, "Towards an Understanding of the Species Called 'Indian Writing in English,'" *The Swan and the Eagle,* 1–18. For an outline of the problems facing Indian writers in English, see Verghese 1971, "Some Aspects of Indian Fiction in English," *Problems of the Indian Creative Writer in English,* 98–125. Interestingly, not only regional writers but also some critics of the West oppose the use of English by Indian writers. See, for instance, McCutchion, *Indian Writing in English,* for a rather pessimistic view of the creative use of English.

2. For an in-depth critical perspective on the novels of Narayan and Rao, please refer to Knippling 1993, 169–86.

3. See Jhabvala 1992, 13–21. Jhabvala makes several tendentious claims about the "intolerable . . . idea" of India for an outsider (20), the "horror" of India's poverty (14), the shallowness of young, Westernized Indian women (16–17), and so on.

4. There may be three groups into which these (predominantly British) literary critics fall. First, one group praises certain Indian writers, often on the basis of a favorable comparison with canonical Anglo-American or classical Russian writers. Thus, for instance, is Narayan touted as India's Gogol or Austen by Western reviewers; Mulk Raj Anand is the country's own Charles Dickens; and Anita Desai is its Chekov. The second group consists of wary readers who often confess ambivalence with regard to the status of English in the literature. Generally speaking, these critics are reluctant to grant the English language its own homegrown legitimacy and literary utility in India. David McCutchion, for instance, warns that Indian literature in English stands to be misread as a curious "phenomenon" rather than a "creative contribution" (McCutchion 1969, 7), because of the colonial legacy of English both for the British and the Indians. The third group is openly critical of the very use of English.

5. Perhaps to underscore her argument, Kirpal consistently capitalizes the word "new," as in "New Indian novel."

Both the global nature of Indian literary production and the constant traffic of writers to and from India create a peculiar difficulty for the bibliographer of indigenous literature in English. The primary bibliography at the end of this chapter reflects this difficulty of including and excluding texts on the unstable premise of a writer's domicile. Generally, I have sought to represent those writers of Indian origin who, in the course of their lifetime, have spent a considerable amount of time in India.

6. See Naik 1984, especially "The Achievement of Indian English Drama" (151–65), "The English Plays of Rabindranath Tagore" (166–81), "Gurcharan Das's *Larins Sahib*" (182–90), and "'From the Horse's Mouth': A Study of *Hayavadana* (by Girish Karnad)" (191–202); Williams 1977, 121–25.

WORKS CITED

Appadurai, Arjun. "Patriotism and Its Futures." *Public Culture* 5:3 (Spring 1993):411–29.

Bhabha, Homi K. "Signs Taken for Wonders: Questions of Ambivalence and Authority under a Tree outside Delhi, May 1817." *Critical Inquiry* 12 (Autumn 1985):144–165.

Foucault, Michel. *Power/Knowledge: Selected Interviews and Other Writings 1972–1977.* Edited by Colin Gordon. Translated by Colin Gordon, Leo Marshall, John Mepham, and Kate Soper. New York: Pantheon Books, 1980.

Jayawardena, Kumari. *Feminism and Nationalism in the Third World.* New Delhi: Kali for Women, 1986.

Jhabvala, Ruth Prawer. Introduction. *Out of India: Selected Stories.* New York: Simon and Schuster, 1992.

King, Bruce. *Modern Indian Poetry in English.* 1987. Delhi: Oxford University Press, 1992.

Kirpal, Viney, ed. *The New Indian Novel in English: A Study of the 1980s.* New Delhi: Allied, 1990.

Knippling, Alpana Sharma. "R. K. Narayan, Raja Rao, and Modern English Discourse in Colonial India." *Modern Fiction Studies* 39:1 (Spring 1993):169–86.

Macaulay, Thomas Babington. "Indian Education." In *Macaulay: Prose and Poetry,* edited by G. M. Young. Cambridge: Harvard University Press, 1952.

McCutchion, David. *Indian Writing in English.* Calcutta: Writers Workshop, 1969.

Naik, M. K. *Dimensions of Indian English Literature.* New Delhi: Sterling, 1984.

Narasimhaiah, C. D. *The Swan and the Eagle: Essays on Indian English Literature.* 1968. Simla: Indian Institute of Advanced Study, 1987.

Rao, Raja. *Kanthapura.* 1938. New York: New Directions, 1967.

Sangari, Kumkum, and Sudesh Vaid, eds. *Recasting Women: Essays in Colonial History.* New Delhi: Kali for Women, 1989.

Spivak, Gayatri Chakravorty. *The Post-Colonial Critic: Interviews, Strategies, Dialogues.* Edited by Sarah Harasym. New York: Routledge, 1990.

Verghese, C. Paul. *Problems of the Indian Creative Writer in English.* Bombay: Somaiya, 1971.

Viswanathan, Gauri. *Masks of Conquest: Literary Study and British Rule in India.* New York: Columbia University Press, 1989.

Walsh, William. "Sweet Mangoes and Malt Vinegar." In *Indo-English Literature: A Collection of Critical Essays,* edited by K. K. Sharma. Ghaziabad: Vimal Prakashan, 1977.

Williams, H. M. *Indo-Anglian Literature 1800–1970: A Survey.* Columbia: South Asia Books, 1977.

SELECTED PRIMARY BIBLIOGRAPHY

Ali, Ahmed. *Ocean of Night.* East Glastonbury: Ind-US, 1973.

———. *Twilight in Delhi.* 1940. Delhi: Oxford University Press, 1991.

———. *The Village.* Delhi: Orient Paperbacks, 1939.

———. *Across the Black Waters.* Delhi: Orient Paperbacks, 1940.

———. *Seven Summers.* Bombay: Kutub-Popular, 1951.
———. *Two Leaves and a Bud.* 1937. Bombay: Kutub-Popular, 1955.
———. *Lament on the Death of a Master of Arts.* Delhi: Orient Paperbacks, 1967.
———. *Morning Face.* New Delhi: Arnold-Heinemann, 1968.
———. *Confessions of a Lover.* New Delhi: Arnold-Heinemann, 1972a.
———. *Coolie.* 1936. Delhi: Orient Paperbacks, 1972b.
———. *Gauri.* East Glastonbury: Ind-US, 1981.
———. *The Big Heart.* 1948. East Glastonbury: Ind-US, 1983.
———. *The Bubble.* New Delhi: Arnold-Heinemann, 1984a.
———. *The Sword and the Sickle.* 1942. New Delhi: Arnold-Heinemann, 1984b.
Anand, Mulk Raj. *Untouchable.* 1935. London: Penguin, 1986.
———. *Pilpali Sahab: The Story of a Big Ego in a Small Body.* New Delhi: Arnold-Heinemann, 1990.
———. *Between Tears and Laughter.* New York: Apt Books, 1991.
Bhattacharya, Bhabhani. *He Who Rides a Tiger.* New Delhi: Hind Pocket Books, 1955.
———. *Steel Hawk and Other Stories.* East Glastonbury: Ind-US, 1968.
———. *Shadow from Ladakh.* East Glastonbury: Ind-US, 1969.
Butalia, Urvashi, and Ritu Menon, eds. *In Other Words: New Writing by Indian Women.* New Delhi: Kali for Women, 1992.
Chatterjee, Upmanyu. *English, August: An Indian Story.* London: Faber and Faber, 1988.
Chaudari, Nirad C. *A Passage to England.* New York: St. Martin's Press, 1959.
———. *The Continent of Circe, Being an Essay on the Peoples of India.* 1965. New York: Oxford University Press, 1967.
———. *Autobiography of an Unknown Indian.* 1951. Reading, Mass.: Addison-Wesley, 1989.
Currimbhoy, Asif. *Plays: Goa, Inquilab, The Doldrummers, The Refugee, "Darjeeling Tea?" Sonar Bangla.* New Delhi: Oxford and IBH, 1972.
da Cunha, Nisha. *Old Cypress: Stories.* New Delhi: Penguin, 1991.
Desai, Anita. *Bye-Bye Blackbird.* Delhi: Hind, 1971.
———. *Games at Twilight and Other Stories.* London: Penguin, 1978.
———. *Clear Light of Day.* London: Penguin, 1980a.
———. *Cry, the Peacock.* 1963. New Delhi: Orient Paperbacks, 1980b.
———. *Fire on the Mountain.* 1977. London: Penguin, 1981.
———. *Voices in the City.* 1965. New Delhi: Orient Paperbacks, 1982a.
———. *Where Shall We Go This Summer?* 1975. Delhi: Orient Paperbacks, 1982b.
———. *In Custody.* New York: Harper and Row, 1984.
———. *Baumgartner's Bombay.* 1988. New York: Penguin, 1990.
Desani, G. V. *All about H. Hatterr.* 1948. New York: McPherson, 1986.
———. *Hali, and Collected Stories.* New York: McPherson, 1991.
Deshpande, Shashi. *The Dark Holds No Terrors.* Delhi: Vikas, 1980.
———. *Roots and Shadows.* New York: Apt Books, 1983.
———. *That Long Silence.* London: Virago Press, 1988.
Dutt, Toru. *Ancient Ballads and Legends of Hindustan.* 1885. East Glastonbury: Ind-US, 1975.
Gokhale, Namita. *Paro: Dreams of Passion.* London: Pan Books, 1985.
Holmstrom, Lakshmi, ed. *The Inner Courtyard: Stories by Indian Women.* London: Virago Press, 1990.
Hosain, Attia. *Sunlight on a Broken Column.* 1961. New York: Viking Penguin, 1989.

Joshi, Arun. *The Foreigner.* 1968. New Delhi: Orient Paperbacks, 1972.
———. *The Apprentice.* East Glastonbury: Ind-US, 1974.
———. *Survivor.* East Glastonbury: Ind-US, 1975.
———. *The Last Labyrinth.* New Delhi: Vision Books, 1981.
Malgonkar, Manohar. *Combat of Shadows.* London: Hamish Hamilton, 1962.
———. *The Princes: A Novel.* New York: Viking Press, 1963.
———. *A Bend in the Ganges.* 1964. New York: Viking Press, 1965.
———. *The Devil's Wind: Nana Saheb's Story.* London: Hamish Hamilton, 1972.
Markandaya, Kamala. *Nectar in a Sieve.* Bombay: Jaico Publishing House, 1954.
———. *A Silence of Desire.* London: Putnam, 1955a.
———. *Some Inner Fury.* London: Putnam, 1955b.
———. *Possession.* Bombay: Jaico Publishing House, 1963.
———. *A Handful of Rice.* New Delhi: Hind Pocket Books, 1966.
———. *The Coffer Dams.* New Delhi: Hind Pocket Books, 1969.
———. *The Nowhere Man.* New Delhi: Orient Longman, 1972.
———. *Two Virgins.* New York: Signet, 1973.
———. *The Golden Honeycomb.* London: Chatto and Windus, 1977.
———. *Pleasure City.* London: Chatto and Windus, 1982.
McDermott, Robert, ed. *The Essential Aurobindo.* Hudson: Lindisfarne Press, 1987.
Mehrotra, Arvind Krishna, ed. *The Oxford India Anthology of Twelve Modern Indian Poets.* Delhi: Oxford University Press, 1992.
Nahal, Chaman. *Azadi.* East Glastonbury: Ind-US, 1979.
———. *Sunrise in Fiji.* Columbia: South Asia Books, 1988.
———. *The Salt of Life: A Novel.* Columbia: South Asia Books, 1990.
Narayan, R. K. *The Bachelor of Arts.* 1937. Chicago: University of Chicago Press, 1980a.
———. *The Emerald Route.* East Glastonbury: Ind-US, 1980b.
———. *The English Teacher.* 1945. Chicago: University of Chicago Press, 1980c.
———. *Swami and Friends.* 1935. Chicago: University of Chicago Press, 1980d.
———. *An Astrologer's Day and Other Stories.* 1964. East Glastonbury: Ind-US, 1981a.
———. *The Dark Room.* 1938. Chicago: University of Chicago Press, 1981b.
———. *The Financial Expert.* 1952. Chicago: University of Chicago Press, 1981c.
———. *Mr. Sampath: The Printer of Malgudi.* 1949. Chicago: University of Chicago Press, 1981d.
———. *Waiting for the Mahatma.* 1955. Chicago: University of Chicago Press, 1981e.
———. *The Man Eater of Malgudi.* 1962. New York: Viking Penguin, 1983a.
———. *The Vendor of Sweets.* 1967. New York: Viking Penguin, 1983b.
———. *Malgudi Days.* New York: Viking Penguin, 1985a.
———. *The Painter of Signs.* 1976. London: Penguin, 1985b.
———. *Under the Banyan Tree.* New York: Viking Penguin, 1987.
———. *The Guide.* 1958. London: Penguin, 1988a.
———. *Talkative Man.* New York: Viking Penguin, 1988b.
———. *My Days: Memoirs.* 1974. New York: Viking Penguin, 1990a.
———. *A Storyteller's World.* 1989. New Delhi: Penguin, 1990b.
———. *The World of Nagaraj.* 1990. New York: Viking Penguin, 1991.
———. *Gods, Demons, and Others.* Chicago: University of Chicago Press, 1993.
Rajan, B. *The Dark Dancer.* London: Heinemann, 1959.
———. *Too Long in the West.* Bombay: Jaico Publishing House, 1961.

Rao, Raja. *The Cow of the Barricades and Other Stories.* Madras: Oxford University Press, 1947.

———. *Kanthapura.* 1938. New York: New Directions, 1967.

———. *The Cat and Shakespeare: A Tale of India.* 1965. Delhi: Hind, 1971.

———. *Comrade Kirillov.* New Delhi: Vision Books, 1976.

———. *The Policeman and the Rose: Stories.* Delhi: Oxford University Press, 1978.

———. *The Serpent and the Rope.* 1960. New York: Overlook, 1986.

———. *The Chessmaster and His Moves.* New Delhi: Vision Books, 1988.

Sahgal, Nayantara. *Rich like Us.* New York: New Directions, 1988.

———. *A Situation in New Delhi.* 1977. New Delhi: Penguin, 1988.

———. *Mistaken Identity.* New York: New Directions, 1989.

The Slate of Life: An Anthology of Stories by Women. New Delhi: Kali for Women, 1990.

Tharu, Susie, and K. Lalita, eds. *Women Writing in India: 600* B.C to the Present. 2 vols. New York: Feminist Press, 1991, 1993.

4

Twentieth-Century Gujarati Literature

SARALA JAG MOHAN

INTRODUCTION

Gujarati is one of the major languages of India, spoken by about 41.3 million people of Gujarat in western India. Originating in the sixth century, it passed through various stages of development, acquiring literary expression by the twelfth century. Since then, literary creation in Gujarati has been an ongoing process.

Gujarati literature has been traditionally divided into (1) an ancient phase up to 1450, (2) a middle phase up to 1800, and (3) the modern phase from 1800 onward. It is customary to trace the roots of modern Gujarati literature to the middle phase.

Middle Phase

The renowned saint-poets Narasingh Mehta and Meerabai, a princess turned poet (fifteenth and sixteenth centuries), were the powerful forces behind the Bhakti movement. Both sang of their love for the god Krishna, but Narasingh Mehta also wrote poetry on the philosophy of the Upanishads. Meerabai, who also wrote in Rajasthani and Braj Bhasha, was lyrical and emotional. Her songs reflected enlightened thinking, though not necessarily profound philosophy. Both used familiar, colloquial language. Narasingh's all-embracing humanism is relevant even today. His famous composition "Vaishnava Jana to tene kahiye" (One Who Feels the Pain of Others Is a True Vaishnav), full of warm compassion, was adopted by Gandhiji and routinely sung during his prayers. Narasingh Mehta has been rightly called the Adi Kavi (the First Poet) of Gujarat. Similarly, Meerabai's devotional songs have remained alive over the centuries. She is ranked with Narasingh as a major poet and is the first woman poet of Gujarat.

Another saint-poet was Akho (1591–1659), a Vedantist and a radical. He chastised false gurus and advocated monistic doctrine. His *Akhegita* and *Anubhavbindu* reveal his deep knowledge of philosophy. The biting satire of his poetry had an underlying humanism. Bhojo Bhagat (1785–1850), Dhiro (1753–1825), and other devotional poets were popular in their time.

The Jain monks also contributed to Gujarati literature through their writings in prose and verse, narrating the life incidents of their Tirthankaras, and also adapted stories from the epics to suit the Jain concepts of life and religion.

Other Poets of the Middle Phase

Gujarati literature of this period was largely religious, but there were exceptions, like Padmanabh's *Kanhadadeprabandh* (1456), a heroic poem. There were also occasional spurts of erotic and romantic poetry. Bhalan (c.1426–1500) adapted Puranic themes to suit his time.

But Premanand (1640–1700) is considered a major nonreligious poet of the middle period because of excellence and abundance of his poetic creations. He first wrote poetry in Hindi, but, on being reprimanded by his guru, he vowed to develop the Gujarati language as a vehicle of fine literary expression and succeeded. His *akhyanas* (long narrative poems), based on epics and plays, had fantastically rich vocabulary and a variety of themes and style. Then came Shamal (1699–1769), who wrote long poems like *Padmavati, Nandbatrisi,* and *Madanamohana,* drawing on tales of wondrous romance.

Dayaram (1767–1852), the last eminent poet of the middle period, was a born lover, uninhibited by conventions. He sang of Krishna as lover in all his poems. He had a special genius for writing *garbis* (lyrical poems with rhythm).

Those were turbulent times in Gujarat. The East India Company had occupied the Surat Fort (1759), and there were frequent Maratha invasions. By 1818, the British were in firm political control in Gujarat. Dayaram's passing away was the end of an era.

Coming of the British: A Turning Point

The arrival of the British marked the beginning of far-reaching political, economic, social, and cultural changes all over India, including Gujarat. A new educational system reached wider sections of the people and encouraged the native languages called "vernaculars." Christian missionaries also played a crucial role in propagating education. However, in Gujarat, the missionaries could mostly influence the deprived and exploited sections of society. With the spread of English education, the educated sections in Gujarat became acquainted and fascinated by English literature and social and political thought of the West. A reaffirmation of Hindu culture took place simultaneously.

Educational Institution and Social Reform

The new currents led to the opening of new schools and establishment of institutions like the Royal Asiatic Society of Bombay, the Elphinstone School and the Elphinstone Institute of Bombay (1835), Gujarat Vernacular Society (1844), which later became the Gujarat Vidya Sabha, the Buddhivardhak Sabha, Bombay (1851), and Manavdharma Sabha, Surat (1844). This brought social, religious, and cultural regeneration, with unmistakable impact on Gujarati literature. With the establishment of the University of Bombay (1857), people with university education became interested in English literature and culture. Some of them felt inspired to try new literary forms in Gujarati and to translate and adapt some literary works from English.

Printing Presses, Newspapers, Periodicals, and Libraries

The coming of printing presses and newspapers like the *Mumabai Samachar Weekly,* later daily (1822), *Amadavad Varatman* (1849) of the Gujarat Vernacular Society, *Amadavad Samachar Weekly* (1860), *Gujarat Mitra,* Surat (1863), and so on, promoted literary activities. More books were written, published, and serialized. Periodicals like the *Buddhiprakash* and *Gujarat Shalapatra,* provided further impetus. With more and more libraries opening up, popular interest in literature steadily grew.

As everywhere in the country, British rule aroused a mixed reaction in Gujarat. To some, it was a blessing, because it had apparently brought stability and introduced modern means of transport and communication and the benefits of scientific and industrial development. Others, though happy to have contact with the West through English education, were dissatisfied with alien rule and started thinking in terms of individual and national freedom. Gujarati literature of the first half of the nineteenth century reflected both these trends. It was the beginning of modern Gujarati literature, and the foundation was laid for all literary developments in the latter half of the nineteenth century and all through the twentieth century.

POST–1850 WRITING

Dalpatram and Narmad

These diverse approaches were reflected in the poets Dalpatram (1820–98) and Narmad (1834–86). Though products of the same age, they were poles apart in their attitudes to British rule. Dalpatram, who knew no English, was encouraged in his literary efforts by an Englishman, Alexander Kinlock Forbes, the magistrate in Ahmedabad, who was interested in the development of the Gujarati language. The Gujarat Vernacular Society was his brainchild. To Dalpatram,

British rule was a blessing. But Narmad, who had the advantage of English education, was possessed with ideas of freedom.

Both shared an awareness of the need for social reforms like opposition to child marriages, encouraging widow remarriages, protecting Indian industries and culture, and education. But even in these matters, Dalpatram favored slow change, while Narmad was more radical.

Further, they were the first to introduce into Gujarati poetry subjects related to common life—a far cry from the predominantly religious and occasionally romantic and narrative poetry of the earlier period. Dalpatram's poetry had commonplace subjects like "trees in a college compound," English law, or even how to write an essay and was replete with his typical sense of humor.

But Narmad's poetry, written in a serious strain, had subjects of direct social relevance, reflecting his impatience and impetuosity. Influenced by English poetry, he also wrote poems about personal love, patriotism, freedom, nature, and so on.

Prose Writing of Dalpatram and Narmad

Dalpatram, an authority on meters, wrote a treatise called *Pingal* (Prosody) a sourcebook for scholars for many decades. Narmad's prose writings included essays, history, autobiography (*Mari Hakikat* 1866), and even a play. Single-handedly, he prepared a Gujarati dictionary (*Narmakosh*). He wrote copiously on education and social reform in the weekly *Dandiyo,* published at his own expense, to propagate his reformist ideas. He was completely devoted to the pen, facing hardships and penury with the courage of a warrior.

Dalpatram and Narmad, in their own different ways, pioneered new literary trends in Gujarat. Poets and writers of the later period did not necessarily imitate them but picked up their threads, to which they added their own strands.

A striking feature of post-British Gujarati literature is the phenomenon of one author's writing in more than one genre.

Development of Gujarati Prose

In the next few years, a number of writers particularly cultivated prose, setting the stage for its further development. The growing influence of the English language, far from subduing the Gujarati language, added new dimensions to it. Efforts were made to evolve appropriate expressions to effectively convey thoughts and human emotions appropriate to Gujarati sensibility.

A notable attempt was the first Gujarati historical novel, *Karanghelo* (1866) by Nandshankar Tuljashankar Mehta (1835–1905). Gujarati prose had not yet developed to suit that genre, but the novel is important as a first step.

His contemporary, Navalram Pandya (1836–88), an educationist and social reformer who edited the then-prestigious journal *Shalapatra,* wrote, in more cultivated prose, Narmad's biography, translated Kalidasa's *Meghdoot,* Molière's play *The Mock Doctor* as *Bhatnun Bhopalun* (1867), and wrote an original play, *Virmati Natak* (1869). He molded Gujarati prose as a vehicle for creative writing and criticism.

Several writers of that period and succeeding decades further developed Gujarati prose with their novels, essays, travelogues, biographies, autobiographies, and journalistic writings. Periodicals like the *Buddhiprakash Satyaprakash, Rastgoftar* also promoted such writing in Gujarati. Durgaram Manchharam (1809–76), a renowned teacher and social reformer, kept a record of his public activities and also wrote his autobiography.

Some time later, Nanilal Nabhubhai Dwivedi, a social reformer and an upholder of women's education, started the monthly *Priyamvada* (1864), later changed into *Sudharshan* (1890), to propagate his ideas about women's education. He recorded his personal experiences in *Atmanimajjan* (1895). But *Kanta Natak* (1882), as the first attempt of a well-structured play, is said to be his most important contribution. He also found the essay form a convenient medium to express his views about education and social reform. His effortless prose bears the mark of his vast scholarship.

Further Strides in Poetry

Gujarati poetry made further strides during this period. Balashankar (1858–99), a bohemian by nature, wrote erotic poetry, combining the Shakta and Persian influences. Balashankar's brief and tempestuous career has remained a subject of curiosity and criticism. His freer diction stands apart from the general tenor of Gujarati poetry of his time.

Balashankar's contemporary Kant (1867–1923) was also an innovative poet, but in a different way. He wrote *khandakavyas* (narrative poems) depicting with intensity sentiments of love and friendship in a picturesque and fluent style. Whenever he glimpsed beauty, he captured it in his words. He also wrote highly subjective lyrics. *Purvalap* (1923), the collection of his poems, was published on the day he died.

Kant, who experienced a long period of religious conflict, remained a Christian at heart. He is remembered most for his metrically perfect and emotionally rich *khandkavyas* and lyrics.

A highly sensitive and romantic poet of this time was Kalapi (1874–1900), who died young but left behind a fairly large number of poems collected as *Kalapino Kekarav* (1931). He started under the influence of Dalpatram and Narmad but was later fascinated by English romantic poets, Narasinghrao's nature poems and lyrics, Balashankar's *ghazals* (verse) and Kant's *khandakavyas.* His highly subjective poetry, full of delicate emotions, reflects anguish of love in his own life. He wrote some *ghazals,* too, combining Sufism and Advita philosophy. His *Kashmirno Pravas* (1912) is the first "creative travelogue" in Gujarati, a specimen of good prose.

A Literary Giant

A new era of creative writing dawned with the coming of Govardhanram N. Tripathi (1855–1907), well known for his novel *Saraswatichandra,* in four parts (1887–1901). He was the "presiding genius" of the age and an "apostle of synthesis" of East and West. His creative writing drew from the Hindu view of life. He was well versed in Sanskrit literature, preceding and contemporary Gujarati literature, and English literature and was guided by patriotism and catholicity of mind. Philosophically inclined, he lived in the thick of worldly responsibilities, albeit suffering from inner tensions.

Drawing inspiration from ancient philosophical heritage, *Saraswatichandra* creates a vivid tapestry of two whose hearts burned with love but were destined to remain unfulfilled. This first truly social novel is considered a modern classic.

Govardhanram's *Snehamudra* (1889) is a long, reflective poem in memory of his first wife, and *Lilavatijivankala* (1905) is a tribute to his dead daughter. In *Saksharajivan,* he propounds his ideals of literary criticism, and *Kavi Dayramno Aksharadeh* (1906) is an appraisal of that poet's works. Whereas *Navalram Lakshmishankaranun Jivanvrittant* is a biography of Nalvalram Pandya, Govardhanram's *Scrap-Book* (1956) is an honest account of his inner experiences, expressing his pet ideal of "practical renunciation." With his profound vision of life and literary creations embodying that vision, Govardhanram became a legend and a precursor of what came to be called the Age of Scholars (Pandit Yug) in Gujarati literature.

Pandit Yug: The Age of Scholars

The Age of Scholars, the period covering the next two and a half decades or so, was characterized by a heaviness of Sanskritized style and thought content in creative critical writings. But what was written in that period has immense value in the development of Gujarati literature, despite the scathing criticism by the latter-day writers.

Among the writers of this period was Ramanbhai Nilkanth (1868–1928), a public figure connected with several social and literary organizations and remembered for his creative and other serious writing. *Bhadrambhandra* (1900), a satirical novel about orthodox social attitudes, *Hasyamandir* (1926), a collection of humorous writing, and the play *Raeno Parvat* (1895) bring out the essence of his thinking in his creative writings. In *Kavita ane Sahitya* (1904), he advocates the view that literary criticism (including *khandakavyas,* lyrics, and devotional songs) leads to an increased interest in quality books.

Another notable writer and critic of the period was Anandshankar Dhruv (1869–1942), a towering figure in Gujarati literature even today. He wrote copiously on religious, philosophical, and literary topics. Dhruv regarded literature as an art and eschewed extremes in his critical writings. He was guided by an enlightened attitude, and his prose was marked by scholarship and a sense of appreciation. He set new standards of criticism in works such as *Kavyatattvavichar* (1939) and *Sahityavichar* (1941). His religious writings include *Hindudharmani Balpothi* and *Apano Dharma* (1916). Though dense reading, his writings have an inherent charm and immense value. His prestigious magazine, *Vasant,* was founded in 1906, and writers considered it an honor to be published in it.

Literary Stalwarts: Narasinghrao and Thakore

Gujarat was invigorated by the emergence of Narasinghrao (1859–1937), a versatile writer of that period. He took Gujarati poetry a step further in the new phase started by Dalpatram and Narmad. His poetic diction was influenced by Sanskrit literature and romantic English poets such as Wordsworth, Keats, and Shelley, relating nature to human emotions. These well-assimilated influences were manifested as his own creative genius, whether his poems were original, translations, or adaptations. In addition to poems of nature, he also wrote *khandakavyas,* lyrics, elegies, and other forms.

Kusumamala (1887), his first collection of poems, is considered a definite advance in modern Gujarati poetry because of its novel use of poetic diction. It was followed by *Hridayaveena* (1896), with *khandakavyas, garbis,* and poems about nature/women, and *Nupurjhankar* (1914), as well as *Smaranasamhita* (1915), an elegy to his son, which contains a sublime expression of emotions. *Buddhacharit* (1934) contains nine poems about incidents in Buddha's life, three original and the rest translations from Edwin Arnold's *The Light of Asia.* Narasinghrao's *Smaranamukur* reveals how the essay may be developed as a literary genre. *Manomukur,* volumes 1–3 (1924, 1936, 1938) contains his appraisals of the works of contemporary and emerging writers. Published posthumously, *Rojnishi* (1954) is a noteworthy work of autobiographical writing, and *Narasinghraono Kavyavichar* (1969) explains his concept of poetry. He made a significant contribution to philology as well. With his multidimensional writings, Narasinghrao greatly enriched Gujarati literature.

Narasinghrao's contemporary, Balawantrai Thakore (1869–1952), was more controversial. He introduced into Gujarati poetry sonnets and the *prithvi* meter, which is closest to English blank verse, and he was the first imagist and formalist poet in the language. Thakore's collections of poems, *Bhanakar* (1917) and *Mharan Sonnet* (1935), demonstrate compositions with his strong sense of individuality and novelty of style, form, and content. He is often criticized for lack of musicality in his poetry, but he had evolved a style suited to his own poetry and became a voice to be reckoned with.

Kavitashikshan (1924), *Apani Kavita Samrioohi* (1931), and *Vividh Vykhyno* (1942–56) in three volumes reveal him as a fearless critic. His prose writings include a collection of short stories, two plays, and his two-volume diary, *Dinky.* Thakore's position as an innovative poet and bold critic is unassailable.

Few Gujarati writers have written literary history. Krishnala M. Jhaveri

(1868–1957) wrote *Milestones in Gujarati Literature* (1914) and *Further Milestones in Gujarati Literature* (1926) in English, both translated into Gujarati. Jhaveri also wrote historical works such as *Aurangazeb ane Rajputs* (1896), *Dayaram ane Hafez* (1895), and others. But his important contribution is as a literary historian. His works in the field are historically important but of specialized interest to students studying Gujarati literature of ancient and middle periods.

A Shift in Emphasis

At the turn of the century, old influences persisted to a certain extent, but there were indications of a shift in emphasis. New literary expressions, free from the influences of Sanskrit or English literature, came into vogue. This trend was encouraged by organizations such as the Gujarat Vernacular Society, Forbes Sabha, Bhikhsu Akhandanand Publishing House, and Gujarati Sahitya Parishad, as well as by the emergence of periodicals such as the *Gujarati, Samalochak, Viami Sadi, Sahitya, Buddhiprakash, Vasant,* and *Sudarshan.* This prepared the ground for developing the Gujarati language to suit the requirements of the age, which rejected heavy scholastic diction. Newspapers also favored simple language. This trend brought some Parsi writers into the field who differed from the mainstream in that they were closer to the public because of their use of daily conversational language.

Among other factors responsible for this change in creative writing in Gujarat and elsewhere in India was the fact that the country was no longer ideologically complaisant to British rule. Organizations such as the Brahmo Samaj, Prarthana Samaj, Arya Samaj, and the Theosophical Society had redirected the attention of the educated classes to Indian culture. There was a tendency to strike a balance between Eastern and the Western thought. The establishment of the Indian National Congress (1885) led to a new awakening in India. Religion-oriented literature did not cease to be written, but poets and writers now did not hesitate to turn their attention from God to man. It was not exactly the end of the Age of Scholars, but literature in Gujarat had entered a new phase.

Arrival of Mahatma Gandhi

The new trend that started at the turn of the century received a further thrust with Gandhi's return from South Africa in 1914. There was change in the air. With the launching of the Satyagraha movement in 1923, there was a surging tide of nationalism in Gujarat, along with the rest of India. Gujarati literature acquired new dimensions. It was the beginning of a literature infused with the spirit of nationalism, concern for the downtrodden, and humanism.

Younger writers were also fascinated by the socialist thought of the West and the success of the Russian revolution. That influence grew stronger during the next two decades, with the formation of the Progressive Writers' Association.

In Gujarat, too, there was a group of progressive writers. Much was written about the downtrodden in quite a revolutionary spirit.

Yet another factor was the writers' interest in Freudian psychology and the stream-of-consciousness technique of James Joyce, then dominating the West. Young Gujarati writers no longer imitated the earlier writers of their own language or even prominent writers like Tagore. Those who started writing in the 1930s strove to bring more psychological content into their creations and themes, with greater emphasis on human relationships. They were more concerned with the inner world of their characters. Even when the freedom struggle figured in their writings, as it often did, they tended to break loose from the inhibitions of the earlier writers. Although not completely free from prevalent moral considerations, they were more considerate toward human beings when their actions did not appear to conform to the accepted social norms. This resulted in a strikingly divergent trend in Gujarati creative writing. But it was not quite the end of the earlier phase of Gujarati literature. Old-time writers continued to write, and there were new entrants who had started writing in the last decade of the nineteenth century but had attracted attention only in the first decade of the twentieth century and were active for the next three or four decades.

Among them was Dalpatram's son Kavi Nanalal (1877–1946). He earned a reputation with his first collection of poems, *Katlank Kavyo* (1903), although he had begun writing more than a decade earlier. Since then, he wrote without interruption almost until he died. His earlier poems were not much different from those of Narasinghrao, Kalapi, and so on, though there was an indication of his own poetic talent. He adopted a distinct diction, with swaying rhythm (*dolanshaili*), and made ingenious use of meter. His poetry had a touch of novelty. His other poetry collections include *Vasantotsav* (1905) and *Harisamhita* (1960) and carry the same level of creativity. His poetry was romantic and classical at the same time, marked with brevity and freshness of expression, lyrics being his most important contribution.

Nanalal wrote several social plays, such as *Indukumar,* volumes 1–3 (1909, 1927, 1942); an imaginary play with an ancient theme called *Jaya-jayant;* a mythological play, *Vishvagita* (1927); historical plays such as *Jehangir-Noorjahan* (1928); *Sanghamitra* (1931), the novel *Sarathi* (1938), which conveys his message of peace among nations; and *Apanan Saksharartno* (1943), containing his introductions and prefaces to books by several writers. Nanalal infused everything he wrote with a streak of poetry and came to be regarded as an outstanding poet of his era.

In contrast, Botadkar's (1870–1924) poetry was about the family life of his days, known for his popular *garba* (folk) songs. His collections included *Shaivalini* and *Srotasvini.* Not a poet par excellence, he was adept at the use of words to suit his medium, and the sentimentalism of his poetry appealed to his readers. Some later poets even imitate him, which lends his reputation certain importance.

Parsi Writing

The Parsis, after their migration from Iran, had accepted Gujarati as their language. Some of them had taken to writing in the language right from the seventeenth century. However, the Parsis came into prominence in the literary field in the third decade of the nineteenth century, essentially through journalism, after the launching of the *Bombay Sanmachar* (1822). That paper published stories in Gujarati, based on Persian themes. Behramji Murzban translated *Gulbankavali* and other works from Persian in the 1850s.

From 1860, Parsis showed interest in plays and theater. They set up the Parsi Natak Mandali (1852), which staged the first play, *Sohrab ane Rustom,* in Bombay that year. Subsequently, the Victoria Natak Mandali, Persian Natak Mandali, and other drama companies were formed. The Parsi plays were mostly translations of Persian or English plays. Kekhushru Kabraji (1842–1904), social reformer of the Parsi society of his time, contributed to the development of the Parsi theater and to the Gujarati novel. Theaters like Victoria Natak Manadi staged translations of Shakespeare's plays, but later the plays were based on Persian history and also Hindu mythology. Khurshadji Maherwanji Baliwala (1852–1913) of the Baliwala Grand Theatre also played a leading role in the development of the Parsi theater, which aimed at entertainment and orienting the Parsi community toward social reform.

But as a creative Parsi writer, Beheramji Malabari stands out, with his Gujarati poems expressing nationalist sentiment. His style was the continuation of the poetic style of Narmad and the Pandit Yug. *Itihasni Aarasi* is his famous patriotic composition. Malabari was the predecessor of the Parsi poet *Ardoshir Faramji Khabardar* (1881–1953). A Parsi poet of considerable merit, Khabardar published several collections, including *Kavyarasika* (1901) and *Vilasika* (1905), with the influences of Dalpatram and Kant. *Bharatno Tankar* (1919) and *Sandeshika* (1925) contained patriotic poems. He also wrote *garba* songs and a eulogy of Gandhiji. While imbibing earlier influences, Khabardar evolved his own musical expression.

Prose Writing in Post-Pandit Yug

The most notable features of prose writing during this period can be found in the works of powerful storytellers like K. M. Munshi (1887–1971), Ramanlal V. Desai (1890–1954), and Dhoomketu (1892–1965).

Munshi wrote five social novels, such as *Verni Vasulat* (1913) and *Swapnadrishta* (1924); seven historical novels, including *Patanani Prabhuta* (1916), *Gujaratno Nath* (1917), *Rajadhiraj* (1918), and *Prithvivallabh* (1920); and four mythological novels, such as *Lopamudra* (1930) and *Bhagwan Parashuram* (1926). His last work, *Krishnavatar* (1963–74), in eight parts, was left incomplete. Munshi's social novels, with their romantic atmosphere and autobiographical touches, were quite popular. But his historical novels, said to have been inspired by Alexander Dumas and Sir Walter Scott, took Gujarat by storm. When charged with distorting history to suit his creative purpose, his defense was that he was writing novels, not history.

Munshi also wrote social plays, including *Brahmacharyashram* (1931) and *Dr. Madhurika* (1936), and mythological plays, *Pausanik Natako, Dhruvaswan-uni Devi and Lopamudra* (1930). Munshi's other prose writings included biographies of Narasingh Mehta and Narmad, autobiographical works like *Adadhe Raste* (1943), *Swapanasiddihini, Shodhman* (1953), and critical writing such as *Ketlak Lekho* (1926). Not comfortable relegated to narrow precincts in life or literature, he covered a vast canvas, including considerable original writing in English, and came to be considered a literary giant.

Ramanlal Desai, equally popular, was admired for his social and political novels, such as *Jayant* (1925) and *Bharelo Agni* (1935), his monumental novel *Gramalakshmi,* in four parts, which deals with the theme of rural resurgence, and *Pralay* (1950), a pessimistic, futuristic novel about the impending annihilation of humankind. Desai's play *Samyukta* (1915) was successfully staged. He aspired to transform the amateur Gujarati stage but felt compelled to write novels, although he did write some more plays. *Jhakal* (1932) and *Pankaj* (1935) are Desai's short story collections. Some of his stories are quite striking, but his novels are more appreciated. *Apsara* (1933–49) in five parts is a study of the life of prostitutes. He published some autobiographical and critical writing and a couple of poetry collections, too. With his copious and variegated writings attractively styled, though subdued and restrained in contrast to Munshi's turbulent style, Desai's romantic depiction of middle-class life in Gujarat held the attention of his readers for a long time.

If Munshi and Desai were at their best in novels, Dhoomketu's forte was the short story. Dhansukhlal Mehta, Malayanil, and Munshi did write short stories before him, but the Gujarati short story is believed to have come into its own with Dhoomketu. His short stories appeared in four successive volumes, *Tanakhamandal* (1926, 1928, 1932, 1934). Dhoomketu enlarged the canvas of the Gujarati short story, depicting characters in their natural habitat, speaking their native language. Dhoomketu also wrote social novels like *Rajmugut* and *Jivananan Khander* (1963) and historical novels such as *Chauladevi* (1940) and *Amrapali* (1954), and a couple of autobiographical works as well. But short stories overshadowed all his other writings.

Another short story writer of this period was Dhansukhlal Mehta (1890–1974). Apparently written in a lighter vein, his short stories in collections like *Hum, Sarala, ane Biji Vato* (1924) and *Ame Bedhan* (1936) have a refined aesthetic sense, deep thinking, and subtle expressions. He regaled his readers and also provided them with an enjoyable literary experience.

Playwriting in Gujarati

Gujarat is rather poor in this particular genre. After Ramanbhai Nilkanth's play *Raeno Parvat,* there were hardly any plays worth mentioning until Randchodbhai Udayram Dave (1837–1923), who reacted against the vulgarities of the folk theater Bhawai and published his *Jekumarno Je* (1866), *Jaikumari Vijaynatak* (1865), and *Nindyashringar Nishedh Rupak* (1920). He formed a drama troupe to eliminate the faulty Gujarati language of the Parsi theater, which was dominating particularly the stage in Bombay. His *Lalita Dukhadarshekk Natak*, dealing with child marriage, is the first tragedy in Gujarati. He also wrote other original plays, like *Nala-Damayanti Natak* and *Harishchandra Natak*. Though not of high artistic quality, Dave attempted to make the theater an instrument of public education.

The next notable playwright, Batubhai Umarawadia (1899–1956), published collections of one-act plays like *Matsyagandha ane Bijar Natako* (1925) and *Maladevi ane Bijan Natako* (1927) and a couple of full-length plays. He added to the Gujarati drama literature but may not particularly impress today's readers.

Chandravadan Mehta (1901–91) was truly a man of drama. His plays, like *Aagagadi*, were a thrill to watch on stage and are a pleasure to read even now. There is an element of satire in his plays. Awarded scholarships by the Sangest Natak Akademi (New Delhi), he spent the best part of his life in studying the theater movements in India and the world and worked hard to infuse life into the Gujarati theater. He published collections of poems, including *Yamal* (1926) and *Ila Kavyo* (1933). However, his poems are not considered on a par with his plays. He has shown himself as a master prose writer in his nine-part autobiography, *Gathariyan* (1954–76).

Humorous Writing

Jyotindra Dave (1901–80) is synonymous with wit and humor in Gujarat, not because of a paucity of humor writers but because of the uniquely healthy and innocent fun one gets from his humorous pieces. *Rantarang*, in six parts (1931–39), is one of the works that have sent the entire Gujarat community into peels of laughter for many decades, and his humor has survived him. He was awarded the prestigious Ranjitram Gold Medal. There have been some other humor writers, such as Mastfakir, but Jyotindra Dave is in a class by himself. However, why Gujarat does not have many humor writers today may well be a subject worth researching.

Gandhiji as a Writer

Gandhiji (1869–1948) wrote abundantly in the course of his historic public life. The bulk of his writing was journalistic, yet he had a literary, at times even poetic touch. Gandhiji began writing with his Gujarati and English columns in the Indian *Opinion* (1830–1914) published in South Africa. In his small tract *Hind Swaraj* (1910), he expounded the idea of Satyagraha and explained the meaning of *swaraj*. Bearing no imprint of any literary tradition, he set a tradition of natural, refined, and direct style with charming simplicity.

Dakshin Africano Satyagrahano Itihas and his autobiography, which he called

Satyana Prayago, Athav Atmakalha (1926), and *Hind Swaraj* are considered his most significant works in Gujarati. The history of *satyagraha* in South Africa is a truthful account of his first experiment in nonviolent resistance. His *Anasaktiyoga* (1930), the translation of the twelfth chapter of the *Gita,* and *Dharmananthan* are his other significant works in Gujarati.

One hundred volumes of the *Collected Works of Mahatma Gandhi,* published by the government of India, give proof of the staggering amount of his writings in Gujarati, Hindustani, and extremely chaste English. Apart from his articles and speeches, these volumes contain an incredible number of letters addressed to the highest dignitaries down to the most modest persons and even children, reflecting his transparent and affectionate heart. Gandhiji's Gujarati writings form an important part of Gujarati prose literature.

Some Gandhian Writers

A number of writers closely associated with Gandhiji soon appeared on the scene with their newfound philosophy and literary expressions. One of them was Kaka Saheb Kalelkar (1885–1980), who entered the field of Gujarati literature with a tremendous flourish. His writings are significant because he wrote abundantly in Gujarati, although his language was Marathi, and also because his prose was well cultivated to convey the profoundest thought as well as to rise to poetic heights.

An eternal traveler, Kaka Saheb has encapsulated in his travelogues, such as *Himalayano Pravas* (1924) and *Purva Africaman* (1959), his experiences during his innumerable sojourns in India and abroad, revealing his profound knowledge of history and culture, apart from giving vivid descriptions. A sense of joy was Kaka Saheb's second nature. *Rakhadvano Anand* (1953) is about joy of wandering, and *Smaranayatra* (1934) contains delightful reminiscences of his childhood and adolescent days.

Kaka Saheb's serious writings include *Jivan Sanskriti* (1939), *Jivanbharati,* and *Jivanvyavastha* (1964). The Sahitya Akademi presented an award to *Jivanvyavastha* as an outstanding work of reflective writing (1964). Even when he wrote heavy prose to suit philosophical subjects, he kept his style free from pedantry. With him, Gujarati prose acquired greater maturity, revealing immense possibilities and inner strength of the language.

Mahadev Desai (1892–1942), Gandhiji's private secretary for many years and described as "Bapu's Boswell," was an outstanding writer, at ease with Gujarati, English, and Bengali. He wrote biographies such as *Vir Vallabhbhai* (1928), *Sant Francis* (1934), and *Be Khudsi Khidmatgar,* about Khan Abdul Ghaffar Khan and his brother Khan Saheb. His most important work is *Mahadevbhaini Diary,* in 15 parts, a record of the contemporary events as well as his inner growth during his years with Gandhiji. Mahadevbhai's translations of Saratchandra's stories (1923) and the little novel *Virajvahu* (1924) from original Bengali and some of Tagore's poems are excellent. He also translated Jawaharlal

Nehru's autobiography (1936). As a writer and translator, he is placed highly in Gujarati literature.

Many other Gandhian writers, like Swami Anand Jugatram Dave and others, have also contributed to Gujarati literature through their biographical and other serious writings. However, a tall figure among them is Indulal Yajnik (1892–1982), originally influenced by Mazzini and Garibaldi but subsequently drawn toward Gandhiji. He started the *Young India* and *Navjivan* weeklies (1915), which he handed over to Ganhiji (1917), and then started the monthly *Yugadharma* and edited the daily *Hindustan.* As a writer, he is known more for *Ganhijina Sahavasman,* in two parts, describing his experiences with Gandhiji. However, his most important work is his autobiography, *Atmakatha,* in five parts (1935–56), an extremely frank account of his life at various stages and a fine human document.

Advances in Creative and Critical Writing

A number of notable writers further enriched Gujarati literature through their abundant output in different fields. Ramanayan Pathak (1887–1955), the founder-editor of the prestigious magazine *Prarathan* (1926), was one of them. Among Pathak's critical works are *Arvachin Kavya Sahityanan Vaheno* (1935) and *Sahityavimarsh* (1939). His *Brihat Pingal* (1956) earned him the Sahitya Akademi Award. A thorough scholar of Indian prosody, Pathak considered criticism an act of social responsibility. Continuing the tradition of Govardhanm, Anandashankar Dhruv, and others, he gave literary criticism during the Gandhian era a solid foundation.

His poems collected in *Sheshnan Kavyo* (1938) reflect his calm and generous bent of mind and sense of humor, combining compassion, seriousness, and playfulness, and display a mature diction and a radiant quality. Pathak's short stories, published as *Dwirefni Vato 1, 2, 3,* (1928, 1935, 1942), have a masterly touch and are emotionally linked with life. *Swairavihar 1, 2* (1931, 1937) and *Manovihar* (1958) contain his serious essays. Though a product of the Gandhian era, Pathak did not mechanically recite Gandhian principles. The whole body of his writings demonstrates Pathak as an eminent literary figure.

After him came Vijayrai K. Vaidya (1897–1974), vigorously protesting the literary criticism during the Pandit Yug, which he felt was unsympathetic. He edited the quarterly *Kaumudi* (1924), which was later turned into a monthly (1930–37) and reemerged as *Manasi,* which continued breathing life into the contemporary literary scene and encouraging rebel writers until 1960. He advocated creative literary criticism in his critical works like *Sahityadarshan* (1935) and *Sahityani Rooprekha.* His other prose writings include satirical articles. In whatever literary capacity, Vijayrai is a name to be counted.

An appreciative reader with an enlightened and refined taste cultivated by the study of great literary works was the critic Vishnuprasad Trivedi (1899–1991).

His works, like *Vivechana* (1939), *Parisheelan* (1941), and *Drumparna* (1963), convey his mature aesthetic sense, catholicity of mind, and original thinking.

As a creative writer, Jhaverchand Meghani (1896–1947) was a rage in his lifetime. His poetry collections, such as *Veninan Phool* (1923) and *Yugavandana* (1935), reflect his vibrant, all-embracing personality. His short stories, following the model of Dhoomketu, are collected in *Vilopan ane Biji Vato* (1944) and others. Among his original novels are *Sorath Taran Vahetan Pani* (1937) and *Tulsikyano* (1940). He also adapted Upton Sinclair's novels *Samuel the Speaker* and *Love's Pilgrimage.* Meghani's *Manasaina Dive* (1946) is based on the experiences of the Gandhian worker Ravishankar Maharaj among the tribals. *Saurashtrani Hasdhar,* in five parts (1923–27), with its stories of valor, sacrifice, and love, *Radhiyali Reat,* in four parts (1925–42), and *Chundadi,* in two parts (1928–29), compilations of Gujarati folksongs and marriage songs, respectively, are the fruit of Meghani's lifetime devotion to Gujarati's folk literature. Meghani still fascinates the reader with his vigorous and passionate writings.

Further Momentum to Nationalist Trend

The nationalist and humanistic trends in Gujarati literature continued during the next two decades or so, because the established writers maintained continuity, and younger writers inspired by Ganhiji entered the field. Many of them were active in the freedom struggle, and, like their immediate predecessors, their writings, fresh with expressions, idioms, and language texture, also embodied a dream of free India and a better world. They can be called the precursors of new Gujarati writing.

One of them was Umashankar Joshi (1911–88), who was instantly recognized as a promising poet with his *Vishwashanti* (1931) and longish *Khandakavya,* followed by several poetry collections, such as *Nishith* (1939) and *Abhijna* (1967), all bearing the stamp of poetic excellence, at times showing social awareness. He is also known as a great poet of nature and love. His dialogue-poems *Prachina* (1944) and *Mahaprasthan* (1965) show his eagerness to seek new modes of expression.

Umashankar's prolific prose writings include short story collections such as *Shravani Melo* (1937) and *Tran Andhun Be* (1938), one-act plays such as *Sapna Bhara* (1936), and the novel *Parkan Janyan* (1940)—all giving intimate portraits of rural life. *Akho: Ek Adhyayan* (1941) and *Klanta Kavi* are in-depth studies of the poets Ako and Balashankar. His critical works, reflecting an appreciative and imaginative approach to literary criticism, include *Samasamvedan* (1948), *Shaili ane Swaroop* (1960), *Nireeksha* (1960), and the Sahitya Akademi winner, *Kavini Shraddha* (1978). Umashankar Joshi brought a fresh approach to all genres in which he wrote and came to be regarded as a literary stalwart who loved all mankind. His monthly magazine, *Sanskirti,* published writings of established and talented young writers. He remained a live force in Gujarati literature and maintained a spirit of the era until his death. His translations of

Abhjnana Shakuntalam and *Anttararamacharikam,* the Sanskrit plays, are also greatly admired.

Umashankar's contemporary Sundaram (1909–90) also started writing under Gandhian and socialist influences, as can be seen in his poetry collections *Koya Bhagatni Kadvi Vani* (1933), *Kavyamangala* (1933), *Yatra* (1951), and others. His poetry also showed concern for the poor and warm sympathy for humankind in general. However, he later turned to the spiritualism of Sri Aurobindo. *Kholki ane Nagarika* (1940), *Piyasi* (1940), *Hirakani* and *Biji Vatu,* and others are Sundaram's short story collections, marking a point of departure from Dhoomketu. *Kholki ane Nagarika* was considered very bold and controversial. Sundaram also authored *Dakshinayan* (1942), as well as a travelogue and a biography of Sri Aurobindo. Sundaram's critical works include *Arvachin Kavita* (1946) and the Sahitya Akademi winner *Avalokana* (1962), among others. He is considered an eminent writer of the Gandhian era.

Another poet in the line was Sneharashmi (1903–90), who was also a freedom fighter. Lyricism, delicate sentiment, captivating rhythm, and concern for the poor marked his poems collected in *Arghya, Panghat,* and so on. He was the pioneer of the Japanese haiku poetry in Gujarati. His prose writings include the short story collections *Tutela Taar* and *Gata Saopalav, Hiranan Latkavian,* the novel *Antarpat,* and his autobiography, *Safalyatanun.* Sneharashmi's poetry, marked by a warm, all-embracing quality, is highly regarded.

Belonging to the same period was the poet Sundarji Betai (1905–89). He did not participate in the freedom struggle, but Gandhian vision is the hallmark of his poetry, which is generally serious and gentle in tone, having the touches of his teacher Narasinghrao's diction and mastery of Sanskrit meters. His poetry collections include *Jyoti-Rekha, Shangali, Shravani Jharmar,* and others, his main contributions being sonnets, *khandakavyas,* and songs. His *Sadgat Chandrasheelane* is regarded as a notable elegy to his wife. Betai's critical works, based on Sanskrit poetics, include *Amod.* His translations include Henry David Thoreau's *Walden,* four cantos of the *Mahabharata,* and the verse rendering of the *Gita.*

A Betai contemporary, poet Badarayan (1905–63), was also Narasinghrao's student and influenced by him. But both regarded Narasinghrao as their source of inspiration and developed their own styles, distinct from one another. Badarayan's output, collected in *Kedi* (1944), was meager, but his sonnets and songs of subjective nature and rare sensibility place him among the important poets of the period.

Mansukhlal Jhaveri (1907–81), deeply rooted in classical Sanskrit poetry, was a Gandhian poet of that era. *Phooldol* (1935), *Anubhuti* (1959), and others are poetry collections containing rhythmic poems about love, nature, and God, with rhythm and master over his medium. He attempted contemporary themes and forms in *Anubhuti* but felt more comfortable in his well-trodden path.

Jhaveri had solid understanding of Eastern and Western concepts of literary criticism, as can be seen in his critical works, *Thoda Vivechanlekhe* (1944),

Paryeshana (1953), *Kavyavimarsh* (1962), and so on. He wrote a history of Gujarati literature for the Sahitya Akademi, and his translated works are *Abhijnana Shakuntalam, Hamlet,* and *Othello*. Jhaveri's creative and critical works, bearing the mark of his individuality and scholarship, place him high among Gujarati writers.

In contrast to most of the writers of this period writing both in prose and in verse, Darshak confined himself to prose. His fiction and nonfiction writings reflect the Gandhian spirit throughout. His most famous novels are *Bandhan ane Mukti* (1939), *Deepnirvan* (1944), *Jher to Peedhan Chhe Jani Jani* (1952), and others, which show his concern for humanity, history, and philosophical thinking and give full expression to his life's ideals of love, peace, and harmony imbibed from Gandhiji, but without sacrificing the structural aspects of the novel as a literary form. Darshak is an exponent of the idea novel in Gujarati. His critical writings are contained in *Wagishwarinan Karnaphoolo* (1985). He is a particular favorite among readers looking for higher life values.

Progressive Writers' Association

About this time, many writers had come under the stronger influence of socialist ideas. Irrespective of being card-carrying communists, some of them were drawn toward the Progressive Writers' Association. Of course, revolutionary idealism had somewhat limited appeal in Gujarat. Still, some younger writers did write in that strain with a fervent desire for a new social order, going beyond the Gandhian concern for the poor.

Swapnastha was one such writer, whose poetry collections, *Achala* and *Vinashna Ansho* and, most of all, *Ajampani Madhuri,* are said to convey his creative imagination with originality. He could weave anything around the sentiment of love with elegant diction. Though belonging to another camp, he was adopted and admired by Gujarati writers. There were also a few others, such as Khaki Praveenchandra Ruparel and Bhogilal Gandhi, in that group who wrote poetry and prose.

Jayanti Dalal (1909–70) was not a camp follower but had socialist leanings. He never used the creative word to propagate his strong convictions, but they were nonetheless the underlying force in his writings. He wrote innovative and excellent one-act plays collected in *Javanka* (1941) and other books that dealt with middle-class intelligentsia with a satirical touch. Dalal wrote striking short stories, as well, collected in *Pagdiviani Pachitethi,* and gripping novels such as *Dhimu ane Vibha* (1947) and *Padarnan Tirath,* with remarkable psychological insight and understanding. He also translated Tolstoy's *War and Peace* thoroughly. Dalal's high-quality writing qualifies him as among the eminent Gujarati writers.

While these writers were active in their respective fields, Gulabdas Broker (1917) entered with a bang with his first short story collection, *Ane Bigi Vato* (1950), followed by several others, including *Ubhi Vate.* He started writing in 1932 in jail during the freedom struggle. He says that he had been inclined from childhood to probe and understand people's inner world and has followed that track all through six decades of writing. He finds the seed of an idea anywhere, not hesitating to treat even the taboo subjects concerning male–female relationships. His stories, depicting mostly middle-class life realistically, are not altogether free from considerations of prevalent social mores. Broker has written some one-act plays, too, but it is the short story with which he forged a new face and meaning.

A writer of totally different ilk was the semieducated, self-taught Pannalal Patel (1914–89). He depicted in his works the rural life of Gujarat artistically, with its good and bad traits. Occasionally, he also wrote against an urban setting, but he was at his creative best in his rural novels. Pannalal's numerous publications include more than 20 short story collections, such as *Sukhdukhnan Sathi* (1940) and *Vatrakne Kanteh* (1952), more than 20 social novels, such as *Malela Jiv* (1941), the Jnanpeeth Award-winner *Manvini Bhavai* (1947), and *Bhangyna Bheru* (1957). The story element in his novels and short stories grows naturally like crops in the field, and the characters fully belong to their social contexts. The most outstanding among his several mythological novels is *Parthene Kaho Chadhave Baan,* based on the *Mahabharata.*

Pannalal has grown with every new book and has delighted Gujarati readers with his gripping power of words. The regional touches and the colloquial expressions made a beautiful blend in his novels and short stories. The novels *Malela Jiv* and *Manvini Bhavai* and the short story *Kanku* have been made into widely acclaimed films. He is "a miracle" in contemporary Gujarati literature, having lost none of his original power to attract readers with the passage of time.

Next came Chunilal Madia (1922–68), who also powerfully depicted rural society in his creative works. *Indhan Ghehhan Padyan* (1951) contains an assortment of short stories. *Vyahno Varas* (1946), *Liludi Dharti* (1960), and others are his novels with rural settings. In view of the critics, he would have put the material at his disposal to a better creative use. While Pannalal wrote about rural life as an insider, Madia is said to have acquired a certain sophistication that does not exactly lead to spontaneity. Nonetheless, he had a powerful pen, and it is a delight to read his works. Madia also wrote well-knit and equally charming novels, such as *Kumjum ane Ashaka* (1962) and *Indradhanushno Althmo Rang* (1967), depicting the psychological conflicts of city life.

Ishwar Patlikar also wrote works with rural settings. His novels, like *Kajalkotdi* and *Janamteep,* written quite effectively, have been fairly popular. But the social reformer in him appeared too prominently in his creations, which was not in keeping with the current style of fiction writing.

Postindependence Literary Output

Gujarati literature during the two decades before independence was inspired writing, on the whole. But the ravages of World War II, though not directly experienced in India, and the communal holocaust before and after the vivisection of the country had a shattering effect on Gujarati writers. The entire value system seemed irrelevant. The excitement of fighting for freedom was replaced by a mood of despair, further intensified by disenchantment with national leadership. Anguish and even cynicism crept into the creations of the new and established writers. Umashankar Joshi came out with a poem expressing his shattered feeling, and this trend was picked up.

Surprisingly, there was also a fresh trend of lyrical poetry and songs. One such poet is Rajendra Shah (1913), who has established himself as a major lyric poet with the collections *Andolan* (1951), *Dhvani, Prasang-Spatak* (1982), and others, which excel in depicting universal love and tender but intense emotions. Seeking beauty and singing of beauty are his main pursuit. He is certainly disturbed by the conditions around him but has responded to society as an artist.

Similarly, Niranjan Bhagat (1926), with poetry collections, compositions, songs, and sonnets, has revealed his concern for human existence. In *Adhunik Kavina Ketlak Prashno* (1972) and *Yantravijnan ane Mentrakavita* (1974), Bhagat has discussed his views on modern poetry with an analytical approach. His acquaintance with world literature has helped his creative process and critical writings.

As a prose writer of this period, Shivkumar Joshi, noted for his one-act plays like *Sonani Hansdi ane Rupani Hansdi* (1958), full-length plays *Andharan Ulecho* (1955) and *Suvarna Rekha,* novels like *Kanchukibandh* (1956) and *Aabh Rune Ehi Navlakh Dhare* (1964), and some short story collections, became popular. In his creative writings, Shivkumar deals with conflicts in contemporary middle-class life without professing to present any profound vision. But he earned a reputation as a creative writer by his mastery of the medium, emotional content, and ability to build up atmosphere.

New Voices, New Forms

While postindependence writing by the older and younger writers continued along these lines, unprecedented changes began taking place in the mid-1950s, with a growing tendency to decry earlier writers for infusing their creations with false idealism. The emphasis was on "pure literature," giving priority to form and freeing the literary word from its traditional meaning. The new writer was overburdened with a sense of the despair, alienation, death, and darkness then prevalent among the Western writers. Interestingly, Western literary influences prevailed during the next two decades or so as in the latter half of the nineteenth century—only the names changed from Wordsworth, Keats, and Shelley to Baudelaire, Camus, and Sartre. In fact, Western writers seemed to have a stronger hold than in the nineteenth century.

The strongest upholder of this new literary trend in Gujarati was the irrepressible Suresh Joshi (1921–86), an unrelenting opponent of the romantic attitude in literature. He was a tireless experimentalist, formalist, and effective prose writer. He was a leading figure to influence the up-and-coming writers of the 1960s and 1970s. He ushered in a new phase in Gujarati literature. Joshi entered the field with short story collections like *Grihapravesh* (1957) and others, exposing Gujarati readers to his newly conceived conception of literary creation with the form as the primary concern, more evident in his novels *Chhinnapatra,* with the theme of "metaphysics of love," and *Maranottar* (1973), depicting existential angst of his characters.

Joshi's personal essays in *Janantike,* demonstrating perfect blending of thought, feeling, and language, are said to have introduced a new prose style in Gujarati. His poetry, too, inspired by Kalidasa and Tagore, on one hand, and Rilke, Baudelaire, and others, on the other, was a departure from the poetry of his immediate predecessors and contemporaries. His poems in collections like the *Upjati* (1956), *Pratyancha* (1975), and others have "suggestive imagery," reflecting his concept of pure poetry, expressed in his critical works *Kindhit* (1960) and *Gujarati Kavitano Aswad* (1962) and about modern fiction in *Shrinvantu* (1972). His *Chintayami Manasa* (1982), for which he declined the Sahitya Akademi Award, also contains his ideas. Existentialism and phenomenology were his primary interests. He promoted small magazines like *Kshilij* and *Manisha* and translated considerably from world poetry and fiction.

Many offbeat rebel poets like Adil Mansoori, Labhashankar Thankar (also a playwright), Ravji Patal, and others formed a group and wrote avant-garde poetry. Painter-poet Gulam Mohammad Sheikh introduced picturesque images in his poetry. Similarly, fiction writers like Prabodh Choksi, Kishore Jadav, and Jyotish Jani completely transformed that genre by resorting to unconventional style, with unconventional symbolism and corresponding approaches to nature, love, and other subjects.

Those Who Did Not Swim with the Current

While the Suresh Joshi wave was still dominating, some writers did not swim with the current. They wrote with modern sensibility and in their own new style, not preoccupied with form as such. They had an unfettered view of reality. Their creations, whether poetry or prose, built into a recognizable whole in spite of their unconventional and impressionistic technique. Their inspiration came straight from the human situation, of which they felt an inseparable part. Free from extraneous influences, there was spontaneity in the depiction of reality, if it acquired varying shades from time to time.

Suresh Dalal (1932), in his several poetry collections, such as *Ekant* (1966) and *Skyscraper* (1980), and his collections of essays, including *Mari Bariethi* (1975), *Chaheraona* (1978), and *Vanman* (1979), with typical symbolism reflecting urban life, shows the creativity with reference to none but himself. He is fully conversant with literary trends in India and abroad, as his critical works like *Apeksha* (1958) and *Prakriya* (1981), guided by a positive approach, indicate. His well-studied and balanced prose writings and poetry, with little sophistication and an inner harmony, placed him among the leading literary figures of the postindependence period.

Dalal's contemporary Harindra Dave (1930) has a quiet charm in lyrical poetry collected in *Asava* (1968), containing *ghazals,* while *Suryopanishad* (1975) has his prose poems, an innovation in poetic diction. The poet Harindra prevails over his novels *Mubhuatu* (1985), *Palnan Pratibimb* (1987), and others. In poetry and prose, Dave has a delicate rhythm, modern and refined sensitivity, controlled expression of intense emotion, and an inner musicality.

Not impressed by the formalist traditions, many writers of this period have sensitively reacted to the human predicament in contemporary society in their well-structured novels and short stories, although their styles and even approaches are dissimilar.

One example is Rahuvir Chaudhari (1938), whose novels, like *Amrita* (1965) and the trilogy *Uparvas, Sahavas,* and *Antarvas* (1975), are reflective and alive to the social and political changes in Gujarat after independence. His short story collections, like *Bahar Koi Chhe* (1972), also give the same impression. His poems in *Tamasa* (1977) have a serious tone, with a fine rhythm in words, absolutely matching the thought and the sentiment.

Then, there is Chandrakant Bakshi (1932), also concerned with humankind in today's world. His view of life is more earthy, and his style is like a river in spate. His social novels, like *Padgha Dubi Gaya* (1958) and *Paralysis* (1978), and historical novels, like *Ayanavritta* (1967), are gripping with the atmosphere he builds up with vivid narration of events, effective dialogues, and forceful language, having a generous sprinkling of Hindu/Urdu words. Bakshi's short stories in *Pyar* (1958) and other collections are marked by brevity. He creates on a limited canvas tiny worlds giving glimpses of real life. He is eminent as a lively and vibrant creative writer.

Bakshi's contemporary Mohammad Mankad (1928) is also a prolific and perceptive writer of fiction. He deals with the urban and rural life of the Saurashtra region as an insider. His novels *Ajanyan Be Jan* (1970), *Bandh Nagar* (1987), *Ashwadod* (1993), and others, with their varied themes and characterizations, show the many sides to his creative urge. Authenticity, appropriate use of colloquial expressions, and convincing depiction of emotions by his characters are the hallmarks of his novels. Their power was further enhanced by the force and fluency of his language. Mankad's short stories, collected in *Tap, Chot* (1970) and elsewhere, also bear his characteristic stamp, equally at ease with urban and rural characters and situations.

In the same category is Bhagwati Kumar Sharma (1938). He has greatly benefited from his longtime journalistic experience but has kept his creative writing amazingly free from its influence. The gentle intensity of diction and well-knit structure with undulating flow of language to suit the situations and characters of his several novels, such as *Urdhvamool, Asooryalok* (winning an award by the Sahitya Akademi), leave a deep impression. This also applies to his short stories collected in *Chhinnabhinna, Adabeed* (1985) and elsewhere.

Sharma is equally comfortable in nonfiction writings, including essays, criticism, and poetry.

Among the critics of this period, Ramanlal Joshi (1932) attracted attention with the publication of *Govardhanram: Ek Adhyayan* (1963), which is considered a major research work on the author of *Saraswatichandra.* His views on literary criticism in *Vivechanani Prakriya* (1978) and *Shabdalokna Yafrio* (1983) are based on an appreciative approach and a desire to fully grasp the purpose of the works under consideration. They also show his acquaintance with Western trends, which have impressed but not overwhelmed him.

Other critics, like Bholabhai Patel, Aniruddh Brahmabhatt, and Bhupendra Trivedi, have contributed to the understanding of Gujarati literature by their perceptive approach and attitude to discover merit. Their works have positive and encouraging impact on creative writers, for the function of literary criticism is not so much to criticize as to elicit merit.

The poet who brought innovation by deviating from tradition in collections like *Ughadti Divalo* (1974) is Chandrakant Sheth. His poems have a calm surface, suppressing violent inner processes. Sheth shows his talent as a creative prose writer in his Sahitya Akademi-winner, *Dhoolmani Paglie* (1984), and in a collection of plays, *Swapnapinjar.*

Post–Suresh Joshi Period

The modernist movement of the sixth decade, leading to extremist literary attitudes and experimental writing, gradually lost its force during the next few years. Not that the circumstances were more congenial for the writers. Actually, the social tensions and revolt against the contemporary situation were stronger in the eighth decade. This revolt manifested itself in literature in the form of dehumanization, shattered feelings, intellectualism, ultrarealism, and a resorting to print gimmickry.

At the same time, some kind of romanticism could also be seen. *Ghasals* and songs and nonmetrical, short poems also became the order of the day among the new generation of writers. During this period, changes in Gujarati literature were frequent and fast, and humor writers, some of whom added fascinating touches with unconventional treatment of unconventional subjects, ended up with intriguing and attractive creations.

One writer, originally charged with incomprehensibility but later admired for his novelty, is Sitanshu Yakeshchandra (1941). Said to be a "pioneer of the surrealist style in Gujarati," he said at the beginning of his career, "I want not a pearl but the whole sea." Like a diver plunging into the depths of the sea, the reader is required to go deep to understand Sitanshu's poetry in *Odeseusnun Halesun* (1974) and the Sahitya Akademi-winner, *Jatayu* (1987).

The poet Sitanshu has also written greatly admired plays, like *As Manas Madrasi Lage Chhe* and *Grahan.* His critical works *Seemakan* and *Ramaniyatano Vagvikalp* (1979) show "penetrating insight in aesthetics," propounding his concepts of literary criticism in the light of fresh understanding of literature. In poetry, drama, and criticism, Sitanshu is the representative of his generation.

Chandrakant Topiwala's critical work and poetry collections, such as *Black Forest,* and Pravin Daryi's poetry in *Pashat* have also nurtured new trends.

A writer of this generation to have completely broken loose from the orthodox family background is Madhu Rye (1942). He rose to quick fame with his short story collections like *Banshi Ramni Ek Chhokri* (1964) and novels like *Kala-sarpa* (1973) and *Kimbles Ravenswood* (1981), the latter achieving uniqueness by depicting characters with ultra-American mannerisms, feeling uncomfortable to speak in Gujarati. His plays *Koi Pan Ek Phoolnun Naam Bolo To* (1974) and *Kumarni Agashi* (1975) have been highly acclaimed.

Around this time, many writers came forward with their experimental creative writing and works of criticism. Radheshyam Sharma's apparently incomprehensible short stories in collections like *Vartavaran* (1987) are characterized by brevity and seemingly unfamiliar subjects. His novels *Phero* (1977) and *Swap-nateerth* (1979) established him as a competent fiction writer of his generation who dramatically brought to the fore the innermost layers of the human mind.

In *Aansu ane Chandaranun* (1983), *Sanchetana,* and other works, Radheshyam emerges as an unusual poet. In his critical works like *Samprat* (1987), he is guided by what are called the contemporary principles of modern criticism. As a creative and critical writer with an urban approach, he has carried forward the modernist trend in literature.

Yaswant Trivedi and Suman Shah, are two of the well-known critics of this period, whose frank interpretations of the works of the writers of previous and present generations are significant.

Parallel Trend

Parallel to this experimental trend, this period has seen the emergence of another type of creative writing, represented by Hemant Desai, Vinesh Antani, Chinu Mody, and others, who have followed more or less the direct technique whereby the intended patterns of their creations automatically emerge in clear focus as one proceeds from page to page. Poetry, fiction, and plays, though by no means traditional in form or content and technique, follow a straight road connecting themselves with the reader.

A new entrant in the field of the short story, Utpal Bhayani, falls in this category. He has brought charming freshness with his collections *Nimajjan* (1978) and *Hallo* (1983), containing intensely told stories that are really short, having straightforward simplicity.

His style has unfrilled modernity absolutely suited to the subjects, drawn from all social levels and having varied cultural backgrounds. He is a creative writer with his feet firmly planted on the solid ground of contemporary reality.

Authentic Regional Element

A welcome development in recent times is the introduction of an authentic regional element in Gujarati novels and short stories of this period, represented by Ujamshi Parmar, Kirit Rhatt, Kanji Patel, and others. Regional touch is not an altogether new feature to Gujarati literature, but it is some kind of "return," since many young writers had been quite preoccupied with the urban life fairly well portrayed in their writings. These new writers who have turned to the village are adopting the forms and techniques of their contemporaries, in the field to depict the changing patterns of the rural life of Gujarat, often inviting the charge of being incomprehensible. However, their writings bear a genuine creative stamp. Yet, some of them could probably do well to be judicious about the use of colloquial expressions without sacrificing authenticity. Its overdose has the danger of defeating its own purpose by creating difficulty in putting their works across to the reader, who is not necessarily familiar with rural dialects. The writers concerned can make a counterargument, but this is a point to consider.

Literature of the Oppressed (Dalit Literature)

The contemporary scene in Gujarati literature also includes Dalit literature, although its tradition is not very strong in Gujarat. But some writers belonging to that section of society have contributed works of good literary standard. Among these few writers, a striking example is Joseph Macwan, who has depicted the anguish and agony in the life of that community. His Sahitya Akademi-winning novel *Angaliat* (1988), based on the life of "untouchables," is remarkable for the faithful re-creation of their life, in which he has successfully kept out his observations as a social reformer.

Then, there are also writers like Anupam Singh Parmar who have effectively written stories and other works about the tribal life of Gujarat.

The Contribution of Women Writers

Strictly speaking, creativity has no gender. Women writers are considered separately not out of feminist consideration but because literary historians tend to treat women's writing casually and, at best, grudgingly appreciate its merit. Putting women's writing together would give a better idea of its bulk and quality.

Women's writing in Gujarat mostly comprises poetry, fiction, and, to a lesser extent, plays and criticism. Its content and expression have a "typical feminine touch," largely due to women's limited world of experience, since they are usually homebound. Still, some women writers are slowly overcoming their constraints, trying to embrace the total human existence in their creative works, although they have still a long way to go.

Women Poets

The first Gujarati woman poet was Meera Bai, unequaled in poetic excellence and popularity over the ages. She was followed by some devotional poets who, within the confines of their social existence, tried to spontaneously express themselves.

Some women poets of the nineteenth century reflected the spirit of the age of social reform that prevailed after the coming of the British. Among them was Narmad's disciple Savitagauri Pandya (1850–1925). Some Parsi and Christian poets like Alibai Palankat and Bai Astor, respectively, also joined their voices.

Diwaliben Nathalal wrote an 18-page poem about injustices to women. Deepakba Desai (1881–1955) wrote some *khandakavyas,* and Munshi's mother, Tapigauri, narrated her lifelong experiences in *Anubhav Tarang* and also wrote devotional songs. Sumatiben Mehta (1890–1911) conveyed her anguish during prolonged illness in *Hridayjharnan* (1912).

Women Poets during Gandhi Era

Concern for the downtrodden, the spirit of nationalism, and the spread of women's education, which had led to the emergence of new Gujarati poetry, were conveyed in women's poetry in the Gandhian era, as in Jyotsna Shukla's (1892–1976) poetry collections *Akashnan Phool* (1941), *Azadinan Geeto* (1947), and others. But a didactic approach marred the aesthetic quality of her poems. Her contemporary Jaimangauri Pathakji (1901–84) showed a gentle quality and realistic and emotional touch in her collections like *Tejacchaya* and *Sonalan.* She also wrote sonnets and *khandakavyas* and attempted verse-dialogues. Poets like Pushpa Vakil (1908–85) wrote few but sensitive poems.

Postindependence Women's Poetry

Women's poetry after independence took a new direction, though some women poets stuck to the conventional type with a somewhat changed diction. Chaitanya Divatia (1919) published her *khandakavyas,* sonnets, and other works in *Nivapanjali.* Anniben Saraiya (1917–83), essentially a children's poet, published 17 poetry collections, like *Noopur* (1958), *Sonalnun Swapna* (1979), and *Culbanki* (1982). Her poetry, on the whole, is of moderate quality, with conventional devotion to Lord Krishna.

A major woman poet of the modern era truly soaked in literature is Heeraben Pathak. With only one collection, *Paraloke Patra* (1976), addressed to her deceased husband, Ramnarayan Pathak, she is ranked among the leading Gujarati poets. In this work, she has objectively narrated the intimate experiences of her married life, which was also a literary companionship. Heeraben is also one of the women to have written highly appreciated critical works, like *Apanun Vivechansahita* and *Kavyabhavan.*

Next is Gita Parikh (1929), whose collections *Purvi* (1966) and *Bhinash* (1979) give full expression to married existence and sentiments of love and philosophical thought. Her strong point is depiction of nature, and she attempted almost all poetic forms.

In subsequent years, some women poets have come out of the proverbially enclosed feminine emotional world. Among them is Jaya Mehta (1929), with her collections like *Venetian Blind* (1978) and *Akashman Tarao Chup Chhe* (1985), which show her concern for the human predicament. Guided more by social awareness and logic than by emotion, she often contemplates life and death without making her poetry heavy with philosophical content. She describes her creative process as a desperate attempt to discover a healthy expression, and she has a sensitivity born out of inner conflict.

Panna Nayak (*Philadelphia* [1980] and *Nisbat* [1988]) has tried to arrive at a meeting point of Indian and American cultures with a modern sensitivity. She considers America responsible for her becoming a poet. She is eager to informally relate herself to the reader. For her, "poetry is the supreme relationship of an individual to another individual" (*Pravesh* 1987). She pointedly brings out the loneliness of modern people. Her poems are soaked in the agony of the individual and the world.

Panna has effectively used a nonmetrical style of poetry, in which she has expressed the anguish of her unfulfilled motherhood, along with the anguish of contemporary life—for she is always conscious of being a woman. Like Jaya, she is not just a woman poet but a poet in the general sense.

The most modern experimental poet is Saroop Dhruv (1948), with her collection *Mara Halthni Vaat* (1982). She believes that the sex of the creative person is irrelevant. Disturbed by the human situation in today's world, she has reacted to it as an individual and honestly tried to express her anguish. Despondency is the prominent note in her poetry. Here is an angry voice against the disharmonies in the world. Saroop is a fresh young voice in Gujarati poetry.

This is not an exhaustive list, but it does indicate the creative world of women poets, which has changed and kept pace with the times. Poets, in any case, tend to be few, and unfortunately there are fewer women poets than men. Moreover, the contemporary idiom of poetry is comparatively new for them, and they are taking their first steps but are sure to go far in the future.

Women Prose Writers

Women entered the field of modern poetry comparatively late, but they started writing prose in the early years of the twentieth century. The humorous articles of Vidyagauri Nilkanth (1896–1958), wife of Ramanbhai Nilkant, were included in his *Hasyamandir*. She also wrote articles pertaining to women, collected in *Grihadeepika* (1931) and elsewhere. She also wrote a biography of Dhondo Keshav Karve. She was an early woman prose writer to have developed a refined style.

Her contemporary Sharda Mehta (1882–1970) wrote a biography of Florence Nightingale and her autobiography, *Jivansamharanan* (1938), regarded as her most significant work.

Around the same time, Hansa Mehta (1897–), a prominent member of the All-India Women's Conference and educationist, entered the field as a competent translator with the Gujarati versions of eight cantos of the Sanskrit *Ramayana,* Shakespeare's play *Merchant of Venice,* plays of Molière, and Swift's *Gulliver's Travels.* She also wrote a couple of original plays.

An eminent prose writer of the following generation was K. M. Munshi's wife, Lilavati Munshi (1899–1978). *Rekhachitro ane Bija Lekho* (1925) instantly established her as a writer in her own right. After a lapse of five decades appeared her collections of short stories and one-act plays in *Jivanani Vatetii* (1977) and collection of articles in *Sanchay* (1975). She wrote little, but her name counts as a leading Gujarati prose writer.

Subsequently, there were not many women prose writers until they began writing novels and short stories. It was a somewhat late beginning, but once the process started, it continued, and today there are a number of women novelists and short story writers of eminence, belonging mostly to the postindependence period—although some, like Labhuben Mehta, wrote novels, reminiscences, interviews with eminent musicians and other works earlier.

One of the important fiction writers of the postindependence period is Kundanika Kapadia (1927), who won first prize for her very first short story, "Premnan Ansu," in the short story competition organized by the *New York Herald Tribune,* and, sometime afterward, her first collection appeared under the same title, followed by the collections *Kagalni Hodi* (1981) and *Java Daishum Tamne* (1983). She subsequently published her novels, *Agan-Pipasa* (1972) and the Sahitya Akademi-winner, *Saat Paglan Akashman* (1984).

Kundanika has a delicate style, often verging on the ornamental. She effectively expresses women's innermost thoughts and feelings, pointing an accusing finger at male domination in family and society. Right from the beginning, she has written against injustices to women and their exploitation. But her anguish becomes anger in *Saat Paglan Akashman,* a totally feminist novel, translated into Hindi and English. Even in her expression of anger, there is her typical linguistic flourish. Despite the suffering woman's being her subject, she is much more than just a woman writer.

Then, there is Dhiruben Patel (1926) with her short story collections like *Vishrambhkatha* (1966). Her novels *Vadvanal* (1963), *Vansno Ankur* (1967), *Andhali Gali,* and others have been widely acclaimed. Dhiruben has also written plays, like *Pahelun Inam* (1957) and *Namani Nagarvel* (1961). She has written a delightful, full-length children's play, children's songs, and limericks.

In her writings, Dhiruben reveals her understanding of the human mind and builds up the characters and situations, forming a natural pattern. She writes with ease and a sense of humor, encompassing in her works the life of men and women at various levels.

Striking an absolutely new note as a fiction writer came Saroj Pathak (1929–88). With her unusual choice of subjects, dealing mainly with disharmony in married life, and inner conflicts with her thrust and irrepressible force of expression, she stands quite apart from other women writers.

Saroj's short stories collected in *Ghata Zuk Aayi* and *Virat Tapakun* (1966) have a tremendous power to hold one's attention, as do her novels *Nihshesh* (1978) and *Priya Punam* (1980), reflecting conflicts and complexities in women's lives. Saroj, with her intense creative upsurge and artistic expression, deserves greater recognition than she has received so far.

Then, there are two sisters, Varsha Adalja and Ila Arab Mehta, who have written fiction without the slightest trace of similarity. Varsha's *Pachhan Faratan* (1979), *Khari Padelo Tahuko* (1988), *Retpankhi* (1985), and other novels deal mainly with middle-class life, with an emphasis on contemporary women. She is not a feminist writer but describes in her fiction women's situation in the best artistic manner possible, with a fairly well-developed idiom.

Ila, on the other hand, has a wider canvas. Even the titles of her novels, like *Shabne ne Naam Nathi Hotun, Ek Cigarette ane Dhoopsali,* and *Ane Mrityu* suggest that her writing is not the usual feminine kind and that a great deal of reflections on life and death have gone into it. Her action-packed, gripping novels and short stories live in the reader's mind.

There are many more fiction writers, like Vasuben Bhatt, Meenal Dikshit, Anjali Khandwala, and Himanshi Shelak, whose works have added to women's creative writing in Gujarati.

The only other woman playwright, apart from Dhiruben Patel, is Rambhaben Gandhi, who held the field for many years with her one-act plays like *Aarati* and *Insaaf,* about contemporary themes dealing with middle-class life in a lively manner, with a touch of humor and satire and easy flow of language.

Women's contribution to critical writing is really meager. Susmita Medh and Tarulala Mehta are the only names that can be mentioned, apart from Heeraben Pathak, who have done critical writing. It is time more women entered this field.

Women's writing in Gujarati, with the exception of a few writers like Savita Ranpura, concentrates mostly on the life and conflicts of the urban middle class, with wealthy characters as and when they form part of that life. It would be a welcome development if rural life also becomes part of women's creative writing.

Similarly, a further dimension would be added to women's prose writings if they venture into experimental writing like some women poets. However, the picture is not very bleak as it is, and there is hope for the future.

CONCLUSION

Thus, looking at the various stages of development of Gujarati literature of the twentieth century in relation to its earlier phases, it is clear that the writers in all genres have responded to the changing times by extending the horizons of their vision of life. They have shown readiness to adopt new themes, new concepts, techniques, and expressions, following their own creative inclinations. Not all that is written is of lasting value, but much of it is the result of genuine responses to the human situation and intense feelings. It has a richness reflecting the typical Gujarati ethos and psyche, enfolding within itself the life of urban, rural, and tribal societies. Of course, Gujarati writers have still to achieve a lot more to reach the higher realms of creativity. But what is done so far is by no means negligible. It is certainly a matter to feel proud about. But rather than feeling complacent, Gujarati writers should take it as a matter of responsibility to create more and better in days to come.

SELECTED PRIMARY BIBLIOGRAPHY

Adalja, Varsha. *Pachhan Faratan.* Bombay: R. R. Sheth, 1979.
———. *Retpankhi.* Bombay: R. R. Sheth, 1985.
———. *Khari Padelo Tahuko.* Bombay: R. R. Sheth, 1988.
Antani, Vinesh. *Anurav.* Bombay: Lokapriya Prakashan, 1984a.
———. *Bijun Koi Nathi.* Bombay: Lokapriya Prakashan, 1984b.
Bakshi, Chandrakant. *Padgha Dubi Gaya.* Bombay: Swati Prakashan, 1958.
———. *Ayanavritta.* Surat: Mudran Prakashan, 1967.
———. *Paralysis.* Bombay: Ashok Prakashan, 1978.
———. *Picnic.* Bombay: Ashok Prakashan, 1980.
———. *Lili Nasaman Pankhar.* Bombay: Ashok Prakashan, 1984.
Betai, Sundarji. *Jyoti-rekha.* Bombay: R. R. Sheth, 1934.
———. *Visheshanjali.* Bombay: R. R. Sheth, 1952.
———. *Sadgat Chandrasheelane.* Bombay: R. R. Sheth, 1959.
———. *Mahabharatnan Chaar Parvo.* Bombay: R. R. Sheth, 1976.
———. *Shravani Jharmar.* Bombay: R. R. Sheth, 1982.
———. *Indradhanu.* Bombay: R. R. Sheth, 1989.
———. *Amod.* Bombay: R. R. Sheth.
Bhayani, Utpal. *Nimajjan.* Bombay: R. R. Sheth, 1978.
———. *Hallo.* Bombay: R. R. Sheth, 1983.
Botadkar. *Srotasvini.* Bhavnagar: Mahila Vidalaya, 1926.
———. *Shaivalini.* 3d ed. Bombay: N. M. Tripathi, 1955.
Broker, Gulabdas. *Lata ane Biji Vato.* Ahmedabad: Jivan Sahitya Mandin, 1950.
———. *Ubhi Vate.* 4th ed. Bombay: Trilochan Printing Press, 1972.
———. *Abhivyakti.* Bombay: Chandra Prakashan, 1985.
Chatterjee, Suniti Kumar. *Languages and Literatures of Modern India.* Calcutta: Bengal, 1963.
Chaudhari, Raghuvir. *Amrita.* Surat: Shri Harihar Pustakalaya, 1965.
———. *Bahar KoiChhe.* Ahmedabad: R. R. Sheth, 1972.
———. *Uparvas, Sahavas, Antarvas* (trilogy). Ahmedabad: R. R. Sheth, 1975.
———. *Tamasa.* Ahmedabad: R. R. Sheth, 1977.
Dalal, Jayanti. *Pagdivani Pachhitethi.* Ahmedabad: Author, 1940.
———. *Javanika.* Ahmedabad: Author, 1941.
Dalal, Jayanti. *Pagdivani Pachhitethi.* Ahmedabad: Author, 1940.

———. *Javanika.* Ahmedabad: Author, 1941.
———. *Dhimu ane Vibha.* Ahmedabad: Maha Gujarat, 1943.
———. *Yuddha ane Shanti* (translation of Leo Tolstoy's *War and Peace*). 4 parts. Ahmedabad: Gurjar Granth Ratna Karyalaya, 1943–44.
———. *Padarnan Tirath.* 2d ed. Ahmedabad: Ravani Prakashan, 1955.
Darji, Pravin. *Pashchat.* Ahmedabad: Kumkum Prakashan; 1982.
Darshak. *Bandhan ane Mukti.* Ahmedabad: Lakshmidas P. Gandhi, 1939.
———. *Deepnirvan.* 3d ed. Sanosara: Author, 1953.
———. *Jher to Pidhan Chche Jani Jani.* 2d ed. Sansosara: Sarvoday Sahakari Prakashan, 1972.
Das, Sisir Kumar. *A History of Indian Literature.* New Delhi: Sahitya Akademi, 1991.
Dave, Harindra. *Palnan Pratibimb.* Bombay: Swati Prakashan, 1966.
———. *Anagat.* Bombay: Swati Prakashan, 1968.
———. *Madhav Kyanya Nathi.* Bombay: Vora, 1970.
———. *Hayati.* Ahmedabad: Chimanlal Literary Trust, 1977.
———. *Mukhvato.* 2 parts. Bombay: N. M. Tripathi, 1985.
Dave, Jyotindra. *Rangtarang.* 6 parts. Surat: Gandhiv Sahitya Mandir, 1931–39.
Desai, Mahadev. *Vir Vallabhbhai.* Ahmedabad: Navjivan.
———. *Sant Francis.* 2d ed. Ahmedabad: Navjivan, 1941.
———. *Be Khudai Khidmatgar.* Ahmedabad: Navjivan.
———. *Mahadevbhaini Diary.* 15 parts. Ahmedabad: Navjivan, 1948–78.
Desai, Ramanlal V. *Apsara.* 5 parts. Bombay: R. R. Sheth, 1933–49.
———. *Gramalakshmi.* 4 parts. Bombay: R. R. Sheth, 1940a.
———. *Jhakal.* 3d ed. Bombay: R. R. Sheth, 1940b.
———. *Bharelo Agni.* 3d ed. Bombay: R. R. Sheth, 1951.
———. *Praylay.* Bombay: R. R. Sheth, 1953.
Dhruv, Anandshankar. Ahmedabad: Gujarat Vernacular Society, 1941.
Dhruv, Saroop. *Mara Haathni Vaat.* Ahmedabad: Nakshatra Trust, 1982.
Gandhi, Mohandas K. *Anasakti Yog.* 2d ed. Ahmedabad: Navjivan, 1949a.
———. *Dharmamanthan.* 2d ed. Ahmedabad: Navjivan, 1949b.
———. *Satyana Prayogo Athava Atmakatha.* 9th ed. Ahmedabad: Navjivan, 1952.
———. *Hind Swaraj.* 2d ed. Ahmedabad: Navjivan, 1954.
———. *Collected Works of Mahatma Gandhi.* 100 vols. Ahmedabad: Navjivan, 1958–94.
———. *Dakshin Africana Satyagrahano Itihas.* Ahmedabad: Navjivan.
Iyengar, K. R. Srinivas. *Indian Literature since Independence.* New Delhi: Sahitya Akademi, 1973.
Jadeja, Dilavarsingh. *Gujarati Sahityaman Pratibimbit Rashtriya Asmita.* Vallabvidyanagar: Author, 1974.
Jhaveri, Mansukhlal M. *Thoda Vivechanlekho.* Rajkot: Author, 1944.
———. *Pholdol.* 2d ed. Bombay: Author, 1950.
———. *Anubhuti.* Bombay: R. R. Sheth, 1956.
———. *Kavyavimarsh.* Bombay: Vora, 1962.
Joshi, Ramanlal. *Abhipsa.* Ahmedabad: Kamalesh Pustak Bhan ar, 1968.
———. *Vivechanani Prakriya.* Ahmedabad: Kumkum Prakashan, 1978.
Joshi, Suresh. *Kinchit.* Baroda: Chetan Prakashan rih, 1960.
———. *Kathopakathan.* Ahmedabad: R. R. Sheth, 1969.
———. *Shrunvantu.* Baroda: Butala, 1972.
———. *Chintayami Manasa.* Ahmedabad: Sadbhav Prakashan, 1985.

Joshi, Umashankar. *Akho: Ek Adhyayan.* Ahmedabad: Gujarat Vernacular Society, 1941.
———. *Abhijnan.* Ahmedabad: Bharati Sahitya Sangh, 1946.
———. *Nishith.* 2d ed. Baroda: Jivan Sahitya, 1947a.
———. *Prachina.* 2d ed. Baroda: Jivan Sahitya Mandir, 1947b.
———. *Samasanvedan.* Baroda: Jivan Sahitya Mandir, 1948a.
———. *Vishwashanti.* 4th ed. Ahmedabad: Navjivan, 1948b.
———. *Parkan Janyan.* Ahmedabad: Lakshmi Pustak Bhandar, 1956.
———. *Shaili ane Swaroop.* Bombay: Vora, 1960.
———. *Mahaprasthan.* Bombay: Vora, 1965.
———. *Nireeksha.* Bombay: Vora, 1972.
———, ed. *Gujarati Sahityano Itihas.* Vols. 3, 4. Ahmedabad: Gujarati Sahitya Parishad, 1978.
Kalapi. *Kalapino Kekarav.* 3d ed. Baroda: Pustakaky Sahayak Mandal, 1952.
Kalelkar, Kaka Saheb. *Himalayno Pravas.* Ahmedabad: Navjivan, 1924.
———. *Smaranayatra.* Ahmedabad: Navjivan, 1934.
———. *Jivta Tahevaro.* Ahmedabad: Navjivan, 1937.
———. *Rakhadvano Anand.* Ahmedabad: Navjivan, 1953.
———. *Purva Africamanan.* Ahmedabad: Navjivan, 1954.
———. *Jivanavyavastha.* Ahmedabad: Navjivan, 1964.
Kant. *Purvalap.* 5th ed. Bhavnagar: Munikumar Bhatt, 1948.
Kapadia, Kundanika. *Agan-Pipasa.* Bombay: Somaiya, 1972.
———. *Java Daishun Tamane.* Ahmedabad: Ashok Prakashan, 1983a.
———. *Kagalani Hodi.* Ahmedabad: Ashok Prakashan, 1983b.
———. *Premnan Aansu.* Ahmedabad: Ashok Prakashan, 1983c.
———. *Saat Pagalan Akashman.* Bombay: Ashok Prakashan, 1984.
Macwan, Joseph. *Angaliyat.* Bombay: R. R. Sheth, 1988.
Madia, Chunilal. *Pawak Jwala.* Joravarnagar: Yashwant Mudranalaya, 1947.
———. *Indhan Ochhan Padyan.* Bombay: N. M. Tripathi, 1951.
———. *Liludi Dharti.* 2d ed. Surat: Shri Harihar Pustakalaya, 1960.
———. *Indradhanushno Athmo Rang.* Bombay: Vora, 1967.
Mankad, Mohammad. *Ajanyan Be Jan.* Ahmedabad: R. R. Sheth, 1970a.
———. *CHOT.* Ahmedabad: R. R. Sheth, 1970b.
———. *Bandh Nagar.* Ahmedabad: Gurjar Granthratna Karyalaya, 1987.
———. *Ashwadod.* Ahmedabad: Gurjar Granthratna Karyalaya, 1993.
Meghani, Jhaverchand. *Saurashtrani Rasadhar.* 3 parts. Ahmedabad: Gurjar Granthratna Karyalaya, 1927–29.
———. *Veninan Phool.* 7th ed. Ahmedabad: Gurjar Granthratna Karyalaya, 1949.
———. *Tulsikyaro.* 4th ed. Bombay: N. M. Tripathi, 1950.
———. *Sorath Taran Vahetan Pani.* 4th ed. Ahmedabad: Gurjar Granthratna Karyalaya, 1954.
———. *Yugavandana.* 5th ed. Bombay: R. R. Sheth, 1955.
———. *Manasaina Diva.* 10th ed. Bhavnagar: Sanskar Sanitya Prakashan, 1969.
———. *Vilopan ane Biji Vata.* 2d ed. Ahmedabad: Prasar Prakashan, 1978.
Mehta, Chandravadan. *Aagagadi.* Surat: Gandiv Sahitya Mandir, 1934.
———. *Gathariyan.* 9 parts. Surat: Gandiv Sahitya Mandir, 1954–76.
———. *Ila Kavyo.* New ed. Ahmedabad: Rupali Prakashan, 1977.
Mehta, Ila Arab. *Shabne ne Naam Nathi Hotun.* Bombay: R. R. Sheth.
———. *Ek Cigarette ane Dhoopsali.* Bombay: R. R. Sheth.

———. *Ane Mrityu.* Bombay: R. R. Sheth.
Mehta, Jaya. *Venetian Blind.* Bombay: Vora, 1978.
———. *Akashman Tarao Chhup Chhe.* Bombay, 1985.
Mehta, Tarulata. *Arvachin Kavitaman Praneynirupan.* Nadiad: Mehta Pradip Books, 1983.
Munshi, K. M. *Pauranik Natako.* 3d ed. Ahmedabad: Gurjar Granthratna Karyalaya, 1943.
———. *Brahmacharyashram.* 2d ed. Ahmedabad: Gurjar Granthratna Karyalaya, 1944.
———. *Adadhe Raste.* 2d ed. Ahmedabad: Gurjar Granthratna Karyalaya, 1946.
———. *Bhagwan Parashuram.* 3d ed. Ahmedabad: Gurjar Granthratna Karyalaya, 1950.
———. *Rajadhiraj.* 5th ed. Ahmedabad: Gurjar Granthratna Karyalaya, 1951a.
———. *Verni Vasulat.* 4th ed. Ahmedabad: Gurjar Granthratna Karyalaya, 1951b.
———. *Gujaratno Nath.* 10th ed. Ahmedabad: Gurjar Granthratna Karyalaya, 1952.
———. *Swapnasiddhini Shadhman.* Bombay: Bharatiya Vidya Bhavan, 1953.
Munshi, Lilavati. *Jivamanthi Jadeli.* Ahmedabad: Gurjar Granthratna Karyalaya, 1944.
———. *Sanchay.* Bombay, 1975.
———. *Jivanani Vatethi.* Bombay, 1977.
Nagendra. *Indian Literature.* Delhi: Prabhat Prakashan, 1988.
Nanalal. *Apanana Saksharartno.* Ahmedabad: Author, 1943.
———. *Indukumar.* 3 parts. 6th ed. Ahmedabad: Manohar N. Kavi, 1951a.
———. *Ketlank Kavyo.* Ahmedabad: Manohar N. Kavi, 1951b.
———. *Vishvagita.* 3d ed. Ahmedabad: Vadilal H. Shah, 1952.
———. *Jaya-Jayant.* 7th ed. Ahmedabad: Manohar N. Kavi, 1955.
———. *Harisamhita.* 3 parts. Ahmedabad: Nanalal Smarak Samiti, 1960.
Narasinghrao. *Smaranasamhita.* 3d ed. Bombay: Jamnadasni, 1940.
———. *Buddhacharit.* 2d ed. Ahmedabad: Gurjar Granthratna Karyalaya, 1947.
———. *Nupurjhankar.* 3d ed. Ahmedabad: Gurjar Granthratna Karyalaya, 1949.
———. *Smaranamukur.* 2d ed. Ahmedabad: Gurjar Granthratna Karyalaya, 1954b.
———. *Narasinghraono Kavyavichar.* Bombay: R. R. Sheth, 1969.
Nayak, Panna. *Philadelphia.* Ahmedabad: Arvind Pandya, 1980.
———. *Pravesh.* Ahmedabad: S. Asar, 1987.
———. *Nisbat.* Bombay, 1988.
Nilkanth, Ramanbhai. *Hasyamandir.* 3d ed. Ahmedabad: Jivanlal Mehta, 1926.
———. *Bhadrambhadra.* 7th ed. K. M. Shah, 1953.
Parikh, Gita. *Purvi.* Bombay: Vora, 1966.
———. *Bhinash.* Ahmedabad: Author, 1979.
———. *Kavya-Spandita.* Ahmedabad: Author, 1989.
Patel, Bholabhai. *Purvapar.* Ahmedabad: R. R. Sheth, 1976.
———. *Kanchanjangha.* Ahmedabad: R. R. Sheth, 1985.
———. *Devoni Ghati.* Ahmedabad: R. R. Sheth, 1989.
———. *Devatma Himalay.* Ahmedabad: R. R. Sheth, 1990.
Patel, C. N. *Gandhiji in His Gujarati Writings.* New Delhi: Sahitya Akademi, 1981.
Patel, Dhiruben. *Vadvanal.* Bombay: N. M. Tripathi, 1963.
———. *Vishrambhakatha.* Bombay: Kalki Prakashan, 1966.
———. *Vansno Ankur.* Bombay: Swati Prakashan, 1967.
———. *Gagananan Lagan.* Bombay: N. M. Tripathi, 1984.
Patel, Pannalal. *Malela Jiv.* 2d ed. Ahmedabad: Bharati Sahitya Sangh, 1950.
———. *Sukhdukhanan Sathi.* 3d ed. Ahmedabad: Bharati Sahitya Sangh, 1955.

———. *Valamanan.* 4th ed. Ahmedabad: Bharati Sahitya Sangh, 1956.
———. *Manvini Bhavai.* 3d ed. Ahmedabad: Bharati Sahitya Sangh, 1957.
———. *Partane Kaho Chadhave Baan.* Rev. ed. Ahmedabad: Sadhna Prakashan, 1976.
Pathak, Heeraben. *Apanun Vivechan Sahitya.* Ahmedabad: Gurjar Granthratna Karyalaya, 1976a.
———. *Kavyabhavan.* Ahmedabad: Gurjar Granthratna Karyalaya, 1976b.
———. *Paraloke Patra.* Ahmedabad: Gurjar Granthratna Karyalaya, 1976c.
Pathak, Ramnarayan V. *Dwirefni Vato.* 3 parts. Ahmedabad: Bharati Sahitya Sangh, 1928–42.
———. *Sheshnan Kavyo.* 2d ed. Ahmedabad: Bharati Sahitya Sangh, 1951a.
———. *Swairavihar.* Ahmedabad: Bharati Sahitya Sangh, 1951b.
———. *Arvachin Kavyasahityanan Vaheno.* Ahmedabad: Bharati Sahitya Sangh, 1955a.
———. *Brihat Pingal.* Ahmedabad: Gujarati Sahitya Parishad, 1955b.
———. *Manovihar.* Ahmedabad: Gurjar Granthratna Karyalaya, 1956.
Pathak, Saroj. *Virat Tapakun.* Ahmedabad: Kumkum Prakashan, 1966.
———. *Nihshesh.* Ahmedabad: Kumkum Prakashan, 1978.
———. *Priya Punam.* Ahmedabad: Kumkum Prakashan, 1980.
Pathakji, Jaimangauri. *Tejchnaya.* Bombay: Author, 1940.
———. *Sonalan.* Bombay: Author, 1957.
Saraiya, Anniben. *Nupur.* Bombay: Author, 1958.
———. *Sonalun Swapna.* Bombay: Author, 1979.
———. *Gulbanki.* Bombay: Author, 1982.
Sharma, Bhagwati Kumar. *Urdhvamool.* Ahmedabad: R. R. Sheth.
———. *Adabeed.* Bombay: R. R. Sheth, 1985.
———. *Asooryalok.* Bombay: R. R. Sheth, 1987.
Sharma, Radhashyam. *Vachana.* Ahmedabad: Trimurti Prakashan, 1972.
———. *Phero.* Ahmedabad: Trimurti Prakashan, 1977.
———. *Samprat.* Ahmedabad: R. R. Sheth, 1978.
———. *Swapnateerth.* Ahmedabad, 1979.
———. *Aansu ane Chandaranun.* Ahmedabad: Trimurti Prakashan, 1983.
———. *Vartavaran.* Ahmedabad: Trimurti Prakashan, 1987.
Sheth, Chandrakant. *Dhoolmani Pagalio.* Ahmedabad: R. R. Sheth, 1984.
Sneharashmi. *Arghya.* Ahmedabad: R. R. Sheth.
———. *Panghat.* Ahmedabad: R. R. Sheth, 1983.
———. *Gata Asopalav.* Ahmedabad: R. R. Sheth.
———. *Antarpat.* Ahmedabad: R. R. Sheth.
———. *Safalyatanun.* Ahmedabad: R. R. Sheth, 1983.
Sundaram. *Piyasi.* 3d ed. Jamnagar Ayurved Mudranalaya, 1946.
———. *Yatra.* Ahmedabad: R. R. Sheth, 1951.
———. *Kavyamangala.* 5th ed. Ahmedabad: R. R. Sheth, 1954.
———. *Avalokana.* Bombay: R. R. Sheth, 1965.
———. *Hirakani ane Biji Vato.* 2d ed. Jamnagar Ayurved Mudranalaya, 1967.
Thakore, Balawantrai. *Kavitashikshan.* Bombay: Author, 1943.
———. *Bhanakar.* Bombay: Author, 1951.
———. *Vividh Vyakhyano.* Baroda: M. S. University, 1956.
Topiwala, Chandrakant. *Black Forest.* Ahmedabad: Parshva Prakashan, 1989.
———. *Vivechanano Vibhajit Pat.* Ahmedabad: Parshva Prakashan, 1990.

Tripathi, Govardhanram. *Saraswatichandra.* 4 parts. Bombay: N. M. Tripathi, 1887–1901.
———. *Snehamudra.* Bombay: N. M. Tripathi, 1889.
———. *Lilavatijivankala.* Bombay: N. M. Tripathi, 1905.
———. *Scrap-book.* Bombay: N. M. Tripathi, 1956.
Trivedi, Vishnuprasad. *Vivechana.* Surat: Author, 1939.
———. *Parisheelan.* Surat: Gandhiv Mudranalaya, 1941.
———. *Dramaparna.* Ahmedabad: Chimanlal Literary Trust, 1983.
Vaidya, Vijayrai K. *Sahityadarshan.* Bhavnagar: Author, 1935.
———. *Manek ane Ateek.* Bhavnagar: Author, 1967.
Yajnik, Indulal. *AtmaKatha.* 6 parts. Mahemdavad: Author, 1955–56.
Yashashchandra, Sitanshu. *Odeseusnun Halesun.* Bombay: R. R. Sheth, 1974.
———. *Aa Manas Madrasi Lage Chhe.* Bombay: R. R. Sheth.
———. *Seemankan ane Ramaniyatano Vagvikalpa.* Bombay: R. R. Sheth, 1979.
———. *Jatayu.* Bombay: R. R. Sheth, 1987.

5

Twentieth-Century Hindi Literature

NANDI BHATIA

INTRODUCTION

One often finds the diverse literatures of India lumped into the unified category of "Indian literature." Given that India has 17 official languages, each with its own script and body of literature, such a categorization is rather simplistic, erasing, as it does, differences in the various literatures. Each language literature is shaped by its own region, politics, cultural traditions, geography, gender, and class and has its own genealogy. An adequate understanding of an "Indian" literature, therefore, requires us to examine the literatures of India in the context of India's linguistic diversity and "the highly diverse historical trajectories [which] may simply not be available for generalizing theoretical practices and unified narratives" (Ahmad 1992, 244). Hindi literature, too, is not an undifferentiated phenomenon but is polyvocal in expressing a range of ideas related to the social fabric from which it emerged. Within Hindi literature, there are multiple voices: radical voices that challenge existing power structures and hegemonies, voices of women and minorities who have often been marginalized, and voices from the center of the discipline that serve to erase these radical tendencies and affirm dominant structures. The latter include writings such as those that Aijaz Ahmad describes as "the High textuality of the Brahaminical kind," albeit writings that have been privileged over other lesser-known works that may be aesthetically or politically important but are excluded from mainstream Hindi literature because of canonical assumptions of "high" literary value (Ahmad 1992, 244). In order to get a glimpse of the multiple voices that constitute Hindi literature, this chapter presents a survey ranging from canonical works to lesser-known works by minority writers that, in spite of their exclusion from the canon, participated in the sociopolitical process and are by no means less significant to Hindi literature.

To understand the multiple strands in Hindi literature, it is necessary to place it against the backdrop of the sociopolitical conditions of Indian society in the twentieth century. The Indian nation witnessed important political changes during the period under consideration: from a colony of the British Empire it became an independent nation in 1947. The violence of colonialism, however, took its toll on the shaping of the nation. The struggle for independence from British colonial rule underwent numerous waves and troughs before the arrival of freedom in 1947. Independence came with a price that was paid by the nation's division into India and Pakistan. During the period of decolonization since independence, the nation has undergone severe upheavals in the form of external aggressions, such as wars with Pakistan and China, and internal aggressions, a most recent example of which is the communal violence that followed the 1992 demolition of the Babri Masjid at Ayodhya by Hindu fundamentalists. Such political ferment, both under British rule and after independence, has played a definite role in the shaping of Hindi literature. We find its manifestation in Hindi literature's multifaceted character, representing a variety of themes. These include the partition of the subcontinent, freedom from colonial oppression, freedom from internal hegemonies, freedom from the struggles of workers against various forms of exploitation, and feminist challenges to oppressive patriarchal structures and social traditions. These multiple themes and trends have been channeled through movements such as *chayavad,* or romantic literature; *pragativad,* or progressive realism; New Criticism; *nai kahani* or new short story; and feminist literature. Although some of these movements have been influenced by similar trends in the West, they emerged from their specific cultural traditions and sociopolitical milieus. The chapter examines the ways in which these multiple voices and movements both contributed to the process of nation building and addressed, at the same time, the sociopolitical problems within Indian society.

Since the survey traces the thematic trends against the backdrop of sociohistorical developments, it is broadly divided into two parts: preindependence and postindependence at 1947, which heralded a new era of national independence as well as the nation's partition into India and Pakistan, serving as a convenient dividing point for the chapter.[1] Part one examines the emergence of nationalist thought and ideology in literary works of the period before independence. The nationalist politics of this era were accompanied by a controversy over the status of Hindi and Urdu, which created communal dissensions that ultimately jeopardized the possibility of a unified struggle against British imperialism. This linguistic controversy is significant, complicating the nationalist struggle against British imperialism by internal communal politics. Configuration of issues such as the partition, the urge for national unity, democracy and secularism in the 1950s, social issues related to village economies, and continuing problems of peasants, workers, women, and other marginalized groups constitutes, to a large degree, the subject matter of Hindi writings after independence and informs the second half of the chapter.

As a broad survey of Hindi literature, this chapter is bound to suffer from certain shortcomings. The chief drawback arises from an inability to define the precise parameters of Hindi literature because of overlaps between Hindi and Urdu. At present, the linguistic differentiation between these languages is rather unsettled.[2] Despite ongoing attempts to settle the differences between Hindi and Urdu since the second half of the nineteenth century, when the debate over linguistic classification first began, it remains difficult to make clear-cut demarcations. Writers who wrote in either of the languages have been co-opted into their respective literatures for political reasons. For example, Premchand, whose works have acquired a very important place in the canon of Hindi literature, wrote some of his works in Urdu before they were transcribed into Devanagari. The choice of the script was forced on him because of the increasingly difficult task of finding publishers for Urdu at a time when Hindi was being propagated as the national language. For the purposes of this chapter, I discuss primarily literature written in Devanagari. Any important work that is left out is the result of an oversight rather than a deliberate omission. Being an overview, moreover, the chapter precludes detailed analyses of specific texts. For this reason, each text, movement, and author deserves further attention.

LITERATURE AND NATIONALISM: THE PREINDEPENDENCE PHASE

Hindi literature during the preindependence period may be usefully read as documents that articulated writers' active political engagement at a time of rising Indian nationalism against British colonialism. We discover, in this period, a unification of culture and politics, in which culture became a site on which was waged the complex struggle for India's freedom. Writers began to carve out an ''imagined'' Indian identity, visualizing a nation free of foreign domination and one in which democracy and brotherhood would prevail.[3] Their search manifested itself in numerous ways: patriotic stories that idealized and glorified India's past, stories urging Hindu–Muslim unity, and stories that exposed and recognized problems relating, among other things, to the exploitation and abuse of peasants, labor, and other marginalized classes under colonial rule.

Hindi–Urdu Divide

The literary manifestation of the nationalistic project was seen as early as 1912 in Maithilisharan Gupta's (1886–1964) poem ''Bharat Bharati'' (''The Voice of India,'' 1912). Gupta's poem contains songs that glorify India's past, deplore contemporary sociopolitical conditions, and suggest a way to a better future on the basis of Hindu–Muslim amity. Emphasis on Hindu–Muslim unity through literature came in the wake of rising Hindu–Muslim animosities around the turn of the century. The communal divide had been set in motion in the nineteenth century, in part, by the debate over the status of Hindi and Urdu as two separate languages. J. B. Gilchrist initiated this separation in the middle of the nineteenth century when he engaged a group of writers at the Fort William College at Calcutta to write Hindustani prose. Hindustani prose was channeled into two distinct styles. One included Hindi without the use of Persianized words, and the other style involved the use of an Urdu that remained as close as possible to Persian (Das Gupta 1970, 52). Such conscious segregation of the two languages made the differences between Urdu and Hindi sharper and became a strong basis for communal divisions between Hindus and Muslims during the nineteenth and twentieth centuries.

As Hindu and Muslim nationalists sought mass support from their respective communities through the propagation of the two languages, the debate intensified. The Hindu leadership stressed the need for popularizing Hindi to serve as a link for interregional communication and rally mass support against imperialism. Efforts to propagate the idea of Hindi as the national language were soon undertaken by organizations such as the Brahmo Samaj and the Arya Samaj, which actively promoted Hindi in North India. Pro-Hindi activism also constituted the introduction of Hindi newspapers in Bengal in the nineteenth century and the introduction of Hindi in law courts and schools in Bihar around 1900 (Das Gupta 1970, 83). Within the Hindi area, many organizations devoted to the cause of Hindi were formed. Of these, the Nagari Prachar Sabha in Benaras in 1893 and the Hindi Sahitya Sammelan, founded in Allahabad in 1910, became the most significant organizations for propagating the use of Hindi. These organizations promoted the Devanagari script and advocated a style that incorporated Sanskrit vocabulary while consciously removing Persian and Arabic words. Mahavir Prasad Dvivedi, the chief proponent of Hindi poetry at the turn of the century and editor of *Saraswati,* encouraged the use of Sanskrit meters in poetry. His own efforts to propagate this style included invitations to poets to write verse in Hindi, which he corrected before publishing in the journal, and he encouraged young poets to imitate his own lyrics published in *Saraswati.* With the publication of this new style of verse in *Saraswati* between 1909 and 1910 by scholars such as Kamta Prasad Guru (1875–1947), author of the first authoritative Hindi grammar, and Ram Chandra Shukla (1884–1941), professor of Hindi in Benaras and historian of Hindi literature, Hindi poetry received further impetus.

Efforts to establish Hindi as the national language and separate it from Urdu aggravated communal tensions. The Muslim community in India saw the advocacy for Hindi and its replacement of Urdu as an exercise of Hindu hegemony that posed a threat to Muslim interests in the subcontinent. Tensions escalated as Hindu revivalists such as Bal Gangadhar Tilak and Lajpat Rai of the Indian National Congress pressured the congress to emphasize Hinduism and Hindi in order to draw support from the Hindu masses. An example of the consolidation of the Hindu–Muslim rift is visible in the simultaneous formation of the Muslim League and the Hindu Mahasabha in 1906. This threat of Hindu domination via propagation of Hindi also resulted in the formation of several organizations for the propagation of Urdu. Of these, the Aligarh movement initiated by Syed

Ahmed Khan in the late nineteenth century was most vocal about asserting the status of Urdu as a national language.[4]

Nationalism and Revival of Hindi

Emphasis on the revival of a Sanskritized Hindi from the orthodox section of the Hindi revivalists led to the development of a highly literate Hindi at the turn of the century and gave a setback to Khadi boli, Braj Bhasha, and Awadhi dialects of Hindustani. Before the language controversy arose, these forms of Hindi or Hindustani were used by Hindus and Muslims alike. For example, Tulsidas's works *Ramcharit Manas* and *Kavitavali* were composed in Awadhi and Braj Bhasha, respectively. However, after the espousal of Hindi, which initiated the purging of Perso-Arabic words from the language, Braj Bhasha was considered unsuitable for poetry. A revised form of Khadi boli that used Sanskrit instead of Persian vocabulary was employed for Hindi verse. Ayodhya Singh Hariaudh, at this time, wrote his epic poems *Priya-pravas* and *Vaidei Banvas* in a Hindi that was highly Sanskritized. Others, such as Ramdhari Singh Dinkar and Shyam Narayan Pandey also utilized Sanskrit meters as opposed to the *dohas, padas,* and *kavittas* (poetic forms) of medieval poetry. Thus, by the first decade of the twentieth century, the language politics motivated by nationalist sympathies largely changed the character of Hindi literature from Hindustani, the standard language, to a highly literate and Sanskritized Hindi. During this period, Hindi received further impetus through *Saraswati,* edited by Shyamsunder Das, which became the most influential literary journal in the first two decades of the twentieth century. Writings in Hindi were encouraged through competitions for which prizes were awarded. By 1916, the number of journals in Hindi in the Uttar Pradesh region had far surpassed the number in Urdu. Between 1900 and 1910, Hindi became the medium of instruction in schools, where Urdu and English were the chief languages. Publishing in Hindi increased, and it became progressively more difficult to find publishers in Urdu.

Accompanying this change from Hindustani to a literate Hindi was a celebration of the past glory of India, as well as a privileging of Hinduism. Hindu intellectuals who advocated Hindi and believed in the glorious Hindu past argued that "only the reform of Hindu society on the basis of *tyag* (asceticism) and patriotism could bring about self-government" (Gaeffke 1978, 21). The revival of a Hindu past was linked to the idea of the vedic "golden age," an idea that had acquired prominence in the late nineteenth century in Bengal as a way of countering British colonialism and had manifested itself in the writings of renowned novelists such as Bankim Chandra (see Chakravarti 1986, 27–87; Kaviraj 1993, 1–39). Evoking images of a "golden Hindu age" was the writers' way of resisting the colonial threat and reminding themselves and their readers of the need to recover what India had lost to its colonizers. Soon it manifested itself in Hindi literature as well. While preaching the ultimate unity of all religions, intellectuals and proponents of Hindi insisted on the superiority of Hinduism and refused any compromise with Muslims or Christians (Gaeffke 1978, 21). Self-government, or *swaraj,* meant the rule of a Hindu majority. Hence, a body of literature poured forth evoking the myth of a glorious Indian past dominated by Hindu kings and philosophers, and a Hindu identity was represented as an "Indian" identity. For example, Shyam Narayan Pandey's epics *Haldighati* and *Jauhar* depicted the heroism of Rajputs in resisting the invasions of the Turks and the Moghuls. Stories of the greatness of Hindu gods were evoked through mythological tales from the *Ramayana* and the *Mahabharata.* Similarly, in *Bhagavad Purana,* Makhan Lal Chaturvedi attempted to reawaken a similar sense of duty in the Indian public as the characters in the *Bhagavad Gita* possessed.

In the field of drama, too, this trend became visible, especially in the historical plays of writers such as Jaishankar Prasad, Badrinath Bhatt, Makhan Lal Chaturvedi, Bechan Sharma Ugra, and Govind Vallabh Pant. Called the most significant playwright of the twentieth century by Dashrath Ojha, Prasad's historical dramas *Ashoka* (1912), *Ajatshatru* (1922), *Chandragupta* (1931), and *Skandagupta Vikramaditya* (1928) dwell on the courage of Hindu kings from ancient India. Shaym Sunder Suman's historical plays, such as *Chanakya Mohan, Haldighati, Padmini,* and *Kunal,* also recuperated themes from history. Plays such as Makhan Lal Chaturvedi's *Krishnarjun Yuddha,* Ugra's *Mahatma Isa,* Govind Vallabh Pant's *Varmala,* and Badrinath Bhatt's *Kuruvan Dahan, Durgavati,* and *Chandrakala Bhanukar* continued to evoke images of a perfect Hindu society.

Hindu texts were also revived by Hindi *nataka mandalis* (play company) to counter the Urdu movement. For example, "Sri Ramlila Nataka Mandali" presented Madhav Shukla's *Sita Swamvara* based on Tulsidas's *Ramcharit Manas, Mahabharata,* and *Maharana Pratap* and plays that satirized Urdu. These performances received immense popularity at the Hindi Sahitya Sammelan conferences at Allahabad and Lucknow (Narayan 1981, 42–43).

Writers' evocation of India's past inspired by a sense of Hindu nationalism was, however, detrimental to Hindu–Muslim relations. Images of a glorious Hindu past smoothed over the internal social and religious conflicts in Indian society, reconstructing a national and cultural identity that was based on upper-caste Hindu notions and values.

National Unity and Reform

In 1906, the Hindu–Muslim conflict culminated in the partition of Bengal. British rulers played up the communal divisions by giving patronage to Hindi and granting in 1909, through the Morley-Minto reforms, separate electorates to Muslims. This phase witnessed the growth of a literature that emphasized Hindu–Muslim unity and evoked India's historical past as an example of solidarity against the foreign powers—a trend that continued into the 1930s and 1940s as writers perceived the designs of British divisiveness of Hindus and Muslims in the interest of consolidating imperial rule. Signs of such an awareness became visible in plays like *Swapan Bhang* and *Rakshabandhan,* which expressed the theme of Hindu–Muslim unity. The aftermath of the partition led to the initiation of the Swadeshi movement in Bengal (1905–8). Swadeshi called for a move toward self-rule and a boycott of foreign goods. The national agitation that initiated the Swadeshi movement after the partition of Bengal spread from Calcutta into rural areas and educational institutions. Poets such as Mahavir Prasad Dvivedi and Lakshmidhar Bajpai articulated their nationalist aspirations by satirizing and ridiculing foreign goods and urging the use of homespun cloth. Their message was that Swadeshi, which aimed at improving the conditions of Indian peasants through the use of indigenous goods, would bring back India's prosperity.

The sociopolitical message of mass unity intensified as Gandhi, upon his return from South Africa in 1915, launched his anticolonial campaigns for suffering peasants in Champaran, Bihar, in 1917 and against the zamindars in the Kaira district of Gujarat in 1918. A combination of Gandhi's campaigns and the Swadeshi movement exerted a great influence on Hindi writers and brought forth a new outpouring of nationalistic literature, with Premchand as the most powerful spokesman of freedom. That Gandhi's influence motivated Premchand's ideas is evident in the writer's resignation of his job as inspector of government schools and increased active participation in Gandhi's movement to teach the villagers how to spin their own yarn and produce indigenous handmade cloth (Gaeffke 1978). The influence of Gandhi's Salt march (1930) and the second noncooperation movement recast itself in his novel *Karmbhumin,* which propagates the effectiveness of public demonstrations. An anti-industrial outlook found its way in Premchand's *Rangbhumin* (1925). In the novel, Premchand interrogates the effects of Western industrialization through a blind beggar's struggles against a cigarette factory owner who establishes his factory next to the beggar's piece of land. Premchand invokes the idea that the consequences of industrialization are brutal: the beggar is killed in his attempts to save his little plot of land that is threatened by the factory. Premchand also expresses the helplessness of the peasants amid rising industrial colonialism by showing the expansion of the factory despite the villagers' protests.

Hindu–Muslim dissensions deepened in the 1940s as the movement for a separate Pakistan became stronger. Hence, Hindu–Muslim unity became a popular theme for writers like Pant, Dvivedi, and Harivansh Rai Bachchan, who lamented the possibility of the subcontinent's breakup and reconstructed in their poems a nation devoid of religious, class, and caste distinctions.

Progressive Realism

Gandhi also propagated Hindu–Muslim unity through his support of Hindustani as the national language instead of Hindi or Urdu, which encouraged Hindu–Muslim separatism and kept the two communities disunited. Gandhi's contention was that, since Hindustani was spoken by both the Hindu and the

Muslim populace, it would prevent dissensions and promote national integration. But while Gandhi emphasized this unity, he made it clear that the script of Hindustani would be Devanagari and not Arabic (Das Gupta 1970). This move caused immense disaffection among progressive intellectuals—both Hindu and Muslim. Disaffection caused by Gandhi's stance on the issue of Devanagari was compounded by disillusionment with Gandhi's strategy of "nonviolence." Even though, largely speaking, Gandhi had, by this time, acquired the image of a *mahatma* (great soul), for many on the Left, his policy of nonviolence had not shown conclusive results. By the 1930s, the "Congress repeatedly aroused expectations and aspirations which it could not satisfy" (Sarkar 1984). Therefore, a challenge from the Left "through trade unions, Kisan Sabhas, radical student organizations, Congress socialists and communists became an important part of the political developments during the mid-1930s. The disillusionment of the radical middle class with Gandhian constraints" also contributed to the growth of the Left by the end of this period, and "revolutionaries abandoned the path of individual violence" to adopt the path of Marxist mass struggle (Sarkar 1984, 255). The upsurge of anticolonial nationalist ideas, World War I, the Great Depression of the 1930s, and continuing colonial exploitation created a mood of active political engagement. Influenced by Marxist ideas and inspired by the success of the Bolshevik revolution of 1917, writers shifted their earlier Gandhian stance in favor of a more revolutionary ideology. A number of disillusioned intellectuals and writers initiated the formation of the Progressive Writers' Association in 1936, with Premchand as its pioneering member. Defining the banner of "progressive" as "[a]ll that arouses in us the critical spirit," writers proposed to turn literature into a weapon in the struggle against colonialism (Pradhan 1979, Vol. 1, 21). The aim of the progressive writers was to portray an "authentic" picture of the problems of marginalized masses through a realistic idiom. This literature was to be expressed in a language easily understood by the masses that initiated a shift from the "high" or Sanskritized Hindi propagated by the orthodox Hindu nationalists to a literature that used Hindustani. A move to realism also established the novel as the chief medium of expressing the political commitment of writers.

In this changing context, Premchand emerged as a key figure in exposing the evils of colonialism through a progressive, realistic style exhibiting the influence of Marxist ideas in stories such as "Katil." "Katil" reveals an ideological shift from the nonviolent path suggested by Gandhi to a revolutionary one. In the story, Dharamvir tells his mother:

> Picketing and squatting crowds do not get us anywhere. You don't make a country free by singing pious songs and parading streets in non-violent batches . . . kill a couple of thousand English today, and you have freedom coming to you on a platter. Yes, mother. That's exactly what happened in Russia, that's exactly what happened in Ireland, and that's exactly what is going to happen in India—I hope. (Savin 1967, 151)

Premchand's novel *Premashram* (1922) also forced open issues concerning colonial exploitation through long descriptions of forced labor and the molestation of poor peasants and their women at the hands of rich landlords. Premchand's answer to freedom lay in collective peasant protest and overthrow of the ruling classes. Frustrated with the oppression from landlords and government officials, Balraj tells the villagers: "The letters that I receive say that in Russia it is the peasants who rule. They do what they want. Close to Russia there is a country called Bulgaria. There, recently, the peasants overthrew the king and now the *panchayat* of peasants and laborers rules" (Premchand 1922, 53; translation mine).[5] Another realistic portrayal of colonial exploitation occurred in Rishabcharan Jain's *Gadar* (The Revolution) in 1930 at the height of the nationalist movement. Not surprisingly, the novel was banned by the British government and reprinted only after independence.[6]

The Progressive Writers' Association also strengthened the Hindi short story, a medium that had already been explored by Premchand and Jaishankar Prasad. As compared to full-length novels, the short story could convey the political message in a shorter space. Seen as a viable means of communicating political messages, some writers, such as Yashpal, adopted this form for expressing their revolutionary views.

While prose remained the dominant form of expression during the 1930s and 1940s, progressive drama, too, played a significant role in attempting to dismantle existing power structures. Upendra Nath Ashk wrote plays such as *Chhata Beta, Jai Parajai, Aadi Marg,* and *Kaid and Udan.* Others, such as Pandit Laxmi Narayan Mishra, expressed their sociopolitical disaffection through "problem plays" such as *Sanyasis, Rakshas Ka Mandir, Mukti Ka Rahasya, Rajyoga,* and *Sindoor Ki Holi* (Nagendra 1988, 645). Protest against problems of farmers, landlords, police, and intercaste marriage, among others, came from Premchand in plays such as *Sangrama* and *Prem Ki Vedi* (1933).

The latter half of the 1920s and the decade of the 1930s saw the proliferation of one-act plays in Hindi, a number of which were also published in various journals, an example of which is Prashad's *Ek Ghunt. Hans,* a journal edited by Premchand, published a special number on one-act plays in 1938. The shift from full-length plays to one-act plays was emblematic of a formalistic struggle that progressive playwrights waged against the power structures. On one hand, it represented a break from the classical, full-length Sanskrit dramas that had acquired popularity because of the efforts to produce Sanskritized Hindi dramas by Hindu nationalist writers. Second, the one-act play in Hindi provided a break from the European full-length plays that dominated metropolitan theaters by the twentieth century. The one-act plays also proved immensely useful for propagating sociopolitical messages: they were both entertaining and instructive, they cut down on the details of a full-length production, they came straight to the point, and they were easy to perform in towns and villages that lacked the requisite theatrical facilities. A number of progressive playwrights, such as Balraj Sahni, K. A. Abbas, and Rasheed Jehan, channeled their attacks on contemporary problems through the Indian People's Theatre Association (IPTA), which was formed on an all-India basis in 1943 to use theater as a vehicle for social change. The IPTA set up a Hindustani squad that performed numerous plays on topics ranging from British imperialism, to fascism in Europe, to landlord problems, to exploitation of workers in factories, to the Bengal famine of 1943 and the cholera epidemic of 1944. Balraj Sahni and K. A. Abbas wrote and produced plays such as *Zubeida, Yeh Amrit Hai.*

The influence of Marxist ideas on Hindi writing continued into the 1940s. With their progressive outlook, writers such as Sohanlal Dvivedi and Sumitrananadan Pant, among others, continued to attack capitalist exploitation and the evils of imperialism and landlordism. The most scathing attack was launched on the imperialists after the Bengal famine of 1943, which, as politically commited writers believed, was created by the British government after the Quit India movement of 1942. The famine had a crippling effect, and millions of lives were affected. Yashpal dealt with these themes in his novels *Dada Comrade, Deshdrohi, Party Comrade,* and *Manushya Ke Rup.*

Chhayavad and Nationalism

Meanwhile, the decades of the 1920s and the 1930s also gave rise to a literature that exhibited a romanticism and mysticism, especially in poetry, a trend that came to be known as *Chhayavad.*[7] *Chhaya,* which literally translates as "a reflection, an image in a mirror," emerged as a revolt against Khadi boli poetry, which had replaced Braj poetry by the beginning of the twentieth century. As mentioned earlier, due to the efforts of orthodox Hindus to propagate the use of Hindi, Khadi boli had experienced a formalistic transformation that imparted a literary character to the language. Poetry born out of Hindu revivalism was replete with images of a lost past. "The ideals of these poets . . . were communal and revivalistic. . . . Their strong feelings of patriotism and nationalism were inspired and coloured by the Hindu ideals which did little to encourage secular ideals for the development of a more progressive Indian society" (Pandey 1975, 82). The *chhayavadis* revolted against this authoritarian control of poetry, which severely curtailed artistic freedom. They propagated the free flow of artistic expression, through which they expressed the problems and disillusionment of the individual in a world gone awry. The shift toward romanticism was also emblematic of writers' protests against British colonialism. By the end of World War I, British exploitation had reached its peak, and the nationalist struggle was at its height. Romantic writers sought an escape from the dreary conditions of life by creating an imaginary world for themselves. To look for solutions to existing political problems, the *chhayavadis* turned to an infinite transcendental reality, holding on to a rhetoric of mysticism and spiritualism. The *chhayavadi* phase emerged from the cultural conditions within Indian society and thus differed from the romantic movement in the West.[8]

The chief proponents of the *Chhayavad* movement were Jaishankar Prasad,

Suryakant Tripathi Nirala, Sumitranandan Pant, and Mahadevi Verma. Nirala's first romantic poem, entitled "Juhi Ki Kali" (The Bud of Jasmine) was published in 1923. Within a short span of time, poets such as Makhan Lal Chaturvedi, Ram Kumar Verma, Bhagvati Charan Verma, Harivansh Rai Bachchan, Narendra Sharma, Uday Shankar Bhatta, and Kedar Nath Bhatta became established as romantic poets. Preoccupied with symbolist experiments, poetic lyricism, and mysticism, the nationalistic themes of the *chhayavadi* writers became replete with such imagery. Nirala's *Anamika* (1937) is the most representative collection of the *chhayavadi* writers. Others, such as Pant's collection of poems *Vani* (1927), *Pallava* (1928), and *Gunjan* (1932), express the loneliness of the poet in a world of chaos.

The revolutionary upsurge in literature and the concern with mass nationalist struggle caused a shift from the individualistic struggles undertaken by the romantics to a depiction of the struggles of the masses. *Chhayavadi* writers such as Jaisankar Prasad, Suryakant Tripathi Nirala (1896–1961), Sumitra Nandan Pant, and Mahadevi Verma started finding their preoccupations with the lyrical charm and pastoral beauty of poetry limited and moved on to overt social themes. Poems such as Mahadevi Verma's "Yama" and "Deepshikha" (1940), Harivansh Rai Bachchan's "Madhushala" (1935), and Pant's "Yuganta" (1939) and "Gramya" (1940) are reflective of this shift. The poems portray poverty, social inequality, and village life. Surya Kant Nirala's *Kukurmutta* (1941) is a powerful attack on the British and Indian ruling classes through the *kukurmutta*'s (mushroom's) chastisement of the rose, which is presented as a metaphor for the capitalistic designs of the rulers.

Gender and Nationalism

Women were always at the center of the nationalist movement, both as historically constituted subjects in the nationalistic schemes of social reformers and political leaders and as constituting their own history through participation in the freedom struggle (see Sangari and Vaid 1986; Chatterjee 1989). Nationalist debates in the nineteenth century on the subjects of sati, child marriage, widow remarriage, and the twentieth-century movement for female enfranchisement were centered around women. Women's issues propelled the national movement forward as Indian nationalist leaders sought to free women from the double burden of colonial and patriarchal exploitation by initiating social reforms and granting them enfranchisement. In so doing, they could show to their colonial masters that they were moving in the direction of a nation that granted equality to all its citizens (see Jayawardene 1986).

Despite these reforms, the narratives of these writers continued to contain women in conservative hegemonic structures. For example, distinguished nationalist writers such as Lajjaram Mehta (1864–1931) did not condemn social problems such as child marriage, widow remarriage, purdah, and so on. As a matter of fact, in *Adarsh Hindu* (The Ideal Hindu, 1915), Mehta celebrated the traditional view that represented an ideal Hindu woman as primarily a mother and a wife who remains dependent on her parents, brother, or husband. Mehta's views were endorsed by Kishorilal Gosvami (1886–1932), another respected writer of the age.

Premchand challenged Mehta's views and attacked the very architecture of the sociocultural system that had negative ramifications on women, through novels such as *Nirmala* (1927) and *Sevasadan.* In *Sevasadan,* Premchand launched an attack on prostitution by exposing the cultural forces that force women into this profession. The principal character, a Hindu lawyer, remains indifferent to the plight of a Brahmin's wife whose husband, on groundless suspicion, turned her out of his house. Her helplessness forces her into prostitution. Integrating the sociocultural structures of caste, family, and colonialism (the Western-educated lawyer represents colonial authority), Premchand reveals the detrimental impact of these features on the position of women in Indian society. Following Premchand's example, a number of writers exposed the social conventions that continued to bind women in the shackles of regressive traditions. Pandey Bechan Sharma Ugra's *Chand Hasinon Ke Khutut* (1927) shows the consequences of Hindu–Muslim bigotry on women. Through a collection of letters, he reveals the inability of a Muslim girl and a Hindu boy, both students in Calcutta, to continue their relationship. Seen as an intruder in the Muslim community because of his love for a Muslim girl, the boy is killed by a Muslim mob at the moment when the girl's father finally agrees to the relationship.

However, even Premchand and his ilk's sympathies with their female protagonists did little to uplift the image of women. In most novels about female exploitation, women remained victims who were either to be pitied for their misfortune or to be admired for their sacrifices in the face of difficulties. In novels such as *Ruthi Rani,* Premchand juxtaposes Indian women with Christian women, through which he constitutes Indian women as having a high moral fiber in contrast with the morally weak character of Christian women. Through the figure of the morally superior Rani, who is a Hindu, Premchand asserts nationalistic pride at a period of the heightening freedom struggle. Such an image of Hindu women as being morally superior to Christian women (Christianity being a marker of complicity with the rulers on account of religion) was a nationalistic attempt on writers' part to show to the West that there were spheres in which India was superior to the West. As Partha Chatterjee argues, the nationalist patriarchy made clear-cut distinctions between spiritual and material spheres, marking the former as Eastern and superior as opposed to Western materialism. It placed women in the spiritual sphere and, in this way, "invested women with the dubious honour of representing a distinctly modern national culture" (Chatterjee 1989, 622). In Rani, we find a woman who upholds traditional Indian values and will thus hold the nation together. Thus, a rather limited portrayal of women emerges in the writings of this period. As in Premchand's *Nirmala* or Rajender Singh Bedi's *Lajvanti,* which deals with the theme of rehabilitation of women abducted during the Hindu–Muslim riots in 1947, women are articulated either as victims of patriarchy or as embodiments of the "ideal" mother or wife.

However, women writers challenged such conventional portrayals of their roles and presented the literary world with empowering images of figures such as the rani of Jhansi. The progressive environment created by the Progressive Writers' Association before independence brought forth an outpouring of texts in which women confronted existing power structures and urged the people's participation in the freedom struggle. Writers such as Subhadra Kumari Chauhan and Mahadevi Verma, among others, spoke openly about the freedom movement in an attempt to solicit the desired nationalist response from their audience. In her poem "Rakhi Ki Chunauti," Subhadra Kumari Chauhan's protagonist is a woman who inspires her brother on the occasion of "Rakhee" to participate in the civil disobedience movement. In Chauhan's *Vida,* a sister joins the disobedience movement herself after learning of her brother's arrest. *Jhansi Ki Rani,* Chauhan's powerful celebration of the queen of Jhansi's participation in the 1857 mutiny against the British rulers, became an example of empowerment of women everywhere.

AFTER INDEPENDENCE

Literature of Partition

The end of the freedom struggle and India's independence from colonial rule in 1947 initiated a new chapter in Hindi literature. Independence was accompanied by the tragedy of the subcontinent's partition into India and Pakistan. Because of the violence that accompanied this geographical division, freedom generated rather mixed feelings. The euphoria of independence soon changed into a mood of gloom as millions of people on both sides of the border were traumatized by the frenzy of communalism, alienation, and despair. Gandhi's assassination in 1948 dealt a further blow and shattered the confidence of the newly independent nation. The trauma of partition affected writers, who started questioning the idea of a nation that was invoked in earlier Hindi writings. While writers depicted the ramifications of the partition on the masses, they reexamined the implications and limitations of a nationalism that caused untold misery and suffering for the teeming millions whom it sought to liberate from foreign oppression. The partition became the predominant theme in the writings of Munto, Rajender Singh Bedi, Bhisham Sahni, and others. Depressing conditions of Lahore slums and the poverty-stricken areas of Jalandhar were portrayed in Upendranath Ashk's *Girti Diwaren* (1947). Other stories, such as Mohan Rakesh's *Andhere Band Kamare* (1961) and Yashpal's *Jhutha Sach* (1960) reevaluated Hindu–Muslim relations against the backdrop of the partition. Agyeya published a collection of stories and poems about the partition called *Sharnarthi* (1948). In the preface to the collection, the author addresses the issue of communal violence, the horrors of war, and the perpetuation of communal strife by the ruling bourgeoisie for their own political gains. A number of writers also found refuge in the literary journal *Hans* (1933–52) for expressing their ideological concerns about the partition and "to draw attention to . . . disadvantaged and neglected groups, the . . . distanced and obscured millions" (Rai 1984, 28).

With escalating communal tensions in India in the decades after independence and the emergence of regional and local nationalisms in different parts of the country, partition narratives continued to be written through the 1980s as a way of conveying the futility of communal dissensions. By depicting the tragedy of the partition, writers such as Bhisham Sahni in recent decades have attempted to enlighten the public about how they are constantly being recast into the ruling class's scheme of a new nation. In *Tamas* (1976), Bhisham Sahni narrativizes the history of partition not as a history of communalism but as a problem that tore the moral and religious fabric of the country beyond repair. Sahni juxtaposes ordinary people from different religious groups with political leaders to show the ways in which the leaders schemed against the people for their own party interests. Sahni's message is that, had the people understood the schemes of the rulers, both British and the Indian elite, they would have never encouraged or participated in the communal violence that ensued. We also find in *Tamas* the interrogation of nationalism, not as a unified phenomenon but in terms of other groups such as the *dalits,* peasants, and women.

Rural–Urban Transitions

In the years immediately following independence, writers also turned to representations of villages after the breakdown of the old order. Phanishwar Renu's *Maila Aanchal* (1954) takes us to a small village in Bihar to show the struggle between a stubborn zamindar and his landless workers. In *Rag-Darbari,* Srilal Shukla shows how new forms of exploitation replaced old ones in the village. Much to his consternation, the protagonist of the story, a research student, goes on vacation to his uncle's village and discovers that his uncle's means of power are money, perjury, and exploitation of the poor. The author lashes out at corrupt politics through the locale of the village, which represents a microcosmic view of the situation at the center. Other stories, such as Nagarjuna's *Balcanma* (1952) and Bhagvati Prasad's *Mother Ganges* (1953), center their plots around village life and the struggle of labor against zamindars.

Fifties and After

In the 1950s and 1960s, the tendencies of New Criticism and modernism that were dominant in the West in the first half of the century infiltrated the Indian literary scene and had a direct influence on the canon of Hindi literature. These configurations emerged in the Hindi Nai Kahani and the Nai Kavita movements of the 1950s. As literature's preoccupation with formalism increased, writers adopted the rhetoric of a "universalist" idiom and became predominantly concerned with purely aesthetic criteria (See Tharu and Lalita 1993, 92). Formalism and ''universalist claims'' of literature became the basis for inclusion of texts into the canon of Hindi literature, resulting in the marginalization of significant writings that came from radical sectors as well as from women.

In the late 1960s and 1970s, the results of independence started to become visible. While the metropolis seemed to progress, unemployment remained high, and large sections of the population remained below the poverty line. Such a climate gave rise to various protest movements, such as the antiprice rise agitation of 1972–73, organized and led primarily by women. The 1970s also saw a vigorous involvement of women in social issues. Several women's organizations were formed that protested against regressive traditions such as dowry and raised their voices against oppression of women. Feminist journals such as *Manushi* raised their voices against the repression of women. In 1975, the government declared a national emergency in the country, which suspended the fundamental rights of citizens until 1977, when the emergency was lifted. ''Slum clearance'' programs were initiated by the government, and the police cold-bloodedly razed ''unsightly'' urban settlements, rendering people homeless and helpless ''with no legal avenues for appeal or protest'' (Tharu and Lalita 1993, 99).

The decade of the 1970s gave birth to a radical new generation of political awareness and engagement. Writers questioned the inadequacies of democracy, which, contrary to its promises, and as the emergency revealed, did not seem to represent the interests of the people. Politically engaged writers made these themes the subjects of their writings, and the protagonists in the writings of the 1970s and 1980s were often lower-class people and women like Basanti, Bhisham Sahni's protagonist in *Basanti,* a novel about slums and slum dwellers in Delhi. *Basanti* (1980) shows the impact of the government slum clearance schemes on lower-class people, especially on women like its protagonist. Basanti belongs to a lower-class and caste community that lost its livelihood during the country's partition and moved to Delhi to revive its lost fortunes. The slum houses in which the community resides are brutally uprooted by police authorities, resulting in the dislocation of its residents without any help or compensation for the loss of their homes. While Sahni's narrative constitutes an attack on repressive government policies, it is significant in showing the impact of the violence caused by national politics on the private space that Basanti occupies.

The political, capitalistic, and physical violence reduces Basanti to a salable commodity and makes her a victim of rape, which ultimately reduces her status to that of a prostitute. However, Sahni does not dismiss Basanti for her open and active sexuality but represents it as being disruptive of patriarchal control. To highlight class and social differences and the ramifications of social policy for different classes, Sahni juxtaposes Basanti with the upper-class Shyama *bibi* (mistress of the house), who remains imprisoned in her middle-class respectability. By virtue of her class affiliation, Shyama has to fulfill the role of the ''good'' wife and mother. Her bourgeois respectability denies her the right to defy the shackles of social convention. Unlike Basanti, Shyama remains submissive to the social order, her husband, and the marriage—a typical model of traditional feminine behavior that is a symbol of governability by a patriarchal colonialist state. Sahni, however, is critical of Shyama for reproducing in her thought the bourgeois ideology that created and now sustains the idea of the "respectable woman." It is the lower-class Basanti, on the other hand, whose courage resists the totalizing portrayals of the passive female subject who seeks to be saved by her fathers and sons.

Women Writing in Hindi

Because of the euphoria created by India's newfound freedom in the immediate postindependence period and the emerging problems of the nation, including the wars with bordering countries of China and Pakistan and preoccupation with the internal communal and political dissensions, problems confronting women are often obscured or rendered invisible. The exploitation that women face in all spheres—economic, physical, and psychological—is ignored under the rhetoric of equal fundamental rights for all citizens. The escalating figures of dowry murders since the 1980s are testimony to the horrifying treatment that women receive. Indeed, one finds, even in the 1990s, that reports of dowry deaths, which should constitute news headlines, are relegated to rather inconspicuous columns in leading newspapers. Female infanticide and, more recently, female feticide, ill treatment of widows, whose worst manifestation was seen in the sati of 17-year-old Roop Kanwar in 1987, and discrimination in education are some other ways in which women are regularly put down. Cultural sanctions for the subjugation of females are also provided by government-regulated, televised renditions of Hindu texts such as the *Ramayana,* which celebrates the most regressive aspects of female subordination through its female protagonist, Sita.[9] Hence, women find themselves caught in a maze of problems stemming from patriarchy, capitalism, tradition, and religion, which, woven around male hierarchies, continue to regulate women's lives.

Although male writers such as Premchand, Jainendra Kumar, Rajender Singh Bedi, and Bhisham Sahni attempted to deal with problems that women face in Indian society, they accorded women spaces that were conceived according to their own social visions. Hence, what was ascribed to women were spaces designated from a male viewpoint. A study of Hindi literature reveals that women carved out their own spaces in order to address issues such as marriage, divorce, sexuality, and women's education, that is, issues that directly affect women's lives. Confronted with such problems, women interrogate in their writings the cultural traditions and the modern uses of patriarchal power in independent India. Many of these women have challenged the power structures that contain them in positions of subordination even while keeping some of the traditions intact. They discuss their frustrations and humiliations stemming from social problems that affect their daily lives. Rajni Pannikar writes:

> [As a child] I used to be very unhappy to see the atrocities committed on women. That time itself, I decided in my heart that I should also write something about the condition of women. And when I started writing, all those situations, all those scenes and pathetic images hit my mind again and again. (''Meri Rachna Prakriya,'' *Gyanoday,* October 1968, 101; cited in Asopa 1987, 51; translation mine)

Krishna Sobti also opposes the traditional moral values imposed on women. She vehemently argues that, to assert our own identity, ''we have to do something that will be different from the past. Something new'' (''Meri Srjan Prakriya,'' *Gyanoday,* November 1968, 55; cited in Asopa 1987, 44; translation mine).

In most of her novels, Shivani opens up numerous windows on the lives of women. She asserts that the tradition-bound, male-dominated system leaves no space for women's individuality. Shivani contends that a woman may be treated as a goddess or as a ''Sati,'' but actually her position is no more than that of a servant. Her novels reveal that even in the contemporary milieu, women's situation is no different from the repressive conditions of the nineteenth century that had urged the need for social reforms. In *Chaudah Phere,* Shivani, through the colonel, his wife, and their daughter Ahilya, problematizes the social system. She posits that in the male-dominated Indian society, a man assumes the rights to behave with a woman in whichever way he likes. Despite Ahilya's protests, her father the colonel forces her to marry the man he chooses as her husband. The colonel himself has an affair with Malika Sarkar, depriving his wife of all her rights in the house. In *Rativilap,* Shivani portrays the difficulties of a widow. In spite of being educated, *Mayapuri*'s Shobha finds herself caught in a web of difficulties. Helpless and trapped, she silently suffers when her poverty, class, and caste prevent her from marrying her lover, Satish, who brings the governor's daughter home as his bride.

Like *Mayapuri*'s Shobha, the protagonist in Usha Priyamvada's *Pachpan Khambe Lal Diwaren* is prevented from marrying the man she loves because it is socially unacceptable. Burdened by poverty and her family's financial crisis, she takes up a job as the warden of a hostel and becomes a prisoner in the building with red walls and 55 pillars.

A number of stories written by women foreground the problems pertaining to marriage. The Indian social system allows little choice to women in the matter of selecting their husbands. For the most part, parents make decisions about matrimony and, in accordance with the Shastras, gift the girl to the groom's family through a ritual called *kanyaadan* (giving of the bride), accompanied by a dowry that serves as a recompense to her husband's family. Unfortunately, the practice of giving dowry has resulted in the commodification of women and encourages, at the same time, mismatched marriages because of economic indigence. While rich men claim an untold price for their sons, the poor are forced to sell their daughters to men because of economic helplessness. Rajni Pannikar vilifies this situation in her novels. Because of her family's inability to give dowry, the heroine of *Do Ladkiyan* remains unmarried. On the night of her wedding, the vows cannot be taken because the prospective groom and his father angrily disrupt the ceremony upon realizing that no dowry will be provided. Helpless, she takes up a job to solve her family's financial difficulties. In the meantime, she meets the wealthy Mr. Kanaudia, who wants to make her his private secretary. In exchange, he offers her a car, a bungalow, and other facilities. She accepts his terms only to later realize his sexual intentions toward her. Kanaudia views her as no more than a female body for his sexual exploits. Pannikar's attempt is to enlighten us about the regressive aspects of a rigidly tradition-bound system.

All too often, the social system ignores women's needs and desires under the garb of traditional values such as *pativrat dharam.*[10] It provides practically no freedom of choice to women, who are expected to be "good" wives and overlook the abuses of their husbands. According to Chandrakiran Saunareksa: "Even today the Indian woman has no freedom of marriage. In our society parents arrange the wedding. And if a woman does not want to marry, she gets no cooperation from society because even today the old traditions are strongly prevalent—how will a woman stay without a protector?" (*Dinman,* July 6, 1975; cited in Asopa 1987, 38; translation mine). This problem of arranged marriage is manifested in Shivani's *Kainja,* whose heroine, Nandi Tiwari, is not allowed to marry the man she chooses, because her father has been told that her horoscope does not predict a happy married future.

The problem of dowry compounded by widowhood is considered in Mrinal Pandey's short story "Hum Safar." Through the thoughts of a young widow, Nirmala, traveling in a train compartment, Pandey illuminates the bitter truth about the ways in which her widowhood denies her whatever little she has left to savor. Nirmala recalls that after her husband's death, her "colored Saris and blouses, her silver anklets and nose ring, all had slowly found their way into her sister-in-law's boxes. Well, she had only a son to bring up, but her sister-in-law had several daughters to marry off. Wasn't her need greater than Nirmala's?" (Pandey 1993, 549). Pandey here is not merely confirming the present-day experiences of widows but also contesting the social structure that continues to shape the widow's world.

The train compartment in Pandey's narrative represents a microscopic version of contemporary India, in which modernization and industrialization attempt to homogenize the social and gendered difference and tend to overlook the complexities of the social structures that continue to confine women to a position of subordination. The train brings "fellow travelers" of both sexes into the space of a common compartment. Despite their inhabiting a common space, the collective "we" (in Hindi, "hum" also translates as "we") in this space of the nation, that is, the train compartment, is divided along gender lines in which the two male companions clearly feel superior and bully the other passengers in the compartment. The space of the train compartment becomes an artificially created space in which sexuality, widowhood, violence, and technology collide. The train journey becomes an allegory of the exploitation of the female, in its various manifestations, under the garb of equal rights. By bringing the segregated dichotomies into a common space, Pandey draws our attention to the fundamental contradictions that have been leveled into an imagined oneness in the interest of making a nation. The tension in the story serves as a reminder of the failed promises (especially for women) made by the custodians of an independent nation.

To confront the violence committed on women in their daily lives, Pandey introduces a language of violence expressed in Nirmala's outrageous beating of her son. Through this violent act, Nirmala conveys to the two loafers that she will no longer put up with their harassment. Perhaps Pandey is also saying that a quiet and nonviolent, passive attitude that society expects from a "virtuous" woman is insufficient to confront the violence inflicted on women through male-dominated structures.

Stories written by women largely reveal women's desires to have the choice to shape their lives, especially marriage—something that existing social institutions do not grant. Although Mannu Bhandari sees marriage as a necessity, she recommends the choice of divorce in an unsuccessful marriage (Bhandari 1971a). At the same time, however, she vivifies the social problems attached to the status of being a divorced woman in *Ap Ka Banti* (1971b).

Most of the stories of Pannikar, Shivani, Mannu Bhandari, and Mrinal Pandey strongly convey the necessity for women's education for achieving social and economic equality. For this reason, their protagonists are often educated women. The heroine of *Do Ladkiyan* is professionally sound because of her education. Similarly, *Kainja*'s Nandi Tiwari fights the system by obtaining a medical degree, which enables her to become a successful doctor. Her education provides her a self-confidence and economic stability that enable her to face the repressive society.

The stories written by these women are strategies for questioning the complex, heterogeneous forces at work in the configuration of the power structures that subordinate women. They introduce old issues, but with new emphases and new orientations. What we get is a textual sense of the struggles through which women's subjectivities are being consolidated in contemporary Indian society.

CONCLUSION

The preceding survey shows the inseparability of literary productions and the lived cultural experiences of society. From the turn of the century until the present, we find, in most texts under consideration, a record of the social milieu that surrounds them. Raymond Williams posits that literary texts are cultural practices that reaffirm the ideologies and experiences of a people (Williams 1990). Therefore, while we may not deny their aesthetic force, it would be unfair to view them only in the light of their aesthetic value and ignore their socio-political affiliations. Hindi writings, as we discovered in this chapter, should not merely be read as "spontaneous overflow of feelings and emotions" of writers but should also be interpreted as testimonials of sociocultural experiences, which include the experiences of imperialism, nationalist aspirations, the struggles of the dominated and their attempts to dismantle hegemonies, and the attempts of the dominant to reinforce hegemonies.

NOTES

I am grateful to Shoba Vasudevan for her invaluable suggestions and editorial guidance and to Sagaree Sengupta for reading the essay.

1. This division is not intended to create absolute categories, nor does it suggest a lack of continuity of certain trends and ideas after independence. The experience of the partition was a major turning point in the history of India and therefore offers a convenient dividing point.

2. Ahmad posits that, starting in the late nineteenth century, the differentiation between Hindi and Urdu has been an ongoing affair. Since then, says Ahmad, many questions have remained unsettled into the present (Ahmad 1992, 247). For statistical details regarding the Hindi-speaking population, see Goel (1990).

3. I use the word "imagined" in the sense that Benedict Anderson uses in *Imagined Communities* where he suggests that communities are created out of the shared desires and meanings of a people bound together by an imagined nationalism (Anderson 1991).

4. For a detailed study of the Hindi–Urdu controversy, see Jyotindra Das Gupta.

5. Premchand admitted the influence of Gandhi, Tolstoy, and Marx on his writing. According to Dharam Paul Sarin, Premchand was inspired by the October Revolution in Russia. For a discussion of the impact of the October Revolution of 1917 on Premchand and some other writers, also see Khullar (1981).

6. Censorship of literary productions was a common phenomenon during British colonial rule. In 1876, for example, the British government in India passed the Dramatic Performances Censorship Act, under which any drama that was viewed as "detrimental to public interest" was barred from performance, its text confiscated, and those involved with the play's production were liable to imprisonment and payment of a fine. For a detailed study of literary censorship during 1907–47, see Gerald Barrier (1974).

7. For a detailed discussion of *chhayavad,* see Schomer; Handa; and Pandey (1975).

8. The *chhayavadis* were also influenced by the English romantics. In *Hindi Literature,* Indu Praksah Pandey (1975) posits that almost all the poets of the Indian romantic school studied English literature. Among other things, translations from English romantic poetry into Hindi laid the foundation for the development of Hindi *chhayavadi* poetry. The earliest of these was Shridhar Pathak's translation of the early poetry of Goldsmith. English romantic poetry also influenced the style of Hindi poetry. Forms such as the ode, the sonnet, and the elegy were used by Hindi writers. Pandey also contends that many Hindi poets confess the influence of Wordsworth, Shelley, Keats, Tennyson, Byron, Browning, Blake, and others. Schomer argues that the Bengali poet Rabindranath Tagore had a tremendous influence on *chhayavadi* poets, such as Sumitranandan Pant and Mahadevi Verma.

9. The fictional character Sita continues to exert tremendous influence on the Hindu mind. In an article on Sita, Sally Sutherland mentions that a "recent survey taken of one thousand men and women in the North Indian state of Uttar Pradesh revealed that from a list of twenty four goddesses, literary heroines and famous women of history, an over-

whelming percentage chose for their ideal female role model Sita, the heroine of *Ramayana*'' (63).

10. *Pativrat dharam* refers to a woman's devotion to her husband, which, according to ancient Hindu legislators, was women's highest duty. See Chakravarti (1986).

WORKS CITED

Ahmad, Aijaz. ''Indian Literature: Notes Towards the Definition of a Category.'' In *Theory: Classes, Nations, Literatures.* London: Verso, 1992.

Anderson, Benedict. *Imagined Communities: Reflections on the Origin and Spread of Nationalism.* London: Verso, 1991.

Asopa, Purushottam. *Mahilaon Ki Drishti Men Purush.* Bikaner: Samask, 1987.

Barrier, N. Gerald. *Banned: Controversial Literature and Political Control in British India, 1907–1947.* Columbia: University of Missouri Press, 1974.

Bhandari, Manu. ''Sex Aur Vivah Kyaa Alag Alag Chizen Hain?'' Paricharcha, *Saptahika Hindustan,* September 24, 1971a.

———. *Ap Ka Banti.* Delhi: Akshar Prakashan, 1971b.

Chakravarti, Uma. ''Whatever Happened to the Vedic Dasi? Orientalism, Nationalism, and a Script for the Past.'' In *Recasting Women: Essays in Colonial History,* edited by Kumkum Sangari and Sudesh Vaid. New Delhi: Kali for Women, 1986, 27–87.

Chatterjee, Partha. ''Colonialism, Nationalism and Colonized Women: The Contest in India.'' *American Ethnologist* 16:4(1989):622–33.

Gaeffke, Peter. *Hindi Literature in the Twentieth Century.* Wiesbaden: Otto Harrassowitz, 1978.

Jayawardene, Kumari. ''Women, Social Reform and Nationalism in India.'' In *Feminism and Nationalism in the Third World.* New Delhi; Kali for Women, 1986.

Kaviraj, Sudipta. ''The Imaginary Institution of India.'' In *Subaltern Studies VII. Writings on South Asian History and Society,* edited by Partha Chatterji and Gyanendra Pandey. Delhi: Oxford University Press, 1993, 1–39.

Khullar, K. K. ''Influence of October Revolution on Urdu Literature.'' *Indian Literature* (March–April 1981): 124–39.

Kumar, Ajit. ''The Hindi Scene: An Indefinite Pattern.'' *Indian Literature* 30:122 (November–December 1987): 71–78.

Nagendra. *Indian Literature.* Delhi: Prabhat Prakashan, 1988.

Narayan, Virendra. *Contours and Landmarks of Hindi Literature. Hindi Drama and Stage.* Delhi: Bansal & Co., 1981.

Ojha, Dashrath. *Aaj Ka Hindi Nataka. Pragati Aur Prabhav.* Delhi: Rajpal and Sons, 1984.

Pandey, Indu Prakash. *Hindi Literature. Trends and Traits.* Calcutta, 1975.

Pradhan, Sudhi, ed. *Marxist Cultural Movement in India. Chronicles and Documents (1936–47).* Vol. 1. Calcutta: National Book Agency, 1979.

Rai, Alok. ''The Trauma of Independence: Some Aspects of Progressive Hindi Literature, 1945–47.'' *Journal of Arts and Ideas,* No. 6 (January–March 1984): 19–34.

Sarin, Dharam Paul. *Influence of Political Movements on Hindi Literature.* Chandigarh: Panjab University Publication Bureau, 1967.

Sarkar, Sumit. *Modern India.* Delhi: Macmillan, 1984.

"Sex Aur Vivah Kya Alag Alag Cheezen Hain?" Paricharcha, *Saptahik Hindustan,* September 24, 1971.

Tharu, Susie, and K. Lalita, eds. "Introduction." *Women Writing in India.* Vol. 2, *The 20th Century.* New York: Feminist Press, 1993.

Williams, Raymond. *Marxism and Literature.* 1977. New York: Oxford University Press, 1990.

SELECTED PRIMARY BIBLIOGRAPHY

Ashk, Upendra Nath. *Girti Diwaren.* Allahabad: Neelabh Prakashan (1st ed. 1947), 4th ed. 1967.

———. *Jai Parajai.* Allahabad: Neelabh Prakashan, 1970.

———. "Kaid." In *Kaid aur Udan.* 1950. Allahabad: Neelabh Prakashan, 1972a, 40–102.

———. "Udan." In *Kaid aur Udan.* 1950. Allahabad: Neelabh Prakashan, 1972b, 103–53.

———. *Chhata Beta.* Allahabad: Naya Idarah, 1981.

Bachchan, Harivansh Rai. *Madhushala* (The House of Wine). Translated by Marjorie Boulton and Ram Swaroop Vyas. Introduction by Jagdish Shivpuri. Delhi: Penguin Books, 1989.

Chaturvedi, Makhan Lal. *Krshnarjun Yuddha.* Allahabad: Vohra, 1967.

Chauhan, Subhadra Kumari. *Jhansi ki Rani.* 5th ed. Allahabad: Hans Prakshan, 1968.

Gupta, Maithilisharan. *Bharat Bharati.* 3d ed. Chirgaon, Jhansi: Sahitya Sadan, 1967.

———. *Saket.* Churgaon, Jhansi: Sahitya Sadan, 1970.

Mohan, Rakesh. *Andhere Band Kamare* (Lingering Shadow). Delhi: Hind Pocket Books, 1970.

Nirala, Suryakant Tripathi. *Anamika* 4th ed. Allahabad: Leader Press, 1963.

———. *Kukurmutta.* Allahabad: Lok Bharati Prakashan, 1969.

———. "Juhi Ki Kali." In *Nirala Rachnavali,* Vol. 1, edited by Nand Kishore Naval. Delhi: Rajkamal, 1983, 31–32.

Pandey, Mrinal. "Hum Safar." In *Women Writing in India,* Vol. 2. New York: Feminist Press, 1993, 547–55.

Pandey, Shyam Narayan. *Jauhar.* 5th ed. Varanasi: Saraswati Mandir, 1970.

Pannikar, Rajani. *Do Ladkiyaan.* Delhi: Pitamber Book Depot, 1973.

Pant, Sumitranandan. *Gunjan.* 12th ed. Allahabad: Leader Press, n.d.

———. *Vani.* 2d ed. Calcutta: Bharatiya Jnanpith Prakashan, 1963.

———. *Pallava.* 4th ed. Delhi: Rajkamal, 1967.

———. *Yuganta.* 5th ed. Allahabad: Lokbharati Prakashan, 1971.

———. *Gramya.* 8th ed. Allahabad: Lokbharati Prakashan, 1972.

Prasad, Jaishankar. *Kamayani.* Translated by Manohar Bandhopadhyay. Delhi: Ankur Publishing House, 1978.

———. *Ajatshatru.* In *Prasad Granthavali.* Vol. 2. Allahabad: Lokbharati Prakashan, 1985, 197–286.

———. *Chandragupta.* In *Prasad Granthavali.* Vol. 2. Allahabad: Lokbharati Prakashan, 1985, 585–739.

———. *Ek Ghoont.* In *Prasad Granthavali.* Vol. 2. Allahabad: Lokbharati Prakashan, 1985, 559–83.

———. *Skandagupta Vikramaditya.* In *Prasad Granthavali.* Vol. 2. Allahabad: Lokbharati Prakashan, 1985, 433–558.

———. *Ashoka.* In *Prasad Granthavali.* Vol. 4. Allahabad: Lokbharati Prakashan, 1986, 36–49.

Premchand. *Ruthi Rani.* Delhi: Lajpat Rai and Sons, n.d.

———. *Godan.* Delhi: Rajpal and Sons, 1959. Translated by Jai Ratan and P. Lal. Bombay: Jaico Publishing House, 1958.

———. *Karmbhumin.* 8th ed. Allahabad: Hans Prakashan, 1960.

———. *Sevasadan.* Allahabad: Saraswati Press, 1973.

———. *Premashram.* Allahabad: Hans Prakashan, 1984.

———. *Rangbhumin.* 13th ed. 1927. Delhi: Saraswati Press, 1986.

———. *Sangrama. Samajika Nataka.* Nai Dilli: Bharatiya Grantha Niketan, 1987.

———. *Nirmala.* Translated by David Ruben. Delhi: Vision Books, 1988.

Premi, Hari Krishna. *Rakshabandhan.* Allahabad: Hindi Bhawan, 1965.

———. *Swapan Bhang.* Delhi: Atma Ram and Sons, 1970.

Priyamvada, Usha. *Pachpan Khambe Lal Diwaren.* Delhi: Rajkamal, n.d.

Renu, Phanishwar. *Maila Aanchal* (The Soiled Border.) Translated with an introduction by Indira Junghare. Delhi: Chanakya, 1991.

Sahni, Bhisham. *Tamas.* Translated by Jai Ratan with an introduction by Govind Nihalani. New Delhi: Penguin Books, 1988.

———. *Basanti.* 4th ed. Delhi: Rajkamal Paperbacks, 1990.

Sharma, Pandey Bechan. "Ugra." In *Chand Haseeno Ke Khutut.* New Delhi: Vani Prakashan, 1987.

Shivani, Gaura Pant. *Mayapuri.* Calcutta: New Age, 1961.

———. *Chaudhah Phere.* 1st ed. Varanasi: Vishwavidyalay Prakashan, 1965.

———. *Kainja.* Delhi: Raj Pal and Sons, 1973.

———. *Rativilaap.* Delhi: Rajpal and Sons, 1974.

Shukla, Srilal. *Rag-Darbari.* New Delhi: Rajkamal Paperbacks, 1985.

Sunder, Shyam "Suman." *Halidighati.* Lucknow: Hindi Sahitya Bhawan, n.d.

———. *Chanakya Mahan.* Mathura: Bhagyoday Prakashan, 1962a.

———. *Kunal.* Mathura: Bhagyaoday Prakashan, 1962b.

———. "Padmini." In *Kunal.* Mathura: Bhagyaoday Prakashan, 1962c.

Tulsidas. *Kavitavali.* Allahabad: Sahitya Bhawan, 1964.

———. *Ramcharit Manas.* Jodhpur: Sadhna Press, 1971.

Upadhyay, Ayodhya Singh "Hariaudh." *Priya Pravas.* 15th ed. Benaras: Hindi Sahitya Kutir, 1973.

Verma, Mahadevi. *Yama.* 5th ed. Allahabad: Bharati Bhandar, 1971.

———. *Deepshikha.* 1st ed., Allahabad: Kitabistan, 1942. 8th ed., Allahabad: Bharati Bhandar, 1976.

Verma, Ram Kumar. *Chandragupta Maurya.* 2d ed. Allahabad: Kitab Mahal, 1964.

Yashpal. *Deshdrohi.* 5th ed. Lucknow: Viplava Karyalay, 1958a.

———. *Party Comrade.* 3rd ed. Lucknow: Viplava Karyalaya, 1958b.

———. *Dada Comrade.* 6th ed. Lucknow: Viplava Karyalay, 1959.

———. *Jutha Sach: Vatan Aur Desh.* Lucknow: Viplava Prakashan, 1960.

———. *Manushya Ke Rup.* 5th ed. Lucknow: Viplava Karyalaya, 1961.

REFERENCES

Aggarwal, Bhagwatsharan. *Hindi Upanyas Aur Rajnitik Andolan.* Ahemdabad: Pasharv Prakashan, 1989.

Aggarwal, Bindu. *Hindi Upanyas Men Nari Chitran.* Delhi: Radhakrishnan Prakashan, 1967.

Ahmad, Aijaz. "Indian Literature: Notes Towards the Definition of a Category." In *Theory: Classes, Nations, Literatures.* London: Verso, 1992.

Anderson, Benedict. *Imagined Communities: Reflections on the Origin and Spread of Nationalism.* London: Verso, 1991.

Asopa, Purushottam. *Mahilaon Ki Drishti Men Purush.* Bikaner: Samask, 1987.

Baranwal, V. K. "Poet Maithilisharan Gupta." *Indian Literature* 30:118 (March–April 1987):9–12.

Barrier, N. Gerald. *Banned. Controversial Literature and Political Control in British India, 1907–1947.* Columbia: University of Missouri Press, 1974.

Chakravarti, Uma. "Whatever Happened to the Vedic Dasi? Orientalism, Nationalism, and a Script for the Past." In *Recasting Women: Essays in Colonial History,* edited by Kumkum Sangari and Sudesh Vaid. New Delhi: Kali for Women, 1986, 27–87.

Chatterjee, Partha. "Colonialism, Nationalism and Colonized Women: The Contest in India." *American Ethnologist* 16:4 (1989): 622–33.

Choudhri, I. N. "Pradesa in Hindi Chhayavad and After." *Indian Literature* 27:2 (March–April 1984): 56–66.

Das Gupta, Jyotirindra. *Language Conflict and National Development: Group Politics and National Language Policy in India.* Berkeley: University of California Press, 1970.

Gaeffke, Peter. *Hindi Literature in the Twentieth Century.* Wiesbaden: Otto Harrassowitz, 1978.

Goel, N. P. *Hindi Speaking Population in India.* New Delhi: Radha, 1990.

Handa, Rajendra Lal. *History of Hindi Language and Literature.* Bombay: Bharatiya Vidya Bhawan, 1978.

Jayawardene, Kumari. "Women, Social Reform and Nationalism in India." In *Feminism and Nationalism in the Third World.* New Delhi: Kali for Women, 1986.

Keay, Frank Ernest. *A History of Hindi Literature. The Heritage of India Series.* Calcutta: YMCA Publishing House, 1960.

Khullar, K. K. "Influence of October Revolution on Urdu Literature." *Indian Literature* (March–April 1981): 124–39.

Kumar, Ajit. "The Hindi Scene: An Indefinite Pattern." *Indian Literature* 30:122 (November–December 1987): 71–78.

Kumar, Jainendra. *Sahitya Aur Sanskriti.* Delhi: Samask, 1971.

Lutze, Lothar. *Hindi Writing in Post-Colonial India: A Study in the Aesthetics of Literary Production.* New Delhi: Manohar, 1985.

———. "Politics and Literature in Post-Colonial India (As Seen by Some Contemporary Hindi Writers)." In *Literature. Social Consciousness and Polity,* edited by Iqbal Narain and Lothar Lutze. New Delhi: Manohar, 1987.

Malik, Yogendra K, ed. "Hindi: From Traditional to Modern Roles of Intelligentsia."

In *South Asia Intellectuals and Social Change.* New Delhi: Heritage, 1982, 119–59.

Maurya, Abhai. *Confluence: Historico-Comparative and Other Literary Studies.* New Delhi: Sterling, 1988.

Misra, Ramdarasa. *Modern Hindi Fiction.* Delhi: Bansal, 1983.

Misra, Ramprasad. *History of Hindi Literature.* Delhi: S. S., 1982.

Nagendra. *Indian Literature.* Delhi: Prabhat Prakashan, 1988.

Narang, Chand-Gopi. *Urdu Language and Literature: Critical Perspectives.* New Delhi: Sterling, 1991.

Narayan, Virendra. *Contours and Landmarks of Hindi Literature. Hindi Drama and Stage.* Delhi: Bansal & Co., 1981.

Ojha, Dashrath. *Aaj Ka Hindi Nataka. Pragati Aur Prabhav.* Delhi: Rajpal and Sons, 1984.

Pandey, Indu Prakash. *Hindi Literature. Trends and Traits.* Calcutta: Firma KL Mukhopadhyay, 1975.

———. *Romantic Feminism in Hindi Novels Written by Women.* Delhi: House of Letters, 1989.

Pandey, Ratnakar. *Hindi Sahitya, Samajik Chetnayen.* Delhi: Samask, 1976.

Phull, Sushil Kumar. "Agyeya: A Moving Force of Modern Hindi Literature." *Indian Literature* 24:5 (September–October 1981): 164–68.

Pradhan, Sudhi, ed. *Marxist Cultural Movement in India. Chronicles and Documents. (1936–47).* Vol. 1. Calcutta: National Book Agency, 1979.

Raghava, Sulochana-Rangeva. "Emerging Trends in the Novels and Contemporary Society." *Indian Literature* 24:2 (March–April 1981): 78–79.

Rai, Alok. "The Trauma of Independence: Some Aspects of Progressive Hindi Literature, 1945–47." *Journal of Arts and Ideas,* No. 6 (January–March 1984): 19–34.

Roadermal, Gordon C. *A Bibliography of English Source Materials for the Study of Modern Hindi Literature.* Berkeley: University of California Press, 1969.

Said, Edward. "Third World Intellectuals and Metropolitan Culture." *Raritan: A Quarterly Review* 9:3 (Winter 1990): 27–50.

Sangari, Kumkum, and Sudesh Vaid, eds. *Recasting Women: Essays in Colonial History.* New Delhi: Kali for Women, 1986.

Sarin, Dharam Paul. *Influence of Political Movements on Hindi Literature.* Chandigarh: Panjab University Publication Bureau, 1967.

Sarkar, Sumit. *Modern India.* Delhi: Macmillan, 1984.

Schomer, Karine. *Mahadevi Verma and the Chayyavad Age of Modern Indian Poetry.* Berkeley: University of California Press, 1983.

"Sex Aur Vivah Kya Alag Alag Cheezen Hain?" Paricharcha, *Saptahik Hindustan,* September 24, 1971.

Shah, Ramesh Chandra. "Not Much to Rave About." *Indian Literature* 27:6 (November–December 1984): 104, 38–48.

Sharma, R. S. "Hindi Writing Today." *Indian and Foreign Review* 17 (July 15–31 1980).

Sprinker, Michael. "Marxism and Nationalism: Ideology and Class Struggle in Premchand's Godan." *Social Text* 23 (Fall–Winter 1989): 59–82.

Srivastava, Parmanand. "The Age of Nehru and Post-Independence Hindi Literary Scene." *Indian Literature* 33:1 (January–February 1990): 71–79.

Sukrita. "Reaction, Acceptance and Rejection Constitute Modernism." *Indian Literature* 32:1 (January–February 1989): 189–97.

Sunder Rajan, Rajeshwari. *Real and Imagined Women. Gender, Culture and Postcolonialism.* New York: Routledge, 1993.

Sutherland, Sally J. "Sita and Draupadi: Aggressive Behavior and Female Role-Models in the Sanskrit Epics." *Journal of the American Oriental Society,* No. 1 (1989): 63–79.

Tharu, Susie, and K. Lalita, eds. "Introduction." In *Women Writing in India.* Vol. 2, *The 20th Century.* New York: Feminist Press, 1993.

Tiwari, Ramesh. *Hindi Upanyas Sahitya Ka Sanskrit Adhyayan.* Allahabad: Rachna Prakashan, 1972.

Verma, Ramesh. *Mahila Upanyason Ki Rachnaon Men Badalte Samajik Sandarbh.* Kanpur: Samask, 1987.

Williams, Raymond. *Marxism and Literature.* 1977. New York: Oxford University Press, 1990.

6

Twentieth-Century Kannada Literature

RAMACHANDRA DEVA

INTRODUCTION

After Sanskrit and Tamil, Kannada has the oldest written literature in India. Pampa, the first major poet to write in Kannada, was born in A.D. 902. In *Vikramārjuna Vijayaṃ,* an epic, he combined contemporary history with myth, thereby creating a new form. For Basava, Allama, Akka Mahādēvi, Dēvara Dāsimayya, and other Virasaivite poets of the eleventh and twelfth centuries, poetry was the outcome of a movement against caste, inequality, falsehood, and injustice. Akka Mahādēvi, who abandoned her husband in search of God, is one of the first major feminist writers in any language. Harihara (c. 1200), Janna (c. 1225), Kumaravyāsa (c. 1400), and Purandaradāsa (c. 1500) were some of the major writers who expanded the possibilities of the Kannada language. They were innovative in technique and deeply responsive to their age. For example, Purandaradāsa, a Bhakti poet, was a witness to the decadence of the Vijayanagara Empire, and his poems record various images relating to the decadence of a culture and lifestyle. For Janna, life is an endless attempt to escape from the consequences of one small act committed unknowingly. Kumaravyāsa gives pictures of the lives of ordinary Kannadigas of the fourteenth century in the course of retelling the story of the Mahabharata.

Among writers in the three centuries after, Muddaṇa (1869–1901) had the potentialities of a great writer, and Śiśunāḷa Śarīpha Sāheba (1819–89) did achieve greatness. But Muddaṇa died young. Moreover, his works gained critical recognition only in the twentieth century, after his death. Śiśunāḷa Śarīpha Sāheba, a Sufi poet, could predict industrialization, emergence of big cities, and the destruction of traditional village culture. But his poetry was edited and published only in the 1970s. Till then, he was known only to the people in and around Dharwad district, where he lived (see Mugali 1953).

There were a few interesting developments at the end of the nineteenth and the beginning of the twentieth centuries. Establishing a printing press and a publishing concern by Basel Mission, a German missionary organization, in the second half of the nineteenth century, played a major role in the development of modern Kannada literature. Rev. Ferdinand Kittel (1832–1903), a German missionary, compiled and published a Kannada–English dictionary, which is still one of the best dictionaries in Kannada. Bengali novels by Bankimchandra and Marathi novels by Harinarayana Apte were adapted into Kannada by B. Venkatacharya (1845–1914) and Galaganatha (1869–1942). M. Govinda Pai (1883–1963), a scholar, was the first poet to give up the traditional second-syllable rhyme pattern to make daring experiments in stanzaic forms. He also wrote poems about the conditions of ordinary people. Hattiyangadi Narayana Rao (1863–1921) and S. G. Narasimhachar (1862–1907) adapted a few English poems, using traditional metrical forms. But none of these writers could establish a new tradition of writing. Govinda Pai was interested more in research than in poetry. The scant body of poetry he wrote is burdened with pedantry. Hattiyangadi Narayana Rao and S. G. Narasimhachar could not create a new idiom to express a new sensibility. Only B. M. Srikantia (1884–1946) and Masti Venkatesha Iyengar (1891–1986) started a new movement in poetry and fiction, respectively.

The Kannada Writer: A Profile

Two factors played major roles in the development of twentieth-century Kannada literature. Almost all Kannada writers have been highly educated. B. M. Srikantia was professor of English in the University of Mysore; Masti had degrees in English literature and was a deputy commissioner and magistrate; V. K. Gokak (1909–92) had degrees in English literature from the University of Oxford; Sriranga (1904–84) and T. P. Kailasam (1884–1946) were educated in London; and Da.Ra. Bendre (1896–1981) and Kuvempu (1904–94) were professors of Kannada, and Kuvempu retired as vice chancellor of the University of Mysore. The tradition continues among modern writers: Gopalakrishna Adiga (1918–92) was a professor of English; U. R. Anantha Murthy (1932) and Shantinath Desai (b. 1929) have postgraduate degrees from the universities of Birmingham and Leeds; Girish Karnad (b. 1938) was a Rhodes scholar in Oxford; A. K. Ramanujan (1929–93) taught at the University of Chicago; and Ramachandra Sharma (1925) has a doctorate from the University of London. These writers chose to write in Kannada instead of in English, as an existential choice of relating themselves to their people. It reflected a realization that a writer cannot write in a language he or she does not hear ordinary people speak in marketplaces and streets.

Naturally, these writers could get good jobs and therefore did not have to either churn out popular writing or eulogize moneyed patrons to make a living. They also had a profound knowledge of English, European, and Sanskrit literatures. As a result, their expectations of Kannada literature were very high. They were fully aware that writings had to be as good as any good literature in English to win a place in world literature. They also borrowed liberally from Sanskrit and European literatures. As a result, twentieth-century Kannada literature is an age of translations, too. Almost all the major European writers have been translated or adapted into Kannada during the last 90 years. They have also been discussed with lively enthusiasm. For example, special issues of little magazines were brought out during the birth centenaries of D. H. Lawrence, T. S. Eliot, and Franz Kafka. In literary circles in Karnataka, it is quite common to hear Susan Sontag or Edward Said discussed with insight or Sappho, the Greek poetess, compared with Akka Mahādēvi and found wanting. Most of the important books published in the West are available in the leading bookshops in Bangalore within a reasonable time gap. In fact, Kannada writers and readers know more about Western literatures than about the literatures in other Indian languages. Recently, this tendency was criticized as another sign of neocolonialism. Encounter with another culture, however, has worked as a catalytic agent to our major writers and helped them overcome their limitations. This was also due to the writers' ability to turn to advantage what was otherwise a disturbing challenge to Indian culture and civilization.

Exploring what was significant in Kannada and Sanskrit literatures of the past also played a major role in shaping twentieth-century Kannada literature. B. M. Srikantia defined the role of a twentieth-century Kannada writer—whom he called a Renaissance man—in the following terms:

> He would absorb the significant knowledge of the past, and reap a new harvest. He is the child of the new world; educated in a new university; and, he is not afraid to expose himself to the knowledge of the West. At the same time, he does not reject his own language. He is the one who shares his knowledge with his people. He is the heir to his ancient culture and the one who values the modern culture. (Srikantia 1973, 276)

Quite a number of important Sanskrit works have been translated or discussed during this period. T. N. Srikanthayya, a scholar, wrote *Bharatīya Kāvya Mimāmse,* a remarkable book on Indian poetics. Almost all the important Kannada works of the past were rediscovered, edited, and published. These include works by major writers like Pampa, Śivakōṭyācārya, and Virasaivite saint-poets. Earlier, their works, considered religious documents, were languishing in palm-leaf manuscripts in caste organizations to which these writers belonged.

Because of this emphasis on Renaissance through English education and rediscovery of the past, preindependence Kannada literature is called Navōdaya Sāhitya, or Renaissance literature.

Another important factor is that Kannada-speaking areas were distributed among Madras, Bombay, Hyderabad, and Mysore provinces in the first half of this century. Only in 1956 were predominantly Kannada-speaking areas united to form the present Karnataka state. Till then, many writers felt that failure to bring the Kannada-speaking areas under one state administration led to the lack of identity of the Kannadigas. Therefore, in Karnataka, the freedom struggle meant not only freeing India from the British but also freeing Kannada-speaking areas from the rules of Tamilians, Telugas, and Marathas. Discovering and propagating the best of Kannada literature of the past and present were the ways of unifying the Kannada-speaking people and helping them find their cultural identity. B. M. Srikantia, Alur Venkata Rao (1880–1930), and their disciples spent a considerable number of years touring different parts of Kannada-speaking areas and lecturing about Kannada language and literature. Thus, Kannada language and culture became important instruments in making people aware of their identity and in helping them regain their self-respect during the freedom struggle.

Probably, writers of the preindependence period felt that only after unifying all the Kannada-speaking areas under one state could Kannada have the backing of political power, which was essential to make their voice heard in the increasing influence of English language and culture.

POETRY

Srikantia, Bendre, and Kuvempu

B. M. Srikantia published his new poems during 1919–24 in various magazines and brought them out in book form under the title *English Gītegalu* (English Songs) in 1926. This was a collection of 62 poems. Except for three original ones, they are Kannada renderings of poems from Palgrave's *Golden Treasury.* Some of these are by Wordsworth ("Written in March," "Rainbow," "The Pet Lamb"), P. B. Shelley ("To a Skylark"), Sir Walter Scott ("Gathering Song"), Tennyson ("Charge of the Light Brigade"), Cowper ("Loss of the Royal George"), Campbell ("Ye Mariners of England"), Byron ("Could Love for Ever"), Robert Burns, Thomas Hood, Charles Lamb, Lady Nairne, Christina Rosetti, Clough, and Sir Henry Wotton.

Obviously, these poems are not the best in English literature. Probably, Srikantia's choice reflects the taste of the English teachers in India and in England at that time. It is interesting that his book does not include any poem by John Keats. Wordsworth and Coleridge are not represented by poems that make greater creative use of the English language. All the poems he chose are simple in structure and theme.

Srikantia was remarkably successful in making use of these poems to write a new kind of poetry. Quite a number of new stanzaic patterns, modeled on English stanziac patterns, were introduced into Kannada. He also used modern Kannada idioms and the language of the ordinary people. Poets like S. G. Narasimhachar and Hattiyangadi Narayana Rao had earlier failed to write new poetry because they used old stanzaic forms and archaic language.

The subject matter also changed. Kings and gods gave place to birds, rainbows, riversides, and ordinary soldiers. "Māda-Mādi," an adaptation of Robert

Burns's "Duncan Gray," depicts Māda and Mādi in their hunting spree. The names Māda and Mādi suggest that they are man and woman of lower caste. Earlier in Kannada poetry, the pleasures of hunting were limited to the royal couple. For the first time, a poet was giving expression to the pleasures of untouchables. The shift was obvious, and the consequences were far-reaching.

Srikantia translated Aeschylus' *Persae* and adapted Sophocles' *Ajax* and Ranna's *Sāhasabhīmavijayaṃ*, a tenth-century Kannada poem. His intention was to introduce the concept of hubris and hamartia. These were the beginnings of poetic drama in Kannada, which was later developed by Kuvempu, Pu.Thi.Narasimhachar (b. 1905), and Ramachandra Sharma. Kuvempu wrote poetic drama by making use of myths from the *Ramayana* and the *Mahabharata.* Pu.Thi.Narasimhachar created a new opera by making use of Carnatic music. Ramachandra Sharma used free verse for poetic drama.

As a poet, Srikantia's was a liberating influence. Many poets now had a new way of expressing themselves. Among them, Da.Ra.Bendre, Kuvempu, Pu.Thi.Narasimhachar, V. K. Gokak, and Kadengodlu Shankara Bhatta (1904–68) are important. Of these writers, Da.Ra.Bendre is considered the greatest.

Da.Ra.Bendre was exposed to the latest developments in Marathi poetry also. Kannada folk songs, one of his dominant interests, also helped him find new idioms. This gave racy vigor to his poetry. But in his major poems, he uses folk idioms and rituals to suggest the difference between folk and urban cultures. For example, in a poem titled "Hubbaḷḷiyāṃva," Bendre captures the longings of a village girl for a man from Hubli, a city. Another poem, "Saṇṇa Sōmavāra," depicts the days of childhood when a folk festival relating to spring was celebrated. Now, both the childhood and the days of folk festival are gone. The only thing that remains is memory and the longing.

Bendre believed that life is a source of joy. In "Beḷagu," he celebrates morning as the time of peace and joy. It is the beginning not of daily routine, but of happiness. Another poem, "Kuṇiyōnu Bārā," suggests that the cosmos is in a state of dance, and the protagonist invites his mate to dance to the rhythm of day and night and to celebrate life.

This has led many critics to remark that evil was alien to Bendre's sensibility. It would be proper to say that Bendre was aware of evil in life but gave it a secondary place in the all-pervading joy of creation. In this respect, his "Jōgi" is a representative poem. The poem creates an atmosphere of darkness and terror. A bird, sitting on the branch of a tree surrounded by snakes, lures the protagonist. Its call is so fascinating and enchanting that it compels the protagonist to ignore the terror created by the atmosphere. He is unable to understand the meaning and the consequences of this call. Probably, it is a metaphysical call, or it is a call of the joys of life hidden behind terror and darkness. But the call is continuous, haunting, and one cannot help responding to it.

Bendre's other writings include plays, literary criticism, and essays. His plays are tragicomedies about the absurd behavior of people in power.

Another influential poet of this period is Kuvempu. His lyrics sing the glory of Karnataka, its culture, and civilization. These are simplistic in structure and theme, very popular, and sung in almost every public function. They also help Kannadigas to feel proud of their past during the freedom struggle. His plays include adaptations of *The Tempest* and *Hamlet.* Both are simplistic versions of Shakespeare's plays. Kuvempu's literary criticism explains Kannada works by using Sanskrit poetics. But his criticism is generally descriptive in nature. His *Śrī Rāmāyaṇa Darśanaṃ,* retelling the story of the Ramayana in verse, is considered the mark of genius by his disciples and an exercise in pomposity by a few critics. His "Niraṅkuśamatigaḷāgi" (Be Free in Thought), a lecture, taught the importance of freedom from superstition to a whole generation of Kannadigas.

Kuvempu and the Novel

Kuvempu's remarkable achievements are his two novels—*Kānūru Heggaditi* (1937) and *Malegaḷalli Madumagaḷu* (1967). *Kānūru Heggaditi* is about the conflict between Hūvayya and the superstitious, ignorant people of his village, to which he returns after education in a city. Hūvayya is a reformer, and he represents the best in Indian and Western traditions. The village Kuvempu depicts, like all the Indian villages of the twentieth century, is in transition. Hūvayya tries to bring about a change in the lives of the villagers by rooting out the negative influence of the West and the past so that they become aware of the best in both traditions. The villagers resist the change; at the same time, they are fascinated by it.

Like *Kānūru Heggaditi, Malegaḷalli Madumagaḷu* is a novel about Indian villages in transition. The cluster of villages Kuvempu depicts in the novel belongs to the nineteenth century, when bicycles and Christianity entered the villages as a consequence of colonization of India by the British. These and other things, like cash instead of bartering, have loosened the hold of traditional values on the lives of the people. As a result, relationships are strained, and families are destroyed. But Kuvempu's attitude to this change is ambiguous. He also notices that these changes have awakened a desire for freedom even in the minds of the low-caste people.

M. G. Krishnamurthi (1931–75), a modern critic who taught Kannada in the universities of Wisconsin and Chicago in the 1960s, says that the novel has too many insignificant details and is therefore a failure. Recently, it has been pointed out that Krishnamurthi considered different levels of consciousness and different kinds of sexual relationships as the major themes of the novel, and therefore many details seemed insignificant to him. But some of the major concerns of the novel are the conflicts between tradition and modernity, Christianity and Hinduism, love and marriage, and the individual and society. Seen in this light, many details that Krishnamurthi thought insignificant gain meaning. The novel is also a profound study of the emergence of capitalism from the hold of feudalism.

NOVEL

The first social novel, *Indirābāyi,* was written by Gulvadi Venkatarav in 1899, and this was followed by Bolara Baburav's *Vāgdēvi* (1905). Baburav depicts Vāgdēvi, a married woman, betraying her husband to have sexual relations with the head of a Hindu religious organization, thereby showing the decadence of both family and the traditional religious organization. *Māḍiddunṇō Mārāya* (1916), the first major novel in Kannada, depicts life in a village near Mysore, the then-capital of the Mysore province. In a traditional Indian society, the temple, the king, the guru, and the Brahmin family are seen as the ''protectors'' of communal values. But in this novel, the temple is occupied by thieves, the guru has become a bully, the Brahmin family has lost its moral right due to internal quarrels, and the king is unable to establish order in the society because of his inability to see corruption among his lieutenants.

The novel gives graphic pictures of decadence of all the traditional ways of living. The king, the Brahmin, and the daughter-in-law, who shape their lives according to traditional values, are unaware that these values are challenged by the changes taking place around them. Ultimately, order is established. But the ending is ambiguous: the question of who establishes order, the British or the king of Mysore, remains unanswered.

Masti Venkatesha Iyengar's works include translations of some of the major plays of Shakespeare, critical works on the *Mahabharata* and the *Ramayana,* poetry, and plays. He was also the chairman of Kannada Sahitya Parishat, a democratic literary body founded by B. M. Srikantia and others in 1915, and the editor of an influential little magazine. Masti was also responsible for publishing the first works of Bendre and Kuvempu.

Masti's writings show remarkable insight into the lives of the ordinary people in the villages. His short story, ''Mosarina Maṅgamma,'' depicts the quarrels in a joint family in a village. Maṅgamma, a curd-seller, is insulted by her daughter-in-law and decides to live separately. But the village is so traditional in its values and lifestyles that she can live peacefully only in a traditional way. Any attempt to upset this system leads to strained personal relationships. His ''Kalmāḍiya Kōṇa,'' another short story, is about the relationships among people, society, and animal. Muniya, who has raised a male buffalo, is forced to sacrifice it to Māri, a goddess. By portraying Muniya's efforts to save the buffalo and the people's insistence on sacrifice, Masti is drawing our attention to the stronghold of superstitions on the minds of the people. Any attempt to bring about a change in the traditional lifestyle leads to its continuation with greater vigor.

His ''Chaṭṭēkāra Tāyi'' depicts the lives of Anglo-Indians. ''Masumatti'' and ''Raṅganahaḷḷiya Rāma'' are about the reactions of Europeans to Indian culture and civilization. Both stories explore the ways the Indian past can become real in the present. In ''Masumatti,'' Indian antiques are used for commercial purposes by all European characters except Emily, who is able to link her personal life to the Indian past. ''Raṅganahaḷḷiya Rāma'' narrates the ways a persuasive

Britisher makes the lost past real to the superstitious, but courteous, Indian villagers. All three stories are important because they show different aspects of the encounters between the East and the West.

His novel *Chikavirarajendra* (1956) depicts the process of colonization of Koḍagu, a small province in Karnataka, by the British. It is colonized because of both the cunning of the British and the decadence of Chikavirarajendra, the king of Koḍagu. Masti powerfully portrays how the goodness and the traditional values of these tribal people turn out to be their weaknesses when it comes to the question of encountering an alien culture and military power. As Masti suggests in the novel, this could be the story of any kingdom in India when it encountered the British in the nineteenth century.

Kākana Kōṭe, one of the plays by Masti, is also about the encounter between two cultures. Kākana Kōṭe, a tribal settlement, is threatened by the king's men, who demand an illegal levy. The tribal settlement can be protected if the headman of the tribes requests the king of Mysore, whose life he once saved, for protection. But then the cultural and political autonomy of the tribe will be destroyed. The headman is ultimately forced to ask for protection. As a result, the tribal settlement comes under the king's jurisdiction and thus loses its identity.

The play is a profound study of the encounter between tribal and urban cultures. In minute details, Masti brings out the psychology of the tribal and urban people when they encounter each other. It is also a study of the colonization of a tribal settlement by the city dwellers. Masti suggests that the change was inevitable. The king's men, who were demanding illegal levy, would have continued to interfere in tribal culture and would have thus changed it. The headman, by requesting the king for protection, has only given official sanction to the change.

Shivarama Karanth (1902) is another major literary figure of the twentieth century. He gave up a college education to participate in the freedom struggle in the 1920s. He has experimented in the areas of education, painting, and music. His experiments in *yakshagana,* folk dance drama, has won him worldwide acclaim. During the last 20 years, he has been active in ecological movements. He has written plays, children's literature, essays, and criticism. But his major contribution is in fiction.

His *Chōmana Duḍi, Sarasammana Samādhi, Maraḷi Maṇṇige,* and *Maimanagaḷa Suḷiyalli,* some of his major novels, depict various aspects of life in rural Karnataka. Chōmana Duḍi narrates an untouchable's attempt to become a farmer. In traditional Indian society, an untouchable is forbidden to till the land. Chōma fails in his attempts. But in the course of narrating Chōma's attempts to become a farmer, Karanth depicts the changes that were taking place in the lives of the untouchables in the twentieth century. He also portrays the ruthlessness of the upper-caste people determined to retain caste distinctions. Karanth's greatness lies in showing how the psychology of both the upper- and lower-caste people is determined by caste considerations.

His *Maraḷi Maṇṇige* is a story of three generations. Rāma Aithāḷa is a traditional Brahmin fascinated by English education. He wants his son to be a lawyer and decides to give him an English education. But his son, Laccha, is alienated from his family, relatives, and the native land due to the negative influence of the West. Rāma, grandson of Rāma Aithāla, is able to use the Western influence creatively to renew himself and the tradition-bound society in which he lives.

Maimanagaḷa Suḷiyalli is also a story of three generations. The woman of the first generation is a *dēvadāsi,* God's bride. She is supposed to entertain chosen men in the name of God. She is famous for her integrity and music. But Karanth knows that she belongs to a dying culture. Her daughter and granddaughter show the negative and positive influences of the Western culture, respectively. The novel also examines the philosophical problem of the unification of body and mind. All the characters satisfy either their mind or their body, not both. As a result, they always remain unhappy.

Karanth's attitude toward change is ambiguous. He thinks that the change brought about by the influence of the West or the East becomes positive only when one links oneself to one's people and their culture. It becomes destructive when it takes one away from one's roots, a result that, for him, seems to be one of the radical problems of colonial India.

Shivarama Karanth's novels were criticized for lack of form in the 1960s. M. G. Krishnamurthi's revaluation sums up his contribution as a novelist:

> The novels of Mr. K. Shivarama Karanth may as well prove to be test cases for the literary critic in Kannada because of their apparent artlessness. One is tempted to say that they are impressive because of their subject matter, and thus beg the question.
>
> It seems to me that Mr. Kurtakoti, like many others, underestimates the art, the organization in Mr. Karanth's novels. It is true that the techniques that Mr. Karanth uses do not draw attention to themselves, and this is probably his strength rather than his weakness. In this he compares with the great 19th century English novelists. (Krishnamurthi 1994, 305)

PROGRESSIVE WRITERS

There was a movement of progressive writers in the 1930s and 1940s. This was led by A. N. Krishna Rao (1908–71). Other important writers of this movement are T. R. Subba Rao, K. S. Niranjana, Basavaraja Kattimani, and Chaduranga. Their favored form was the novel.

All these writers were influenced by Marxism. They propagated that literature should serve the needs of social revolution. Accordingly, they wrote about the downtrodden, the exploited class. One of their favorite topics was the problem of prostitution. All were prolific writers. A. N. Krishna Rao, leader of the movement, wrote more than 100 novels. They sold very well, chiefly because of the nonmoralistic writing when it came to questions like prostitution. However, the limitations of Euro-Marxism in theorizing caste become apparent.

These writers believed that Indian reality could be explained in terms of class struggle, and they ignored the dominant role played by caste in determining human relations. The result was oversimplification (see section on Lohia).

Gopalakrishna Adiga gave expression to the realities of postindependent India. Adiga's *Bhāvataraṅga* (1946), the first collection of poems, shows the influence of Bendre. He also had a stint with the progressive writer's movement in *Kaṭṭuvevu Nāvu* (1949), his second collection of poems. But his *Caṇḍe-Manddaḷe* (1956), the fourth collection of poems, marked a definite break from Navōdaya literature. He used free verse instead of metrical forms. He also wrote about urban experiences, which hitherto had been considered unfit for poetic treatment. The broken sentences, sudden jolts, and use of irony to show the pomposity of rhetoric, juxtaposing mythical characters and situations with present-day reality, are some of the characteristics of his new poetry. He rebelled against Kuvempu's poetry of statements and Bendre's musicality. He emphasized that any experience not realized in concrete terms cannot become literature. Like T. S. Eliot, from whom he learned his art, he also argued that poetry is the outcome of intellect as much as of emotion. He wrote in an epic mode instead of Bendre's and Kuvempu's lyrical mode. He argued that poetry should give expression to all levels of experience. The high ideals and dreams people had during the freedom struggle remained unfulfilled, and Adiga's poetry gave expression to this disillusionment. It was also a great attempt toward the unification of sensibility.

His "Bhūmigīta" (1958), "Vardhamāna" (1972), and "Idannu Bayasiralilla" (1975) show full realization of the promises shown in *Caṇḍe-Maddaḷe.* "Bhūmigita" and "Bhūta" are two of his representative poems. In "Bhūmigīta," earth is no longer the mother interested in the welfare of her offspring. Instead, she is a stepmother continuously engaged in copulation and childbirth. An individual is left alone to find his or her way in the darkness by the indifferent mother and unknown father. The contrast among the poems of Srikantia, Bendre, and Kuvempu, where earth is considered the mother, is striking. Adiga also suggested that the fate of humankind is that of blinded Oedipus. In "Bhūta," another great poem, Adiga considers the past something that haunts like a ghost. (In Kannada, *bhūta,* a Sanskrit loanword, means both past and ghost.) In the process of escaping from it, we have gone West. Now, we have to learn the ways of digging up the significant things of the past as one digs up the golden ore and molds them to suit our personal gods. The poem ends with the great image of the stagnant water of the well evaporating to form clouds. Then it rains, and the land becomes green. Thus, past, present, and future combine to make life whole. In almost all his major poems, Adiga returns to this theme of fragmentation of life in modern times and the ways of making it whole.

Adiga was actively involved in the problems of society and contested, unsuccessfully, both for the Parliament and Karnataka Assembly seats. He edited

Sākśi, an influential literary quarterly, for 10 years. His influence on the younger generation was as great as Srikantia's influence on the previous generation of writers. He recognized the changed sensibility after independence and created a new idiom to express it. His poetry also led to the reevaluation and reinterpretation of poetry written by Virasaivite saints of the eleventh and twelfth centuries.

NAVYA SĀHITYA

This new movement founded by Adiga is called Navya Sāhitya or New/Modern literature. This phrase was first coined by V. K. Gokak. He also wrote some new poems. But they are chiefly versifications of ideas borrowed from others and can hardly be called poetry. He thought modernity was a question of technique. For Adiga, it was a question of sensibility.

P. Lankesh (1935), U. R. Anantha Murthy, Shantinath Desai, Yashwanth Chittal (1928), Purnachandra Tejaswi (1938), Girish Karnad, A. K. Ramanujan, Ramachandra Sharma, and Gangadhara Chittala are other important writers of Navya literature.

Shantinath Desai's *Mukti* (1962) was the first major attempt to express modern sensibility in fiction. Gowrish, the hero of the novel, is a weak man with high ideals. This leads to a split in his personality that ultimately drives him to suicide. Desai's short story "Kśitija" portrays the predicament of a traditional Hindu woman traveling to England for higher studies. Yashwanth Chittal and P. Lankesh portray the changing Indian society in urban and rural settings. Lankesh's short stories, plays, and novels portray the psychology of weak people caught in the labyrinth created by the people in power. His poetry has influenced younger poets like K. V. Thirumalesh and B. R. Lakshmana Rao. He is also a filmmaker and journalist. Ramachandra Sharma's poetry has details taken from both the West and the East. Purnachandra Tejaswi's novels and short stories depict life in very backward villages. His two novels, *Nigūḍha Manuṣyaru* and *Karvāllo,* are about an encounter between educated people and uncivilized villagers. K. S. Narasimha Swamy's poetry upholds the importance of familial relationships in modern times.

U. R. Anantha Murthy's *Saṃskāra* (1966) received considerable praise. It portrays the decadence of traditional Brāhmanic society and the changes facing it. Conflict between traditional and modern societies is one of the major themes of Anantha Murthy's novels and short stories. His *Bhāratīpura* (1972), a novel, depicts the changes a Western-educated person tries to bring about in a feudal town built around a temple. *Avasthe* (1978), another novel, explores the same theme in the larger context of politics in a state capital. His "Akkayya," a short story, depicts the relationships between a traditional Hindu woman of a village and her brother, who now lives in America. The portrayal of the relationships between this earthy woman and her brother symbolizes the relationships between Indian and American cultures determined by precapitalist and capitalist forces, respectively. Anantha Murthy's writings are remarkable for their portrayals of different kinds of rebels against tradition. Through them, he portrays Indian society in transition.

A. K. Ramanujan's Kannada writings include three collections of poems, three short stories, and a novel. His poetry showed a new way out when younger poets were trying to escape from Adiga's influence. He concentrated on the little details of daily life. His writings are also about the problems of migration. His short story "Aṇṇayyana Mānavaśāstra" is about an Indian academic living in America. This academic is so far removed from India and the past that he can now know about his relatives, including his mother, only through a book on anthropology. Ramanujan's casual narrative method saves it from melodrama. Such method marks his poetry, too. He is capable of writing about some of the profoundest experiences in a casual, matter-of-fact manner. For example, his "Aṅgula Huḷuvina Parakāya Pravēśa" is about a small bird trying to save its identity among big birds and animals. Ramanujan's casual way of narration makes one feel that he is telling a children's story. But subsequent readings make one realize the political and metaphysical undertones of the poem.

Ram Manohar Lohia (1910–67), a Parliamentarian and one of the founders of the Samyuktha Socialist Party, was a strong influence on Navya writers. Adiga, Anantha Murthy, Lankesh, and Purnachandra Tejaswi were actively associated with the Socialist Party. Adiga and Tejaswi translated Lohia into Kannada, and Anantha Murthy and Lankesh have written extensively.

Lohia was one of the important writers to question Marx's concept of history. According to Lohia, the movement of history toward progress is cyclical and not linear. If it is linear, he asked, why was the West in a state of barbarism when India was at an advanced material stage, say, during the Buddha's time, or in the Guptha period? Why is India backward now, when the West is at the height of its glory? Lohia suggests that Marx's concept of linear development takes into account only the European countries after the Renaissance and ignores Asia. His other contributions include analysis of the caste system, some of the Hindu myths, and Mahatma Gandhi's contribution to Indian thought. He was a strong advocate of decentralization and opposed Jawaharlal Nehru's attempts toward centralized rule. He also opposed multinational companies investing in India.

Lohia helped Navya writers to understand Indian society with greater insight than Marxism did. Most of the social ideas of Navya writers, which sometimes have forced the government of Karnataka to change its policy, are influenced by Lohia. His influence on Adiga is seen in poems like "Nehru Nivruttarāguvudilla" and "Śrī Rāmanavamiya Divasa."

NAVYA THEATER

Girish Karnad, a major playwright of the Navya movement, uses historical and mythological stories for plots. In *Yayāti* (1961), his first play, he uses the

Mahabharata story to dramatize the conflict between old and younger generations. *Tughlaq* (1964), a historical play, mirrors Indian society of the Nehru era. His *Taledaṇḍa* (1990), based on the life of Basava, eleventh-century Virasaivite saint-poet, also dramatizes the conflict between castes. His *Hayavadana* (1971) and *Nāgamaṇḍala* (1989) use the techniques of folk theater. Another important playwright who uses the techniques of folk theater is Chandrashekhara Kambara. But his plays lack the remarkable insight into mind and society that mark Girish Karnad's plays.

The tradition of using history to write plays on contemporary issues began with Samsa (1898–1939). He dramatized the history of the Mysore royal family. He learned this technique by reading the plays of Shakespeare.

Samsa's plays also show the decadence of the royal family. In all his plays, he looks for an ideal king who can be a link between God and people. He thought that only an ideal king could oppose British rule. But he was so aware of reality that, in all his plays, one comes across an empty throne symbolizing the absence of an ideal king. He was also the first Kannada writer to portray characters disturbed by the loss of faith in people, God, and religion.

The first major playwright to write in Kannada was T. P. Kailasam. The locales of his plays are the middle-class homes of cities in Karnataka. He also used Kannada—mixed with English words—in his plays. Thus, he was the first writer to make creative use of the kind of Kannada spoken by members of the educated middle class. His *Baṇḍvāḷvillada Baḍāyi* is about the shallowness of a Westernized lawyer. He pretends to be knowledgeable by speaking English-mixed-Kannada with other semiliterate members of his family. But this leads only to laughter and contempt. °*Toḷḷugaṭṭi,* another play, brings out the contrast between two sons of a government employee. One is bent upon an English education and climbing socially. The other, indifferent to academic learning, is attached to other members of the family. When a fire breaks out in the house, the English-educated son is interested only in saving himself, whereas the not-so-educated son saves all the others without bothering about his own safety.

The play is a simplistic one. Kailasam, like his contemporaries, was responding to the rootlessness caused by Westernization. Writers like Shivarama Karanth and Adiga wrote about the same theme with greater insight.

Kailasam's *Bahiṣkāra* represents the inhumanity of a middle-class Brahmin family. Raṅgaṇṇa, a government employee and a Brahmin by birth, is banished from his caste for not marrying off his daughter before she attained puberty. Ultimately, his daughter is left with no option but suicide. Even though the play is melodramatic, it focused attention on the inhumanity of some of the practices of Hindu religious organizations.

Shriranga (1904–84) has written more than 45 full-length plays. Most of his plays are marked by hasty or indifferent writing. He refused to revise them. Therefore, out of his vast body of writing, only 4 or 5 plays can be considered significant. Till 1960, he wrote with reformistic zeal. His *Harijanvāra* (1934) can be considered a representative play of this period. It is about the conflict between upper-caste Hindus and untouchables. Ultimately, the humanity of an upper-caste widow gains victory over rigid caste rules. His *Sandhyākāla* (1939) and *Śōkacakra* (1957) are also about the importance of reformation. But *Kēḷu Janamējaya* (1960) shows a remarkable change in his method of writing. It combines techniques from absurd and realistic drama. Everyone in the play seems to be groping for something in darkness. The play is considered a powerful dramatization of the helplessness of people before their rulers.

A Hindi translation of this play was staged in New Delhi in 1963 by the National School of Drama. This began a new era in Indian theater. Till then, it was believed that one had to look toward the West for modern plays. It was the first time that theater personalities became aware of an Indian play with modern technique and theme. This opened new doors in writing and staging of plays in India.

Shiranga was actively involved in developing theater activities in Karnataka. He has also written novels. His other publications include a Kannada translation of Bharata's *Nāṭyaśāstra.*

Theater is very active in Karnataka. Prasanna (1951), a young leftist director, began a movement of staging street plays in the 1970s. B. V. Karanth (1929), another important director, uses techniques of folk theater in his plays. He also stages plays in Hindi and is one of the very influential directors. Karanth's influence can be seen behind Girish Karnad's and Chandrashekhara Kambar's experiments with folk theater. The plays Karanth directed include Shakespeare's *Macbeth* and Sophocles' *King Oedipus.*

K. V. Subbanna is another important theater personality. He was influenced by Lohia's ideas about cultural decentralization and started a theater movement in Heggōḍu, a small village with a population of around 500, in the late 1960s. Now he runs a theater center training around 20 students every year and a repertory. It tours Karnataka every year with three plays, which include classics from a European language and Sanskrit. As a result, theater activities have developed even in small towns and villages in Karnataka. Before Subbanna started this movement, cultural activities of this type were limited to big cities like Bangalore and Mysore.

WOMEN'S WRITING

Triveni (1928–63) wrote novels chiefly about the emotional repressions of middle-class women. This suppression becomes necessary for them to gain respectability in a middle-class family. But it leads to various psychological problems, as in the case of Kaveri in *Śarapanjara* or Malathi in *Haṇṇele Ciguridāga.* Kaveri suppresses her love for one person and marries another approved of by her parents. This ultimately leads her to madness. Malathi, a widow, decides to suppress her feelings for a man in order to please her orthodox father. Triveni suggests that no change in the condition of women is possible until men recognize their problems. She is the first Kannada writer to recognize the specificity of women's psychologies, but one gets the feeling that she sentimentalizes women's problems.

Rajalakshmi N. Rao's *Saṅgama* (1954), a collection of short stories, is also about the emotional repression of women. Her "Illa Illa" is a story about a middle-class woman who dons the mask of a faithful wife in order to gain respectability. She now represents the class against which her former lover, a communist, rebelled. She cannot admit that she is still secretly in love with him, because she cannot break off from the society in which she now lives. The only thing left for her is to suppress her feelings and lead a double life. Parvathi, the heroine of "Phedra," another story, also resorts to daydreaming in order to give expression to her feelings. She also cannot break off from the society and live a separate life.

N. V. Bhagyalakshmi's *Beraḷa Sandiya Baduku* (1976), a collection of poems, is about the suppressed feelings of unmarried women. This was the first collection of poems that unhesitatingly told Kannada readers that unmarried Indian women suppress their feelings in order to make themselves acceptable to men in the marriage market. This collection of poems started a new trend in Kannada poetry because Bhagyalakshmi had created a new idiom to express women's feelings.

Both Rajalakshmi and Bhagyalakshmi have stopped writing after their first books. Bhagyalakshmi is married and lives in Delhi. Rajalakshmi married in the 1950s, was disillusioned, and has been living as a *sanyasin* (ascetic) somewhere near the Himalayas during the last 30 years. In an interview she gave to a magazine when she visited Karnataka in 1983 to attend the birth centenary of B. M. Srikantia, her grandfather, she admitted that renouncing writing in Kannada was the most difficult thing to do. A writer who gave expression to suppressed sexual feelings of women, in the interview she admitted that she hated sex after marriage, which ultimately led her to *sanyasa.*

Other important women writers are Vaidehi (1947), Tejaswini Niranjana, S. Usha, Pratibha Nandakumar, and Vina Shanteshwar (1945). The women characters that Vaidehi and Vina portray are freer emotionally than earlier. Vina's "Hīgondu Kathe" portrays an unwed mother who feels that giving birth to a child is the right of every woman. Vina's protagonist and Vaidehi's Akku, another woman character in a recently published story with the same title, are female characters who feel that their lives do not have to be determined by the requirements of men. The connection of this freedom to economic factors is also significant. All the characters in Triveni's and Rajalakshmi's fiction are housewives, dependent on their husbands for income. Vina's and Vaidehi's characters who show freedom of choice have independent sources of income. The difference also indicates the change that has taken place in the status of middle-class women in the last 20 years. Many of the contradictions in women's position still need to be addressed.

There were women writers among Virasaivite saints of the tenth and eleventh centuries. Apart from Akka Mahādēvi, a writer like Sūḷe Saṅkavva expressed what she felt while working as a prostitute to make a living. The women writers of recent times have been able to link themselves to this tradition of Virasaivite poetry. Women's writings have also led to a new interest in the writings of some of the ignored aspects of Virasaivite poetry.

PROTEST LITERATURE

There was a movement against Navya literature in the 1970s and 1980s. This movement, led by Baraguru Ramachandrappa (1945), a Marxist, is called Bandaya (Protest) literary movement. Other writers of this group include Kalegowda Nagavara, Ramjan Darga, R. K. Manipal, and Hosuru Munishamappa. Protest writers criticized Navya literature as too complex to be understood by ordinary people. They propagated the view that writers should write in such a way that their writings are easily understood by the people. Bandaya writers also linked themselves to progressive writers of the 1930s and 1940s. Unfortunately, none of the Bandaya writers have shown interest in the nuances of words. Quite often, their poetry is versification of Marx's or Lohia's ideas. Bandaya writers, however, raised some fundamental questions about inequality and exploitation. They also attracted the attention of the exploited people, who were looking for opportunities to express themselves. While their contribution is significant in the field of social activity, its poetic aesthetic content remains questionable.

Devanura Mahadeva (1949) and Siddhalingaiah (1954) come from the untouchable caste. Devanura Mahadeva's publications are limited to a collection of short stories and two short novels. He writes about his experiences as an untouchable. His writings usher in a totally new world in Kannada literature. He has also used language in a new manner. There is almost no young writer who is not influenced by his use of language. Siddhalingaiah's poetry has also given expression to the conditions of untouchables in present-day society. While occasionally propagandist, he has introduced a new world of experience to Kannada literature.

KANNADA LITERATURE AND TRADITIONAL POETICS

There was also a new movement in the 1980s to go back to the traditional narrative methods of the *Ramayana,* the *Mahabharata,* and other writings of ancient India. All the Kannada writings of the twentieth century consist of logically verifiable details. But writings of ancient India are not based on logically verifiable details. In these writings, a squirrel's speaking or a mountain's flying is as real as a human being's taking a bath or eating. The argument is that the tradition of Indian writing can be continued to create a totally new way of writing, hitherto unknown in twentieth-century Kannada literature. But this theory has not yet given birth to any important creative writing.

Writers belonging to different movements write in Kannada at one and the same time. Till recently, Kuvempu or Adiga, two writers belonging to two completely opposite literary movements, were writing along with Devanura Mahadeva, another totally different kind of writer. As a result, one comes across varieties of literary expression in Kannada. This has also resulted in the interpretation of reality through different viewpoints. One can say that all these viewpoints help in understanding Indian reality. They have also added significant chapters to the history of Kannada literature, which began with Pampa in the tenth century A.D.

WORKS CITED

Krishnamurthi, M. G. (Kṛti Saṃskṛti). *M. G. Keyavara Samagra Lēkhanagaḷu.* Mysore: Rujuvathu Prakashana, 1994.

Srikantia, B. M. (Śrīsāhitya). *Ācārya Bi.Eṃ.Śrīkaṇṭhayyanavara Samagra Kṛti Saṃpuṭa.* Mysore: Kannada Adhyayana Saṃsthe, University of Mysore, 1973.

SELECTED PRIMARY BIBLIOGRAPHY

Adiga, Gopalakrishna. *Samagra Kāvya, 1937–1976* (Collected Poems, 1937–1976). Bangalore: Sakshi Prakashana, 1974.

———. *Samagra Gadya* (Collected Prose). Bangalore: Sakshi Prakashana, 1977.

Ananthamurthy, U. R. *Saṃskāra* (Rite for a Dead Man). Dharwad: Manohara Granthamala, 1966.

———. *Prajñe mattu Praisara* (Consciousness and Environment). Sagara: Akshara Prakashana, 1971a.

———. *Pūrvapara* (East-West). Sagara: Akshara Prakashana, 1971b.

———. *Bhāratipura.* Sagara: Akshara Prakashana, 1973.

———. *Avasthe* (Condition). Sagara: Akshara Prakashana, 1978.

———. *Eraḍu Daśakada Kathegaḷu* (Short Stories of Two Decades). Sagara: Akshara Prakashana, 1981.

Bendre, D. R. *Gari* (Feather). Dharwad: Manohara Granthaprakashana Samithi, 1932.

———. *Muktakaṇṭha* (Open Throat). Dharwad: Samaja Pustakalaya, 1956.

———. *Nāku Tanti* (Four Strings). Dharwad: Samaja Pustakalaya, 1964.

———. *Nāṭaka Saṃpuṭa* (Collected Plays). Dharwad: Samaja Pustakalaya, 1982.

———. *Nādalīle* (Melody Play). 1938. Dharwad: Ambikatanayadatta Vedike, 1987.

Bhagyalakshmi, N. V. *Beraḷa Sandiya Baduku* (Life between Fingers). Bangalore: Christ College, 1976.

Chittala, Gangadhara. *Samagra Kāvya, 1948–1983* (Collected Poems, 1948–1983). Mysore: Githa Book House, 1985.

Deva, Ramachandra. *Mūgēla Mattu Itara Kathegaḷu* (Mugela and Other Stories). Bangalore: Chairade Prakashana, 1985.

———. *Indraprastha Mattu Itara Kavanagaḷu* (Indraprastha and Other Poems). Bangalore: Granthavali, 1994a.

———. *Muccu Mattu Itara Lekhanagaḷu* (Hiding and Other Essays). Bangalore: Granthavali, 1994b.

———. *Shakespeare: Eraḍu Saṃskṛtigaḷalli* (Shakespeare in Two Cultures). Bangalore: Granthavali, 1994c.

Indira, M. K. *Phaṇiyamma.* Dharwad: Manohara Granthamala, 1974.

Kailasam, T. P. *Kailāsam Kṛtigaḷu* (Collected Works). Mysore: Kannada Adhyayana Samsthe, 1987.

Karantha, Shivarama. *Chōmana Duḍi* (Choma's Drum). Mangalore: Shenoy Brothers, 1933.

———. *Maraḷi Maṇṇige* (Back to Soil). Dharwad: Manohara Granthamala, 1942.

———. *Beṭṭada Jīva* (Man of the Hills). Dharwad: Manohara Granthamala, 1943.

———. *Sarasammana Samādhi* (Sarasamma's Tomb). Dharwad: Manohara Granthamala, 1948.

———. *Aḷida Mēle* (After the Death). Putturu: Harsha Prakatamalaya, 1960.

Karnad, Girish. *Tughlaq.* Dharwad: Manohara Granthamala, 1964.

———. *Añju Mallige* (Frightened Jasmine). Dharwad: Manohara Granthamala, 1971.

———. *Tale-Daṇḍa* (Death by Beheading). Dharwad: Manohara Granthamala, 1990.

———. *Agni mattu Maḷe* (Fire and Rain). Dharwad: Manohara Granthamala, 1994.

Krishnamurthi, M. G. *Kṛti-Saṃskṛti* (Work-Culture). Mysore: Rujuvathu Prakashana, 1994.

Kurtakoti, Kirthinath. *Da.Ra.Bēndre.* Bangalore: Prasaranga, Bangalore University, 1982.

———. *Yugadharma Hāgu Sāhityadarśana* (Sensibility of the Age and Literature). Bangalore: Visva Kannada Sammelana, 1983.

Kuvempu. *Kānūru Heggaḍiti.* Mysore: Udayaravi Prakashana, 1936.

———. *Malegaḷalli Madumagaḷu* (Bride in the Forests). Mysore: Udayaravi Prakashana, 1967.

Lankesh, P. *Biruku* (A Crack). Sagara: Akshara Prakashana, 1967.

———. *Talemāru* (Generations). Sagara: Akshara Prakashana, 1973.

———. *Mussañjeya Kathāprasanga* (Twilight Story). Mysore: Nelamane Prakashana, 1978.

Mahadeva, Devanura. *Oḍalāḷa* (Depth of the Heart). Mysore: Nelamane Prakashana, 1981a.

———. *Kusumabāle.* Bangalore: Sangathi Sahakari Prakashana, 1981b.

Mangesh Rao, Panje. *Pañjeyavara Kṛtigaḷu* (Collected Works). Bombay: Orient Longman, 1973.

Mokashi Punekar, Shankara. *Gangavva-Gangamāyi* (Gangavva and the River Ganges). 1956. Mysore: Suruchi Prakashana, 1975.

Mugali, R. S. *Kannaḍa Sāhitya Caritre* (History of Kannada Literature). Mysore: Usha Sahitya Male, 1953.

Narasimhachar, D. L. *Pīṭhikegaḷu Lēkhanagaḷu* (Prefaces, Essays). Mysore: D.V.K. Murthy, 1971.

Narasimhachar, Pu. Thi. *Samagra Kavanagaḷu, 1933–1988* (Collected Poems, 1933–1988). Bangalore: Lipi Prakashana, 1988.

Narasimha Swamy, K. S. *Malligeya Māle, 1942–1994* (Collected Poems, 1942–1994). Bangalore: Lipi Prakashana, 1994.

Rajaratnam, G. P. *Ratnana Padagaḷu* (Rathna's Poems). 1934. Bangalore: Sakya Sahitya Mantapa, 1984.

Ramanujan, A. K. *Hokkuḷalli Hūvilla* (No Flower in the Navel). Dharwad: Manohara Granthamala, 1967.

———. *Mattu Itara Kavanagaḷu* (And Other Poems). Dharwad: Manohara Granthamala, 1977.

———. *Mattobbana Ātmacaritre* (Another's Autobiography). Dharwad: Manohara Granthamala, 1978.

———. *Kuṇṭōbille* (Hopscotch). Dharwad: Manohara Granthamala, 1990.

Rao, Rajalakshmi N. *Saṅgama* (Coming Together). 1954. Bangalore: Kannada Mattu Samskriti Ilakhe, 1985.

Ravabahaddura. *Grāmāyaṇa* (Saga of a Village). Dharwad: Manohara Granthamala, 1956.

Samsa. *Saṃsa Nāṭakagaḷu* (Collected Plays). Bangalore: Nataka Akademi, 1988.

Shivarudrappa, G. S. *Samagra Kāvya* (Collected Poems). Bangalore: Sneha Prakashana, 1987.

Srikantia, B. M. *Śrī Sāhitya* (Complete Works). Mysore: Kannada Adhyayana Samsthe, 1983.

Sriranga. *Āyda Nāṭakagaḷu* (Selected Plays). Hampi: Kannada Visvavidyanilaya, 1994.

Tejasvi, Purnachandra. *Karvālo.* Mysore: Nelamane Prakashana, 1978.

———. *Ella Kategaḷu* (Collected Short Stories). Bangalore: Patrike Prakashana, 1983.

Venkatesha Iyengar, Masti. *Cikavīra Rājendra.* Bangalore: Jivana Karyalaya, 1956.

———. *Samagra Kategaḷu* (Collected Short Stories). 2 vols. Bangalore: Purogami, 1987–88.

REFERENCES AND TRANSLATIONS

(*Anikethana,* quarterly journal published by Karnataka Sahitya Akademi, Bangalore, is meant exclusively for English translations of Kannada works. *Accessions List,* a serial, published by U.S. Library of Congress Office, New Delhi, contains annotated bibliography of works published in Kannada and other Indian languages.)

Adiga, Gopalakrishna. *Song of the Earth and Other Poems.* Translated by A. K. Ramanujan et al. Calcutta: Writers Workshop, 1967.

Amur G. S., ed. *Selected Kannada Short Stories.* New Delhi: Sahitya Akademi, 1993.

Anantha Murthy, U. R. *Samskara: A Rite for a Dead Man.* Translated by A. K. Ramanujan. Delhi: Oxford University Press, 1976.

Bendre, D. R. *Four Strings.* Translated by K. Raghavendra Rao, V. D. Bendre, and K. S. Sharma. Dharwad: Kavyadhara Prakashana, 1975.

Bhyrappa, S. L. *Parva: A Tale of War, Peace, Death, God, and Man.* Translated by K. Raghavendra Rao. New Delhi: Sahitya Akademi, 1994.

Chittal, Yashwanth. *The Boy Who Talked to Trees.* Translated by Padma Ramachandra Sharma and Ramachandra Sharma. New Delhi: Penguin Books, 1994.

Desai, P. B. *Basavesvara and His Times.* Dharwad: Kannada Research Institute, Karnataka University, 1968.

Gubbannanavara, Sivananda. *Shishunala Sharif Saheb.* New Delhi: Sahitya Akademi, 1989.

Hayagrivachar, Kadambi, ed. and trans. *Masumatti and Other Stories.* Bangalore: Pranesh Prakashana, 1992.

Jussawalla, Adil. *New Writing in India.* Harmondsworth: Penguin Books, 1974.

Kambara, Chandrashekhara. *Jokumaraswami.* Translated by Rajiv Taranath. Calcutta: Seagull, 1989.

———. *Samba Shiva: A Farce.* Translated by Padma Ramachandra Sharma. Calcutta: Seagull Books, 1991.

———. *Siri Sampige: A Play in Sixteen Acts.* Translated by Rowena Hill with K. P. Vasudevan and N. S. Ramaswamy. Calcutta: Seagull Books, 1992.

Kanavi, Channaveera, and K. Raghavendra Rao, eds. *Adhunika Kannada Kavya* (Modern Kannada poetry). Dharwad: Karnataka University, 1976.

Karnad, Girish. *Tughlaq: A Play in Thirteen Scenes.* Translated by author. Delhi: Oxford University Press, 1972.

———. *Hayavadana.* Translated by author. Calcutta: Oxford University Press, 1975.

———. *Tale-Danda.* Translated by author. Delhi: Ravi Dayal, 1993.

Krishnamurthi, M. G., ed. *Modern Kannada Fiction: A Critical Anthology.* Madison: Department of Indian Studies, University of Wisconsin, 1967.

Kulkarni, N. K. *Shiranga.* New Delhi: Sahitya Akademi, 1989.

Kurtakoti, Kirthinath. *Kumaravyasa.* New Delhi: Sahitya Akademi, 1989.

Nadiga, Sumatheendra, ed. and trans. *20th Century Kannada Poetry: Selections.* Bangalore: Vishwa Kannada Sammelana, 1983.

Narasimha Swamy, K. S. *The Buddha Smile: A Collection of Poems.* Translated by P. Sreenivasa Rao and Sumatheendra Nadig. Mysore: Kavyalaya Prakashana, 1993.

Niranjana, K. S. *Coming Forth by Day.* Translated by Tejaswini Niranjana. Hyderabad: Disha Books, 1994.

Nisar Ahmed, K. S., ed. *10 Years of Kannada Poetry.* Bangalore: Karnataka Sahitya Akademi, 1983.

Ramanujan, A. K. *Speaking of Śiva.* Harmondsworth: Penguin Books, 1973.

Sharma, Ramachandra, ed. *BMS: The Man and His Mission.* Bangalore: BMS Memorial Foundation, 1983.

———. *From Cauvery to Godavari.* New Delhi: Penguin Books, 1992.

Sheshagiri Rao, L. S., and T. P. Kailasam. New Delhi: Sahitya Akademi, 1990.

Shivarudrappa, G. S., and L. S. Seshagiri Rao. *Sixty Years of Kannada Poetry.* Bangalore: Kannada Sahitya Parishat, 1977.

Sitharamiah, V., and Panje Mangesh Rao. New Delhi: Sahitya Akademi, 1985.

Tejaswi, K. P. *Purnachandra. Carvalho; Men of Mystery.* Translated by Padma Ramachandra Sharma. New Delhi: Penguin Books, 1990.

Varadaraja Rao, G. *Purandaradasa.* New Delhi: Sahitya Akademi, 1983.

Venkatesha Iyengar, Masti. *Chikavirarajendra.* Translated by Ramachandra Sharma. New Delhi: Penguin Books, 1992.

7

Twentieth-Century Malayalam Literature

THOMAS PALAKEEL

Often misguessed as the language of Malaysia, the Malayalam language of the southwestern state of Kerala (population 28 million) is a member of the Indo-Dravidian family. Kerala itself is a new political entity, as it was formed only in 1956, incorporating the Malayalam-speaking kingdoms of Travancore, Cochin, and Malabar, which was ruled directly by the British.

Throughout its three hegemonic phases—Dravidian, Aryan, and European—Malayalam language assimilated new genres and styles and gradually built up a rich regional literary tradition, an integral part of Indian literature. However, it is only in the twentieth century, with the advent of social modernity, that Malayalam literature has completely transformed itself into a truly independent literature that can encompass all classes and communities. Now, as Malayalam literature responds to the cultural trends of other prominent literatures in the East and the West, it is also able to contribute exemplary works of poetry and fiction, in return, to the larger world beyond the geographical boundaries of Kerala.

ORIGINS OF THE LANGUAGE

Endless debates about the origins of the Malayalam language mark one aspect of the Kerala public culture. Of the many theories of origin, the most popular ones claim that Malayalam was born out of the confluence of Tamil and Sanskrit, that it originated out of Sanskrit alone, and that both Malayalam and Tamil came out of a single protolanguage. In his *Comparative Grammar of Dravidian Languages* (1875), Bishop Robert Caldwell argued that Malayalam evolved out of Tamil and that the process took place during the Sangam period (first five centuries of the Common Era), when Kerala belonged to the larger political unit called Tamilakam, the apogee of Dravidian civilization.

After the waning of the Sangam Age, the Kerala region went through a prolonged "Dark Ages" (500–900 C.E.), when Sanksritization (influx of Aryan culture from the north) of the dialect was completed, which helped the emergence of Manipravalam (a mixture of the local dialect and Sanskrit), which, in turn, helped the formation of Malayalam as an independent language. Several poetic works written in this mixed style have survived; highly erotic and decadent in nature, they express the worldview of the feudal class that monopolized the Kerala culture until the first decade of the twentieth century.

The first Malayalam prose work, *Bhashakautiliyam,* a commentary on Kautilya's *Arthasastra,* was written in the twelfth century. The first Malayalam grammar/literary treatise, *Lilathilakam,* compiled in the fourteenth century, is considered the culmination of Manipravalam style. While the region continued to produce important works of literature in Sanskrit and Tamil, by the fifteenth century, Malayalam had its first classic in Cherusseri's *Krishna Gatha,* and the sixteenth century produced the father of modern Malayalam literature, Thunchath Ezhuthachan, whose renderings of *Adhyatma Ramayana* and *Mahabharata* employed the narrative device of *kilipattu* (Bird Song). Until the end of the eighteenth century, Malayalam literature was closely allied with *kathakali,* a complex operative dance form dependent on the literary quality of the text. The nexus between *kathakali* and poetry helped the growth of literary Malayalam.

Almost exclusively poetic in form, the post-Sangam literature was in the mythical mode, whereas the Sangam literature (35,000 lines of poetry by 400 authors have survived) tended to be realistic portrayals of common people and their domestic and personal experience, which we have come to expect from modern literature. Only in the eighteenth century, with the work of poets like Kunchan Nambiar, do we begin to see the return of such literary expressions of domesticity. A gradual departure from the mythical to a satirical mode of writing becomes evident at this juncture. By the nineteenth century, prose forms enter the tradition with the translations of the Bible, and many works of European prose literature become widely available.

Literary journals like *Vidya Vinodini* and *Bhasha Poshini* opened up the language for the larger public, while several prolific writers and scholars belonging to the different royal families patronized literature. Translations from Sanskrit and English helped the foundation of a broader base for Malayalam writers. This period is marked by the trailblazing work by the Text Book Committee of Travancore (1866), which functioned like a literary movement. Valiya Koyil Thampuran and A. R. Rajaraja Varma were champions of this movement, even though these two royals were basically part of the orthodox literary establishment.

European education and Christian missions had already created a suitable environment for journalism, historical writing, and prose in general. The first travelogue (a native Catholic's journey to Rome) was written as early as 1786. The first history of Kerala was published in 1860, and its author, Pachu Moothathu, also wrote the first autobiography in Malayalam in 1871. The first Malayalam novel was published in 1887, and two years later, one of the greatest contributions to the genre was made by Chandu Menon, whose novel *Indulekha* ushered in the modern period of Malayalam literature.

Triumph of Social Modernity

After a long history of caste and class oppression, Kerala underwent radical cultural transformation in the 100 years that followed the Travancore Education Bill of 1817, promulgated by Queen Rani Gauri Parvathi Bhai. In 1853–54, both Travancore and Cochin kingdoms passed laws emancipating bonded laborers. In the year 1888, during the reign of Maharaja Srimulam Thirunal, for the first time ever in the history of an Indian kingdom, a legislative assembly began to participate in the administration. In the following decades, several schools, colleges, public libraries, and newspapers were founded all over the region, so that the rise of a modern sensibility was inevitable. Unlike in the previous centuries, prose literature came to play an increasingly important role in the new era.

However, poetry was enjoying its modern golden age. While the novelists were quickly building up their new genre by following the romantic tradition of the novel set by Chandu Menon (1847–99) and C. V. Raman Pillai (1858–1922), the poets, mainly Kumaran Asan (1871–1924) and Vallathol Narayana Menon (1878–1958), produced great masterpieces and set a clearly modernist taste; their work made a radical break from the mythical and pseudophilosophical themes that had obsessed the poets of the ruling class up to that point. This aesthetic shift was a natural extension of the social modernity made possible by reform. Enlightened institutions of education, the law, the press, and several reform movements imbued the people with a robust optimism about the future of Indian society.

MODERN POETRY

The rise of modern Malayalam poetry began with the Venmani group, whose members started experimenting with new forms and subject matter, abandoning the classicist mode, using simple diction and Dravidian meters, and, above all, daring to deal with taboo subjects. Ironically, this was also an era when the literary orthodoxy was the most active in public culture. For instance, the elite Brahmin poets (with last names like Iyer, Sharma, Moothathu, Varma, Namboothiri) and Nair poets (Menon, Pillai, Marar, Panicker) frequently indulged in poetic combats such as *akshara sloka* (recitation) and *samasya* (poetic riddles). A poetry feud of the period led to the historic "rhyme dispute," during which the entire literary community of Kerala came to be divided on the question whether rhyme enhanced or hindered poetry. The lively literary environment also enabled many new poets to start resisting the orthodoxy to produce unrhymed verse, consequently freeing the language from the traditional epic poetry limited to endless veneration of the Hindu pantheon. While the orthodox poets had been evasive about the harsh social and economic realities prevalent in the land for over a millennium, the new generation became emboldened to seek out new forms and contents for their poetry.

With the publication of K. C. Kesava Pillai's *Asanna Marana Chinta Satakam* (Verses on Imminent Death) and V. C. Balakrishna Panicker's *Oru Vilapam* (A Lament, 1909), Malayalam poets began to proclaim their Romantic aspirations; the revolutionary spirit of the English Romantics appealed to these poets. Panicker's short life was similar to that of Shelley and Keats. Having established himself as a major poet at the age of 19, he died at the age of 27. The poets of his generation defied mythological subjects and emphasized individual experience, altruism, and cultural renaissance, and motifs of sacrificial suffering became central poetic images. This late arrival of the romantic spirit quickly transformed Malayalam literature as a whole, and out of the ferment emerged the three poets known as the Great Trio.

The Great Trio of Poets

Three of the most prolific poets of the first half of the twentieth century, Kumaran Asan (1871–1924), Ullur Parameswara Iyer (1877–1949), and Vallathol Narayana Menon (1878–1958), are collectively known as the Great Trio (*mahakavitrayam*). Their work provided Malayalam with a truly native tradition in literature, nationalist in spirit, romantic in style, and modernist in outlook. They freed the language from having to depend on the Sanskrit heritage. Together, their works have acquired the status of a "school of poetry," even though each of them was unique and seldom stable in his aesthetic.

While the classicism of Cherusseri, Poonthanam, and Ezhuthachan derived mainly out of their allegiance to the Brahmin culture of *Ramayana* and *Mahabharata,* the Great Trio produced a massive corpus of literature drawing on the Buddhist, Christian, and Islamic, as well as Hindu, traditions, in essence creating a new mythos for the modern age. Much of the poetry and criticism of twentieth-century Malayalam literature is actually an extended response to the work of the Great Trio.

Kumaran Asan: The Poet of New Humanity

The oldest and the most important member of the Great Trio, Kumaran Asan belonged to the Ezhava caste, which was discriminated against by the upper castes that monopolized the literary and cultural life of Kerala throughout history. Influenced by the teachings of the philosopher/cultural activist Narayana Guru, Asan sought to create a new cultural ethos for Malayalam based on English liberal education. Narayana Guru and Kumaran Asan also preached an increased adherence to the Sanskrit tradition—this helped them in effectively outwitting the proponents of caste supremacy on every level of culture and politics.

While most of the prominent poets wrote classical epics, in the year 1909, Kumaran Asan published his long elegiacal poem *Vina Poovu* (A Fallen Bloom) and provided a metaphor for the tragedy of human life in modern times. In many ways, much of the poetry of previous generations ignored human life, if it dealt with it at all; those poets seemed to treat everything as an illusion and spoke in the idioms of the Hindu philosophers. Asan's poetry moved away from the glib philosophizations and started to capture the contemporary experience of bondage. He wrote repeatedly about the dehumanizing experience of the individual who has been deprived of fundamental human dignity. His new style of writing, characterized by unprecedented clarity and romantic rage, cried out for the freedom of the individual. Asan's individualism was not a solipsistic, bourgeois ideal. A low-caste individual's assertion of identity and self-respect was an act of subversion in the eyes of the higher castes, which, for centuries, refused to acknowledge such individuality; Asan's poetry rendered, for the first time, the essence of the "low-caste" individual who possessed a higher moral authority than the oppressors; in effect, Asan's poetry was affirming the essence of the collectivity that was historically denied.

In conjunction with Asan's nationalist aspirations, his poetry proclaimed freedom from the bondage of ignorance and political and personal silence. He developed a consistent vision that included not only those who were oppressed but also the oppressors. In his *Duravastha* (The Tragic Plight, 1923), Kumaran Asan exhorted: "Remove the bonds of your effete tradition/ Or it will ruin you within your own selves." Asan's poetry brought into the culture a plea for a revolution of the heart. In *Duravastha,* his most celebrated *khanda kavya* (miniature epic), a Brahmin woman named Savithri marries Chathan, an untouchable, after he gave her refuge when her family home was destroyed in the Muslim revolt of Malabar (1921). This event takes place during a period when many Brahmins still considered lower-caste people untouchables. Having accepted the kindness of an untouchable, Savithri reciprocates his generosity by marrying him. This was incendiary material in the eyes of the orthodoxy; even distinguished critics like A. R. Rajaraja Varma, a part of the orthodoxy, sought to chastise Asan's great work for faulty Sanskrit style. But Kumaran Asan's poetry found the right audience among the nationalists and the new, educated class.

That Asan was able to create human drama without succumbing to didacticism provided unusual strength to his poetry, as well as his romantic vision. Having transformed Malayalam poetry from the stale, quotidian, cultural environment, Kumaran Asan was able to make his readers experience the horror of bondage, both external and internal; this was also the philosophical strategy of his mentor, Narayana Guru, whose followers became a ready audience for Asan's poetry.

In his miniature epics such as *Nalini* (1911), *Leela* (1914), *Chandalabhikshshuki* (The Beggar Woman, 1923), *Chintavishtayaya Sita* (Brooding Sita), and *Karuna* (Mercy, 1924), Kumaran Asan sang eloquently about such issues as class oppression, feudalism, imperialism, materialism, untouchability, and unapproachability. Though there existed no gender-based cultural critique at this point, most of his works displayed a great understanding of womanhood. His heroines continue to inhabit the language as if they are actual human beings.

His work drew much strength from Buddhism, which challenged the iniquities of caste while offering realistic materials suitable to make his romantic art. For instance, *Chandala Bhikshuki* is about a low-caste woman named Matangi who offers, with misgiving, a drink of water to a young Buddhist monk, Ananda. His acceptance of it is in defiance of caste. She undergoes a conversion experience and becomes a Buddhist nun. In *Karuna,* the courtesan Vasavadatha is attracted to the Buddhist monk Upagupta, who keeps telling her that it is not yet time for him to enter her life. After the courtesan had murdered a merchant, she was apprehended, and her limbs were dismembered in punishment. For Asan, Vasavadatta is a metaphor of alienation and decay, and the poet seems to suggest that her longing for the monk's presence is that of society's desire for renewal. Upagupta the monk does arrive to comfort her with the compassion of the Buddha.

It is important to note that Kumaran Asan chose a Buddha figure (as a religion, Buddhism is almost nonexistent in India because of its resistance to caste) instead of a Hindu ascetic (even contemplative life is prohibited for the lower castes) as a harbinger of renewal. The Buddhist conversion rhetoric here is not meant for proselytization at all; the poet uses it as a trope of dissent to all levels of cultural decay characteristic of Indian society of the times. Of the many poets of this romantic tradition who invoked Buddha and Jesus metaphors, the most significant figure was Vallathol, a member of the Great Trio.

Vallathol Narayana Menon: Lyrical Nationalist

Among the Great Trio of modern poets, Asan's style was roughly hewn, and Ullur's was pedantic, but Vallathol wrote as the consummate lyrical stylist. A poet who transformed himself from a traditional classicist poet to a popular romantic bard, Vallathol also outlived the other two members of the Great Trio to become one of the most recognized poets of modern India. Published in 1910, Vallathol's first major work, *Badhira Vilapam* (A Deaf Man's Lament), dealt with the poet's loss of hearing, his sense of deprivation of the world. The poet seeks to transcend the world of frightening silence in the same manner Milton resigned himself to the reality of darkness in his sonnet "On His Blindness."

In 1916, when the first of his eight-volume masterpiece *Sahitya Manjari* (A Bouquet of Literature), appeared, he was immediately recognized as a significant voice, particularly because of his use of both the Sanskrit and Dravidian meters in his lyrical poetry. Even though his earlier poetry, like much of the poetry of Asan and Ullur, was rooted primarily in the Sanskrit tradition and in religious themes, Vallathol changed with the times, becoming an integral part of the nationalist consciousness sweeping the land. He sought to reach beyond the regionalism of the Kerala tradition and the orthodoxy of the Sanskrit heritage. The Gandhian movement transformed him into a modernist with broader nationalist aspirations. His poem "Ente Gurunathan," an eloquent testimonial of a Gandhi disciple's trust in the teacher, pointed at the direction his future poetry was to take. His celebrated works such as *Bandanasthanaya Anirudhan, Viras-*

rinkala, Divaswapnam, Achanum Makalum, and *Magdalana Mariam* reiterated the poet's commitment to larger human issues. His *khanda kavya* on the life of Mary Magdalene continues to be popular; it also paved the way for a new tradition of Christian symbolism in Malayalam. A literary tradition attempting to disengage itself from the mythical mode found an easier transition in the figures of the gospel and in Gandhi and Buddha. Though Vallathol did not have the benefit of the English education that Asan and Ullur had, he did try to imbibe Western traditions. Through his efforts to bring Kathakali out of feudal control, Vallathol also modernized a theater that had dominated the literary scene for at least four centuries.

Ullur S. Parameswara Iyer: Versatile Genius

The prolific Ullur was a scholar-poet. Though his position as one of the Great Trio is often questioned, his overall contribution to Malayalam literature is beyond dispute. He is known for his versatility, his lyricism, his innovative techniques of prosody, and, of course, his productivity. Ullur's five-volume history of Malayalam literature is still the best work on pretwentieth-century Sanskrit, Tamil, and Malayalam. Though many critics eventually sought to attack Ullur as a member of the ruling class, the service he rendered to modern Malayalam literature through such works as *Umakeralam, Karnabhushanam, Bhakthi Deepika,* and *Kiranavali* ensured his position among the Great Trio. His most memorable poem is "Prema Sangitam," a beautiful, ornate, pre-Raphaelite lyric about the aesthetics of love.

The author of the epic on Kerala, *Umakeralam,* Ullur was the most classical of the three poets. In midcareer, he abandoned some of his classicism and joined the new movement that was being popularized by Asan and Vallathol. As a first step, he adopted Dravidian meter and enriched it with his impeccable technical skill. His main contribution was to develop a sense of pride about the Indian identity of Malayalam-speakers. Being a top official in the government and an orthodox Brahmin himself, he predicated his works upon a lofty ideal of eternal India of Sanskrit culture and provided the best fusion of the Aryan and Dravidian cultures.

Ullur's zeal for asserting cultural identity is most evident in *Chithrasala* (The Art Gallery), in which the poet takes the American writer Katharine Mayo for a demonstrative tour of the eternal India. In her *Mother India,* Mayo had attacked Indian culture and made many cynical, myopic remarks on Indian womanhood. Ullur took it upon himself to set the record straight by revealing to the American writer the gallery of portraits of men and women of the Indian tradition, describing their greatness, showing how the women often emerged nobler and wiser than their consorts.

Late Romantics

The late Romantics were not merely a group of decadent aesthetes creating art for art's sake. Extreme idealists and dreamers, they seemed to be obsessed with death and the awareness of transience and the futility of life. Among the Romantic poets who followed in the footsteps of the Great Trio, the most important figure was Nalappat Narayana Menon (1887–1955), but his poetic output was limited. From his early poetic phase, he shifted his attention to criticism, psychology, and ancient Indian philosophy; he also published translations from European writers. His best-known poetic work, *Kannunirthulli* (Teardrop), is an elegy on the death of his wife. Written in a terse, lucid style, the poem is still popular, as it possesses a rare nostalgic intensity and a new brand of metaphysical reflection. For a literature that thrived on glib invocations of fatalism, Nalappat's poetry opened up a new way of looking at the experience of suffering.

Two younger late Romantics of equal importance, (both passed away early in their careers) stand out: Changanpuzha (1914–48) and Idappally (1909–36). *Ramanan,* the former poet's Lycidas-like pastoral elegy about the latter's suicide at a young age, continues to spawn generations of younger poets who freely exhibit their lofty idealism and passion of romantic suffering. Though Changanpuzha himself died at the age 34, he left behind a large volume of intensely lyrical, romantic poetry. His *Vazhakkula* (A Stalk of Plantains) is a small poetic gem; the poet narrates the story of an untouchable tenant who nurtures a plantain tree in his backyard; their father's work enables the children to dream about the sweet nourishment the tree will render them when the fruit is ripe. But the landlord arrives. He claims the fruit. The fruit of the poor man's labors is snatched away because the rich landlord claimed ownership on the patch of land.

In many ways, Changanpuzha's *Vazhakkula* exemplifies the core of Malayalam Romanticism, which begins with the Great Trio and ends with the late Romantics: a profound sorrow about the human failure in acknowledging the dignity of all, even though all individuals must face the certainty of death. This poetic knowledge emboldens the poet to speak for a revolution of the heart.

Romantic poetry weakens with the death of Changanpuzha, whom Vallathol outlived by a whole decade. Romanticism in Malayalam contributed greatly toward developing a native poetic voice that is modern, yet nonimitative of Western models. Post Romantic and late Romantic poets, in general, sought to strike a truly Malayalam note in their poetry.

Among the dozens of poets who did hit the right note, the most important poet was G. Sankara Kurup. Writing in the 1950s and 1960s, Sankara Kurup attained a voice independent of the one set by Europeans. Kurup's collection of symbolist lyrics, *Odakkuzhal* (Bamboo Flute, 1950), won him the first Jnanpith Award in 1965, India's top literary honor. Inspired more by Tagore than Wordsworth, G. Sankara Kurup played an important role as a poet of the Indian independence movement, and he championed a poetry of humanism. He is probably the only poet of Kerala who is known as a bard of science, for he refers to the advancements in science in his meditations of the human potential, but his approach has to be understood as the beginnings of a postmodern sensibility, and the best example of this trend is his famous narrative poem "The Master Carpenter," in which he uses a Kerala legend about a master carpenter's envy for his son, who excels in the father's art; to give a postmodern spin to the Western notion of the oedipal story, the poet offers a vivid character study of a father who kills his rival in art, his own son.

The legacy of the poets of the first half of the twentieth century (Kunjikuttan Thampuran, Rajaraja Varma, Kattakkayam, K. V. Simon, the two Naduvath poets Oravankara and Kundoor, and K. C. Kesava Pillai) was enhanced by the poets of the post Romantic period. Among the large number of the post-Romantics who have made significant contributions are Kunjiraman Nair, Balamani Amma, Edassery, Mary Benigna, Mary John Koothattukulam, Palai Narayanan Nair, Vennikulam, Vayalar Rama Varma, Mathan Tharakan, Vailoppilli, Krishna Warrier, M. P. Appan, Nalankal Krishna Pillai, G. Kumara Pillai, O.N.V. Kurup, P. Bhaskaran, Kadavadu Kuttikrishnan, K. V. Ramakrishnan, Sugatha Kumari, and Yusuf Ali Kecheri. It is interesting that Romantics like O.N.V. Kurup (*Ujjaini,* 1995), Sugatha Kumain (*Ambalamani,* 1993), and Naiv Madhusudhan (*Naranath Bhranthan,* 1995) are best sellers.

The Postmodernism of the Poets

As varied as their backgrounds and contributions, some of the late Romantics continued the Vallathol school of poetry; conservative and lyrical in style, yet progressive in terms of the poetic vision, their poems were region-specific and not easily translatable. Some of their work seemed like products of a region that was too distant from the larger world.

The postmodern poets and fiction writers connected Malayalam literature to a world larger than Kerala. With the death of Sankara Kurup, Idassery, and Kunjiraman Nair, what was known initially as a strange generation of "ultra-moderns" came to take Malayalam poetry in a new direction. They were actually the postmoderns, and their landmark publication was Ayyappa Paniker's long poem *Kuruskhetra* (1961). With its resonances of *The Waste Land* and *The Bhagavat Gita,* this long poem gathers together varied strands of Indian postmodernity: the East and the West merge in this era of late capitalism; poverty lingers; revolution has failed; no certainties are left to offer us solace, not even the old tribal rhythms, because our modernity has disturbed them. Paniker's poem voices the sense of guilt and terror an individual has to bear with living in an unbounded historical moment in which, according to Panikker, the World Bank becomes the custodian of truth.

In spite of the wide difference in terms of their age, the postmodernist poets like Kadammanitta Ramakrishnan, M. Govindan, A. Ayyappan, O. V. Usha, Satchidanandan, Balachandran Chullikkad, Chemmanam Chacko, Cherian K. Cherian, N. N. Kakkad, Madhavan Ayyppath, K. G. Sankara Pillai, Vinayachandran, and three dozen other poets have created a sustained poetic culture in Kerala. Some of these poets have also brought poetry into the public culture through street performances and campus readings, ushering in a new golden age of poetry.

PROSE LITERATURE COMES OF AGE

Though the first prose treatise in Malayalam, *Bhasha Kautiliyam,* was written as early as the twelfth century, the development of prose literature was slow. Poetic works and *kathakali* texts had a ready audience throughout the history of Malayalam literature, but prose readership began to grow only with the growth of printing in the 1850s—the first press was established in 1563, at a seminary in Cochin. One of the famous early prose pieces, Velu Thampy's *Kundera Proclamation* of 1809, a battle cry against British colonialism, had moments of literary brilliance:

> Taking over the realms of others by treachery is their [British] hereditary tradition; when thus a land passes into their hands, their soldiery will take over palace and fort under their guard . . . then land and hut, field and orchard will become their monopoly.

During the last quarter of the nineteenth century, we also begin to see a gradual decline of such traditional and unique Malayalam genres as *attakatha* (poetic narratives), *ithihasas* (sagas), *kavyas,* and *khanda kavyas* (miniature epics), which were all replaced by the mainstream European genres.

The Rise of the Novel

Though the semifeudal modes of production continued to play an important role in literature and life, a sufficiently independent class of readers and writers emerged, making possible what Ian Watt called (in the context of eighteenth-century England) the "rise of the novel." Appu Nedungadi's *Kundalatha* (1887) is arguably the first original novel in Malayalam. Chandu Menon's *Indulekha* (1889) is certainly the first significant Malayalam novel; the English lineage of the novel is acknowledged in the novel's subtitle: *Englishnovel Matiriyilulla Oru Katha* (A Story in the Manner of the English Novel).

Chandu Menon has written that he initially meant to translate Benjamin Disraeli's *Henrietta Temple* (1836) into Malayalam, but, having struggled with the subtleties of an alien culture, he abandoned the project in favor of writing one on his own, depicting a familiar story. The fact that Chandu Menon's novel deals with the decline of the feudal, Brahminical culture in Kerala also explains the rise of the novel form in Malayalam, as one of the necessary preconditions for the flourishing of the novel genre is the emergence of an educated middle class. Menon's *Indulekha* dramatizes the resistance of a progressive woman named Indulekha, who is being pressured into marrying the lecherous Brahmin Suri Namboothiri, who represents the decadence of feudalism, its caste oppression, and polygamy.

While feudalism controlled art and kept it limited to self-serving ritual forms, caste prohibited literary production because education itself was prohibited to the lower castes. The Brahmins maintained a belief that the untouchables would pollute the sacred language, Sanskrit. The gradual breakdown of such structures of oppression opened up the culture and made the rise of the novel possible. Chandu Menon's heroine persists in her educated convictions (she is an ardent student of the English language!) and eventually weds her lover, Madhavan, in the process defeating the Brahmin, who is shown as an effete oppressor. Many of the social evils depicted in the novel have disappeared in independent India, partly due to the forceful representation of these problems in new literary forms.

Chandu Menon's *Indulekha* set the tone for the future development of the novel in Malayalam: novelists began debating social issues through their elaborate probing into the individual experience of characters who were drawn from contemporary society. This literary trend had shown its first signs in Malayalam as early as during the eighteenth century (as it did in Europe), when the poet Kunchan Nambiar satirized society and its mannerisms and inequities. Had he written a prose narrative, we would have called it a novel. In the absence of the print culture, prose fiction had to wait until the final years of the nineteenth century.

The second major novelist to emerge in Malayalam was C. V. Raman Pillai. His Walter Scott-inspired historical novels about the Travancore dynasty, *Marthanda Varma* (1891) and *Dharmaraja* (1911), made up for the late blooming of the genre. He produced grand historical romances about the different Travancore kings and war heroes who stood up to British imperialism. In his *Dharmaraja,* actually a sequel to *Marthanda Varma,* C. V. Raman Pillai follows up on the historical events that ended with the execution of a clan of King Marthanda Varma's enemies.

In *Dharmaraja,* two descendants from the clan return disguised as wandering monks seeking revenge at the new king and to usurp the throne of Travancore, but the conspiracy is spoiled by the king's lieutenant, Kesava Pillai, who himself becomes the central character in the third part of the saga, *Rama Raja Bahadur.* The historical context is that of the incursions of Tippu Sultan into the kingdom and the persistence of clannish dissent, which leads Travancore into accepting the hegemony of the British. Very much in the manner of Walter Scott's romances, C. V. Raman Pillai also creates an elaborate human drama grounded in history, yet peopled with realistic characters.

Following in the tradition of C. V. Raman Pillai, several historical novels were written. Pallath Raman's *Amrita Pulinam* and Appan Thampuran's *Bhoota Rayar* and *Bhaskara Menon* (the first detective novel) deserve mention. Sardar K. M. Panikkar's *Paranki Padayali* (The Portuguese Soldier), *Dhumakethuvinte Udayam* (The Comet of Ill Omen), and *Kerala Simham* (The Lion of Kerala) are also important works of subaltern sensibility in presenting Kerala's encounter with the colonizers and imperialists. The range and popularity of the early novels helped the construction of a culture of the novel in Malayalam literature.

When C. V. Raman Pillai wrote his first satirical novel, *Premamrutam,* it also spawned yet another series of imitations. At this time, translations of novels from world literature began to appear, further enhancing the credibility of the genre. Besides Nalappat's classic translation of *Les Miserables,* several other translations of John Bunyan, Maxim Gorky, Thomas Hardy, Dostoevsky, Tolstoy, and Tagore elevated the position of the novel in Malayalam.

The Malayalam Novel in Transition

If Malayalam poetry was revitalized the moment it parted company with the rigidities dominating South Indian literatures after the waning of the Sangam period, the resurgence of the novel as the preeminent literary genre followed the social and political transformations taking place in response to Western humanist tradition, increasingly drawing its energy from Marxist philosophy and aesthetics.

By the 1930s, a whole new school of writers, known as progressive writers, had come into existence. Three young critics, Kesari Balakrishna Pillai, M. P. Paul, and Joseph Muntasseri, became the theoreticians of the school. Having understood the great potential of realistic fiction, these critics theorized about the new role of Malayalam literature in an era of Western literary and cultural paradigms. Through the many critical introductions he contributed to the works of emerging writers, Kesari Balakrishna Pillai affirmed the literary and aesthetic qualities of prose fiction. The mature theoretical synthesis of M. P. Paul's critical monographs, *Novel Sahityam, Cherukatha Prasthanam,* and *Gadyagathi,* defined the novel, the short story, and the essay, respectively, and aligned Malayalam literature with international aesthetic trends. Joseph Muntasseri spoke primarily as a Marxist aesthete grounded in Indian literary traditions.

The Progressive Writers

The progressives acquired the label as they started out as socialist realists. Most of them gradually transcended all such "isms" even as Kerala was becoming the first state in the world to bring a communist government to power through electoral process. A famous critical work of the period, Guptan Nair's *Isamgalkkapuram,* advocated artistic freedom reaching beyond "isms" and agendas. Kuttikrishna Marar's critical essays, eventually collected in 1965 as a single volume, *Kala Jeevitham Thanne,* took issue with both the socialist realists and the proponents of "art for art's sake," pointing at the unique path an Indian writer could take independent of Western prescriptions. Again, the aesthetic independence of leftist writers might have been a result of the peculiar mutations of Marxism itself as it won followers from upper and lower castes alike, forming, in essence, a regionalist coalition against the mainstream Congress Party and its bourgeois, sectarian allies.

In 1956, the three Malayalam-speaking regions, Malabar, Cochin, and Travancore, were united to form the state of Kerala, bringing an environment of political and linguistic unity to the culture of Malayalam-speaking people. Many members of the new communist cabinet were literary personalities; the critic and novelist Joseph Muntasseri himself became the minister of education, and the chief minister was E.M.S. Namboothiripad, a prolific writer on history and Marxist aesthetics. Vaikom Muhammad Basheer, Thakazhi Sivasankara Pillai, Kesava Dev, S. K. Pottekkat, Lalithambika Antharjanam, Uroob, and Cherukad are prominent novelists of this generation. The novelist who typifies the generation of the progressive is Thakazhi Sivasankara Pillai; he started out as a leftist and matured into a true Kerala original.

Thakazhi Sivasankara Pillai

The best-known Malayalam writer, both nationally and internationally, is Thakazhi Sivasankara Pillai (1914). His fame is partly on account of the United Nations Educational, Scientific, and Cultural Organization (UNESCO) translation of his masterpiece *Chemmeen* (The Prawn) and its classic film adaptation made in 1966 by Ramu Kariat. Though Thakazhi is often considered a hardcore socialist-realist, his major works, like *Chemmeen* and *Enippadikal,* are intense portrayals of love and tragedy, and they have little to do with socialism or realism. Very few Indian novelists have explored the nature of passion the way Thakazhi has in *Chemmeen,* in which the social and economic exploitation is mostly a subtext. Taken as a whole, his voluminous works present a proletarian position. Like Basheer's work, Thakazhi Sivansankara Pillai also captured the living language of the underclass and traced the waxing and waning of its hopes in modern India.

In the novel *Thottiyude Makan* (Scavenger's Son, 1947), we witness the story of three generations of *thottis,* cleaners of night soil. The first two generations struggle to attain individuality; they suffer and die unfulfilled, oppressed and ostracized, but their struggles enable Mohanan, the third-generation *thotti,* to assert his individual dignity and lead his fellow untouchables to rise against oppression and prejudice. The landscapes of Thakazhi's novels are peopled with thousands of characters who represent a cross-section of Kerala: fisherfolk, toddy tappers, clerks, small farmers, landlords. He also tries to capture the peculiar social and mythical codes that continue to sustain their lives, making his works very much a part of the Indian tradition. In his voluminous novel *Kayar* (1978), through recapitulating the history of 200 years of the life of the working class and landowners, he also raised the scope of socialist realism by including the nuances of Kerala's regional culture. Among the two dozen novels of this prolific writer are *Enippadikal* (Rungs of the Ladder), *Randidangazhi* (Two Measures of Rice), and nearly 100 short stories. His works have been translated into about 25 languages.

Vaikom Muhammad Basheer

Basheer (1910–94) is arguably the most significant novelist of the latter half of the century. He spent his youth wandering all over India and the Middle East when he was not incarcerated by the British. Having begun his writing career during the final phase of Gandhi's struggles, he became a popular novelist after independence in 1947. Though one would suspect great revolutionary spirit in his works, what he offered were simple pictures of life in the poor, illiterate Muslim community of Kerala, trying to adjust to modernity, religious pluralism, and socialism. Though a tragic sense of life is prevalent in his early work, his characters learn to accept the tragic; they live in a spirit of profound love for their neighbors and fellow beings, including animals and birds and all the creatures of the natural world. His 30 or so novels and short story collections include *Prema Lekhanam* (Love Letter, 1943), *Balyakala Sakhi* (Childhood Playmate, 1944), *Sabdangal* (Voices, 1947), *Pathummayude Aadu* (Fathima's Goat, 1959), and *Mantrikapucha* (Magic Cat, 1968). None of these works were overt commentaries about social and economic inequities, but Basheer captured the life of a whole underclass and helped it appropriate the culture that had been monopolized by one elite group for too long.

Kesava Dev and His Contemporaries

Another novelist who started out along with Thakazhi was Kesava Dev, whose novels *Odayil Ninnu* (From the Gutters) and *Ulakka* (The Pestle) are typical examples of socialist realism. Unlike Basheer and Thakazhi, Dev did not evolve and grow as a novelist; he even became a strident voice of the socialist orthodoxy. His tireless polemic against the postmodernist generation indicated the limitations of the original position of the progressives, and the literature of commitment came to be somewhat discredited in Malayalam.

Among other significant novels produced by the frontline progressives are Uroob's *Sundarikalum Sundaranmarum* (Beautiful People) and *Ommachu,* S. K. Pottekkat's *Oru Desathinte Katha* (The Story of a Land) and *Visha Kanyaka* (The Venomous Virgin), the military novelist Parappurath's *Ara Nazhika Neram* (Half an Hour More) and *Ninamaninja Kalpadukal* (Blood-Stained Steps), Ponjikkara Rafi's *Daivadoothan* (The Angel), and Lalithambika Antherjanam's *Agnisakshi* (Witness by Fire), a milestone work, written toward the end of her writing career; she harmonized both the spiritual and the social realms in this novel, as did the other thoughtful progressives who allowed themselves to be transformed by new ideas and voices.

There is also a transitional generation of younger novelists who distance themselves from the progressives. The best representative of this generation is M. T. Vasudevan Nair, whose novels *Kalam* (Time), *Nalukettu* (The Mansion), and *Manj* (Mist) are profound explorations of the northern Kerala characters startled by the abrupt changes in the traditional way of life. Equally important are his short stories and screenplays and his work as the editor of the foremost literary weekly, *Mathrubhumi.* N. P. Muhammad's *Arabiponnu* (Arab Gold), Unnikrishnan Puthur's *Anappaka* (The Elephantine Revenge); the late psychological novelist Vilasini's 4,000-page, four-volume modern-day *Mahabharata* called *Avakasikal* (The Claimants); Malayatoor's *Verukal* (Roots); C. Radhakrishanan's *Ellam Mayikunna Kadal;* the various novels of G. Vivekanandan, E. Vasu, G. N. Panikkar, Perumbadavam Sreedharan, Joseph Mattom, Vettoor Raman Nair, Pamman, V. T. Nandakumar, and P. Valsala (*Nellu* and *Agneyam*); and K. Surendran's *Kattu Kurangu* (The Wild Ape) are among the best works in a vast category of authors.

Postmodernism and the Prose Writers

A literary historian who categorizes the writers of the twentieth century will have to relabel the progressives as modernists. Their worldview and their realistic style make them part of a broader phenomenon of modernity through which writers and thinkers around the world have tried to move away from the traditional cultural paradigms into the certainties of the age of the scientific temper. While, in modernity, such notions as democracy, socialism, global market, empiricism, rationalism, nationalism, existentialism, and other beliefs construct its certainties, in postmodernism, at least in its literary version, the writers tend to subvert some of these certainties from within.

Postmodernism in the West is primarily an engagement with form, but in Malayalam, besides its subversion of form, novelists and poets appear to be reinstating some of the irrationalities and tribalisms that modernism worked so hard to get rid of. In many ways, this trend is an extension of social postmodernity. The persistence of caste consciousness, the puzzling coexistence of tribalism and individualism, the ascent of consumerism and liberalization of capitalist enterprise, the rise of religious fundamentalism, the decline of the Left, and various anxieties about the future of modernity and nationality (all these are seen from the region, from Kerala's peripheral position) are factors that are yet to be played out fully. However, the immediate trajectory for postmodernist writing has been the habitualization of modern literary forms (socialist realism). Among the more profound cultural reasons we can include the general breakdown of idealism, the excesses of political organizations (Marxist Party, the Naxalites), and the rise of communal and fascist organizations.

Two Postmodernists: O. V. Vijayan and Zacharia

The central figure in the postmodernist generation is O. V. Vijayan. He confronts the Marxist Party on a regular basis as he confronted, early on, the preeminent socialist realist Kesav Dev about his generation's outmoded aesthetics and their suspicion toward the expressions of the younger generation. It must be remembered that, in both cases, it was the younger modernist revolting against the older modernist on issues of form and content, literary and social. Vijayan, who is also one of the leading English-language cartoonists in India, exploded into the literary scene with his dark, brooding, profoundly unsettling novel *Khasakkinte Ithihasam* (The Legends of Khasak, 1965, 1994). His writing was immediately identified as *athyadunikam* (ultramodern), as the term "post-modern" had not come into vogue in the critical vocabulary in Malayalam. Vijayan continued to write masterly short stories and social critiques until the national emergency in 1975, when his second novel, the scatalogical masterpiece *Dharmapuranam* (The Saga of Dharmapuri), was prevented from publication. *Dharmapuranam* seems to have been influenced by the existentialists as well as by Jonathan Swift and Laurence Sterne, but his vision and style, in general, spring out of the archetypal experience of the premodern India, vestiges of which have managed to survive in the remote village and tribal cultures of Kerala. The nascent postmodernist sensibility enabled him to bring out the essence of the premodern in a scorching, flaming narrative style, much to the confusion of the modern progressives, who claimed certainty in the matters of life and art. His dissent to modernism was evident in his early short stories and parodies. For instance, in the story "The Progressive Classic," a woman sitting under the full moon asks her beloved, "Darling . . . have you read Karl Marx's *Das Kapital?*" As the man begins to undo the woman's blouse, she insists they read *The Das Kapital* right away. The author asks us to fill in the blanks with the four volumes of Marx, claiming that it would make his short story the lengthiest socialist-realist novel.

O. V. Vijayan has remained a thoroughly Indian writer by sustaining a certain continuity of the tradition established by Vaikom Muhammad Basheer. This he achieves through delving deeper into the subcultures and the subtle dialectal variations of Malayalam and simultaneously connecting his work to the post-modern condition. Ravi, the young protagonist in *Khasakinte Ithihasam,* is an educated young man who loses himself in an isolated village where he volunteers to teach in an elementary school. Earlier, he had fled from the octopus clasp of modernity: city, college, intellectual life, a future career as an astrophysicist in the United States. When the village falls apart on account of the intrusion of the outside world, Ravi departs, seeing himself as an intruder, but, as he waits for the bus to take him back to the city, he allows a snake to bite him. At the close of the novel, we still see him awaiting his final journey. In his 1986 memoir about the writing of *Khasakinte Ithihasam,* Vijayan has explained that his art has nothing to do with Western forms of existentialist philosophy, as has been suggested, and that he receives his sustenance from postindependence Indian realities. This intentional rejection of Western modernity is actually a mark of Malayalam postmodernism.

Another significant postmodernist writer is Zacharia, whose style and posture are also comparable to the work of the novelist Basheer. Zacharia's tightly drawn short stories possess a Borgesian inventiveness and the precision of Flannery O'Connor. The self-conscious narrative voice in his stories parades and parodies several recognizable styles, often within a single sentence. At the end of each story, he manages to collapse the whole edifice with a naughty nudge. His collections *Oridath* (1978) and *Arkariyam* (1986) also provide a unique Syrian–Christian texture to his stories. His characters are modern individuals, like Mr. Chacko, who has all the trappings of a Westernized pseudointellectual, but he also possesses a postmodernist sense of entrapment in the labyrinth of Indian culture that convinces Mr. Chacko to commit suicide, but he fails: he couldn't quite open the poison bottle no matter how hard he tried. So he is condemned to live! Zacharia's famous novella *Bhaskara Pattelar and My Life* (made into a film, *Vidheyan,* by Adoor Gopalakrishnan) provides us insights into his constant and evolving themes as the servile narrator lives his life to quench the master's ruthless thirst for violence and deprivation. In spite of his introspective awareness about serving the devil, the narrator (like the fascist's butler in Kazuo Ishiguro's *Remains of the Day*) cannot act as a conscientious individual until the master is murdered, which leaves the servile man rather perplexed by the newly gained freedom.

The category of modernists and postmodernists encompasses a large number of poets, novelists, short story writers, critics, and historians. Among the most significant contemporary fiction writers who are making lasting contributions are Madhavikutty (*Manasi*), Anand (*Alkoottam, Marana Certificate, Marubhmikal Undavunnathu Engane*), Sethu (*Pandava Puram*), Punathil Kunjabdulla (*Smaraka Shilakal, Marunnu*), Kakanadan (*Ushna Mekhala, Parankimala, Arudeyo Oru Nagaram*), M. Mukundan (*Mayyazhippuzhayude Thirangalil, Elokam Athil Orun Manushyan*), Padmarajan (*Nakshatrangale Kaval*), M. P. Narayana Pillai (*Parinamam*), V. K. N. (*Pithamahan* and *Payyan Kathakal*), C. V. Balakrishnan (*Ayusinte Pusthakam*), Gracy (*Padiyirangippoya Parvathi*), Sarah Joseph (*Papathara*), U. A. Khader (*Khuraissikoottam*), and K. L. Mohana Varma (*Nakshatrangalude Thadavukari).* A list of important emerging writers to watch for in the years to come includes Nalini Bakal, Unnikrishnan Thiruvazhyodu, Madambu Kunhikuttan, K. B. Sridevi, M. D. Ratnamma, Sarah Thomas, T. V. Kochubava, Harikumar, N. S. Madhavan, V. G. Maramuttam, U. K. Kumaran, Jayanarayanan, C. V. Sreeraman, Ipe Paramel, P. T. Rajalakshmi, Thomas Joseph, K. P. Nirmal Kumar, and Joseph Vytilla.

Women Writing in the Age of Modernity and Postmodernity

Much of the good modernist and postmodernist fiction and poetry published over the second half of the century has been by women, mostly upper-caste women and Christians. During the first half of the century, fiction writers like Lalithambika Antherjanam, K. Saraswati Amma, and Annie Thayyil and poets like Balamani Amma, Mary John Thottam (Sister Benigna), Mary John Koothattukulam, and Muthukulam Parvathi Amma had emerged as major figures in a largely upper-caste, male-dominated world of Malayalam literature. Even Christian and Muslim male writers did not find favorable critical attention because cultural production was monopolized too long by the upper-caste Hindus. When Kattakkayam Cheriyan Mappila published his great epic on the life of Christ (*Sreeyesu Vijayam*), the critical establishment mocked the work, saying that, in the manner a moccasin might be called the king of snakes in an abandoned pond, Kattakkayam may be a Kalidas of the Christians! Women writers faced exclusionism of the worst kind: the social structure simply didn't allow them to write, for they had "no room of their own" to engage in creative act. However, *Kavitharamam* (1929), a collection of poems by a Catholic nun named Sister Mary Benigna, became a best-seller (over 100,000 copies), and one of the poems in the collection, "Lokame Yatra" (Farewell, World), a brooding, funereal poem justifying her decision to abandon the material world in favor of the cloister, remains a classic among Romantic poems.

Of the women writers who persisted in their calling in spite of the oppressive environment, Lalithambika Antherjanam (1909–87) and Madhavikutty are the best examples of a fulfilled literary career. Lalithambika's last name, "Antherjanam" (those who live inside the house), offers us a clue about the level of social incarceration women faced in her orthodox Brahmin community, but she was fortunate to be born in a Gandhiyan family actively involved in fighting the many social and political battles of the day. Even after her marriage to a farmer, with whom she raised a large family, she was able to pursue her career in fiction and to emerge as one of the greatest writers of the century. She published her first collection of stories in 1937 and followed it up with a wide range of books in different genres, culminating with her most famous novel, *Agnisakshi* (Witness by Fire), which appeared as late as 1976. From the romanticism of her early poetry, she quickly switched to a realist mode at the time of the progressive writers and became known for her craft of the short story, which retained the stylistic elegance and control of her poetry and brought in new elements of anger and commitment. Her work provided insights into the many levels of alienation women of her powerful orthodox community experienced, much of it resulting from pointless rituals and the burden of tradition and caste, which served only the family patriarch and harmed practically everybody else. In the wake of social modernity, the Brahmin community lost much of its power, and Kerala society, as a whole, became radicalized in conjunction with the nationalist struggle. Large-scale women's participation in the Gandhiyan movement helped to bring more women into the public culture, particularly into the political, literary, and academic fields. The transformation was not always easy. The case of Rajalakshmi (1930–65) illustrates the persistence of the suffocating domestic milieu a woman has to encounter in spite of the fact that Kerala is now known for its traditional acceptance of women's equality, its matrilineal heritage, the history of women's participation in education and politics, and its commendable male–female ratio. Rajalakshmi wrote about father–daughter relationships and the choking effects patriarchal figures could have upon women, particularly those who were accomplished and imaginative. The serial publication of her novel *Uchaveyilum Ilam Nilavum* (Midday Sun and Tender Moonlight) was canceled because of protest from readers who found her attack on the hypocrisy of idealist men too close to home. She found it impossible to continue her writing career and took her own life. K. Saraswati Amma (1919–75), the author of *Purushanmarillatha Lokam* (A World without Men), did not take her own life, but she lived single and isolated, her work applauded only after her death. Her last book, *Cholamarangal,* was published in 1958 and virtually disappeared from the scene.

The most important feminist writer to emerge in the last 30 years is Madhavikutty (Kamala Das), who is known nationally for her profoundly feminine, lyrical English poetry and for her short stories in Malayalam. Like Lalithambika Antherjanam, she comes from a distinguished literary family of northern Kerala. Her mother, Balamani Amma, is among the most significant poets to emerge after the Great Trio. The late Romantic poet and translator Nalapatt Nayaraya Menon was her maternal granduncle. However, her marriage and urban experience living in Calcutta and Bombay inspired her work in English and Malayalam. She began publishing fiction in the mid-1960s with such collections as *Mathilukal, Oru Pakshiyude Manam,* and *Thanuppu,* and immediately she was received as one of the key figures in the "ultramodern" (postmodern) literary movement, but her controversial memoir *Ente Katha,* published in both Malayalam and English (*My Story,* 1975), brought her national attention and some international notoriety (*Time* magazine featured her as an Indian confessional writer). The memoir was a watershed event for women writers in Kerala, as the work made it possible for women to write more candidly about sexuality as a structure of oppression. Over a decade after *Ente Katha,* Madhavikutty followed it with *Balyakala Smaranakal* (1987) and *Nirmathalam Poothakalam* (1994); the three memoirs are increasingly perceived as documents about constructing a feminist self. Though written in a gentle, lyrical style, her memoirs are charged with much rebellious anger aimed at her aristocratic background and at many of the illustrious literary and cultural figures born in her ancestral family. In her short stories and novellas, she discusses women's inner lives in an age when their traditional lifestyle has been altered radically in the wake of social modernity. Many women who grew up in the dual worlds of tradition and modernity increasingly found themselves vulnerable and unprepared to face the world, which is still controlled by patriarchal values.

In terms of her double existence as a bilingual writer who also runs for election and participates in the active public culture of Kerala, Madhavikutty is a product of postmodernity and postcoloniality, whereas Lalithambika Antherjanam wrote as a consummate modernist who possessed many certainties and convictions about the condition of women who were under the yoke of a male-dominated tradition and hypocrisy. In these final years of the century, many new women writers of fiction and poetry have begun to publish their first books, and their works are characterized by gender consciousness and the politics of desire; they are also conscious of the metafictionality of their work. The short short stories of Gracy (*Padiyirangippoya Parvathy*) is a case in point. In her one-page story about the ''Parable of the Sower,'' Gracy brings in a broad narrative context of contemporary drug culture and the pseudoreligious cults of Westernized gurus. The guru quotes the biblical parable, but his disciples fall at his feet, asking for the esoteric meaning of the parable. The guru tells them:

> We are the sowers. The seeds sown into barren women are eaten away by their barrenness. Virgins abort the seed before they begin to sprout. Seeds sown in whores are choked by the pills they take. But, alas, it is the seed sown in thy neighbor's wife that sprouts and come to fruition.

In a short story called ''Maranantharam'' (After the Death), the narrator, a young woman who has committed suicide, begins to chastise all those hypocrites who wait around her coffin, mourning for her. She opens her eyes and then asks her father why he was struggling so to pretend sorrow. The question makes him withdraw from the scene. To her lazy brother she says, Go on eating and sleeping, for my share of land is now secure in your hands. After talking likewise to all her relatives, she sees her lover, who kissed her and pretended much love, but, when he got a job, he wished to go separate ways. She speaks out to him and to all the other mourners: ''You're all nobody for me. Why go on pretending sorrow? Please, shut my coffin and go.'' The longer pieces in the collection also have layers and layers of sarcasm and irony and gender-conscious critique of the lingering power of traditional ways to force women to internalize their rebellion instead of bringing it out into the public, as we see in the voice of the suicide.

The future looks very promising for women writers of poetry and fiction, and, already, some of the best writing in Malayalam is done by gender-conscious women writers. Besides, the woman writer of today is an active public figure, as we see in the case of the poet Sugatha Kumari, who has become the preeminent voice against environmental exploitation in India. In her famous poem *Ratrimazha* (Night Rain), she merges the private and the public, and, in much of her work, we hear a woman's lamentation as she immerses her whole being into the metaphor of nature, which is being driven to the brink of death. The novelist Sarah Joseph is involved with the feminist movement, and P. Vatsala's fiction seldom deviates from the social and political context of women, tribals, and the Kerala working class. Similarly, the poet O. V. Usha, like her contemporaries Sugatha Kumari, Kanammanitta, and Chullikad, exemplifies the unique postmodern sensibility in Malayalam poetry by attempting to link the mystical and modern, political and domestic, philosophical and religious to capture the puzzle of human experience in the second half of the century. A coherent feminist aesthetics (pennezhuthu) has many adherents.

REVOLUTIONARY THEATER AND THE THEATER REVOLUTION

Though Sanskrit literature had a distinguished dramatic literature, and a school of Sanskrit plays known as Trivandrum Plays was written by playwrights from different regions of Kerala, theater in modern Malayalam literature did not begin to flourish until late into the nineteenth century. Since the dominant Hindu culture had elaborate traditions of temple theater such as Koodiyattam, Thullal, and Kathakali, realistic drama failed to receive respectability or audience.

The Portuguese contact had helped the development of a Christian theater, and the Christians who lived primarily in central Kerala staged plays on the history of Charlemagne, Jacob of the Old Testament, and the lives of various saints. Most churches produced passion plays and gospel enactments, which went unnoticed by the mainstream culture. Only after Valia Koyil Thampuran's translation of Kalidasa's *Sakuntala* (1882) did drama begin to get the proper attention of Malayalam writers. The Kalidasa play set off a stream of translations and borrowings from Sanskrit and English, and, following Varghese Mappilai's adaptation in 1893 of *Taming of the Shrew,* Shakespeare plays began to appear.

The novelist C. V. Raman Pillai also produced adaptations of English neo-classical dramas of Sheridan and Goldsmith. His *Kurupilla Kalari* (A Chaotic Place, 1909) provided a model for the future development of comedy, and E. V. Krishna Pillai's farces filled the lacuna of a dramatic tradition in Malayalam. At this point, Thottakkat Ikkavamma, the first woman dramatist in Malayalam, introduced her play *Subhadrarjunam* with a proclamation that it was not to the glory of the Muse that women were incompetent in writing plays.

With the rise of communism, drama became popular as an expression of the revolutionary zeal of the emerging political culture. The progressive writers were at the vanguard of the new theater movement. With Thoppil Bhasi's socialist-realist play *Ningalenne Kammunistakki* (You Made Me a Communist, 1952) performed by the Kerala People's Arts Club in every village and town in the state, Malayalam theater came of age. C. J. Thomas ushered in the modernist phase with his *Avan Vintum Varunnu!* (Behold! He Comes Again, 1949) and *Crime 27* (1954). Krishna Pillai's adaptation of Ibsen, especially in his *Bhagna Bhavanam* (Broken Home), helped the refinement of the theater and led to further adaptations and translations from Continental drama. With the enormous success of a dozen plays written and produced by N. N. Pillai (*Easwaran Arrestil* [God under Arrest, 1967]), the psychological and existential drama became a dominant part of Malayalam literature. With Thoppil Bhasi, N. N. Pillai, and K. T. Muhammad, touring theater companies became a major cultural factor in Kerala, but in the late 1960s, the artistic theater declined with the rise of the popular, commercialized theater, performed by groups like Alleppey Theaters and Kalanilayam and by dozens of smaller professional and amateur companies located throughout the state. That most of these performing groups are still patronized by Hindu temples and church organizations explains the general weakness of modern Malayalam drama.

Other important playwrights of the midcentury include Ponkunnam Varkey, C. N. Srikantan Nair, Kainikkara Kumara Pillai, Thikodeeyan, Idassery, T. N. Gopinathan Nair, K. T. Muhammad, P. R. Chandran, and C. L. Jose. Though television and the film industry have weakened the theater, a new wave of postmodernist drama has begun to take root, rivaling the mainstream theater. Again, like the fiction writers and poets, their formal approach is determined by a new anchoring in precolonial cultural forms, reinterpreted for a world that has lost much of the certainties of modernism. This new generation is led by G. Sankara Pillai, Vayala Vasudevan Pillai, Vasu Pradeep, Kadavoor Chandran Pillai, S. Ramesan Nair, Narendra Prasad, and Kavalam Narayana Panickar. They have begun to relink theater with Kerala's ancient traditions of ritual theater. Theater has been used by promoters of scientific temper, by extremist socialist groups, and, more important, by Malayalam-speaking people settled elsewhere—the postmodern reality of geopolitical displacement to other parts of India and in the United States and Arab countries. A *fatwa* (religious edict) was declared upon an amateur group that performed in Abu Dhabi, for daring to portray Mohammad in a play along with Jesus and Buddha and other religious figures. The entire cast has been jailed; the playwright Vayala Vasudevan Pillai, who lives in Kerala, has allegedly denied its authorship. In the past decade, the state government has banned the production of several plays in Kerala, the most recent one being P. M. Antony's adaptation in 1986 of *The Last Temptation of Christ.*

CRITICISM, THEORY, AND OTHER PROSE WRITINGS

We discussed the influence of criticism and aesthetic theory (M. P. Paul, Kesari Balakrishna Pillai, and Joseph Muntasseri) on modern writers who came to be known as the progressives. Critical activity at the turn of the twentieth century was limited to delineations of two primary Indian classical notions of *rasa* (mood, aesthetic pleasure, reader response) and *dhvani* (suggestion, tone, intentionality) and their variants *anumanam, riti, alamkaram, gunam, ouchityam,* and *vakrokthi* codified in classical Sanskrit texts composed between the sixth and seventeenth centuries.

Even after the flood of European criticism, a small group of critics has continued to write primarily on the basis of Indian literary theories. The best example of such an approach is Kuttikrishna Marar, whose classical scholarship and dense Sanskritized prose performance, notably in his 1950 classic *Bharatha Paryadanam* (A Journey through *Mahabharatha*), dazzled readers and elevated the status of critical writing. His works, such as *Sahitya Vidya* (On Literary Technique), *Hasasahityam* (On Humor), and his selected critical essays "Kala Jeevithan Thanne" (On the Purpose of Literature), have enabled Malayalam literature to keep itself grounded in the Indian traditions. A writer with greater range in both Indian and European traditions is Nityachaitanya Yati. Among his dozens of philosophical works, his two critiques of Kumaran Asan's poetry, *Nalini Enna Kavya Shilpam* and *Duravastha: Oru Patanam,* demonstrate the continuing relevance of the Indian aesthetic approach.

As a continuation of the legacy of both critical traditions, a new generation of younger critics capable of developing a postmodern critical practice seems to be emerging. They seem to be attempting to harmonize the Western avant-garde criticism and the Indian traditional aesthetics to create a new critical methodology. Notable among this group are V. C. Sreejan and Asha Menon, whose writings are highly poetic and Sanskritized; their first books are fastidious explorations of our literature and culture in the context of postmodernist, postcolonial world writing.

Major Critics and Prose Writers

A survey of a century of critical prose in Malayalam should at least name the following writers and the areas they have enriched. Sardar K. M. Panikker's work in politics and the history of Western dominance is internationally known. The prolific historical and philosophical output of the Marxist leader E.M.S. Namboothiripad and K. Damodaran will continue to have national relevance. The Montaignesque essays of Sanjayan and E. V. Krishna Pillai will go down in literary history as the best prose works of the century. Kottarathil Sankunni's eight-volume work on Kerala mythology and Vettom Mani's voluminous philological and lexicographical works will be difficult to replace. The philosophical work of Narayana Guru, Chattambi Swamikal, and Nityachaitanya Yati will become part of our great tradition.

Among those who made lasting contributions to criticism and prose writings, the following writers deserve mention: P. K. Parameswaran Nair's biographies of Gandhi and Voltaire, I. C. Chacko's work on linguistics, K. P. Kesava Menon's life of Christ, K. Raghavan Pillai's work on existentialism, M. Achuthan's monumental studies in Western literary theory and the history of the short story in Malayalam, K. M. Tharakan's work on the novel, M. Mukundan's essays on modernism, K. T. Rama Varma's historical survey of Western art, Ayyappa Paniker's collections of essays on English and Malayalam literature, Sukumar Azhikode's work on literature and Vedanta, S. K. Nair's literary memoirs, K. M. George's philological studies and comparativist approach to Indian regional literatures, Sebastian Kappen's seminal book on liberation theology for the Indian context, K. Venu's theoretical speculations on a Marxist–Leninist revolution for the Kerala working class, Ajitha's memoir about her failed experiments with that revolution, K. P. Appan's provocative essays on European modernist writers, Mathew Kuzhiveli's work on children's literature, P. K. Balakrishnan's critical works on the Western novel and Kerala historiography, Ponjikkara Rafi and Sabina Rafi's reflections on counterculture, Chummar Chundal's work on folklore, Krishna Chaitanya's monumental literary histories and cultural critiques, the psychological criticism of M. Lilavathy, and, of course, the personality of M. Krishnan Nair, the columnist who has been publishing a weekly almanac of the literary world for over a quarter of a century. He has been provoking writers and entertaining readers by assessing the week's literary output after comparing them with his usual touchstones: Borges, Garcia-Marquez, Foucault, and Carl Jung. Considered an enemy of every writer in the land, his column, although glib, has brought Malayalam readers and writers closer to an awareness of our existence as part of two larger categories, Indian literature and world literature.

NOTE

Though Kerala has an active publishing culture, several bibliographical problems still persist, most important a lack of consistency in citing sources; writers tend to avoid citations in general. The most important publishing phenomenon of the century was the formation of Sahitya Pravarthaka Sahakarana Sangham (SPCS), an authors' cooperative with a network of bookstores all over Kerala (National Book Stall). SPCS remains a significant publishing house, even though D. C. Books, owned by D. C. Kizhakemuri, one of the founders of SPCS, has emerged as an equal, if not a superior, force, with the purchase of the esteemed Current Books and other smaller imprints. In spite of the decline of the Kerala library movement, which arranged funds for village libraries throughout the state, the strength of book publishing is evident in the number of houses in business. Among the following list of active publishers, many have come to prominence in the past decade: Mulberry, Little Prince, Purna, Prabhath, Vidyarthi Mithram, Mulberry, Chinta, Deepika, CICC, Kairali Book Trust, Mathrubhumi, Sahitya Akademi, Jeevan, Janatha, CLS, Kerala Bhasha Institute, P. K. Brothers, Vidyarambham, D. C. Books, Current, and SPCS. The top two publishers bring out an average of 200 titles a year. SPCS (National Book Stall) is said to be giving 35 percent royalties to its authors, but it is unlikely that more than a dozen writers in Kerala make a living out of their vocation. Almost all the novels, stories, and poems first appear in such commercial periodicals as *Mathrubhumi, Kalakaumudi, India Today, Kumkumam, Deshabhimani, Chandrika, Kerala Sabdam, Manorama Weekly, Bhashaposhini, Mangalam, Manorajyam Deepika,* and *Vanitha* before they are released as books, mostly in trade paperback format. Some of the lowbrow periodicals serialize as many as 10 novels simultaneously. Children's publishing and religious publishing are also important elements of the book industry in Kerala.

SELECTED PRIMARY BIBLIOGRAPHY

Anand. *Marubhoomikal Undaakunnathu.* Kottayam: D. C. Books, 1990.
———. *Alkkoottam.* 1970. Kottayam: D. C. Books, 1991.
Antherjanam, Lalithambika. *Agnisakshi.* Kottayam: National Book Stall, 1976.
Appan, K. P. *Maarunna Malayalam Novel.* Alleppey: Gautama, 1988.
———. *Varakalum Varnangalum.* Kottayam: D. C. Books, 1994.
Asan, Kumaran. *Selected Poems.* Edited by P. C. Gangadharan. Trivandrum: University of Kerala, 1975.

———. *Kumaranasante Sampoorna Padyakritikal* (Complete Poetical Works). 1st SPCS Edition. Kottayam: National Book Stall, 1982.

Asher, R. E. *Malayala Sahitya Patanangal.* Edited by S. Velayudhan and M. M. Basheer. Kottayam: D. C. Books, 1989.

Basheer, Vaikom Muhammad. *Enruppuppakoranentarnnu.* Kottayam: National Book Stall, 1951.

———. *"Me Grandad 'ad an elephant!": Three Stories of Muslim Life in South India.* Translated by R. E. Asher and Achamma Coilparampil. UNESCO Indian Translation Series. Edinburgh: University of Edinburgh Press, 1980.

———. *The Love-Letter and Other Stories.* Translated by V. Abdulla. Madras: Sangam Books, 1983.

———. *Basheer Sampoorna Kritikal* (Complete Works). 2 vols. Kottayam: D. C. Books, 1992.

Chaitanya, Krishna. *Samskrutathile Sahitya Thatwachinta.* 2 vols. Kottayam: National Book Stall, 1973.

Changanpuzha, Krishna Pillai. *Raktapushpangal.* Palai: St. Joseph's Press, 1942.

Cherian, K. Cherian. *Palazhimadhanam.* Kottayam: D. C. Books, 1994.

Chullikad, Balachandran. *Pathinettu Kavithakal.* Cochin: Rasana, 1976.

Damodaran, K. *Keralacharithram: Pracheenakeralam.* 1962. Trivandrum: Prabhath Book House, 1991.

Joseph, Sarah. *Papathara.* Kottayam: Current Books, 1993.

Kakanadan. *Arudueyo Oru Nagaram.* Kottayam: National Book Stall, 1994.

Kavalam, Narayana Panikkar. *Kavalam Kavithakal.* Vaikom: Tirusadas Samskarika Vedi, 1993.

Kecheri, Yousuf Ali. *Alila.* Trichur: Kairali, 1994.

Kesavadev, P. *Otayilninnu.* Kottayam: National Book Stall, 1942.

———. *Novel Novelistinte Kazhchappadil.* Trivandrum: Kerala University Press, 1973a.

———. *Ormayude Lokathil.* Kottayam: National Book Stall, 1973b.

———. *From the Gutter.* Translated by E. M. J. Venniyoor. Trichur: Kerala Sahitya Akademi, 1978.

Khader, U. A. *Khuraisikoottam.* Kottayam: Vidyarthi Mithram, 1973.

Koduppunna. *Kalaghattathinte Sahityam.* Kottayam: National Book Stall, 1975.

Koodapuzha, Xavier. *Bharatasbhacharithram.* Kottayam: Oriental Institute, 1980.

Krishnapillai, N. *Kairaliyude Katha.* Rev. ed. Kottayam: National Book Stall, 1975.

Kurup, O. N. V. *Karutha Pakshiyude Pattu.* Kottayam: Current Books, 1993.

Leelavathi, M. *Varnaraji.* Kottayam: National Book Stall, 1977.

Madhavan, N. S. *Hygwitta.* Kottayam: D. C. Books, 1993.

Madhavikutty. *Neermathalam Poothakalam.* Kottayam: D. C. Books, 1994.

Madhusudhan, Naiv. *Naranath Branthan.* Kottayam: D. C. Books, 1995.

Maramuttam, V. G. *Anantham.* Kottayam: National Book Stall, 1994.

Marar, Kuttikrishna. *Bharathaparyadanam.* Kottayam: National Book Stall, 1950.

———. *Kala Jeevitham Thanne.* Kottayam: National Book Stall, 1965.

———. *Terenjedutha Prabandhangal* (Selected Essays). Trichur: Kerala Sahitya Akademi, 1990.

Mar Gregorios, Paulose. *Darsanathinte Pookkal.* Kottayam: Current Books, 1992.

Menon, Asha. *Kaliyugaranyakangal.* Kottayam: National Book Stall, 1982.

Mukundan, M. *Mayyazhipuzhayude Theerangalil.* Kottayam: National Book Stall, 1972.

———. *Eelokam Athil Oru Manushyan.* Calicut: Purna Books, 1992.

———. *Adityanum, Radhayum, Mattu Chilarum.* Kottayam: D. C. Books, 1993.
Muntasseri, Josep. *Professor.* Trichur: Mangalodayam, 1946.
Nair, Parameswaran P. K. *Malayala Sahitya Charithram.* New Delhi: Sahitya Akademi, 1977.
Padmanabhan, T. *Sakshi.* Kottayam: National Book Stall, 1973.
———. *Prakasam Parathunna Oru Penkutti.* Kottayam: Current Books, 1993.
Panicker, Ayyappa. *Selected Poems of Ayyappa Panicker.* Trivandrum: Modern Book Center, 1985.
Paul, M. P. *Novelsaahityam.* Kottayam: National Book Stall, 1963.
Rajakrishnan, V. *Rogathinte Pookkal.* Kottayam: National Book Stall, 1979.
Sachidanandan. *Anchu Suryan.* Kottayam: National Book Stall, 1971.
———. *Kavithayum Janathayum.* Kottayam: D. C. Books, 1982.
Sanjayan. *Hashyanjali* (1943). Calicut: Mathrubhumi, 1985.
Sankarakurup, G. *Odakuzhal.* Kottayam: National Book Stall, 1950.
———. *Selected Poems.* Translated by T. C. Sankara Menon. Trichur: Kerala Sahitya Akademi, 1978.
Sankunni, Kottarathil. *Eithihyamaala.* 1909–34. 8 vols. Kottayam: Current Books, 1992.
Sreejan, V. C. *Chintayile Roopakangal.* Kannur: Sameeksha, 1991.
———. *Ya Devee Sarvabhudeshu.* Calicut: Mulberry, 1992.
Surendran, K. *Sathyamapriyam.* Kottayam: D. C. Books, 1944.
Thakazhi, Sivasankara Pillai. *Thottiyude Makan.* Trichur: Mangalodayam, 1947.
———. *Randitangazhi.* Trichur: Mangalodayam, 1948.
———. *Chemmen.* Kottayam: National Book Stall, 1956.
———. *Chemmeen.* Translated by Narayana Menon. UNESCO Indian Translation Series. New York: Harper, 1962.
———. *Enippatikal.* Kottayam: National Book Stall, 1966.
———. *Kayar.* Kottayam: D. C. Books, 1982.
———. *Oru Kuttanadan Katha.* Kottayam: D. C. Books, 1992.
———. *Scavenger's Son.* Translated by R. E. Asher. London: Heinemann, 1993.
Ullur, Parameswara Iyer. *Bhaktidipika.* Trivandrum: Ullur, 1973.
———. *English Essays and Poems of Mahakavi Ulloor.* Edited by N. Vishwanathan. Trivandrum: University of Kerala Department of Publications, 1978.
Vallathol, Narayanna Menon. *Sahityamanjari.* 3 vols. Cheruthuruthi: Vallathol Grandhalayam, 1963.
———. *Achanum Makalum.* Cheruthuruthi: Vallathol Grandhalayam, 1973.
———. *Selected Poems.* Translated from the original by Ayyappa Panicker et al. Edited by K. M. Tharakan. Trichur: Kerala Sahitya Akademi, 1978.
Vasudevan Nair, M. T. *Nalukettu.* Kottayam: National Book Stall, 1958.
———. *Therenjedutha Kathakal* (Selected Short Stories). Trichur: Current Books, 1968.
Vijayan, O. V. *Khasakkinte Ithihasam.* Kottayam: National Book Stall, 1969.
———. *Dharmapuranam.* Kottayam: D. C. Books, 1985. *The Saga of Dharmapuri.* Trans. by the Author. New Delhi: Penguin, 1988.
———. *Ithihasathinte Ithihasam.* Kottayam: D. C. Books, 1986.
———. *After the Hanging and Other Stories.* Translated by author. New Delhi: Penguin, 1989.
———. *The Legends of Khasak.* Translated by author. New Delhi: Penguin, 1994.
Vilasini, M. K. Menon. *Avakasikal.* 4 vols. Kottayam: National Book Stall, 1980.

Vinayachandran, D. *Narakam Oru Premakavitha Ezhuthunnu.* Kottayam: National Book Stall, 1991.

Yati, Nityachaitanya. *Bharathiya Manasastrathinu Oramukham.* Kottayam: Current Books, 1988.

———. *Nalini Enna Karyasilpam* (1975). Kottayam: D.C. Books, 1995.

Zacharia. *Oridathu: Zachariayude Kathakal.* Kottayam: National Book Stall, 1978.

———. *Arkariyam.* Kottayam: Current Books, 1986.

———. *Bhaskara Pattelar and Other Stories.* Translated by Gita Krishnankutty, A. J. Thomas, and the author. Madras: Manas Books, 1994.

———. *Govindam Bhajah Modamathe:* Kottayam: D. C. Books, 1994.

8

Twentieth-Century Marathi Literature

SHRIPAD D. DEO

INTRODUCTION

Marathi, a language spoken by more than 50 million people in western parts of India, can trace its literary history to about the eleventh century. In spite of such a long literary history, Marathi language and literature began to change with the British expansion and domination in western India. The decline of the Maratha Empire, degeneration during the latter part of the Peshava rule, and British colonization have had an impact in shaping educated, urban, middle-class Marathi culture and character during the nineteenth and twentieth centuries. In the postcolonial years, the political movement to establish a separate state for Marathi-speaking people and its successful culmination in the establishment of the state of Maharashtra in 1960, with Bombay as its political and economic center, played a significant role in shaping Maharashtrian identity.

Maharashtra is geographically located between the north and south divide of the Indian subcontinent. In spite of its physical homogeneity, Maharashtra can be divided into four regions: the Konkan includes Bombay and the western coastal region; the Deccan includes Pune and the inland plateau; Marathwada includes Aurangabad and its vicinity; and Vidarbha includes Nagpur and the adjacent region.[1] These regions of present Maharashtra were parts of different political entities before the British rule and thereafter.

This aspect of the history of these regions is important in understanding the divisions that existed before the establishment of the Maharashtra state in 1956. The fissiparous tendencies to break away from the domination of one region over others, to assert separate regional identity, or to establish independent status of their language have been observed throughout the postcolonial history of Maharashtra. The diaspora of Marathi speakers outside Maharashtra has a strong sense of cultural history. This is observed in large clusters of Marathi speakers in erstwhile states ruled by Maratha aristocrats, such as Indore, Gwalior, and Baroda.

The apparently strong sense of linguistic unity makes the underlying social and economic divisions as well as an almost continuous history of conflict between the Brahmans and the non-Brahmans. These conflicts encompass the use and control of economic resources, political power, and cultural domain. There have been attempts to homogenize Marathi culture, and they have been consistently resisted by the fragments of Marathi culture. The non-Brahmans comprise castes of artisans and cultivators, tribals and the *dalits* (untouchables). The expansion of the capitalist mode of production, incorporation into the global capitalist economic system, and modernization through planning have developed economic classes in addition to the urban–rural division. It is necessary to be aware of these fragments, as this chapter seeks to provide an overview of development of Marathi literature from the early years. The focus of the chapter, however, is on the contemporary period. The chapter is divided into four time periods with distinct characteristics. The discussion of major writers and their works in various genres during each time period is contextualized in their socioeconomic, cultural, and political structures and relations.

PRE–NINETEENTH-CENTURY MARATHI LITERATURE

The earliest known Marathi inscription, dated around A.D. 983, is at the foot of the statue at Shravanbelgola in Karnataka.[2] During the thirteenth century, a great variety of literature, such as treatises in astrology and medicine, folktales, stories for children, folksongs, and poetry, flourished in Marathi. The domination of orthodox Hindu traditions, rituals, and institutions through Sanskrit was pervasive. It was a period of change, when representatives of heterodox religious movements were challenging cultural hegemony of the Brahmans (Omvedt 1976, 53; Thapar 1966, 167).

The *bhajans* (religious songs) written by members of these cults were part of the oral traditions observed in many societies before the advent of the printing press. The major part of written Marathi literature was accessible to only high-caste Hindus who were either Sanskrit scholars, professional scribes, or rulers. Oral religiocultural presentations were commonly used for communicating literature to the masses or for religious and philosophical discourse.

The cultural challenge to Hindu orthodoxy was continued through the *bhakti* (popular religious) movement and its popular expression in the *Vārkari* (pilgrim) movement in Maharashtra. As Omvedt argues, the currency of the Vārkari movement since the thirteenth century partly reflects attempts by Brahmans to incorporate the cultural challenge within the bounds of the caste system (Omvedt 1976, 54–55). It is necessary to bear in mind that the Vārkari movement itself subsumed many contradictory trends representing a compromise between caste orthodoxy and anticaste forces. Another important element in its continuous popularity was the royal patronage received by the Vārkari movement.

Dnyaneshwar (1275–1306), Namdev (1270–1350), and Tukaram (1598–1649) are the major representatives of the Vārkari tradition in Maharashtra. Dnyaneshwar's *Dnyaneshwari* (1290), a long and lucid Marathi commentary on the *Bhagvad Gita,* has been represented both as an attempt at Sanskritization of the movement (Omvedt 1976, 55) and as a step toward making Sanskrit works accessible to the masses. Namdev is considered by many as the true founder of the Vārkari movement and its ambassador (Deshpande and Rajadhyaksha 1988, 16).

From the times of Dnyaneshwar and Namdev till the seventeenth century, Maharashtra saw the decline of the Yadav dynasty and the emergence of Muslim rule. The new Muslim rulers consolidated their political and military domination for the next three centuries. During this period, Maharashtra's cultural and spiritual integrity was sustained by the teachings of Dnyaneshwar, Namdev, Eknath, and other poet-saints of the Vārkari movement. The commonsense understanding of Hindu doctrines diffused throughout the population through the works of these poets and provided the necessary armor against the Muslim rule. The spontaneity of their poetry, philosophical message, and simplicity made it amenable to oral rendering by the masses.

During the first half of the seventeenth century, the cultural challenge of the Vārkari movement became stronger through the poetic works of Tukaram. For three centuries, Muslim rulers became more autocratic, the caste system became more rigid, and the society became more segregated. Tukaram's *Gatha* exposed the hypocrisy of the contemporary religious leaders and opened the minds of common people to the deeper meanings of their life and to the path toward self-realization.

The rise of Shivaji (1627–80) and his successful efforts to forge a Maratha nation mark the beginning of a period of resurgence in the history of Maharashtra. During Shivaji's times, Ramdas (1608–81), a poet-saint, came to prominence. He did not belong to the Vārkari movement. His work is different from that of other writers in Vārkari tradition in that he provides a strong militant expression to Hindu nationalism as a means of protection against the Muslim rule. The domain of political affairs was renounced by the Vārkaris because it would draw one into an arena of futile conflicts and lure one to pursue fame, adulation, and power. Ramdas, on the other hand, advocated the unity of Marathas to propagate Maharashtra dharma.[3] An important point here is that the change in sociopolitical conditions, with Shivaji's rule, is reflected in the literary works of the period. In that sense, Tukaram and Ramdas can be perceived as "organic intellectuals" of their times, attempting to maintain cultural influence of intellectuals while inoculating their ideas in the fundamental processes of social transformation. It is also important to bear in mind that the orality and simplicity of the poetry, simple *ovees* (songs) sung by women while doing their household work, the spiritual songs—*bhajans, abhangas,* and *shlokas*—and the *pōwadas,* or ballads, describing real and mythical battles and conquests, facilitated the commonsense understanding of the times.

The prose of the times did not develop beyond the form of *bakhar*, which was used to record accounts of battles and administrative and political orders and events. These *bakhars* provide us with contemporary accounts of the times in clear and precise terms. This form flourished later during the times of the Peshwas (Deshpande and Rajadhyaksha 1988, 29; Kulkarni 1988a, 329–31).

The period after Shivaji's death in 1680 is marked by social and political turmoil in Maharashtra. It also saw the paradox of stagnation and vigor. The followers of Ramdas did little new writing on their own and contented themselves in either replicating or idolizing the work of their guru. On the other hand, the Vārkari movement continued to maintain its appeal to the masses and retained its creativity. During this period, *akhyan kavya,* a form of poetry started by Eknath, flourished. Wamanpandit (1608–95), a contemporary of Ramdas, wrote translations of Sanskrit classics. He was notable for his command over language, philosophical erudition, and conscious literary artistry. This denotes resurgence of pedantic works emphasizing knowledge rather than inspiration and emergence of the elitist impulses in literature focusing on form and nuances unsullied by the social and political disquiet of the times.

The death of Auragazeb, the last of the powerful Mughal emperors, in 1707, provided the Maratha kingdom with much needed respite from the continuous struggle to maintain the integrity of its freedom. A sense of security and stability that began to spread throughout the kingdom was also accompanied by tendencies to expand geographically. The Maratha power, wielded by the Brahman *peshawas* (prime ministers) initially in the name of Shahu Maharaj and later almost independently, became a dominant force on the subcontinent. This political and military domination brought an era of relative prosperity in Maharashtra. Pune became the center of learning, culture, colorful social life, and political power. In spite of this, the rule of *peshawas* was not a particularly peaceful time because of intrigues and rifts within the kingdom, military attacks on the fringes of the empire, and personal ambitions of the *peshawas* and their noblemen who controlled parts of the empire.

Moropant (1729–93) is the dominant poet of this period, representing the tradition of Eknath, Wamanpandit, and Raghunathpandit. He read verse stories from the *puranas* (ancient texts) in temples, explaining them to lay audiences. The emphasis was on keeping the audience attracted through clarity of narration embellished with poetic elan, craftsmanship, and lyricism.

The expansion of the empire and the rise of the *peshawas* gave boost to the *powadas.* The balladeers sang about the military exploits and tragedies of the Maratha warriors. These *powadas* were sung before a variety of gatherings from courts to the villages. If *powadas* presented the heroism and exploits of Maratha soldiers on the battlefields, *lāvani* (romantic songs) gave expression to their love of sensual pleasure. Both these forms, popular even today, have a genuine folk flavor reflecting the speech and rhythms of the masses (Deshpande and Rajadhyaksha 1988, 39).

EARLY NINETEENTH CENTURY

Even though 1818 can be a useful marker to denote the beginning of British rule in Maharashtra, the signs of the end of the Maratha Empire were visible for some time. Shivaji's attempts to establish a centralized bureaucracy with control over revenues were intended to establish discipline over his unruly feudatories. Later, the *peshawas* tried to reverse this tradition by allowing the Maratha *sardars* (chiefs) to collect revenues on their own and establish their semiautonomous states in return for allegiance to fight against the Muslims.

The nature of relations between the state and society is also noteworthy for its consequences for the reach, structure, and form of political power (see Kaviraj [1991], 74–76). The "sovereignty" of the state was two-layered. There was the distant, all-encompassing empire, but actual political suffering was inflicted on an everyday basis by the local autocrats. The communities themselves had considerable powers of self-regulation. Kaviraj makes a cogent point that these self-regulatory powers need not be interpreted in a romanticized image of democratic or unchanging communities. The "peculiar segmentary social arrangement" of these communities represented a mix of caste, religious denomination, and occupation. The economic relation of the state with these communities was in terms of tax and rent. The demands for rent or tax would vary depending on the military needs and the state's ability to plunder, but it could not restructure the productive or occupational organization of these social groups. In short, the state could not claim to act on behalf of the society as a whole.

The feeling of unity among the Marathi speakers was lost as the *peshawas* restored the caste divisions of the society. Some of the Maratha aristocrats sought help from the British to bolster their personal power. After the conquest of Maharashtra was completed, the British made conscious efforts to win over the upper castes by providing protection of their personal property rights. It was not difficult for these groups to slip into a life of moral and intellectual degeneration while Brahmans asserted their domination over other groups through ritualism.

In such a sociopolitical situation, the British began the process of reconstituting India in their imagination. Their immediate objective was to consolidate their hold over the subcontinent and establish an administrative structure that could be run with willing cooperation of Indians.[4] To achieve this objective, the education of Indians, to create "a class who may be interpreters between us and the millions whom we govern, a class of persons, Indian in blood and color but English in taste, opinions, in morals and in intellect" (Macaulay in de Bary et al. 1958), became an urgent need. To impart education, books written in English and Marathi became necessary. The British officers felt it necessary to learn Indian languages for communication and effective control of administration, for which they employed the services of Indian scholars as language teachers.

American and Scottish missionaries were the other group interested in learning Indian languages to spread Christianity, which relies heavily on the teachings in the Bible. This necessitated translation, as well as knowledge, of Indic languages. William Carey, a professor at the Fort Williams College in Calcutta, played an important role in preparation of a grammar and dictionary of Marathi. The missionaries in Maharashtra, as in other parts of the subcontinent, were trying to deprecate Hindu culture, practices, superstitions, and gods to prepare for the spread of Christianity.

The language and style of books produced by the British differed markedly from the prose works written by the Marathi authors at the time or earlier. There was a clear disjuncture from earlier traditions in Marathi literature. The language took on the English avatar with a new diction and syntax. The introduction of the printing press, establishment of schools and colleges, and school textbook production contributed to the objectives of the colonizers.[5] The emphasis on written form and reading skills once again put the upper castes in a relatively advantageous position vis-à-vis new rulers.[6] The standardization of both the written and spoken form of Marathi by the British put *devanagari* as a script and a variety of Marathi spoken in and around Pune by educated people in dominant positions.

If printing technology helped the missionaries and administrators in diffusing their ideas and objectives, Maharashtrians began to explore new possibilities in the changed sociopolitical milieu. The periodicals in English provided a useful model for the educated Maharashtrians and an opportunity to revive interest in older Marathi poetry and other classics (Deshpande and Rajadhyaksha 1988, 48). Along with literary periodicals, there were other periodicals countering the attacks of the missionaries on Hinduism.

While upper-caste, educated Hindus were countering the missionaries, through writings on social, political, religious, and philosophical issues, they were also translating literary works from English. Printing technology and education enabled the non-Brahmans to forge alliances with the reformist elements among the Brahmans and later pave an independent path to reject the caste system. The revolutionary work of Mahatma Jyotiba Phule (1827–90) in educating women and persons from lower castes is important in this period. It is discussed in the chapter on Dalit literature. Gopal Hari Deshmukh (1823–92) was an important reformist writer of this period. Through his contribution to the weekly *Prabhakar,* he criticized the superstition, indolence, and ignorance widespread in Maharashtra of his times and extolled the virtues of the British, namely, learning, efficiency, industriousness, and scientific knowledge.

The emergence of new forms of fiction, especially the novel, is attributed to political domination by the British, English education, and exposure to Western literature through English, as well as several indigenous narrative traditions that survived through constant mutation (Mukherjee 1985, 3). It is interesting to note that the word *kadambari* is used for ''novel'' in Marathi, acknowledging Banabhatta's literary work in Sanskrit as the first of its kind in this genre. Following Nemade (1980), we can identify three strands of prose fiction in Marathi, specifically the novel, that have evolved and transmuted in different patterns since this time. The first strand is exemplified by Baba Padamanji's *Yamuna Paryatana* (1857). Padamanji, a convert to Christianity, represents reformist impulses in a functional way. The second is represented by Lakshman Halbe's *Muktamala* (1861), denoting the imaginative-romantic urge. The third strand is exemplified by R. B. Gunjikari's *Mochanagad* (1871), incorporating the revivalist-historical spirit. The story of *Mochanagad,* for example, is set in a hill fort in Maharashtra. Shivaji's capture of the fort and the lives of imaginary characters enable the author to weave a happy, romantic tale. This pattern has been repeated since to depict Maratha history.

One literary form that managed to remain outside the sphere of influence of the British at the time was drama. Early Marathi drama retained its basis in Sanskrit or folk forms for some time. But dramas, along with periodicals, provided an effective means to resist the influence of the missionaries and infuse a new spirit of self-respect. As the first few generations graduated from colleges, the impact of, and exposure to, English literature was clear.

LATE NINETEENTH AND EARLY TWENTIETH CENTURIES

The period between the demise of the *peshawa* rule, establishment of the British administration, and 1874 was characterized by the paradox of vigor and vulnerability. The introduction of an education system and printing technology, the spread of periodicals, and exposure to Western social, economic, and political thoughts brought a new vigor to the stagnated Maharashtrian society. The new class of educated people, exposed to Western ideas, began to see the problems and limitations of traditional social structure and relations. The attacks on Hindu culture, rituals, and philosophy by the missionaries also forced this class to reconsider many of the issues, social and spiritual, affecting their lives. Politically, the British rule had brought order and stability. This had also led this class to think about possibilities of social change in a decadent society. Their initial, tentative attempts to articulate the nature and possibilities of change exposed new cleavages in the society: orthodox and reformist, educated and uneducated, Brahman and non-Brahman, rulers and the ruled.

The year 1874 provides a useful benchmark in the history of Maharashtra to examine the change in character and tenor of an apathetic society. Vishnushastri Chiplunkar (1850–82), the son of an eminent scholar, started his own periodical, *Nibandhamala,* during that year. He single-handedly galvanized the educated middle class with a series of essays on a range of topics, such as literary criticism, need to rehabilitate the Marathi language, social problems and prevalent attitudes, political issues, and philosophical questions.[7] He represents the conservative reaction to the reformist tendencies manifesting in the society. He wielded his pen like a rapier to attack educated people displaying servile attitude and mimicking the British. He brought precision, refinement, polish, ease, and compact writing style to the Marathi language. Even though he represents the conservative reaction to Westernization, he himself was consciously emulating Western authors and philosophers. He was inspired by Macaulay, Mill, and Johnson. He wrote a biography of Johnson and completed the translation of his *Rasselas,* started by his father. He, through his essays in *Nibandhamala,* laid the foundation of literary criticism in Marathi.[8]

Chiplunkar's impact on social, political, literary, and intellectual spheres of Maharashtra goes beyond his writings. He understood the importance of periodicals, printing, publication, and education in mobilizing public opinion and cultural reproduction. To achieve those objectives, he started his own printing press, a publishing house, periodicals—a magazine and two newspapers, *Kesari* (in Marathi) and *Maratha* (in English)—and the New English School in Pune. He attracted able, dedicated, and distinguished collaborators like B. G. Tilak, G. G. Agarkar, and M. B. Namjoshi. He deplored the tendency of the English education system to undermine the faith of the people in their own religion and culture. To redress the situation, the school, the periodicals, and the appeal to the glory of Maratha hegemony were arrayed.

Chiplunkar accomplished a great deal during his short life and left an enduring legacy of self-confidence for a people who seemed lost, self-expression through service to the society, and political radicalism for the educated Marathi middle class. His tendency of social conservativism, inherited and perpetuated by Bal Gangadhar Tilak, persisted and shaped social thinking in Maharashtra for a long time. He influenced a whole generation, which included Tilak, Agarkar, H. N. Apte (novelist), S. M. Paranjape (journalist), V. K. Rajawade (historian), K. K. Damle (poet), and litterateurs like N. C. Kelkar and L. R. Pangarkar. The revolutionary influence of Chiplunkar was, however, restricted to the middle-class, educated Brahmans. In 1873, a year before *Nibandhamala* began publication, Mahatma Jyotiba Phule had started his *Satyshodhaka* movement. He had started his schools for women and the untouchables in 1851 and 1852, respectively. Chiplunkar started his New English School in 1880. *Dinbandhu,* a weekly, was started by Phule and K. P. Bhalekar in 1877. Phule's revolutionary work was "lost, stole, or strayed" in history books.[9] Chiplunkar used his publication to viciously attack both Phule and Gopal Hari Deshmukh, the reformer, for allegedly borrowing from the Christian criticism of Hinduism.

In the period after Chiplunkar's death, the existing schisms became more pronounced. Bombay, for example, by now an important commercial city, became a center of Western-educated, reform-minded, careerist middle class, while Pune symbolized the pride of traditional culture and idealism of the educated class, which believed in the possibility of social and cultural reproduction through nationalist education. Marathi society remained vulnerable to the perpetuation of the caste system and domination of the Brahmans, who were now the educated middle class. Even though the hegemony of the Brahmans in matters religious and spiritual was abating, their new position provided the measure of social change. The new middle class was reinventing reality: political, social, cultural, and literary.[10]

Another important division that emerged in Maharashtra during the last decade of the nineteenth century was about the objectives of nationalist movement. Gopal Ganesh Agarkar (1856–95), a colleague of Chiplunkar and Tilak, argued, along with M. G. Ranade (1842–1901), that social emancipation should precede the struggle for political freedom. Their liberal views on social and cultural renaissance were at odds with those of Chiplunkar and Tilak. Agarkar broke away from the *Kesari* organization dominated by Tilak to start his own periodical, *Sudharak,* in 1887. His reasoned and rational views on social issues, his humanism, and his deep understanding of historical processes left a profound mark on the middle class and higher castes.

The intellectual ferment and social change left a profound impression on literature of the period. At the same time, developments in literature reflected and contributed to the process of change under way and mirrored different tendencies manifested during this period. Hari Narayan Apte (1864–1919), the first major Marathi novelist, wrote his first novel, *Madhali Sthiti,* in 1885. It is an adaptation of W. M. Reynold's *Mysteries of London.* In his novel, Apte depicts the paradox of Western notions of modernity and the depravity of orthodoxy in the Pune of his times. The title of the novel has been explained as "state of middle classes" or "the transitional stage." In it, Agarkar's influence, his spirit of social reform, is more visible than Chiplunkar's revival of the Marathi spirit. His *Pan Lakshyat Kon Gheto?* (1890) blends realism and idealism to trace the life of Yamuna, the narrator, from childhood to maturity. Though clearly a tragedy of Yamuna's life, it is also an attempt to show the efforts to change women's lives through education. In this 700-page, meandering story, the first-person narrative is used to ensure authenticity. Through a conscious design, Apte develops narrative in a halting, recursive style to indicate the limited verbal resources of an uneducated and unsophisticated girl. As the character grows older, she is ready to discuss social conditions and social injustices facing women (Mukherjee 1985). The differences in the social surroundings of Bombay and Pune also delineate the contradictions of middle-class Marathi life. Bombay represents, in the novel, a world of social freedom, revival, and individualism while Pune is an orthodox and closed community. Yamuna moves to Bombay with her husband for two years. Those are the two happy years of her life. There she experiences being herself, away from the constant scrutiny and intrigue of her joint family in Pune. Through this novel, Apte depicts the subtle interpenetration of the social and the individual in nineteenth-century Maharashtra, embroiled in Brahman orthodoxy and reform movements.

Apte's other novels, like *Ganapatrao* (1883), *Mee* (1893–95), and *Jag He Ase Aahe* (1897–99), show his maturity as a novelist attempting to react, reflect, and record the changing social and political milieu of Maharashtra. His contribution to the development of the historical novel in Marathi is equally significant. The educated middle class was showing an interest in the history of Maharashtra. It was the reaction of a people who had lost power and had yet to learn to deal with it. It was a moment when the story of the loss of power was to be told, not merely "how it happened" but with a theoretical perspective. As the educated class learned how the Maratha Empire was defeated, it was necessary to restore its "will to power" (Deshpande 1992). V. K. Rajawade's historical research in Maratha history facilitated this process. The emergent nationalist ideology helped in the reinterpretation of the history. Apte's historical novels need to be examined in this context. His first historical novel, *Mysoracha Wagh* (1890), was a sloppy adaptation of an English novel by Meadows Taylor on Tipu Sultan. His *Ushakkal* (1896) matches the merit of his social novels.

Apte develops splendid images of life during the Maratha period. The historical materials relating to the period were yet to be organized. He relied on folklore, legends, gossip, and whatever factual material was available to him to develop the ethos of those times. His *Ushakkal* is distinct as a historical novel in that it depicts a touching picture of the traditional values and norms dominating the lives of an older generation of the Deshmukh family. It also portrays the picture of a younger, idealistic generation with new ideas of self-respect, freedom, and loyalty within that same family. This intergenerational struggle within the family surpasses the intensity of clashes between the Muslims and the Marathas. Other novelists of the time did not match Apte in his craftsmanship, style, and social consciousness. K. R. Mitra (1871–1920) stands out for his translations of Bengali novels and stories in Marathi. He successfully introduced the gentle emotionalism of Bengali works in Marathi. It was a new element that enriched Marathi fiction (Deshpande and Rajadhyaksha 1988, 96). It is also an indication of the process of development of "national" consciousness under way.

If Marathi prose established itself as an effective instrument of communication and mobilization, poetry was liberated from the domination of Sanskrit poetics and the orthodoxy of the Marathi pandit poets of the seventeenth and eighteenth centuries. K. K. Damle, *Keshavsut* (1866–1905), the son of an ill-paid schoolteacher with a large family, is the one who opened new horizons for Marathi poetry. A contemporary of Hari Narayan Apte, he, too, was influenced by Agarkar's passion for social reform. His early poetry was influenced by the style and imagery of Sanskrit poetry. As he encountered English poetry, his own work began to reflect new style, words, and expressions. He began to blend the *shloka* structure in Marathi to the ode. Later, he also experimented with the sonnet and other forms to suit the expression. He was influenced by the English romantic poets, especially Wordsworth. This influence is to be seen in his choice of words, his ability to express his intense feelings as he experienced them and to look at the world from his own perspective. This subjective element was new to Marathi poetry. It is also a reflection of a society that was moving away from group consciousness and identity to a more individualized, self-centered identity. A new awareness of the presence of nature was being expressed in a simple and contemplative manner without resorting to stylized imagery and details. His poems like "Pushpaprat," "Satareeche Bol," "Nairutyekadil Waryas," and "Ek Khede" exhibit these qualities (Deshpande and Rajadhyaksha 1988, 102).

The other facet of his poetry reflects reformist impulses. He felt an urgent need for social reform and for equality among men. His call to action is expressed in his poems like "Tutari" and "Nava Shipai." If Keshavsut was breaking the molds of traditional poetry, his contemporaries followed different paths. Narayan W. Tilak (1862–1919) was a deeply religious person who rejected Hindu religious orthodoxy and wrote against social injustices, resonating his faith in God and humanity. Vinayak J. Karandikar's (1872–1909) poetry represents the conservative, romantic reaction rejoicing in the glory of Maratha and Rajput history. As the nationalist movement became stronger, his sentiments enjoyed a wide appeal in Maharashtra. Ram Ganesh Gadkari, *Govindagraj* (1885–1919), T. B. Thombre, *Balakavi* (1890–1918), and Narayan M. Gupte, *Bee* (1872–1947), were other prominent poets of the period, but they did not necessarily follow the lead of Keshavsut.

Between 1885 and 1920, Marathi theater gained respectability, popularity, and maturity. From the early unscripted plays of Vishnudas Bhave in Sangli through translations and adaptations of Sanskrit and English plays, Marathi drama began to adapt to the new needs and times. The adaptations were now oriented toward performance and were influenced by commercial considerations. G. B. Deval's (1855–1916) *Sharada* (1899) is his only original play that truly reflects the concerns of his times. Child marriage, especially very young girls marrying old men, was a burning issue at the time. *Sharada* uses this issue as its theme not only to criticize this practice and advocate social reform but also to paint a touching picture of the girl's plight. Deval's translations of Shakespeare's *Othello* as *Zunzarrao* and Molière's *Sganarelle* as *Sanshayakallol* remained popular for a long time.

Shripad K. Kolhatkar's (1871–1934) versatility as a humorist, essayist, novelist, critic, and playwright is commonly acknowledged by critics. His *Mookanayak* (1897) and *Mativikar* (1906) deal with social problems like drinking and widow marriage, but their popularity owed more to music and wit than to the themes. K. P. Khadilkar (1872–1948) was another successful playwright who skillfully blended theme, music, and dialogue in his plays. His *Sawai Madhavravacha Mrutyu* (1893) is a historical play, while *Kichaka-vadha* (1907) is an adaptation from a story in *Mahabharat.* The play gained publicity because of the ban by the British. It was argued that the villain of the play resembled Lord Curzon. His *Bhaubandaki* (1909) uses an episode in history to comment on the rift between the moderate and radical factions at the Surat session of the Indian National Congress (Deshpande and Rajadhyaksha 1988, 113). R. G. Gadkari's *Ekach Pyala* (1919) and *Bhavabandhan* (1920) were popular for decades for their dialogues, songs, and humor. Marathi theater was already under the control of producers, who were able to assert their will on the playwrights to ensure commercial success. Formulaic use of classical music, humor, and crisp dialogue was emphasized to the detriment of theme and social content. Marathi theater soon slipped into a long period of decadence and stagnation.

NATIONALISM AND MODERNIZATION

Bal Gangadhar Tilak died on August 1, 1920. His death marked the end of an era in the history of Maharashtra. Not only had his conservative social views and radical nationalist politics shaped Maharashtrian society during that period, but his legacy has persisted over the years. The nationalist discourse that he shaped created a "national consciousness" heavily influenced by concessions to scriptural or canonical authority. He did not subscribe to the progressive views embedded in liberal, secular, and rational attitudes that tended to look to the West for a model. The urban, educated middle class could not develop a broad social base for the national movement. He seemed to mobilize upper castes to transform society and stamp their hegemony. He did not make sustained overtures either to non-Brahman groups, to the peasants, or the burgeoning industrial working class to build real alliances.[11] Partha Chatterjee has argued that "it is the content of nationalist ideology, its claims about what is possible and what is legitimate, which gives specific shape to its politics. The latter cannot be understood without examining the former" (Chatterjee 1986, 40).

The dichotomy of revivalist and reformist trends within the nationalist movement became fairly pronounced during this time.[12] How to reach the goal of national independence, the methods, and the strategies became a contested terrain. India as "an imagined political community" superseding the one based on religion and dynasty had to be thought out and created. This idea of India as a nation, an "imagined political community," was a fundamental change in the modes of apprehending the world that "made it possible to 'think' the nation" (Anderson 1983, 14–28). A group among nationalists believed that as long as the British had an edge over the Indians in the development and application of science and technology, the standard in religion, culture, and politics was set by the industrially advanced nations (Hutchins 1967, 124). Those Indians who were close to the colonial rule and its reward system shared the values and aspirations of the raj. To them, British rule in India was the first essential step toward a just, equal, and "modern" world (Nandy 1983, ix).

The nationalist thinkers began to assert that backwardness is not an inherent quality of their culture but the result of their subjugation by the attributes of "modernity" associated with the West. Our "nation," acting as a collectivity, can adopt science, technology, and quest for progress from Western culture and combine it with the "spirituality" of the Eastern culture to forge a superior culture. This synthesis and quest for new "modernity" implied an elitist program. The limitations of elitist politics were clear by the 1920s. The necessity to maneuver between Western and Eastern notions in the ideological creation of the nation opened contradictory possibilities within the nationalist movement. Gandhi was involved in maneuvering a national political movement toward independence.

Labor unrest, unionization, and peasant agitations were on the rise in both Bengal and Maharashtra during 1920–21. The influence of Marxist ideas and the impact of the Bolshevik revolution were visible in industrial centers of Maharashtra.

The impact of the Bolshevik revolution and the appeal of Marxist views were quite widespread among the elite. They certainly appealed to the younger generation, which viewed Gandhian ideas as retrogressive. Even Jawaharlal Nehru found Marxist–Leninist ideas more interesting in the 1930s (Chandra 1975). It is no surprise that Marathi litterateurs found ideas like classless society or economic equality as a basis for organizing society refreshing. In Maharashtra, it was possible to see the impact of industrialization or economic inequality inherent in capitalist development in Bombay, the leading industrial center in India. Another reason for the attraction of Marxist ideas was that they went beyond the reformist ideas of Agarkar and Ranade. It is possible to see the contest between different ideologies to assert their hegemony. Gandhism did not influence the writers and their writings directly, but Mahatma Gandhi's program for national reawakening struck a responsive note in Marathi literature, prominently in drama.[13] Similarly, Marxist ideas also inspired many Marathi writers, but the mainstream of Marathi literature during this period remained under the sway of the urban, educated middle class.

In poetry, there was no dominant poet to set new directions. The innate relationship between sociopolitical changes taking place in the country and literary activity was beginning to atrophy. This was no accident. The educated, urban middle class in Maharashtra, which had dominated the literary scene as consumer and producer, was experiencing a loss of power in the Gandhian moment of nationalist movement. The dramatic changes in social, economic, and political life had left many youths confused. The new alternatives were drawing them in different directions. In 1925, Rashtriya Swayamsevak Sangh (RSS) was established with an objective of reasserting the identity of the Hindus with the nationalist movement. It emerged in a period when the anti-Brahman movement started by Phule had found an articulate and powerful voice in B. R. Ambedkar. By the mid-1920s, the Congress and Khilafat alliance had collapsed, and there were riots between Hindus and Muslims in many parts of the country. In Maharashtra, the Muslims were a small minority. The anti-Brahman movement and greater participation of other castes in Gandhi's nationalist agitation had left the middle-class Brahmans in a precarious position. Tilak's influence had lasted for more than a decade after his death, but his followers were wary of Gandhi and the Congress. The formation of the RSS "was an upper caste bid to restore a slipping hegemony" (Basu et al. 1993, 10–11).

The retrogressive tendencies in Maharashtra's political and social life are reflected in literature in different ways. C. S. Gorhe (1871–1937), *Chandrashekhar,* could be placed as a contemporary of Keshavsut, but his poetry belonged to an even earlier period. His poetry is a strange blend of the romantic and the classical. He was influenced by the works of Scott and Wordsworth. The technical virtuosity in his longer poems like "Kunjkunjana," "Kavitaratri," or "Godagaurava" are evocative of the pundit poets in Marathi. B. R. Tambe

(1874–1941) had a much larger following. The musicality of his poetry was helped by the popularity of gramophone and radio. Poetry recitals had become a popular form of cultural event. The emphasis on sweet-sounding words, cadence, and lyricism was soothing to his predominantly Brahman readers and audience in a disturbed world. His influence on Borkar, Padgaonkar, and Bapat can be seen in their early works.

Ravikiran Mandal, formed in 1923, was a group of young poets in Pune that dominated the scene for some time. These middle-class, educated poets tried to avoid the verbal and emotional profligacy of Gadakari and social activism of Keshavsut in poetry. They favored romantic; mildly reformist; to some extent, nostalgic; and escapist views of life. If Yashwant D. Pendharkar, *Yashwant,* and Shankar K. Kanetkar, *Girish,* preferred to depict yearning pictures of the simple, virtuous life of rural Maharashra, Madhav T. Patwardhan, *Madhav Julian,* preferred to write love poems in the form of *ghazals* (lyrics) with a liberal blend of Arabic, Persian, and Sanskrit words. His collection of poems, *Gajjalanjali,* was published in 1933. Many critics thought that his love poems were too personal, but they also signify a shift toward a self-oriented view, to be seen in later poetry. Kusumavati Deshpande has described this period as "an era of mediocrities" (Deshpande and Rajadhyaksha 1988, 138). This description fits the middle-class conformism obvious in the poetry and fiction of the time.

The Ravikiran Mendal faded slowly, but its presence remained through parodies of its style. P. K. Atre (1898–1969) published his collection of parodies, *Jhenduchi Phule,* in 1925. Atmaram R. Deshpande (1901–82), *Anil,* began to write poetry as a conscious reaction against the mediocrity and sweet unreality of Ravikiran Mandal.[14] Anant Kanekar (1905–80) was another important poet who contributed to this process. Anant's poetry represents an important convergence of romanticism and a profound sense of social inequality and moral indignation. His initial collection, *Phulwat* (1932), resonates a sensitive, precise, subjective, and delicate expression of love. His next two collections were *Bhagnamurti* (1940) and *Nirvasita Chini Mulasa* (1943). In *Bhagnamurti,* he employs *muktachhanda,* or free verse, to contemplate the decline and fall of civilization. This musing does not show despair but concentrates on causes of the decline. Here we see the return of passion for social change and a call for critical social consciousness. *Nirvasita Chini Mulasa* is a poem about an orphaned Chinese boy fleeing Japanese oppression. It clearly shows the poet's ability to evoke powerful reactions: compassion, indignation, and humanity. An incessant experimenter, he developed a new form of sonnet, *dashapadi,* or a 10-line poem. He titled his collection by the same name in 1976, which received the Sahitya Akademi Award in 1977. His other collections include *Perte Vha* (1947) and *Sangati* (1961).

Anant Kanekar's collection of poetry, *Chandarata* (1933), shows awareness of incongruence of an industrial society that was coming into existence. The moonlight is juxtaposed with smokestacks (Deshpande and Rajadhyaksha 1988); rejection of religion by the worker is paired with a wealthy owner's conspicuous idol worship. The poems are full of satire, protest, atheism, and socialist visions. Later, he concentrated on essays and travelogues, but his social commitment remained deep.

Two other important poets of Anil's generation are B. B. Borkar (1910–84) and V. V. Shirwadkar (1912), *Kusumagraja.* Berkar's initial poetry was swayed by B. R. Tambe, but he went beyond that mellifluousness to incorporate influences of poetry in several languages, the Portuguese culture of his native Goa, Bhakti poets, and Gandhian ideas. His important collections include *Jeevan Sengeet* (1937), *Dudhasagar* (1947), *Anand Bhairavi* (1950), *Chitraveena* (1960), and *Chaitra Punav* (1970). He remained a classical poet by following the traditional patterns of rhyme and rhythm. He was a consummate craftsman of words that were chaste and delightful. He also wrote some novels, with the same facility for language and narration. His *Bhavin* (1950) depicts a compassionate picture of the life of a *devadasi* (temple dancer).

Kusumagraj established himself as a major port during the Quit India movement in 1942 with his first collection, *Vishakha.* His poems mirror the genuine nationalist spirit of the times. His other books, *Jeevan Lahari* and *Kinare* (1952), show "his humanism, revolutionary zeal and metaphysical probings" with "a powerful and lively expression" (Kanadey 1991, 66).

Two novelists, N. S. Phadke (1894–1978) and V. S. Khandekar (1898–1976), dominated the two decades before independence in terms of popularity; however, other novelists made significant contributions to the development of the genre. They included V. M. Joshi (1883–1943), S. V. Ketkar (1884–1937) and B. V. Warerkar (1883–1943) (see Karhade 1981; Deshpande and Rajadpadhyaksha 1988). Joshi took the Marathi novel beyond the thematic of Apte's novel: social reform and nationalist refashioning of history. His novels have women with a sense of identity as main characters. Joshi's *Ragini* (1915) deals with the rights of women and the tension felt by middle-class, educated women of the time: an aggressive advocacy of women's rights or traditional family ideal. Even though the novel is weak in structure, the contemporaneity of the theme is refreshing. Women who had begun to acquire education and were able to participate in the Gandhian moment of national struggle faced these questions. His other novels, *Ashram Harini* (1916), *Nalini* (1920), and *Sushilecha Deva* (1930), explore similar social themes. In *Sushilecha Deva,* he raises the issue of the conception of God and takes the discussion beyond the notion of an idol to interpret it as an ideal of service to humanity. The influence of Gandhian thinking is visible, as is the reason for unease among those who had assimilated Western rationalist thinking.

Ketkar was an iconoclast who, in 1920, became the first person to edit and publish an encyclopedia, *Maharashtriya Dnyanakosha,* in Marathi modeled after *Encyclopedia Britiannica.* He used novels as vehicles for his social thoughts. His novel *Brahmakanya* (1930), for example, takes up the issue of the status of a child in society from the marriage of a Brahman and a prostitute. In *Paraganda* (1926) and *Gavasasu* (1930), he picks up the theme of emigration to a foreign country and marriage there. The choice of settings for his novels, for example, Vidarbha, England, and the United States, also reveals his reaction to dominant tendencies in literature to focus on Pune and Bombay (Deshpande and Rajadhyaksha 1988). He bared the cloistered, middle-class minds to decaying social institutions and problems beyond their limited experiences.

Warerkar's novels present angry women characters reacting against their social circumstances. In his *Vidhava Kumari* (1928), for example, we see a rebellious child widow, and in *Godu Gokhale,* the heroine reacts strongly against social injustices and the subservient position of women in the institution of marriage.[15] Warerkar's *Dhavata Dhota* (1933) presents with authentic realism the life of a textile millworker facing an imminent strike. In *Saat Lakhatil Eka* (1940), he paints a somber picture of life oppressed by poverty and superstition in Konkan. Gandhi's philosophy of dignifying simple village life and his message "back to the village" rekindled reformist awareness among middle-class writers. It later developed into a subgenre, *gramin sahitya,* or rural literature.

N. S. Phadke was a prolific writer who handled novels, essays, and short stories with equal facility. His literary output is steeped in the lives of educated, urban, middle-class people. As more educated Maharashtrians pursued remunerative and prestigious occupations, the middle class diverged into a relatively small section of upper-income professionals and a large lower-income, white-collar group. The first group claimed the mantle of intelligentsia and showed more affinity to the West. The lower middle class aspired to move up, but its objective economic condition remained close to that of the working class. These classes provided large and sustained readership for Phadke and Khandekar for different reasons. The upper middle class found itself setting the social norms and fashions through Phadke's characters. The lower middle class found very enticing the happy love stories situated in beautiful settings where the couples are young and smart, economically secure, and accomplished in music, painting, or sports. His characters, at times, indulge in political activities but do not have to deal with oppressive or intractable issues. Phadke himself did not believe in an overt social role of literature. The function of literature, to him, was to provide an escape from harsh realities of everyday life and make readers feel good about themselves and their lives in this facile, imagined world. Phadke's novels may have lacked social commitment, but they were always well crafted. That may also be a reason for his popularity. His novels *Jadugar* (1928), *Daulat* (1929), *Atakepar* (1931), *Akherch Band* (1944), *Kalanka Shobha* (1933), *Bharari* (1967), and *Kulabyachi Dandi* (1971) are representative of his work.

V. S. Khandekar represents the other side of the same coin. He represents the idealistic streak borrowed from Gandhism and faintly colored by socialistic concern for the downtrodden. His writings are characterized by an excessive sentimentality, compassion, and fragility. His belief in selfless service to uplift the wretched and to usher in a world without oppression and injustice is evident in his work. This romantic idealism is underscored in contrast to Phadke's epicurean, romantic view of life. However sincere and idealistic Khandekar's work may be, it does not insist that the reader act according to it. If his work does not induce the reader to social action, then it is not too far apart from Phadke's work. Middle-class readers may have found his illusory world more socially acceptable than Phadke's indulgent romanticism.

Khandekar's early novels, like *Hrudayachi Haaka* (1930) and *Kanchanamruga* (1931), differ from the subsequent *Ulka* (1934) or *Dona Dhauva* (1934) in organization. But they have "artificial and complicated plots, sugary and fine sounding sentiments, uncomplicated characters, the writing laden with lavish fancy and the right touch of moral ardour" (Deshpande and Rajadhyaksha 1988, 158). Khandekar was not as prolific as Phadke, but he enjoyed a wider appeal, even outside Maharashtra. His novel *Yayati* was given the prestigious Jnanapith Award.

During the decades before independence, women writers made their mark on Marathi literature. Malatibai Bedekar (1904), *Vibhawari Shirurkar,* published her *Kalyanche Nishwas* (1933), a collection of stories, with an introduction by S. V. Ketkar (Deshpande and Rajadhyaksha 1988). In her stories, she raised complex social issues like women and marriage, or frustrations and mental anguish of educated, middle-class women. She argued that women's education had neither made them happy nor helped them in facing newer problems. In her novel *Hindolyawar* (1934), she discusses the issue of extramarital love and a woman's yearning to bear a child out of that relationship. This novel represents the defiant mood of educated women of the time, yet her use of a pseudonym indicates the fear of orthodox retaliation. Her maturity as a novelist is evident in *Bali* (1950), a sympathetic story of inmates of a criminal tribal camp. Other women writers of the period included Geeta Sane (1907), Prema Kantak (1906), and Girijabai Kelkar (1886–1980).

Marathi theater's sunny days were clouded by the economic depression of the 1920s and 1930s. The dependence of theater groups on general economic conditions became clear during this period, when urban unemployment had increased, and the small town and rural patrons, facing declining prices of agricultural produce, could not continue their support. Development of motion pictures proved to be a more popular visual entertainment and contributed to the dismal picture. Wararkar's plays provided some fillip during these dismal days through realism in production and social context back to the stage. His *Kunjavihari* (1908), *Haach Mulacha Baap* (1916), and *Bhvomikanya Seeta* (1955) are noteworthy. M. N. Joshi's *Municipality* (1925) caricatured the activities of newly established local governments. The efforts to rejuvenate theater led to the formation of an organization called Natyamanvantara in the early 1930s. The effort did not last too long, but it brought S. V. Vartak (1885–1950) to prominence as a playwright. His adaptations of Henrik Ibsen and Björnstjerne Björnsen were produced with little success. This experiment also introduced, for the first time, a woman to play a female role on the professional stage (Deshpande and Rajadhyaksha 1988).

If formulaic Ibsen did not catch on, a farcical and satirical treatment of social issues did. Vartak's *Takshasheela* (1933), M. N. Joshi's *Municipality,* S. P. Joshi's *Khadashtak* (1927), and P. K. Atre's *Sashtang Namaskar* (1933) were popular until the mid-1950s. Atre's play makes fun of many social fads of the time, like physical exercise as a cure-all for problems, physical and sociopolitical; the effeminate stereotype of romantic poets; belief in astrology; and newly developed passion for movies. After a successful debut, Atre wrote *Gharabaher* (1934) and *Udyacha Sansar* (1938), focusing on the plight of women in middle-class, joint families. His *Lagnachi Bedi* and *Bhramacha Bhopala* were well-written comedies. His adaptation of Molière's *L'Avare* as *Kavadichumbak* and Brandon Thomas's *Charley's Aunt* as *Moruchi Marashi* were also successful on stage (Deshpande and Rajadhyaksha 1988; Malshe 1988, 264–65). M. G. Ranganekar (1907) entered the scene as Atre shifted to successful careers in cinema, journalism, and politics, especially during the Samyukta Maharashtra agitation. Ranganekar's *Kulavadhu* (1942) is a watered-down adaptation of Ibsen's *Doll's House.* It brought the urban, middle-class audience back to the stage. It established a pattern of "crisp dialogues spiced with humor, that scrupulously avoided exaggeration and verbal subtlety, plausible realism in the action and characters, and nimble movement" of story line, for subsequent plays (Deshpande and Rajadhyaksha 1988; 187).

Anant Kanekar was one of the founders of Natyamanvantar. He successfully adapted from the works of Henrik Ibsen, John Galsworthy, James Barrie, and Oliver Goldsmith. He also contributed to the introduction of a new form to the theater, one-act plays. During this period, popularity of writers in English had increased in Maharashtra. The educated class took pride in reading and keeping up with trends in the West. In this milieu, one-act plays were introduced and established. Many prominent dramatists, like P. L. Deshpande, Shamrao Oka, M. G. Ranganekar, Madhav Manohar, and Vijay Tendulkar, began their literary careers by writing one-act plays.

INDEPENDENCE, MODERNITY, AND POSTINDEPENDENCE LITERATURE

Background

Political independence of India was an occasion of mixed hope, despair, and anxiety in Maharashtra. The signs of a better future for the nation had raised the spirits of the people. The massacre in Panjab and other parts of the country following the partition, including Maharashtra, had created an atmosphere of fear and anxiety. It was further exacerbated by the assassination of Mahatma Gandhi by a Brahman from Maharashtra. The anti-Brahman sentiment peaked, resulting in reprisals against Brahmans, especially in rural areas and small towns. Hindu Mahasabha and the RSS drew wrath and animosity because both these organizations were predominantly Maharashtrian and Brahman. This tension remained in Maharashtra for decades.

At independence, there was the Bombay state, made up of Gujarat and Maharashtra, but no separate state for Marathi speakers. The domination of Bombay as a commercial metropolitan area distorted the economic development of the state and increased the influence of the bourgeoisie made up of the Gujaratis, the Marwaris, and the Parsis. The movement demanding a linguistic division of the state reached its peak after 1956, culminating in the present Maharashtra state in 1960. If nationalism had undertaken the task of reconstructing the history of India to suit its problematic, a similar project was under way for Maharashtra. The interpretation of Shivaji's work and legacy has remained a contested terrain, over which both Brahmans and non-Brahmans have tried to interpret the history to suit the exigencies. The remnants of feudal and religious prerogatives were now being converted into the new democratic framework.

In the countryside, the landlord class was very much in command at independence, but not for too long. The land reforms changed the pattern of landownership from predominantly, Brahman control to Maratha and other intermediate castes. They were "a class of capitalist farmers in embryo, in the womb of the old order" (Byres 1974, 235). The Green revolution, development of agricultural cooperatives and control of rural cooperative credit, helped this class to consolidate its political and economic gains. Also important to our understanding of the times and literature in the postcolonial period is the character of the middle class that was now in control. It had taken on the mantle of the British. It has also assumed the position of organic intellectuals of the new regime chanting the mantras of modernization, industrialization, scientific frame of mind, technological development, economic planning, and progress. The intellectual discourse of the period was so dominated by Western notions of progress that progressive deterioration in the living conditions of workers, both agricultural and nonagricultural, and the rapacious profits made by the upper middle class and businessmen had made the masses wonder about the new era. As Kosambi writes in his review of Nehru's *Discovery of India,* "The gain [made by this class] may be camouflaged by the ostentatious simplicity of white *khaddar* (homespun) and the eternal Gandhi cap" (1946, 395).

It was becoming clear even before 1947 that the Gandhian critique of modernity and his alternative vision for India were being garbled and appropriated by the modernizing, Westward-looking middle class. The problem was that Gandhi was seen by "the vast multitude of semi-naked masses as 'a great soul.' Nehru being the political heir to Gandhi could justify his appropriation or rejection of Gandhism without remorse by saying that Gandhi was "utterly sincere," "a great and unique man," "a glorious leader," but his vision of independent India was "impossible of achievement" (1938, 510).[16] Gandhi's methods were revolutionary, and his vision was religious and metaphysical, but it is not desirable or sufficient for state-building activities. This Nehruvian appropriation contributed to certain interrelated tendencies. For example, it reinforced the notion that to be modern is to look to the West and that the spirit of the age was described in terms of secularism, rationality, scientific curiosity, technology, and so on. The educated middle class and the bourgeoisie took it as a signal to reject the *swadeshi* and uncritically accept what was a historical presentation of the West. Partha Chatterjee has pointed out: "Nationalism sets out to assert its freedom from European domination. But in the very conception of its project, it remains a prisoner of the prevalent European [and American] intellectual fashions" (1976, 10).

B. S. Mardhekar (1909–56) is acknowledged as the originator of the "modernist" trend in Marathi literature. His early poetry was in the footsteps of the Ravikiran Mandal and Balkavi Thombre. His initial collection of poems, *Shishiragama* (1939), mirrors those influences. However, in 1947, he published his second volume, *Kahi Kavita,* which changed the tenor of Marathi poetry. In this collection, he expresses the disillusionment, irony, and incongruity of human life in contemporary society (Deshpande and Rajadhyaksha 1988, 143–44). As society undergoes change, the earlier established structures, modes of relations, and interactions go through changes, too. Classical European sociologists had analyzed this occurrence in the last century in the wake of the Industrial Revolution. What is perplexing is the fact that the period during which he wrote it did not show any more perceptible degradation of human life in India than before. Development of science, technology, and industry remained distorted and restricted. The capitalist mode of production was not yet the dominant one. The dehumanization, disillusionment, and uncertainties that he expresses through this volume are more reflective of the postwar European situation. This is not to suggest that conditions in Maharashtra or in India were better. It has been suggested that "[t]he impact of the West, especially, the example of T. S. Eliot and Ezra Pound and the modern European attitude of sardonic disillusionment shaped his poetic sensibility" (Kanadey 1991, 65).

In his *Anakhi Kahi Kavita* (1951), there is a conscious attempt to go beyond human destitution. There is an attempt to reconcile the Western values imbibed through education and the spiritual discourse of the native saints. As Deshpande and Rajadhyaksha (1988, 144) put it, "the spiritual strain that had been dormant came alive." Even in his turn to the spiritual understanding of the modern world, he seems to cling to the rationalist approach. He strove for precision of expression in his poetry. Mardhekar's poetry did not create a tradition in Marathi poetry, but it certainly changed its direction and form. It also marked a decline of romantic-humanist tradition in Marathi poetry.

P. S. Rege (1910–78) is acknowledged as an important poet of contemporary Marathi poetry. He, along with Mardhekar and Muktibodh, is credited for revitalization of poetry in the postcolonial period. Yet, his approach to poetry is quite different from that of the other two. He is more focused with form, style, rhythm, lyricism, and sensual expression. His poetry eschews time and space dimensionality. As Deshpande and Rajadhyaksha (1988, 145) put it, his poetic world is "utterly, almost forbiddingly, private," and his language, which could have provided access to that world, is also very compendious.

He published his first collection of poems, *Sadhana ani Itar Kavita,* in 1931.

Himaseka (1943) is acknowledged as his first major collection. He has published steadily since. A consistency in the theme has haunted his imagination, namely, woman in love. The multidimensionality of femininity, in his conception, is not restricted to the human, the emotive, or the individual. It embodies not the emotional needs of an individual but the essence of love that transcends time and event. "Radha is Rege's paragon of such beloved. She is not just woman: she is the distilled essence of womanhood" (Deshpande and Rajadhyaksha 1988, 145).

His later collections of poetry include *Dusara Pakshi* (1966), *Priyala* (1972), and *Suhrudgatha* (1975). He also wrote three novels, two volumes of essays and literary criticism, and several plays. His poetry is compared to an exquisite piece of hand-carved ivory, and, hence, it is criticized for its lack of social context (Soman 1989, 11). It is also true that Rege could not have much impact on Marathi poetry.

Govind V. Karandikar (1918) started along the path paved by Keshavsut, Madhav Julian, and Savarkar but later turned to Mardhekar and Rege for inspiration (Deshpande and Rajadhyaksha 1988). His *Mrudgandha* (1954) and *Dhrupada* (1959) brought him recognition as an innovative poet.

Sharatchandra Muktibodh's (1921–84) work was also influential in charting the modernist trend in Marathi poetry. It is influenced by Marxist ideas. He, too, confronts modern society, but his work projects a clarity and resolve to bring about social justice to all people. The inner loneliness and fragility of Mardhekar's work are not to be seen in Muktibodh. There is a conviction of inherent human abilities and creativity, as well as an awareness of contradictions and inequalities of modern industrial societies. His first volume of poetry, *Navi Malawat* (1949), attracted attention because of the expression of genuine social commitment and concern for the exploited classes of the industrial age. *Yatrik* (1957), his next collection, continued along the same path, unmasking the pretensions of the middle class. His poetry discomposed those segments of the middle class comforted by the conformist poetry of Tambe and the Ravikiran Mandal.

It is noteworthy that his poetry, in spite of its overt and genuine concern for the working classes, is not blaring. It is vivid, sensitive, intelligent, and imaginative. The recurring images of fire in his poetry denote both the destruction of the oppressive and exploitative social order and resurrection of just society (Kanadey 1991, 139).

His trilogy of novels began with *Kshipra* in 1954 and followed with *Haddapar* and *Jan He Voltu Jethe.* The characters in the trilogy are involved in the Quit India movement in 1942. The intellectual journey of the main character, Bishu, in search of a cohesive framework to understand social contradictions, enables Muktibodh to provide bold interpretation of social changes while reflecting on the interaction of individual and society (Kanadey 1991, 140).

Vasant Bapat's (1922) poetry reveals his early association with a socialist organization. His patriotic songs charmed the youth of Maharashtra during the

Quit India movement in 1942. His first collection, *Bijali* (1952), was followed by *Setu* (1957), *Akravi Disha* (1962), *Sainya Chalale Pudhe* (1965), *Sakina* (1975), *Manasi* (1977), and *Pravasachya Kavita* (1982). His poetry shows his sustained development and maturity as a poet.

Novel and Short Story

Gangadhar Gadgil (1923), with Arvind Gokhale, Vyankatesh Madgulkar, and P. B. Bhave, ushered in what Deshpande and Rajadhyaksha (1988) call the "new short story." The newness implied in the label refers to the return of realism. Gadgil led the charge against the contrived romantic-imaginary world exemplified in the works of Phadke and Khandekar. The dehumanizing industrial world, horrors of war, the partition, and changing social reality provided the writers of his generation with many themes to explore in their works. The newness of short stories of Gadgil and his contemporaries lay in their willingness to experiment with new techniques and themes with a sense of purpose.

Gadgil has experimented with the stream-of-consciousness technique in his novel *Liliche Phul* (1955) to explore the inner conflicts of a person's sexual tendencies. Gadgil has published many collections of short stories over his long literary career. His *Manaschitre* (1946), *Kadu ani Goad* (1948), *Navya Wata* (1950), *Talawatila Chandane* (1954), *Vegale Jaga* (1958), *Gunakar* (1965), *Athavana* (1978), and *Uddhvastava Vishva* (1982) are representative of his work. Gadgil also firmly established travelogue as a genre in Marathi literature. Earlier, Anant Kanekar wrote his *Dhukyatun Lal Taryakade* (1940), noting his impressions of travel in the Soviet Union and Western Europe. The informal, impressionistic sketches of people and places were refreshing. His *Amachi Mati, Amache Aakash* (1950) was about his travel in India with Dinanath Dalal, the artist. Gadgil's *Sata Samudrapalikade* (1959) is a chronicle of his travels in Europe and the United States. It is more impressionistic than documentary, reflecting on places and individuals he encountered. In *Gopuranchya Pradeshat* (1952), he writes about his travels in south India. His descriptions of places reflect a sensitive and keen mind (Sheorey 1988, 1336–37).

Arvind Gokhale (1919) has earned his literary reputation through his contribution to the Marathi short story in the postindependence period. He has stayed with the genre throughout his career when his contemporaries ranged over other modes. As is common with many postindependence writers, an individual is the focal point of his stories. Both men and women, severally and in their relationships, have been the subjects of his stories. They are examined in different locales and situations. His stories are characterized by elegance, economy, restraint, and structure. His first collection, *Nazarana,* was published in 1944. He has written at a steady pace to produce more than 25 collections, of which *Maher* (1949), *Mithila* (1959), *Anamika* (1961), and *Nakoshi* (1977) are notable. Gokhale also made a conscious effort to sustain the short story as a genre in recent years. He brought out anthologies of short stories by other authors in

Marathi. He has written about the work of well-known short story writers in other regional languages as well as in Pakistan and Bangladesh (Sheorey 1988, 1437–38).

P. B. Bhave (1910–80) was a productive writer, with 26 collections of short stories, 17 novels, eight plays, and 12 collections of articles. He was among the early writers who rejuvenated the short story in Marathi. His strong orthodox views color his work, his characters, and their relationships.

Novels and short stories by Vyankatesh Madgulkar (1927) contributed to the popular interest in literature after the 1950s. His novel *Bangarwadi* (1955) revolves around the experience of a young schoolteacher who moves into a small village. The initial feeling of being out of place gives way to an affinity for the people and the village. The novel is notable for its deceptively simple and direct style. In his later works, like *Mandeshi Manase* (1972) and *Goshti Gharakadila* (1977), he continues to draw on his knowledge of rural Maharashtra. He, along with D. M. Mirasdar and Shankar Patil, have popularized storytelling as a literary event. Shankar Patil's stories are also situated in rural Maharashtra, but his subjects show greater variety, and his treatment of his characters and situations goes beyond the apparent dissonance.

G. A. Kulkarni (1923–87), who brought new strength and vitality to the Marathi short story, is admittedly the most distinguished exponent of that genre. A contemporary of Gangadhar Gadgil, Arvind Gokhale, and Vyankatesh Madgulkar, he did not subscribe to the cause of modernism in literature. He charted his own separate course and cultivated new acuity and taste for a class of faithful readers. He has written at a steady pace over the years. His well-known collections of short stories include *Nila Sawala, Parwa, Hirave Rawe, Raktachandan, Sanjashakun, Ramalkhuna,* and *Kusumgunja.* His *Kajalamaya* received the Sahitya Akademi Award.

G. A. Kulkarni, too, has created a world of his own where his characters are in pursuit of the unknowable destiny. A dark mood reflects the inscrutable ways in which destiny shadows his characters, male and female. His use of symbolism, allegory, and irony provides his stories a unique texture and ethos. His world encompasses a wide diversity of locales, situations, characters, and experiences; yet, it is demarcated by the region bordering Maharashtra and Karnataka. His characters generally live in small towns, villages, and settlements in this region, but his stories cannot be classified under "rural literature," because the mythic, allegorical experiences make it difficult to sort out the realities from dreams, themes, and meditations. Yet, it is possible for the reader to identify with his characters, places, and experiences because of his keen observation of human, animal, and social worlds in their beauty and deformity. Gadgil (1980) observes that characters in Kulkarni's world are multifaceted, but they are not independent. They lead their lives as if they are puppets guided by an unseen hand and are unable to change the direction. Why they follow that path to their demise or why they cannot change it by their volition is not known. In that sense, his work is a reversal of direction fostered by the modernist short story in Marathi.

Gauri Deshpande (1942) is one of the important women writers in contemporary Marathi literature. She has also published three collections of her poetry in English. She has made her mark on the Marathi short story and novel with themes and concerns that are closer to upper-middle-class cosmopolitan women (Raykar 1988, 932–33). Her *Eka Paan Galavaya* (1980) is a collection of three long stories. "Turungatil Patre" is a story of an urbane and sensitive young woman who is trying to comprehend her relationships to men in her life. The second story in the collection, "Madhya Latapatita," is again a story of a happily married woman in that anxious transitory phase of approaching middle age. She is unsure of the meaning and purpose of her married life. She leaves her husband, with whom she is living in a foreign country, and returns to Bombay to reassess the meaning she was seeking. The last story in the collection, "Eka Paan Galavaya," is about Radha, a woman past her middle age who has lost her husband recently. With a remarkable sensitivity, Deshpande depicts her struggles to free herself from the bonds of her children and friends to face her life ahead. Her recent novels, *Teruo ani Kahi Dooraparyant* (1985), *Ahe He Asa Ahe* (1985), and *Chandrike Ga Chandrike* (1987), show her quest to explore different dimensions of life in a refreshing way.

Regional Literature

The body of literature recognized in Marathi as "regional literature" owes much to the work of S. N. Pendse (1913). His novels have focused on lives and circumstances in a specific region of Maharashtra, namely, northern Konkan. His intimate knowledge of the economy, environment, and culture helps him re-create it with authenticity in his novels (Deshpande and Rajadhyaksha 1988). In his maiden novel, *Elgar* (1949), he handles the sensitive theme of communal discord in the wake of tragic events of Noakhali in a coastal village. *Haddapar* (1950) and *Garambicha Bapu* (1951) established his reputation in the Marathi literary world. His characters of school teacher Raje and Bapu are memorable. In *Garambicha Bapu,* he utilizes the natural environment of Konkan and the tradition-bound ways of the village community to narrate a romantic story. *Hatya* (1954) and its sequel, *Kalandar* (1959), *Yashoda* (1957), *Rathachakra* (1962), *Lawhali* (1966), and *Octopus* (1972) are representative of his work. He focuses on realistic pictures of the region and its people.

Jayawant Dalvi (1925) is a prolific writer who has handled short story, novel, humor, and drama proficiently (Govilkar 1988a, 843). He has more than 14 novels, 10 collections of short stories, eight plays, and more travelogues and collections of humorous stories. He writes with sensitivity, vigor, and compassion for human beings in contemporary society and their varied life-worlds. He has relied on the experiences of the middle class for his themes. However, in his novel *Chakra* (1963), he portrays the stark reality of slum life in a very provocative manner. This novel helped him in establishing his reputation as a competent writer. His other novels, *Sare Pravasi Ghadiche, Vedagala, Swagat,* and *Adhantari* are noteworthy. His play *Sandhya Chhaya* explores the problems and inner turmoil of an old couple. His other plays reflect his interest in contemporary social and political issues.

M. M. Karnik's (1933) stories are situated in South Konkan. Through his stories, he brings out the warmth and humor of people as well as the natural beauty of this coastal region.

G. N. Dandekar (1916) is a prolific writer who has written on history, religion, literature, culture, and mythology. He has also contributed to various literary genres but is known for his historical novels set in Marathi history, like *Kadambarimaya Shivakala, Baya Daar Ughada, Harahar Mahadeva,* and *Jhunjhar Machi.* He continues the tradition of romantic portrayal of Maratha history as part of cultural revivalism. The transitional period from colonial control to political independence and the waning traditional values in the wake of modern industrial society have helped him to sustain that tradition. His reaction to social change is to romanticize traditional society and its ways. The remorseful and nostalgic antimodern attitude reverberates in his *Shitu* (1955), *Padghavali* (1956), *Pawanakathacha Dhondi* (1958), and *Machiwarala Budha* (1958).

Gramina Sahitya

Gramina sahitya, or rural literature, focuses on life in rural Maharashtra (Yadav 1988, 1467–68). The focus is on the ways of life, traditions, and values of common people in villages. There is also a concern about the impact of urbanization and urban lifestyles, economic development, democratization and its influence on traditional hierarchies, and so on. It is interested in the conflict of two different worldviews: urban and rural, modern and traditional.

After independence and more so after Maharashtra state became a linguistically unified state and after the spread of education, economic planning, cooperatives, transportation and means of communication, *panchayati raj* (village government), and so on, a group of writers came forth from rural Maharashtra who could articulate the ethos of the countryside better. For more than 100 years, the literary output of the urban, middle-class, educated society was identified with Marathi literature. It represented their values, concerns, ideologies, and class consciousness almost to the exclusion of people from rural areas.

Rural literature has drawn attention to the distinctive features and problems of rural life. It has shown the wide diversity in dialects, customs, natural environment, and so on that exists in rural parts of Maharashtra. The folk literature and its forms that have flourished for centuries are less often employed as preferred modes of expression. R. V. Dighe is known for his realistic portrayal of rural life in Maharashtra, with which he was familiar from his childhood. He is recognized as the first to introduce this category, *gramin sahitya,* in Marathi. His major novels include *Panakala* (1939), *Sarai* (1943), and *Pada Re Panya*

(1958). He also wrote short stories depicting lives of rural people. Though influenced by the works of H. N. Apte, Thomas Hardy, Sir Walter Scott, and Feodor Dostoyevsky, he delved deep into his own experiences and observations to sketch rural lives and its problems like untouchability, land tenure, and landlessness (Dhere 1988, 1044–45).

Raosaheb Borade (1940) is credited for bringing the realities of Marathwada to mainstream Marathi literature (Manchankar 1988, 561). He is among the first generation of authors after independence who brought a new awareness and realism from their personal experiences of life in rural areas. His novel *Pachola* (1971) is a story of emotional stresses created in the lives of village craftsmen because of modernization. Narration by Parvati, the wife of a tailor, brings out the human dimensions of social change. The entire novel is written in Usmanabadi dialect, which lends it authenticity and charm. He has published more than 14 collections of short stories exploring different facets of rural life. Even the titles of his collections reflect his roots in rural life, for example, *Perani* (Sowing), *Malani* (Threshing), *Valvan* (Drying), and *Rakhan* (Guarding the Crop). He focuses on family as a unit and the emotional ties that fuse its members. He has focused on tensions in these relationships by privations, especially those felt by women. The impact of social institutions, customs, and traditions on individuals and community is explored with deep sympathy.

Historical Novel

Ranjit Desai (1928) is a versatile writer who excels in portrayal of historical times and figures (Govilkar 1988, 927–28). His novels *Swami* (1965) and *Shriman Yogi* (1968) established him as a premier writer of historical novels. As in earlier novels in this category, the attempt is to resuscitate the grandeur and glory of the times of Shivaji and the Peshavas. He succeeds in that enterprise. He is very meticulous in detailing sociopolitical conditions of the times. His craftsmanship, development of characters, and attention to structure are notable. In his *Shriman Yogi,* based on the life of Shivaji, is a chapter on the relationship between Ramdas and Shivaji as the teacher and the pupil. This relationship, as mentioned earlier, has been challenged on the basis of historical documents. His other historical novels, including *Lakshyawedha* (1980) and *Pawankhinda* (1980), also show his proclivity to research his themes, times, and characters. In preface to his novel *Lakshyawedha,* he writes that historical facts and research are not adequate; the author has to let his imagination play a role. He has been criticized for his propensity to exaggeration and sentimentality in his work. He has written several plays, including *Tansen, Bandha Reshamache, Ramashastri, Kanchanmruga, Garudajhepa,* and *Varasa,* but his play based on the novel *Swami* has proved to be more popular.

Among other prominent historical novelists, N. S. Inamdar (1923) ranks high. Inamdar, too, digs into Maratha history for his characters and settings. His *Jhep, Jhunja, Mantravegala, Rau, Shahenshah, Shikasta,* and *Rajeshri* deal with the life and times of Shivaji, his son Sambhaji, and Aurangazeb. His work is characterized by attention to detail and skillful use of narration to develop his heroes. Shivaji Sawant (1940) has written novels using both historical and mythical characters. His *Mrutyunjaya* depicts the life of Karna, a character from *Mahabharata,* but symbolically expresses the plight of the *dalits.* His *Chhava* is based on the life of Sambhaji.

New Trends

Bhalchandra Nemade's first novel, *Kosla,* came out in 1963. It represented the beginning of a new trend in the Marathi novel. It is a story of Pandurang Sangavikar, a young man with rural upbringing who moves to Pune for higher education. This young man is alienated in his new social setting. Experiencing a persistent feeling of estrangement, he returns home, only to encounter further disillusionment. Pandurang's acute experiences of his sister's death, his father's domination, and his own financial dependence are combined in a powerful way. The book marks the beginning of existentialist literature in Marathi and a reduced influence of the Phadke-Khandekar paradigm. *Kosla*'s literary success provided an impetus to literature based on existentialist philosophy, which was influential in Europe through the works of Sartre and Camus. His subsequent novels, *Bidhar* (1975), *Jarila,* and *Jhul* (1979), have not been able to sustain the promise. However, many others took their cues to write within the existentialist mode at that time and since then. Notable among them are Bhau Padhye, Vasant Abaji Dahake, Kiran Nagarkar, T. V. Sardeshmukh, and C. T. Khanolkar (Machwe 1988, 1245–46).

Dilip Chitre took on the cause of modernism in Marathi poetry after Mardhekar. He is known for his poetry, short stories, and literary criticism. He acknowledges his affinity with surrealism and expressionism in Europe, which has made a deep impact on his literary work. There is a meditative quality congruous with the *bhakti* poets like Tukaram and Dnyaneshwar. In his work, there is a continuous search for the warp and irrationality of contemporary life. Over the years, literary critics have had no qualms about his sensitivity and intellect, but they have criticized him for his elitism and deliberate abstruseness.

Chitre was one of the leaders of the little magazines movement in the urban Marathi literary world (Hatkanagalekar 1988, 737). His publication *Shabda* was influential among those who were looking to the West, especially the United States, for new ideas and inspiration in the 1960s. He remained an icon for those who were advocating modernity in literature in the Western conception. His initial collection of poems, *Kavita* (1960), is representative of this period. After that period, he has been diligently attempting to mediate the Western aesthetic and literary traditions with the indigenous. His collection of short stories, *Orpheus* (1968), his travelogue, *Sheba Ranichya Shodhat* (1970), and his later works, *Kavitenantarchya Kavita* (1978), *Kavya* (1982), *Tirakasa ani Chaukasa*

(1990), and *Ekuna Kavita* (1991), reflect his conscious search for identity, a dilemma facing every sensitive, educated Indian laid exposed to Western culture.

Manik Godghate (1940), *Grace,* is one of the important contemporary poets. Like many of his contemporaries, he is trying to convey the experiences of struggles to comprehend the meaning of existence. Grace's refined and perceptive mind draws on traditional images to express the poignancy of human existence. The lyrical quality, wondrous imagination, and sensuous, colorful poignancy characterize his literary work (Machwe 1988, 1432). His first collection of poems, *Sandhyakalachya Kavita* (1967), brought him recognition and honor. His *Rajaputra and Darling* (1974) and *Chandramadhavicha Pradesh* (1977) were well recognized by critics and readers. He has also published collections of essays, *Churchbell* (1974) and *Mitava* (1987).

C. T. Khanolkar's (1930–76) multifaceted talents in literature were lost by his premature death.[17] He wrote poetry, novels, and plays with distinction and received critical acclaim. His world is shaped and circumscribed by the natural and social environment of his native Konkan. The social world that is intrinsic to his world is essentially rural and traditional. He blends realism with highly imaginative and symbolic re-creations. The urban images that he creates in his poetry are simultaneously vapid and destitute and remind one of the Mardhekerian landscape. In his poetry, he tends to ask philosophical questions to which there are no answers, or puzzles to which there are no solutions, and with lucidity he delves into a meditation on the meanings of life. A simplicity of expression distinguishes his poetry from that of his contemporaries.

Besides his three collections of poetry, Khanolkar also wrote six original plays and more adaptations. His *Eka Shoonya Bajirao* (1966) is a memorable play for its exploration of surreality. His *Abhogi, Rakheli, Avadhya,* and *Sagesoyare* take place at a level of reality that is neither symbolic nor phantasmic nor psychoanalytic. There is a reflective thought informed by deeply held values that has interpreted the reality. His 10 published novels depict the grinding lives of lower-middle-class people. Arrogant and moneyed people provide the counterpoise within the established traditions. Social customs and traditions dominate social interaction in his novels, but there is a conscious attempt to analyze their impact.

The literary reputation of P. L. Deshpande (1919) rests on his plays, humorous stories, and one-man performances. He has attracted urban, middle-class audiences with his versatility as an entertainer. His humorous stories primarily draw on experiences and responses of the urban lower middle class to everyday situations. His early collections, *Khogir Bharati* (1949), *Nasti Uthatheva* (1952), and *Gola Berij* (1960), have been popular.

He has adapted works of Western playwrights in Marathi over the years (Manohar 1988, 934), for example, Gogol's *Inspector General* as *Amaladar* (1952), Rudolf Basier's *Barrets of Wimpole Street* as *Sundar Mi Honar* (1958), Shaw's *Pygmalion* as *Ti Phularani,* Brecht's *The Three Penny Opera* as *Teen Paishancha Tamasha* (1978), and Sophocles' *Oedipus Rex* as *Raja Oedipus* (1979). His original play, *Tujhe ahe Tujapashi* (1957), presents two contrasting worldviews, indulgence of Kakaji and Gandhian idealism of Acharya. The younger characters attracted to the Gandhian message of simple life are finally converted to a life of comfort and enjoyment. The play has proved extremely popular with urban, educated audiences. Its message helped them to repulse Gandhian ideals for their hypocrisy and idiosyncracies. It was a variant of Nehruvian repudiation of Gandhism as inappropriate for the modern world.

Durga Bhagwat (1910) symbolizes the conscience of intellectuals and intellectual traditions in contemporary Maharashtra. A noted anthropologist and folklorist, she has made a mark on Marathi literature through her creative and critical work. Her *Rutuchakra* (1956), *Bhava Mudra* (1960), *Vyasaparva* (1962), *Ruparanga* (1967), and *Pais* (1970) well represent her creative contributions, and *Lokasahityachi Ruparekha* and *Ketakari Kadambari* (1967) represent her critical works. She writes in a remarkably simple and informal style (Kulkarni 1988, 426). Her *Rutuchakra* is unique in Marathi literature for its sensitive and informed description of nature in different seasons, its influence on, and relation to, human lives, folklore, and customs. She has brought her scholarship and mature understanding to explore many new subjects; for example, *Aswal* (1982) is a study of Indian bears. She was elected the president of Marathi Sahitya Sammelan (an annual conference of Marathi writers) at Karad in 1975 during the emergency. From her position, she spoke out against the censorship and restraints on freedom of speech imposed on writers. *Mukta* (1977) is a collection of her speeches on many topics germane to writers. This collection reflects her dedication and unequivocal commitment to freedom of expression.

Drama

Vijay Tendulkar (1928) has remained the preeminent dramatist in Marathi for the last three decades. With his plays translated and staged in other regional languages, he has gained wider recognition and reputation. Both Tendulkar and other younger playwrights wanted to give theater "a new form" and experiment with all aspects of it, including content, acting, decor, and audience communication (Nadkarni 1990, 9). He started writing plays in the 1950s, but they remained within the experimental and theater groups. Here the term "experimental theater" can be interpreted as a synonym for "modern" and "Western." In his early one-act plays, he used the techniques common in contemporary European and American theater. His *Shrimant* (1955) deals with the familiar theme of the conflict between the rich and the poor in a capitalist society. It also explores the predicament of a lower-middle-class family with the problem of premarital pregnancy. Both *Shrimant* and the subsequent *Gharate Amuche Chhan* deal with the corrupt, money-driven, and selfish lives of the rich who are morally vacuous. Many of his early plays are fairly conventional in dramatic form and style, but in his later ones he has experimented with both, but not in a contrived fashion.

Gangadhar Gadgil (1980, 48–78) divides Tendulkar's work in two periods,

1953–68 and 1968–80, for convenience of analysis. The plays included in the first period are *Shrimant, Manus Nawache Bet, Ashi Pakhare Yeti, Saree Ga Saree, Mi Jinkalo, Mi Haralo, Shantata, Court Chalu Ahe,* and *Madhalya Bhinti.* The plays written during the first period focus on the lives and concerns of lower-middle-class characters: financial strains, specter of joblessness, inadequate income of those with jobs, problems of housing and high rent, marriage and oppression of women, and so on. The stark realism of his work is accentuated by his use of humor and satire, with telling effect. He has an uncanny ability to develop a complete image of the characters with relative ease through few but cogent details. In *Shantata* and *Court Chalu Ahe,* he has interwoven the rehearsal of a play and a real life story to produce intense dramatic encounters where reality and fiction become difficult to separate.

The plays in the second period break away from the milieu of the middle class and probe the sociopolitical and historical realm. *Gidhade* (1971), *Sakharam Binder* (1972), *Ghashiram Kotwal* (1973), *Bhalyakaka* (1974), *Bhau Murarrao* (1975), and *Bebi* (1975) are, in Gadgil's judgment, better conceived compared to some of the first period. *Ghashiram Kotwal,* his most popular play, was published in 1973, but it was performed in December 1972. This play, a dance and musical spectacle, on one level, is a biting commentary on the hypocrisy of the dominant castes/classes in society, on another level. Its characters are historical figures, and it is set in the Peshwa period, but it is not a historical play. It is a fictional account of the social circumstances that can create characters like Ghashiram. The theme of the play, the debauchery of the orthodox Brahmans of Pune and impoverished Ghashiram's willingness to offer his daughter to the demands of lecherous Nana Phadanavis, created a storm of social protest in Pune. Tendulkar's play makes use of chorus as well as *kirtan,* a folk music form used primarily to narrate religiomythical stories, with incisive effect.

Barve (1990, 22–25) has argued that Tendulkar "can rejoice in the beauty and nobility in the world but he is not blind to the ugly and ignoble in it. . . . [H]is literary tendency is of realistic, soft but poignant expression." Gadgil (1980) has argued that Tendulkar's work is wanting in many ways by literary standards when compared to his reputation and popularity. Barve (1990, 23), on the other hand, asserts that Tendulkar is interested in "individual identity of man and his social existence." Tendulkar's work may not seem to carry the "burden of intellectual speculation," but it offers "something, beyond words." There is little doubt that Tendulkar's work has taken Marathi theater away from the clichéd and contrived work of earlier generations.

Anil Barve (1948–84) was a political activist in the Naxalite movement in Andhra Pradesh and other parts of India. His journalistic reports brought him to prominence. His first novel, *Thank You, Mr. Glad* (1975), is a story of an encounter between Virbhushan Patnaik, a Naxalite prisoner, and Mr. Glad, the British superintendent of the jail. Patnaik is awaiting his execution in the Rajmahendry jail for his political activities. The conversion of the autocratic jailer, who shoots his ward at his request and takes his place in the cell, is riveting.

He adapted the play in 1977 with success. His other novels, *Dongar Mhatara Jhala* (1977) and *Akara Koti Gallon Panee* (1978), deal with tensions between an aging communist and a retired army officer and between a corrupt mine owner and a decent engineer, respectively. His play *Hamidabaichi Kothi* (1979) is a tale of a prostitute, Hamidabai, whose *kothi* (brothel) has fallen on lean days. The play captures the suffering of the woman and her attempts to escape the brothel life. Barve goes beyond the transient emotional or subjective elements to focus on the social origins of the tragedy. Barve has brought realism with all the starkness back to the Marathi novel and drama (Manohar 1988, 399–400).

Mahesh Elkunchwar (1939) and Satish Alekar (1949) represent the new generation of playwrights who followed, like Tendulkar, the path away from the professional Marathi theater. Elkunchwar's plays have drawn social criticism throughout his career. He has shown willingness to take on topics that go against middle-class moral values and orthodox social norms. His plays have been translated into English and Hindi. He has been publishing plays since 1970, and his plays have been staged by prominent producers (Machwe 1988, 1160). His first play, *Sultan,* was followed by *Garbo* (1973), *Rudravarsha* (1974), *Vasanakand* (1975), *Yatanaghar* (1977), *Party* (1981), and *Wada Chirebandi* (1987). In his quest to explore interaction between human relationships and the morality that supposedly holds society together, he projects the conflictual outcome. His one-act plays, starting with *Sultan,* brought new intensity to the genre in Marathi. Critics have faulted him for focusing on sex and violence to attract audiences (Kanadey 1991, 28–29) or for openly discussing social taboos like the incestual relationship between brother and sister in his *Vasanakand.* Others have praised him for bringing to light the practices that society does not want its members to discuss or practice and thus pushing the limits of social discourse.

Satish Alekar also has stayed primarily with experimental theater. His plays *Micky ani Memsaheb* and *Mahanirvan* (1974) established him as a promising young playwright. His other plays include *Mahapur* (1977), *Begum Barve* (1979), and *Shaniwar, Raviwar* (1982). His *Mahanirvan* is a satire of the practices and morality of the urban, lower-middle-class Brahmans. The death of a tenement dweller provides a platform to launch his black comedy, which alternates between a farce and tragedy.

SUMMING UP

The economy, polity, and society of Maharashtra were influenced by the British colonial rule, as was the literature. The relative impact varied in different periods in the past, depending on the larger forces at work. Throughout the period, the label "Marathi" was predominantly defined by the Brahman, educated, and middle class, which subsumed many divergent, congruent, and contradictory social structures and relations. Orthodoxy, progressive groups, revivalism, and reformist forces have contributed to this discourse, but non-Brahman groups were treated as marginal to this process.

Since the first decades of this century, those who promoted and articulated the cause of modernity in the name of change, newness, and universality were borrowing from the West. This was to be seen in adaptations and translations of literature from Europe and North America. The anxiety to become modern, with few exceptions, has led to mimicry or withdrawal into an illusory or torpid outlook on life. One has to read annual reviews in Sahitya Akademi's journal, *Indian Literature,* to confirm the uninspired literary output in Marathi.

In this enervated condition, the *dalit* writers have been infusing some passion, but their work is downplayed by the dominant groups. This has led to the formation of various literary organizations representing disparate interests pursuing different goals, leaving modernity's project in Marathi literature with an uncertain prospect.

NOTES

1. The regions of present Maharashtra have been identified by various authors in different ways. All of them emphasize the impact of political rule, topography, and natural resources on socioeconomic conditions and cultural identity (Karve 1968; Omvedt 1976; Surana and Bedakihala 1988, 210–13).

2. This section is largely based on Deshpande and Rajadhyaksha (1988), Karhade (1981), and Nasirabadkar (1976).

3. A controversy surrounds the interpretation of his call to unity and formation of Maharashtra. Did he imply unity of all Marathi speakers or of Marathas, a cluster of artisan-cultivating castes? Was he providing orthodox interpretation of the Maratha upsurge under the leadership of Shivaji in his *Dasbodha* (1632–82)? What role, if any, did he play during Shivaji's rule? The nationalist historians, mostly Brahmans, have insisted that Ramdas met Shivaji in 1649 and that Ramdas was his spiritual and political guru, who guided him in the formation of the Hindu nation. On the other hand, others have argued that Shivaji had no idea till 1658 about Ramdas's existence. A. G. Pawar has asserted, on the basis of historical evidence, that "Ramdas was not the political guru of Shivaji. For that matter Shivaji had no political guru at all. He received no inspiration, no guidance from anyone in creating 'a new Maharashtra.' He was, indeed, his own guru" (cited in Nasirabadkar 1976, 141). This controversy reflects the tensions between Brahmans and non-Brahmans that have persisted in Maharashtra till today.

4. K. S. Rajyashree (1991) is a useful source for understanding the dynamics of British needs, response by Maharashtrians, and changes in Marathi language.

5. The attempts by the British colonizers to impose an education system on the natives of the Indian subcontinent in the nineteenth century were intended for ideological pacification and reformation of a potentially mutinous population. Vishwanathan (1989) argues convincingly that this system was transferred to England for a different but related exercise.

6. Rajyashree (1991) provides a fascinating account of how printing, technology, and the colonial rule led to the standardization of Marathi language. He points out that the emphasis by the British on precision in the use of language created uniform rules in writing, which, in turn, created the impression that there was a standard form of spoken Marathi.

7. In the initial years of *Nibandhamala,* he dealt only with literary themes. He had to close his earlier magazine, *Shalapatrak,* started by his father, because he was openly critical of the British government (Deshpande and Rajadhyaksha 1988; Nanda 1977).

8. Vishnushastri Chiplunkar "fancied he was doing for Marathi literature in the nineteenth century what Dr. Samuel Johnson had done for English literature in the eighteenth. His Marathi style, with its rhetorical and colorful prose, was consciously modelled after Macaulay. He wanted to infuse something of the sharpness, vigor and flexibility of the English language into Marathi prose. 'The English language,' he wrote, 'is the nourishing mother of the Marathi tigress' " (Nanda 1977, 28).

9. The phrase is borrowed from a documentary on black history produced by California Newsreel, 1968.

10. Historians of Maharashtra have focused exclusively on developments in Pune and Bombay and neglected the sociocultural or political happenings in Kolhapur, Nagpur, Nanded, or Ratnagiri.

11. N. M. Lokhande, an associate of Jyotiba Phule, had started organizing activities in the 1880s among textile millworkers in Bombay (Sarkar 1983, 133).

12. Sarkar (1983) Chatterjee (1986), Karhade (1981), Brown (1986), Hutchins (1967, and 1973) were useful sources in understanding socioeconomic issues discussed in this section.

13. Karhade (1981) has appendixes listing different plays written during this time influenced by Gandhism and Marxism.

14. V. R. Kanadey's essay on Anil and Sharatchandra Muktibodh was very useful in understanding their work (1991, 131–43).

15. The women characters of Joshi, Ketkar, and Warerkar presented the predicament of women in Maharashtra and their efforts to overcome their plight, but they were not received with understanding or sympathy by society at large.

16. Chatterjee (1986) is a helpful book in understanding the nationalist project in India.

17. Gadgil (1980) was a useful resource for the works of G. A. Kulkarni, Vijay Tendulkar, and C. T. Khanolkar.

WORKS CITED

Anderson, B. *Imagined Communities: Reflections on the Origin and Spread of Nationalism.* London: Verso, 1983.

Barve, C. "Vijay Tendulkar: The Man Who Explores the Depths of Life." In *Studies in Contemporary Indian Drama,* edited by S. Pandey and F. Taraporewala. New Delhi: Prestige Books, 1990, 22–25.

Basu, T., et al. *Khaki Shorts, Saffron Flags: A Critique of the Hindu Right.* New Delhi: Orient Longman, 1993.

Bhave, P. "Experimental Marathi Theatre" In *Studies in Contemporary Indian Drama,* edited by S. Pandey and F. Taraporewala. New Delhi: Prestige Books, 1990, 16–21.

Brown, J. *Modern India: The Origins of an Asian Democracy.* Delhi: Oxford University Press, 1986.

Byres, T. J. "Land Reform, Industrialization and the Marketed Surplus in India: An Essay on the Power of Rural Bias." In *Peasants, Landlords and Government,* edited by D. Lehmann. New York: Holmes and Meier, 1974, 221–61.

Chatterjee, P. *Nationalist Thought and the Colonial World: A Derivative Discourse?* London: Zed Books, 1986.

———. *The Nation and Its Fragments: Colonial and Postcolonial Histories.* Princeton, NJ: Princeton University Press, 1993.

Das, S. K. *A History of Indian Literature, 1800–1910.* Vol. 8. New Delhi: Sahitya Akademi, 1991.

Datta, A., ed. *Encyclopaedia of Indian Literature.* Vols. 1, 2. New Delhi: Sahitya Akademi, 1988.

de Bary, W. T., et al., eds. *Sources of Indian Tradition.* New York: Columbia University Press, 1958.

Deshpande, Kusumavati, and M. V. Rajadhyaksha. *A History of Marathi Literature.* New Delhi: Sahitya Akademi, 1988.

Dhere, A. *Encyclopaedia of Indian Literature.* Vol. 2. New Delhi: Sahitya Akademi, 1988.

Gadgil, G. *Aajakalache Sahityika.* Pune: Utkarsha Prakashan, 1980.

Govilkar, L. *Encyclopaedia of Indian Literature.* Vol. 1. New Delhi: Sahitya Akademi, 1988.

Hatkanagalekar, M. D. *Encyclopaedia of Indian Literature.* Vol. 1. New Delhi: Sahitya Akademi, 1988.

Hutchins, F. *The Illusion of Permanence: British Imperialism in India.* Princeton, NJ: Princeton University Press, 1967.

———. *India's Revolution: Gandhi and the Quit India Movement.* Cambridge: Harvard University Press, 1973.

Kanadey, Vishwas R. *Contemporary Marathi Literature.* Delhi: D. K., 1991.

Karhade, S. *Arwachin Marathi Sahityachi Sanskrutika Parshwabhumi.* Bombay: Lokasahitya Gruha, 1981.

Karve, Irawati. *Marathi Lokanchi Sanskruti.* 2d ed. Pune: Deshmukh, 1962.

———. *Maharashtra State Gazetteer: Maharashtra, Land and Its People.* Bombay: Directorate of Government Printing, Stationery and Publications, Maharashtra State, 1968.

Kaviraj, S. "On State, Society and Discourse in India." In *Rethinking Third World Politics,* edited by James Manor. London: Longman, 1991, 72–99.

Kosambi, D. D. "The Bourgeoisie Comes of Age in India." *Science and Society* 10: 4 (1946): 392–98.

Kulkarni, B. *Encyclopaedia of Indian Literature.* Vol. 1. New Delhi: Sahitya Akademi, 1988.

Machwe, P. *Encyclopaedia of Indian Literature.* Vol. 2. New Delhi: Sahitya Akademi, 1988.

Malshe, S. G. *Encyclopaedia of Indian Literature.* Vol. 1. New Delhi: Sahitya Akademi, 1988.

Manchankar, R. B. *Encyclopaedia of Indian Literature.* Vol. 1. New Delhi: Sahitya Akademi, 1988.

Mande, Prabhakar B. *Lokasahityache Swarupa.* Aurangabad: Parimal Prakashan, 1978.

Manohar, M. *Encyclopaedia of Indian Literature.* Vol. 1. New Delhi: Sahitya Akademi, 1988: 399–400.

Mukherjee, M. *Realism and Reality.* Delhi: Oxford University Press, 1985.

Nadkarni, D. "Contemporary Marathi Theatre" In *Studies in Contemporary Indian*

Drama, edited by S. Pandey and F. Taraporewala. New Delhi: Prestige Books, 1990, 9–15.

Nanda, B. R. *Gokhale: The Indian Moderates and the British Raj.* Princeton, NJ: Princeton University Press, 1977.

Nandy, A. *Intimate Enemy: Loss and Recovery of Self under Colonialism.* Delhi: Oxford University Press, 1983.

Nasirabadkar, L. R. *Prachina Marathi Wangamayache Itihasa.* 2d. ed. Kolhapur: MV Phadke, 1976.

Nehru, J. *An Autobiography with Musings on Recent Events in India.* London: Bodley Head, 1938.

Nemade, B. "Marathi Kadambari: Prerana va Swaroopa." *Anushtubh* (September–October 1980).

Omvedt, Gail. *Cultural Revolt in a Colonial Society: The Non-Brahman Movement in Western India: 1873 to 1930.* Bombay: Scientific Socialist Education Trust, 1976.

Pandey, S., and F. Taraporewala, eds. *Studies in Contemporary Indian Drama.* New Delhi: Prestige Books, 1990.

Rajyashree, K. S. "Consequences of Printing on the Written Marathi." *Indian Journal of Applied Linguistics* 17:1 (January–June 1991): 109–25.

Raykar, S. *Encyclopaedia of Indian Literature.* Vol. 1. New Delhi: Sahitya Akademi, 1988.

Sarkar, S. *Modern India 1885–1947.* Delhi: Macmillan India, 1983.

Sheorey, I. *Encyclopaedia of Indian Literature.* Vol. 2. New Delhi: Sahitya Akademi, 1988.

Soman, A. *Sahitya ani Samajik Sandarbha.* Pune: Pratima Prakashan, 1989.

Surana, Pannalal, and Kishor Bedakihala, eds. *Ajacha Maharashtra.* Pune: Shrividya Prakashan, 1988.

Thapar, Romila. *A History of India.* Harmondsworth: Penguin, 1966.

Vishwanathan, G. *Masks of Conquest: Literary Study and British Rule in India.* New York: Columbia University Press, 1989.

Yadav, A. *Encyclopaedia of Indian Literature.* Vol. 2. New Delhi: Sahitya Akademi, 1988.

SELECTED PRIMARY BIBLIOGRAPHY

Agarkar, G. G. *Agarkar-Lekha Sangraha.* 2d ed. Edited by G. P. Pradhan. New Delhi: Sahitya Akademi, 1971.

Alekar, Satish. *Jhulata Pula.* Pune: Nilkanth Prakashan, 1973.

———. *Mahanirvana.* Pune: Nilkanth Prakashan, 1974.

———. *Mahapura.* Pune: Nilkanth Prakashan, 1976.

———. *Begam Barve.* Pune: Nilkanth Prakashan, 1979.

———. *Shaniwar, Raviwar.* Pune: Nilkanth Prakashan, 1982.

Apte, H. N. *Pan Lakshat Kon Gheto?* 10th ed. Pune: Ramyakatha Prakashan, 1972a.

———. *Suryodaya.* 5th ed. Pune: Ramyakatha Prakashan, 1972b.

———. *Shakespearechya rupantaranchi praikshane.* Bombay: Mumbai Marathi Granthasangrahalaya, 1979.

Atre, P. K. *Jhenduchi Phule.* Bombay: Parchure Prakashan, 1972.

———. *Nivadaka Atre.* Edited by Bal Samant. Pune: Continental Prakashan, 1978.

———. *Gudde ani Gudagulya.* Bombay: Divine Prakashan, 1980.

Bapat, Vasant. *Pravasachya Kavita.* Bombay: Mauj Prakashan, 1982.

Barlingay, S. S. *Mi-pana Majhe*. Pune: Shrividya Prakashan, 1982.

Barve, Achyut. *Shobhechi Phule*. Pune: Menaka Prakashan, 1964.

———. *Kalideoscope*. Bombay: Majestic Book Stall, 1977.

———. *Sukhada*. Bombay: Majestic Book Stall, 1981.

———. *Hangover*. Bombay: Majestic Book Stall, 1983.

Barve, Anil. *Dongara Mhatara Jhala*. Bombay: Majestic Book Stall, 1977a.

———. *Thank You, Mister Glad*. Bombay: Popular Prakashan, 1977b.

———. *Hamidabaichi Kothi*. Bombay: Popular Prakashan, 1979.

Bhagwat, Durga. *Purva*. Pune: Nutan Prakashan, 1957.

———. *Roopranga*. Bombay: Popular Prakashan, 1967a.

———. *Rutuchakra*. 3d ed. Bombay: Popular Prakashan, 1967b.

———. *Athavale tase*. Bombay: Nana Joshi Prakashan, 1991.

Bhanage, S. *Dura Ghara Majhe*. Pune: Joshi Pustak Bhandar, 1972.

———. *Are Ashvatthama!* Pune: Continental Prakashan, 1975.

Bhave, P. B. *Dewhara: Kathasangraha*. 2d ed. Pune: Menaka Prakashan, 1977.

———. *Catai: Kathasangraha*. Pune: Menaka Prakashan, 1982.

———. *Nivadaka Pu. Bha. Bhave*. Edited by V. K. Varhadpande. New Delhi: Sahitya Akademi, 1987.

Borkar, B. B. *Kanchansandhya*. Bombay: Mauj Prakashan, 1981a.

———. *Vasavadatta: Eka Pranaya Natya*. Priyola: Jag Prakashan, 1981b.

———. *Samudrakathachi Ratra*. Pune: Suresh Agency, 1981c.

———. *Anuragini*. Pune: Suresh Agency, 1982a.

———. *Chandanyache Kavadase*. Bombay: Majestic Book Stall, 1982b.

———. *Pavalapurata Prakasha*. Kolhapur: Aloka Prakashan, 1983.

Buva, V. A. *Chori Kiya to Darana Kya?* Pune: Menaka Prakashan, 1966a.

———. *Pudhe Chalu Thevu*. Pune: Menaka Prakashan, 1966b.

Chiplunkar, V. *Nibandhamala*. 3d ed. Edited by V. V. Sathe. Pune: S. N. Joshi, 1926.

———. *Vishnupadi*. 2d ed. Edited by S. N. Banahatti. Pune: Suvichara Prakashan Mandala, 1974.

Chirmulay, S. W. *Kogja*. Bombay: Mauj Prakashan, 1973.

———. *Pool*. Bombay: Majestic Book Stall, 1991.

Chitre, Dilip. *Shiba Ranichya Shodhata*. Bombay: Majestic Book Stall, 1971.

———. *Kavitanantarachya Kavita*. Aurangabad: Vacha Prakashan, 1978.

———. *Kavya*. Bombay: Prasa Prakashan, 1982.

———. *Punha Tukarama*. Pune: S. K. Belvelkar, 1990a.

———. *Tirakasa ani Chaukasa*. Bombay: Lokvangmaya Gruha, 1990b.

———. *Ekuna Kavita*. Bombay: Popular Prakashan, 1992.

Dahake, Vasant A. *Pratibaddha ani martya*. Bombay: Mauj Prakashan, 1981.

———. *Shubhavartamana*. Bombay: Mauj Prakashan, 1987.

Dalvi, Jayawant. *Nivadaka Thanathanapala*. Bombay: Majestic Book Stall, 1969.

———. *Chakra*. Bombay: Majestic Book Stall, 1974.

———. *Athanga*. Bombay: Majestic Book Stall, 1977a.

———. *Barrister*. Bombay: Majestic Book Stall, 1977b.

———. *Gamatichya Goshti*. Bombay: Majestic Book Stall, 1983.

Damle, K. K. (*Keshavasut*) *Keshavsutanchi Kavita*. Bombay: Keshavasut Janmashatabdi Samiti, 1967.

Dandekar, G. N. *Purnamayechi Lekara*. Bombay: Majestic Book Stall, 1972.

———. *Mogara Phulala*. Bombay: Majestic Book Stall, 1975.

———. *Kille.* Bombay: Majestic Book Stall, 1979.
———. *Tambadphuti.* Bombay: Majestic Book Stall, 1982.
Desai, Kamal. *Kala Surya.* Bombay: Mauj Prakashan, 1975.
Desai, Ranajit. *Shrimana Yogi.* Poona: Deshmukh Prakashan, 1968.
———. *Lakshyavedha.* Belagaum: Navasahitya Prakasan, 1980a.
———. *Majha gava.* Kolhapur: Ajab Prakashan, 1980b.
Deshmukh, G. H. *Lokahitavadinchi Sata Patre.* Aundha: Usha Prakashan, 1940.
Deshpande, A. R. (*Anil*) *Bhagnamurti.* 2d ed. Pune: Vinash Prakashan, 1965.
———. *Dasapadi.* Bombay: Mauj Prakashan, 1976.
Deshpande, Gauri. *Ekaeka Paana galavaya.* Bombay: Mauj Prakashan, 1980.
———. *Ahe he asa ahe.* Bombay: Mauj Prakashan, 1985a.
———. *Chandrike ga Chandrike.* Bombay: Mauj Prakashan, 1985b.
———. *Teruo ani kahi duraparyanta.* Bombay: Mauj Prakashan, 1985c.
———. *Niragathi ani Chandrike ga, Sarike ga.* Bombay: Mauj Prakashan, 1987.
———. *Mukkama.* Bombay: Mauj Prakashan, 1992.
Deshpande, P. L. *Vyakti ani Valli.* Pune: Deshmukh Prakashan, 1962.
———. *Purvaranga.* Pune: Deshmukh Prakashan, 1963.
———. *Ganagota.* Pune: Deshmukh Prakashan, 1966.
———. *Hasavanuka.* Pune: Deshmukh Prakashan, 1968.
———. *Batatyachi Chaala.* Bombay: Mauj Prakashan, 1969.
———. *Teena Paishacha Tamasha.* Pune: Vishvakarma Sahityalaya, 1978.
———. *Raja Oedipus.* Bombay: Mauj Prakashan, 1979.
———. *Pu. La. Eka Saathavana.* 2d ed. Edited by J. Dalvi. Bombay: Majestic Book Stall, 1980.
Deval, G. B. *Sangeet Sharada.* New ed. Bombay: Balwant Pustak Bhandar, 1969.
Dhere, Aruna. *Urvashi.* Pune: Suresh Agency, 1989.
Dighe, R. V. *Sonaki: Adivasi Jivanavaril Kadambari.* Pune: Shrilekha Vachan Bhandar, 1979.
———. *Hirava Sana.* Pune: Thokala Prakashan, 1980.
Dnyaneshwar. *Amritanabhava.* Eng. ed. Pune: Ajay Prakashan, 1981.
———. *Sri Jnanadeva's Bhavartha Dipika: Otherwise Known as Jnaneshwari.* Eng. ed. Madras: Samata Books, 1979.
Eknath. *Sribhavartharamayana.* Edited by S. V. Dandekar et al. Bombay: Government of Maharashtra, 1982.
Elkunchwar, Mahesh. *Rudravarsha.* Nagpur: Ameya Prakashan, 1974.
———. *Vasanakanda.* Bombay: Mauj Prakashan, 1975.
———. *Party.* Bombay: Mauj Prakashan, 1981.
———. *Vada Chirebandi.* Bombay: Mauj Prakashan, 1987.
———. *"Atmakatha" ani "Pratibimba."* Bombay: Mauj Prakashan, 1989.
Gadgil, Bal. *Bashinga.* Pune: Omkar Prakashan, 1978a.
———. *Chimanaravacha nava avatara.* Pune: Indrayani Sahitya, 1978b.
———. *Lakhatila eka.* Nagpur: Ameya Prakashan, 1978c.
———. *Sukhi Manasacha Sadara.* Pune: Indrayani Sahitya, 1978d.
———. *Vashilyache Tattu.* Pune: Indrayani Sahitya, 1979.
———. *Konala hi thodakyat paduna deu.* Kolhapur: Minal Prakashan, 1980.
Gadgil, Gangadhar. *Khadaka ani Pani.* Bombay: Mauj Prakashan, 1966.
———. *Gopuranchya Pradeshata.* Pune: Suvichar Prakashan, 1971.
———. *Aathavana.* Pune: Inamdar Bandhu Prakashan, 1978.

———. *Panyavarachi Akshare.* Pune: Suvichar Prakashan Mandal, 1979.
———. *Aajakalache Sahityaka.* Pune: Utkarsha Prakashan, 1980.
———. *Palana.* Pune: Suparna Prakashan, 1981.
———. *Amhi Aaple Dhaddhopanta.* Pune: Shaana, 1982.
———. *Aasa ani Tasa.* Pune: Suparna Prakashan, 1983.
———. *Nivadaka Gangadhar Gadgil.* Pune: Suresh Agency, 1986.
Gadkari, R. G. *Poems of Govindagraj.* Eng. trans. by Sarojini Namjoshi and Suniti Namjoshi. Calcutta: Writers Workshop, 1968.
———. *Pimpalapana.* Pune: Continental Prakashan, 1970.
———. *Anakhi Gadkari.* Nagpur: Vidarbha Sahitya Sangh, 1981.
———. *Sampurna Gadkari.* Bombay: Maharashtra Rajya Sahitya Sanskruti Mandal, 1984.
Ghate, V. D. *Vicharavilasate.* Bombay: Mauj Prakashan, 1973.
Godghate, M. (*Grace*) *Churchbell.* Bombay: Popular Prakashan, 1974.
———. *Rajaputra ani Darling.* Nagpur: Ameya Prakashan, 1974.
———. *Chandramadhavicha Pradesh.* Bombay: Popular Prakashan, 1977.
———. *Mitava.* Bombay: Popular Prakashan, 1987.
Gokhale, Aravind. *Janma Khuna.* Pune: Continental Prakashan, 1963.
———. *Ekanta.* Pune: Pune Sahitya Vitarana, 1981a.
———. *Jagarana.* Pune: Pune Sahitya Vitarana, 1981b.
———. *Kanamantra.* Pune: Pune Sahitya Vitarana, 1983.
Gokhale, Vidyadhar. *Bavankhani.* Bombay: Majestic Book Stall, 1983.
Inamdar, N. S. *Shahenshah.* Pune: Continental Prakashan, 1976.
Kanekar, Anant. *Chowkoni Akash.* Pune: Suvichar Prakashan Mandal, 1975.
———. *Anantika.* Pune: Shrividya Prakashan, 1979.
Kanetkar, Shankar K. (*Girish*) *Ambarai.* Edited by V. Kane. Pune: Venus Prakashan, 1975.
Kanetkar, Vasant. *Ithe Oshalala Mrutyu.* Bombay: Popular Prakashan, 1968.
———. *Gaganbhedi.* Bombay: Parchure Prakashan, 1982.
———. *Divyasamora Andhar.* Pune: Indrayani Sahitya, 1986a.
———. *Mala Kahi Sangayachaya.* Bombay: Popular Prakashan, 1986b.
Karandikar, G. V. *Parampara ani Navata.* 2d ed. Bombay: Popular Prakashan, 1980a.
———. *Virupika.* 2d ed. Bombay: Popular, 1980b.
Karnik, Madhu Mangesh. *Uttarayana.* Kolhapur: Meenal Prakashan, 1980.
———. *Kalavita.* Kolhapur: Meenal Prakashan, 1982.
Khandekar, V. S. *Nivadaka Katha.* Pune: Marathi Pocket Books, 1976.
———. *Dipagraha.* Edited by V. V. Patki. Pune: Venus Prakashan, 1980a.
———. *Hiravala.* Kolhapur: Ajab Pustakalaya, 1980b.
———. *Ekapanachi Kahani: Atmacharitra.* Pune: Deshmukh, 1981.
Khanolkar, C. T. *Jogava.* Bombay: Mauj Prakashan, 1959.
———. *Dipamala.* Pune: Shri Prakashan, 1974.
———. *Asahi Eka Ashvatthama.* Pune: Pramod Prakashan, 1977.
———. *Dushtachakra.* Pune: Nilakanth Prakashan, 1979.
———. *Apule Marana.* Bombay: Mauj Prakashan, 1990.
Kulkarni, G. A. *Ramalakhuna.* Pune: Continental Prakashan, 1975a.
———. *Sanjashakuna.* Bombay: Popular Prakashan, 1975b.
———. *Pingalavela.* Bombay: Popular Prakashan, 1977.
———. *Manase.* Bombay: Parchure Prakashan, 1988.

———. *Kusumgunja*. Bombay: Parchure Prakashan, 1989.
———. *Sonapavale*. Bombay: Parchure Prakashan, 1991.
Madgulkar, Vyankatesh. *Pudhacha Paula*. Pune: Indrayani Sahitya Prakashan, 1950.
———. *Manadeshi Manase*. Bombay: Mauj Prakashan, 1972.
———. *Banagarwadi*. 7th ed. Bombay: Mauj Prakashan, 1974.
———. *Goshti, Gharakadila*. Solapur: Deepak Prakashan, 1977.
———. *Pandhari Mendhare, Hiravi Kurane*. Pune: Indrayani Sahitya, 1979.
———. *Sattantara*. Bombay: Majestic Book Stall, 1982.
———. *Chitre ani Charitre*. Pune: Utkarsha Prakashan, 1983.
Marathe, H. M. *Devachi Ghanta*. Bombay: Majestic Book Stall, 1980a.
———. *No Sentiments, Please!* Bombay: Majestic Book Stall, 1980b.
———. *Ghoda*. Bombay: Majestic Book Stall, 1982.
Mardhekar, B. S. *Mardhekaranchya Kadambarya*. Bombay: Mauj Prakashan, 1962.
———. *Natashreshtha ani chara sangeetika*. Bombay: Mauj Prakashan, 1965.
———. *Mardhekaranchi Kavita*. Bombay: Mauj Prakashan, 1969.
Matkari, Ratnakar. *Andharavada*. Pune: Shrivishakha Prakashan, 1977.
———. *Ashvamedha*. Pune: Shrivishakha Prakashan, 1980.
———. *Chi. Sau. Ka. Champa Govekara*. Pune: Shrivishakha Prakashan, 1981.
———. *Ratnakar Matkarinchya nivadaka goodhkatha*. Kolhapur: Minal Prakashan, 1982.
———. *Sattandha*. Bombay: Majestic Book Stall, 1986.
———. *Ghara thinagicha hava*. Bombay: Majestic Book Stall, 1991.
Menjoge, Sitaram P. *Amhi Postateela Manase*. Thane: Dimple Prakashan, 1985.
Mirasdar, D. M. *Makadameva*. Ahmednagar: Mohak Prakashan, 1970.
———. *Bhutancha Janma*. Ahmednagar: Mohak Prakashan, 1971.
———. *Pharmasa Goshti*. Solapur: Deepak Prakashan, 1976.
Mokashi, D. B. *Deva Chalale*. English trans. by Pramod Kale. Delhi: Hind Pocket Books, 1972.
———. *Anandaovari*. Bombay: Mauj Prakashan, 1974.
———. *Aamhi Marathi Manasa*. Pune: Utkarsha Prakashan, 1981.
———. *Paalakhi*. English trans. by O. C. Engblom. Albany: SUNY Press, 1987.
———. *Jara Jauna Yeto: Nivadaka Katha*. Pune: Pratima Prakashan, 1987.
Muktibodh, S. *Srushti, "Saundarya" ani Sahityamulya*. Bombay: Lokavangmaya Griha, 1978.
Nemade, Bhalchandra. *Jhula*. Bombay: Popular Prakashan, 1979.
———. *Dekhani: Meladi ani nantarchya kavita*. Bombay: Popular Prakashan, 1991.
Padgaonkar, Mangesh. *Vatratika*. Bombay: Mauj Prakashan, 1964.
———. *Salam*. Bombay: Mauj Prakashan, 1978.
———. *Gajhal*. Bombay: Mauj Prakashan, 1981.
Padhye, Bhau. *Vasunaka*. Bombay: Popular Prakashan, 1965.
———. *Thalapitha: A-vyabhichara katha*. Thane: Dimple Prakashan, 1984.
———. *Thodisi Jo Pi Li!* Thane: Saras Prakashan, 1986.
———. *Gurudatta*. Bombay: Lokavangmaya Gruha, 1990.
Patil, Shankar. *Lavangi Mirachi Kolhapurachi*. Pune: Kulkarni Granthagara, 1969.
———. *Beimana*. Kolhapur: Karmavir Prakashan, 1976.
Patil, Vishwas. *Panagira*. Bombay: Granthali, 1990.
———. *Jhadajhadati*. Pune: Rajahansa Prakashan, 1991.
Patwardhan, Vasundhara. *Devagharache Lene*. Pune: Shrivishakha Prakashan, 1974.

———. *Paithani.* Pune: Prapancha Prakashan, 1979.
Pendse, S. N. *Elgar.* Bombay: Mauj Prakashan, 1949.
———. *Garambicha Bapu.* Bombay: Mauj, 1951.
———. *Chakravyuwha.* Bombay: Mauj Prakashan, 1970.
———. *Octopus.* Bombay: Mauj Prakashan, 1972.
———. *Pandita! Ata Tari Shahane Wha!* Bombay: Mauj Prakashan, 1978.
———. *Rathachakra.* Bombay: Mauj Prakashan, 1980.
———. *Akanta.* Bombay: Mauj Prakashan, 1982.
———. *Hattya.* Bombay: Majestic Book Stall, 1983.
———. *Tumbadache Khota.* Pune: Continental Prakashan, 1987.
———. *Garambichi Radha.* Bombay: Mauj Prakashan, 1993.
Phadke, N. S. *Jadugar.* Pune: Kulkarni Granthagara, 1962.
———. *Kulabyachi Dandi.* Pune: Kulkarni Granthagara, 1971.
———. *Kalanka-shobha.* Pune: Kulkarni Granthagara, 1972.
———. *Hira jo Bhangala.* Pune: Kulkarni Granthagara, 1975.
———. *Bajirao.* Pune: Kulkarni Granthagara, 1976a.
———. *Marathi Laghunibandhacha Janaka Kona?* Pune: Kulkarni Granthagara, 1976b.
———. *Nivadaka Katha.* Pune: Marathi Pocket Books, 1976c.
———. *Jugara.* Pune: Kulkarni Granthagara, 1978.
———. *Shidori: Kathasangraha.* Pune: Kulkarni Granthagara, 1979.
———. *Nivadaka Na. Si. Phadake.* Edited by Indiara Sant and Prahlad Vadera. New Delhi: Sahitya Akademi, 1987.
Pitale, D. M. (*Nathmadhav*) *Swarajyantila Duphali.* 7th ed. Pune: Ramyakatha Prakashan, 1971.
———. *Swarajya Karbhar.* 7th ed. Pune: Ramyakatha Prakashan, 1971.
———. *Swarajyavarila Sankata.* 7th ed. Pune: Ramyakatha Prakashan, 1971.
Pundalik, Vidyadhar. *Charvaka.* Pune: Continental Prakashan, 1979a.
———. *Devachapha.* Bombay: Mauj Prakashan, 1979b.
———. *Mala.* Bombay: Mauj Prakashan, 1979c.
Rajadhyaksha, Vijaya. *Anolakhi.* Bombay: Majestic Book Stall, 1973.
———. *Akalpita.* Pune: Prapancha Prakashan, 1976a.
———. *Parambya.* Solapur: Sant Buddhisagar, 1976b.
———. *Chaitanyache Una.* Kolhapur: Minal Prakashan, 1981a.
———. *Jivhara Svanandiche.* Bombay: Dinapurusha Prakashan, 1981b.
Ramdas. *Shri Samartha Ramdasanchi Karunashtake.* Nagpur: Ameya Prakashan, 1978.
Ranganekar, M. G. *Rambha.* Bombay: Bombay Book Depot, 1965.
Rege, P. S. *Priyala.* Bombay: Mauj Prakashan, 1972.
———. *Renu.* Bombay: Mauj Prakashan, 1973.
———. *Eka Pidhiche Atmakathana.* Bombay: Mumbai Marathi Sahitya Sangha, 1975a.
———. *Suhrudagatha.* Poona: Continental Prakashan, 1975b.
———. *Matruka.* Bombay: Mauj Prakashan, 1978.
———. *Aniha.* Bombay: Mauj Prakashan, 1984.
Sadhale, Anand. *Chanakya.* Bombay: Priya Prakashan, 1979.
———. *Ananddhvajachya katha.* Bombay: Majestic Book Stall, 1985.
Sadhu, Arun. *Mumbai Dinanka.* Bombay: Majestic Book Stall, 1973.
———. *Sinhasana.* Bombay: Granthali, 1977.
———. *Bahishkruta.* Bombay: Majestic Book Stall, 1978a.
———. *Sphota.* Bombay: Majestic Book Stall, 1978b.

———. *Bin Pavasacha Divasa.* Bombay: Majestic Book Stall, 1983.
Samant, Anant. *M. T. Aywa Maru.* Bombay: Majestic Book Stall, 1989.
Sant, Indira. *Mrunmayi: Indira Sant yanchi nivadaka kavita.* Edited by Ramesh A. Tendulkar. Pune: Suvichar Prakashan Mandal, 1981.
———. *Garbhareshima.* Belgava: Navasahitya Prakashan, 1982.
Sarang, Vilas. *Soledad.* Bombay: Mauj Prakashan, 1975.
———. *Enkichya Rajyata.* Bombay: Mauj Prakashan, 1983.
———. *Kavita, 1969–1984.* Bombay: Mauj Prakashan, 1986.
Savant, Shivaji. *Mrutyunjaya.* Pune: Continental Prakashan, 1968.
———. *Chhava.* Pune: Continental Prakashan, 1979.
Shelke, Shanta. *Anubandh.* Pune: Mehta Publishing House, 1980.
———. *Anandache Jhad.* Bombay: Majestic Book Stall, 1982.
Shirwadkar, V. V. *Kavya Vahini.* Edited by R. S. Joag. Pune: Continental Prakashan, 1971.
———. *Eka Hoti Vaghina.* Bombay: Popular Prakashan, 1975.
———. *Ananda.* Bombay: Popular Prakashan, 1976.
———. *Appointment.* Poona: Vishvakarma Sahityalaya, 1978.
———. *Mukhyamantri.* Bombay: Popular Prakashan, 1979.
———. *Chandra Jethe ugawata Nahi.* Bombay: Popular Prakashan, 1981.
———. *Ekaki Tara.* Poona: Inamdar Bandhu Prakashan, 1982.
Surve, Narayan. *Majhe Vidyapitha.* Bombay: Popular Prakashan, 1970.
———. *Jahirnama.* Bombay: Popular Prakashan, 1975.
Tendulkar, Priya. *Jyacha Tyacha Prashna.* Thane: Dimple Prakashan, 1987.
———. *Panchatarankita.* Thane: Dimple Prakashan, 1989.
Tendulkar, Vijay. *Ashee Pakhare yeti.* Bombay: Mauj Prakashan, 1970.
———. *Sari ga Sari.* Bombay: Mauj Prakashan, 1971a.
———. *Shantata! Korta Chaalu Aahe.* 2d ed. Bombay: Mauj Prakashan, 1971b.
———. *Sakharam Binder.* Pune: Nilkanth Prakashan, 1972.
———. *Dambdwipacha Mukabala.* Nagpur: Ameya Prakashan, 1973a.
———. *Ghashiram Kotawala.* Pune: Nilkanth Prakashan, 1973b.
———. *Bhalyakaka.* Nagpur: Ameya Prakashan, 1974.
———. *Bebi.* Pune: Nilkanth Prakashan, 1975.
———. *Bhau Murararava.* Pune: Nilkanth Prakashan, 1975.
———. *Pahije Jaatiche.* Pune: Nilkanth Prakashan, 1977.
———. *Saamana.* Pune: Nilkanth Prakashan, 1978.
———. *Mitrachi Goshta.* Pune: Nilkanth Prakashan, 1982.
———. *He Sarva Kothuna Yete?* Bombay: Chauphera Prakashan, 1992.
Tilak, B. G. *Samagra Lokmanya Tilak.* Pune: Kesari Prakashan, 1974–76.
Tilak, Lakshmibai. *Smruti Chitre.* Nasik: A. D. Tilak, 1973.
Tukaram. *Shri Tukarambuvanchya Abhangachi Gatha.* 2d ed. Bombay: Shasakiya Madhyavarti Mudranalaya, 1973.
Varde, Mohini. *Teaser.* Bombay: Dimple Publication, 1987.
Yadav, Anand. *Ekalakonda.* Pune: Mehta Publishing House, 1980.
———. *Davarani.* Pune: Mehta Publishing House, 1982.
———. *Paana Bhavare.* Bombay: Mauj Prakashan, 1983.
———. *Ghara Javai.* Pune: Mehta Publishing House, 1987a.
———. *Jhombi.* Pune: Mehta Publishing House, 1987b.

———. *Mati Khalachi Mati.* Pune: Mehta Publishing House, 1991a.

———. *Nangarani.* Pune: Mehta Publishing House, 1991b.

Yadav, Anand, and Baba Patil, eds. *Tisarya Pidhichi Gramina Katha.* Pune: Mehta Publishing House, 1981.

9

Twentieth-Century Panjabi Literature

ATAMJIT SINGH

HISTORICAL PERSPECTIVE

Modern Panjabi literature, like other regional literatures, has been shaped by Western influences percolating in Panjabi life and letters from the middle of the nineteenth century. For many years, the Panjabi people could not counter the cultural effects of British colonization. The English rulers thought poorly of Asian cultures and literature, as evidenced in Macaulay's 1831 Minute on Indian Education, and wanted them to adopt the European way of life. The first generation of Indians internalized this judgment and began to lose contact with Indian tradition and learning.

In Panjab, while the elite accepted the impact of the British imperialist masters, common people retained a living relationship with their land. The next generation, however, made conscious efforts to assert their past heritage and transmit it to their descendants.

MOVEMENTS OF RELIGIOUS REVIVALISM

As a reaction to the Christian missionaries, the Arya Samaj and the Singh Sabha launched movements in order to preach and propagate their own respective religions by reviving Vedic learning of ancient times and preaching Sikhism as originally propagated by Sikh gurus. These movements of revival and reform started later here than in other parts of the country. Hindi and Urdu were linked through the medium of *madrassas, anjumans,* journals, translations, and publication staffs. But in Panjab, Persian continued to reign supreme during the Sikh rule and retained its supremacy for a considerable period of time under the aegis of the British. Later, they introduced Urdu as the medium of instruction at the school level and also at the lower rungs of administration and judiciary. This explains the relatively late emergence of a renaissance in Panjabi writing.

The Christian missionaries in Panjab had begun their proselytizing activities by converting Hindus, Muslims, and Sikhs to Christianity. This triggered resentment among these communities, which, in turn, launched their own movements of religious revival. In their earlier stages, these movements attempted to insulate their respective communities against other beliefs and practices, but, with the passage of time, each of them became an instrument of religious and social reform. This was responsible for the rise of the Singh Sabha movement among the Sikhs, who were especially involved in Panjabi writings and support for the development of the Panjabi language.

WRITERS OF THE SINGH SABHA MOVEMENT (1900–1935)

The major writers of the Singh Sabha movement (such as Bhai Mohan Singh Vaid, S. S. Charan Singh Shaheed, Bhai Jodh Singh, Bhai Kahan Singh Nabha, Bhai Dit Singh, Charan Singh [Father of Bhai Vir Singh], Bhai Sewa Singh, Bhai Koer Singh, and Balbir Singh) not only propagated the message of the Sikh gurus and initiated a movement to reform the religious and ethical life of the Sikhs but also made efforts to develop Panjabi language and literature. Bhai Vir Singh was committed to the use of literature to forge a Panjabi cultural identity.

The Singh Sabha movement's primary aim was to establish a separate cultural identity for the Sikhs. It started in 1870, but it found its institutionalized existence in 1873. Bhai Vir Singh (1872–1957), its chief exponent, contributed significantly to the understanding of Sikhism by the Sikh masses. More, he established a distinct literary tradition, both in the literary and in the ethical or social-historical sense. He wrote fiction, poetry, prose of ideas, and learned commentaries on the old sacred texts. He also wrote tracts and launched a weekly in Panjabi, *Khalsa Smachar,* in order to propagate and disseminate the teachings of the Sikh gurus and to restore Sikhism to its traditional glory. He wrote semi-novels to depict the most trying conditions for the Sikhs when they were being ruthlessly persecuted by the Mughal rulers in the latter half of the eighteenth century.

His first three novels, *Sundari* (1898), *Bijay Singh* (1899), and *Satwant Kaur* (1900), deal with the theme of Sikh valor and chivalry in their battles against the local Mughal chieftains and also against foreign Pathan invaders from Kabul, who would return after loot and plunder from Panjab. In *Baba Naudh Singh* (1921), he epitomizes the highest virtues of a Sikh. It seeks to portray the ideal character of a Sikh who has imbibed the true teachings of the Sikh gurus and who, through his conduct, reforms the religious life of all those who come into contact with him. The characters of these novels became household figures in Sikh homes for several years. Bhai Vir Singh's fictional writings, which are more like historical romances, serve a special purpose, which he had predetermined. He tried to present the image of Sikhs as men without hate, without fear, always at the service of the people, ever ready to fight for noble causes. In his hands, the story, therefore, was merely a vehicle to throw light on the various social customs and religious beliefs of the Sikhs.

Bhai Vir Singh's poetry is deemed his major contribution to Panjabi literature. Though much of his poetry is essentially religious in content, he introduced new themes in his poems that did not conform to the known models of the past. His poetry works include *Rana Surat Singh* (1905), *Lehran de Har* (1907–21), *Matak Hulare* (1920), and *Bijlian de Har* (1922–27). His *Mere Sayian Jio* (1953), the final volume of his poems, won the Sahitya Academy Award in 1955, two years after his death. His poetry portrays the longing for a mystic consummation. In his long poem *Rana Surat Singh,* written in blank verse, the poet attempts a search for an inner poise, tranquility, and freedom from anxiety through Sikh spirituality. Bhai Vir Singh's poetry achieves the sublime height of mysticism. Every poem is steeped in the love of the Supreme Being, to which he gives expression in different metaphors, such as lightning suffusing spheres, a river merging into the sea, and an ever-moving brook seeking its beloved Lord.

Bhai Vir Singh also made a splendid contribution to scholarship and as an explicator of the Sikh scriptures. He edited and annotated *Guru Pratap Suraj Granth* (1926–33) and completed the compilation of *Guru Granth Kosh* (1927). It was followed by a biography of *Bhai Gurdas* (1940) and *Asht Guru Chamtkar* (1951). In short, Bhai Vir Singh in his lifetime assumed the role of father figure of twentieth-century Panjabi literature and won universal admiration, which turned into an abiding reverence. In recognition of his services to Panjabi life and letters, he was conferred the degree of Oriental learning honoris causa by the Panjab University in 1949 and was nominated to the Panjab Legislative Council in 1952. He was also nominated to the National Academy of Letters in 1954, thus achieving national eminence. He was a powerful influence on contemporary writers, such as Bhai Kahan Singh Nabha, Mohan Singh Vaid, Charan Singh Shaheed, Dhani Ram Chatrik, Puran Singh, Balbir Singh, and Bhai Jodh Singh.

Among the writers who came under the influence of Bhai Vir Singh, Puran Singh (1881–1931) broke all traditional barriers and chose free verse for his poetic composition, following the style of the American poet Walt Whitman. He wrote three volumes of Panjabi poetry, *Khule Maidan* (Free Meadows, 1923), *Khule Ghund* (Free Veils, 1923), and *Khule Asmani Rang* (Boundless Blue Colors of the Sky, 1926). His poetry is characterized in letter and spirit by transcendence of the limits of self, home, and country. A mood of abandon permeates his whole verse.

The most important feature of his verse is its passionate preaching of the importance of common people. The hardworking and patient farmers of Panjab and the passionate heroes and heroines of love stories have been portrayed with such a sincere sentiment that they gain a special significance in the world of the poet. They become symbols of universal love and freedom. He talks about the poor and the hungry and idealizes them, seeing in their eyes a peace and contentment that he misses in the vulgar rich. In some of his poems, he has reinterpreted the medieval romances of Hir Ranjha, Sohni Mahival, Sassi Punnu, and Puran Bhagat and made them the true representatives of the free human spirit. He sings the praises of the rather less known humble trees of the land and sees untold beauty in obscure flowers. He draws the poetic sketch of a poor village woman who is making cow-dung cakes and tries to project her as a kind of great artist. He creates scenes from everyday life of Panjab and portrays some immortal Panjabi characters. He sings in praise of Sikh gurus, particularly focusing on the 10th master, Guru Gobind Singh, whose philosophy had struck him as majestic.

Though he was saturated with an intense feeling of the life and teachings of the Sikh gurus, he strove to live a universal religion transcending barriers of various established faiths. In one of his poems, he calls on God not so he may worship him, but with an appeal that he may break all instruments of worship with his own hands so that people can be free from the shackles of man-made religions.

In Puran Singh, Panjabi literature took a firm step forward toward modernity. Other poets who flourished as contemporaries of Bhai Vir Singh were Dhani Ram Chatrik and Lala Kirpa Sagar. Both had a close, personal relationship with Vir Singh, but in their verse they strove to bring a variety to the tradition promoted by him. Chatrik identified with the Persian tradition of romance but later wrote lyrics with a mystical strain of Panjabi Sufi poets, bringing them closest to the Panjabi folk songs. In his adaptation of the narrative by Sir Walter Scott, "The Lady of the Lake," Lala Kirpa Sagar introduced a secular theme of a Western romance into the poetic tradition of Sikh religious poetry nurtured by Bhai Vir Singh.

Whereas Puran Singh liberated Panjabi poetry from the limits of religious preaching and didacticism and made his verse intense, uncontrolled emotion, he also, for the first time, focused his attention on the common people and identified his sympathies with common people of Panjab. New Panjabi poetry follows Puran Singh in recognizing the down-to-earth problems of the common masses. His rejection of the idea of an organized religion and promotion of democratic and egalitarian self-reliance also gave strength to the progressive poetry written under the Marxist creed of writing. Among the forerunners of the new poetry, the name of Diwan Singh Kalepani (1894–1944) deserves mention, along with Puran Singh, because he, too, wrote poetry in free verse. He took an active interest in the national struggle for freedom. Despite being a government medical doctor, he supported the noncooperation movement in the 1920s. He was punished with a transfer to Andeman in 1927, where he was tortured by the British and killed. Andeman at that time was the most difficult place to live, and those who were sent there were supposed to live in very inhumane conditions. Diwan Singh chose his pen name Kalepani (black waters) because he was a victim of the British high-handedness and inhumane, barbarous treatment. He contributed two collections of poems, *Vagde Pani* (Running Waters, 1938) and *Antim Lehran* (Winding Waves, 1962), later published posthumously by his son. Some of the ideas in his poetry include revolt against the established religion and its elaborate rituals as well as political slavery and the attainment of freedom from the oppressive British colonial rule. He also champions women's rights in Indian society. Diwan Singh's use of free verse in his poetry is not as successful as that of Puran Singh because he lacks the latter's freshness of imagery and vitality of expression.

THE NEW PANJABI POETRY (1935–47)

The appearance of Mohan Singh (1905–78) and Amrita Pritam (1919) on the Panjabi poetic scene marks a revolt against the three-decade-old poetic tradition. The writers who had derived their inspiration from the religious renaissance under the Singh Sabha movement used Panjabi as a poetic medium. They also restated the mysticism of the Sikh gurus that flourished in the previous century. To these poets, ideas and feelings already expressed by the medieval religious poets provided guiding principles to creative writing, but the new poet was finding ways to admit new ideas and create new forms. Both Mohan Singh and Amrita Pritam struggled to devise unconventional verse patterns and to develop distinct, individual styles, though in their early writings they were influenced by the medieval Qissa tradition.

Mohan Singh, who, during his 50-year poetic career, contributed more than a dozen collections of poetry, stands out as one of the greatest poets of his time. His major works include *Sawe Pattar* (Green Leaves, 1936), *Adhwate* (The Midway, 1939–40), *Kach Sach* (Illusion and Reality, 1944–50), *Awazan* (The Calls, 1950–54), *Wada Vela* (The Dawn, 1954–58), *Jandre* (The Locks, 1964), and *Jaimir* (Long Live the Peace, 1968). In addition, he translated into Panjabi verse Matthew Arnold's *The Light of Asia* and wrote *Nankayan* (1971), the life story of Guru Nanak in epic form to celebrate the guru's quincentenary.

Mohan Singh sings about his personal love in his early writings, but soon his growing faith was seized by the dilemma between the social and the literary. The poet made a promising start with his early poems, which still remain popular with Panjabi readers, but in his later works, beginning with *Kach-sach,* he shows a strong bias in favor of progressive writing, which had become a dominant movement in the regional-language literature of northern India. The poet's so-called progressive poems are not as striking or memorable as his poems that bring together personal and social themes. In fact, Mohan Singh, under the influence of Marxist criticism, is torn in two directions, his heart clinging to tradition and his intellect pulling toward revolutionary expression. In fact, over some period, he remains irresolute and is not able to decide which direction to follow. Later, after he himself realized that by following his head he had lost poetic finesse, he again reverted to the call of his heart and was once more able to recapture the spontaneous beauty of his earlier poetry. In his *Jandre* and *Jaimir,* the last two collections of poetry, he composed a few of the finest ghazals showing a delicacy comparable to that of the Urdu *ghazal* (lyric). Mohan

Singh was a love poet, and he sang its immortality in varied musical forms, variations, and notations. His lyrics still enthrall Panjabi hearts.

Amrita Pritam, another versatile poet, like Mohan Singh, developed her poetic art in stages. She began writing poetry at a very tender age under the guidance of her father, Kartar Singh Hitkari, himself a poet and a scholar of *Braj Bhasha.* Her important collections of poems include her first publication, *Amrit Lehran* (Immortal Waves, 1936), which appeared when she was just 17, followed by *Jiunda Jiwan* (The Exuberant Life, 1939), *Lok Peeran* (The People's Anguish, 1944), *Pathar Geetey* (The Pebbles, 1946), *Sunehre* (Messages, 1953), *Ashoka Cheti* (1956), *Kasturi* (The Musk, 1958), *Kagaz te Canvas* (The Paper and the Canvas, 1970), and *Kala Gulab* (The Black Rose, 1973). In her first book, she gave expression to her personal love in a rather traditional idiom, but later, with maturity, she became more conscious of harsh social realities around her, and her poetry turned into an informed commentary on urgent social and political complexities.

Amrita's poetry is known for giving powerful voice to the theme of women's agony and shame in the world dominated by man. She considers this world made sacrosanct by man's clever laws not conducive to the growth of love. Still, this harsh and crude world of man becomes a measure of her inner strength. The metaphor of love pervades most of her poetry collections. She underlines the uniqueness of each individual love and says that a love of one person is never a repetition of the other. She is bold enough to admit the carnality of her love and does not want to hide it behind any kind of mystical or metaphysical metaphor. In fact, she believes that only when one has attained fulfillment in physical love does one attain spiritual accomplishment.

Amrita Pritam is perhaps the only modern Panjabi poet who is very popular with both Indian and Pakistani Panjabs. Her poem "Aj Akhan Waris Shah nun" (Today I Invoke Waris Shah), written at the time of partition of India, is equally appealing to the people of the two countries and has become symbolic of the nostalgic days when Hindus, Sikhs, and Muslims lived together like good neighbors. It portrays the barbarity and lunacy of the Panjabis, who forgetting the message of love of the great poet Waris Shah in his immortal *Heer,* indulged in senseless killing rampages that spurred large-scale migration, which saw both sides abandoning their homes. Without a doubt, Amrita Pritam holds a preeminent place in Panjabi poetry. She is the only Panjabi writer who has been honored with the Jnan Peeth Award, besides numerous national and international recognitions. She also edits a poetry magazine, *Nagmani,* which, over the years, has become a rallying point for many budding writers.

Both Mohan Singh and Amrita Pritam as poets have some common features. Both, in their early writing, give voice to feminist feelings in a cruel, man-dominated world. Their poetry is firmly rooted in Panjabi folk idiom. In their love lyrics, both of them draw on the oral rhythms of Panjabi folk songs and dances. Even the imagery is rural, bringing into its fold the sensitive rituals of birth, marriage, memories of paternal home, departure of a daughter from her parent's home, pangs of separation and distant living. They also share in common images based on agricultural operations, spinning, sewing, and embroidery, the domestic chores investing their poetry with an aura of romance and realism.

OTHER POETS

Besides Mohan Singh and Amrita Pritam, the two major figures, a number of other poets achieved distinction in this period. Pritam Singh Safeer (1916), now a retired Delhi High Court justice, wrote mystical poems using a mixture of Eastern and modern Western mystic thoughts. He has contributed to Panjabi poetry about half a dozen collections of poems, including *Katak Kunjan* (The Pelicans of Winter, 1941), *Pap de Sohile* (Appraises of Sin, 1942), and *Rakat Bundan* and *Ad(i) Jugad* (The Beginnings, 1958). His latest book is an epic on the life of guru Gobind Singh (1991).

Whereas Safir could not remain a significant voice in modern Panjabi letters, Bawa Balwant (1915–68), who belonged to the progressive stream of poetry, made his mark as an original and creative artist. He was profoundly influenced by Persian and Urdu poetry, as well as other contemporary, progressive writers of Urdu, and had fairly good command of Urdu prosody. He was influenced by Iqbal's concept of "perfect man" (*mard-e Kamil*). In his poem "Zindgi hi Zindgi" (Life and Only Life), he gives a forceful voice to this idea of a superman. Bawa's lyrics reflect a mystical strain. "Pippal dian Chhawan" (Shades of the Peepal Tree) is one such composition. Some of his major collections of poems are *Kav Sagar* (1955), *Mahan Nach* (1941), *Amar Geet* (1942), *Jawala Mukhi* (1943), *Bandargah* (1951), and *Sugandh Sameer* (1959).

The other poets who made their mark in this period are Avtar Singh Azad (1906–79), Piara Singh Sehrai (1915), and Santokh Singh Dhir (1920). Another tall figure, Mohan Singh Diwana (1899–1984), also made an impact on this period. Some of his well-known works include *Neel Dhara* (The Blue Ocean, 1935), *Jagat Tamasha* (The World—A Fair, 1942), *Masti* (Ecstasy, 1946–49), and *Dhup Chhan* (Sunshine and Shade, 1932).

EMERGENCE OF PANJABI NATIONALISM

Through Panjabi poetry, a Panjabi nationalism, cutting across denominational and religious boundaries, started emerging. The grip of metaphysical speculation loosened, and interest in secular and worldly pursuits emerged. Almost all the writers at this time supported the national struggle for independence, which was in full swing. Some of them, like Diwan Singh Kale Pani, Gurmukh Singh Mussafir, Hira Singh Dard, Master Tara Singh, Principal Niranjan Singh, Bhai Jodh Singh, and Prem Singh Prem, were actively involved in it and had been imprisoned several times. The political turmoil in Panjab made its impact on contemporary writing by bringing into the fore problems of the common people. It also aroused protest and resentment among the masses in Panjab. The *kisan* movement of 1907 and development of canal colonies gave fillip to patriotic sentiment. The *khilafat* movement and then the *akalii* movement for Gurdwara reform contributed to awaken the masses politically. In its early stages, the *kisan* movement received support from poets like Prabh Dayal and Banke Bihari (1880–1920), who composed popular verses such as *Pagri Sambhal Jatta* (Watch Your Turban! O My Peasant Friend!), which became very popular with Panjab peasants and later were sung as patriotic songs by the youth involved in the freedom movement. Poetry symposia played a significant role in spreading the political message to the Panjabis, who participated in the fight against the colonial rulers without consideration of any religious affiliations. The publication of literary magazines and growth of vernacular press further helped in the development of Panjabi literature, which could not be considered of much poetic worth but contributed to the creation of a feeling of sharing a common Panjabi identity. The *ghadar* movement, which was launched from overseas, started making its impact at home, giving impetus to patriotic writing in Panjabi. *Ghadar di Gunj* (The Echo of Revolt, 1914), published in many volumes, exhorted the people of India to fight the unjust imperial British rule. All these developments together brought about change in thinking and promoted secular values by breaking the barriers of narrow sectarian ways.

PANJABI POETRY AFTER INDEPENDENCE (1947–70)

Secularism soon gave way to communalism. As a prelude to the partition of India, communal riots between the Muslims, on one hand, and Hindus and the Sikhs, on the other, took place on a very large scale. Reckless destruction of human life and property ensued. The migration of large populations from both sides seriously disturbed the demographic pattern and created serious problems of rehabilitation of millions of people uprooted in the process. It was an agonizing experience for the creative artist. The Panjabis on both sides of the international border saw their friends alienated, families divided, and the country dismembered. The large-scale killings, loot and plunder, rape and shame shook the conscience of every sensitive being on both sides. The trauma of partition gulfed the experience of independence.

Whereas in the prepartition Panjab literature the Sikh revivalist movement remained dominant in spite of pressure from the progressive movement starting in the early 1940s, after independence, Panjab literature under the impact of *pragtivadis* brought into fore the themes of revolution, violence, death, and devastation. This continued until the early 1960s.

In the late 1960s and early 1970s, the *naxalite* movement in Bengal was at its peak. It was an ultraleftist, militant movement, which was ruthlessly crushed by the then-Bengal government. The young writers from rural Panjab, often from landless peasant families, particularly from the Malwa belt, wrote fiery verses in support of revolution. Known as *jhujarvadi* or *nakasalvadi* verse, it attracted a few committed political workers who wrote verses to arouse the landless farmworkers to take to arms against the big landlords. The Panjab government suppressed this movement with a heavy hand. The poets went underground, but they had the sympathy of the common people in the villages. Their poetry during this period remained close to the hearts of a few, but now it is being published. This poetry was committed to progressive ideology, but its relationship with rural ethos was much pronounced. There is also a tendency in this poetry to reinterpret Sikh history, myths, and legends in the modern social and cultural contexts, investing Sikh lore and its traditions with new meanings. This poetry doesn't have much poetic or intellectual maturity, but still it has considerable mass appeal. Some prominent names of this movement are Avtar Singh Pash, Lal Singh, Darshan Khatkar, and Harbhajan Halwarvi.

PROGRESSIVES VERSUS EXPERIMENTALISTS

Until the late 1960s, Panjab poetry was dominated by the progressive movement. The major preoccupation of these poets was to focus on the problems of workers and landless peasantry and project their pain and suffering. They showered praise on those countries ruled by communist ideology and condemned capitalist countries for their inhumane policies. The Panjab poet repeated these subjects and reduced his or her verse to mere propaganda. As a matter of fact, the phenomenon of "progressive" writing was widespread and attained an interlanguage character. In Panjabi, it acquired more or less a communist "closed"-shop organization, and its writing became politically more explicit. This resulted in a widespread feeling that progressive, or *pragtivadi,* poetry was avowedly propagandist. Some of the poets who were otherwise strongly committed to the Marxist ideology reacted against it and, under the leadership of Jasbir Singh Ahluwalia, wrote as experimentalists. They concentrated on the search for a distinct idiom for their verse. They were inspired by the Hindi experimentalists, or *pryogvadins.* They were also influenced by the English poet T. S. Eliot. Ahluwalia, supported by one or two other poets of his group, wrote on the functions of poetry. The poets who were attracted by this reaction against progressive poetry included Sukhpalvir Singh Hasrat and Sohan Singh Misha. But this movement did not last long and in no way influenced future Panjabi poetry. Only two poets of the *prayogvadi* group deserve special mention. Jasbir Singh Ahluwalia, with his two collections of poems, *Koor Raja Koor Parja* (False Is the King and False Are His Subjects) and *Kagz da Ravan* (The Paper Ravan), had limited success in his attempt to evolve a new poetic idiom. His main quality is that he takes most of his imagery from the Holy *Granth* but, interprets it in the context of contemporary situation. Sukhpalvir Singh Hasrat's collected poems, *Hasrat Kav* (1975), are considered a major work of writing in Panjabi. He is largely declamatory in tone and is recognized for his cult of Shaktivad (Strength).

This account cannot be considered complete without mention of a few poets who also deviated from the progressive stream and established their own distinct identity. These were Haribhajan Singh (1920), Jaswant Singh Neki (1925), Shiv Kumar (1937–73), Sukhbir (1926), Tara Singh (1929–93), Surjit Rampuri (1931–90), and Jagtar (1931). These poets laid the foundations of a new aesthetics rooted in ordinary speech. Among them, Haribhajan Singh is the most prominent. He came into the limelight with his first collection, *Lassan* (Lashes, 1958), which departed from established taste. He has about a dozen collections of poems to his credit. A few of them are the most discussed works of this period, such as *Tar Tupka* (A Hanging Drop, 1961), *Adhraini* (Midnight, 1965), *Na Dhupe Na Chhaven* (Neither in the Sun nor in the Shade, 1966), *Mein Jo Bit Gaya* (Me, the One Who Is Past, 1970), *Sarak de Safe te* (On the Page of a Road, 1973), *Alaf Dupehar* (The Naked Midday, 1973), *Tukian Jibhan Wale* (Those with Cut Tongues, 1976), *Mathe wala Deeva* (The Forehead's Light, 1989), *Tar Tupka* and a new form of a poem, "Ik Patri Kavita" (A Poem with One Interlocutor).

Jaswant Singh Neki has published five books of poetry, which include his long autobiographical poem "Simriti de Kiran Ton Pehlan" (Before the Dissolution of Memory). His other collections of poems are *Asle te ohle* (Illusion and Reality, 1955), *Eh Mere Sanse eh Mere Gee* (Here Are My Fears, Here Are My Songs), and *Karuna Di Chhoh ton Pichhon* (After the Benevolent Touch). Neki's short poems revolve around themes based on spiritual values and are of a perennial nature. Though the poet deals with values related to a kind of mystical experience, a scientific approach may be discerned that gives new content to his poetry. In his *Karuna di Choh ton Pichhon,* he narrates his spiritual experience in a very personal and sensitive style. *Samriti de Kiran ton Pehlan* is also a narrative of his intense experience, born out of his encounter with near death following a frightful car accident.

Shiv Kumar, known widely as Shiv Kumar Batalvi and a major poet of this period, is considered a rare phenomenon in Panjabi literature. He distinguished himself as a poet of rare lyrical intensity. No other poet in this period attained so much popularity. He is known for his lyrics expressing acute agony and personal pain of an individual in an idiom closest to the hearts of the people. He was very much rooted in the soil of the Panjab and imbibed the exuberance of Panjabi culture. The early works of Shiv Kumar, collected in the first volume of his complete works, *Birhan Tun Sultan* (O Separation, You Are Supreme), represent a varied specimen of his painful and sad lyrics. This work became less important in light of the popularity attained by his later work, a verse play called *Loona.* In this poem, he uses the mode of the lyric to delve deeply into the folklore of Panjab, revealing the depth of human experience in personal love from the vantage point of pain and suffering. In this epic, Shiv Kumar imparts a new meaning to a popular tale, immortalizing an oft repeated folktale with new depth.

S. S. Misha, who is known for his ironic mode, added a new dimension to contemporary Panjabi poetry. He is incisive and, at times, biting in exposing the inconsistencies of the social system. He uses prose rhythms of common speech for effective communication, welding them into his artistic verbal expression. His most popular collection of poems is *Kach de Vastar* (The Dress Made of Glass.) Tara Singh, another Sahitya Academy Award winner, for his collection of poems *Kehkshan* (The Milky Way), has depicted in his poems a total erosion of faith. He is also known for his satire and wit.

The Pragti Vadi poets, such as Santokh Singh Dhir Surjit, Rampuri Jagtar, and Prabhjot Kaur, attained a considerable achievement in writing verse with a message. Prabhjot Kaur also composed some lyrics that have the flavor of folk songs. Santokh Singh Dhir is still on his ascendancy, but he no longer writes in a Marxist slant. Only Jagtar, with whom we have come a long way in the tradition of Panjabi poetry, has walked abreast with all the major poetic movements, such as romanticism, Pragtivad, experimentalism, and militant poetry of Jhujarvad. He has six collections of poetry to his credit, which demonstrate his deep mastery of classical Persian poetry. A keen awareness of modern Urdu poetry being written both in India and in Pakistan has enabled him to exercise a dexterous rhythmic control over his compositions, which are replete with delicate Urdu poetic imagery. *Chhangya RuKh* (Pruned Tree) is one of his very popular collections of poems.

POSTINDEPENDENCE PANJABI POETRY (1970–94)

During the 1970s, along with the old masters, rose new poets who have shown great promise such as Harnam (1934–90), Mohanjit (1938), Tarlok Singh Kanwar (1931–94), Sutinder Singh Noor (1939), Surinder Gill (1942), Joga Singh (1942), Harbhajan Halwaravi (1943), Minder (1944), Surjit Pattar (1945), Parmindejit (1944), Manjit Tiwana (1947), Awtar Singh Pash (1950–88), Santokh Singh Shehar Yar (1947), Ravinder (1946), S. Balwant (1946), Savinderjit Savi (1947), Ravinder Bhathal (1946), Ajaib Hundal, and Gian Singh Sandhu (1936). They have shown not only a deep social awareness but also intellectual and artistic maturity in the small body of their best work. Pattar's *Hawa vich likhe Harf* (The Words Scribbled in Air), *Likhtam Parminderjit* (Parminderjit Writes), and *Uneenda Vartman* (Sleepless Present) have rightly been deemed first-rate poetry. Pattar, a master of the form of *ghazal,* not only is aware of surrounding realities but also possesses a fine poetic sensibility for the beauty and import of the word. Irony and a highly delicate and sensuous imagery, along with lyricism, lend his poems a rare charm. Surjit Pattar, as well as Manjit Tiwana, are both recipients of the coveted Sahitya Academy Award.

PANJABI POETRY IN PAKISTAN

In Pakistan, classical Panjabi poetry of medieval times remained quite popular for a long time, and Waris and Sufi poets are still in much demand. Curbs on the freedom of expression, particularly during the days of military rule, affected creative writing throughout Pakistan, including Panjab, where Panjabi literature suffered censure. As a result, most poets composed in an indirect way, using symbols and images as an aid. The old guard like Ustad Daman, Faqir Ahamed, Maula Bakhsh Kushta, Hakim Nasir, Hayat Pasruri, Akbar Lahori, Janab Jatoi, Pir Fazal, and Ghulam Haidar Yateem, continued writing traditional verse in Panjabi.

Along with them, some new poets of a new sensibility, such as Ahmed Rahi, Najm Hossain Sayad, Munir Niazi, Nasreen Anjum Bhatti, Majid Siddiqui, Baqi Suddiqui, Zaffar Iqbal, Munnoo Bhai, and Masud Anwar, became trendsetters. Most of them started their poetic career in Urdu or English but later turned to their mother tongue. Leading names in Urdu include Faiz Ahmed Faiz, Sufi Tubbassam, Ahmad Nassem Qasimi, Habib Jalib, Raza Hamdani, Qateel Shifai, Jamel Maik, and a host of others. The *ghazal,* a traditional form of poetry in Urdu, was popularized in Panjabi by most of them. It is estimated that more than 200 poetry collections have been published during the last 38 years.

PANJABI POETRY IN THE WEST

A large number of poets flourish in the Western countries. Some are Gurcharn Rampuri, Ravinder Ravi, Ajmer Rode (1940), Darshan Gill (1943), Surjeet Kalsey (1944), Iqbal Ramuwalia (1946), Sukhinder (1947), Sadhu (1947), Surinder Dhanjal (1950), and Charan Singh (1950), all from Canada; Niranjan Singh Noor (1933), Avtar (1937), Santokh Singh Santokh (1938), Mushtaq Slngh (1939), and Amarjit Chandan (1946), from the U.K.; Dev (1947), who settled in Switzerland; Satti Kumar (1936) of Sweden; Ajaib Kamal (1932) in Kenya; and Gurmel (1943), Jang Singh Giani (1920), Shashi Samundra, and Sukhminder Kamboj, from the United States.

YOUNG NEW POETS

The decade of the 1980s has produced at least two dozen young new poets, covering a wide range: college teachers, farmers, political workers, students, and homemakers. Though a few have one or two books published, some have so far published only in literary magazines but show a good deal of promise. An anthology of three to five poems from each poet, entitled *Naven Dishadian Di Tlash* (The Search for New Horizons), has been recently released by Gursharan Singh, the noted Panjabi playwright, on behalf of the Balraj Sahni Memorial Publications, Chandigarh. Some of the poets included in the volume are Amarjit Kaunke, Amardeep Gill, Avtarjit, Asi, Swarnjit Savi, Swarajbir, Surjit Judge, Suhinderbir, Dharam Kameana, Nirupma Dut, Prvesh, Harmeet Vidyarthi, Pal Kaur, Balbir Parwana, Lakhvinder Johal, Rajbir, Ram Singh Chahal, Madan Vira, and Jaswant Deed. Their poetry is marked by the liberation of feeling from predetermined ideological prejudices, many displaying rare skill and ingenuity.

PANJABI NOVEL (1900–1947)

The Panjabi novel was born with Bhai Vir Singh, Mohan Singh Vaid, Charan Singh Shaheed, Joshua Fazal Din, and others. These works can, at best, be accepted as a first tentative exercise in Panjabi fiction. Vir Singh used the novel form for didactic purpose, and so did the other writers. Though the Panjabi novel developed under the direct influence of the Western novel, its early form was somewhat deficient in literary value. Yet, these fiction writers did receive Western influence through Hindi and Urdu translations.

With Nanak Singh (1897–73), the beginning of the Panjabi novel can be traced. As the first Panjabi author of fictional works that could be called novels in the modern sense, he chose his field wisely; most of his characters come from the people he knew well—the lower middle class in the urban setting of Panjab. He also depicted the struggle of the worker against the capitalistic order, the decaying feudalistic aristocracy, and the rising intellectual. He depicted the life of the Panjabi lower middle class faithfully and with great sympathy; his novels have well-constructed plots. In his reformist zeal, he tended to sentimentalize Panjabi society, but with growing maturity he became more detached and critical, and his writing gained considerably in power. He wrote during the period when Marxist criticism had the foremost place, and, in the misguided belief that "progressive" writing necessarily meant writing about the militant worker, the so-called Pragtivad established the stock character in stock situations of conflict. As such, the works of Nanak Singh lost their storytelling charm and were reduced to mere communist propaganda. He consciously tried to free himself of this impeding influence in his later works.

Nanak Singh, is, perhaps, the first writer who made the medium of the novel an instrument of social reform, and, over his long career of more than 50 years, he reflected on the pressing problems of the growing Panjabi society. He wrote around 50 novels. A few of them became very popular with Panjabi readers. Many of his works have been translated into other Indian languages. In his first phase of writing, he brought to the fore the problems of communalism, religious hypocrisy, untouchability, widow marriage, illiteracy, and social and economic backwardness. Some of his most popular novels are *Chitta Lahu* (The White Blood, 1932), *Kagtan di Beri* (The Paper Boat), *Pavitter Papi* (The Pious Sinner), *Agg di Khed* (The Play of Fire), and *Chiterkar* (The Painter). After partition, he took up the problems of the independence of women. He has depicted woman fighting for her rights and gaining economic self-reliance. *Katti Hoi Patang* (The Kite with Cut String) and *AdamKhor* (Cannibals) represent this period of his writing. Nanak Singh remained active till the mid-1960s, mostly repeating the same themes. In brief, Nanak Singh is a giant among novelists. He is realistic and has portrayed the anguish of the downtrodden throughout his life. He has given voice to those who could not express their feelings and invested them with the grandeur of simple humanity.

SOCIALIST REALISM IN THE PANJAB NOVEL (1947 ONWARD)

After Nanak Singh, the Panjabi novel developed under the impact of movements of socialist realism. Surinder Singh Narula (1919) is the most consistent exponent of Marxist ideology in his fiction. His first novel, *Peo Pvtter* (Father and Son, 1946), accepted as a major work of fiction, narrates the story of the city of Amritsar and its significant phases of development in the first two decades of the twentieth century, bringing into focus successive religious and political movements in the Panjab. In *Rang Mahal* (The Palace of Enjoyment, 1949), the writer, using Marxist and Freudian critique, draws the picture of a retired, corrupt bureaucrat and his equally corrupt wife, who live in a *shish mahal* (a glass palace) with four mentally retarded daughters. The couple is tormented with mental agonies, resulting in a prosperous house turning into a virtual hell. His novels also depict the duality of class disputes.

Narula has also written a historical novel, *Nili Bar* (1956), depicting the life of the people in one of the canal colonies developed by the British in West Panjab. It reproduces with sympathy and sensitivity the life of the tribes inhabiting the areas between Chenab and Jhelum and foreshadows the sufferings and exploitation they were likely to undergo from the local aristocracy with the help of the rulers. In another novel, *Lok Dushman* (The Enemies of the People, 1953), he attempts to depict the conflict between the feudal lords and the peasants. Narula, in short, is responsible for introducing intellectual realism in Panjabi fiction supported by documentation of facts. As a result, his novels turned into more or less dry accounts of social and historical facts, and the story interest in them took a back seat. Some of his novels written after independence made some attempts to liberate them from the puritanical and reformist frame given by Nanak Singh. Another feature of his works is that it shifted the domestic scene to which the Panjabi novel was confined earlier and broadened its sphere to meaningful socioeconomic perspective.

Sant Singh Sekhon with his *Lahu Mitci* (Blood and Soil) narrates the story of a Panjabi peasant with a background of vast agricultural and economic changes. Sekhon's major contribution to Panjabi fiction is in the field of the short story. In fact, he inaugurated the era of experiment in the field of the Panjabi short story. He brought a whirl of fertilizing ideas, pleading for a new society, new humanism, and a "new hero." He is responsible for introducing into the short story the pattern, technique, and realistic methods of Chekhov and Katherine Mansfield. Jaswant Singh Kanwal, who wrote profusely, like Nanak Singh, is very sentimental in his storytelling and is a committed Marxist. He is, however, puritanical in his approach while depicting love themes and also preaches revolution for fulfillment of the total human personality. Whereas Nanak Singh depicted mostly the urban life of Panjab, Kanwal moved the scenario to rural settings in which his heroes and heroines are involved in romance. He attempts to invest a charm in the rural life of Panjab. His novel *Puranmashi*

(The Night of Full Moon, 1954), a work of his early phase, depicts village life in an exquisite manner by combining the elements of romance, mystery, and beauty. In his later novels, he becomes more and more political, and in most of his novels he superimposes abstract polemical discussion on Marxist ideology and mixes the same with Indian religious philosophy. Only in *Civil Lines* (1956) does he sustain fictional interest and give a realistic picture of the modern culture. He also wrote some short stories.

SIKH LEGEND, MYTH, AND HISTORY WELDED INTO THE NOVEL

Narinderpal Singh, who wrote on the lines of Nanak Singh, attempted some novels based on Sikh history. *Khanion Ti~bi* (Sharper than Blade, 1960) deals with the period of Sikh history when Baba Banda Bahadur rose to power, crushing the Moghul rulers in Panjab. In *Walon Nikki* (Thinner than Hair, 1960), he depicts the period when the Sikh Missels were fighting with one another to gain political power. *Et Marg Jana* (This Path to Be Followed, 1960) deals with the rule of Maharaja Ranjit Singh. *Ik Sarkar Bajhon* (In the Absence of the Emperor, 1961) portrays the conditions that led to the downfall of the Sikh rule and the battles fought by the Sikhs against the British during 1845–49. These are based on a good deal of historical research and provide interesting reading. His other novels, *Ik Rab Ik Para* (A Path and a Stage, 1953), *Shakti* (Power), *Tria Jal* (The Spell of Women, 1957), and *Aman de Rab* (The Paths of Peace), either are biographical or portray the effects of war on youth.

Kartar Singh Duggal started writing novels soon after independence. He gave to the Panjabi world before the beginning of the 1960s three novels, namely, *Andran* (Intestines, 1949), *Naunh te Mas* (The Nails and the Flesh, 1957), and *Eh Dil Vikau Hai* (This Heart Is for Sale, 1959). Then, after about 10 years, in the late 1960s, he published a trilogy entitled *Hal Muridan Da* (The Poor Plight of the Pupil), with three novels in a series depicting in a marvelous detail and sensitivity the story of three generations of a family uprooted from West Panjab and resettled in Delhi after partition. This novel presents a vivid picture of Panjabi life and culture in a sociocultural and historical perspective that brings out its diversity. One of his novels of the trilogy, *Man Pardesi,* (Mind, the Foreigner), was very well received among the Panjabi readership.

Duggal primarily wrote short stories, but after partition his interest switched to novels. Many others who established themselves as story writers, such as Dalip Kaur Tiwana, Gurdial Singh, Jaswant Singh Virdi, and Sukhbir, found novel writing more satisfying for development of their genius. This is a significant tendency in the postpartition Panjabi literature which shows that most of the older-generation fiction writers chose to devote their energies to novel writing, and this provided an opportunity to the younger writers to take to story writing. Duggal has contributed more than a dozen collections of short stories, among which are *Saver Sar* (The Morning Time, 1941), *Nawan Ghar* (The New Home, 1951), *Karamat* (The Miracle, 1957), and *Pare Mere* (1967).

TURN TOWARD DEPICTION OF THE RURAL CULTURAL ETHOS OF MALWA

Dalip Kaur Tiwana, who started writing in the early 1960s, has published more than half a dozen novels, but her most outstanding work till now remains *Eh Hamara Jiwana,* a very moving tale of a poor peasant girl who becomes a victim of reckless human lust. It narrates the tragedy of a woman belonging to a landless peasant family who, despite her best effort to preserve herself, becomes victim to circumstances in which she and her family remain caught. She wielded the regional dialect of Malwa in this novel for the expression of deep inner feelings with minimum use of words. Another novel, *Rin Pittran Da* (Ancestral Debts), is the depiction of suffering undergone by the Panjabis in the wake of Operation Blue Star. Bikram, an offspring of a Sikh father and an English mother, is the hero of this novel. His father dies in a road accident when he returns from England to his home in the Panjab soon after Operation Blue Star, and Bikram's English mother dies in England, leaving him alone in this world. He wishes his stepmother in India would own him as her son, but she refuses to do so. Ultimately, his stepsister, Simmy, accepts him as her brother, thus allowing him entry into his ancestral roots. In this novel, too, she uses the dialect of Bhathinda, a district in the Malwa belt of Panjab, and minutely depicts regional cultural ethos in a charming manner. Tiwana is also a Sahitya Academy Award recipient, and her novel *Pile Pattian Di Dastan* (The Story of Dried Yellow Leaves) also needs special mention as an outstanding piece of fictional art. Dalip Kaur Tiwana, along with Ajti Caur (1934), Gurbachan Bhullar (1935), and Gulzar Singh Sandhu (1935), wrote very delicate stories in their own individual styles.

Gurdial Singh, whose name links him with the last 30 years of contemporary Panjabi literature, is a leading figure of the new Panjabi novel. The publication of his *Marhi da Diva* (The Earthen Lamp of a Tomb, 1962) marks the beginning of a new era of the Panjabi novel. It brings out in a significant manner the rural cultural ethos of a region of the Malwa area of Panjab. It, therefore, establishes an altogether different identity of the Panjabi novel, assigning it the features of both a regional novel and a pastoral parable. His other two novels, *Anhoye* (Nonbeings) and *Adh Chanai Rat* (Midnight Lit with Moon), written successively after *Marhi da Diva,* also portray effectively the fate of the nonperson "hero" in different settings.

Sohan Singh Sittal, now in his late 80s, earlier composed ballads and charmed large Panjabi audiences by performing them on the stage over half a century. He turned to novel writing in his late 50s. His *Tutan Wala Khuh* (A Well by the Mulberry Trees) displays a maturity of approach and skillfulness in weaving a story around the aftereffects of the country's partition in the background of

Panjab's rural environment. The writer brings out the feelings of remorse in the wake of partition of Panjab, where both Hindus and Muslims were living in an atmosphere of communal amity. The village well becomes a symbol of the past life marked by mutual understanding and hope, cruelly dismembered by the forces of communalism and hatred. Another novel, *Jang Ke Arnan* (War or Peace), brings out forcefully the adverse impacts of war on human society. He has published nearly a dozen novels, which are marked by a very compact organization of the narrative, with a keen sense of observation of details and well-drawn characters. He, to a great extent, follows Nanak Singh in form and style, though he does make some innovations here and there in the fictional form. His *Jug Badal Gaya* (The Times Have Changed) also represents an ideal piece of a mature, humanistic sensibility.

THE NOVELS OF GUJJAR AND MACHHIARA TRIBES

Mohan Kahlon, another Panjabi novelist of note who carved out a distinct place in this art form, is known for portraying tribal life on the bank of the river Ravi on the border of Panjab and Jammu. He also focuses on the life of Gujjars living on the Himalayan hills in the same area. His very popular novel *Ret te Breta* (The Sand and the Sandbank, 1969) portrays in fair detail the cultural and social life of the tribal herdsmen (Gujjars) who raise cattle in the hills and sell their milk to the people living in the surrounding plains to earn their livelihood. Likewise, his *Machhli Ik Dariya Di* (A Fish out of a River) highlights the life of boatmen of the riverine area on the western banks of the Ravi at the point where it enters the plains of Panjab. He has given, in a very lively manners, customs, manners, rituals, folk songs, and enormous wealth of information, which are significant anthropologically and charming as a part of the fictional world. Kahlon has given a vivid picture of the inner intricacies of their social organization and their intratribal relationships. Kahlon has also thrown light on the corruption and inefficiency of the police and judicial system that is responsible for oppression of these innocent people. The story of his second novel, *Ret te Breta,* revolves around the character Qadir, an outcaste, who struggles to fight the injustice done to him by his society but who finally gives way to the might of the established system. Another novel, *Kali Mitti* (The Black Earth, 1986), has attracted critical attention for its depiction of promiscuity. Mohan Kahlon, by capturing the conflicts lying underneath the surface of the life of these tribes of Panjab, assigns a dramatic quality to his novels.

PANJABI NOVEL ABROAD

Some novelists who were living in India but later settled in other countries have also distinguished themselves in this field. At least two names deserve a special mention. Giani Kesar Singh (Canada) and Swarn Chandan (U.K.), who have been writing regularly, have established themselves as representatives of two different areas of novel writing. Whereas Giani Kesar Singh has devoted himself to writing historical novels based on the lives of those who sacrificed their lives in foreign lands during the freedom movement of the country, Swarn Chandan through his novels portrayed the lives of those Indians who are living in the U.K. He throws light on the economic and social life of Indians in England who have no sense of belonging to that land and are also conscious of the historical colonial background of the British. In his more than half a dozen novels, he has narrated the woes of those who work day and night shifts to earn their livelihood and save something for their kith and kin at home. He brings out the pains of the racial discrimination that they have suffered at the hands of the whites. Swarn Chandan also represents the winds of change sweeping over them. While constructing his fictional world, he has made experiments in form and employed a number of techniques and ideas. Strong feelings of rootlessness, disorientation, nostalgia, depersonalization, and isolation are replete in his novels. *Kakb, Kan, Te Darya* (The Straw, the Chaff and River, 1980) is his most popular work of fiction. Swarn Chandan also wrote some short stories, but due to the contribution of Ravinder Ravi (Canada) and Raghbir Dhand (U.K.), the Panjabi short story by diaspora writers acquired a distinct identity.

Giani Kesar Singh published his first novel, *Lehar Vadhdi Gayi* (The Current Went on Swelling), in the mid-1960s, in which he depicted the anti-imperialist struggle of the Indian community in Canada and within the country. In 1970, he published his second novel, *Jangi Qaidi* (The Prisoner of War), in which, besides narrating the horrors of World War II, he described the experience of Panjabis in the war and its impact on the sociocultural life at home. He later shifted his interest in writing fiction to the lives of the heroes who laid down their lives for the independence of the country. Some of his novels, such as *Shaheed Udham Singh* (The Martyr Udham Singh), *Amar Shaheed Madan Lal Dhingra, Baba Hari Singh Usman, Shaheed Mewa Singh Lopoke,* and so on, have been popular with Panjabi readers. Most of these novels are written in the style of Nanak Singh. But their merit lies in the fact that they preserve the history of the freedom movement in India, which has otherwise been neglected till now. In 1986, Giani wrote *Waris Shah di Maut* (The Death of Waris Shah), depicting the cultural crisis of Panjabis living abroad. He shows how the younger generations of Panjabis are forgetting their heritage and losing their own distinct identity.

STREAM OF CONSCIOUSNESS

Surjit Singh Sethi, a dramatist, theater artist, novelist, and short story writer, wrote a couple of novels on the lines of stream of consciousness as practiced in the West by James Joyce and others. His experiment with this form is very bold, indeed, but in his *Ik Khali Piyala* (An Empty Cup) he did not achieve much success. However, in his second novel, *Kal Vi Suraj Charhega* (The Sun Will Rise Even Tomorrow), the story based on the Jallianwala Bagh tragedy, he is able to establish better communication with his readers. Sukhbir, another fiction writer settled in Bombay, has written novels on the life of the metropolis and has described the elements of the alienation in this life with a good measure of success. He has also experimented with stream of consciousness with much maturity and skill. Other examples of the experimental novel are Narinderpal Singh's *Pvniya ke Masya* and Jagjit Brar's *Dhup Darya di Dosti* (The Friendship of Sunshine and the River), in which novel techniques of building a fictional image have been tried with unequal success.

INDIVIDUAL IN THE CRISIS OF VALUES

Niranjan Tasneem, Surjit Hans, Joginder Kairon, Ram Saroop Ankhi, and a host of young writers have written novels of new sensibility. They portray a picture of the harassed individual enmeshed in the crisis of values. They express various facets of the same theme with different techniques and varying levels of symbolic and allegorical expressions. Along with the new, some of the old novelists continued to write. Harnam Dass Sehrai, who started writing fiction in the mid-1960s, is still actively engaged in writing novels on Sikh history saturated with sentimentalism. He has published more than 40 novels eulogizing the Sikh gurus and heroes, but they lack authentic historical facts and are largely based on stories preserved in oral tradition.

FICTION IN PAKISTAN

In Pakistan after 1947, the Panjabi novel received some encouragement at the hands of a number of writers who were earlier writing in Urdu. There were only three Panjabi novels written by Muslim authors before partition. Joshua Fazal Din and Miran Bakhsh Minhas wrote a few more novels even after Pakistan came into existence. Mohmmad Bakir and Abdul Majeed Bhatti also wrote one novel each. The main theme of these novels was social reform. They later were joined by the young writers, Afzal Ahsan Randhawa, Fakhar Zaman, Saleem Khan Gimmi, Zafar Lashari, Ismail Ahmadani, Razia Noor Mohammad, Raja Mohammad Ahmed, Nadim Asari, Kehkshan Malik, Ahmed Saleem, Muneer Ahmed Alvi, Ehsan Batalvi, and many others. Some of the novels written, notably by Rajinder Singh Bedi, Amrita Pritam, and Nanak Singh, were published in Persian script. Afzal Randhawa translated into Panjabi in Persian script Chinua Achebe's African novel, *Things Fall Apart.* The novel depicts the tragedy of Okankwo, an important man in the Obi tribe in the days when white men first came on the scene. This novel tells the series of events by which Okankwo, through his pride and his fears, becomes exiled from his tribe and returns, only to be forced into the ignominy of suicide to escape the results of his courage against the white man. Randhawa selected this novel for translation into Panjabi because it looks like the story of Panjab when it fell in the last century. The story, which the British wrote on the bones of an African hero, was the same as the story written on the bones of Panjabi heroes of that period. There is marked identity in the sociocultural values of the African tribes and the Panjabi society. The motive is to rediscover the Panjab, which has been lost due to the centuries of subservience. Randhawa, in the same manner, has tried to rediscover the lost Panjabi identity in his novel *Doaba.*

Fakhar Zaman, a poet, novelist, and intellectual, wrote three novels, *Ik Mare Bande di Kahani, Sat Guacbe Lok,* and *Bandiwan.* In the first two, he attempts to rediscover the roots of Panjabi life. The third is the gruesome story of the execution of Zulfiqar Ali Bhutto, a former prime minister of Pakistan. The protagonists in these novels reflect his intense desire to search for Panjabi roots in the archetypal and imaginative world of Panjab. They make a voyage into the depths of their being and search for their authentic self. The third novel, *Bandiwan,* is interspersed with poetry, symbols, and allusions to the depths of the inner being of Panjabi character, which form an integral part of the emotional and technical development of the story. These novels have been transcribed into the Gurmukhi script in the Indian Panjab and are well received there. Randhawa's *Doaba* has also been rendered into Gurmukhi and warmly applauded by Panjabi readers in India. The search for roots is also visible in another powerful novel, *Taee* (Aunt) by Farzand Ali. Most of these writers have also tried their hand at story writing and have depicted lively pictures of rural Panjabi life and its personality in an uninhibited manner. There is a long list of young Pakistani short story writers who are well equipped to practice this art form because of their sensitivity and keen eye for detail.

During the last two decades, the short story in Panjabi has grown as a modern literary form identified by the presence of a conscious narrative, foregrounding a particular incident, situation, or moment of emotional intensity. The Panjabi writer has used this form with great flexibility and seriousness. The most significant feature of Panjabi fiction—both novel and short story—can be seen in its strength of foregrounding the common person.

PANJABI DRAMA AND THEATER

Panjabi drama, from the very beginning an admixture of the characteristics of English and Sanskrit drama, bears a greater impact of English drama—particularly of Shakespeare—than of traditional Sanskrit drama. In fact, Sanskrit drama and poetics, though they flourished in this land in ancient times, ironically, did not have much influence in shaping the drama developed in the twentieth century.

Though Bhai Vir Singh, a Panjabi (*Raja Lakhdata Singh,* 1910), Kirpa Sagar (*Maharaja Ranjit Singh* and *Dido Jamval*), Bawa Budh Singh (1878–1931) (*Chander Hari* and *Mundri Chhall* [The Magical Ring]), Charan Singh (1853–1908) (Rani Sarab Kaur), Gurbax Singh Barrister (*Mohan Bhaia,* 1912), Brij Lal Shastri (*Puraan Natak,* 1919, *Partigya, Vasva Datta,* 1925) started writing Panjabi plays in the early part of this century, Ishwar Chander Nanda (1892–

1966) wrote the first successful plays in Panjabi in a realistic style on the model of Western drama. His predecessors did follow models of Sanskrit plays, but Nanda started writing under the direct influence of Western drama. He came in contact with Norah Richards and Philips E. Richards of Dayal Singh College, Lahore, during his student days and started writing short plays in Panjabi. *Dulhan* (The Bride) and *Bebe Ram Bhajni* were Nanda's two one-act plays, which pioneered modern Panjabi drama.

Nanda's first one-act-play was staged in 1914, and his full-length play *Subhadra* was published in 1920. He has written two other full-length plays, *Var Ghar jan Lily da Viah* (1938) and *Social Circle* (1953), and a Panjabi adaptation of Shakespeare's *Merchant of Venice* entitled *Shamu Shah* (1928). Besides these, he wrote over a dozen one-act plays, published in two collections, *Jhalkare* (Reflections, 1949) and *Lishkare* (Flashes, 1956).

In all his works, Nanda wrote about social problems of his day. In *Subhadra,* he deals with the problem of widow remarriage; in *Var Ghar Jan Lily da Viyah,* he contrasts love marriage and arranged marriage; and in *Social Circle,* he portrays the urban, middle-class elite who arrange their "social meets" merely to promote their narrow commercial interests.

The most important contribution of Nanda's plays is that, with them, Panjabi drama is freed from religious and mythological themes. He propagated new values through young men and women educated in schools and colleges. That is why he highlights mutual conflict between the two generations of the Panjabi middle class. To Nanda's credit, while adopting Western techniques of drama, he made full use of the folk theater tradition of Panjab, blending the two in a vivid pattern. His presentation of marriage scenes, religious ceremonies, superstitions, the ignorance of the village folks, folk songs and folk dances, and so on invests his plays with a Panjabi character. Nanda greatly influenced the later playwrights who were responsible for shaping the future Panjabi drama into a theater molded and motivated by Western drama on realistic lines. Those who followed him included Joshua Fazal-ud-din (1903–73), Harcharn Singh (1914), Sant Singh Sekhon (1908), Balwant Gargi (1916), and a few others. The writers who were almost contemporaries of Nanda were Gurbakhsh Singh Preet Lari (1895–1978), Mohan Singh Dewana (1899–1984), Harcharn Singh, Gurdial Singh Khosla (1912), Roshan Lal Ahuja (1904–87), and Gurdial Singh Phul (1911–88). Some of the writers of this generation were writing in other genres, and so drama and theater were not their mainstay. They were primarily writing drama only for enriching this form also; otherwise, they distinguished themselves in other forms of literature. For example, Dewana gained fame in poetry and literary scholarship, Gurbakhsh Singh in prose, and Sant Singh Sekhon in fiction and literary criticism, but a few of them devoted themselves wholeheartedly to drama. Except for Sant Singh Sekhon, most of these playwrights contributed to the growth of popular drama nurtured by Harcharn Singh. It was taken forward by Gurdial Singh Khosla, Roshan Lal Ahuja, and Gurdial Singh Phul, all playwrights of the first generation. These playwrights wrote on topical social, historical, and mythological themes. The dramatization of Sikh cultural ethos was also a favorite subject of these playwrights. The audiences who were not conscious of any quality theater were swayed by their religious sentimentality. However the plays of this generation gained popularity, their art remained untouched by modernism. The defining feature of these playwrights was their farcical or melodramatic impact, which did not rise above the level of Ram Lila performances.

PROGRESSIVE TRENDS—PANJABI DRAMA BETWEEN 1931 AND 1947

There is no doubt that Harcharan Singh and the playwrights who followed his lead added quantitatively to the body of dramatic literature in Panjabi, but they have offered little by way of quality, which appeared only when stalwarts like Sant Singh Sekhon, Balwant Gargi, and Amrik Singh (1921) made their contribution. These writers have brought vigor and freshness to Panjabi drama. With them began the trend of progressive writing. Sekhon has given a new dimension to Panjabi drama by committing the genre to a dialectical interpretation of contemporary reality. He is responsible for evolving a form of Panjabi drama that is called intellectual drama. Instead of presenting matter-of-fact details, Sekhon, in this type of play, subjects themes to intellectual insight and philosophical scrutiny. Sekhon, in his more than a dozen plays, raised exciting debate on various themes of contemporary social and cultural relevance, which has made some of his plays very controversial. Some of his very well known plays include *Kalakar* (The Artist, 1946), *Moyian Sar na Kai* (Gone and Forgotten), *Bera Bandh Na Sakyo* (You Did Not Bind the Logs of the Float), *Narki* (Denizens of Hell, 1952), *Damyanti* (1962), and *Mitter Pyara* (The Dear Friend). It is generally believed that Sekhon has failed to write plays meant to be staged, and his works do not go beyond intellectual discussions, which, of course, are stimulating. His characters are automatons and devoid of any physical action, but still his writing offers an exciting fare for mature and lively debate.

During this period, there seemed to have developed a cleavage between literary drama and drama meant for the stage. The plays of Sant Singh Sekhon, though impressive, were scarcely staged. Defending his plays, he argued that they could not be staged for they represented times ahead of him. The existing theater was not adequate to produce his plays because of its limitations. On the other hand, some Panjabi critics characterized these plays as literary plays at best, having no potential to turn into a stage reality. Roshan Lal Ahuja accepted that there could be both kinds of plays—literary meant for reading only and others worthy of stage production. Thus, for some time, there existed a state of isolation between the literary, on one hand, and stage drama, on the other, in Panjabi. Balwant Gargi, one of the most distinguished names in Panjabi drama and theater arts, brought an end to this controversy by laying the foundations of a mature, professional theater in Panjabi. His plays are a happy synthesis between the requirements of stage and the demands of literature. The dialogue of his plays has a literary grace and poetic charm. Panjabi folklore in its diverse manifestations lends meaning to his plays and makes them memorable.

His earliest work, *Loha Kut* (The Blacksmith, 1944), created a stir in Panjabi literary circles for its unusual theme and distinct form. It is a very sensitive play with an equally unusual theme: the problem of suppressed passions. In it, the inner dreams and aspirations of both mother and daughter are ruthlessly crushed in the suffocating atmosphere of the blacksmith Kaku's home. The daughter revolts against the orthodoxy and oppression and elopes with her sweetheart. The mother follows the example of her daughter and leaves Kaku, even though they have been married 18 years. At a symbolic level, the play deals with the elemental and primordial in human nature.

Gargi, under the impact of pragtivad (progressive movement), wrote a number of plays with a Marxist slant. Notable among them are *Ghuggi* (The Dove), *Biswedar* (The Feudal Lord), *Sail Pathar* (Still Stones), *Kesro* (Name of Woman), and *Girjhan* (Vultures, 1951). These plays are on themes such as the world peace movement, the agrarian struggle, national reconstruction, and polemics on committed art. In his *Dhuni di Agg* (The Dark Ritual), he breaks with the realistic tradition and represents love and hatred as primeval forces through the symbolism of red flames of fire contrasted with the darkness of night. Among his plays based on Marxist ideology, *Kanak di Bali* (Stem of Wheat) departs from realistic tradition and introduces an element of lyricality from the indigenous folklore. He attains a rare height in *Sultan Razia,* a historical play that deals with an action-packed period of Indian history, from the dying Iltumish to the death of Sultan Razia. It is a period of uncertainty and conspiracies resulting in ruthless killings for the throne. This play in its Hindi version was staged by the National School of Drama under the directorship of E. Alkazi and thus brought Gargi to national fame. In another play, *Saunkan* (The Other Wife, 1979), he deals with the triple relationship among mother, son, and daughter. He presents the sexual rivalry between the daughter and the mother at the psychological level. This is rather a disappointing work, for it does not give rise to any powerful dramatic conflict. Gargi is also an author of a scholarly treatise on Indian stagecraft entitled *Bharti Drama,* which won him a Sahitya Academy Award.

Among the older generation, Kartar Singh Duggal, a leading fiction writer, wrote plays that have been produced mainly by All India Radio. He is credited with developing a form of the radio play in Panjabi. To meet the needs of the radio play, he uses his characters as symbols. His play *Puranian Botlan* (The Old Bottles) is a meaningful critique of the unscrupulous behavior of the urban middle class. His other notable plays include *Auh Gaye Sajjan Auh Gaye* (There Goes Our Good Friend, 1942), *Ik Siffer Siffer* (One Zero Makes Zero, 1941), and *Mitha Pani* (The Sweet Water), all of which have been produced successfully several times over the radio. Duggal in these plays seems to have been impressed by the technique of T. S. Eliot and Christopher Frye in the matter of the use of rhythmic prose in his plays.

POSTINDEPENDENCE PERIOD (1947–70)

Most of the playwrights of the preindependence period continued writing after independence, and some, like Gurdial Singh Khosla, Harcharan Singh, Kartar Singh Duggal, and Sant Singh Sekhon, wrote plays on the problems of rehabilitation of refugees following in the wake of partition of the country, yet a group of new young writers, namely, Amrik Singh, Harsaran Singh (1929–94), Gurcharan Singh Jasuja (1925), Surjit Singh Sethi (1928), Kapur Singh Ghumman (1927–84), and Paritosh Gargi (1923), introduced a few new themes and techniques in their plays.

IPTA and Panjabi Drama

During the freedom movement before independence, theater activity had assumed a far greater relevance than before, and links between the Indian arts, especially theater arts and the resurgence of Indian people, had become stronger. The Indian Progressive Theater Association (IPTA) movement in the realm of drama and theater was responsible for greater participation of the masses in different art activities, particularly in theater, as a result of which drama went closer to the day-to-day routine of the life of people. The theater arts were no longer conceived as mere means of entertainment, but they were reoriented toward playing a greater role as instruments of social awakening. IPTA also worked for obliterating the link between the theater and audience and bringing it closer to their hearts. It also brought about a significant change in the Panjabi theater in the sense that it extended its area of operation by making possible its convergence with theater activity in the rest of the country. This resulted in the liberation of Panjabi theater from inhibitions of academicism and middle-class prudery, and the IPTA movement in Panjab made it possible for appearance on the theater scene of artists like Shiela Bhatia, the well-known film star Balraj Sahni, Balwant Gargi, Tera Singh Chan, Joginder Bahrla, Pandit Khalili, and others, who made serious efforts to take Panjabi theater to the masses and evolve a powerful idiom of dramatic conflict.

Exploration of Inner Recesses of the Mind

In contrast, some of the new playwrights started introducing experiments in their plays under the influence of some Western dramatists and theater artists. Their focus of interest shifted from the portrayal of economic and social problems to the exploration of inner recesses of the human mind. Amrik Singh, in his *Parchhavian Di Pakkar* (The Grip of Shadows), makes use of episodic technique in building to a sharp climax the crippling grip of past events on the life of an innocent victim of circumstances. In *Atit de Parchhaven* (Shadows of the Past), the design of the play is clearly influenced by August Stindberg, the Swedish playwright. In *Bujharat* (The Riddle), he again plunges into experimentation of form while dramatizing the life of Stindberg. Here, he makes use of the dream technique and symbolism of the sea to unfold the inner workings of his protagonist's mind.

Harsaran Singh, another experimentalist, in his plays *Jigra* (Courage) and *Udas Lok* (The Dispirited People), has shown unusual vitality by bringing to bear critical realism on contemporary social problems. He brings out forcefully in *Udas Lok* the tensions in a joint family and its gradual disintegration. In his historical play *Nizam Sakka,* he presents in dramatic form the brief rule of Nizam, a water carrier, on whom the Mughal emperor Hamayun had bestowed kingship for one day in reward for saving him from drowning. The writer has tried to make this incident relevant to the contemporary situation by projecting Nizam Sakka's rule as concretizing the dreams and aspirations of a socialist democratic welfare state.

Surjit Singh Sethi, another playwright, started writing social plays with a realistic slant and soon turned into an experimentalist. His *King Mirza te Spera* (King Mirza and the Snake Charmer) is reminiscent of Samuel Beckett's *Waiting for Godot.* It is an attempt to find meaning in the futility of existence. In another play, *Nangi Sarak Rat da Ujala* (The Naked Road and the Light of Night), Sethi attempts to focus on the experience of alienation and loneliness being suffered by modern individuals. In yet another play, *Eh Zindgi Hai Dosto* (This Life, O Friends), he wrote a powerful satire on corruption in contemporary social life. He profitably makes use of Artaud's theater of cruelty in its production. Sethi is a bold experimentalist and has been able to translate Western ideas into playwriting and stage production in Panjabi.

The experimental drama received a further fillip from Paritosh Gargi. His *Luk Chhip Jana* (Ay! Hide You Yourself) and *Chhleda* (Illusion) are authentic pieces of experimental structuring. The former recalls Eugene Ionesco's *The Chairs* and later focuses on a social problem using experimental techniques.

Gurcharan Singh Jasuja, who stands out prominently among the new dramatists, writes his plays with down-to-earth common sense. By remaining away from all kinds of theories and fashions, he is able to dramatize small-time conflicts of the lackluster middle class. Still, he has made some significant innovations and a meaningful analysis of the inner self in his plays. In *Kandhan Ret Dian* (The Walls of Sand) and *Andhkar* (The Mist), he moves from visual symbols to verbal symbols, which not only help to unfold meaning but also intensify the action in the plays. One of his recent plays, *Rachna Ram Banai* (God Made the Creation), a play based on the verse of Guru Tegh Bahadur, implies that the Lord is the creator of this world and that every object in it takes its shape according to his will. The play, a fine example of the dramatization of an idealistic theory creation, is a distinguished work possessing literary grace and artistic excellence.

The quincentenary of the first Sikh guru, Baba Nanak was celebrated in the year 1969. In 1966, the 300th birth anniversary of the 10th master, Guru Gobind Singh, was celebrated with great fanfare. In 1977, the 300th anniversary of the founding of the city of Amritsar by Sri Guru Ram Das was celebrated. During these anniversaries, the art of drama and theater was used to pay tributes to these Panjabi heroes, and many aspects of their life and teachings were projected in various theatrical performances. A lot of dramatic literature was produced during this period. Some critics give a name to this period as *shatabdi kal* (centenary period) of Panjabi drama and theater, when a large number of playwrights and theater artists devoted themselves to the task of writing religious plays around the legends and history of the Sikh gurus. It was a challenge for a playwright to write a play about the Sikh gurus without their presence on the stage. The Sikh religious sentiments cannot tolerate any flesh-and-blood character portraying the great guru. Some plays revolve around an idea or a character that appears but briefly on the stage, but any play based on Sikh history depicting the gurus and their times has to present the main character only as a reported speech. In these plays, Panjabi playwrights drew the character of the off-stage hero in a superb manner. Balwant Gargi, in his *Gagan Mien Thal* (The Sky, the Worship Plate), presents, in absentia, guru Nanak as its hero. A bulk of drama literature produced in this category lacked quality and overwhelmed large audiences due to religious fervor. Some of the titles that became popular during this period are *Sabh Kichh Hote Upaye* (Everything Could Be Possible) and *Jin Sach Pale Hoye* (Those Who Possess the Truth, 1969) by Gurdial Singh Phul, *Itihas Juab Mangda Hai* (History Demands Answer, 1967), *Zafarnama* (1969), and *Chamkaur Di Garhi* (The Fortress of Chamkaur, 1969) by Harcharan Singh, and *Amritsar Sifti da Ghar* (Amritsar—the House of Praise) by S. S. Amole.

Some very eminent poets have written memorable verse plays in Panjabi. Haribhajan Singh wrote *Tar Tupka* (A Drop Hanging by a String, 1957); Ravinder Ravi of Canada, *Bimar Sadi* (The Ailing Century); Shiv Kumar, *Luna* (Name of a Woman); and Ajaib Kamal of Kenya, *Langra Asman* (The Lame Sky).

On the other side of the border, some efforts have been made to promote the genre of drama by some Pakistani writers. Some of them wrote for radio and television. Ashfaq Ahmad, Sajjad Haider, Nawaz Sheikh Iqbal, Baqi Siddiqui, Saleem Rafiqui, Akram Butt, Agha Ashraf, and, above all, Rafi Peer made important contributions in this regard. Those who wrote for television and made a mark in this sphere are Safdar Mir, Munnoo Bhai, Younis Javed, Ashfaq Ahmed, and Bano Qudsia. Munnoo Bhai's serial "Jazeera" (Island) was very popular with viewers on both sides of the border. Later, it published in book form.

There has been some stage activity in the cities of Pakistan, particularly at Lahore, which had grown into an excellent center of Panjabi theater arts before partition. There has been a spurt in the commercial theater, but very little can stand out as a genuine art. *Pug* (The Turban) and *Aj Akhan Waris Shah Nun* (I Address Waris Shah Again) are rare exceptions.

There have been some very good plays in Panjabi written over the years on this side of Panjab. The late Ishaq Mohammad's *Mussali* (Water Carrier) and *Quqnus* (name of a mythological bird), Najm Hussain Sayad's *Takhat Lahore* (The Throne of Lahore) and *Ik Raat Ravi Di* (A Night on the Banks of the River Ravi), and Sarmad Sehbai's *Punjwan Chiragh* (The Fifth Earthen Lamp) and *Shak Shubhey da Vela* (The Time for Doubt and Suspicion) all deal with the history of Panjab and attempt to identify and rediscover Panjabi "roots." Najm Hussain Sayad's plays are already translated into Gurmukhi in the Indian part of Panjab and are quite popular with Panjabi readers. Ishaq Mohammad's *Mussali* is also available to Panjabi readership on the Indian side in Gurmukhi script. The play has been staged successfully a number of times in Chandigarh, Ludhiana, and Amritsar by Kala Mandir Mohali and has received great applause from large audiences. It has been produced and directed by the noted author and theater artist Atamjit. The play charms audiences for its dialect of the Bar area in West Panjab. Its story goes back to the times when the Aryans invaded the subcontinent and destroyed Harrapa. It is the sad story of Mussallis who were subjugated by the Aryans, being labeled as *daso achhoots* (untouchables) and made to do low, menial work in the farms without home and hearth.

Experimental drama made its presence felt in the hands of a couple of young playwrights and directors, like Atamjit (1950) and Ajmer Aulakh (1949). Atamjit's *Rishtian da Ki Rakhiye Nan, Ajit Ram, Seenan,* and *Farash Vich Ugiyya Hoya Rukh* are very popular with Panjabi audiences. His short plays *Murghi Khana* and *Pallu di Udik Vich* are equally well known to the Panjabi world. Aulakh has become a household name in the world of Panjabi theater with *Begane Bohar di Chhan, Ik Ramayan Hor,* and *Bhajian Bahin.*

PANJABI THEATER AND ITS PRESENT POSITION

The early Panjabi theater catered primarily to the urban middle class, and its intent was to bring about social reform. Whatever the conflicts presented, these plays focused on the domestic and the romantic. The characters were generally stock types, and the denouement proceeded on familiar lines. According to Sant Singh Sekhon, Panjabi theater in its early days was rhetorical, with emotions and sentiments having great importance.

During the 1940s, there emerged a significant Panjabi theater in Lahore. But the partition of the country was responsible for checking its growth. Uprooted from its nuclear cultural center of Lahore, theater activity received a serious setback when it dispersed to Shimla, Jullunder, Patiala, Amritsar, Delhi, and, later, Chandigarh. Nowhere could it make its presence felt. In all these places, Panjabi theater remained a localized affair with no distinctive character of its own.

National School of Drama (NSD) and the Panjabi Theater

Only in the 1960s did the theater movement in the regional languages attain maturity and professional skill. The National School of Drama, established in Delhi in the early 1960s, became a strong center for bringing about a purposeful dialogue among theater folks of the different regions of India. With coming into contact with the theater being done elsewhere in India, Panjabi theater found a new orientation in the Panjab and Delhi and Bombay. It had an opportunity to avail itself of the services of well trained professional theater artists like Harpal Tiwana and his talented wife, Neena, Bansi Kaul, Suresh Pandit, Gurcharan Singh Channi, Devinder Daman, Sonal Mann Singh, Balraj Pandit, Kewal Dhaliwal, Kamal Tiwari Mahender, Navnindra Behal, and Rani Balbir Kaur, who have brought into it a new vitality and vigor. The establishment of the departments of Indian drama and Asian theater at Panjab University, Chandigarh, and speech and drama at Panjab University, Patiala, under the guidance of two theater stalwarts, Balwant Gargi and Surjit Singh Sethi, respectively, has led to some bold experiments in theater. Some playwrights, such as Gursharan Singh and Atamjit, though they did not have formal training in theater arts, are absolutely so slick in their profession that they are bringing a professional touch to Panjabi theater.

In the 1970s, Prem Julundry, with his Sapru House shows, regaled middle-class Panjabi audiences in Delhi. These shows, a craze of those times, offered what may be termed "hilarious adult comedy," which were also called "laugh-a-minute sex comedies." These Panjabi farces with salacious titles have been attacked, defended, even threatened, yet they were big box office hits.

In this very period, Panjabi theater started having its impact, for some of the theater groups made a serious effort to free themselves from the bonds of tradition. The Delhi Art Theater of Shiela Bhatia, Gursharan Singh's Amritsar School of Drama, which later took the name of Chandigarh School of Drama after his moving to Chandigarh, Balraj Pandit's Natakwala, and Atamjit's Kala Mandir, first at Amritsar and now at Mohali, have combined dramatic dexterity with ingenious devices while exploring new modes of expression on stage. Ajmer Aulakh has evolved a new, robust theatrical idiom from the folklore of Panjab. Devinder Daman and Jaswant Damanthe, a director–actress, husband–wife team, have, through their Norah Richards's *Rang Manch,* introduced new modes of action in religious-historical plays.

PANJABI DRAMA AND THEATER FROM 1980 ONWARD

From 1980, Panjabi drama and theater passed through most difficult times. In this period, the people of Panjab suffered the most painful conditions of reckless killings and tensions between the two major religious groups of Panjab—Hindus and Sikhs. There was an atmosphere of total darkness and dissolution, with ever-increasing terrorist activity of looting and killings and fake police encounters, with women widowed and children orphaned. The killings were not confined to only one community, as the men, women, and children of both communities were being shot dead in cold blood. The people, terrified by the harrowing atmosphere, dared not stir from their homes at night. Mothers prayed for the safe return of their children; the shrieks of widows and orphans continued to rend the sky. Ironically, theater activity was triggered by militancy. Most of the theater groups concentrated on the Panjab problem and churned out scripts and staged plays on this problem. Gursharan Singh, the most notable of the artists, took his crisp, message-oriented plays from village to village and, in a loud voice, warned the masses of the dangers of religious fundamentalism. His plays written and enacted during this period were repeatedly applauded, enjoyed, and reenjoyed by the common people. *Ik Kursi, Ik Morcha te Hawa vich Latkde Lok* (A Chair, an Agitation and People Hanging in Midair), *Curfew, Hitlist, Baba Bolda Hai* (The Old Man Speaks), *Bhai Manna Singh, Chandigarh Puare di Jarh* (Chandigarh, The Root Cause of Discord), and others were being staged at every corner of the state, and people in large numbers would witness these plays. There was no artistic quality in them, nothing that would make them a good example of professional theater, yet they had a sway on the people. Gursharan Singh himself does not boast their finesse, but he measures his success in terms of their delivery of a message. He represents the *Janvadi* (the people's) movement in Panjabi theater. Other theater artistes, such as Atamjit, took a different position. They do recognize the importance of a message, but for them theater is a unique art: it must be conceived in terms of dramatic metaphor, it must be transformed into a metaphorical mode of existence, and these metaphors should unfold meaning in a future-oriented movement of time. Therefore, there must be a significant experiment in form. His *Seenan* (Stitches) and *Ajit Ram* are not just tear-jerkers; they are mature pieces of new experimentation in form. Even his *Rishtiyan da Ki Rakhiye Nan* (How to Name the Kinship Relationships), staged by a number of theater groups, is found to be relevant to the communally charged atmosphere of the 1980s and early 1990s. An adaptation of Sadat Hassan Manto's short story "Toba Tek Singh," it presents in spectacle the story of the country's partition in an ironic mode. Happily, it is still a powerful story with which the people can identify even after 40 years. It will be interesting to note that, in spite of disturbed conditions, some good theater has also been possible. Sonal Mann Singh, Atamjit, Charan Das Sidhu (Delhi) Kewal Dhaliwal, Navnindra Behal, and a host of other directors and producers are engaged in widening the vision. But still, drama and theater remain the weakest link in twentieth-century Panjabi literature. Panjabi theater is still not flourishing due to paucity of scripts, and very few playwrights can write good scripts. In their absence, the theater has to depend on adaptations and translations from other languages. There is no doubt that the new interest in theater in Panjab is here to stay, yet there is much to be done to improve the future of Panjabi theater.

SHORT STORY

The short story came into existence in the late 1930s, the stories of Nanak Singh, Naurang Singh, Lal Singh Kamla Akali (1889), Gurbakhksh Singh (1895–1978), Sujan Singh (1909–91), and others of an earlier period being either bald narratives or abbreviated novels developed on similar lines as novels. These stories were written on themes of social reform. They dealt largely with the domestic scene and poverty through sentimentality. Though Nanak Singh distinguished himself as a major novelist, his five collections of short stories also charmed the Panjabi reader for their simplicity and directness. He touched upon themes such as communalism, untouchability, litigation, innocence of childhood, the sometimes rather embarrassing affection and hospitality of Panjabi elders, wasteful expenditure on weddings, and evils of dowry, and he treated them from an idealistic point of view. Some of his popular stories are "Bhua" (Aunt), "Chhota Doctor" (The Little Doctor), and "Rakhi" (A Hindu Festival). The name of his popular short story book is *Hanjhuan de Har* (The Necklaces of Tears, 1949).

Gurbakhsh Singh Preetlari, who wrote in all genres of literature, wrote some short stories on social reform, portraying the evils of Panjabi society. He upheld the values of traditional morality. His ideas revolve around the philosophy of love not as possession but as understanding. Many of his stories impressed the reader of those times and had a great impact on society. "Anokhe te Ikale" (The Strange and the Distinct) "Bhukhi Atma" (A Hungry Soul), "Bhabi Maina" (Maina—the Sister-in-Law), and "Veena Vinod" are some of his stories in which he illustrated his idea of an ideal love. Some of his stories shower praise on American life as he saw it in the early 1930s. He contributed seven collections of stories to Panjabi literature, namely, *Preet Kahanian* (Love Stories, 1940), *Anokhe te Ikale* (The Strange and the Unique, 1940), *Veena Vinod* (Veena and Vinod, 1941), *Nag Preet da jadu* (The Magic of Serpent Love, 1949), *Bhabi Maina te hor Kahanian* (Bhabi Maina and Other Stories, 1949), *Preetan di Pehredar* (The Guard of Loves, 1950), and *Shabnam* (Dewdrop, 1950).

Sujan Singh, who remained active till the early 1990s, started writing short stories under the influence of socialist realism. He made his debut in the early 1940s with "Dukh Sukh" (Pain and Pleasure, 1941). Those were the days when the Panjabi people witnessed an awakening caused by consciousness about the liberal democratic setup in the West. It lent a new awareness of realities to Panjabi writers. Even earlier, Panjabi writers were portraying social and cultural realities, but with Sujan Singh and Sant Singh Sekhon, socialist realism came into prominence. The Progressive Writers' Association was set up in 1936. A majority of short story writers who later became very eminent grew under its influence. Sujan Singh in his stories, which were closer to the form of the novel, depicted the misery of the underdog. He has eight collections of short stories to his credit, of which *Sabh Rang* (All Color, 1950), *Manukh te Pashu* (The Man and the Beast, 1958), *Khumban da Shikar* (The Hunt for Mushrooms), and *Shehar te Gran* (The City and the Village) are quite popular. His stories, along with those of Gurbakhsh Singh and Sant Sekhon, held their spell on Panjabi readers until the early 1960s. Later on, they failed to retain their tenderness of treatment and plasticity of structure that marked their earlier works.

Sant Singh Sekhon (1908) is, by all measures, the father of the Panjabi short story. He inaugurated the era of experiment in the field of the Panjabi short story and brought a whirl of fertilizing ideas that pleaded for a new society, new humanism, and a "new hero." Marxist realism, the inspiration of young intellectuals working in colleges during those days, assigned a new content to the short story. Sant Singh Sekhon led the vanguard of this brand of young writers. He introduced the pattern, technique, and realistic methods of Chekhov, Katherine Mansfield, and Edgar Allan Poe to his writing. He presented small incidents of life and expressed the delicacy, beauty, and importance of ordinary incidents of life. Though a die-hard communist, Sekhon, at least in the stories of his early period, does not preach communist dogma. Instead, he narrates small incidents of life in such a manner that they become meaningful creations from the ordinary life of common people. His first collection, *Samachar* (The News, 1943), held out great promise, and some of the stories in it attracted keen critical attention. His "Pemi de Niane" (The Children of Pemi) became a classic. Likewise, "Anaukh Singh di Vohti" (The Wife of Anaukh Singh) is considered unique as a character sketch. Sekhon abandoned the straightforward narrative and made dexterous use of allusion, understatement, situation, psychology, and suggestion. His best-known books of stories include *Kame te Yodhe* (The Workers and Warriors, 1950), *Adhi Wat* (The Half Way, 1954), and *Teeja Pehar* (The Late Afternoon, 1958).

Sekhon is a prolific writer who wrote extensively in the fields of poetry, drama, novel, short story, poetics, literary criticism, and journalism. He is a recipient of the Sahitya Academy Award for his play *Mitter Piara* (Our Beloved Friend). He also made an important contribution to the area of translation, his notable work being the English translation of Waris Shah's *Hir*.

Devinder Satyarthi (1908) made his contribution to the Panjabi short story by writing lyrical stories modeled on folk songs. His persistent interest in the study of folk literature has provided him ground to write about events in regional color, which, at the same time, takes a universal meaning. His stories are collected in three volumes, *Kungposh* (Kungposh), *Sona Gachi* (Cake of Gold), and *Devta Dig Piya* (The Fallen God).

During this period, the Panjabi short story echoes and reechoes the manifesto of the "progressive" school. Besides Sujan Singh and Sekhon, Santokh Singh Dhir, Hari Singh Dilber, and Navtej Singh (1925–80) were all committed Pragtivadi writers who wrote on themes related to the evils of capitalist society, under which humanity was groaning with poverty, ignorance and superstition, hunger and starvation, and it appealed to the poor, the have-nots, the workers to unite to give a fierce fight to the existing regime of bigotry and exploitation.

Yet, some of them, like Dhir and Navtej Singh, each in his own way, contributed to the development of Panjabi short story. Their imaginative energy breaks through all the dikes of customary form and style and has helped them to carve out new channels. They are concerned with the inner movements of impulse as much as social and sociological problems. Santokh Singh Dhir's "Ik Sawar Hor" (One More Passenger, Please) and "Desh Vapsi" (Returning Back Home) are the best specimens in point. Here we find art and life artistically blended. But, in many cases, the stories, unfortunately, are adolescent in their sex appeal and are overbold and loud.

Yet, Kartar Singh Duggal, one of the finest Panjabi short story writers who took his cue from Sekhon, is still the best-known master of this genre. In his earliest writings, he was profoundly influenced by Maupassant and Chekhov. He also opened his doors to Urdu writing and was in a fruitful dialogue with contemporary Urdu short story writers like Krishan Chander, Rajinder Singh Bedi, and Sa'dat Hassan Monto, dialogue that developed in him the touch of delicate expression. Monto, himself a master practitioner of this art, inspired him to take to the naturalist trend. His forte is his knowledge of the Pothohari dialect of the area around Rawalpindi, which he uses in his fiction with remarkable ease and felicity. He made his debut with *Sver Sar* (The Morning Time, 1941) and till now has contributed more than a dozen collections. Some of his short story books, written over a period of 40 years, include *Pippal Pattian* (The Leaves of Peepal Tree, 1941), *Kuri Kahani Kardi Gayee* (The Girl Continued Narrating the Story, 1946), *Dangar* (The Cattle, 1946), *Agg Khan Vale* (The Fire Eaters, 1948), *Nawan Ghar* (The New Home, 1951), *Karamat* (The Miracle, 1957), *Aje Mhaja nahin Moya* (Mhaja Is Not Yet Dead, 1960), *Phul Torna Manah Hai* (No Plucking of Flowers, 1964), and *Pare Mere* (1967).

Duggal's writings have depicted the tragedy of the country's partition with detached irony. His "Nawan Ghar" and "Tun Khah" (You Eat) are good specimens of this kind. Some other writers, such as Mohinder Singh Sarna (1925) and Kulwant Singh Virk (1921–88), wrote powerful pieces on this theme. "Ladhewala Varaich" (The Varaich of Ladhewala) by Sarna and "Khabal" (A Wild Grass) by Virk are still fresh in the memory of Panjabi readers. These stories may not have attained the popularity of Urdu stories on the same theme such as Krishan Chander's "Hum Wahshi Hain" (We Are Barbarians) and Ismat Chughtai's "Sone ka Anda" (The Golden Egg), which are intense appeals for sanity and toleration. Still, Duggal's stories have lyrical humanism and are artistically successful.

Kartar Singh Duggal wrote on many themes, but the dominant themes of his stories are sex, nudity and the ugliness of society. Under the influence of Freud and Jung, he attempts to portray the inner mind of his characters and unravel the causes of their abnormal behavior. He emphasizes the forces of sexual repression in human beings and tries to show how this suppression of the natural flow of feelings has led to abnormality in some individuals due to inflexibility of social rules. "Meera Mussali" is an example. In his "Vadh Vich Ik Saver" (A Morning in the Harvest), he has also portrayed the rather immature adolescent sex attraction of young boys and girls toward one another. Duggal's leaning toward too much sex and pornography has been, by and large, disapproved by critics. Its effect, however, has been not so unpleasant due to the fact that he consciously depicts negative character in his stories like "Main Bhukkha Han" (I Am Hungry), "Ho Sauhri" (Go to Hell), and "Nawan Admi" (The New Man).

Duggal is still very active and writes short stories occasionally, though his major interest has shifted to novel writing. His stories offer the most readable examples of technical virtuosity in themes. Later writers in the 1970s through the 1990s have grown maturer in experience and have tried to weave symbol and theme upon a groundwork of naturalistic detail, which we examine in some detail in the section on postpartition literature. Kartar Singh Duggal played a major role in shaping the development of new trends in the contemporary Panjabi story.

Mohindyer Singh Sarna, another prominent fiction writer, has written some good short stories in Panjabi. His focus is on the depiction of the inner realities of the human mind, and he has tried his hand at depicting "durational flux" in both his novels and stories. Most of his stories that have attracted critical attention are psychological and employ stream-of-consciousness technique. Two of his collections, *Patthar de Admi* (The Stone Men, 1950) and *Shagnan Bhari Sver* (The Auspicious Morning, 1951), were very well received by Panjabi readership. Since the late 1980s, his major interest has moved to poetry, and he has recently composed a long narrative on the life of guru Gobind Singh, the 10th guru of the Sikhs.

Some of the leading writers who attained eminence in other forms of writing also wrote short stories. Amrita Pritam in her stories tries to awaken a social consciousness. She not only denounces outworn traditions but also draws a realistic and lively picture of the conflict of life of the urban middle class. Her famous story entitled "Shah di Kanjari" (The Prostitute of the Shah) is an example in which a strumpet who was an old concubine of a quickly grown rich businessman is invited to his house to give a singing performance at the wedding of his son. Amrita, in an ironic mode, builds a meaningful tension between the traditional and the new moral values. Similarly, her "Panj Warhe Lammi Sarak" (A Road Five Years Long) is a remarkable story with a keen sense of detail. Mohan Singh, a prominent poet, was an equally proficient practitioner of the art of the short story. His story entitled "Nikki Nikki Washna" (The Sweet Smell), until now, remains a landmark in Panjabi short story writing. Balwant Gargi, who established himself as one of the best playwrights and a theater artist, also wrote stories, which are immaculate in their form. His "Budhi di Peepi" (The Tin Container of the Old Woman) is an excellent vignette of narration and character sketching in ironical contrast.

POSTPARTITION PANJABI SHORT STORY (1947–70)

After partition, some of the major short story writers, such as Gurbakhsh Singh, Sant Singh Sekhon, and Sujan Singh, either switched over to some other form of literature or became lackluster and started marking time, repeating what they had achieved earlier. Kartar Singh Duggal, a major short story writer, turned to novel writing. Some others who established themselves as story writers some time after him also transferred their allegiance to the novel because writing merely short stories was proving rather inadequate for their genius. Kulwant Singh Virk, Dalip Kaur Tiwana, Gurdial Singh, Jaswant Singh Virdi, Sukhbir and others found novel writing more satisfying for them to flourish. Sekhon turned to writing literary criticism. Gurbakhsh Singh and Sujan Singh did not do much writing in this period. This provided the opportunity to younger writers to take to the field of story writing. A number of young writers shone in the art of the short story, some of them becoming prominent in the 1970s and 1980s. The majority of the new writers who entered the field of short story writing, such as Gurbachan Bhuller, Ajit Kaur, Rajinder Kaur, Sukhwant Kaur Mann, and Mohan Bhandari, made their mark in the practice of this art. These young people who entered the field of the short story through literary journals were uninspired by the ideals of social reform or revolution and had very little in common with the progressive ideals of their ancestors. To most of them, didacticism was taboo. Influenced as they were by the tensions generated by the speedy industrial development, they attempted to focus on creating meanings from changing patterns of life. Social commitment to them was not an axiom, for their very relationship with the social environment was ambivalent. Hence, the entire problem of the social significance of their themes was thrown open.

Kulwant Singh Virk was the first among the comparatively younger writers to establish himself as a significant name in the field. His stories were marked by a simplicity of structure and sensitivity of approach. With a few light strokes, he was able to write stories with profound human interest, defying a socialist realist's tendency of providing a social message. On one side, he could see the dying civilization and, on the other, a glittering town life, and his experience between the two led him to write stories depicting tension, disappointment, and yearning. In his Sahitya Academy-winning book *Nawen Lok* (The New People, 1959), he responds in a subtle manner to the stresses and strains of increasing urbanization in Panjab. His other well-known books are *Chah Vela* (The Breakfast Time, 1952), *Dharti Te Akash* (The Earth and Sky, 1953), *Turi Di Pand* (The Truss, 1954), and *Ekas Ke Hum Barik* (We, the Children of One God, 1955). Virk dominated the Panjabi writing scene till the 1970s.

Santokh Singh Dhir, who dealt with rural themes, added tragic dimension to the depiction of the social life of the poor and the landless in the villages. Some of his stories, like "Saver Hon Tak" (Till Dawn), "Ikk Hor Swar" (One More Passenger, Please!), and "Sanjhi Kandh" (The Common Wall), are known for their pathos and economy of expression. Among other writers who shot into prominence in the 1950s and 1960s were Lochan Bakhshi, Davinder, Mohinder Singh Sarna, Mohinder Singh Joshi, Amar Singh, and a few others who tried to bring technical refinement to their art and enjoyed a high reputation as sophisticated artists. But, occasionally their art became too arty, resulting in the loss of purposeful discourse. These writers turned toward a highly urbanized city life, ignoring rural realities, creating, thus, some kind of imbalance.

Soon after, a crop of new practitioners of this art form, some with an orientation for the rural, also made their appearance. Ajit Kaur (1934), Gurbachan Bhuller (1935), Gulzar Singh Sandhu (1935), Gurdial Singh (1930), and Dalip Kaur Tiwana (1933) carved a new and individual form and style of their own. Some of them focused on urban life and its conflicts, and some concerned themselves with Panjabi rural life. Whereas the first two dealt with the complexity of urban problems, the rest depicted glimpses of rural life. Gulzar Singh Sandhu makes lively pictures of village life and its personality in an uninhibited manner. Gurdial Singh, as in his novels, portrays simple, nonhero characters who are corroded due to economic deprivation. He portrays poverty in its various manifestations without being sentimental or a preacher. Dalip Kaur Tiwana in her stories attempts to depict the decline and fall of feudal values against the changing rural life of the Malwa region. She has also presented the psychological study of human characters in urban settings.

Gurbachan Bhullar in his stories portrays common people who are unable to fulfill their dreams and aspirations for better treatment. He is very well equipped to practice this art form because of his sensitiveness and keen eye for detail. He deals with situations both in city life as well as in villages. Bhullar is known for his skillful and chiseled finish of his pieces. *Wakhtan Mare* (The Oppressed, 1974) is his collection of stories, which has a few memorable pieces of short fiction. In another collection entitled *Main Ghaznavi Nahin* (I Am Not a Ghaznavi, 1985), he offers a meaningful commentary on the plight of the modern individual who is a victim of the strains and stresses of urban life. *Car Khidauni* (Car—The Play Toy) and *Dhund te Suraj* (The Fog and the Sun) throw light on the widening schism between the haves and have-nots. The story lending its name to this collection expresses the view that the beautiful images that get enshrined in someone's mind during the period of youth must be protected from the ravages of time. To be an iconoclast like Gaznavi in this respect would be committing a sacrilege.

Ajit Kaur Kaur, a recipient of the Sahitya Academy Award, is perhaps the most outstanding practitioner of this art form among this generation of writers. She deals with the complex phenomenon of the man–woman relationship in a bold manner with rare frankness and incisiveness. Her stories on these themes, written from the vantage point of a woman, focus on mutual hatred, suspicion, and frustration of the man–woman relationship, which very often appears quite smooth outwardly. She is completely free from the traditional moral overtones of romantic love of the previous generation and attempts to depict the problems of primordial man–woman relationships in a rather allegorical manner. She has more than six collections of short stories to her credit. Her stories with the titles "Hot Water Bottle" and "Maria Hoya Pal" (The Dead Moment) are considered the best pieces in the language for giving an effective expression to feminine feeling with poignancy and restraint.

Gurdev Singh Rupana, Navtej Puadhi, Bachint Kaur, Rajinder Kaur, Prem Prakash, Mohan Bhandari, Jaswant Singh Virdi, Davinder, Jasbir Bhullar, Dilbir Chetan, Sukhwant Kaur Mann, Prem Gorki, and many others who are engaged in writing short stories till now have extended the frontiers of this literary form. Virdi, better known for his collection of short stories *Apo Apni Seema* (Limitations of Each One), throws light on the sensibilities of the Panjabi lower middle class living in urban areas in their period of trials and tribulations.

Maheep Singh, who had earlier earned a name in the field of the Hindi short story, took to writing stories in Panjabi since the mid-1960s. His focus is on the life of the people of Delhi and Bombay. He portrays the life of the lower middle class, gnarled and defeated by years of despair. His stories are characterized by an acute power of observation, tender poetic touches of characterization, and a sensitive style of expression.

Among the latest young short story writers of Panjabi, mention may be made of Waryam Sandhu, Nachhatar, Joginder Kairon, Mukhtiar Gill, and Mohinderjit, who, over the years, have given evidence of remarkable freshness of approach and great complexity of skill. Many of them have written very touching stories on the theme of the Panjab problem. Notably, Waryam Sandhu seems to be the most powerful artist in this regard, and his "Bhajian Bahin" (The Fractured Arms) offers a penetrating analysis of a poor peasant's family crumbling under the weight of communal tensions resulting from the sociocultural and political situation. This story became extremely popular with Panjabi readers and received dramatic form at the hands of Ajmer Singh Aulakh, one of the most talented young playwrights and theater artists.

Whereas some of the short story writers who flourished during the last decade have been able to develop their own distinct personalities, a few are showing considerable promise. A couple of writers deserve special mention for contributing to this form of literature while living in foreign countries. Of those, Raghbir Dhand in the U.K. and Ravinder Ravi in Canada have been in the field for more than two decades. Raghbir Dhand's collection entitled *Uss Par* (Yonder) is focused on the problems of nonwhites settled in the U.K., who are the worst victims of racial discrimination. They are made to work in the most humiliating and inhuman conditions and feel very much alienated there. They feel the pangs of separation from their families back home. Yet, they are determined to fight for their rights, however fierce the struggle may be. Some of his stories, such as "Nawin Qism de Nag" (The New Kind of Serpents), "Ganda Rang" (The Dirty Color), and "Lal Lakir" (Red Line), eloquently portray these problems. Ravinder Ravi, who is known for his contribution to other genres, wrote stories on the life of Panjabis settled in Kenya, where he lived for a long period before moving to Canada. He is a short story writer of considerable accomplishment who, in his collection of short stories entitled *Kon-Pratikon* (View—Counterview), depicts the problems of Panjabis in the context of East African life. His stories are marked by objective analysis and convincing art. Ravi has also portrayed the life of the tribals of East Africa and accentuated the human element in them.

The short story in Panjabi developed on the other side of the international border with equal enthuasism. Sajjad Haider, Agha Hameed, and Nizam Tawakkli were already established short story writers at the time of partition. They continued writing short stories even after partition. Nawaz was another fiction writer who turned to story writing and published a collection of short stories entitled *Doonghian Shaman* (Deep Evenings), which impressed his contemporaries. Riffat, now an Urdu columnist, also switched to writing short stories in Panjabi. Some women writers, such as Khalida Malik, Kehkshan Malik, Farkhanda Lodhi, Nasreen Bhatti, Naheed Akhtar, and at least two dozen more writers have contributed to the art of the short story, and some of them have made significant contributions to it. Some of the writings, such as *Akbar Kahanian* by Akbar Lahori, *Charkhe di Maut* (Death of the Spinning Wheel) by Hanif Bawa, *Sitian Akhan Wale* (The Men with Sewn Eyes) by Nasir Balauch, *Mitti Ute Leek* (A Line on the Earth) by Rashad Javed Ahmed, and *Shehar te Sufne* (The City and Dreams) by Hasin Shad, are outstanding collections of Panjabi short stories. *Chaunvin Kahani* (*The Selected Short Story,* 1986) by Sajjad Haider offers a fairly broad spectrum of Pakistani Panjabi short story in a historical perspective and includes some of the most sensitive pieces of varied human experience.

To conclude, Panjabi literature of the twentieth century reflects the experience of trauma and dissent, reconstruction and cohesion. It reflects connections with other literatures such as Urdu, Dogri, and Sindhi, with which it has had connections since medieval times. It evolved in new directions in Pakistan, where large proportions of Panjabis settled. While preindependence Panjabi was under the great influence of the Sikh religion, it is now more cosmopolitan. Earlier, it attempted to resolve sectarian issues but now attempts to counter fanaticism and revivalism. It reflects the modernization, under the influence of scientific development, of the Panjab.

WORKS CITED

Attar, Singh. *Secularization of Modern Panjabi Poetry.* Chandigarh: Panjab Prakashan, 1988.

Dewana, Mohan Singh. *An Introduction to Panjabi Literature.* Amritsar: Nanak Singh Pustak Mala, 1951.

Duggal, K. S. *Literary Encounters.* Delhi: Marwah, 1980.

Harbans, Singh. *Aspects of Panjabi Literature.* Ferozepore Cantt: Bawa Publishing House, 1961.

Maini, Darshan Singh. *Studies in Panjabi Poetry.* New Delhi: Vikas Publishing House, 1979.

Mirza, Tanveer Shafqat. *Resistance Themes in Panjabi Literature.* Lahore: Sange Meel, 1992.

Talib, Gurbachan Singh, and Attar Singh, eds. *Bhai Vir Singh—Life, Times and Works.* Chandigarh: Publication Bureau, Panjab University, 1973.

SELECTED PRIMARY BIBLIOGRAPHY

Atamjit. *Kabarastan.* Amritsar: Amol Sahit Prakashan, 1975.

———. *Chabian te Hor Ikangi.* Amritsar: New Age Book Centre, 1976.

———. *Hava Mahal ate Hor Natak.* Amritsar: Jaideep Prakashan, 1980a.

———. *Natak Natak Natak.* Amritsar: Jaideep Prakashan, 1981.

———. *Rishtian Da Ki Rakhiye Nan.* Amritsar: Jaideep Prakashan, 1981.

———. *Puran.* Sirhind: Lokgeet Prakashan, 1987.

Aulakh, Ajmer Singh. *Arbad Narbad Dhundukara.* Amritsar: Balraj Sahni Ghrelu Pustakmala, 1978.

———. *Begane Bohar di Chhan.* Amritsar: Lokayat Prakashan, 1979.

Duggal, Kartar Singh. *Eh Dil Vikau Hai.* Delhi: Navyug, 1957.

Gargi, Balwant *Loha Kut.* 1943. Amritsar: Sikh Publishing House, 1950.

———. *Kesro.* Amritsar: Kasturi Lal and Sons, 1952.

———. *Sultan Razia.* Delhi: Navyug, 1974.

———. *Dhuni Di Agg.* Delhi: Navyug, 1976a.

———. *Kanak Di Balli.* 1954. Delhi: Navyug, 1976b.

———. *Saunkan.* Delhi: Navyug, 1979.

Ghumman, Kapur Singh. *Atit de Parchhaven.* Amritsar: Panjabi Sahit Prakashan, 1967.

———. *Bujharat.* Jullunder: New Book, 1970.

———. *Muk Sansar.* Jullunder: New Book, 1973.

———. *Rani Koklan.* Jullunder: New Book, 1979.

———. *Pagal Lok.* Amritsar: Ravi Sahit Prakashan, 1982a.

———. *Roda Jalali.* Jullunder: New Book, 1982b.

Jasuja, Gurcharn Singh. *Goumukha Shermukha.* Jullunder: Dhanpat Rai and Sons, 1955.

———. *Andhkar.* Delhi: Bishan Chand and Sons, 1968.

———. *Charhiya Sodhan Dhart Lokai.* Ludhiana: Sahitya Academy, 1969.

———. *Kandhan Ret Dian.* Ludhiana: Central, 1973.

———. *Rachna Ram Banai.* New Delhi: Author, 3A/83 W. E. A., 1977.

———. *Umra Lammi Daur.* Delhi: Panjabi Writers Cooperative Society, 1980.

Kanwal, Jaswant Singh. *Hani* 1952. Delhi: Navyug, 1977.

———. *Bebe Ram Bhajni.* 1914. In *Nanda De Sare De Sare Natak,* edited by Harcharn Singh. Patiala: Panjabi University, 1974a.

———. *Subhdran.* 1920. Patiala: Panjabi University, 1974b.

———. *Var Ghar Jan Lily Da Viah.* 1928. Patiala: Panjabi University, 1974.

Nanda, Ishwar Chander. *Social Circle.* Delhi: Sahit Bhavan, 1953.

Phul, Gurdial Singh. *Chanan Di Mehk.* Jullunder: Dhanpat Rai and Sons, 1951.

———. *Sabh Kichh Hot Upaye.* Jullunder: Hazuria and Sons, 1967.

———. *Nanak Nadari Nihal.* Jullunder: Hazuria and Sons, 1969.

———. *Asin Doon Swaye Hoye.* Amritsar: Singh Brothers, 1972a.

———. *Tatti Vau Na Laagi.* Jullunder: Hazuria and Sons, 1972b.

———. *Anokhe Te Ikale.* Lahore: Lahore Book Shop, 1940.

Prit Lari, Gurbakhsh Singh. *Preet Kahaniyan.* Lahore: Preet Nagar Shop, 1938.
Pritam, Amrita. *Amrit Lehran.* Lahore: Amolak Rattan Bhandar, 1936.
———. *Jioonda Jiwan.* Lahore: Commercial Printing Works, 1939.
———. *Lok Pir.* Lahore: Lahore Book Shop, 1944.
———. *Main Twarikh Han Hind Di.* Delhi: Navyug, 1950.
———. *Lammian Vatan.* Amritsar: Lok Sahit Prakashan, 1951.
———. *Pathar Geetey.* 1946. Delhi: Navyug, 1952a.
———. *Sarghi Vela.* Amritsar: Lok Sahit Prakashan, 1952b.
———. *Sunhere.* Delhi: Navyug 1955.
———. *Ashoka Cheti.* Amritsar: Lok Sahit Prakashan, 1957.
———. *Kasturi.* Delhi: Navyug, 1958.
———. *Kala Gulab.* New Delhi: Nagmani, 1967.
———. *Kagaz te Canvas.* Delhi: Navyug, 1970.
Sekhon, Sant Singh. *Chhe Ghar.* 1941. Ludhiana: Lahore Book Shop, 1950a.
———. *Narki.* Amritsar: Sikh Publishing House, 1950b.
———. *Kalakar.* 1945. Ludhiana: Lahore Book Shop, 1954.
———. *Damyanti.* Delhi: Kasturi Lal and Sons, 1960.
———. *Moian Sar Na Kai.* Ludhiana: Lahore Book Shop, 1969.
———. *Mitter Piara.* Ludhiana: Lahore Book Shop, 1970.
Sethi, Surjit Singh. *Bharia Bharia, Sakhna Sakhna.* Amritsar: Lok Sahit Prakashan, 1964.
———. *King Mirza Te Sapera.* Jullunder: Navin Sahit Prakashan, 1965.
———. *Eh Zindagi Hai Dosto.* Ludhiana: Lahore Book Shop, 1976a.
———. *Qadar Yar.* Jullunder: New Book, 1976b.
Sidhu, Charan Das. *Bhajnon.* New Delhi: Panjabi Writers Cooperative Society, 1981.
Singh, Amrik. *Rahan de Nikher Te.* Amritsar: Sikh Publishing House, 1953.
———. *Parchhavian Di Pakkar.* New Delhi: Sikh Publishing House, 1954.
Singh, Gurdial. *Marhi Da Deeva.* New Delhi: Navyug, 1967.
Singh, Harcharn. *Kamla Kumari.* Amritsar: Likhari Book Depot, 1937.
———. *Dur Durade Shehron.* Amritsar: Panjabi Piare, 1939.
———. *Anjor.* Lahore: Singh Brothers, 1941.
———. *Khedan De Din Char.* Lahore: Lahore Book Shop, 1942.
———. *Jivan Lila.* Lahore: Lahore Book Shop, 1944.
———. *Raja Porus.* 1938. Ludhiana: Lahore Book Shop, 1946.
———. *Dosh.* Delhi: Nawan Panjab, 1951.
———. *Tera Ghar So Mera Ghar.* Delhi: Panjabi Prakashan, 1954.
———. *Shobha Shakti.* Delhi: Navyug, 1967.
———. *Itihas Juab Mangda Hai.* Jullunder: New Book Company, 1968.
———. *Chamkaur Di Garhi.* Amritsar: Singh Brothers, 1969a.
———. *Punnian Da Chan.* Amritsar: Singh Brothers, 1969b.
———. *Hind Di Chadar.* Ludhiana: Lahore Book Shop, 1977a.
———. *Ratta Salu.* Delhi: Arsee, 1977b.
Singh, Harsarn. *Apradhi.* Jullunder: Manjit, 1962.
———. *Jigra.* Bishan: Chand and Sons, 1968.
———. *Lammen Samay Da Narak.* Jullunder: Seema Prakashan, 1975.
———. *Nizam Sakka.* Delhi: Arsee Prakashan, 1977.
———. *Raja.* Chandigarh: Raghbir Prakashan, 1981.
Singh, Kesar Giani. *Baba Hari Singh Asman.* Amritsar: Singh Brothers, 1977.
Singh, Nanak. *Ik Mian Do Talwaran.* Delhi: Navyug, 1967.

Singh, Puran. *Khule Lekh.* 1929. Ludhiana: Lahore Book Shop, 1951.
———. *Puran Singh Di Chaunvin Kavita.* New Delhi: Sahitya Academy, 1962.
———. *Khule Ghuund.* 1923. Ludhiana: Lahore Book Shop, 1981.
———. *Khule Maidan.* 1923. Ludhiana: Lahore Book Shop, 1989.
Singh, Vir Bhai. *Rana Surat Singh.* Amritsar: Khalsa Smachar, 1905.
———. *Raja Lakhdata Singh.* Amritsar: Wazir Hind Press, 1910.
———. *Baba Naudh Singh.* Amritsar: Wazir Hind Press, 1921a.
———. *Lehran de Har.* Amritsar: Khalsa Smachar, 1921b.
———. *Matak Hulare.* Amritsar: Khalsa Smachar, 1922.
———. *Bijlian de Har.* Amritsar: Khalsa Smachar, 1927.
———. *Lehar Hulare.* (Devnagri Script). Amritsar: Khalsa Smachar, 1946.
———. *Lehar Hulare.* (Gurmukhi Script). Amritsar: Khalsa Smachar, 1948.
———. *Mere Sainyan Jio.* Amritsar: Khalsa Smachar, 1953.
———. *Sundri.* 1897. Amritsar: Khalsa Smachar, 1966.
———. *Bijay Singh.* 1900 (pt.1) and 1920 (pt.2). Amritsar: Khalsa Smachar, 1967.
———. *Satwant Kaur.* 1922. Amritsar: Khalsa Smachar, 1968.
Tasneem, Niranjan. 1977. *Jadon Swer Hoi.* Amritsar: Singh Brothers, 1983.
Tiwana, Dalip Kaur. *Eh Hamara Jiwana.* Amritsar: Durbar Publishing House, 1969.

10

Twentieth-Century Tamil Literature

P. S. SRI

The Dravidians, in particular, the Tamils, have made many magnificent contributions to the cultural heritage of the world, such as the temple architecture of the Pallavas and the Cholas, the bronze sculpture of the Cholas, the picturesque dance form of *bharatha natyam,* and the Carnatic school of music. Perhaps their most significant achievement is the outstanding efflorescence of Tamil literature over the past 2,300 years.

The Tamil literary tradition can be traced clearly to at least the third century B.C. This tradition, moreover, is "independent, not derived, not imitative . . . pre-Sanskritic" (Zvelbil 1973, 11). Hence, Tamil language and literature are distinct and stand apart from all the other languages and literatures of India. Indeed, it is a well-established scholarly maxim that "there exist in India only two great specific and independent classical and historically attested cultures—the Sanskritic culture and the Tamil culture" (Zvelbil 1973, 11). It is also an indisputable fact that Tamil writing is vigorously alive even today. Consequently, Tamil has a unique, unbroken literary tradition stretching from the very ancient to the most modern times.

Not surprisingly, modern scholars, both Indian and Western, are unanimous in their regard for Tamil literature, for it is "the only Indian literature which is both classical and modern" (Zvelbil 1973, 11). On one hand, it is as ancient and classical as the very best Sanskrit or Greek literature, while, on the other, it is as modern and vibrant as the most significant English and American literature.

By a conservative estimate, Tamil literature spans at least 2,000 years. It includes the exquisite lyricism and the "interior landscapes" of the Sangam poetry, its treatment of love and war, the panoramic sweep of great epics such as *Silappadikaram* (The Tale of the Anklet), and the aphoristic wisdom of *Tiruk Kural* (Sacred Couplets). It also contains the devotional poetry of the Saivite *Nayanmars* and the Vaishnavite *Alwars,* the grand *bhakti* (devotion) and finely wrought poetry of *Kamba Ramayanam,* and the enigmatic aphorisms of the *Siddhars,* such as those found in *Thiru Manthiram.* Indeed, these and other outstanding works of the past form a splendid backdrop against which are enacted the ever-fascinating twists and turns of modern Tamil literature.[1]

In the course of the twentieth century, Tamil literature has not only made tremendous strides in its traditional field of poetry but also attained remarkable heights in the imported and new forms of the short story and the novel. A bird's-eye view of these developments could, therefore, be very useful.

POETRY

Subramanya Bhárathi (1882–1921) at once modernized and rejuvenated Tamil poetry by discarding the complex vocabulary and convoluted sentence structure of his nineteenth-century predecessors and by preferring simple words and rhythms drawn from the everyday lives and activities of ordinary people in Tamil Nadu. ''Simple terms, simple style, simple meters, popular melodies—the poet who combines these in a modern epic breathes fresh life into our Tamil language,'' writes Bhárathi (quoted by Poo Vannan 1992, 318) in his Preface to his masterpiece of dramatic poetry, *Pánchálíyin Sabadham* (Pánchálí's Vow). He practices this principle of simplicity in everything he writes. For example, in the central section of the poem that deals with the game of dice between the upright and righteous Yudhishtra and the crooked and cunning Shakuni, Bhárathi infuses terrific vitality and suspense into the verses describing the treacherous play by adapting the stirring rhythms of Gypsy women hawking multicolored beads and sewing needles down the streets of Tamil Nadu.

Bhárathi's fame as a poet rests primarily on his numerous fiery songs of freedom—collected and published under the title *Sarva Désa Geethangal* (Songs for All Nations)—through which he sought to kindle the flames of patriotism and nationalism in the hearts of his fellow Tamilians. ''Tamil,'' declared the magazine *Chentamizh* in 1908, ''has innumerable poems, epics and legends focusing on God and divine love. But it lacks nationalistic songs capable of fulfilling our present need to evoke patriotic feelings in people's hearts. By turning his poetic talents to this high purpose, Bhárathi has done us all invaluable service'' (quoted by Poo Vannan 1992, 322).

Nevertheless, Bhárathi is justly celebrated not only for the simplicity of his well-crafted poems and the intense national feelings in his songs but also for the novel ideas and techniques in his devotional *(bhakthi)* lyrics to God. For example, when he prays to Shakti, he is simultaneously yearning for three kinds of freedom: the liberation of his motherland from the British yoke, the emancipation of women from superstition and centuries-old male dominance, and the release of the human soul from the bondage of *maya* (illusion). When Bhárathi expresses his rapturous love for Krishna, he does not follow the example of countless *azhwars* (devotees of Krishna) who adorn the annals of Tamil poetry in the centuries before him and sing of Krishna as mother, father, guru, king, and protector. Instead, Bhárathi revolutionizes Tamil poetry by imagining Krishna as his servant—one who reforms him through loving and tender service! Again, he feminizes Kannan into Kannamma and pours his love out for her in several beautiful love lyrics that have come to be cherished and adored by all through the length and breadth of Tamil Nadu.

The cool caress of summer breezes, the quiet calm of clear streams, the honeyed sweetness of children's lisps are all at once experienced in the lyrics of Kavimani Désika Vinayakam Pillai. They are full of breathtaking beauty, heartwarming love, and endearing, childlike simplicity. Kavimani began writing his lovely little poems for children as early as 1901. All these poems were collected and published by 1941 under the title *Ilam Thendral* (Gentle Southern Breeze). Later, they became part of his collected poems, *Malarum Malaiyum,* which included all the mature poems he intended for adults as well. Eventually, his poems for children were republished in a separate volume called *Kuzhandai Chelvam* (Child's Treasure) and won the government of Tamil Nadu's Literary Award for children's literature.

Kavimani had the rare ability to render foreign classics into Tamil so adeptly that his translations read like original Tamil lyrics. His *Asiya Jyothi* and *Umar Khaiyam Padalgal* were exact yet melodious renditions of Edwin Arnold's *The Light of Asia* (a poetic depiction of the life of the Buddha) and *The Rubiayyat of Omar Khayyam.* That incomparable Tamil critic T. K. Chidambara Natha Mudaliyar, known as Rasikamani, has paid a lyrical tribute to Kavimani's poetic talent. "The songs of Dé-si-ka Vi-na-ya-kam Pil-lai," he wrote, "are an invaluable legacy to the Tamils. Like a nectar of everlasting sweetness or a lovely bouquet of unfading flowers, they are to be cherished life-long by every Tamil soul" (quoted by Poo Vannan 1992, 325). Those who plunge even briefly into the limpid stream of Kavimani's poetry will soon realize that these words of appreciation are no exaggeration.

"In all his thoughts, words and deeds, he constantly served his Motherland" (quoted by Poo Vannan, 1992, 325)—such was the praise lavished on V. Ramalingam Pillai of Namakkal, familiarly called Namakkal Kavignar (the poet from Namakkal), even during his lifetime.

Author of about 30 volumes of poetry and prose, Namakkal Kavignar was most known for the popular nationalistic songs he wrote about the greatness of freedom during the famous Salt march of Mahatma Gandhi in his *satyagraha* (nonviolent, truthful aggression) against the British raj. Apart from these passion-fired songs of patriotism, Namakkal Kavignar also composed a wonderful lyric called "Avanum Avalum" (He and She), which was extremely well received in his own day.

"The torrential force of a mountain stream, the rapidity of a lightning strike, the vitality of life-giving food, the purity of a dew-drop, the piercing sweetness of honey, the heady fragrance of a jasmine flower, the never-failing sense of humour—the creative combination of all these qualities form the poems of *Puratchi Kavignnar* (Poet of Revolution) Bhárathi Dasan," wrote N. D. Sundara

Vadivélu (quoted by Poo Vannan 1992, 327), former vice chancellor of the University of Madras, in praise of the output of the extraordinary poet Bhárathi Dasan. (We may note the connection of the romantic with the radical.)[2]

Calling himself *Bhárathi Dasan* (Disciple of Bhárathi), he waged a lifelong war of fiery poetry against the evils he saw in Tamil society, such as the divisive caste system, the ruthless exploitation of hardworking laborers, and the conflicts between the haves and the have-nots. At the same time, he experimented with a variety of literary forms and subjects. If his *Pandiyan Parisu* (Gift of the Pandiyan King) is a historical romance casting a nostalgic look at the glorious past of the Tamils, his *Kudumba Vilakku* (The Lamp of the Family) is a psychological masterpiece focused on the travails of family life in the average modern Tamilian household. His *Azhagin Chirippu* (The Smile of Beauty) captures the splendors of nature, while his *Tamizh Iyakkam* (The Tamil Movement) is a poetic manifesto for the elevation of Tamil language and culture. Because of the sociopolitical-economic relevance of these themes and the captivating rhythms of his verses, Bhárathi Dasan earned the title *Pa Véndar* (King of Poetry), and his poems sold in the millions all over Tamil Nadu.

Every hamlet, village, town, and city in Tamil Nadu knows the name of Kanna Dasan, the first Tamil poet to gain immense fame by writing thousands of film songs, which remain popular to this day and are hummed by millions of Tamil-speaking people in India as well as abroad. It is noteworthy that, apart from his well-known film songs, Kanna Dasan wrote a number of poems with a literary flair. These poems have been collected in six parts under the title *Kanna Dasan's Poems.* Also, he authored a small epic called *Mangkani* (Mango Fruit) and a long lyric on two star-crossed lovers called *Attanaththi Adimandi.*

The term *puthuk kavithai* (new poetry) was first applied to the works of a particular group of "new poets" who appeared approximately after 1958–59 and whose poems were collected by C. S. Chellappa, who was himself one of the new poets, in October 1962 in a slim, trailblazing volume called *Puthuk Kuralkal* (New Voices). Besides five poems by the "revolutionary" Pichamurthi and Rajagopalan, the book featured 58 other poems by 22 younger poets—the poems were all written between 1959 and 1962—as well as a very important introduction by Chellappa.

The new poets are markedly different from other "modern poets," who, despite their sometimes fiery espousal of novel political ideologies and use of contemporary idioms, continue to compose poems in orthodox meters and traditional rhythms. In fact, the new poets are set apart by certain distinct features: first, their poems are, historically speaking, in the "revolutionary" groundbreaking manner and style of the four outstanding poets Subhramanya Bhárathi, Puthumai Piththan, K. P. Rajagopalan, and Pichamurthi; second, they embody a radical break with the past history and ancient traditions of Tamil Nadu, though they do not deny the richness of the cultural heritage of the Tamils; third, they break free from traditional forms and prosodic structures and delight in innovation; fourth, they experiment with language and form in ways suggestive of an acquaintance with modern trends in French, English, and American poetry; and fifth, they focus on contemporary matters and include hitherto ignored subjects as well as unorthodox treatment of traditional motifs. While the prose poems and vers libre of Bhárathi and Puthumai Piththan ushered in the new poetry, the decisive turning points in the development of the genre came with Pichamurthi's poem ''Kattu Vaththu'' (Wild Duck) in 1959 and the publication of Chellappa's avant-garde anthology *Puthuk Kuralkal* in 1962.

The young poets featured in Chellappa's anthology wanted to dissociate themselves from the hackneyed words, well-worn themes, and all-too-familiar forms of traditional poetry. By eschewing the elaborate diction and expansive imagery of medieval poetry, the new poets were essentially carrying out a ''revolt'' (*puratchi*), as Chellappa sees it, and expressing an obsessive concern with everyday realities in forceful language that paradoxically mirrored the unsurpassed brevity, terseness, and directness of the early classical poetry. Indeed, in the writings of the new poets, ''a clash between 'tradition' and 'modernity' takes place in contemporary Tamil literature'' (Zvelbil 1973, 318). Still, the basic characteristics of traditional poetry can be discerned even in the avant-garde poems of the most ''rebellious'' new poets, simply because the new features are intimately connected with the intrinsic rhythms of Tamil language and speech.

Nevertheless, there is a definite break with tradition in the new poetry on two levels. From the bardic poetry of the classical age to the lyrics of Bhárathi, literature and music have been closely associated, so that Tamil poems have most often been *sung* with a great deal of emotion, with *bhakthi* (love of God) predominating; in dramatic contrast, the new poems strive consciously after a unity of meaning (*porul*) and form (*uru*) in their patently sincere attempts to map out the contemporary scene of Tamil Nadu.

Three and a half decades have passed since the new poets broke all traditional metrical rules, experimented with free verse, and wrote uninhibitedly about unconventional and even forbidden subjects in an effort to create a fresh and truly modern Tamil idiom in their poetry. Initially, they were shunned by traditionalists and ignored by many Tamil academics; there was also hardly any response from ordinary readers. Today, however, innumerable young poets are exercising their considerable skills in this fresh mode, and almost a hundred New Wave poetic collections are published every year. Among the numerous talents that adorn the fascinating field of New Wave poetry, the names of Vaira Muththu and Mu. Mehta stand out because of their deft use of colloquial speech, arresting imagery, and memorable rhythms. One may justly say, therefore, that Tamil poetry has taken gigantic steps toward modernity and has come to prevail.

Though the tradition of storytelling has prevailed in Tamil literature from time immemorial, the specific forms of the short story and the novel were imported from the West via the English language and its literature.

SHORT STORY

Va. Vé. Su. Iyer (1881–1925) was the earliest writer to introduce the short story in Tamil. In all the short stories in his collection *Mangaiyerkkarasiyin Kadal* (The Love of Mangaiyerkkarasi, 1910–20), Iyer exploited the now well-known techniques of beginning his narrative in medias res (or of plunging his readers right into the middle of the action) and of offering psychological insights into the actions of his characters in order to infuse feeling and versimilitude into his short stories. Iyer introduced two of the most famous love stories in the world—those of "Laila Majnu" and "Anarkali"—through the medium of the short story to the Tamil-speaking world. Iyer also pioneered the tale of social satire and reform through his short story "Kulaththangkarai Arasa Maram" (The Arasu Tree at the Edge of the Temple Tank).

Following the footsteps of Iyer, Pudumai Piththan (1906–48) wrought a revolution in the world of the Tamil short story. Employing subtle sarcasm and outright mockery, he highlighted the social evils and shortcomings of contemporary Tamil society with such devastating realism that he invited a host of negative criticisms from all and sundry. But even those he outraged by his sympathetic yet convincing depiction of society's underdogs, such as prostitutes, could never stop reading his short stories! Most notable among his creations are gems such as "Kadavulum Kandasami Pillaiyum" (God and Kandasami Pillai) and "Sabha Vimochanam" (The Curse Repealed).

The short stories of Kalki—pseudonym of R. Krishnamurthi (1809–1954)—captivated all sorts and conditions of people because of their irresistible combination of high ideals and rich humor. A number of his short stories even campaigned effectively against prominent social evils such as drinking and untouchability. "Kédariyin Amma" (Ké-da-ri's Ma) and "Thirudan Mahan Thirudan" (Thief's Son's a Thief) are two of his outstanding stories.

Among the writers who followed the robust example of Kalki, the most outstanding was Akilan. His short stories such as "Ganga Snanam" (A Dip in the Ganges), "Kuraththi" (Gypsy Woman), and "Kuzhandai Chiriththathu" (The Child Laughed), reinforced the wholesome ideals of the Tamil culture without underplaying the realistic struggles in modern Tamil society.

While T. Janaki Raman (1921), author of innovative short stories such as "Chilirppu" (Shiver) and "Sivappu Riksha" (The Red Riksha), was a fine craftsman who was skilled in plumbing the dark depths of the human heart and bringing out hidden feelings to make them glisten like pearls in broad daylight, K. Raja Narayanan was remarkable for his exploitation of colloquial speech rhythms and Tamilian village traditions in his short stories.

No other modern short story writer in Tamil has explored the lives of slum dwellers with such fidelity and sympathy as Jaya Kanthan (1934). To him also belongs the credit of introducing, à la D. H. Lawrence, explicit sex into the world of the Tamil short story, with the ultimate aim of providing psychological insights into some dark corners of the human mind. "Agni Pravésham" (The

Test of Fire) and "Suya Darisanam" (Self-Recognition) are among his best short stories.

Among women writers, R. Choodamani is outstanding for the vivid imagery and intuitive delicacy of her short stories, while Siva Sankari is known for her concern with women's privations and rights.

Today, the short story is a fast-growing phenomenon in Tamil. Many fine male writers, like Chu. Samudiram and Bala Kumaran, as well as female writers, such as Ambai and Vasanthi, are enriching the world of the Tamil short story.

Popular magazines like *Ananda Vikatan, Kalki, Kalaimagal,* and *Kumudam,* as well as literary journals like *Kanaiyazhi, Chemmalar,* and *Subha Mangala,* provide outlets for writers of every kind, from those promoting lofty ideals to those with crass commercial motives. Short story collections, too, appear regularly and generally sell well.

A nonprofit organization called Ilakkiya Chinthanai even scrutinizes the short stories published in Tamil magazines and selects the best one every month. Next, it sifts the resulting 12 and selects the best short story of the year. Finally, it brings out all 12 short stories in a single volume. Since the organization has brought out these yearly anthologies fom 1970 onward, it is possible to assess the growth and development of the Tamil short story with reasonable accuracy. It is certain that the short story in Tamil has come a long way from its humble beginnings and is now capable of challenging the very best short stories in any of the world's major literatures. It is also clear that Tamil short stories not only are increasing in numbers every day but also have a bright future ahead of them as a literary form.

THE NOVEL

Like the short story, the novel has been transplanted from the West. In spite of its alien form, though, the novel has taken deep roots in the rich soil of Tamil literature.

The seed was sown by Véda Nayakam Pillai (1826–89) of Mayavaram, the author of the first Tamil novel, called *Pratapa Mudaliyar Chariththiram* (The Story of Pratapa Mudaliyar), which was published in 1876. Narrated in the first person by the chief protagonist, Pratapa Mudaliyar, the novel brings to life two unforgettable characters in Pratapa Mudaliyar and his wife, friend, philosopher, guide, and helpmate, Gnanambal.

P. R. Rajam Iyer's creation *Kamalambal Chariththiram* (The Story of Kamalam-bal, 1896) was the second novel in Tamil and represented a major step forward in sophistication, since the author consciously employed irony and contrast to underscore the shortcomings of his characters.

Since they employ nail-biting suspense and provide thrilling entertainment, detective novels are always popular with most readers. Not surprisingly, detective novels flourished in Tamil from the very beginning. In the early part of the twentieth century, authors like Vaduvur Dorai Swamy Iyengar, Arani Kuppu

Swamy Mudaliyar, and K. R. Ranga Raju wrote countless tales of mystery and imagination containing intriguing elements of detection. Sadly, most of them were imitations or adaptations of English detective novels. By the mid-1950s, however, talented writers like Chiranjeevi, Dévan, and Tamizh Vanan began to turn out quality detective fiction in Tamil with originality and sophistication. The 1970s yielded a major writer of spellbinding detective fiction in Sujatha. Freely borrowing and adapting English expressions and motifs in his tales, such as *Nylon Kaiyiru* (Nylon Rope), *Gayathri,* and *Kanavuth Thozhirtchchalai* (Dream Factory), Sujatha managed to infuse a tremendous excitement into his stories. Soon, he became the idol of young readers who liked fast-paced stories that made their flesh creep and kept them on the edge of their seats. He retains that enviable status to this day.

By portraying realistic characters and focusing on their daily problems and conflicts, Tamil novels of social realism create an aura of authenticity and capture their readers' hearts. Some of these novels are openly didactic, while others are satiric and reformist in content and intention.

Kalki (1899–1954) occupies a unique place in the world of the Tamil novel of social realism. The early decades of the twentieth century come convincingly to life in his masterpieces *Thyaga Bhoomi* (The Land of Sacrifice, 1938–39) and *Alai Osai* (The Sound of Waves, 1948–49). The freedom struggle was depicted so graphically in *Thyaga Bhoomi* that it was banned for its incendiary political ideas by the British raj.

In fact, Kalki has, with great dexterity, woven into the very texture of his social novels a number of historic events connected with the Indian struggle for independence, such as the Sepoy mutiny (1857), the noncooperation movement (1929), the Salt *satyagraha* (1930), the Gandhi–Irwin Pact (1931), the Second Roundtable Conference (1931), the arrest of Gandhi and Nehru (1931), the Quit India movement (1942), the Independence Day celebrations (1947), the Hindu–Muslim conflict subsequent to partition (1947–48), and the assassination of Gandhi (1948).

Among the novelists who captivated the reading public in the postindependence era, Akilan stands foremost. Novel after novel of Akilan won a prestigious award. *Penn* (Woman) won the Narayana Swamy Iyer Prize, and *Nenjin Alaigal* (The Waves of the Mind) won the Tamil Valarchi Kazhagam's Prize. *Chiththirap Pavai* (The Picturesque Woman) obtained the Gnana Peedam Prize, while *Pavai Vilakku* (The Lamp of the Lady) gained national recognition by securing the Sahithya Academy Award. The secret of Akilan's continued success was simple: he paid scrupulous attention to the creation of arresting characters and gripping plots, used a straightforward yet enchanting style, and instilled lofty ideals into his narratives without compromising their realism.

Na. Partha Sarathy's *Kurinchi Malar* (The Rarest Flower) and Indira Partha Sarathy's *Kurudhip Punal* (Blood Stream) are two postindependence novels memorable for their characterization and plot. Among recent novelists, Balakumaran is noteworthy. Serialized simultaneously in several popular Tamil magazines, his novels, such as *Irandavathu Suryan* (The Second Sun), *Payanikal Gavanickavum* (Travelers, Watch Out!), and *Thoppul Kodi* (Umbilical Cord), have become immensely popular.

Among the novels that concentrate on a particular region of Tamil Nadu and bring its speech and culture lovingly to life, Koththa Mangalam Subbu's masterpiece *Thillana Mohanambal* (Mohanambal the Unique Dancer of *Thillana*) and K. Raja Narayanan's magnum opus *Gopalla Puraththu Makkal* (The People of Gopalla Puram) are outstanding and have carved themselves a permanent niche in Tamilian hearts worldwide. While Subbu's novel captures with affectionate care the picturesque lifestyle that prevailed in the preindependence Tanjore district of Tamil Nadu, Raja Narayanan's saga relates the deprivations and fulfillments of ordinary villagers in the dry districts of present-day Tamil Nadu. Among contemporary works, Jayamohan's novel *Rubber,* which won the Akilan Memorial Prize in 1990, is outstanding for its graphic depiction of the agrarian community in south India. When the community abandons its long-standing traditional crop of plantains and cultivates rubber trees, unsuited to the climate and environment, disaster follows. The novel thus underscores the importance of living in tune with nature.

Several women writers, too, are contributing to the growth of the Tamil novel. The works of Anuththama, such as *Oru Veedu* (A Home), *Kétta Varam* (The Sought-After Boon), and *Manal Veedu* (House of Sand), and of Lakshmi, such as *Penn Manam* (Woman's Heart), *Kanchanaiyin Kanavu* (Kanchanai's Dream), and *Aththai* (Aunt), revolve around domestic problems and emphasize values of love and self-sacrifice as means of resolution. Rajam Krishnan's novels often explore uncharted sections of Tamil society. For instance, her *Kurinchith Thén* (The Rarest Honey) focuses on an aboriginal tribe of Tamil Nadu and deals with the conflicts they experience between their age-old traditions and modern innovations. Siva Sankari is another unusual novelist who handles controversial yet timely ideas in her works. For example, her novel *Avan Aval Adhu* (He She It) deals with artificial insemination and shows how it plays havoc with the peace and harmony of a typical south Indian family.

No other writer of historical novels in Tamil handled famous characters and poignant themes from the rich Tamilian cultural heritage so brilliantly and movingly as Kalki. His epic delineations of the great Mahéndra Varma Pallava and his illustrious son Narasimha Varma Pallava in *Sivakamiyin Sabadam* (Sivakami's Vow—4 parts, 1944–46) and *Parthiban Kanavu* (Parthiban's Dream, 1941–43), as well as his monumental odyssey of the young Raja Raja to the Chozha throne in *Ponniyin Chelvan* (The Beloved Offspring of the River Ponni, 1950–54), are enduring historical romances that bring to life the splendor of the Pallava and Chozha kingdoms of bygone ages and have thus come to dominate the Tamilian imagination. It is no exaggeration, therefore, to say that Kalki not only created among the Tamils a taste for history but also satisfied it with a superb feast of historical novels.

Akilan was second only to Kalki. His gripping evocation of the times of that incomparable conqueror and administrator Rajendra Chozha in *Véngaiyin Maindan* (The Tiger's Son) garnered him the Sahitya Academy Award. The magnificence of the Vijaya Nagara Empire comes thrillingly to life in another of his novels called *Vetrith Thiru Nagar* (Vijaya Nagara, the City of Victory).

Among contemporary historical novels, Prapanjan's award-winning *Manutam Vellum* (Humankind Will Triumph) is a notable achievement. Based on the diaries of Anandarangam Pillai, a translator in Pondicherry under General Dupleix, governor of French colonial possessions, the novel depicts in fascinating detail the daily vicissitudes of living in eighteenth-century India.

That the alien imported form of the novel has become an integral part of Tamil culture goes without saying. The fact that it has sprouted forth from its obscure origins and branched out so rapidly in several distinctly different directions suggests that there are greater things in store.

DRAMA

The dramatic tradition in Tamil literature is as old as the language itself. In fact, drama is so integral to the tradition that Tamil is often spoken of as *mutthamizh* (threefold Tamil) in which poetry, drama, and music are inseparably interwoven. Not surprisingly, there are references to drama even in *Thol Kappiyum* (Oldest Commentary), the first and most ancient treatise on grammar in Tamil. In the great *Silappadikaram* (The Tale of the Anklet)—often called a dramatic epic—there are detailed descriptions of the setting of the stage as well as expositions of the role of music and dance on the stage. Only after the eighteenth century did prose slowly begin to make inroads into drama. Nevertheless, folk poetic drama such as *Kutrala Kuravanchi* (Gypsy Dance of Kutralam) and *Rama Natakam* (The Drama of Rama's Life) reigned. Even during the nineteenth century, hundreds of verse plays drawing upon the stories in the great national epics *Ramayana* and *Mahabharatha* made their appearance. The most notable of these were *Madurai Veeran Vilasam* (The Saga of Madurai Veeran) and *Sita Kalyanam* (The Wedding of Sita). Muslim and Christian traditions, too, found outlets in verse plays such as *Ali Padusha* and *Gnana Soundari Ammal.* Perhaps the most outstanding historical play of this period was Sundaram Pillai's *Manonmaniam.*

The transformation of traditional poetic drama into modern prose drama was eventually accomplished in the early twentieth century by stalwarts such as Sankaradas Swamigal, Nawab Govindasamy Rao, and Pammal Sambanda Mudaliyar. Since then, Tamil drama has proliferated in various genres.

Mythological Plays

In the first half of the twentieth century, pioneers such as Kannaiya Naidu and Nawab Raja Manickkam Pillai staged countless plays based on age-old Hindu myths and epics and stimulated *bhakti* in the hearts of those who witnessed them. In fact, it was quite common for people to pay respect with folded hands to the "gods" whenever they appeared on stage during performances of *Dasavatharam* (Ten Avataras of Vishnu), *Iyappan* (Lord Iyappan), *Sampoorna Ramayanam* (The Complete and Wholesome Ramayana), *Bhagavat Gitai* (The Bhagavad Gita), and *Rama Das* (Saint Rama Das). It was also not unusual to see the audience in tears over the trials of Karna or the privations of Panchali (from the *Mahabharatha*) when they were movingly depicted by the veteran director-actor S. V. Sahasranamam, in his performance of P. S. Ramaiah's *Therotti Makan* (The Charioteer's Son) or Bharathi's poetic drama *Panchaliyin Sabadam.* The mythic-epic trend is still very much alive in Tamil drama. For the past two decades, R. S. Manohar has been staging extremely popular and critically acclaimed plays such as *Ilankeswaran* (Lord of Lanka), *Surapadman* (Demon Sura), and *Viswamithra* (Sage Viswamithra).

Historical Plays

Staging historical plays in Tamil is a costly and daunting proposition, for the background scenery, costumes, events, and dialogues have to be accurate and authentic. Nevertheless, the challenge has been courageously met time and again. In the 1950s and 1960s, the well-known T.K.S. brothers staged immensely popular historical plays such as *Raja Raja Chola* (The Great Chola King Raja Raja) and *Kappalottiya Tamizhan* (The Tamilian Who Plied Ships), a play based on the life and achievements of V. O. Chidambaram Pillai, who fought for freedom from British rule during the 1930s and became famous throughout the country as the first Tamilian to challenge the British merchant navy on the high seas. The T.K.S. brothers were not totally alone in launching historical plays. The famous cinema actor Sivaji Ganesan brought the heroic life of a pioneer freedom fighter to the stage and into the hearts of the Tamil people in *Veera Pandiya Katta Bomman.*

But R. S. Manohar must be credited with the establishment of historical plays on rock-hard foundations of historical research and realistic dramatization over the past 25 years. By combining split-second timing, dazzling special effects, moving dialogues, and powerful acting, Manohar mesmerized audiences by recreating famous and even controversial historical figures in *Chanakya Sabadam* and *Malik Kafoor,* so that Chanakya and Malik Kafoor imprinted themselves indelibly in Tamilian minds. Manohar's dramatic productivity shows no signs of abatement. Even today, his latest play *Thirunavukku Arasar* (Saint Thirunavukku Arasar)—a dramatization of the life of the Saivite saint Appar, who came into conflict with, and triumphed over, Mahendra Varma Pallava—thrills audiences all over Tamil Nadu and Southeast Asia.

Plays of Social Realism

Though Tamil prose plays that dealt convincingly with the ups and downs in the life of ordinary people began to be written and produced as early as the last decades of the nineteenth century, not till the mid-twentieth century did social realism come into its own domain. Again, the T.K.S. brothers and S. V. Sahasranamam did yeomanly service to the Tamil stage by dramatizing classic novels by literary greats such as Kalki, Akilan, and T. Janakiraman. Thus, literary works such as Kalki's *Kalvanin Kadali* (The Thief's Beloved), Akilan's *Vazhvil Inbam* (Happiness and Life), and Janakiraman's *Vadivelu Vaddhiyar* (Vadivelu Teacher) and *Nalu Veli Nilam* (Four Acres of Ground) came to the stage and captured a permanent place for themselves in the Tamilian imagination. At the same time, plays by C. N. Annadurai—who led the anti-Brahminical DMK movement and eventually became the chief minister of Tamil Nadu—also came to the fore. Annadurai's plays, such as *Velaik Kari* (Servant Maid), *Or Iravu* (One Night), and *Needhi Devan Mayakkam* (The God of Justice's Bewilderment), forcefully attacked social evils such as bribery and casteism and unmasked the hypocrisies of the powerful. In the 1960s and 1970s, K. Balachandar's extremely well received plays such as *Malliyam Mangalam* (Mangalam of Malliyam) riveted the attention of theatergoers by zeroing in on the problems, dilemmas, bonds, and affections that beset ordinary, middle-class households in Tamil Nadu. When Balachandar went over to cinema and became a famous director of box office hits, the Tamil stage lost a fine and extraordinary talent.

Comedies

The pioneer Sambanda Mudaliyar first invoked laughter onto the Tamil stage through his full-length humorous play *Sabhapathi.* Following his footsteps, Devan created humorous masterpieces such as *Thuppariyum Sambu* (Detective Sambu) in the 1950s. A decade later, K. Balachandar made Tamilians laugh, made them think, and made them cry through his mildly satiric plays such as *Server Sundaram* (Waiter Sundaram) and *Edhir Neechal* (Swimming against the Current). Meanwhile, Cho's polemical plays were not only providing sidesplitting theatrical entertainment to the Tamil public but also provoking them to subject self-serving politicians to relentless scrutiny and scathing criticism. Cho's play *Mohammed Bin Tughlak,* for example, received rave reviews and played to packed audiences all over Tamil Nadu. It is probably one of the finest political satires in modern Tamil drama. Recently, however, the trend on the Tamil stage is toward plays that are merely absurd and invite the belly laugh. Dramatists like Crazy Mohan, S. V. Sekhar, and Mouli are busy churning out such "entertainers."

Clearly, Tamil drama has made, and is making, tremendous strides in several directions. There is no doubt that its future looks promising. However, the sad fact is that Tamil plays seldom appear in print in paperbacks or anthologies. In the absence of such "literary" backup, it is quite possible that even masterpieces such as *Raja Raja Chola* might be permanently lost to Tamil literature.

To sum up, modern Tamil literature has evolved so rapidly in the past 100 years and shows such vitality and vibrancy that it is clear it will go from strength to strength in the coming century. One cannot do better than to pray to whatever powers there be to send the "roots" of modern Tamil literature "rain" so that its various forms continue to thrive, grow, and come to fruition.

NOTES

1. The aesthetic-popular aspects of Tamil literature highlighted in this survey connect provocatively with the sociopolitical. It is important to note, in any consideration of Tamil literature, that the "Tamil Renaissance" in literature in the twentieth century weaves in and out of Gandhian nationalism, "Dravidian" identity politics, caste politics, and social reform movements (see Ryerson 1988, esp. Chapter 4). For example, Ryerson notes that the romantic nationalism of poets such as Bharatidasan was connected to a radical socialism, which highlighted a new (classless, casteless) identity based on a literary-linguistic affiliation to Tamil (referring to Bharatidasan's *Puratchikavi,* Ryerson 1988, 82). Tamil literature's role in the caste politics of Tamil Nadu is ambivalent—uniting castes in a common participation in the production and appreciation of Tamil literature, yet giving rise to acrimonious debates (see Ryerson 1988, 83). As regards women's roles, Tamil literature through the century has redrawn ideological borders even as it has sought to extend women's possibilities. C. S. Lakshmi traces the trajectory from the romantic representations of femaleness as Shakti in reformist poets such as Bharatiyar, to the "pulp fiction" heroines catering to a mass-market and "filmic" culture (see Lakshmi 1984)—*Ed.*

2. See note 1.

WORKS CITED

Lakshmi, C. S. *The Face behind the Mask.* New Delhi: Vikas, 1984.

Poo Vannan. *Tamizh Ilakkiya Varalaru* (Tamil Literary History). Madras: Varthamanan, 1992.

Ryerson, Charles. *The Tamil Renaissance and Popular Hinduism.* Madras: Christian Lit. Society, 1988.

Zvelbil, Kamil. *The Smile of Murugan on Tamil Literature of South India.* Leiden: E. J. Brill, 1973.

SELECTED PRIMARY BIBLIOGRAPHY

Poetry

Bhárathi, Subramanya. *Bhárathiyin Kavithaikal.* Madras: Vanathi Pathippakam, 1991.

Bhárathi Dasan. *Bharathidasan Kavithai Thokuppu* (Anthology of Bharathidasan's Poems). Tiruchirapalli: Bharathidasan University Press, 1991.

Chellappa, C. S., ed. *Puthuk Kuralkal.* Madras, 1962.

Pichamurthi, N. *Kattu Vaththu* (Forest Duck). Madras, 1959.

Pillai, Kavimani Désika Vinayakam. *Ilam Thendral* (The Fragrant Southern Breeze). Madras, 1941.

Short Story

Akilan. *Tamizh Chiru Kathaikal* (Tamil Short Stories). New Delhi: Sahitya Academy, 1959.
———. *Puthiya Vizhippu* (Fresh Awakening). Madras: Tamizh Putthakalayam, 1986.
Iyer, Va. Vé. Su. *Mangaiyerkku Arasiyin Kathal* (The Love of Mangaiyerkku Arasi). Madras, 1910–20.
Janakiraman, T. *Thi Janakiraman Chirukathai Thokuthi* (T. Janakiraman's Short Stories: An Anthology). Madras: Ainthinaip Pathippakam, 1991.
Jayakanthan. *Chiru Kathaikal* (Short Stories). Madras: Vanathi Pathippakam, 1986.
Kalki. *Chiru Kathaikal.* Madras: Vanathi Pathippakam, 1990a.
———. *Otrai Roja* (Solitary Rose). Madras: Vanathi Pathippakam, 1990b.
Krishnan, Rajam. *Kanavu: Chiru Kathaikal* (Dream: Short Stories). Madras: Thakam, 1978a.
———. *Uyirppu: Chiru Kathaikal* (Breath of Life: Short Stories). Madras: Pari Putthakap Pannai, 1978b.
———. *Kálam: Chiru Kathaikal* (Time: Short Stories). Madras: Pari Putthakap Pannai, 1985.
———. *Aval: Chiru Kathaikal* (She: Short Stories). Madras: Tamizh Putthakalayam, 1992.
Pudumai Piththan. *Pudumai Piththan Kathaikal* (Pudumai Piththan's Stories). Madras: Star Piracuram, 1966, 1977.
———. *Pudumai Pitthan Padaippukkal* (Works of Pudumai Pitthan). Madras: Ainthinai Pathippakam, 1987.
———. *Stalinkkuth Theriyum* (Stalin Knows). Madras: Iyinthinai Pathippakam, 1991.
Raja Narayanan, K. *Pinjukal* (Seedlings). Sivagangai: Akaram, 1979.
———. *Appa Pillai, Amma Pillai: Chiru Kathaikal* (Pa's Darling, Ma's Pet: Short Stories). Sivagangai: Akaram, 1980.
———. *Oru Thani Veedu* (A Solitary House). Kovai: Samudayam Pirasuralayam, 1984a.
———. *Thatha Chonna Kathaikal* (Stories Grandpa Told). Sivagangai: Annam, 1984b.
———. *Kottaip Paruththi: Chiru Kathaikal* (Choice Cotton: Short Stories). Sivagangai: Annam, 1985.
———. *Vayadhu Vandavarkalukku Mattum* (For Adults Only). Kovai: Vijaya Pathippakam, 1992.

Novel

Akilan. *Putu Vellam* (Fresh Flood). Madras: Pari Puttakapannai, 1964.
———. *Palmarak Káttinilé* (In the Milkwood Forest). Madras: Porkoti Vilayudhyu, 1977.
———. *Sakotarar Andro* (Aren't They Brothers?) Madras: Paari Puthakap Pannai, 1981.
———. *Vánama Bhoomiya?* (The Sky or the Earth?) Madras: Pari Putthaka Pannai, 1983.
———. *Véngaiyin Maindan* (The Tiger's Son). Madras: Tamizh Putthakalayam, n. d.

Anuththama. *Nainda Ullam* (Frayed Heart). Madras: Amuda Nilayam, 1977.
———. *Srudhi Bhedam* (Out of Tune). Madras: Amuda Nilayam, 1979.
———. *Jayanthipura Thiruvizha* (Jayanthipura Festival). Madras: Amuda Nilayam, 1982.
———. *Alai Páyudhe* (The Restless Wave). Madras: Tamizh Ezhuththalar Sangam, 1988a.
———. *Ondru Pattal . . .* (If We Unite . . .). Madras: Tamizh Ezhuththalar Sangam, 1988b.
Balakumaran. *Kalyana Murungai* (The Wedding Tree). Manyan, March 1982.
———. *Irumbu Gudiraigal* (Iron Horses). Madras: Vanathi Pathippakam, 1984.
———. *Endrendrum Anbudan* (Forever with Love). Madras: Vanathi Pathippakam, 1986.
Iyer, P. R. Ra-jam. *Kamalambal Chariththiram* (The Story of Kamalambal). 1986. Tiruchirapalli: Indira Pathippakam, 1990.
Janakiraman, T. *Karunkatalum Kalaikkatalum* (The Black-Hued Sea and the Artistic Sea). Madras: Vachakar Vattap Piracuram, 1974.
———. *Brahmam* (Reality). Madras: Vanathi Pathippakam, 1983.
Jayakanthan. *Indha Nerathil Ival* (At This Time—She). Madras: Meenatchi, 1977.
———. *Oru Manidanum Chila Erumai Madukalum* (A Man and a Few Buffaloes). Madurai: Meenakshi Putthaka Nilayam, 1979.
———. *Jaya Jaya Sankara* (Victory, Victory to Sankara). Madras: Aintinaip Pathippakam, 1984.
———. *Pukai Natuvinile* (Amid Smoke). 1984. Madurai: Meenatchi Puththaka Nilayam, 1990.
Kalki. *Thyaga Bhoomi* (Land of Self-Sacrifice). Madras, 1938–39.
———. *Alai Osai* (The Wave's Sound). Madras, 1948–49.
———. *Ponniyin Chelvan* (The Beloved Offspring of the River Ponni). Madras: Vanathi Pathippakam, 1950–54.
———. *Mada Thevan Chunai* (Mada Thevan's Tarn). Madras: Vanathi Pathippakam, 1957.
———. *Makutapathi* (Crowned Head). Madras: Vanathi Pathippakam, 1979a.
———. *Thiruvazhunthur Sivakozhundhu* (Sivakozhundu of Thiruvazhunthur). Madras: Vanathi Pathippakam, 1979b.
———. *Sivakamiyin Sabadam* (Sivakami's Vow). 1944–46. Madras: Vanathi Pathippakam, 1982.
———. *Kalvanin Kathali* (Thief's Beloved). Madras: Vanathi Pathippakam, 1985a.
———. *Párthiban Kanavu* (Parthiban's Dream). 1941–43 Madras: Vanathi Pathippakam, 1985b.
———. *Mayilvizhi Mán* (The Beautiful One). Madras: Vanathi Pathippakam, 1986.
———. *Arumpum Anbukal* (Budding Loves). Madras: Bharathi Pathippakam, 1988.
Krishnan, Rajam. *Chetril Manidarkal* (Humans in the Mud). Madras: Pari Putthaka Pannai, 1982.
———. *Pudhiya Chiragukal* (New Wings). Madras: Pari Putthaka Pannai, 1985.
———. *Chuzhalil Midakkum Deepankal* (Lamps Afloat in a Whirlpool). Madras: Thakam, 1987.
———. *Ankalodu Penkalum* (Men and Women Together). Madras: Thakam, 1988.
———. *Gopura Bommaikal* (Toy Figures on a Temple Tower). Madras: Thakam, 1993.

Parthasarathy, Indira. *Agni Charukukal* (Burnt Leaves). Madras: Tamizh Putthakalayam, 1983.
———. *Akasa Thámarai* (A Lotus in the Sky). Madras: Tamizh Putthakalayam, 1991.
Parthasarathy, Na. *Kurinchi Malar* (Rarest Flower). Madras: Tamizh Putthakalayam, 1966.
———. *Pookalai Yarum Midhika Koodadhu* (None Must Trample on the Flowers). Madras: Tamizh Putthakalayam, 1979.
Raja Narayanan, K. *Gopalla Puraththu Makkal* (People of Gopalla Puram). Sivagangai: Annam, 1990.
Sivasankari. *Oru Apparum Irantu Penkalum* (A Pa and Two Daughters). Madras: Tirumakal Nilaiyam, 1992.
———. *Katal Enbathu Ethuvarai?* (How Far Does the Sea Extend? Madras: Tirumakal Nilaiyam, 1993.
———. Ini (Hereafter). Madras: Gangai Puttaka Nilaiyam, 1994.
Vasanthi. *Káthalenum Vánavil* (Love's Rainbow). Madras: Gangai Puththaka Nilayam, 1992a.
———. *Nizhalattam: Oru Návalum Kathaikalum* (Shadow Play: A Novel and Stories). Madras: Narmada Pathipakam, 1992b.

Tamil Fiction Translated into English

Our thanks to Arasu Balan for his assistance with this bibliography.
Akilan. *Flower of Gold.* New Delhi: Sterling Paperbacks, 1978.
———. *Portrait of a Woman* (Chittirapavai). Delhi: Macmillan, 1981.
Ambai. *A Purple Sea: Short Stories by Ambai.* New Delhi: Affiliated East-West Press, 1992.
Ashokamitran. *Water* (Tannir). Oxford: Heinemann, 1993.
Balakrishnan, P. *The Pageant of Tamil Literature.* Madras: Sekhar, 1966.
———. *The Gold Bangle and Other Stories.* Bombay: Bharatiya Vidya Bhavan, 1968.
Janakiraman, T. *The Sins of Appu's Mother.* Translated by M. Krishnan. Delhi: Hind Pocket Books, 1972.
———. *Wooden Cow* (Marap Pasu). Madras: Sangam, 1979.
———. *Eternal Kaveri: The Story of a River.* New Delhi: Penguin, 1993.
Jayakanthan. *Game of Cards and Other Stories.* Madras: Asia Books, 1972.
———. *Pebbles from the Sea.* Gandigram: Gandigram Rural Institute, 1987.
Kannan, Lakshmi. *India Gate and Other Stories.* London: Sangam, 1993.
Lakshmi. *Ripples in the River.* New Delhi: Sahitya Akademi, 1992.
Modern Tamil Stories. 2 vols. Edited and translated by M. S. Ramaswami. Calcutta: Writers Workshop, 1991.
Parthasarathy, Indira. *Free Land* (Suthandira Bhoomi). New Delhi: Arnold Heinemann, 1975.
———. *Blood Stream* (Kuruthip Punal). New Delhi: Vikas, 1979.
———. *Beyond Veils* (Thiraikalukku Appal). New Delhi: Sterling, 1983.
Parthasarathy, N. *Society's Path* (Samudaya Veedhi). New Delhi: Sahitya Academy, 1990.
The Plough and the Stars: Stories from Tamilnadu. Edited by K. Swaminathan. Bombay: Asia Publishing House, 1963.

Santhanam, K. *Eight Seers of Rice and Other Stories of Indian Life.* Madras, 1958.
Sivasankari. *Tyagu: Oru Manithanin Kathai.* New Delhi: Affiliated East-West Press, 1990.
———. *The Trip to Nowhere* (Avan). Calcutta: Rupa, 1992.
Tamil Short Stories. New Delhi: Authors Guild of India Cooperative Society, 1978.
Varadarajan, M. *Was It Liberation? A Collection of Tamil Short Stories.* Madurai: Madurai University, 1972a.
———. *A Mother's Heart.* Madurai: Madurai University, 1972b.
Vasanthi. *The Silent Storm.* Translated by Gomathi Narayanan. New Delhi: Affiliated East-West Press, 1989a.
———. *When Bamboo Blossoms.* Translated by Gomathi Narayanan. Gauhati: Span, 1989b.

REFERENCES

Dandayutham, R. *Tamizh Chirukathai Munnotikal* (Forerunners of the Tamil Short Story). Madras: Tamizh Puththakalayam, 1972.
———. *Tharkala Tamizh Ilakliyam* (Comtemporary Tamil Literature). Madras: Tamizh Puththakalayam, 1973.

11

Twentieth-Century Telugu Literature

G. K. SUBBARAYUDU AND C. VIJAYASREE

INTRODUCTION: HISTORY AND CONTEXT

Many modern Indian languages drawing from Sanskrit as well as Dravidian roots establish their literary traditions and history between the eleventh and the fourteenth centuries. Telugu, the language of the *Trilinga Desa*—at some stage turned synonymous with the *Andhra Desa*—also establishes its earliest literary credentials in the eleventh century. Nannayya Bhattu's Telugu translation of a portion of the Sanskrit *Mahabharatha* is the earliest available work. The development of Telugu literature between the twelfth and the sixteenth centuries describes two distinct phases: (1) the age of the *puranas,* during which several *puranic* stories were rendered into Telugu. These works conformed to the traditional stylistic modes, and their prime objective was propagation of the *vedic dharma* (faith); (2) the age of the *prabandhas* wherein the literary subjects were still drawn from the *puranas,* but an elaborately ornate style replaced the classical simplicity. Telugu literature describes a sharp decline in the seventeenth and the eighteenth centuries with mediocre limitations of *prabandhas* ruling the day. The revival came in the nineteenth century through the efforts of Charles Philip Brown, the Orientalist lexicographer, who brought many Telugu classics into edition and print and gave Telugu its first authoritative dictionary as well. Besides, the contribution of Vavilla Ramaswami Sastrulu, printer and publisher of easily 1,000 titles, is worth recording.

Turn of the Century: The Rise of Modernism

The rise of a modern sensibility around the turn of the century had a profound impact on the growth of Telugu literature in the twentieth century. The two factors that influenced this development were the colonial history and consequent exposure to the West, and a growing spirit of nationalism. Modernism in the context of Telugu literature may be further identified with four interrelated trends: (1) a review of the existing sociocultural institutions and practices, resulting in a movement away from orthodoxy toward a liberal system of thought and living; (2) a reform of language, that is, a shift from the classical to the *vyavaharik* (colloquial); (3) a quest for freer and more malleable forms of literary expression; and (4) the growing significance of prose forms, including essay and journalism, as direct means of dissemination of ideas and ideologies.

Kandukuri: The Pioneer

Kandukuri Veeresalingam is the central personality in this period of literary activity and is generally acknowledged the founder of modern Telugu literature. Though Kandukuri was a traditional scholar brought up in the orthodox tradition, he was a rationalist and revolutionary by temperament. He responded to the social and religious issues of the time with an uncommonly critical rigor. He was inspired by the social reform movement launched by Raja Ram Mohan Roy in Bengal and soon enrolled himself as a member of the Brahmo Samaj. He started a journal, *Vivekavardhani,* which became a forum for active deliberations on the social issues of the time, which included the evils of the caste system, the practice of sati, the dowry system, the need for women's education, and the desirability of widow remarriage. Telugu prose acquired a new force and vigor in Kandukuri's writings and became adequately equipped for the tasks of a new era. Kandukuri launched a movement for a revival of Telugu literature. He condemned the degeneration of poetic form into a banal, rule-minded exercise in his long poem, *Saraswati Narada Samvadam* (1887). A great scholar of world literature, he introduced several new forms in Telugu literature: essay, biography, autobiography, and novel, and thus he heralded a new era in Telugu literature.

Modernization of Telugu Language

The modernization of the Telugu language started by Kandukuri developed into a movement for linguistic reform under the stewardship of Gurajada Appa Rao and Gidugu Ramamurthy Panthulu. Stressing the need for adapting the Telugu language to the changing ethos, they urged the extensive use of *vyavaharik* (colloquial) idiom in place of the *grandhik* (classical) style. They advocated the adoption of the colloquial Telugu as the chief mode of spreading literacy and, with that, the possibility of enlightenment. The twin objectives of the language reform movement, therefore, were to make language accessible to the common person and turn literature into a reflection of quotidian reality. This, of course, meant that the colloquial idiom was not only to replace the classical in literature but also to be introduced in educational institutions. Gurajada believed that colloquial language work would reach the common people and shake them out of their complacent acceptance of the givens with which they had lived for very long.

POETRY: DEVELOPMENTS

Against this background of the modernization of language, the spread of English education, and the increasing publication and popularity of periodicals, modern poetry in Telugu emerged as a genre distinct from the traditional poetic style. Salient features of this new poetry are emergence of short poetic texts (*khanda kavyas*), subjectivity, originality in the choice of poetic subject, stylistic and technical experimentation, and the use of common idioms. This modern Telugu poetry, since its beginnings around 1900, manifested itself in three chief forms—*bhava kavitvam* (lyrical poetry), *abhyudaya kavitvam* (progressive poetry), and new experimental poetry, including *viplava kavitvam* (revolutionary poetry). However, it is interesting to note that traditional verse forms exhibit a surprising resilience and survive alongside the new forms.

The Early Phase

C. R. Reddy's *Musalamma Maranam* (1900), though written in traditional metrical form, testifies to his modern outlook in his choice of social subject and option for tragic closure and is regarded as an important transitional event. The distinguished poetic duo Divakarla Tirupati Sastry and Chellapilla Venkata Sastry also made vital contributions to the shaping of modern Telugu poetry. Though they continued to write in traditional metrical forms, they anticipate a modern trend in their concern with social issues in works such as *Panigrihita* (1909) and *Sravananandam* (1909). In their performances of *satavadhanams* (spontaneous responses, often in verse, to 100 queries), they struck a note of freshness, vigor, and simplicity, perforce due to the need for direct communication with the audience; such a linguistic reformation had a salutary impact on the contemporary language of poetry.

The grand entry of modern poetry in Telugu may be said to have been heralded by the publication of *Mutyala Saralu* (1910) by Gurajada Appa Rao and *Lalitha* (1909) by Rayaprolu Subba Rao. Together, they form the vital force behind the modernist movement. *Mutyala Saralu* presents a new poetic vision and ushers in an era of lyrical poetry in Telugu. Traditional meter is replaced by a new lyrical and four-beat balladic rhythm that is close to folk meter and has resonances from the *ghazal*. Though initially Gurajada wrote in traditional style, his exposure to English romantic and Victorian poets and an awareness of the general social transformation then under way in India brought about a change in his view of literature. This change is reflected in his narrative poems such as *Lavanaraju Kala* (1911), *Kanyaka* (1912), and *Purnima* (1912), all of which were written in the new four-line stanzaic form. Such poems could be distinguished from traditional poetry not only through the distinct metrical form but also through features such as (1) an emphasis on the experience of common folks; (2) language approximating common idiom; and (3) the use of poetic imagination to highlight the novel in the commonplace. Gurajada's philosophy of poetry, along with Rayaprolu's new ideas, provides the basis for a new wave of poetry, *bhava kavitvam.*

Rayaprolu Subba Rao dominated the Telugu literary scene for nearly five decades. He created memorable works in a variety of poetic forms: lyric, love poetry, pastoral verse, and patriotic songs. The two dominant influences on Rayaprolu's work can be traced to his acquaintance with British poetry of the nineteenth century and to his exposure to the literary movements of Bengal. In fact, he spent some time at Shantiniketan with Tagore around 1915. A romantic in vision, he dealt with the theme of love with rare sensitivity and sophistication in *Trinakankanam* (1912), *Snehalatha* (1914), and *Swapna Kumaram* (reprint, 1969). His philosophy of love, which highlighted the essential beauty of the emotion in its various forms—friendship, affection, tenderness, love—is popularly known as *amalina sringara,* a love that is abstract and spiritual, being centered on *vipralambha,* that is, the nonpossibility of physical union, leading to an eternal love (somewhat like Keats' bold lover in "Ode on Grecian Urn"). The chief expression of his credo comes through *Ramyalokam* and *Madhuri Darsanam* (1956, 6th ed.), both of which must be regarded as his aesthetic philosophical statements.

Bhava Kavitvam

The term *bhava kavitvam* was first used to describe the distinctive poetic compositions of Rayaprolu in 1920. It is generally agreed that this movement was chiefly inspired by the English lyric. *Bhava kavitvam* manifested itself in different forms in different poets. A love of freedom in choice of subject and mode of expression is the wellspring of *bhava kavitvam.* However, it is not so much a difference of metrical and prosodic features that distinguishes this poetry from classical Telugu poetry; rather, the emphasis on *bhava* (emotion) marks it apart from the *rasa-pradhana* (sentimental) poetry of the classical mold. Some striking features of this poetry are interiorization of experience; greater focus on spiritual beauty than on the merely physical; worship of the metaphysical rather than material nature; celebration of *prapatti,* or total surrender to the Divine. *Bhava kavitvam* takes different forms, such as love poetry, patriotic verse, poetry of social reform, nature poetry, and *bhakti,* or devotional poetry. Running through all these manifestations is the thread of musicality, the feature that enabled these lyrics to be sung. This seems a major reason for the popularity of the movement.

The theme of love received a novel treatment in the hands of *bhavakavis* (sentimental poets). It is not the fulfillment of love, but the eternal waiting of lovers, that is celebrated in these poems. Abburi Ramakrishna Rao's *Mallikamba* (1915) and Duvvuri Rami Reddy's *Kadapati Veedkolu* (1924) exemplify this trend. Poets often describe an imaginary beloved and elevate her above and beyond the familiar, circumscribing, familial roles—woman as the symbol of *viswaprema* (universal love), as friend, philosopher, and as impalpable yet alluring divinity. Devulapalli Krishna Sastry's Urvasi (1926–29), Adivi Bapriraju's *Sasikala* (1939), and Tallavajjula Sivasankara Swamy's *Hridayeswari* (1926) belong in this category. Some poets celebrate marital love and treat the man–woman relationship as the objective correlative of *atma-paramatma* (lower self and higher self) union. Viswanatha Satyanarayana's *Girikumaruni Prema Geethaalu* (1953) is a striking instance of this kind.

As *bhava kavitvam* developed against the backdrop of the Indian nationalist movement, patriotic verse and poetry of social reform emerged as an important branch of this poetry. Songs of anti-imperial protest urging freedom, written in vers libre, gained immense popularity in the 1930s and 1940s. Chilakamarti Lakshmi Narasimhan's *Bharatha Khandam,* Duvvooris's *Naivedyam* (1921), and Grimella Satyanarayana's *Ma koddee thella dorathanam* are some of the most powerful patriotic verses of this school. Biographical verses written on the lives of heroes from the past and contemporary life form a part of this kind of poetry. Gadiyaram Venkata Sesha Sastri's *Sivabharatham* (1953, 3d ed.) on the life of Shivaji and Jandhyala Papayya Sastry's many short lyrics on the life of the Buddha are good examples of this form. Gandhiji was the subject of countless Telugu poems written during this period; Devulapalli's *Gandhiyugam*, Tummala Sitarama Murthy's *Bapuji Atmakatha* (1951), and Basavaraju Appa Rao's lyrics on Gandhi merit special mention. *Bhava kavitvam* urged social change and reform. Gurram Jashuva's *Gabbilam* (1941) is a powerful critique of caste/class structure in Indian society; Tripuraneni Ramaswamy Chaudhuri's *Suthapuranam* (1954) makes a strong plea for the abolition of caste distinctions; Katuri Venkateswara Rao's *Gudigantalu* demands that temple doors be thrown open to untouchables. Poetry thus became a social act.

Nature poetry evoking and celebrating the landscape of the Telugu land constitutes yet another important strand of *bhava kavitvam.* Devulapalli seeks total identification with nature in his *Krishna Paksham* (1925); Jandhyala empathizes with floral maidens in *Pushpa Vilapam;* Abburi shows how nature spurs love in *Oohaganam* (1918). Viswanatha's *Kinnerasani Patalu* (1924) and Nanduri Subba Rao's *Yenki Paatalu* (1925) are examples of the beautiful pastorals and moving rural romance that *bhava kavitvam* created. Poets composed lyrics to folk tunes that were popular among different regions of Andhra. Duvvuri captured the rhythms of farmers' lives in *Krisivaludu* (1919). Nandoori's *Yenki* and *Naidu bava* have become living legends in Telugu literature.

Finally, *bhakti kavitvam,* or devotional poetry, forms an important tributary in the streams of *bhava kavitvam.* Poetry became an act of self-surrender, and the poets submitted themselves totally to the will of God. Puttaparthi Narayanacharyulu's *Sivathandavam* (1940) is a powerful poetic tribute to Lord Shiva; Devulapalli pays homage to a universal God in *Mahathi;* Jandhyala invokes the myth of Radha-Krishna to express his devotion to Krishna; Basavaraju's *Gopika Geethalu* (1921), too, invokes Lord Krishna through dedication and devotion. These form a part of the philosophy of *Krishna tatvam,* in which the devotee takes the place of Radha the beloved and views God as Krishna, the "universal lover."

Abhyudaya Kavitvam (Progressive Poetry)

Bhava kavitvam, which reigned supreme on the Telugu literary scene for three decades, started playing itself out by the 1940s, though its influence continued well into the second half of the twentieth century. It declined into a blind imitation of Rayaprolu and Devulapalli; subjectivity now was shrouding social purpose; and a countermovement to *bhava kavitvam* began. Poets such as Sistla Umamaheswara Rao, Srirangam Srinivasa Rao (Sri Sri), Pattabhirami Reddy, and Srirangam Narayanababu, who started in the vein of *bhava kavitvam,* turned away from that form. Their quest for novelty, exposure to Western literature, and the sociopolitical climate of their times influenced their poetry profoundly. The result was the rise of a new wave of poetry—*abhyudaya kavitvam,* or progressive poetry.

The first Andhra Progressive Poets (Abhyudaya Rachayitala Sangham [ARASAM]) conference, held in Tenali in 1943, was presided over by Tapi Dharma Rao. The 1943 conference, however, must be seen as only the first organized effort of ARASAM. By 1933, progressive writings were being published in Telugu. Such developments were, of course, the result of exposure to socialist-communist literature and ideology. The years 1928–29 witnessed the underground distribution of socialist-communist ideological texts in Madras and Andhra districts. Bhagat Singh, who, through 1929–31, had evolved into a leading Marxist revolutionary, was executed in 1931; his martyrdom had a profound influence on the thinking of young men who later became important figures in the progressive poetry movement. In 1933, S. Muddukrishna started publishing *Jwaala,* a periodical journal, as a forum for progressive writers and thinkers to express their ideas of socialism and equality. The year 1934 saw the formation of the Congress-Socialist Party and the Communist Party of India. Working-class ideologies were becoming popular among the intelligentsia, and the universities and colleges in the composite Madras state (including the districts of Andhra) often became the centers of new, revolutionary thought.

Some of the recurrent themes of this poetry are class conflict, legends of heroes of the past, realization of a socialist state. *Abhyudaya* poetry incites the weak and the lowly to shake off their complacency and resignation and fight for their rights. Progressivism spread the message of freedom and equality and an aversion to wars, which always result in large-scale massacre. Its dream is a classless society based on the principles of liberty and equality. The most important aspect of the *abhyudaya* movement was the emergence of Sri Sri as a powerful voice. Sri Sri, who may be seen as Gurajada's intellectual heir, had moved away from *bhava kavitvam* and made his poetry a tool of progressivism.

He struck his first note of revolution in a poetic fragment, *Supsthasthikalu,* in 1929. After that, he made revolution the major thrust of his work and declared his ideological commitment to socialism in *Jayabheri* (1933). His *Mahaprasthanam* (a long poem, 1934) is a landmark work in the development of *abhyudaya kavitvam* and encodes the manifesto of progressive writers. Sri Sri pledged himself to the task of working-class welfare and the uplift of laborers in *Pratigna* (1937). A socialist utopia beckoned him and the others who followed in his wake; Sri Sri became the ideological role model for many Telugu poets.

Pattabhirami Reddy demonstrated his dissent through *Fidelu Ragaala Dozen* (1939). He carried his dispute with tradition so far as to assert the dismantling of traditional meters and the grammar of Chinnaya Suri. Sistla proclaimed his revolt against *bhava kavitvam* through *Navami Chiluka* (1938), which, he hoped, would pave the way for a new, people's poetry. Narayanababu opposed the idealism of *bhava kavitvam* and made a strong case for realistic and naturalistic modes of presentation. *Abhyudaya kavitvam* soon became a powerful movement and attracted a large number of poet practitioners. Chief among these were Puripanda Appalaswamy and "Papa," whose lyrics anticipate the experimental poetry of a later period.

The publication of *Niagara* (1944), an anthology of progressive verse, gave voice to many *abhyudaya* poets, including Kundurthi Anjaneyulu, Bellamkonda Ramadasu, and Yechuri Subramanyam. Others who drew influence from Sri Sri and the movement published their progressive verses. Dasarathi's *Agnidhara* (1949) and *Rudraveena* (1950), Somasundar's *Vajrayudham* (1949), Arudra's *Tvamevaham* (1949), Anisetti's *Agniveena* (1949), and Gangineni's *Udayini* (1950) are some notable examples of this phase.

One important strand of *abhyudaya kavitvam* concerns itself with the liberation of Telangana. Even after independence of India, Hyderabad remained under the feudalistic rule of the Nizams, through Paigahs, Zamindars, Jagirdars, and Inamdars. Poets of this region urged the freedom of Telangana from this oppressive regime. This movement was supported by the Communist Party. Dasarathi is the most important figure in this movement. Among other poets who spearheaded the Telangana movement through their stirring poetry, Kundurthi Anjaneyulu and Kaloji Narayana Rao are prominent.

Strands of Tradition

Even as the winds of *bhava kavitvam* and *abhyudaya kavitvam* were blowing across the Telugu land, traditional poetry continued to be in vogue, and good poetry written in classical style did not altogether lose its place or significance. One of the major literary figures who belonged to the traditionalist school was Jnanpith Award-winning Viswanatha Sathyanarayana. Though he handled both the traditional and modern forms with equal ease and felicity, he wrote his magnum opus, *Srimad Ramayana Kalpa Vruksham* (1962), a major text of our times, in traditional meter and style. Among the other traditionalists, Madhunapanthula Satyanarayana Sastri is well known for his *Andhrapuranam* (1954), history of Andhra written in verse. Vajjala Kalidasu's *Andhra Mahavishnuvu* (1928) is a historical poem written in *dvipada,* or couplet form. Vaddadi Subbrayudu's *Bhakta Chintamani* (1893) is a devotional work of 100 poems, *satakam.* Tirupati Venkata Kavulu wrote *Buddha Charitra* (1902), the life history of Buddha in verse. Other writers, such as Puttaparthi Narayanacharyulu, Sripada Krishnamurthy Sastry, Janamanchi Seshadri Sarma, and Vavilakolanu Subba Rao, continued to use the traditional poetic forms with remarkable felicity.

New Experimental Poetry

Although the progressive movement lost some of its momentum by 1955, it may be said to continue as long as there are social problems and poets who raise their banners of revolt. There was some disenchantment with the progressive movement, mainly because of a general disappointment with communism. While Dasarathi and Somasundar abandoned the progressive movement more or less completely, Sri Sri and Arudra remained steadfast in their adherence to the movement. In 1965, C. Vijayalakshmi wrote *Vishadabharatham,* which may be identified as the last important work of the progressive movement. A number of new trends developed in the post-1955 period, primarily due to the influence of European avant-garde writing.

Prose poetry, or *vachana kavitvam,* became significant, mainly because of the efforts of Kundurthi Anjaneyulu, who became its leading exponent. *Vachana kavitvam* thematizes the problems of common people in colloquial idiom. Here, rhythm that carries the reader through to the end of the poem on the wave of cadence is more important than metrical uniformity. Tilak, Narayana Reddy, Aluri Bairagi, Varavara Rao, and Guntur Seshendra Sarma wrote poetry of this kind.

In 1965, one midnight in the month of May, a group of angry young men came out with a collection of poems and got it released by a rickshaw puller. These young men, who called themselves *digambara kavulu* (naked poets), assumed symbolic names: Nagna Muni (Naked Saint), Jwala Mukhi (Volcano), Mahaswapna (Great Vision), Nikhileshwar (the Omnipotent) Bhairvavayya (the Hound), and Cherabanda Raju (Raju, Turned to Stone in Prison). Digambara poets set out to startle society with naked truth. They were deeply agitated by the mechanical existence of humans and felt that such drab routine reduced human beings to an animal level. Their anguish turned to anger, and much of their work, written in the white heat of fury, displayed more aggression than poetry.

The year 1970 saw the founding of the Revolutionary Writers' Association (Viplava Rachayitala Sangham [VIRASAM]). Sri Sri became the president of this association of poets, who believed in Marxism and armed struggle against the establishment. VIRASAM used poetry and literature as a tool to propagate this ideology and further the struggle. Some *digambara* poets also joined this movement. In yet another development, an organized group, Kavisena, came into existence in 1977. Led by Guntur Seshendra Sarma, Kavisena opposes sloganism and aggressiveness and evinces faith in organized leadership. Intellectuals, the group believed, should provide proper direction to the masses through their creative work.

A Class Apart

It is difficult to label some of the contemporary writers as romantics or revolutionaries, as they do not write poetry strictly of one kind or another. They may generally be called neoclassicists. Of these, C. Narayana Reddy is the most outstanding. He tried his hand successfully at different forms of verse—romantic, revolutionary, traditional. His masterpiece *Viswambhara* (1980), dealing with the theme of universal brotherhood, is one of the most powerful works of our times. Reddy, who won the Jnanpith Award for his meritorious work, may well be described as the representative poet of contemporary Telugu literature. Thus, Telugu poetry in the twentieth century is rich and varied, with tradition and innovation jostling with each other in their search for appropriate form of expression.

DRAMA: DEVELOPMENTS

Of all literary forms, drama is considered the most impressive and powerful by ancient Indian aestheticians. Strangely, it is the least developed and most neglected form in Telugu. Many indigenous (*desi*) dramatic modes such as *yakshaganam, veedhi natakalu,* and *bhagavàtha melalu* were in vogue in Andhra, but these did not develop into sustained theatrical movements. Till about the 1860s, there is no history of dramatic writing in Telugu. Korada Ramachandra Sastry's *Manjari Madhukareeyam* (1860) is the first original drama to be written in Telugu, but most of the early plays that appeared in Telugu were translations either from Sanskrit or from English.

Translations from Sanskrit began with Kokkonda Venkataratnam's *Narakasura Vijaya Vyayogamu* (1872), followed by translations of work of several renowned Sanskrit dramatists, such as Kalidasa, Bhasa, Bhavabhuti, Sudraka, and Harsha. Alongside appeared Telugu translations of English plays as well. In 1890, Kandukuri translated *Comedy of Errors* under the title *Chamatkara Ratnavali,* and it was staged by his students. Among the other Western playwrights to be rendered into Telugu were Goldsmith, Sheridan, Molière, and Gibbon. The influence of these translations on Telugu drama was rather limited, but the newly formed English Dramatic Associations aroused keen interest in play performance among Telugus. Besides, Parsi and Dharwar drama troupes touring Andhra around 1880 staged plays in Hindi that were enthusiastically received. This also gave a boost to dramatic writing in Telugu. Some of the important Telugu dramatic associations to be founded around the turn of the century were Sarasavinodini Sabha, Sumanorama Sabha, Surabhi Company, and Hindu Nataka Samajam. These contributed immensely to the emergence of Telugu drama into a distinct genre and the popularization of performance in Andhra.

The Early Phase

The early phase in Telugu drama is marked by an adaptation of mythological plots for theatrical performance. Sri Rama's exemplary life, Sri Krishna's pranks, and Kaurava-Pandava strife were among the popular themes. The most important writer of this phase was Dharmavaram Krishnamacharyulu, the founder of Sarasavinodini Sabha. He wrote over 30 plays and actively participated in the performance of these plays. He blended the conventions of Sanskrit classical drama with those of the Western theater and produced several stageable plays. *Chitranaleeyam* (1894), the story of Nala and Damayanti, was his most successful work. His *Sarangadhara* (1897), with its tragic closure, breaks the conventions of ancient Indian aesthetics and marks a revolutionary change in Telugu drama. In 1897, Vedam Venkataraya Sastry brought yet another innovation in his play *Pratapa Rudreeyam* by introducing character-specific speech for the first time. Prominent among the other writers of this period are Kolachalam Srinivasa Rao and Vaddadi Subbarayudu.

Kanyasulkam and the Secularization of Drama

Telugu drama entered a new phase with the staging of Gurajada Appa Rao's *Kanyasulkam,* the first social play in 1892. The play had several successful performances in the state before it was published in 1897. Gurajada's work can be placed in the tradition of *prahasanam,* one of the 10 dramatic modes used in Sanskrit literature. *Prahasanam* is a satirical play that exposes social foibles and absurdities in a humorous vein. Kandukuri used this form to attack the social evils of his time and arouse apathetic masses. Drawing from these sources, Gurajada wrote the first full-length social play dealing with one of the most urgent issues of his time—bride price, the practice of selling minor girls to old men. Gurajada's play becomes a landmark in the evolution of twentieth-century drama in several ways: the theme is secular and not mythological, characters are fully developed and lifelike, and the language used is the simple, everyday idiom. Above all, the gentle and sophisticated humor Gurajada brought to dramatic dialogue and situation made it an unprecedented success both on stage and in print. The trend started by Gurajada, however, found no immediate followers, and the Telugu social play as a subgenre took long to emerge. Kallakuri Narayana Rao revived the social play almost two decades later in his *Varavikrayam* (1921) and *Madhuseva* (1926).

Verse Drama

Verse dramas continued to dominate the scene in the first two decades of the twentieth century, and mythological plays retained their prime position. Chilakamarthi Lakshmi Narasimham's *Gayopakhyanam* (1909) and Panuganti Lakshmi Narasimha Rao's *Paduka Pattabhishekam* (1909) were among the most popular plays of the period and had several successful performances all over the state. The stories of the *Mahabharatha* have a very special attraction for Indian people. The stories of their culture-heroes—Krishna, Harischandra, and Pandava kings—rendered into the dramatic mode with the added interest of popular poems from the epics set to impressive musical scores never ceased to interest the Telugu public. Some of the most popular mythological plays based on the *Mahabharatha* tales include *Pandavodyoga Vijayam* (1911) by Tirupathi Venkata Kavulu, *Satya Harischandreeyam* (1922) by Balijepalli Lakshmikantham, and *Sri Krishna Tulabharam* (1922) by Mutharaju Subba Rao.

Another form of verse drama that developed into an important trend during 1900–20 is the historical drama. These plays offered an imaginative rendering of certain important historical incidents in the dramatic mode. Sripada Krishnamurthy's *Bobbili Yudhdham* (1908), Kolachalam Srinivasa Rao's *Rama Raju* (1920), and Duvvuri Rami Reddy's *Kumbha Rana* (1921) exemplify this trend. Kopparapu Subbarao's *Roshanara* (1921), a very successful yet controversial play, triggered a sectarian stir and was banned. Around this time, a number of historical plays apparently dealing with centuries of Islamic rule were actually camouflaging resentment against the British rule. The British government soon discovered the political motives behind these plays and ordered the closure of theaters. The era of historical plays, which began around 1910, thus came to a halt by 1925.

The Independence Movement and Revolutionary Drama

The historical drama of the earlier period began to acquire echoes of political innuendo, and political drama emerged as an important trend in the 1920s and 1930s. Some of the earliest plays to contain political messages in poetic dialogue were Kallakuri Narayana Rao's *Padmavyuham* (1919) and Damaraju Pundarikakshudu's *Gandhiji Vijayam* (1921). The writers often used historical or mythological frameworks to allegorize contemporary reality. Damaraju's *Panchala Parabhavam* (1922), Somaraju Ramanuja Rao's *Tilak Rayabaram* (1921), and Budhdhavarapu Pattabhiramayya's *Matrudasya Vimochanam* (1924) exemplify this trend. Under the impact of the widespread anticolonial movement and the upsurge of a nationalist spirit, the writers felt the need for re-creating a national history and sculpting a national identity. This accounts for a fresh renewal of interest in historical themes, which provided the suitable terrain for dramatizing patriotic fervor and nationalist emotions. Sripada Kameswara Rao's *Kalapahad* (1913), Muttaraju Subba Rao's *Chandragupta* (1932), Viswanatha Satyanarayana's *Venaraju* (1934), and Gundimeda Venkata Subba Rao's *Khilji Rajya Patanam* (1935) form a part of this development. There was a rereading of the history of Andhra as well, as seen in Grandhi Venkata Subbaraya Gupta's *Andhramatha* (1913) and Kavuluri Hanumantha Rao's *Andhra Patakam* (1939).

The next set of political plays came around the time of the Quit India movement (1942), with which the Indian independence movement entered its final and most forceful phase. The years 1943–46 witnessed the publication of a large number of plays revolving round the theme of political liberation: Vedantakavi's *Telugu Talli* (1940), Utukuru Satyanarayana Rao's *Sapa Vimochanam* (1943), Jasti Venkata Narasayya's *Congress Vijayam* (1946), and Pattigodupu Raghava Raju's *Delhi Kota* (1946) dramatize the political struggle for freedom and celebrate the liberation of the Indian people. The purpose of these plays was to spread the message of liberation to common folk and consolidate the nationalist movement.

The progressive movement in the 1940s provided further impetus for the political drama. The Praja Natya Mandali (people's theater movement) provided the forum for the performance of revolutionary plays. Sunkara Satyanarayana and V. Bhaskara Rao jointly brought out two plays: *Mundadugu* (1945) and *Ma Bhoomi* (1947), dealing with the atrocities of zamindars and the autocratic rule of the Nizam of Hyderabad, respectively. This movement adopted folk forms such as *burrakatha* (storytelling) to reach out to the masses with their political messages. The establishment banned the performance of these plays; besides, the propagandist slant of these works lost the movement its audiences.

The Emergence of Modern Drama

Gurajada's *Kanyasulkam,* as seen earlier, marked a departure from the traditional dramatic forms and the beginning of a new era. However, the traditional forms continued to dominate the scene, and modern drama as an established form took long to emerge. Modernism in the context of Telugu drama implies secularization of dramatic subjects, contemporization of dialogue, and formal/technical experimentation. Here again, the impact of Western literature is an important factor. The novelty of Ibsen's work impressed the Telugu playwrights so much that there were serious attempts to revolutionize playwriting and play production along the lines of Ibsenian drama. Writers tried to replace the conventional lies of the stage with some necessary though bitter truths of life and bring the plays close to actual life. P. V. Rajamannar's *Tappevaridi* (1929), written under the influence of Ibsen, is considered the first modern play in Telugu. This play dramatizes the liberation of a much-harassed woman from the shackles of an unhappy marriage. It called age-old traditions into question and underscored the need for a reevaluation of traditional sociocultural institutions. P. V. Rangaram's *Dampathulu* (1931) and Ballari Raghava's *Saripadani Sangathulu* (1938) both belong to the same trend and center round marital and familial problems. The stage became a forum for an intellectual debate of social problems in this phase. As a part of this theatrical revolt, a new brand of mythological plays emerged around the same time. Muddu Krishna's *Asokamu* (1934), Chalam's *Harischandra* (1937), and Amancharla Gopala Rao's *Hiranya Kasipudu* (1937) attempt revisionist reinterpretations of mythological stories. However, these plays could not be staged for a long time, because people considered it a sacrilege to meddle with the sacred texts.

The revival of Andhra Nataka Kala Parishad in 1941 was an important attempt to sustain the theater movement. The Parishad conducted regular competitions and made awards to talented playwrights. Acharya Atreya, Muddu Krishna, and D. V. Narasaraju established their credentials through these competitions. In the 1940s and 1950s, the thematic range of plays widened significantly, and a realistic drama addressing contemporary social issues such as caste system, class structure, and gender discrimination emerged as the dominant trend of this period. Acharya Atreya's *NGO* (1949) dramatized the problems of a meagerly paid clerk, and its success on the stage proved that the ordinary and the commonplace could be turned into powerful drama. Kopparapu Subba Rao's *Inapa Teralu* (1950), Kodali Gopala Rao's *Peda Raithu* (1952), and Pinisetti Srirama Murthy's *Kulam Leni Pillalu* (1951) are all written in the same vein. Rachakonda Viswanatha Sastry's *Tiraskriti* (1957) and Bellamkonda Ramadasu's *Panjaram* (1956) deal with the emancipation of women and address specific women's issues. Buchibabu's *Atmavanchana* (1951) and Bhamidipati Radhakrishna's *Keertiseshulu* (1960) focus on the paradoxes of the human condition and dramatize psychological conflicts and complexes. Telugu drama thus tapped a variety of thematic tropes and widened the horizons of its concern by the end of the 1960s, after which it described a steady decline. The growing popularity of television and film practically rang the death knell of Telugu drama.

The Contemporary Scene

Despite sporadic efforts to revive and sustain Telugu theater, drama in Telugu has not been able to secure a significant place either in Telugu literature or in the tradition of performance. Andhra University established an open-air theater and later started a Department of Theatre Arts. So did the Osmania University subsequently. The efforts of the university departments and the state-financed institutions have barely managed to keep the tradition alive, but a total lack of popular patronage blocks the revival of drama in Andhra. What revival there is in recent Telugu drama comes mainly from Western enthusiasts but has not met with much success. Very few good plays appeared in the last 25 years: R. S. Ramaswami's *Galivana* (1968), N. R. Nandi's *Maro Mohenzadaro* (1969), Rentala Gopala Krishna's *Rajani* (1972), Arudra's *Radari Banglow,* and Gollapudi Maruthi Rao's *Kallu* merit special mention. These plays show the influence of the Western avant-garde movement and ably adapt the new dramatic techniques to Indian themes.

Telugu drama is more than a century old now. There have been several significant changes in the themes and forms of drama in these 100 years, but the essential structure of the play has not altered. Mythological subjects were replaced by social and secular themes; verse yielded place to prose, which, in the course of time, turned into colloquial idiom; the long play with elaborate scenes and several characters gradually became condensed into short and often one-act plays; new modes of presentations, including realist, symbolic, and expressionist techniques, were attempted, but no new forms with indigenous roots have yet emerged.

NOVEL: DEVELOPMENTS

A variety of narrative forms and storytelling habits existed in the oral tradition of Indian literatures. *Katha, gatha, akhyayika,* and *nitikatha* are terms and forms related to narration one comes across in Sanskrit as well as regional literatures of India. So *katha,* or storytelling vital to the novel form, was nothing new to the Indian aesthetic experience. But the novel as an original story written in prose largely to be read by and for oneself is a concept that grew out of a complex network of sociocultural factors: spread of literacy, popularity of the print medium, English education, rise of the middle class, emergence of newspapers and magazines in regional languages, increase in the size of the reading public, and the influence of the English novel.

The Beginnings

The first novel in Telugu, *Sri Rangaraju Charitra,* was written by Narahari Gopalakrishnama Setty in 1872. When Kandukuri Veeresalingam published *Rajasekhara Charitram* in 1878, he was obviously not aware of the earlier work and hence claimed that his was the first attempt at "novel" writing. Kandukuri did not use the word "novel" but chose to call his work *vachana prabandham.* His purpose in writing this work was to fight superstition and obscurantism in contemporary society. The Telugu equivalent for novel, *navala,* was first used in a review of Kandukuri's work and declared the arrival of a new genre in Telugu. *Chintamani,* a literary magazine in Telugu, conducted annual competitions and gave awards to talented novelists. This provided the impetus for the growth of this new literary form. Some of the nineteenth-century novels that received the Chintamani Award were Chilakamarthi Lakshmi Narasimham's *Ramachandra Vijayam* (1894), *Hemalatha* (1896), *Saundaryatilaka* (1899); Tallapragada Suryanarayana's *Sanjeevaraya Charitra* (1893); and Khandavalli Ramachandrudu's *Malathi Raghavam* (1895).

The Early Phase

A number of publishing houses that came into existence in the early twentieth century lent tremendous support to the growth of the novel. Saraswathi Granthamala (1898), Vignanachandrika Granthamala (1903), Andhra Pracharini Granthamala (1911), and Veguchukka Granthamala (1911) were, to a large extent, responsible for the consolidation of narrative tradition in Telugu. The spread of English education brought Telugu youth into contact with nineteenth-century novelists like Scott and Goldsmith. More important, the novel in Bengal had already grown into a powerful literary form and began playing a vital role in the cultural revival, and this had a definite impact on the developments of the Telugu novel in its formative phase.

One of the most important developments of this phase is a sudden spurt of translations of Bengali novels. Venkata Parvateesa Kavulu rendered several of Bankim Chandra Chatterjee's novels into easy and readable Telugu. These include *Rajasimham* (1912) and *Krishnakanthuni Marana Sasanam* (1914). Chaganti Seshaiah's *Durgesa Nandini* (1911) and *Navab Nandini* (1915), too, were received with great enthusiasm by Telugu readers. Among the other Bengali novelists to be translated into Telugu were Sarat Chandra Chatterjee and Rabindranath Tagore. These translations not only aroused a keen interest in novel reading but also provided inspiration and a sense of direction to Telugu novels.

In this phase, the Telugu novel widened the scope of its thematic interests but made little progress in terms of technical sophistication. A number of social and historical novels were written during this phase. The social novels of this period, such as *Matru Mandiram* (1920) by Venkata Parvateesa Kavulu and Chilakamarti's *Ganapathi* (1920), focus on the customs and cultural conflicts of Telugu Brahmin families during the transitional period. Although the writers urge social reform, they do not look to the experience of the socially deprived for their fictional subjects. The historical novels by far outnumber the social novels during this phase. The cultural revival of the early twentieth century, the nascent spirit of nationalism, and love of freedom filled the writers with a patriotic fervor. Narrating history may be viewed as a part of the retrieval of the past and a revival of lost glory. Chilakamarthi's *Vishnuvardhanudu* (1927), Ketavarapu Venkata Sastry's *Rayachuru Yudhdham* (1914), and Bhogaraju Narayana Murthy's *Vimala* (1910) are some notable examples of this trend. Even in historical novels, the writers rarely let go an opportunity to urge change and social reform.

Changes, Challenges, and Narration

The period between 1920 and 1950 was marked by hectic political activity, rapid social change, and intense cultural conflict. The Telugu novel, coping with these changes and challenges, came of age during this period. This phase produced major novelists and their masterpieces. Colonial rule, consequent cultural conflicts, and anticolonial movement form the sociopolitical context of these texts; but the narrative discourses that developed are so diverse that they cannot be grouped into a general category like "anticolonial novel" or "national allegories," to use a more recent critical label. Two important trends, however, may be identified: (1) a discourse of critical realism that calls into question not only the dominant imperial authority but all forms of authoritarian systems, including feudalism, caste system, class structure, and patriarchal ideology, and (2) fictionalizing the traditional ethos of a vanishing past and exploiting the textual space for the conservation of cultural values.

Unnava Lakshminarayana's *Malapalli* (1922), one of the major novels of this phase, inaugurates the former trend. Unnava was a close associate of Kandukuri and lent the latter strong support in his reform activities for child widows. The political upheavals of the time drew him into the vortex of political activity. He was influenced by the political philosophy of Bala Gangadhara Tilak, socialist ideologies of the Soviet Union, and the idealism of the Mahatma Gandhi. For his involvement in the nationalist movement, Unnava was arrested, and the epic novel *Malapalli,* encompassing the entire sociopolitical situation of the times, was written while he was in prison. *Malapalli* is a trendsetter in a number of ways: for the first time, the social underdog becomes the subject of a literary work; the life of the inhabitants of a Harijan hamlet is rendered in the local dialect used by those people; a work of fiction is turned into a powerful forum for foregrounding social tension and ideological conflicts. Another important writer who was motivated by a strong sense of rejection of the existing socio-cultural institutions was Gudipati Venkata Chalam, popularly known as Chalam. His focus was on the here and the now, and he protested against the oppression of women in unequivocal terms. The question of political freedom was never an isolated issue in Andhra; it was invariably linked with the liberation of the peasant and the worker, freedom of the untouchable, and the emancipation of women. Chalam's works, *Daivamichina Bharya* (1923), *Maidanam* (1927), *Aruna* (1935), and *Ameena* (1942), all offer a critique of patriarchal power structures, including family and marriage, that reduce women to a subordinate position. These novels celebrated female sexuality and aroused resentment in orthodox circles.

Viswanatha Satyanarayana, a scholar of Sanskrit and Vedic texts, a traditionalist in outlook, was skeptical of the forces of Westernization and modernization gripping contemporary society, and his work is an earnest effort to conserve the indigenous culture against this onslaught. Viswanatha, a gifted writer and a mature thinker, wrote 57 works of fiction, and there was hardly any aspect of life that was left out of his fictional universe. His magnum opus, *Veyi Padagalu* (1961), is an epic novel covering the lives of three generations and unfolding alongside the political and social history of the Telugus for over half a century. The writer upholds the ancient Hindu dharma and underscores the spirituality that forms the basis of Hindu life and thought. Adavi Bapiruju re-creates the history of Andhras in a series of historical romances such as *Gona Gannareddy* (1958) and *Himabindu* (1960). More of a romantic, he brings the past alive through symbolic representation and sensitive images. Rewriting history, political or cultural, was a part of the celebration of the past, a movement of cultural nationalism.

The Age of Experimentation

The Telugu novel enters the age of experimentation in the 1950s because the writers have, by this time, come under the influence of some of the important intellectual and ideological developments of the time, such as Freudian psychoanalysis, Marxian socialism, and European existentialism. Besides, the modernist writings of the West, too, have had considerable impact on the creative minds of the time. Furthermore, the writers of the 1950s, coming after the literary giants like Unnava and Viswanatha, needed to do something different and original in order to emerge out of the shadows of their predecessors. A quest for form and penchant for experimental constructs, hence, become the most dominant features of the Telugu novel in this phase.

The psychological novel, probing the inner conflicts and complexes of the human psyche, found favor with a number of writers of this time. Gopichand's *Asmardhuni Jeevayatra* (1960) is a powerful fictional rendering of the tragic strife of a common man to come to terms with the society around him. Buchi Babu's (S. Venkata Subba Rao) *Chivaraku Migiledi* (1946) traces the predicament of a sensitive young man struggling to grow out of a strong oedipal complex. Rachakonda Viswanatha Sastry's (Ravisastry) *Alpajivi* (1981), Naveen's *Ampasayya* (1982), and Latha's *Prema Rahityamlo Stree* (1978) are some of the other successful attempts at the psychological novel, and the authors use the interior monologue and stream-of-consciousness techniques for recording the psychological processes and unraveling the deeper layers of the human psyche.

As in the case of all postcolonial literatures, political satire became the mainstay of the Telugu novel in the postindependence phase. The writers focus on the aftermath of the colonial rule and offer a satirical delineation of the new bourgeois government. Kodavatiganti Kutumba Rao's *Chaduvu* (1952) deals with the social and cultural changes that took place in middle-class families during the colonial times and exposes the incongruity and absurdity that arose out of a collision of dissimilar cultures. Viswanatha, who continued to write well into the experimental phase, produced delightful satires in *Vishnu Sarma English Chaduvu* and *Pulula Satyagraham.* Ravisastry's *Govulostunnai Jagrata* and Palagummi Padmaraju's *Bathikina College* are among the other notable examples of this trend.

The more overtly political novel, fielding specific political issues, is yet another significant development of this period. The writers, who came under the influence of the progressive writers movement found the novel an extremely effective medium for communicating messages of revolution and progress. A strong faith in the Marxist socialist ideology inspires these writers and their works. G. V. Krishna Rao's *Keelu Bommalu* (1952) and Balivada Kantharao's *Dagapadina Tammulu* (1961) merit special mention in this category. Novels that thematized the Telangana struggle for freedom form a part of this trend. Bollimunta Sivaramakrishna's *Mrutyunjayulu* (1947), Vattikota Alwar Swamy's *Gangu* (1965), and Dasarathi Krishllamacharyulu's *Chillara Devullu* (1970) offer a moving account of the sufferings of poor farmers under the zamindari system and urge revolutionary action.

Women's Writing

A notable feature of the Telugu novel is that this genre has encouraged many women writers. Women's writing, in fact, forms a distinct and considerable segment. Writers like Jayanti Suramma, Suram Subhadramma, and Kanaparthi Varalakshmamma were among the earliest to have used the fictional mode to project women's issues. Between 1960 and 1980, a number of women writers took to the novel form and achieved considerable success through serialized periodical publication. There is an impressive thematic variety in their writing, which covers practically every aspect of women's experience: the position of women in the Hindu joint family; problems faced by career and single women; the dowry system; marital maladjustments; pleasures and problems of motherhood; and female sexuality.

A close study of women's texts reveals two distinct trends. Writers like Muppala Ranganayakamma, V. Sitadevi, and Lata show that women should break the shackles of social and familial bonds and seek freedom, whatever the price may be. On the other hand, Illindala Saraswatidevi, Ramalakshmi, Parimala Someswar, and Dvivedula Visalakshi, who are equally sensitive to the problems faced by women, advocate not total rejection of the existing systems but a thorough overhaul. Another group of women writers, including Yeddanapudi Sulochanarani, Madireddy Sulochana, and Koduri Kausalyadevi, are all gifted storytellers with evident predilection for romance and popular fiction. The major contribution of women's writing is the emergence of an alert and alive woman with vibrant passions and a strong voice to articulate them. The new women created in these stories deconstruct the conventional "stereotypes" of virtuous women and declare their autonomy. Women writers, however, have not gone beyond the traditional modes of narration and expression, which become clear restrictions on their writing. They are yet to find their own idiom and language and write themselves into their texts.

The Contemporary Scene

The novel continues to be the most popular form in the 1980s and 1990s, particularly through periodical serial publications. Thematically, we can identify two important trends in the vast corpus of fictional writing in the last decade and a half: progressive writing addressing the problems of the socially deprived and underprivileged, as in Ravi Sastri's *Sommulu Ponayandi* (1980), Allam Rajaiah's *Vooru* (1982), and Beena Devi's *Captain Katha* (1984), and the feminist novel, offering a systematically worked out feminist ideology, as in Muppala's *Janaki Vimukti* (1981) and Volga's *Swechcha* (1987). In both these movements, the hitherto marginalized sections are brought into focus, and the privileged centers of the past—the bourgeosie and the male—are displaced. The anxiety to sound different and original resulted in a great deal of contrived and mediocre writing. A large number of novels written according to popular formulaic structures depend heavily on sex, violence, superstition, and exorcism. The value of much of this writing is questionable. However, the comprehensive hold that the novel has on the Telugu literary scene is an undeniable fact.

SHORT STORY: DEVELOPMENTS

As with the novel, the short story is a popular prose form that finds a symbiotic sustenance in the relationship with periodical publications. Of the many periodicals that gave encouragement and support to the short story, special mention must be made of *Bharathi* (1924) for the service it rendered to this genre. Besides, Sahiti Samithi, a literary organization founded by Tallavajjhala Sivasankara Sastry, also encouraged the writing of short stories.

The Beginnings

Gurajada Appa Rao's ''Diddubaatu,'' published in 1910, is regarded as the first short story in Telugu. He published a slim volume of stories entitled *Animutyalu,* addressing different social problems. The potential of the short story form to address various issues without the constraints of the verse form or the diffusion of the novel form attracted a number of able practitioners. Among the pioneers of the Telugu short story, Chinta Deekshitulu, Veluri Sivarama Sastry, Viswanatha, Munimanikyam Narsimha Rao, and Chalam figure prominently. Veluri wrote interesting stories about the social life of the middle class. His well-known story ''Depression Chembu'' ridicules the vanities of educated youth. Chinta Deekshitulu's stories, written in a humorous vein, expose the absurdities of obscurantism and orthodoxy. Chalam addresses women's issues, and his ''Hampikanyalu'' is considered an important work. Munimanikyam recreates the rhythms of middle-class domestic life in ''Kantham Kathalu.'' Stories of these writers are anthologized as *Tolinati Telugu Kathalu* (1936–45) by the Andhra Pradesh Sahitya Akademi. Adavi Bapiraju, Karuna Kumara, Tripuraneni Gopichand, and Kodavatiganti Kutumba Rao also figure among the pioneers whose work was reviewed and assessed through *Aksharabhishekam* by Gorrepati Venkata Subbaiah in 1952. Many of these writers continued to write well into the decades that followed.

Consolidation

Technical sophistication, the use of colloquial language, and international recognition mark this phase. A fairly representative selection of stories from 1946 to 1955 published by the Andhra Pradesh Sahitya Akademi under the title *Oka Dasabdi Telugu Kathalu* (1980) testifies to this fact. These stories demonstrate an ability to combine formal, technical accomplishment with social awareness and responsiveness; the skill and sensitivity that went into the work, surely, proclaim the maturity of the genre. Palagummi Padmaraju's *Galivana* won second prize in an international competition held by the *New York Herald Tribune* in 1952. Puranam Subrahmanya Sarma's ''Neeli'' won first prize in the Telugu section of the 1953 version of this competition. Such achievements indicate that the gains of the early period had now been consolidated.

Wide thematic variety is the chief feature of the stories of this period. The lives of the socially deprived classes are mirrored in Puranam's ''Neeli'' and Karuna Kumar's ''Rickshaw Wallah.'' Jamadagni's ''Marupurani aa Vooru,'' Kavikondala Venkat Rao's ''Zamindaru,'' and Veluri's ''Arachakam'' depict the life and landscape of the various regions of Andhra Pradesh and reflect village politics while re-creating rural life. The complex inner life of an average person is powerfully portrayed in the psychological stories that probe the depths of human thought, emotion, and experience. Palagummi's ''Galivana,'' Hitasri's ''Nijanijalu,'' and Amarendra's ''Panjaram'' belong to this category. Women's issues figure prominently in Balivada Kantha Rao's ''Paadulokam, Paadumanushulu,'' Gopichand's ''Karyasurudu,'' and Buchibabu's ''Thananu Gurinchina Nijam.'' Such stories reflect the changing relationship between man and woman and debate the validity of marriage as an institution. The common person's dream of an egalitarian society and the struggle of an emergent new society with the forces of stasis and corruption find expression in stories such as Kalipatnam Rama Rao's ''Palayithudu,'' Ravisastri's ''Puvvulu,'' and Munipalle Raju's ''Bicchagalla Jenda.''

Continuity

Even as the established writers of the 1940s and 1950s continued to be prominent, other writers entered the field, adding variety and experiment to it. R. Vasundhara Devi, Seela Veerraju, and Saurees exploit a wide range of narrative possibilities in their stories. In general, the newer writers continued to build on the foundations provided by the established writers. The thread of continuity, however, also gives some glimpses into certain common weaknesses of the Telugu short story: a tendency to make explicit end statements or an option for some contrivance to make a closed ending possible, prolongation of the narration beyond a good technical ending, and a weakness for purple prose. Such weaknesses mar the impact of many a good story. Yet, to read Ravuri Bharadwaja's ''Paristhitula Varasulu,'' Ravi Sastri's ''Lakshmi,'' or R. S. Sudarsanam's ''Madhura Meenakshi'' is to become aware of superb craftsmanship, excellent plotline, fine sense of ending, engagement with contemporary society, and aesthetic refinement. Such stories affirm that the Telugu short story is equal to the best practice anywhere in the world.

CONCLUSION

What may be said by way of a summing up about Telugu literature in the twentieth century? It would be most appropriate to observe that we are, at the turn of the century, too close in time to make an objective assessment. It is well worth remembering the maxim that what has been long preserved has been subjected to repeated scrutiny. Twentieth-century Telugu literature is yet too young to pass this test of time. But there are indications that, as a literature fully alive to human developments, both at home and abroad, it will surely find its niche in the history of world literature.

SELECTED PRIMARY BIBLIOGRAPHY

Abburi, Ramakrishna Rao. 1949. *Oohaganam.* New Delhi: Kavita, n.d.

Acharya, Atreya. *NGO.* Vijayawada: Kurukuri Subbarao and Sons, 1952.

Adivi, Bapiraju. *Gona Gannareddy.* Machilipatnam: Triveni, 1946.

———. *Sasikala.* 1939. Vijayawada: Jayanthi, 1978.

———. *Himabindu.* 1924. Vijayawada: Jayanthi, 1986.

Arudra. *Tvamevaham.* 1949. Vijayawada: Visalandhra Publishing House, 1971.

Avanthsa, Somasunder. *Vajrayudham.* 1949. Vijayawada: Visalandhra Publishing House, 1979.

Balijepalli, Lakshmi Kantham. *Satya Harischandreeyam.* 1912. Rajahmundry: Kondapalli Veeravenkaiah and Sons, 1958.

Balivada, Kantharao. *Dagapadina Tammulu.* 1961. Machilipatnam: M. Seshachalam, 1976.

Basavaraju, Apparao. *Gopika Geethalu.* 1921. Vijayawada: Udai Bhaskar, 1962.

Bollimuntha, Sivaramakrishna. *Mruthunjayulu.* 1947. Vijayawada: Visalandhra Publishing House, 1968.

Buchibabu. *Chivaraku Migiledi.* 1946. Secunderabad: M. Seshachalam, 1970.

Chilakamarthi, Lakshmi Narasimham. *Gayopakhyanam.* 1909. Rajahmundry: Kondapalli Veeravenkaiah and Sons, 1955.

———. *Ganapathi.* 1920. Machilipatnam: M. Seshachalam, 1975.

C. Narayana Reddy. *Nadaka Naa Thalli.* Manaswi Prachurana, Hyderabad: Master Art Printers, 1983.

———. *Viswambhara.* Hyderabad: Mauktika Prachuranalu, 1990.

D. Ramalingam, ed. *Telugu Katha.* New Delhi: Sahitya Akademi, 1982.

Dasaradhi, Krishnamacharyulu. *Agnidhara.* 1949. Secunderabad: Chandra Narayana Sreshti, 1963.

———. *Chillara Devullu.* 1970. Hyderabad: Desi Prachuranalu, 1978.

Devulapalli, Krishnasastry. *Krishnapaksham.* 1925. Madras: Rajahamsa, 1983.

Dharmavaram, Krishnamacharyulu. *Sarangadhara.* 1897. Hyderabad: A. P. Sahitya Akademi, 1983.

Divakarla, Trirupathi Sastry, and Venkatasastry Chellapilla. *Panigrihita.* 1909. Kadiyam: Venkateswara, 1956.

———. *Sravananandam.* 1909. Vijayawada: Visalandhra Publishing House, 1972.

———. *Pandavodyoga ViJayam.* 1911. Rajahmundry: Venkateswara, n.d.

Duvvuri, Rami Reddy. *Kadapati Veedkolu.* 1924. Pemmareddy Palem: Kavikokilagranthamala, 1957.

———. *Krishivaludu.* 1919. Pemmareddy Palem: Kavikokilagranthamala, 1957.

Gollapadi Maruthirao. *Kallu.* Vijayawada: Aruna, n.d.

Gudipati, Venka-tachalam. *Hampi Kanyalu.* Vijayawada: Desi Kavitha Mandali, 1955.

———. *Aruna.* 1935. Secunderabad: M. Seshachalam, 1976a.

———. *Daivamichina Bharya.* 1923. Machilipatnam: M. Seshachalam, 1976b.

Gurajada, Apparao. *Gurjada Rachanalu Kavitala Samputam.* Vijayawada: Visalandhra Publishing House, 1984.

———. *Kanyasulkam.* 1897. Vijayawada: Jayanthi, 1992.

Gurram, Jashua. *Gabbilam.* 1941. Vijayawada: Hemalatha Lavanam, 1987.

Jandhyala, Papayya Sastry. "Pushpa Vilapam." In *Udayasri.* Vijayawada: Rama, 1953.

Kallakuri, Narayanarao. *Madhuseva.* 1926. Vijayawada: Kurukuri Subbarao and Sons, 1937, 1953.

———. *Varavikrayam.* 1921. Vijayawada: Jayanthi, 1988.

Kandukuri, Veerasalingam. *Rajasekhara Charitram.* 1878. Machilipatnam: M. Seshachalam, 1969.

Kodavatiganti, Kutumbarao. *Chaduvu.* 1946. Vijayawada: Visalandhra Publishing House, 1982.

Kokkonda, Venkataratnam. *Narakasura Vijaya Vyayogamu.* 1872. Madras: Vavilla Ramaswamy and Sons, 1950.

Kundurti, Anjaneyulu. *Telangana.* 1956. Vijayawada: Visalandhra Publishing House, 1995.

Madhunapanthula, Satyanarayana Sastry. *Andhrapuranam.* Pallipalem: Madhunapanthula Surayyasastri, 1954.

Madhuranthakam, Rajaram. *Oka Dasabdhi Telugu Kadhalu.* 1946–55. Hyderabad: Andhra Pradesh Sahitya Akademi, 1980.

Nanduri, Subbarao. *Yenkipatalu.* 1925. Hyderabad: Sairam, 1991.

Naveen. *Ampasayya.* Hyderabad: Navayuga, 1982.

N. R. Nandi. *Maro Mohenzadaro.* 1969. Vijayawada: Navodaya, 1975.

Panuganti, Lakshmi Narasimharao. *Paduka Pattabhishekam.* 1909. Vijayawada: Kurukuri Subbarao and Sons, 1932, 1955.

Puttaparthi, Narayanacharyulu. *Sivatandavam.* 1940. Mahaboobnagar: Gayatri Prachuranalu, 1969.

Rachakonda, Viswanatha Sastry. *Alpajivi.* Vijayawada: Vijaywa Books, 1981.

———. *Sommulu Ponayandi.* 1980. Vijayawada: Karuna Publishing House, 1981.

Rayaprolu, Subbarao. *Trinakankanam.* 1912. Guntur: Navya Sahitya Parishad, n.d.

———. *Snehalatha.* Guntur: Navya Sahitya Parishad, n.d.

———. *Swapnalokam and Madhuridarsanam.* Vol. 2 of *Abhinavakavita.* Hyderabad: Navodaya, 1949.

Samineni, Muddukrishna. *Asokamu.* 1934. In *Natikalu.* Madras: M. Seshachalam, 1964.

Sistla, Uma Maheswar Rao. *Navami Chiluka.* N.P., n.d.

Sripada, Krishnamurthy Sastry. *Bobbili Yudhdham.* 1908. Rajahmundry: Kondapalli Veeravenkaiah and Sons, 1953.

Srirangam, Srinivasa Rao. *Mahaprasthanam.* 1934. Vijayawada: Visalandhra Publishing House, 1984.

Tallavajjula, Sivasankara Swamy. *Hridyeswari.* 1926. Tenali: Devuluru Venkata Subbarao, n.d.

Tenneti, (Hema) Latha. *Premarahityamlo Street.* Vijayawada: Jayanthi, 1978.

Tikkavarapu, Pattabhirami Reddy. *Fidelu Ragala Dozen.* 1939. Nellore: Vardhamana Samajam, 1973.

Tripuraneni, Gopichand. *Asamarthuni Jeeva Yatra.* Vijayawada: Deluxe, 1960.

Tripuraneni, Ramaswam Choudhary. *Sutapuranam.* 1954. Vijayawada: Sutasrama Granthamala, n.d.

Tummala, Sitarama Murthy. *Bapuji Atmakatha.* Vijayawada: Ramamohana Granthamala, 1951.

Unnava, Lakshminarayana. *Malapalli.* 1922. Vijayawada: Jayanthi, 1968.

Vedam, Venkataraya Sastr. *Pratapa Rudreeyam.* 1897. Madras: Vavilla Ramaswarny and Sons, 1927.

Viswanatha, Satyanarayana. *Vishnusarma English Chaduvu.* Vijayawada: Sarvodaya, 1972.

———. *Srimad Ramayana Kalpa Vruksham.* 1972. Vijayawada: Viswanatha, 1992.

———. *Veyipadagalu.* 1939. Vijayawada: Viswanatha, 1992.

REFERENCES

Arudra. *Samagra Andhra Sahithyam.* 13 vols. Vijayawada: Prajasakthi Book House, 1991.

C. Narayana Reddy. *Adhunika Andhra Kvithvamu: Sampradayamulu, Prayogamulu.* Hyderabad: Author, 1967.

D. Ramanuja, Rao, P.S.R. Appara Rao, and G. V. Subramanyam, eds. *Telugulo Parisadhana: Essays on Research in Telugu.* Hyderabad: Andhra Pradesh Sahitya Akademi, 1983.

G. Subhbirami Reddy. *Aadhunika Telugu Natakam.* Secunderabad: Praveen, 1991.

K. Venkatarama Narasimham. *Aadhnika Andhra Kavitha Sameeksha.* Vijayawada: Ganyadhara, 1982.

M. Kulasekhara Rao. *A History of Telugu Literature.* Hyderabad: Master Art Printers, 1988.

M. Sujatha Reddy. *Telugu Navalanuseelanam.* Hyderabad: Santha Art Printers, 1990.

P. T. Raju. *Telugu Literature (Andhra Literature).* Bombay: International Book House, 1944.

Poranki Dakshinamurthy. *Nuru Samvatsaralu.* Hyderabad: Andhra Pradesh Sahitya Akademi, 1973.

Telugu Sahitya Kosamu. *Adhunika Sahityam 1851–1950.* Hyderabad: Telugu Akademi, 1986.

Utukuri Lakshmikanthamma. *Andhra Kavayitrulu.* Rajamahendravaram: Sanskrita Kalasala, 1953.

V. Mandeswara Rao. *Noorella Sahityamlo Konni Dhoranulu Dhrukpadhalu.* Hyderabad: Padmavathi Art Printers, 1991.

V. Narayana Rao. *Telugu Kavitha Viplava Swarupam.* Vijayawada: Visalandhra, 1978.

12

Twentieth-Century Urdu Literature

OMAR QURESHI

This introductory summary, of the course of Urdu literature in the twentieth century must continuously refer to the nineteenth century. This becomes necessary because, depending on one's point of view, it was Urdu's destiny or misfortune to gradually become identified as the lingua franca of the Muslims of India in the latter half of the last century. Consequently, the still-unresolved dilemmas of the politics of Muslim identity in South Asia are difficult to separate from their expression in and through the development of Urdu.

For our purposes, then, the most significant consequence of the failed rebellion of 1857 was the gradual emergence of group identity among the recently politically dispossessed and culturally disoriented Muslim elite of north India. This effort to define Indian Muslim nationhood in the new colonial environment placed issues of past, present, and future identity at the center of elite Muslim concerns. Not only were these concerns expressed largely in Urdu, but the literary legacy of Urdu formed the terrain through and on which some of the more significant debates were conducted. The Muslim leadership that emerged after 1857 looked to this precolonial literary legacy as an authentic, but highly problematic repository of the Indian Muslim identity and the Urdu language itself as the most effective medium for the renewal and reform of the Muslims of British India. As Muslim identity politics gathered strength in colonial India, and Urdu was turned into the print language of the emerging nation, discussions of an apparently purely literary nature became a veritable mirror of ideological and sociopolitical change among India's Muslims. For example, calls for the reform of precolonial Urdu poetics mirrored analogous reform initiatives in the religious, social, and political spheres. This relationship has continued, in different ways, since the division of British India into India and Pakistan in 1947. It is this ongoing dialogue between the reform of Urdu and issues of Muslim identity that I highlight here as the major literary trends, works, and writers in Urdu in the twentieth century are surveyed.

ORIGINS

The origins of Urdu are a matter of some dispute among scholars. Depending on which of the numerous linguistic, historical, literary, and geographically diverse sources scholars make use of, many plausible speculations are possible. The minimal explanation on which most scholars agree and which is probably the least misleading is that a literary written language similar to what we now call Urdu gradually began to replace Persian in importance in early eighteenth-century Delhi and, "while still resting firmly on its Indic grammatical and lexical base, was steadily enlarging its repertoire of Persian genres and imagery" (Pritchett 1994, 4). From Delhi and nearby Agra, this literary Urdu spread to Avadh, Panjab, the Deccan, and Bihar. In time, Lucknow, Lahore, and Hyderabad, as well as Delhi, became major centers of Urdu publishing and scholarship. Before the eighteenth century, various dialects of a proto-Urdu were probably widely spoken over a very wide geographic area across India.

In other explanations, the emergence of Urdu has been traced as far back as the first arrival of Persianized Muslims into north India in the eleventh century; to the introduction of Arabic, Persian, and Turkish expressions into the local Indian languages over the centuries; and to areas as diverse as the Deccan, Gujarat, the Ganga-Jamuna region, and Panjab.[1] Still others hold the view that the mixture of West Asian and Indic linguistic and literary traditions took place at the Mughal court, especially in the military camp and marketplace on the environs of the Delhi fort and the court of Shahjahan (r. 1628–58) (Sadeed 1991, 41). The word "Urdu" itself is of Turkish origin and refers to a military camp. It came into sole usage only at the end of the nineteenth century. Until the nineteenth century, Urdu was also known by a number of other names, including Khari Boli, Braj Bhasha, Zaban-i Urdu-yi Mu'allah, Rekhtah, Dehlavi, Dakkani, Gujri, Lahori, Hindavi, Hindi, and Hindustani (Sadeed 1991, 51). In its literary variant, Urdu is most commonly written in the *nasta'liq* style of the Arabic alphabet, which was borrowed from Indo-Persian.

In short, by defining Urdu essentially in terms of the grafting of West Asian and classical Islamic linguistic and literary traditions onto Indic, local, and largely colloquial languages, Urdu scholars agree to place Urdu firmly at the points of Muslim interaction with, and experience in, South Asia. For example, the Urdu literary canon, with its emphasis on works of West Asian expression and its exclusion of works in local dialects, is an apparent but little-examined reflection of this view. The process of formation of this now generally accepted canon in the nineteenth century holds important implications for Urdu's close ties to Muslim nationalism in South Asia (Naim 1978, 5–12).

CONSEQUENCES OF 1857

The failure of the rebellion against British rule by sections of the north Indian populace resulted in incalculable loss and tragedy for Delhi's Muslims, in particular, and for large sections of the Muslim elite of north India generally. Delhi had served as the symbol of local sociopolitical autonomy and as the cultural capital of Mughal India. After their victory over the rebels, the British mainly held the Muslims of Delhi and surrounding areas responsible for the revolt. Many Muslim notables were executed. Muslim institutions in Delhi, including libraries, were destroyed, while the majority of the Muslim population was expelled from Delhi. According to one commentator, ''[t]he savage British suppression of the Mutiny and Rising, with its destruction of Delhi as a center of Muslim culture, and the dispersion of the descendants of Akbar and Aurangzib by execution and exile, at last forced educated Muslims to realize not only that the British were in India to stay, but also that they intended to stay on their own terms'' (Hardy 1972, 61). The traumatic events of that summer represented the final passing away of an age for the Muslim elite and initiated moves to adjust to European rule, with its technological superiority and efforts to rule over India through the introduction of administrative and educational reforms. For the next half-century, Urdu's fortunes were intertwined with moves to come to terms with the colonial regime and with efforts at Muslim reform.

ALIGARH MOVEMENT AND ITS CRITICS

Muslim efforts to adopt Western knowledge while attempting to retain traditional values were led by Sayyid Ahmad Khan (d. 1898) and his successful movement to set up a college for Muslim gentlemen at Aligarh along modern educational lines (1877).[2] Through his writings and political activity and, later, through the Muhammadan Anglo-Oriental College at Aligarh, Sayyid Ahmad attempted to convince fellow Muslims that, if they hoped to reverse their declining fortunes, they must assimilate European thought and understand that the bases for Western worldly success lay in nineteenth-century rationalism. He argued that Muslim religious beliefs, if rationally understood, did not necessarily conflict with Western insights, but Muslims must still reform their political, social, cultural, and moral values when contradicted by more rational and ''natural'' Victorian modes of thought and conduct.

Sayyid Ahmad was of the view that a selective adoption of Western science and rationality would allow the depressed Muslim elite to begin to improve its lot. To this end, he adopted a clear, precise, and functional language for his forceful reformist essays and avoided the ornate and plastic language of the Mughal court. Precedents for Sayyid Ahmad Khan's style exist in the large number of translations from European languages into Urdu that took place at Delhi College (founded in 1825) and in the Urdu works compiled under the supervision of John Gilchrist (d. 1841) at Fort William College in Calcutta (founded in 1800) (Sadiq 1984, 290–91, 315–18). Sayyid Ahmad's writing may also have been inspired by the unaffected prose of the letters of Mirza Asadullah Khan Ghalib (d. 1869) and the religious tracts of Shah Isma'il (d. 1831). Moreover, his utilitarian views of language, in turn, influenced a whole generation of writers in Urdu. Sayyid Ahmad Khan was a prolific writer and produced works on a wide range of topics, including theology, architecture, archaeology, politics, and apologetics. *Tahzeeb-ul Ikhlaq,* the journal he started in 1870, which remained in publication for 12 years, contains the best examples of his writing style and views.

To resist Sayyid Ahmad Khan's Westernizing influences among Muslims, a group of Muslim *'ulama,* or learned scholars, founded a religious seminary in the small district town of Deoband, north of Delhi, in 1867.[3] While Deoband accepted the reality of British political rule, it sought to preserve correct Muslim belief and practice in the face of a rapidly changing society. Its devotion to a revival of Islamic practice and learning soon manifested itself in a mushrooming of similar institutions in north India, and Deoband itself attracted students from all over India. Since the language of instruction in these *madaris,* or schools, was Urdu, and much of the popular religious proselytizing and debate against Aligarh or competing religious groups was also conducted in Urdu, these religious institutions (and other religious reform movements) should also be credited with the rapid spread of Urdu in the nineteenth century. Deoband's founder, Muhammad Qasim Nanautavi (d. 1880), matched Sayyid Ahmad in the sobriety of his argumentation and writing style. He counted among his followers Mahmudul Hasan (d. 1920), who participated in the founding of Jamiah Miliyah in Delhi in 1920, which combined elements of Aligarh and Deoband and became a center of language instruction in Urdu; and Ashraf Ali Thanvi (d. 1943), who, in turn, influenced a whole generation of followers, largely through his careful pedagogic style and religious charisma. His influence was spread by his copious writings, which were learned and easy to understand. His *Bihishti Zevar* (1906), a reform manual for women, is a classic and best-selling example of his style.[4]

HAI I'S REVOLUTION

Before Altaf Husain Hali (d. 1914) unleashed his wide-ranging condemnation of Urdu literature in his *Muqaddamah-i Sher o Sha'iri* in 1893, Muhammad Husain Azad (d. 1910) had already shown the way through his influential history and anthology of Urdu poetry, *Ab-i Hayat* (1880). Azad was not directly connected with the Aligarh movement but had come under the influence of reformist ideas through his association with the Anjuman-i Panjab in Lahore, where he had moved from Delhi in 1864. As part of his activities for the Anjuman, Azad wrote and lectured extensively on the need to reform Urdu literature so that it would be better able to bear the demands of the new society. "Azad made a passionate appeal for the avoidance of abstract themes, high flights of imagination, and complex traditional metaphors which he saw as outworn" (Faruqi 1992, 422). Sayyid Ahmad Khan also praised Azad for his efforts to bring Urdu closer to a simpler and natural style and for his critique of the artificiality of traditional poetry (Pritchett 1994, 38).

Like Azad, Hali was also influenced by the British educators associated with the Anjuman-i Panjab during his brief stay in Lahore. This reformist zeal combined with a deep admiration for Sayyid Ahmad Khan and his reform movement to ensure that Hali would go even beyond Azad, whose work he admired, in his call for a new poetics that would serve the interests of the emerging Muslim community. The one continuous strand in the *Muqaddamah* is the call for a poetry that is able to reflect changes taking place in Indo-Muslim society and that can be true and natural. Hali stood for a careful editing of the literary tradition to save only those elements that were morally uplifting and socially useful.[5] While Hali did not call for a complete rejection of traditional poetry,

> [d]rawing upon what he thought were reliable sources for western literary theory, and also making abundant reference to Arabic and Persian where it suited his argument, [he] created a literary theory which was an odd combination of Platonic idealism and Benthamite utilitarianism. He found much in Urdu literature that was morally unsatisfactory, artistically weak, and almost utterly useless as an instrument of social change. . . . But the reason for the tremendous influence of Hali's thought was not so much the power of his logic as the emotional and mental state of his audience. (Faruqi 1992, 424)

Hali's ideas were widely discussed and largely accepted, and the subsequent history of Urdu literature became an endeavor to come to terms with Hali's vision in myriad ways.[6]

One of the major consequences of Hali's critique was a devaluation of the lyric, or *ghazal* form, in Urdu poetry, which is fundamentally concerned with the concept of *'ishq,* or love in the widest sense. The *ghazal* had been the major component of Urdu literature, and poets such as Mir Taqi Mir (d. 1810), and Ghalib had produced *ghazal* poetry of the highest standards. Moreover, the universe of the *ghazal* form apparently contained within it the ideals of Indo-Muslim culture that had developed in the Mughal period and that were now being viewed with ambivalence by the Muslim community, which saw them as impotent and debilitating in the face of the colonial onslaught.[7] Probably for this very reason, Azad and Hali picked on the *ghazal* as the major target of their criticism and, through it, of the precolonial legacy as a whole. Yet, the ambivalence of the reformists about modernizing, while retaining traditional values, was also visible here. For example, the attraction of the *ghazal* was such that neither Hali nor Azad could quite escape its charms; and Hali, for instance, continued writing traditional *ghazals* of a high order. Hali also tried to write *ghazals* based on his recommendations for the reform of poetry and was the first to introduce overtly reformist themes into the *ghazal.* Nevertheless, his poetic genius really showed in his long narrative poems after the Western fashion, especially his immortal *Musaddas-i Madd-o Jazr-i Islam* (1879), which traced the rise and decline of the Muslims and tried to exhort them to change their old ways. The *Musaddas* also condemned past literature for its decadence.

HALI'S CONTEMPORARIES

Prose

Shibli Nomani (d. 1914) was associated with Sayyid Ahmad Khan's reformist efforts, and, like other nineteenth-century Indian Muslims, he, too, was internally ambivalent about the wholesale rejection of the precolonial heritage. He eventually became a powerful critic of the excesses of Aligarh and tried to steer a middle path between Deoband and Aligarh through his association with the Nadvat-ul 'Ulama in Lucknow (founded in 1894). Although he wrote scholarly works of literary criticism, they never commanded as much influence as Hali's seemingly more relevant views.[8] Nevertheless, his literary work is important for the emphasis it places on the centrality of classical Islamic literature, especially Persian, as the model for a reforming Urdu. In Shibli, we observe a demotion of Urdu as the Indian Muslims' language of identity in favor of an imagined West Asian golden tradition. Instead of rejecting the literary heritage completely, Shibli divides it into the non-Indic older and the more recent decadent Indic and views the former as more properly constitutive of Indo-Muslim identity. Therefore, while Shibli complicates Hali's blanket critique of the tradition by viewing earlier portions of it as more progressive, he does so by strengthening the distinction between the West Asian and Indic parts of Indo-Muslim identity. Finally, Shibli's great contribution lies in his introduction into Urdu of Western methods of research and historical criticism through his writings on Islamic history, which are still valuable as much for their content as for their style.[9]

The didactic novels of another contemporary, Nazeer Ahmad (d. 1912), are straightforward application of the Aligarh philosophy of "productive work, socially responsible behavior, frugality, and a code of conduct which had very little place for pleasure, and none for levity" (Faruqi 1992, 425). His novels are the first in Urdu and were instantly successful, especially *Mir'at-ul Uroos* (1869), *Taubat-un Nusuh* (1877), and *Banat-un Na'sh* (1873), but were paradoxically accompanied by *Ibn-ul Vaqt* (1888), which savagely satirized the imitation of English manners and customs and the excesses of reform.[10] Both Hali and Nazeer Ahmad were particularly interested in the reform of Muslim households through the education and proper training of women.[11]

Like them, the novelist Rashidul Khairi (d. 1936) also wrote against useless customs and superstitious beliefs on the part of women, exhorted them to serve as sensible guardian-educators of their households, and saw the home as the sanctuary of the Muslims' identity.[12] In contrast to Nazeer Ahmad's satire, Khairi adopted a more emotional style.

Nazeer Ahmad was also followed by Ratan Nath Dar Sarshar's (d. 1902) attempts to mold the oral romance (*dastan*) tradition into the novel form, by the historical novels of Abdul Halim Sharar (d. 1926), and by the social novels of Mirza Muhammad Hadi Rusva (d. 1931), especially *Umrao Jan Ada* (1899), a novel about the experiences of a reformed Lucknow courtesan.

Poetry

Paradoxically, the efforts of Hali and Azad to reform the Urdu poetic tradition gave rise to a new breed of poets who used their newly acquired, socially responsible literary talents to criticize Sayyid Ahmad's political loyalty to the Crown and reformist excesses. They did this precisely within the modern framework of Hali's reformed and reformist spirit. As already noted, Hali himself continued to write *ghazals* in the traditional mode while composing his ameliorative poems. Similarly, the colonial government service had in its employ Urdu's greatest satirical poet, Akbar Allahabadi (d. 1921). Akbar also wrote traditional *ghazals* of great worth but adopted the Halian poem to point to deeper philosophical inconsistencies in the reformist movement. Akbar's vitriolic wit made his poetry instantly popular and allowed him to express his opposition to colonial rule, coupled with telling criticisms of modernization.

Like Akbar, Hasrat Mohani (d. 1951) was an inconsolable opponent of colonial rule, but his objections to Hali's aims were of a more literary nature. Hasrat sought to defend Urdu poetry from Hali's criticisms, but without the latter's theoretical sophistication. Rather, Hasrat's real contribution was to struggle with the legacy of the *ghazal* in his own poetry. He saw the *ghazal* as fundamentally love poetry and stressed its continuing ability to appeal to people's emotions with great facility. Hasrat is a *ghazal* poet of some distinction and was the first "to introduce overtly political themes in the ghazal," as well as revivifying it more generally (Faruqi 1992, 427). Hasrat was also active in compiling and editing the works of poets of the classical period. Braj Narayan Chakbast (d. 1926) and Isma'il Mairthi (d. 1917) adopted the new narrative or descriptive poem and experimented with form and theme to pave the way for the powerful populist poetic expression of opposition to colonial rule during the Khilafat movement.

KHILAFAT MOVEMENT

Although the movement to safeguard the caliphate in Istanbul was fundamentally misguided, the Khilafat movement represented a great moment of hope and optimism in the India of the early 1920s. This period was marked not only by great shows of Hindu–Muslim unity but also by anticolonial fervor and pan-Islamic idealism. The first great mass struggle against the colonial regime resulted in a renewal of Urdu journalism. Muhammad Ali Jauhar (d. 1931), a leader of the Khilafat and a product of Aligarh, produced patriotic prose and poetry of great popularity that exhorted the Muslims of India to unite against the Western powers. Meanwhile, Abul Kalam Azad (d. 1958) combined a conservative religious view with an openly anticolonial attitude to produce moving editorials of great passion in his newspapers, *al-Hilal* and *al-Balagh.* Azad also served as Shibli's factotum for a time but differed from the latter's scholarly style by producing Urdu prose of almost poetic inspiration. Zafar Ali Khan (d.

1956), editor of the newspaper *Zamindar* and an accomplished satirist, also produced poetry and prose of some power and served as an important popularizer of Urdu in the Panjab.

The massive support provided to Urdu scholars by the government of the Nizam of Hyderabad also deserves mention. Not only did the Hyderabad state government provide scholarships and stipends to countless Muslim writers and scholars all over India (among them, Iqbal and Shibli), but it also established Usmania University in Hyderabad in 1919, which became a great center of Urdu scholarship, employing the noted Urdu scholar Abdul Haq (d. 1963), among many other luminaries.[13]

IQBAL

The Khilafat movement's failure to comprehend the internal politics of the Middle East should not distract from the immense impact it had on the psyches of colonial India's Muslims. The Khilafat represented the first time since 1857 that Muslims had come out in large numbers against British rule. One way to understand the Khilafat movement's consequences is in terms of its resistance to the modern idea of nationalism. Through the Khilafat, Indian Muslims seemed to be making two points. By stressing their transnational loyalties, they marked their disagreement with the international system of nation-states then emerging in Asia under colonial rule. Second, by garnering Hindu support for what was considered a Muslim minority issue, they seemed to be registering their refusal of a corporate minority status within the nationalist struggle against colonial rule or in a future Indian state. The Khilafat's immense sense of community also indicated a distrust of the idea of the modern, legal individual and citizen.[14] Urdu literature of the Khilafat period reflects a new appreciation of the historical and cultural heritage of Indian Muslims in the face of disenchantment with wholesale Westernization.

The Khilafat was the formative period for the poetry of Muhammad Iqbal (1877–1938), who is undoubtedly the towering figure in Urdu poetry this century. In addition to a deep knowledge of the traditional Indo-Islamic sciences, Iqbal was also well versed in, and deeply influenced by, European philosophy. His knowledge of the latter meant that Iqbal understood the Western economic and political systems with considerably more depth than did the generation preceding him. This, of course, meant that he was also conversant with the critique of European thought and practice attempted by European thinkers from Marx to Nietzsche. Partly with the assistance of these philosophies, Iqbal was able to think through the rationality that was leading to the increasing brutalization of humankind in a supposed age of progress. From Marx, Iqbal learned to distrust unchecked capitalism as an economic system, and Nietzsche helped him to recognize the spiritual and existential emptiness of modernity. Moreover, as Iqbal himself claimed, the English and German romantics helped him to look to religion as a source of possible alternatives to the abuses of capitalist modernity.

Subsequently, Iqbal turned to the Indo-Islamic tradition to examine its potential as basis for a critique of, and for an alternative imagining to, colonial modernity. Like Hali and Shibli, Iqbal was insistent in holding large portions of the textual legacy responsible for the decline of the Muslims, but, following Akbar, he saw other parts of it as dynamic exhortations to creative activity that did not always participate in dominant European definitions of subjectivity. Similarly, Iqbal questioned the bases on which Muslim reformers had, up to now, attempted to define the Muslims as a nation and, instead, tried to outline a pragmatic ethics that would limit, but deepen the claims of community. Iqbal subsequently developed his idea of *khudi,* or dynamic selfhood, as a response to what he saw as the dehumanizing results of virulent nationalism and unbridled capitalism. Through the idea of *khudi,* Iqbal tried to visualize a self-defining individual who accomplished the task of resisting and reforming totalizing modernity (and a fatalistic, decadent tradition) through will rooted in an ethical community.

Iqbal's genius lay in combining these disparate elements in such a fashion that they seemed inherently and organically connected. Iqbal's censure of the West and his explicit disagreements with admired European thinkers demonstrated his confident and nondeferential attitude toward his European sources, and his rediscovery and respectful utilization of the Indo-Islamic spiritual tradition gave it new vibrancy and relevance. In Iqbal's poetry, it becomes impossible to separate the Western or Indo-Islamic content from his own interpretations, and these from their expression in language. Thus, it is no accident that he admired the Muslim mystic Rumi and Nietzsche, both of whom are similarly considered great stylists of their respective languages, as well as important thinkers.

Iqbal's accomplishments are important for several reasons. First, without really adopting new poetic genres, Iqbal took the traditional forms and revived them by his use of new constructions and imagery. This made his poetry instantly recognizable and popular but also made the familiar strange by radically expanding the subjects and language usage these genres could handle. Iqbal's use of Urdu (and Persian) for his message gave the language the depth and the expanse to be able to manage newer and larger issues, some raised so explicitly for the first time. Second, Iqbal continued Hali's example of using poetry for pedagogic purposes, but he deepened the concerns that this poetry addressed and made the use of language itself an essential element of his project of renewal. Thus, Iqbal is explicitly not a utilitarian, as Faruqi would have it (1992, 427–28).[15] Rather, Iqbal is advocating an existential and sociopolitical reimagining, instead of the very limited goal of practical means-ends efficiency. Third, Iqbal's greatest contribution is his success in making the Indo-Islamic tradition relevant as a fruitful source of artistic creativity in Urdu through which modern human issues could now be adequately explored.[16]

IQBAL'S CONTEMPORARIES

Iqbal's stature is such that other exceptional writers who happened to be producing at the same time that he wrote are eclipsed. This is unfortunate. Some of his contemporaries we have already mentioned; others are listed later. What has now become known as the age of Iqbal saw a reassertion of the *ghazal* as a result of new appreciation of the tradition and consequently produced many *ghazal* poets of note. That is not to say that the *ghazal* had ever really ceased being written, read, or heard with great enthusiasm. After Ghalib and his contemporaries, there had been several good *ghazal* poets, including Dagh (d. 1905), Ameer Meena'i (d. 1900), and Hali himself. Yet, these poets, by and large, continued to write within the framework of traditional poetics. With Akbar and Hasrat, the *ghazal* had begun to change under the influence of modernization. This change became even more apparent in the *ghazals* of Mirza Yas Yaganah Changezi (d. 1956) and Firaq Gorakhpuri (d. 1982).

Yaganah expressed skepticism both toward the new socially useful poetry and toward the return of the *ghazal* to more traditional topics (Hasrat had combined both trends). Yaganah also thought Iqbal's all-encompassing vision vacuous. Thus rejecting all options, Yaganah turned inward to express the desolate loneliness of a lover, whose traditional relationship with his beloved had forever vanished but who continued to resist the new, legal self imposed by the colonial regime and the more pragmatic self devised by Iqbal. The egocentrism and inflated pride that resulted from Yaganah's radical individualism moved him closer to his imagined nemesis, Ghalib, than to Mir. But while Ghalib's claustrophobia was often due to external circumstances, Yaganah's was self-imposed. Yaganah's poetry provides unflinching insight into a frightful aspect of the modern individual.

In some ways, Firaq was the opposite of Yaganah. Devoted to the Indian National Congress's struggle for Indian independence, associated with the Progressive Writers' Group (see later), Firaq attempted to go back beyond Ghalib to Mir to try to imitate his style and revive his conception of love. In some ways, this was an important step. Ever since Hali's biography of Ghalib (*Yadgar-i Ghalib,* 1897) and Abdur Rahman Bijnori's (d. 1918) influential and adulatory study of Ghalib (*Mahasin-i Kalam-i Ghalib,* 1921), Ghalib had become established as the representative of the classical tradition. As Hali had recognized, Ghalib's poetry had already anticipated the deeper changes that would be brought about by modernization in a colonial environment.[17] The move toward Mir meant that a more objective view of the classical tradition would emerge. In his literary criticism and in his poetry, Firaq attempted to learn from Mir and, in turn, to enrich the "traditional framework of the ghazal by incorporating into it themes untried before" (Sadiq 1984, 516). As a result, a sensuous and earthy view of the beloved marks Firaq's *ghazals* and poems, which present *'ishq* as fulfillment of body and soul.[18] In an attempt to bridge the divide between Indic and Islamic elements within Urdu, Firaq also invested his poetry with insights from the Hindi literary tradition. His influence on Urdu criticism and poetry has been significant, but increasingly he is being viewed critically, especially for his careless use of language (Sadeed 1991, 356).

Other noteworthy poets of this period who were more traditional but nevertheless informed by modern sensibilities to some degree are Shad Azeemabadi (d. 1927), Asghar Gondvi (d. 1936), Safi Lakhnavi (d. 1950), Aziz Lakhnavi (d. 1935), Arzu Lakhnavi (d. 1951), Fani Badayuni (d. 1941), Jigar Muradabadi (d. 1961), Seemab Akbarabadi (d. 1951), and Vahshat Kalkatvi (d. 1965).

1936–47

While the tension between traditional poetics and a perceived Western and modern sensibility characterized the period before Iqbal, after Iqbal, a return to an unmodified tradition seemed impossible. Faruqi makes a telling point when he writes that

> because Iqbal's utterances about the nature of poetry were cast very much in . . . Hali's mold, he also helped strengthen the notion that our classical ideas about poetry were inadequate, not to say *inutile*—embarrassing baggage, that we had luckily jettisoned in the course of our "progress" . . . classical poetics was all but gone. . . . In many ways, Iqbal's poetry can be taken as the fulfillment of Hali's mission. Hali inaugurated modern style theoretical and practical criticism in Urdu. He taught us comparative literature; he made us look beyond our immediate literary and cultural environment. There is no one writing in Urdu who is not in his debt. But he also gave us a terrible guilt complex. . . . By shaking our once-firm belief in the superiority of our literary values, he broadened our perspective—but also narrowed it. For after Hali it became very difficult for an Urdu writer to value poetry for its own sake. (Faruqi 1992, 429)

Thus, instead of the old debates, Urdu writers began to explore new avenues, among them a critical appraisal of the potential of Iqbal's vision. Partly through Iqbal's example, Urdu writers began to delve more deeply into Western philosophies like those of Nietzsche, Bergson, Darwin, Marx, and Freud and into Western literary criticism and social theory (Sadeed 1991, 423). For facility rather than for any analytical value, post-Iqbal literary trends in Urdu are usually divided into three tendencies: romantic, progressive, and those of the group around the Halqa-yi Arbab-i Zauq (Circle of Connoisseurs). It is very important to remember that these are not absolute categories, and obviously many writers are inclined toward more than one tendency; in fact, many are not bound by any category.

THE ROMANTICS

To date the beginnings of the romantic movement in Urdu would be difficult, as there were similar inclinations in the writings of the pre-Iqbal generation, and Iqbal's poetry itself contained strong elements of romanticism. The romantics were extremely sensitive to their surroundings, especially to nature, and used that as a means to free their imaginations and feed their spirit. There were certainly utopian tendencies within the movement. The romantics quickly gave way to the progressives and others, all of whom were heavily indebted to romantic ideas.

If we exclude Iqbal, the romantics produced only a few poets of note. Probably the best of them was Ihsan Danish (d. 1982), whose poetry is "born of the rarity of happiness and the excess of disappointment" (Sadeed 1991, 437). Ihsan Danish's poems and *ghazals* reveal a sensitive individual who is able to feel the grief of humankind and who is still surprised by the moral decline of society.

Josh Malihabadi (d. 1982) liked to think of himself as a political and religious revolutionary, but his feudal background often reduced him to a nostalgia for the old order. Probably as a consequence of this conflict, Josh was never able to maintain a philosophy of life that would inform his poetry. His best poems are characterized by infectious rhythms and evocative images, and the worst tend to be overlaid by unnecessary verbiage. He had great facility in composing poetry; consequently, there is much that is mediocre. But, at times, his protest against the injustices of colonial rule and religious superficiality can be quite precise. He will probably be remembered more for his prose autobiography, *Yadon ki Barat* (1970), which is a stylistic masterpiece, even if it is not always completely truthful.

Hafeez Jalandhari (d. 1982) was influenced by Hali, Iqbal, and the Bengali poet Rabindranath Tagore and made nature and religion his topics. Musicality, lyricism, and a degree of evocative power mark his poems. Although Hafeez's long poem about the glories of Islam, *Shahnamah-i Islam,* enjoyed some popularity, he is now chiefly remembered as the author of the Pakistani national anthem and a handful of other poems. Akhtar Sheerani (d. 1948) wrote adolescent, pulp romantic poetry of some talent. He invented for himself a repertoire of beautiful, virginal young women to whom he addressed his verses. He found it hard to face his poetic beloved (or much else) and found it safer to dream about her in imagined heavenly surroundings. Nevertheless, he remains an influential Urdu poet.

THE PROGRESSIVES

Under the influence of socialist ideas, the progressive writers' movement was formally launched in 1936.[19] In the context of rampant class oppression prevailing in Urdu-speaking societies, progressive views understandably enjoyed considerable influence and popularity among Urdu writers. The progressives have provided the valuable service of keeping Urdu writers sensitive to their sociopolitical environment and its injustices. "[T]hey shifted the centre of literary experience from *afaq* (the universe in the abstract) to *anfus* (people and things). In the Islamic and Indo-Muslim traditions, the stress was on *afaq*. That is why our classical literature has so little nature poetry of the 'concrete' type, and our traditional narrative so little 'characterization' " (Faruqi 1992, 432). However, the movement produced good rather than exceptional poets. Its inability to accept that ideologically correct literature is not inevitably good or that non-Marxist literature may be of some worth results in doctrinal nit-picking and periodic purges. Its contributions to literary criticism and prose fiction are more substantial.

Poetry

The only progressive poets deserving mention are Faiz Ahmad Faiz (d. 1984), Ali Sardar Jafri (b. 1913), and Asrarul Haq Majaz (d. 1955). Faiz is arguably the best-known Urdu poet. His imprisonment by military authorities in Pakistan and periodic martial law in that country, combined with Faiz's doctrinal correctness, adolescent romanticism, and use of modified traditional imagery, have ensured that he is read in both India and Pakistan with much enthusiasm and self-righteous, bourgeois indignation against the oppression of the poor. Faiz's heavy use of Arabic and Persian expressions also ensures that his poetry evokes an image of Urdu as a courtly, cultured language among those who show a predilection for such sensations. Faiz's poetry moves one to wallow in an individualistic and ultimately self-defeating oppositional mode and breeds a sense of superiority over a society that refuses to reform and thus ultimately leads to inaction. Like Josh, Faiz takes a voyeuristic view of the beloved, but without Josh's aggressive eroticism. Faiz is more passive and prefers watching the beloved disrobe through the haze of a drunken stupor and a smoke-filled room, all the while discussing revolution with fellow comrades. Ultimately, the poet is merely self-involved and refuses to problematize any relationship, including that with the working class (Ahmad 1962, 65–75). At best, the working class exists so that the poet may wax eloquent about his quixotic attempts to save it. When the beloved gets too demanding, Faiz invokes the oppressed, and, when that reality gets too overwhelming, he returns to the beloved, never really able to connect with either. Faiz began as a romantic, and his best collection is his first, where he still seems to be working out his poetic impulses. The instant popularity that followed the publication of *Naqsh-i Faryadi* (1942) encouraged Faiz to continue with its successful formula, which had a debilitating effect on Faiz's language and technical abilities. He has been devastatingly criticized for verbosity and nonsensical use of Arabic, Persian, and other constructions (Khan 1959, 50–101). However, Faiz has produced a few *ghazals* and poems of rare beauty, especially those that problematize his relationship with the beloved and with the coming revolution and its aftermath. His stylistic manner has proved irresistible to many. He has been quite influential among younger poets, the best of whom have succeeded in avoiding some of the more blatant pitfalls.

Majaz, like Faiz, is torn between revolutionary and romantic impulses, although his romanticism includes naturism and active rebellion. Hence, his poetry is abundant with nature themes and with an equation of anti-British nationalism and revolution. He also seems to have a fascination with revolutionary violence. Majaz's poetry is direct and lyrical but tends toward monotony. Ali Sardar Jafri is guilty of some of the same faults as Faiz, although he is more experimental in form and theme and has contributed nuanced criticism of some value (Khan 1959, 263–87). Since his initial espousal of unflexible socialist themes, Jafri has adopted a more realistic view of the individual. Majrooh Sultanpuri (b. 1919) remains a good *ghazal* poet for his nuanced treatment of socialist themes. Other progressive poets include Makhdum Mohiuddin (d. 1969), Sahir Ludhyanvi (d. 1980), Jan Nisar Akhtar (d. 1976), Ahmad Nadeem Qasmi (b. 1916), Kaifi Azmi (b. 1918), Salam Machhlishehri (d. 1973), Safdar Mir (Zeno), Farigh Bukhari (b. 1917), and Moeen Ehsan Jazbi (b. 1912).

Short Stories and Novels

In prose, the progressive movement has made immense contributions to Urdu literature, although, as Faruqi indicates, some of the best writers were expelled for failing to conform to the party line (Faruqi 1992, 434). Faruqi speculates that because "fiction lends itself more easily to social concerns, the Progressives' greatest achievements were in fiction, especially realistic fiction" (Faruqi 1992, 432). Premchand (d. 1936) preceded the progressives and was one of the earliest writers of short stories in Urdu. Social realism, a taut plot, and good character development are reliable features of his novels and short stories. He is equally good at evoking the atmosphere of a city, town, or village, using a simple and versatile language. Premchand's fiction has a progressive and reformist message and points to the poverty and injustice of the Indian city and countryside and the human tragedy that result from this under colonial capitalism. His novels include *Bazar-i Husn* (1917), *Chaugan-i Hasti,* and *Gosha-yi Afi'at,* and among his short stories are "Kafan," "Mantar," "Kaffara," "Kashmakash," and "Najat." Premchand remains one of the better fiction writers in Urdu, although he switched to writing in Hindi in 1914.

The controversy caused by the publication in 1932 of *Angare,* a collection of short stories by four writers, probably also encouraged the Urdu short story. For supposedly containing blasphemous and obscene material, the book was banned by the government in 1933. The authors included Ahmad Ali (d. 1994), Rasheed Jahan (d. 1952), Mahmuduzzafar (d. 1956), and Sajjad Zaheer (d. 1973). The stories were not particularly sophisticated but attempted to handle class oppression, women's issues, sexuality, and religious obscurantism in a more open manner.[20] These themes became standard fare for the progressive writers.

Krishan Chandar (d. 1977) was a prolific writer of short stories, and his fiction is characterized by a mixture of realism and romanticism, modernism, and a nostalgia for the past (Sadiq 1984, 586). He is a good stylist but often becomes artificial and verbose and cannot be easily typecast. His best stories are "Firdaus," "Ta'i Isree," "Muskurane Valian," and "Phir Mujhe Deeda-yi tar Yad Aya." He produced many shrill stories about partition, for instance, "Peshavar Express", in which he was unable to suppress his nationalist prejudices and was widely criticized.

Rajinder Singh Bedi (d. 1984) was a short story writer of great subtlety and social realism. His best stories include "Garam Kot" and "Lajvanti," the latter a masterpiece of psychological insight concerning the abduction of women during partition. His novelette *Ik Chadar Maili Si* (1962) remains important.[21]

Ismat Chughta'i (d. 1991) depicts the world of middle-class Muslim women with great sensitivity combined with a willingness to treat delicate subjects, especially women's sexuality. She employs women's idiomatic spoken language, as well as her sharp wit, to great effect. Her short stories include "Chauthi ka Jora," "Do Hath, Choten," and "Lihaf," the last about a lesbian relationship. Other progressive short story writers and novelists include Upindar Nath Ashk (b. 1910), Ahmad Nadeem Qasmi, Balvant Singh (d. 1986), Akhtar Husain Raipuri (d. 1992), Suhail Azeemabadi (d. 1979), and Mohinder Nath (d. 1974).

OTHER FICTION WRITERS

By far the greatest Urdu short story writer is Sa'adat Hasan Manto (d. 1955). Manto was a great observer of human nature, and, through his use of a reticent language or through reproduction of the idiom of his various characters, he was able to convey his characterizations with great effect. Manto wrote about the individual in extreme situations and attempted to discover and communicate her or his underlying humanity. Many of his stories are about prostitutes, criminals, violence, and sex, in which he succeeds in conveying the motives of the characters with disturbing detachment. His portrayals of less appealing aspects of human nature remain unsurpassed in Urdu. Manto was an important innovator and experimented with form and technique till the end of his life. Partition violence and the red-light areas and slums of Bombay inspired some of his greatest stories. His masterpieces include "Thanda Gosht," "Khol Do," "Dhu-'an," "Lazzat-i Sang," "Hatak," "Kali Shalvar," "Toba Tek Singh," "Yazeed," "Blouse," "Phaha" and others. Both Manto and Ismat also produced insightful and frank character sketches of their contemporaries that are a pleasure to read.

Ghulam Abbas (d. 1982) is also an author of great distinction. His fiction, which examines society with sympathetic detachment, conveys its understanding through understatement and by attempts to make the insignificant significant. His most important short stories are "Anandi" and "Ovar Kot." Other important writers include Aziz Ahmad (d. 1978), Mumtaz Mufti (b. 1905), and Qudratullah Shahab (d. 1986). All are important novelists as well. Shahab has also posthumously published an important and best-selling autobiography. Muhammad Hasan Askari (d. 1978) also wrote important short stories and remains an influential critic.

HALQA-YI ARBAB-I ZAUQ

Although the Halqa was not formed in opposition to the progressives, it did attract many disaffected writers. It was devoted to an exploration of the inner self and eschewed politics, while the progressives, complementarily, concentrated on social involvement. Nonetheless, the circle was critical of the progressives' one-dimensional view of human nature and, instead, encouraged the asking of new questions. Members of the group have often been accused of advocating "art for art's sake" views, but this seems an oversimplification. They were, however, drawn to the psychological exploration of the modern, urban, middle-class individual in their poetry and, in the process, produced works of a very high standard, indeed.

Still, it seems a shame to restrict Meeraji (d. 1949) and N. M. Rashid (d. 1975) to this category, as is traditionally done, since they rank as the two most profound Urdu poets since Iqbal. Meeraji was well acquainted with Indic and European literary traditions, especially with *bhakti* poetry (Meerabai) and Sanskrit poetics and the French symbolists. He was also well read in European literary criticism and was a critic and translator of distinction who introduced Urdu writers to new points of view, especially to psychology. Meeraji has a more Indic expression than most Urdu poets. His poems also show considerable influence of Baudelaire and Poe and are similarly deceptively easy to grasp. In his poems, Meeraji attempted to disentangle the various strands of the sexual psychoses of the South Asian Muslim male and his inability to either understand or overcome his exile from woman. To this end he examined "the mystery of human desires, the sorrows and pains of loving, the sin and rapture of sex" and coupled these with meditations on time and death (Faruqi 1992, 435).[22] Meeraji's great accomplishment was to tie these concerns with the psychological health or sickness of the individual and society and thus provide us with insights into other psychosocial problems as well. Unfortunately, Meeraji still awaits proper appreciation and elucidation in Urdu scholarship.

Rashid began with concerns akin to Meeraji's but quickly moved on to a more metaphysical treatment of them. Rashid saw the modern, colonized individual as not only sexually damaged but also lacking a meaningful, rooted existence generally. While Rashid viewed the latter condition as an opportunity for greater freedom, he was also aware of its schizophrenic potential and nihilistic attractions. Rashid tried to question the ungraspable yet remembered past, deceased gods, and fellow colonized societies in an attempt to understand the political and psychic predicaments of men of color and to point a way toward a more authentic and meaningful existence.[23] In addition, he remained concerned with the imperatives of creativity in art, and his style progressively becomes more symbolic (Hassan 1985, 23–34). Rashid's style differs from Meeraji's in his reliance on Arabic and Persian, rather than Indic, elements and on his complete avoidance of the *ghazal* and other traditional genres.

Other poets associated with the Halqa include Yusuf Zafar (d. 1972), Qayyum Nazar (d. 1989), Ziya Jalandhari (b. 1923), Anjum Rumani (b. 1920), and Hafeez Hoshiarpuri (d. 1973). Ziya is interesting for his attempt to combine elements of Meeraji and Rashid.

OTHER POETS

Among poets not associated with either the Halqa or the progressives, the most important is Majeed Amjad (d. 1974). His poetry apparently contains a mood of desolation and grief but, on closer examination, presents the poet as someone who accepts, nay, is thankful for, whatever life has to offer him or her, with sober serenity. Majeed Amjad has the ability to connect the most mundane details to an experiential universe and vice versa, with profound introspection accompanied by slight surprise. In the mood of his poems and in his less self-absorbed attitude to nature, Majeed Amjad presents a strange contrast to Rashid and Meeraji.

Despite being influenced by the progressives, Akhtarul Iman (b. 1915) has fashioned his own subjects and style. He writes about the impossibility of fulfilling relationships within the increasing isolation of the urban environment. His recognition that unsatisfactory relationships are unavoidable gives his verse a bitter edge. At times, he fashions almost Kafkaesque (surreal, as well as material) images, probably as a result of his keen sensitivity to industrialization. His poems seem surrounded by an atmosphere of gloom and a sense of futility (Sadiq 1984, 565).

Shad Arifi (d. 1964) is an important but undervalued poet who went even further than Hasrat Mohani in introducing more realism into the *ghazal.* In contrast to the formally idealized beloved of the *ghazal,* the beloved in Shad's poetry is ordinary and familiar, and the relationship with the beloved is rooted in everyday social and domestic reality and remains unfulfilled. He was also a good satirist and produced many sharp poems on day-to-day problems and events that rival the progressives' concern with similar topics.[24]

PARTITION AND INDEPENDENCE

The year 1947 is an important date in the development of Urdu. In that year, Pakistan and India became independent nation-states, with Pakistan adopting Urdu as its national language and India still containing a substantial number of Urdu-speakers within its borders. Therefore, this seems a particularly good point to pause to assess the implications of Partition for Urdu, within the general argument of this chapter about the increasing identification of Urdu as the language of the politics of Muslim identity in South Asia. I do this through a dialogue with Shamsur Rahman Faruqi's comments on partition's effects and attempt to argue for a different view (Faruqi 1992, 435–36).

Many Urdu critics have viewed the division of British India as an unmitigated calamity for Urdu.[25] While it is certainly true that, in many ways, partition was a disaster for independent India's Muslims, and the accompanying violence was unbearably tragic, the effects on Urdu may not have been as severe as is usually noted. For one, the decline of Urdu in India due to the defensive insecurity of India's Muslims, coupled with the discriminatory attitude of the Indian state, was balanced by the flourishing of Urdu in Pakistan due to official patronage and the arrival of Urdu-speaking refugees from India. Also, partition violence turned out to be an unhappy blessing for Urdu, as it inspired a flurry of good writing. Nonetheless, what is most noticeable in the postindependence period is the remarkable affinity between critical and literary trends in Urdu on both sides of the border, despite some interesting differences.[26]

Why is this? I propose that Urdu scholarship should concentrate for a possible answer on the decade preceding partition, which witnessed profound ideological and socioeconomic changes in colonial India. For instance, the two world wars caused substantial physical and social dislocation among the native population, especially through increasing urbanization. At the political level, all hopes of Hindu–Muslim unity seemed ended, with Muslims arguing for some degree of autonomy and the Congress insisting on a strong, centralized state. In this environment, the generation of Urdu writers immediately following Iqbal attempted to describe and diagnose the condition of the contemporary individual and society. We must remember that almost all the authors and poets whom we have previously mentioned above and whose formative period was the decade preceding partition also produced a substantial corpus after independence, but, despite the ideological demands of the two nation-states' official nationalisms, the best Urdu writers (e.g., Manto, Bedi, Meeraji, Rashid, Firaq) continued to look beyond nationalistic controversies and produced good literature. Without ignoring politics, these authors successfully unmasked more fundamental human issues.

In my opinion, this was possible largely because of Iqbal's influence. He is the transition figure between two very different literary periods in Urdu. While Hali's challenge had been specifically directed toward the Muslims (as his *Musaddas* makes clear), Iqbal interrogated issues of identity at more fundamental levels. Iqbal was forced to concede that modernization had created a new human being, against whom he sought to present an alternative. Islam and Muslims are merely allies in this quest. Hali had sought to save Islam and Muslims from the consequences of 1857, while Iqbal's desire was to understand and rescue the modern human. The generation following Iqbal inherited his romanticism and his antimodernism and applied that to a more complex understanding of the individual formed by colonial modernization. In other words, since Iqbal, Urdu has been preoccupied with the contradictions of modernity and with understanding the modern individual and society at a more basic level, rather than only at the level of identity politics or the nation-state. This is one reason for the similarity of Urdu writing in India and Pakistan. Urdu critics themselves acknowledge the differences between the pre- and post-Iqbal period when they usually map the Hali-to-Iqbal period in historical and political terms and the period following in terms of literary categories.

Faruqi, then, is quite mistaken when he writes about Pakistan that "a people who cannot make up their minds whether they should include the likes of Ghalib and Premchand, the *Kathasaritsagara* [an Indic work] and the *Dastan-i Amir Hamza* [a work of West Asian inspiration], in their literary heritage, cannot be too far along toward achieving a viable cultural consciousness" (Faruqi 1992, 436). It is not our purpose to scrutinize Faruqi's assumptions or to ask what he could possibly mean by "a people" and "their literary heritage" and "a viable cultural consciousness." Neither is it our purpose to point to the sort of philosophical and political assumptions that make these terms operative.

Rather, the more important question is about the politics of formation of the Urdu canon that precedes both the formation of Pakistan and the coming into being of the Muslims of independent India as a minority corporate group. If we assume that the formation of this canon is, at least broadly, connected to the politics of Muslim identity in South Asia, as I have schematically tried to show, then the ideological assumptions behind the formation of the Urdu canon inform both Pakistani nationalism and the identity politics of India's Muslims. This is the second reason for the similarity of Urdu writing in Pakistan and India. After all, the questions that Faruqi accuses official Pakistan nationalism of burdening Urdu with have been asked of Urdu in various forms since the nineteenth century: What is and has been the nature and place of Islam and Muslims in South Asia? For instance, as Askari has observed, the Musaddas of Hali and the *na't* of Muhsin Kakorvi (d. 1905) contain fundamentally different views of the Prophet (Askari 1977, 238–66). Muhsin's prophet seems more culturally indigenous, while Hali's is more Arab/foreign. Even before partition, Hali's image of the prophet is canonized, not Muhsin's. Consequently, while it is true that Urdu in Pakistan has been involved in rather tiresome debates about the nature of the Pakistani identity, Askari's "traditionalist Islamism" (Faruqi's description) and the Pakistani Urdu scholar Jameel Jalibi's (b. 1929) somewhat confused book on Urdu's relationship with a specifically Pakistani identity still seem much more within the established Urdu tradition than the platitudinous nods toward Indian secularism attempted by Indian Urdu writers.[27] In other words, the Islamization of Urdu began much before the search for an Islamic Pakistani identity and remains more hegemonic.

Furthermore, how true is it, in fact, that "Indo-Muslim culture . . . had been shared by Hindus and Muslims alike in most of pre-Partition India"? (Faruqi 1992, 436). By this, does Faruqi mean that Urdu was not made into a Muslim language in colonial India? Conversely, does he also mean to suggest that there was no movement for Hindi to be recognized as the language of north Indian

Hindus? If the contribution was ''alike,'' why was there a need to construct Hindi and Urdu as separate languages, and what made the postpartition rupture so possible? Furthermore, what Faruqi must really be claiming is that Hindu *men* have contributed to Urdu. As far as I am aware, Hindu women have not particularly written in Urdu, and there are inherent and interesting connections between nineteenth-century attempts at Hindu women's reform and the Hindu language movement. The real question that should be asked is about the different ways in which Hindus and Muslims participated in, and contributed to, Urdu and how those have changed over time.[28] Otherwise, Faruqi's statement is patently inaccurate and represents another disingenuous attempt at espousing a superficial secularism.

Urdu scholars should be careful about overemphasizing the importance of debates about official nationalism conducted through the medium of Urdu and, instead, pay some attention to the lack of debate about the Urdu canon, which has been uncritically accepted, at least since Iqbal. This is the more fundamental issue. In the same essay, Faruqi praises the novelist Intizar Husain (b. 1925) for tapping the *Kathasaritsagara* (ancient fables) as a source. Now, Intizar Husain writes in Pakistan, and all the debates about the propriety of using the *Kathasaritsagara* in Pakistan do not prevent him from writing or his many readers from reading him. Nor for that matter is Vazeer Agha (b. 1922), another respected Pakistani critic, prevented from advocating the superiority of an indigenous Indic aesthetic.[29] Conversely, Nayyar Masood (b. 1936), the Indian writer, looks to classical Islamic romances and Persian literature for inspiration. Good Urdu writers have been remarkably resilient in resisting serving a parochial Pakistani nationalism (or, for that matter, an unthought Indian secularism and a centralizing pan-Indian nationalism), and this is probably because Pakistani nationalism has not had an advocate as sincere as Hali or a theoretician of Iqbal's profundity. Also, according to Faruqi's view, Urdu speakers in India would be less resistant to the evocation of elements of ''purely Indic'' origin. Is this really true? Has the Urdu canon changed so much in India over the past 50 some years? As long as Urdu speakers and writers on both sides of the border are in general agreement about the literary legacy of Urdu, they are immersed in the politics of Muslim identity, and their more immediate, separate concerns will not much affect the status of Urdu.

Similarly, I do not want to equate Urdu completely with Muslim identity politics. As I have argued earlier, we should thank Iqbal both for sidelining Urdu as the repository of Muslim identity and for secularizing Urdu by forcing it to deal with larger and more fundamental human questions to some extent, rather than being solely concerned with the defining of Muslims, as Urdu was in the period between Hali and Iqbal. The Urdu-speaking Muslim elite of north India had made Urdu an essential element of Indo-Muslim identity, and Pakistani nationalism is merely one variant of an identity that Muslims on both sides of the border share, largely through Urdu—for better or for worse. I believe Iqbal tried to escape this linguistic definition of the Indian Muslim.

Finally, in Faruqi's terms, traditional literature is concerned with the abstract universal (*afaq*), and the post-Iqbal generation is concerned with people and things (*anfus*). Therefore, the significant point to make is that in the period between traditional poetics and the post-Iqbal period, that is, the Hali-to-Iqbal period, what was Urdu poetics concerned with if not the intermediate questions of Muslim identity? Only when this question was in some ways settled by Iqbal, did Urdu turn to more important questions. Thus, one way to make sense of Iqbal's concept of *khudi,* or dynamic selfhood, is precisely to understand it as an attempt to bring together the two seeming extremes of *afaq* and *anfus* in a new aesthetic.

To summarize, I have tried to argue that Urdu is powerfully joined, rather than divided, across the border between Pakistan and India by its prepartition participation in Muslim identity politics and, paradoxically, by the moves toward exploring more fundamental human concerns by the generation immediately preceding partition. Struggling with the former in its Pakistani or Indian Muslim variant, at the same time as recognizing the essential truth of the latter, is the story of the dynamism of Urdu literature after 1947.

POST–1947

The nearly 50 years since independence are marked by the proliferation of experiments in poetry and prose as a response to the experience of postcolonial state-building in Pakistan and India and rapid socioeconomic changes. In poetry, there have also been more attempts to renew contact with the tradition of the *ghazal* and other traditional genres.

Ghazal

The *ghazal* has maintained its popularity and has increased its expanse to include even more subjects of concern to poets. *Ghazal* poets may be divided into three groups: progressives, traditionalists, and others. Among the competent progressive poets are Arif Abdul Mateen, Muhsin Ihsan (b. 1932), Khatir Ghaznavi (b. 1925), Ahmad Faraz (b. 1931), Zaheer Kashmiri (d. 1994), and Qateel Shifa'i (b. 1919). Those who have remained within the traditional *ghazal* to exploit its possibilities include Raees Amrohvi (d. 1988), Jagannath Azad (b. 1918), Shanul Haq Haqqi (b. 1917), Mehshar Badayuni, and Murtaza Barlas.

Poets belonging to neither of these two groups have been the most innovative. They have attempted to expand the *ghazal* form so that it is able to express a variety of contemporary concerns. Nasir Kazmi (d. 1972) is influenced by Mir and Firaq and wrote *ghazals* that are stylistically traditional and modern at the same time. His *ghazals* present a bohemian protagonist saddened by the weight of nostalgia, the experience of exile, and the thirst of loneliness. Ibne Insha (d. 1979) adopts the guise of a wandering minstrel to express a certain critical indifference toward the world. Khalilur Rahman Azmi (d. 1978) was a pioneer of "new" poetry (*jadidiyat*) in Urdu and wrote insightful poems as well as *ghazals.* His sensitive portrayal of unrealized potential in the complexity and fragmentation of modern existence gives his poetry a wistful air. His *ghazals'* underlying concern with life's more mundane dilemmas betrays his progressive origins. Muneer Niyazi (b. 1928) attempts to make the familiar surreal, especially in his use of words, and describes a world of fear and mistrust. Mustafa Zaidi (d. 1970) created a character who compensates for other disappointments by aggressively pursuing the embrace of the beloved, while remaining self-centered. Shikaib Jalali (d. 1966) tries to formulate a new relationship between the individual and nature that is not bound by space and time. Shahzad Ahmad (b. 1932) attempts to will meaning in the face of hopelessness. Zafar Iqbal (b. 1933) is a great experimenter of the *ghazal* and has written some excellent *ghazals.* He fashions an easily irritated, sarcastic protagonist who refuses to be satisfied with the finiteness of human relations. He has also been a pioneer of the "anti-*ghazal.*" Ahmad Mushtaq (b. 1929) is able to convey innocence and surprise amid ruin with great affect. Some other notable *ghazal* poets include the literary critic Saleem Ahmad (d. 1983), Rajindar Bani (d. 1981), Baqi Siddiqi (d. 1972), Saifuddin Saif (d. 1994), Jameeluddin Aali (b. 1926), and Bimal Krishan Ashk (d. 1982).

Non-*Ghazal* Poetry

Non-*ghazal* poetry in Urdu has also made great leaps since 1947. Its various forms have proven ideal in conveying the increasing mechanization and alienation of the contemporary condition. It has been equally effective in dealing with issues of the inner self, as well as conveying the social and natural world. Vazeer Agha's use of unfamiliar nature imagery in his poems serves as a means to expose the spiritual needs of the self. He is also a good *ghazal* poet. Ameeq Hanfi's (d. 1988) poems present the dissatisfaction and unhappiness of the present and seem to be searching for an affirmation of human existence. Other important poets include Mazhar Imam (b. 1930), Balraj Komal (b. 1928), Jeelani Kamran (b. 1926), Saqi Farooqi (b. 1936), Shaz Tamkinat (d. 1985), Himayat Ali Sha'ir (b. 1930), Kumar Pashi (d. 1992), Shaharyar (b. 1936), Nida Fazli (b. 1938), Anees Nagi (b. 1939), Iftikhar Jalib (b. 1936), Muhammad Alavi (b. 1927), Afzaal Ahmad Sayyid (b. 1946), Iftikhar Arif (b. 1940), and Zeeshan Sahil.

Short Stories and Novels

After being sidelined by poetry for most of its career, Urdu fiction has come into its own in the years since independence. A strong base had already been prepared by the writers we have previously indicated, who also of course, continued to write after 1947. As mentioned, fictional prose received a boost from the shock of communal violence during partition, and subsequent writing continued to examine issues of communal and national identity. The condition of postcolonial nationality was examined from both psychological and progressive points of view, and special emphasis was placed on the dystopia that quickly set in after independence. Short stories have usually been of better quality than the novels.

Qurratul Ain Haidar (b. 1927) and Intizar Husain are probably the most highly regarded authors of the postindependence period. Haidar writes about the dilemmas of middle-class existence, and her work is marked by sensitivity toward issues of cultural and social constraints, the legacy of history, the devaluation of values, and the predicament of women in the Indo-Muslim familial milieu. She has complete control over her language and has produced worthwhile short stories as well as novels. Her most important contribution remains her groundbreaking novel *Aag ka Darya* (1959), which tried to examine issues of identity in the context of the civilizational history of South Asia.

Intizar Husain's novels and short stories have made important contributions toward further developing these genres in Urdu. His work is marked by the experience of migration and exile. He laments the passing away of a more holistic and integrated civilizational world and is pessimistic with regard to the current ethical decline. Intizar Husain foregrounds the decline of humanity against the backdrop of myth and history. His short stories include "Kaya Klap," "Voh Jo Deevar Chat Nah Sake," "Akhri Admi," "Intizar," and "Shajrah-i Nasab." His novel *Basti* (1979) is justly praised for its creative use of a traditional worldview to comment on contemporary social and personal predicaments.[30]

Abdullah Husain (b. 1931) appeared on the literary scene with the publication of his prizewinning novel *Udaas Naslen* (1963), which attempted, with some success, to excavate the characteristics of the individual under colonial rule and the socioeconomic changes brought in its wake. He also writes short stories. Ahsan Faruqi (d. 1978) depicted the old culture of Lucknow in his popular novel *Sham-i Avadh.* Shaukat Siddiqi's unblinking depiction of the poverty, brutality, and injustice of a postcolonial urban sprawl prevents his novel *Khuda ki Basti* from becoming a mere statement of progressive ideology. Other important novelists and short story writers are Zameeruddin Ahmad (d. 1990), Ashfaq Ahmad (b. 1924), Bano Qudsiyah (b. 1928), Altaf Fatimah (b. 1929), the sisters Khadeejah Mastoor (d. 1982) and Hajirah Masroor (b. 1929), Ram Lal (b. 1923), A. Hameed (b. 1935), Jogindar Pal (b. 1925), Mumtaz Shireen (d. 1973), Jameelah Hashmi (d. 1988), and Ibraheem Jalees (d. 1977).

Still other writers have been more courageous in their explorations and have conducted interesting experiments. Their writing makes use of fantasy, myth, magic, and hallucination. One drawback is that they create "highly wrought but very nearly opaque stories which refuse to observe the conventions of plot and character" (Faruqi 1992, 439). Good examples of such allegorical writing are provided by Anvar Sajjad (b. 1936), Khalidah Husain (b. 1938), Nayyar Masud, Surendar Prakash (b. 1930), Ahmad Hameesh (b. 1941), Balraj Komal, Asad

Muhammad Khan (b. 1938), Zahidah Hina (b. 1946), Mansha Yad (b. 1937), and Mazharul Islam.[31]

Compared to short stories and novels, Urdu plays have been of poorer quality. On the other hand, Urdu prose is abundant with the following relatively more developed genres: essays, autobiography, letters, travelogues, journalism, humor, and literary criticism.

WOMEN POETS OF PAKISTAN

In at least one important respect, Faruqi is quite wrong that "[t]he Pakistani quest for new ideas on literature ended with the advance of fundamentalism in the late seventies" (437).[32] This was precisely the period in Pakistan that produced some of the most powerful protest poetry from many excellent poets who are women.[33] Although important women writers had appeared before that, this period saw a proliferation of poetry by women that critiqued the patriarchal cultural, social, and political system with profound insight and great passion. In contrast to the progressives, this poetry also represents an instance where overtly sociopolitical concerns have also generally led to good literature. Moreover, the work of women writers may be viewed as a complement and response to Meeraji and Rashid's enterprise. Women's writing insists that any adequate treatment of the important issues raised by these two poets will be futile until and unless the concerns of women are addressed.

Speculatively, the reason for the many fine women poets in Pakistan, as compared to almost none in India, may have something to do with the different ways in which women in Pakistan and Muslim women in India are members of civil society and participate in the public sphere. It is beyond the scope of this chapter to indicate the aspects in which their sociopolitical status differs, but it is probably safe to say that, to the extent that women are part of civil society in Pakistan, they are so as women rather than as Muslims. For example, during the colonial period, women were viewed as keepers of the tradition, but, after the creation of Pakistan, this function in many ways shifted to the state. While this liberated Pakistani women from quite a burden, it also made them more vulnerable to state laws directed against them. In India, it may be argued, Muslim women continue to be held as guardians of a Muslim identity. Furthermore, social conservatism, plus the state imposition of Islamic laws, has meant that the position of women as women is, in some ways, particularly tenuous in Pakistan. Their subsequent greater ability to participate in public debate in Pakistan has also empowered them in interesting ways.

The first major poet to write as a woman appeared soon after independence. Ada Jafri (b. 1924) wrote of her experiences as a wife and mother in a modified traditional idiom but also noticed the lack of fulfillment that accompanied these relationships. She also protests against society's dehumanization of women by its reduction of them to sexual objects and is keenly aware of discrimination.

Ada Jafri's poetry explores women's identity, rather than concentrating on them as a romantic ideal, as poetry up to now had usually done.

She was followed by Zehra Nigah, who attempts to portray a desire for a degree of equality of emotional expression in women's relationships. Zehra Nigah, while staying in a generally progressive framework, is also keenly aware of the specific exploitation of women in society. Her poetry explores the schizophrenic existence of women that results from social taboos. Therefore, she attempts to give voice to the woman within the one who is forced to compromise with patriarchal society.

The two most influential and important women poets writing today are Kishvar Naheed (b. 1940) and Fehmeedah Riyaz (b. 1945), both of whom started writing in the 1960s. Kishvar Naheed rebels against the agreement among religion, society, and state to fix the place of woman and determine her personality and desires. Employing a gentle tone or the voice of bitter protest, she can effectively communicate the pain of the truncated spiritual, sociopolitical, and physical existence of women in an oppressive society. For her, the poem becomes a weapon with which to undermine such a society. Kishvar Naheed can communicate the contradictions of patriarchal society with a measure of profundity, including questioning the very category of gender as the basis for social and political organization. She has examined all aspects of women's lives, from their place in the politics of nation and state-building, to their sexual exploitation. She has also translated women's writings from other languages into Urdu and writes *ghazals* and poems with equal facility. Lately, her poetry has become more overtly political.

Fehmeedah Riyaz is a poet of woman's emotional reserves, which she transforms into critique of patriarchal relations. She writes about the unfulfilled sexuality of women, their creative power, and their closeness to earth with outspoken candor and sometimes anger. Fehmeedah Riyaz is keenly aware of the manner in which social relationships, like marriage, serve to mold women's personalities. Like Kishvar Naheed, she implicitly takes up Iqbal's idea of a constantly self-forming self and utilizes this idea to undermine attempts by the state to define and fix the gendered boundaries of official nationalism. She has recently published a widely acclaimed novelette and a travelogue of Bangladesh. Her poetry has also become more apparently political over the years.

A younger generation of women took their cue from these predecessors but more closely examined the subtleties of human and social relations. From the most mundane activities of women to the contradictions of family and nation, these women explore women's lives and, in the process, also tell us much about men. Women poets have also experimented in form and style so that they are better able to convey their views. Parveen Shakir (d. 1994) is conscious of her grief as a woman but examines her attraction for exploitative relationships that result from a need for emotional support and fulfillment. Her poetry may be read as an attempt to complicate the vision of Kishvar Naheed and Fehmeedah Riyaz. Sara Shuguftah (d. 1984) is a profound chronicler and analyst of women's psychological states in a claustrophobic society that provides them with no escape. Azra Abbas (b. 1950) is particularly concerned with exploring the relationship of women's bodies to their emotions. Ishrat Afreen examines the tension between her newfound confidence as a woman and a patriarchal reality. Fatimah Husain writes about the disagreements within the women's movement. Other good poets include Tanveer Anjum (b. 1956), A'ishah Aslam, Mahmoodah Ghaziyah, Yasmeen Hameed, Shahidah Hasan, and Parveen Fana Sayyid. Zahidah Zaidi (b. 1930) writes in India.

"NEW" POETRY

Somewhat implicitly, this survey has viewed the genre of the *ghazal* as the common thread that binds contemporary Urdu literature to its immediate past and to the more distant classical tradition. A more detailed examination of the literary debates surrounding the *ghazal* will help us to review the development of Urdu literature to the present and hopefully provide us with some insights into future prospects.

As previously detailed, Hali's project laid the foundations for modifying the traditional *ghazal* to serve the interests of reform. This trend was accompanied by the denigration of the *ghazal* as a pleasurable but nonserious form of poetry, especially when the precolonial legacy of the *ghazal* became too constricting or seductive. Instead, the narrative poem was utilized to preach the reformist message. Similarly, Iqbal essentially continued the tradition of the non-*ghazal* poem. Taking Hali's logic further, the progressives criticized the *ghazal* as a reactionary and feudal genre, while they paradoxically continued to write *ghazals* in an attempt to make the *ghazal* conform to ideological imperatives. The opposition to the creative straitjacket of progressive ideology came from poets associated with the Halqa-yi Arbab-i Zauq, but they also chose to express themselves largely through the non-*ghazal* poem. The more effective challenge to the near monopoly of the *ghazal* by the progressives came in the aftermath of partition, which had dealt a severe blow to the optimism of the progressive view.

Pioneers like Nasir Kazmi in Pakistan and Khalilur Rahman Azmi in India reacted against the inability of the progressives to adequately explain the post-independence dystopia and the massive psychological and social changes brought in its wake. These poets and others now attempted to use the *ghazal* form to continue to examine issues like the devaluation of values, increasing mechanization, and alienation already raised by Rashid and Meeraji in their non-*ghazal* poetry. Through the example of *ghazal* poets like Yaganah and Firaq, among others, they also looked to the precolonial *ghazal* tradition as a source of ideals that would inform their endeavor to understand their present situation. This resistance to the hegemony of the progressives in the late 1950s in Pakistan and somewhat later in India was inspired by the very different nature of the problems of the postcolonial nation-state and individual and represented a move toward understanding the disintegrating *inner* self. The move to write what was now being called the ''new'' *ghazal* paralleled similar attempts to move beyond progressive-influenced fiction and non-*ghazal* poetry.

This literary trend of newness, or *jadidiyat,* was marked by two opposing tendencies. On one hand, there was a rejection of the ideological surveillance of art and a celebration of a newfound freedom from restrictions on creative activity. On the other hand, these new writers also wanted to utilize the tradition represented by the formal and restrictive form of the *ghazal* for inspiration and insight. The question that this tension raised was the extent to which one should free oneself from the classical tradition and from the legacy of Hali, Iqbal, and the progressives. Some poets followed the example of Rashid and basically rejected the *ghazal,* but most have made important contributions both to the new *ghazal* and to non-*ghazal* poetry.

The new *ghazal* can be characterized by four areas in which it has made important contributions. One, it takes the idea of *'ishq,* or love, from the traditional *ghazal,* where it served as the basis of a holistic system, and via Iqbal transforms it into a dynamic force that maintains itself as a response to, and despite the angst of, contemporary existence. The new poets reject the progressive reinterpretation of *'ishq* and other components of the *ghazal* as instruments to express political concerns and, instead, use the *ghazal* imagery to analyze the internal psychic state of the fractured individual embedded in the contingency of modern existence. Furthermore, the new *ghazal* attempts to highlight the social and psychological dislocation caused by political, economic, and societal changes that are no longer easily diagnosed or solved. It particularly rails against the ethical cynicism of the age caused by political expediency and materialism. Third, the new *ghazal* is characterized by its creative use of language. New poets tend to stay away from the formally precise language usage of the classical tradition and from the ideological usage of the progressives. Rather, they use words to create an atmosphere, evoke a sensation, or tease a personal or historical memory. Through the use of unfamiliar idiom, new poets attempt to make the form of expression conform to its content, which emphasizes the anxious disturbance of the contemporary self. Last, the new *ghazal* attempts to satirize and undermine the claims to coherence of the traditional *ghazal* form, later developments, and itself, by use of jarring or comical words and phrases and unsettling imagery.[34]

This development of the new *ghazal* and analogous developments in non-*ghazal* poetry and prose fiction seem to have broken the hold of the progressives, and literary trends are now marked by more openness, eclecticism, and a willingness to experiment. Nevertheless, the increasingly allegorical nature of many poems and short stories raises questions about the lack of comprehensibility of these writings and their increasingly unverifiable value either as art or as social critique. Furthermore, new poets are also characterized by an escalating specialization of idiom and by a fetishization of the historical and literary tradition. The nostalgia for a holistic past and discomfort at the unrooted present that mark the work of many of these writers also seem to indicate a suppressed regret of a loss of manhood. In this sense, the new poets have not yet come to terms with the issues raised by women's writing. Moreover, for some other writers, a tension with the tradition remains and, to the extent that they explicitly write outside any reference to the tradition or some other worldview, also raises the issue of the lack of ontological and epistemological basis for their critique and reimagining.[35] But this may be too much to expect from Urdu or any other literature. On the other hand, Urdu literature, as always, seems eager to take on all these debates, which have contributed to its remarkable energy since the nineteenth century.

NOTES

I wish to thank Professor C. M. Naim for his comments on an earlier version of this chapter. I am also grateful to Faisal Devji, Osman Qureshi, and Mustafa Ulucan for their helpful remarks. Of course, I alone am responsible for the views expressed herein.

1. For a detailed discussion, see Annemarie Schimmel, *Classical Urdu Literature from the Beginning to Iqbal* (Wiesbaden: Otto Harrassowitz, 1975), and Sadeed, 1991.

2. For dates of birth and death, I have relied on Shamsur Rahman Faruqi and Frances W. Pritchett, comps., ''A Date List for Urdu Literature—A Work in Progress,'' *Annual of Urdu Studies,* No. 9 (1994): 173–211. When the date of birth is given, it indicates that the person is living; otherwise, only the date of death is used.

3. On Deoband's services to Urdu, see Barbara Daly Metcalf, *Islamic Revival in British India, Deoband, 1860–1900* (Princeton, NJ: Princeton University Press, 1982).

4. For an abridged translation, but an informative introduction and commentary, see Barbara Daly Metcalf, *Perfecting Women: Maulana Ashraf Ali Thanvi's ''Bihishti Zevar''* (Berkeley: University of California Press, 1990). See also her ''Maulana Ashraf Ali Thanvi and Urdu Literature,'' in *Urdu and Muslim South Asia,* edited by Christopher Shackle. (Delhi: Oxford University Press, 1991).

5. Laurel Steele, ''Hali and His *Muqaddamah:* The Creation of a Literary Attitude in Nineteenth Century India,'' *Annual of Urdu Studies,* No. 1 (1981): 1–45. Steele appends a summary of the *Muqaddamah* in English translation.

6. See Pritchett (1994) for an excellent discussion of the views and legacy of Hali and Azad. See also Saleem Ahmad, ''The Ghazal, A Muffler, and India,'' translated by John A. Hanson, *Annual of Urdu Studies,* No. 2 (1982): 53–83.

7. This appears to be Askari's thesis. For instance, see Muhammad Hasan Askari, ''Mazedar Sha'ir,'' in *Sitarah ya Badban* (Aligarh: Educational Book House, 1977, original ed., Karachi, 1963), 197–229. Faruqi seems to be making a similar point in the introductory material to his monumental selection of, and commentary on, Mir's *ghazal* poetry. See Shamsur Rahman Faruqi, *Sher Shor Angez,* 4 vols. (Delhi: Taraqqi-yi Urdu Bureau, 1990–94).

8. The two most important being *Mavazanah-i Anees o Dabeer* (1907) and the five-volume *Sher-ul Ajam* (1906–8).

9. For example, *Al-Faruq* (1899), the incomplete *Sirat-un Nabi,* and a collection of essays, *Rasail-i Shibli* (1898).

10. For a discussion of Nazeer Ahmad, see C. M. Naim, ''Prize-Winning *Adab:* A Study of Five Urdu Books Written in Response to the Allahabad Government Gazette

Notification,'' in *Moral Conduct and Authority: The Place of ''Adab'' in South Asian Islam,* edited by Barbara Daly Metcalf (Berkeley: University of California Press, 1984), 290–314.

11. For details, see Faisal Fatehali Devji, ''Gender and the Politics of Space: The Movement for Women's Reform in Muslim India, 1857–1900,'' *South Asia* 14:1 (1991): 141–53. For Hali's views on women, see Altaf Husain Hali, *Voices of Silence: English Translations of ''Majalis-un Nisa'' and ''Chup ki Dad,''* edited and translated by Gail Minault (Delhi: Chanakya, 1986).

12. For details, see Gail Minault, '''*Ismat:* Rashidul Khairi's Novels and Urdu Literary Journalism for Women,'' in *Urdu and Muslim South Asia,* edited by Christopher Shackle (Delhi: Oxford University Press, 1991).

13. Abdul Haq was instrumental in recovering Dakkani poetry.

14. I am indebted to Faisal Devji for this suggestion.

15. Nothing could be more misleading than to view Iqbal as a Benthamite, as Faruqi does.

16. In this sense, the poetry of Rashid and the fiction of Intizar Husain are possible only after Iqbal. In some ways, this can also be said of Meeraji and Qurratul Ain Haidar (see following sections).

17. Even before 1857, Ghalib had written: ''Sambhalne de mujhe ai na-umeedi kiya qayamat hai / keh daman-i khayal-i yar chhoota ja'i hai mujh se;'' and ''Ba-qadr-i shauq nahin zarf-i tangna-yi ghazal / kuchh aur chahiye vus'at mire bayan ke liye.''

18. For a discussion of love and eroticism in classical and modern Urdu poetry, see Zameeruddin Ahmad, *Khatir-i Masoom: Urdu Sha'iri Men Mehboob ki Jinsiyat ka Mutali'ah* (Karachi: Ahsan Matbu'at, 1990).

19. For details, see Carlo Coppola, ''Urdu Poetry, 1935–1970: The Progressive Episode,'' 2 vols. (Ph.D. diss., University of Chicago, 1975).

20. For details, see Carlo Coppola, ''The *Angare* Group: The *Enfants Terribles* of Urdu Literature,'' *Annual of Urdu Studies,* No. 1 (1981): 57–69.

21. For a discussion of an important aspect of Bedi's corpus, see Jamila Feldman, ''To Be or Not to Be a Goddess: Rajinder Singh Bedi's Women Characters,'' *Annual of Urdu Studies,* No. 7 (1990): 67–75.

22. See also Geeta Patel, ''Re-Naming Oneself: Meeraji and the Politics of Gender,'' *Annual of Urdu Studies,* No. 8 (1993): 109–18.

23. I say ''men'' because of the following quote about the important feminist poet and author Fehmeedah Riyaz attributed to Rashid by Saqi Farooqi. Asked to evaluate Riyaz's work, Rashid commented, ''A tiny girl with a tiny pain'' See Saqi Farooqi, ''Hasan Kooza-gar,'' translated by Rafey Habib and Faruq Hasan, *Annual of Urdu Studies,* No. 5 (1985): 3–17; the comment appears on p. 9.

24. For a reappraisal of Shad, see Muzaffar Hanfi, *Shad Arifi: Shakhsiyat aur Fan* (Delhi: Maktabah-i Jamiah, 1977).

25. Faruqi entitles his section on partition ''The Trauma of Independence.'' Interestingly, this heading is missing from a version of the same essay entitled ''Images in a Darkened Mirror: Issues and Ideas in Modern Urdu Literature,'' printed in *Annual of Urdu Studies,* No. 6 (1987): 43–54, an American publication.

26. One difference is in the number of important women writers in Pakistan. Another is the different ways in which Urdu has been, and will continue to be, influenced by the various languages in India and Pakistan. Also, not only has Urdu become involved in different ideological debates in India and Pakistan (Faruqi mentions only Pakistan), but

Urdu in Pakistan has become complicit with actual state policy and regional linguistic reassertions. For example, Bengali nationalism, which led to East Pakistan's becoming independent Bangladesh, was opposed to the imposition of Urdu as the sole national language.

27. Jalibi explicitly places his discussion within the context of pre-Pakistan Muslim nationalism. See Jameel Jalibi, *Pakistani Kalchar: Qaumi Kalchar ki Tashkeel ka Mas'alah* (Karachi: Mushtaq Book Depot, 1964).

28. A starting point would be a critical assessment of the place and contribution of Chakbast and Premchand and of Urdu's treatment of them. Chakbast is a particularly interesting figure because of his attempt to employ Urdu for reform among Hindus. For Premchand's complaints about the discriminatory treatment of Hindu Urdu writers by the Urdu establishment, see Premchand, *Premchand: Adabiyat* (Patna: Khuda Bakhsh Oriental Public Library, 1993).

29. For details, see Vazeer Agha, *Urdu Sha'iri ka Mizaj* (Aligarh: Educational Book House, 1974).

30. For details, see Muhammad Umar Memon, ''Partition Literature: A Study of Intizar Husain,'' *Modern Asian Studies* 4:3 (1980): 377–410, and ''Reclamation of Memory, Fall, and the Death of the Creative Self: Three Movements in the Fiction of Intizar Husain,'' *International Journal of Middle East Studies,* No. 13 (1981): 73–91.

31. For a brief survey of the modern Urdu Short story, see Muhammed Memon, ''Introduction: The Colour of Nothingness,'' in his *Modern Urdu Short Stories* (Delhi: Penguin, 1991), xi–xxx.

32. Faruqi devotes a total of three sentences to women poets!

33. Space does not permit a discussion of women's prose writings. Important writers are listed in the previous sections.

34. For a good discussion of the ''new'' *ghazal,* see Shameem Hanfi, *Ghazal ka Naya Manzar Namah* (Aligarh: Educational Book House, 1981).

35. For a nonprogressive critique of ''new'' poetry, see Saleem Ahmad, *Na'i Sha'iri, Na Maqbool Sha'iri* (Karachi: Nafees Academy, 1989).

WORKS CITED

Ahmad, Saleem. *Na'i Nazm aur Poora Admi.* 1962. Karachi: Nafees Academy, 1989.

Askari, Muhammad Hasan. ''Muhsin Kakorvi.'' 1963. In *Sitarah ya Badban.* Aligarh: Educational Book House, 1977.

Faruqi, Shamsur Rahman. ''Modern Urdu Literature.'' In *Modern Indian Literature: An Anthology* Vol. 1, edited by K. M. George. Delhi: Sahitya Akademi, 1992.

Hardy, P. *The Muslims of British India.* Cambridge University Press, 1972.

Hassan, Faruq. '' 'Beyond Blasphemy and Prayers': The Concept of God in Rashed's Poetry.'' *Annual of Urdu Studies,* No. 5 (1985): 23–34.

Khan, Rasheed Hasan. ''Faiz ki Sha'iri ke Chand Pehlu.'' In *Talash o Tabeer.* Delhi: Urdu Academy, 1988a.

———. ''Zaban o Bayan ke Baz Pehlu.'' In *Talash o Tabeer.* Delhi: Urdu Academy, 1988b.

Naim, C. M. ''Urdu in the Pre-Modern Period: Synthesis or Particularism?'' *New Quest,* No. 6 (1978): 5–12.

Pritchett, Frances W. *Nets of Awareness: Urdu Poetry and Its Critics.* New York: Columbia University Press, 1994.

Sadeed, Anvar. *Urdu Adab ki Mukhtasar Tareekh.* Islamabad: Muqtadirah Qaumi Zaban, 1991.

Sadiq, Muhammad. *A History of Urdu Literature.* Delhi: Oxford University Press, 1964; 2d rev. ed., 1984.

SELECTED PRIMARY BIBLIOGRAPHY

(For reasons of space, the following selection is, regrettably, restricted to books in Urdu. For translations, Pritchett's bibliography of Urdu literature in English translation may be usefully consulted. Unfortunately, her survey stops at 1978. Since then, numerous English translations of Urdu prose and poetry have appeared in India, Pakistan, the United Kingdom, and the United States (especially in journals and magazines) and may also be consulted.)

Abbas, Azra. *Mez Par Rakkhe Hath* (Poems). Karachi: Jadeed Classic, 1988.

Abbas, Ghulam. *Zindagi, Niqab, Chihre* (Selected short stories). Karachi: Daniyal, 1984.

Ada Jafri. *Ghazalan Tum To Vaqif Ho* (Poems). Lahore: Ghalib, 1982a.

———. *Men Saz Dhoondti Rahi* (Poems). Lahore: Ghalib Publishers, 1982b.

———. *Shehr-i Dard* (Poems). Lahore: Ghalib, 1982c.

———. *Saz-i Sukhan Bahanah Hai* (Poems). Lahore: Maqbool Academy, 1988.

Agha, Vazeer. *Vazeer Agha ki Nazmen* (Selected poems). Edited by Ghulam Husain Azhar. Lahore: Nami Press, 1974.

———. *Aadhi Sadi ke Bad* (Poems). Lahore: Maktabah-i Urdu Zaban, 1981.

———. *Ghazlain* (Selected poems). Lahore: Maktabah-i Fikr o Khayal, 1988.

Ahmad, Aziz, and A. A. Suroor, eds. *Intikhab-i Jadeed* (Anthology of poetry, 1914–42). Karachi: Anjuman-i Taraqqi-yi Urdu, 1973.

Ahmad, Nazeer. *Mira't-al Uroos* (Bride's Mirror). Karachi: Sultan Hasan and Sons, 1963.

———. *Taubat-un Nusuh* (Nusuh's Repentance). Lahore: Majlis-i Tarraqi-yi Adab, 1964.

———. *Ibn-ul Vaqt* (The Opportunist). Lucknow: Uttar Pradesh Urdu Academy, 1983.

Akbar Allahabadi. *Kulliyat-i Akbar* (Complete poetry). Allahabad: Shan-i Hind, 1991.

Akhtar Sheerani. *Kulliyat-i Akhtar Sheerani* (Complete poetry). Edited by Yunus Hasani. Lahore: Nadeem Book House, 1993.

Akhtarul Iman. *Sar o Saman* (Collected poems). Bombay: Rakhshandah Kitab Ghar, 1983.

Ali, Ahmad, et al. *Angare* (Smoldering Coals). Lucknow: Sajjad Zaheer, 1932.

Anjum, Tanveer. *An Dekhi Lehrain* (Poems). Karachi: Shakeel, 1982.

Anvar, Vaheed, ed. *Kahaniyan* (Anthology of short stories). 2 vols. Bombay: Urdu Classic, 1980, 1985.

Azad, Abul Kalam. *Mazameen-i al-Hilal* (Essays of al-Hilal). Delhi: Idara-yi Isha'at-al Qur'an, n.d.

Azad, Muhammad Husain. *Ab-i Hayat* (Water of Life). 2d ed. Lucknow: Uttar Pradesh Urdu Academy, 1982.

Azmi, Khalilur Rahman. *Intikhab-i Kalam: Khalilur Rahman Azmi* (Selected poetry). Edited by Shaharyar. Lucknow: Uttar Pradesh Urdu Academy, 1991.

Bedi, Rajinder Singh. *Bedi ke Afsane* (Selected short stories). Edited by Muhammad Imran. Lahore: Nazeer Sons, 1991.

Beg, Mirza Hamid, ed. *Urdu Afsane ki Rivayat* (Anthology of short stories). Islamabad: Academy of Letters, 1991.

Chandar, Krishan. *Krishan Chandar ke Numa'indah Afsane* (Selected short stories). Edited by Parvez Akhtar. Karachi: al-Muslim, 1990.

Chughta'i, Ismat. *Ismat Chughta'i: Shakhsiyat aur Fan* (Selected short stories). Edited by M. Sultanah Bakhsh. Islamabad: Word Vision, 1992.

Faiz, Faiz Ahmad. *Nuskha ha-yi Vafa* (Complete poetry). Lahore: Maktabah-i Karvan, 1986.

Faruqi, Ahsan. *Sham-i Avadh* (Avadh's Twilight). Karachi: Sindh Urdu Academy, 1957.

Firaq Gorakhpuri. *Ghazal* (Selected poetry). Edited by Nasir Kazmi. Lahore: Naya Idarah, 1971.

———. *Jahan-i Firaq* (Selected poetry). Taj Saeed, ed. Lahore: Sang-i Meel, 1991.

Ghalib, Mirza Asadullah Khan. *Khutoot-i Ghalib* (Letters of Ghalib). Ghulam Rasool Mihr, ed. 2 vols. Lahore: Panjab University, 1969.

Hafeez Jalandhari. *Shahnamah-i Islam.* Islamabad: Government of Pakistan, 1982.

Haidar, Qurratul Ain. *Aag ka Darya* (River of Fire). Delhi: Urdu Kitab Ghar, 1984.

Hali, Altaf Husain. *Muqaddamah-i Sher o Sha'iri* (Introduction to poetry and poetics). Edited by Vaheed Quraishi. Lahore: Maktabah-i Jadeed, 1953.

———. *Musaddas-i Hali* (Hali's *Musaddas*). Karachi: Sindh Urdu Academy, 1985.

———. *Divan-i Hali* (The poetry of Hali). Delhi: Urdu Academy, 1991.

Hameesh, Ahmad, ed. *Asr-i Hazir ki Behtareen Kahaniyan* (Anthology of short stories). Karachi: al-Baqiriyah, 1980.

Hasrat Mohani. *Kulliyat-i Hasrat* (Complete poetry). Lahore: Khayyam, 1987.

Husain, Abdullah. *Udas Naslen* (Sad Generations). Lahore: Naya Idarah, 1963.

Husain, Intizar. *Basti* (The Town). Lahore: Naqsh-i Avval Kitab Ghar, 1979.

———. *Intizar Husain aur Un ke Afsane* (Selected short stories). Edited by Gopi Chand Narang. Aligarh: Educational Book House, 1986.

Ibne Insha. *Is Basti ke Ik Kooche Men* (Poems). Lahore: Lahore Academy, 1978.

———. *Chand Nagar* (Poems). Lahore: Lahore Academy, 1988a.

———. *Dil-i Vahshi* (Poems). Lahore: Lahore Academy, 1988b.

Iqbal, Muhammad. *Kulliyat-i Iqbal: Urdu* (Complete Urdu poetry). Lahore: Shaikh Ghulam Ali and Sons, 1986.

Ishrat Afreen. *Kunj Peele Phulon Ka* (Poems). Karachi: Daniyal, 1985.

Jafri, Ali Sardar. *Pairahan-i Sharar* (Poems). Bombay: Halqah-i Adab, 1966.

Josh Malihabadi. *Yadon ki Barat* (Procession of Memories). Lahore: Maktabah-i Sher o Adab, 1975.

———. *Uroos-i Adab* (Selected poetry). 2 vols. Edited by Ainulhaq. Karachi: Bazm-i Josh, 1983.

Kamal, Ajmal, ed. *Aaj ki Pehli Kitab* (Anthology of short stories and poetry). Karachi: Aaj ki Kitaben, 1981.

Kanjahi, Roohi, ed. *Bemisal Afsane* (Anthology of short stories). Lahore: Shu'a-yi Adab, 1988.

Khan, Sayyid Ahmad. *Maktoobat-i Sar Sayyid Ahmad Khan* (Sayyid Ahmad Khan's Writings). Edited by Shaikh M. Isma'il Panipati. Lahore: Majlis-i Taraqqi-yi Adab, 1959.

Majaz, Asrarul Haq. *Kulliyat-i Majaz* (Complete poetry). Lahore: Maktabah-i Urdu Adab, n.d.

Majeed Amjad. *Kulliyat-i Majeed Amjad* (Complete poetry). Edited by Khwajah Muhammad Zakriya. Lahore: Mavara, 1989.

Manto, Sa'adat Hasan. *Manto Namah* (Selected short stories). Lahore: Sang-i Meel, 1990a.

———. *Manto Rama* (Selected short stories). Lahore: Sang-i Meel, 1990b.

———. *Manto Numa* (Selected short stories). Lahore: Sang-i Meel, 1991.

Masud, Nayyar. *Simiya* (Short stories). Lahore: Qawsain, 1987.

Meeraji. *Kulliyat-i Meeraji* (Complete poetry). Edited by Jameel Jalibi. London: Urdu Markaz, 1988.

———. *Baqiyat-i Meeraji* (Poems not included in the *Kulliyat*). Edited by Sheema Majeed. Lahore: Pakistan Books and Literary Sounds, 1990.

Muneer Niyazi. *Kulliyat-i Muneer* (Complete poetry). Lahore: Mavara, 1990.

Mushtaq, Ahmad. *Majmuah* (Complete poetry). Lahore: Tanseer and Brothers Printers, 1993.

Naheed, Kishvar. *Fitnah Samani-yi Dil* (Collected poems). Lahore: Sang-i Meel, 1985.

———. *Siyah Hashiye Men Gulabi Rang* (Poems). Lahore: Sang-i Meel, 1986.

———. *Khiyali Shakhs se Muqabilah* (Poems). Lahore: Sang-i Meel, 1992.

Nasir Kazmi. *Kulliyat-i Nasir* (Complete poetry). Lahore: Maktabah-i Khayal, 1990.

Parveen Shakir. *Sad Barg* (Poems). Lahore: Ghalib, 1981.

———. *Khushbu* (Poems). Lahore: Ghalib, 1983.

———. *Khud Kalami* (Poems). Lahore: at-Tehreer, 1988.

———. *Inkar* (Poems). Islamabad: Murad, 1990.

Premchand. *Premchand ke Sau Afsane* (Selected short stories). Edited by Prem Gopal Mittal. Delhi: Modern Publishing House, 1990.

Pritchett, Frances W. *Urdu Literature: A Bibliography of English Language Sources.* Delhi: Manohar, 1979.

Qudsiyah, Bano. *Rajah Gidh* (Royal Vulture). Lahore: Sang-i Meel, 1981.

Rashid, N. M. *Kulliyat-i Rashid* (Complete poetry). Lahore: Mavara, 1988.

Riyaz, Fehmeedah. *Main Matti ki Moorat Hoon* (Collected poems). Lahore: Sang-i Meel, 1988.

———. *Apna Jurm Sabit Hai* (Poems). Lahore: Nigarishat, n.d.

Rusva, Mirza Muhammad Hadi. *Umrao Jan Ada* (Courtesan of Lucknow). Delhi: Maktabah-i Jamiah, 1971.

Saqi Farooqi. *Zindah Pani Sachcha* (Complete poetry). Lahore: Sang-i Meel, 1992.

Sara Shuguftah. *Ankhen* (Poems). Karachi: Shakeel, 1985.

Shad Arifi. *Kulliyat-i Shad Arifi* (Complete poetry). Edited by Muzaffar Hanfi. Delhi: National Academy, 1975.

Shaharyar. *Ism-i Azam* (Poems). Aligarh: Indian Book House, 1965.

Shahzad Ahmad. *Deevar Peh Dastak* (Complete poetry). Lahore: Sang-i Meel, 1991.

Shibli Nomani. *Maqalat-i Shibli* (Shibli's essays). Several vols. Edited by Sayyid Sulaiman Nadvi. Azamgarh: Ma'arif Press, 1938.

Shireen, Mumtaz, ed. *Zulmat-i Neem Roz* (Anthology of partition literature). Karachi: Nafees Academy, 1990.

Siddiqi, Shaukat. *Khuda ki Basti* (City of God). Karachi: Maktabah Naya Rahi, 1962.

Thanvi, Ashraf Ali. *Bihishti Zevar* (Heavenly Ornaments). Lahore: Taj, n.d.

Tufayl, M., ed. *Nuqoosh: Afsanah Nambar* (Anthology of short stories). 2 vols. Lahore: Idarah-i Farogh-i Urdu, 1982.

Yaganah Changezi, Mirza Yas. *Yaganah* (Selected poetry). Edited by Sahil Ahmad. Allahabad: Urdu Writer's Guild, 1986.

Zafar Iqbal. *Zafarnamah* (Complete poetry). Lahore: Pakistan Books and Literary Sounds, 1991.

Zaidi, Mustafa. *Kulliyat-i Mustafa Zaidi* (Complete poetry). Lahore: Mavara, n.d.

Zehra Nigah. *Sham Ka Pehla Tara* (Poems). Karachi: n.p., 1980.

Ziya Jalandhari. *''Sar-i Sham'' se ''Pas-i Harf'' tak* (Complete poetry). Lahore: Sang-i Meel, 1993.

13

Dalit Literature in Marathi

VEENA DEO

INTRODUCTION

The term "Dalit" literature has been in use since 1958, the year of the first Conference of the Maharashtra Dalit Sahitya Sangha (i.e., Maharashtra Dalit Literary Society) in Bombay, and is a marker for a numerous and exciting literary production.[1] Its advent and persistent output shook the Marathi mainstream literary tradition to its core by its representation of the lives of the most marginalized—the previous untouchable communities of the Hindu caste system. The Marathi literary reader, scholarly as well as casual, heard a new language; a new, direct, angry, accusatory, and analytic voice; and a literary production that dared to question centuries-old myths, traditions, and practices. Despite some initial defensive critical moves by the literary establishment, Dalit writing has found its readers and supporters in Maharashtra and is now commonly used in school textbooks and college curricula in Marathi literature departments.

This brief survey of Dalit Marathi literature attempts to understand and outline interconnections of liberal humanism, Marxism, and Hindu reform/Buddhism in Dalit writing's advent and proliferation as an integral part of the tensions of modernity.

Phule and Ambedkar: The Two Visionary Anchors

Even a brief attempt to situate Dalit writing in its historical context necessitates the mention of two very forceful thinkers from Maharashtra's past—Mahatma Jyotiba Phule (1828–90) and Bheemrao Ramji Ambedkar (1891–1956). We need to remind ourselves here to consider the importance of struggles for social reform and individual rights in the complex and changing context of colonial rule, struggles for home rule, nationalist movements, and the establishment of a new independent India in the midst of several interests contesting for power.

Mahatma Jyotiba Phule—reformist, activist, critic of the Hindu caste system, advocate of individual rights for men and women, and writer—is important to Dalit activism and writing, even if his work and its influence were obscured for a while in the early part of the twentieth century. His own life and work are testimony to his considerable passion for reform of Hindu society during colonial times. Influenced by the ideas of Thomas Penn and others, he advocated equal rights and education for women and the untouchable communities and critiqued the caste Hindus and their penchant for exploitative policies long before other reformers did in the twentieth century. As a writer, his poetry; his play *Tritiya Netra* (The Third Eye); and his interpretation of the myths of the 10 incarnations of Vishnu (as historical evidence of the Aryan rewriting of indigenous history and demonization of indigenous peoples and their struggles) in *Gulamgiri* (Slavery) are treasured volumes that became available to Dalit writers only after 1969. His followers carefully steered his organization, Satyashodhak Samaj (Society of Truth Seekers), away from the untouchable communities for which Phule himself had fought. As a result, his influence was somewhat hidden from view in a wider arena, although Ambedkar acknowledged and respected it. More recently, his work has been rehistoricized. If Mahatma Phule's direct influence on Dalit writing was somewhat limited, Ambedkar's has been quite extensive.

Most Dalit writers understand Bheemrao Ramji Ambedkar to be the primary impetus for their self-conscious, socially critical, political art. Ambedkar provided a vision of an egalitarian society where birth/caste determinants would become obsolete. He did this by inspiring outcaste communities to struggle for their own human and civil rights. As an important leader—a brilliant legal mind, a shrewd social critic, and political activist for Dalits before India's independence—Ambedkar also played a major role as chairperson of the drafting committee in the writing of the Indian Constitution, in which he initiated, negotiated, and supervised a reserved quota system for the scheduled castes and scheduled tribes of India. Thus, opportunities for advancement and participation in all spheres of life, ranging from the educational to the political, were ensured and became available to Dalit and *adivasi* (indigenous tribal) communities. Reconstruction of a modern, postcolonial India dedicated to secular and democratic principles of equality was his primary goal.

Both Phule and Ambedkar understood the role of Hindu religious emphasis on karma and *moksha* (salvation) in the perpetuation of the caste system, so they fought to eradicate its influence. Disappointed by the actual implementation of constitutional rights, however, Ambedkar modified his secular position and led more than 4 million Indians (most of them from his Mahar caste) into Buddhism in a mass conversion ceremony in Nagpur in 1956. He reinterpreted Buddhism as a religion to emphasize its investment in improving life on earth, in the here and now of the social world. Religious conversion seemed to him significant for Dalits to sever ties from the pressures of Hindu traditions, to forge social and cultural cohesion, and to foster a sense of pride and identity. On one hand, this was a clear rejection of the Hindu social structure based on caste, religious texts, and traditions; on the other, it was an articulation of a nationalist position for a new India based on a reinterpretation of indigenous ideas from India's past. A significant number of Dalit writers are also Buddhists. Even though their literary output cannot be dubbed Buddhist literature, references to Buddhism emerge in the subject matter and may provide an impetus in the future for a different sort of self-representation (see Zelliot 1992).

Although Mahatma Gandhi was a well-known critic of untouchability in the Hindu caste system, and he saw a need for reform before people could be united in the struggle for Indian independence, he was often at odds with Ambedkar's ideas for Dalit struggle for human and civil rights. The very term *harijan* (people of God) that he used in reference to Dalits was considered patronizing rather than respectful. Ambedkar considered his alliances with capital and upper-caste interests with suspicion as well. There is, therefore, a greater sense of reverence for Ambedkar and his clearly envisioned social and political work for Dalits among Maharashtrian communities, but especially among those whose lives were touched and forever transformed by his activism and vision.

Marxism provides yet another very strong rubric for Dalit literary production and has been favored for systemic analysis as well as political alliances. However, it has often split members in their attempt to define the goals and thrust of Dalit writing and activism. Who this struggle is for, who should be considered Dalit, whether the Hindu caste system should be the primary target, what methods suit best for whom, whether differences and degrees of differences among various oppressed groups should be addressed under the same headings, whether revolutionary violence is acceptable—these are some of the difficult questions that make for disagreements and mark the internal politics of the organization.

Hence, philosophical discussions regarding Buddhism, Marxism, and democracy as values guiding lives and social, economic, and cultural policies are continuously conducted in Dalit writing. The trust that Ambedkar's writings evoke invariably affects the outcome of these discussions in his favor.

"Dalit": Defining the Term

Before we consider some representative Dalit writers and their works, however, it is important to define what constitutes "Dalit" literature and understand some of the issues that are debated around the term itself. One of the primary aspects that most Dalit writers would agree on is that this is a literary movement emerging from struggles for social change. The connection between the struggle of Dalits for their rights and their literary output is seen by many Dalit writers as a parallel struggle to that of the black communities in the United States. Black literature and the work of Martin Luther King are vastly respected and emulated. The word "Dalit" as a general word comes from the word *padadalit* (slave at one's feet) and refers to people in the underclasses—the ex-untouchables of the Hindu caste system as well as other oppressed communities, including the *adivasis,* the poor, the laborers, and so on, as Datta Bhagat explains it (1992). He further clarifies that such a broad definition, however, is *not* applicable to the word "Dalit," as in Dalit literature. The term is more limited in this case to refer to the outcaste communities of India that were discriminated against on the basis of birth. This literature registers protest; uncovers hypocritical double standards of behavior among caste Maharashtrians; acquaints readers with, and expresses anger at, the inhuman treatment experienced by such communities; and is committed to an incisive critique of the social, cultural, and political world the writers experience with a view to raise a voice for justice and equality. It does not automatically follow, Bhagat says, that only certain communities (defined Dalit by birth) can write Dalit literature, nor should it suggest that Dalit literature will become obsolete if/when experiences of Dalits change (Bhagat 1992, 40–46). Some non-Dalit writers' works are acclaimed and found acceptable because the Dalit writers trust their intellectual integrity and admire their critical positions and commitment to social change—here the names of well-known non-Dalit poets like Narayan Surve, Sharatchandra Muktibodh, and Keshavsut come to mind.

Any writing, literary or critical, that comes out of formulaic Marxist ideologies, sentimentality, and/or a patronizing attitude is immediately critiqued and roundly denounced. Dalit readership is expected to be inspired for activism by this writing, while non-Dalit readership is expected to be informed, educated, warned, and/or encouraged to change and critically examine its perspective. Dalit writers who have moved up the social ladder and are interested in dissociating themselves from the label "Dalit" and prefer a more universal title of writer are dismissed as "Dalit Brahmins." One of the inherent contradictions that Dalit intellectuals wrestle with is a well-meaning policy of reserved quotas, on one hand, that continues to encourage people, for practical reasons, to invest energy in identity politics and caste self-definitions, while, on the other, aspiring for a more egalitarian social and political system where such divisions would be permanently broken down.

DALIT LITERARY PRODUCTION

Dalit literary production has gained ground steadily over the years from the turn of the twentieth century onward, more particularly, since India's independence. The period of the 1960s and thereafter has seen considerable outpouring of works. Among many genres, poetry seems to be a more favored vehicle used by Dalit writers. However, prose fiction—novels and short stories—has also been influential. Essays of social and literary criticism are steadily produced in order to define and redefine Dalit writing and/or critique literary production, as well as critical reception of Dalit writing. Considerable talent is also invested in autobiographical writing, drama, and feminist writing with specific focus on Dalit women's issues.

The Role of Magazines

As in any movement, magazines and journals have played a significant role in Dalit writing, although some have had a very short life. Such magazines and journals as *Prabuddha Bharat, Asmitadarsha, Magova, Amhi, Satyakatha,* and *Vidroha* (to mention a few, with *Asmitadarsha* still being distributed and read widely) have been vital to the publication and dissemination of Dalit writing among Maharashtrian readers. Among some others, *Maitarani* should be mentioned as a new venture by Dalit and Buddhist women who started their quarterly publication in Bombay in 1992 with a special issue dedicated to Phule and Ambedkar, celebrating Ambedkar's birth centenary year (1990–91). Attempts to invigorate conversations among Dalit writers and scholars of Dalit writing across regions and countries are also made by a more current journal edited by Kashinath Ranveer, *The Downtrodden India: Journal of Dalit and Bahujan Studies,* published at Dr. Babasaheb Ambedkar Marathwada University, Aurangabad, in English (its first volume was published in January 1994).

Raising Issues of Classification

Dalit writing, with its multivalent emphasis on journalism, history, critical essays, literature, and literary criticism, brings to the forefront the idea that any social change involving groups of individuals would have to address all necessary issues at once through all available means. If journalistic writing helps disseminate ideas and mobilize support for social change to a wide audience within and without the Dalit groups, literary production and its success ensure cultural value and facilitate social mobility. What is significant, however, is that Dalit writing, which is part of a massive struggle for social and political change, consistently blurs boundaries between established genres in its attempts to clarify and critique social realities of the Dalits.

Hence, for the purposes of this short survey chapter, the Dalit Panther movement (1972) and women's movements in India are considered significant markers that provided and continue to provide momentum to Dalit writing rather than specific periods or genres. Dalit writing is considered here under three broad headings: Pre-Panther Dalit Writing; Dalit Panther Movement and After; and Dalit and Buddhist Women's Writing. Instead of compiling a long list of names and dates for this survey, I highlight a few representative works in order to look at texts more closely. Two important issues for Dalit writers are addressed primarily in this survey of Dalit writing: negotiations with language and identity, although these issues are only a part, albeit important, of many others, as mentioned before. The selected bibliography that follows this chapter attempts to cover more writers and their works than this brief survey can address with deserved care.

PRE-PANTHER DALIT WRITING

Whether one wishes to trace Dalit writing back to the Buddhist period; to the saint-poet of the Bhakti movement, Chokhamela (fourteenth century); or to Mahatma Jyotiba Phule, critical writing against the Hindu caste system with reference to the plight of those marginalized and oppressed by Brahminical traditions is not entirely new to India. Not until the twentieth century, however, is a concerted effort made to define a separate Dalit identity and a Dalit literary movement within the context of social change and modernity as India takes its place among modern nations. Among the outstanding early twentieth-century Dalit writers were Gopalbaba Valangkar, Kisan Phagoji Bansod, Ghanashyam Talwatkar and Shankarrao Kharat. The mainstream literary scene was dominated by middle-class, Brahmin writers such as N. S. Phadake and V. S. Khandekar. A prominent and prolific Dalit fiction writer like Annabhau Sathe wrote under the influence of Marxism. His novels *Phakira* and *Varanecha Vagha* are very well known as sensitive portraits of individual Dalit heroism within conflictual and complex social realities of their village communities.

Issues of Language and Representation

Baburao Bagul is a significant name among this early group of writers who propelled Dalit writing to a different height. As a senior writer who gave impetus to the younger generation led by Dhasal, his work first stood out in a collection of Dalit poems titled *Akar* (Shape, 1967).

His collection of short stories *Maran Swasta Hot Ahe* (Death Is Getting Cheaper, 1968) is considered a significant landmark in Dalit writing. This book is dedicated to Martin Luther King and his civil rights struggle for African Americans. The seventh story in this collection with the same title as that of the book provides a good example of its import. The story emerges through a conversation between two literary friends, a fiction writer and a poet, who are struggling to forge a new kind of writing. They find it difficult to capture precisely their ideas or find a shape and form for them. In frustration, they walk out of the apartment of the narrator, who seems to know stories of every slum dweller he is greeted by as they walk. The narrator/writer and poet are thus presented as being sympathetic observers of life in Bombay slums and as also closely connected to those experiences. The narrator has clearly conversed with the people whose stories he narrates and is familiar with their environment. Therefore, he can be a reliable and convincing narrator. He is, at once, a part of that world and apart from it. The world that emerges from the narrator/writer's narrations is a world of brutality and dubious survival—of humans preying upon humans; of fathers prostituting their own daughters; of the young competing for work with older folks without any qualms; of children without childhood who are aged beyond years; of wives being raped in the presence of their husbands; of broken hearts, aspirations, and hopelessness; of casual and senseless violence. The narrator's poet friend, who is attempting to compose a poem about Bombay, freedom, modernity, and so on at the beginning of this story, is so shaken by these experiences/narratives that he decides to throw all his words out and keep only one line—"This is Bombay. Humans eat humans here, and death gets cheaper . . . !" (Bagul 1980, 88; translation mine).

The literary issues raised in Bagul's short story illustrate a Dalit writer's struggle with form and language. All human experience is clearly considered appropriate subject matter for poetry. No concession is made to the Marathi literary mainstream on that issue. But the difficulty that a Dalit writer/poet faces with language use is clearly emphasized. An insider as well as an outsider (unaffected by the brutalizing effects of this world he lives in and writes about), the writer or poet and his consciousness become central to the way the story gets written. Photographic realism is necessary to show readers (probably middle-class) an unfamiliar world. Yet, as insiders, these writers are also affected by a strong mix of emotions—anger, compassion, hatred—that have to be kept at bay for the writing to take "acceptable" shape. The story needs to be told without polemics, but with unmistakable social criticism and a clear political agenda. The writer and poet are, thus, as much observers as they become characters whose creative process is itself under observation and made part of the subject of the story itself. Effecting appropriate intellectual distance and control in order to create a desired effect on the reader is a continuous challenge. The strength of the writing in Bagul's collection, its stark reality, its reflectiveness, its compassion make his collection very valuable. Bagul's work exemplifies a Dalit writer's effort to challenge and collapse boundaries between the old-fashioned imaginary world of literature and the everyday "reality" of the dispossessed, which was even further beyond the bounds of literary realism marked by the genre of the novel and the short story in the mainstream.

These issues are consciously explored by several other poets and novelists as well. Particular mention among early significant works should be made here of Daya Pawar's collection of poems *Kondvada* and Keshav Meshram's works *Hakikat Ani Jatayu* (1972), a novel, *Chayaban* (1973), a collection of short stories, and his volume of poems *Utkhanan* (1977).

Experiment with Form

Yeshwant Manohar, in his volume of poems titled *Utthangumpha* (1977), experiments with a parody of the classic verse form of *ovi* used in Marathi poetry by saint-poets of the Bhakti movement. One of the poems, "Chorpurushano," is a challenge to translate into English, but even a brief mention helps to illustrate one Dalit writer's various experiments with language use. An attempt to explain the title should reveal its complexity and difficulty. The title is addressed to thieves and/or hypocrites by the use of one word that rhymes by association with *thorpurushano* (great/good men) by simply substituting "thor" with "chor." The poem is addressed with mock respect to great thieves or hypocrites who claim patriotism, godliness, and respectability while scapegoating and demeaning Dalits permanently in social roles, such as that of cleaning latrines. Indirection works here at many levels. The use of the *ovi* form allows for a tone of respect, while the references and words themselves allow for severe mockery and provide an undertone of anger and disgust. Beyond that, the reader is quite taken by the clever reversal of the form—clearly, a Caliban-like move, that is, turning the language of the master against him—thereby also showing one's own control and mastery of it.

Arjun Dangle's volume of poems *Chavani Halte Ahe* (1977), Tryambak Sapkale's poetry in his volume titled *Surung* (1976), and Pralahd Chedvankar's poetry volume *Audit* (1976) are some other examples of works that experiment with form.

DALIT PANTHER MOVEMENT AND AFTER

The changing economic scene in Maharashtra in postindependent India with land development, modernization of agriculture, sugar factories, cooperatives, and so on continued to oppress the outcaste communities, even further increasing conflicts in rural Maharashtra as well as urban centers, where droves from villages came looking for better working conditions. Baburao Bagul, the senior writer and activist involved with labor issues in urban Maharashtra, influenced many young Dalit writers, such as Daya Pawar, Arjun Dangle, Namdeo Dhasal, Raja Dhale, J. V. Pawar, and others who felt a need for a new militant and radical momentum for Dalit activism and writing. Influenced by radical leftist ideologies and emulating the Black Panthers of the United States, the Dalit Panthers established themselves as a group on July 9, 1972. Frustration with inaction of earlier attempts at social change was expressed through black flag demonstrations to mark the 25th anniversary of India's independence in 1972. Provocative poetry and incendiary writing were to be coupled with radical activism. Poetry was to be written in the service of society. Namdeo Dhasal, one of the more provocative and most famous of the Panthers, had said in an interview with Sudhir Sonalkar in *The Sunday Observer* of August 8, 1982 that if the aim of social struggles was the removal of unhappiness, then poetry was necessary because it expressed that unhappiness vividly and powerfully (Hovell 1991, 77). By 1982, the Dalit Panthers had split over ideological differences trying to negotiate Dalit identity between Ambedkarism and Marxist ideas that insisted on allegiances across caste for philosophical and practical purposes. Yet, the effect of their radical stance was very powerful.

The challenge Dalit writing offered the established literary traditions in subject matter and language use was further sharpened and made even more militant. Namdeo Dhasal shocked the literary scene in 1973 with his collection of poems *Golpitha.* Here he wrote about his experiences of Bombay's brothels and, slums shocking the middle-class reader. Baburao Bagul's generation challenged many literary conventions, but they also saw themselves as writers who were dedicated to "good" writing, that is, writing that followed the conventions of genre and literary language. Dhasal, on the other hand, was self-consciously iconoclastic and known to use vocabulary deliberately to violate literary tastes and to force the reader to acknowledge that literary language would not be allowed to distance readers from horrific human experiences and man's inhumanity to man. Literary language went places where it had never been before. *Murkh Mhataryane Dongar Halavila* (1975) and *Tuhi Iyatta Kanchi* (1981) are Dhasal's other well-known collections of poetry. He also has a novel, *Hadki Hadwal,* to his credit. Dhasal's poems are written with great force. He never minces words and was often critiqued for his use of vulgarisms. Sexuality, for instance, is not romanticized but is starkly related to power and domination in the area of intimate human experiences. His title poem of *Tuhi Iyatta Kanchi* (1981) displays all of the taboo subjects for the prudish caste Hindus—explicit sexual references, intercourse with a menstruating woman, dragging dead cattle and eating their beef—for whom ideas of pollution and impurity organize their world of experience, and the question is asked mockingly, "What grade are you in?"—in other words, What use is your education if some parts of human experience are unknown to you?[2] A Brahmin's claim to superiority based on knowledge and birth is repeatedly called to question by mocking at traditions that restrict and oppress expressions of basic humanity. Even personally, he would do unconventional things such as use his mother's name as his middle name rather than his father's, as is the tradition in Maharashtra. Thus, he called himself Namdeo Salubai Dhasal (since knowledge of one's mother is a greater certainty, in general, and Dhasal did not know his father), implying also that he was not afraid to overturn traditions nor to question and examine rigorously any idea that is considered ordinary and normal. Dhasal's political views have never been tied down to a single perspective. He has explored different leftist ideologies as well as Buddhism and Ambedkarism. In all, he has struggled with the issue of Dalit identity and what exactly it means and how it can be represented.

A sociocultural study done by G. M. Kulkarni and Vidyadhar Pundalik titled *Dalit Sahitya: Ek Samajik-Sanskritik Abhyas* (Dalit Literature: A Sociocultural Study, 1992), based on responses to an elaborate questionnaire answered by 62–65 Dalit writers, shows that, although the Dalit Panther movement did not last very long, 69.3 percent of the respondents answering a series of questions in the section about their political views said that they considered the movement to be significant. The authors of this study ascribe such a response to the strong impact of the Panther movement on literary style and language use.[3]

Use of Spoken Dialects

Another area of negotiation for Dalit writers has been the use of spoken dialects in written form, challenging notions of "aesthetics" among the mainstream writers. Careful distinction is made between writers who use local dialects as pastoral romanticists, who have very little respect for village folk they write about, and those who have lived experiences that make the use of dialect part of the aesthetics of their storytelling.

Lakshman Mane's autobiographical narrative *Upara* (Outsider, 1980), among many others, illustrates this issue well. He speaks of his first experiences at school. His family speaks the Kaikadi language, which he transcribes and translates for Marathi readers. The entire narrative uses *kaikadi,* spoken Marathi dialect from his village, as well as standard written Marathi in a seamless weave. The narrator/speaker/character emerging from this text explains the particular problems of his situation as a Dalit in an alien environment in an educational institution in two separate ways. First, he is the first one from his family to go to school; hence, he is new to the culture of book learning; second, he is a bilingual who is forced into written Marathi as a third language because the spoken version he knows as a second language is different from the one he is later educated to use. The narrative documents the irony of a society that thrusts egalitarian values through its educational and progressive uplift programs but also perpetuates, through family and village structures, caste identity that discourages social change. Ambedkar had mentioned in his work intercaste marriage as perhaps the only sure solution for dismantling the rigid Hindu caste system. When Mane marries out of his caste (in accordance with his newly learned values), all of his family and his wife's family refuse to accept his intercaste marriage, forcing activism on individuals who may not want to be so heroic in everyday life. It comes as a surprise that the upper castes are not the only castes that are fearful of collapsing caste boundaries. Consolidation of groups at all levels of the social strata makes individual activism that much more difficult. This insider knowledge of the writer makes the narrative come alive in all three languages with which he works. Literary Marathi is thus enriched and extended. This language also exercises some power over its middle-class and caste Hindu reading public by effectively alienating it from the narrative perspective through a variety of language use and forcing the reader to stay in that role of the outsider where control of the narrative as a reader would become difficult. The effect of literary writing on readers thus gets politicized.

Narratives of Self-Fashioning

The 1980s have seen a considerable development of autobiographical works by Dalit men and women that capture the nuances of their struggles through a wide variety of regional, experiential, and linguistic means. There is considerable discussion among the critical community about whether to label these narratives autobiographies or narratives of self.[4] Kusare-Kulkarni notes in these narratives a distinction between testimony and something of deeper personal and cultural import. These narratives are more than an account of, or a testimony to, achievements in one's individual life; instead they help articulate for the writer a social, as well as a personal, identity. To that extent, they fashion a self in the articulation as much as they situate this self within a larger social and cultural context. They speak not merely to an individual identity, but to a collective identity. The struggles in that articulation are as much those of an individual as of a group.

The narratives themselves experiment with form and language use in a variety of ways. Daya Pawar's *Balut* (1989), for instance, is told as a story by Dagdu Pawar to the more literate Daya Pawar, both Dagdu and Daya being the same person in different situations. P. E. Sonkamble's *Athvaninche Pakshi* (Birds of Memory, 1979) documents vignettes of experiences, as if they were short stories, rather than a continuous narrative. The second edition of this text has almost twice the number of vignettes as the first and suggests a continuum along which this narrative could keep moving in its articulation of self. Madhav Kondvilkar's *Mukkam Post Devache Gothane* (Postal Residence Devache Gothane) is recorded as a diary from the years 1969–77. Lakshaman Mane's *Upara,* discussed earlier, reads like fiction. These writers use particular spoken dialects connected to the region, locality, and caste from which they narrate. Moving between dialect and standard Marathi, these accounts of self create unique opportunities for these writers for self-fashioning.

Gaze Turned Within

The critical gaze of the Dalit writer has always been sharply attentive to traditions, myths, and practices—social, political, cultural, and literary. It often turns inward as well in self-criticism. A more recent poet, Loknath Yeshwant, in his *Teen Kavita* (Three Poems), published in the 1992 Diwali issue of *Asmitadarsha,* critiques with bitterness three different groups important to Dalit activism—members of Ambedkar's Republican Party; a political leader whose image as leader is only that of a crowd pleaser and different from what it was when he was a young idealist; and a soliloquist. The speaker/poet identifies with all three very closely. Ambedkar asks the Republican why he cannot carry on the struggle for which Ambedkar gave him powerful weapons of knowledge. The young Republican has no answers and only keeps standing like a question mark. In the second poem, a tired brother asks the political leader what has happened to the struggle. The leader shoots this brother in anger and finds he has only shot the mirror image in the glass in front of him. In the third poem, the soliloquist lashes out at himself because he participates in locating people by their caste, even though he knows that to be wrong. Each of the sections, titled "Republican," "Leader," "Soliloquy," shows a split within generations and within the individual and acutely captures the frustration, anger, and sense of hopelessness and inaction a young Dalit writer and activist experiences today.

It is this kind of impasse that critics talk about when they comment on the direction Dalit writing is taking. Datta Bhagat in *Dalit Sahitya: Disha Ani Dishantar;* Arun Kamble in his preface to his mother's autobiography, *Majya Jal-*

machi Chittarkatha (Moving Pictures of My Life); as well as Arjun Dangle in *Poisoned Bread,* among others, record a concern expressed by some critics that Dalit writing is losing its edge or that it is losing its dynamism and becoming static. These writers indicate their strong belief that the work started by Dalit writers will continue as long as people are fighting battles for social change. Arun Kamble even suggests that the readership that complains does not show the necessary insight into nuanced use of language. Considerable impact can be seen in a variety of areas of research, dramatic forms, women's writing, and so on that readers need to notice.

WRITING BY DALIT AND BUDDHIST WOMEN

Mahatma Phule and Ambedkar had both involved women closely in their struggle for individual rights and social reform. Dalit women acknowledge their contributions with respect. Meenakshi Mun and Urmila Pawar's joint writing of the history of women in the Ambedkar movement, titled *Amhihi Itihas Ghadavala* (We Too Made History, 1989), should be mentioned here particularly for that reason. Educational opportunities for all women in postindependent India have had an impact in the concerted efforts being made by women and women's organizations to define their roles and issues. Particular efforts by Dalit women can be seen as well. Shantabai Kamble's *Majya Jalmachi Chittarkatha,* published as a complete book in 1986 but presented to readers and television audiences in serial form through the early 1980s, is considered the first autobiographical narrative by a Dalit woman writer. Autobiographical writing has since become an important genre for women writers. Dalit women have written poems for a longer time. Meena Gajbhiye, Surekha Bhagat, Hira Bansode, and Jyoti Lanjewar are some names that must be mentioned in this context.

Dalit women writers' late coming to the written world of literature can be understood in many ways. Women have always occupied a lower step in the social ladder in all patriarchal societies. Nineteenth-century reform movements for women (Mahatma Phule's efforts, for instance) in Maharashtra affected middle-class women, to some extent leaving Dalit women out, for the most part. In addition, for Dalit women, work responsibilities for family support added another hurdle to overcome. Even with educational opportunities in place now, situations among Dalit women vary widely from village to urban communities. Dalit struggle for civil and human rights became a priority for many women who first affected a change for the younger generations and more particularly for their sons before the daughters also got a chance. Many Dalit writers in their autobiographies speak of the hardships their mothers undertook to provide them with opportunities.

Dalit Women: Orality and Literacy

Asha Mundale in her discussion/article "Dalit Streecha Va Tichya Baddalcha Bhashavyavahar" (The Language of and about Dalit Women [Bhagwat

1987,161–174]) makes some important observations. She cites several reasons to explain how a Dalit woman's personality is shaped by her environment. She is exploited sexually by any number of caste men and has never been able to voice her complaints about that. This has made her relationship with her husband somewhat ambivalent, and she becomes a target of his abuse and/or frustrations. Her children revere her and have compassion for her because they see her always working hard to keep the family fed. Mundale clearly recounts a Dalit woman's social history to explain what her expressive language is like. A Dalit woman is not afraid to express herself; she can be very sharp and quick-witted with her words. She is open about her sexuality, expressed in song and dance forms such as the *lavani* or the *tamasha.* Mundale's primary argument is that the written tradition is not the appropriate yardstick to measure Dalit women's expressive forms. So one should not speak about the Dalit woman's silence in the same way as one speaks about middle-class women's silence. A Dalit woman is articulate and forceful, even though written literary expression is a relatively new avenue for her (Bhagwat 1987, 161–74).

Several important poets and writers have emerged in the past few years. Meena Gajbhiye, Surekha Bhagat, Babytai Kamble, Mallika Amarshekh, Kumud Pawade, Mukta Sarvagod, Meenakshi Mun, Urmila Pawar, and Hira Bansode are names that immediately suggest a growing concert of voices.

Dalit woman writer Urmila Pawar, in her collection of short stories *Sahav Bot* (Sixth Finger), highlights the modern, urban, working woman's problems. In doing so, she gives us a glimpse of women in every age group, but she does not focus on Dalit women only. Women's relationships with men and other women are of greater interest to her, which she explores in a wide variety of contexts of interpersonal or generational power relationships. Pawar's short stories collected in *Sahav Bot* and *Chauthi Bhint* (Fourth Wall) provide a glimpse into a wide range of women's experiences across caste, class, and age. Her ear for nuances of language, rural, regional, and urban, and her sense of the dramatic and the humorous make her stories very valuable.

Hira Bansode, primarily a poet, has explored the implications of urban sisterhood in her poem "Sakhi" (Friend—the *i* at the end of the word makes it feminine) from her collection *Phiryad* (1984). A girlfriend from work comes to a Dalit woman's house for the first time—a momentous event that moves the poet to record and celebrate it. The friend has taken a giant step for justice when she agrees to visit a Dalit woman's home and share her food. But she cannot resist criticizing the way the Dalit woman serves the food. The plate is arranged very differently, the last course of rice is not served with yogurt (a Brahmin custom), and the Brahmin friend remarks that "your caste is never going to learn and improve" (Bansode 1984, 22–23; translation mine). Bansode ironically records the Dalit woman's sense of shame and her plea for understanding because poverty has never allowed her to know the varieties of food that would make a multicourse meal possible. Anger is not recorded here, but shame is, and the reader is troubled by the responses of the host as well as the visitor.

Solidarity and alliances across castes may be a desirable objective but are not devoid of problems.

Bansode also explores in her poems the psyche of legendary or historical women whose voices have not been recorded. Her tribute to Buddha's wife in the poem titled "Yashodhara" (first published in a women's popular magazine, *Stree,* in 1979 and later published in her volume *Phiryad* [Appeal for Justice]) attempts to understand with great compassion the depth of Yashodhara's experience after she is abandoned by her more famous husband. Other abandoned women, like Sita from the Hindu epic *Ramayana,* have been written about in revisionist texts. The poet laments and tries to seek answers for why Yashodhara might be forgotten (Bansode 1984, 5–7). Her offering to Shabari, who tasted every berry, hoping to find her salvation before she offered it to Rama, is a mixed message in her poem "Shabarees" (To Shabari). On one hand, she wants to acknowledge her as a sister and as an outcaste, although a devotee of Rama. On the other hand, she reprimands her for making a mistake by not confronting and upbraiding Rama with the story of the unfortunate Ekalavya or her own outcaste situation.

Hira Bansode offers in her poems a variety of her concerns as a Dalit woman, thereby emphasizing the need of Dalit women writers to articulate their concerns equally as Dalits and as women. She, too, struggles with language as a Dalit poet. Her poem "Shabdanno" (To Words) urges her words to represent adequately the suffering that Dalits have borne for centuries. Beautiful language seems to be a problem. The poet asks a series of questions toward the end of the poem that may be roughly translated as follows: Doesn't the ocean cross boundaries, swallow and destroy land when his heart is in turmoil? Doesn't the earth destroy large cities when she cannot bear sins anymore? Doesn't even a little ant sting back sharply when someone's foot hurts her? Then our silence about awful acts of inhumanity against us is our mistake, and heinous acts against us continue because our words have forgiven too much. Dear words, dawn will not rise until you become weapons and strike (Bansode 1984, 49).

Under the awareness and impact of Dalit writing, activism, and the women's movements in Maharashtra, some very interesting research has been undertaken. One such is Roopa Kulkarni's translation into Marathi and critical discussion of the Sanskrit text *Vajrasuchi* (1992) by a Buddhist scholar, Ashwaghosh, who is supposed to have lived between A.D. 75 and 150. She argues that Ashwaghosh was the first thorough textual critic of Manusmriti and the Brahminical tradition, whose text, however, was deliberately suppressed. She brings a considerable scholarship to bear on her argument.

Dalit activism and writing continue to provide a challenge and a critical perspective to Marathi readers and are a significant contribution to Marathi language and literature, as well as to the self-formulations of Maharashtrians in the modern world.

NOTES

Thanks to Eleanor Zelliot for her support.

1. I have translated for this chapter some titles and names in parentheses whenever I thought it would be useful for general readers unfamiliar with Marathi.

2. It is important to remember that one of the former untouchable communities lived only by scavenging and accepting leftover food from caste Hindus. Dragging away the dead village cattle was considered one of their responsibilities. This meat was often something that provided nourishment to their families—a testimony to the poverty that was endorsed and perpetuated by caste Hindus of the villages. Under Ambedkar's influence, considerable effort through educational work among village Dalit communities was undertaken to help them understand social practices that continued to oppress and abuse them. Political protests were organized where Dalits refused to participate in those practices that the whole village benefited from while they were demeaned by them.

3. This study provides some quantitative information; however, the questionnaire also suggests some important problems. The authors openly describe some of these in the study. Of the 150 questionnaires sent, 60–70 were returned, and the published writers who were chosen to participate did not answer all the questions with enthusiasm. Many were somewhat suspicious of the intent of such a study conducted by caste writers and were unwilling or reluctant. Repeated reminders were necessary to get the surveys back. Those who agreed and/or considered this study to have value mostly represented the older generation of writers. Only four women writers were among the respondents. One of the women asked why specific questions addressing women's issues were not in the questionnaire. The questionnaire that is attached as an appendix to the published study clearly shows that the questions are addressed to men specifically. Class/caste and gender bias is very much in evidence here. This study clearly has a limited appeal to Dalit writers and reflects a reserve and/or mistrust toward these authors, as well as toward this kind of survey and analysis that proposes objectivity. Using this study for the specific information used here is not invalid, but it also highlights the problems attached to scholarship in this area. It reemphasizes the need for rigorous and critical reading, as well as providing a glimpse at the literary world in which Dalit writers operate.

4. Particular mention should be made here of Arati Kusare-Kulkarni's study titled *Dalit Swakathane: Sahityaroop* (Dalit Self-Narratives: Their Literary Qualities, 1991).

WORKS CITED

Bagul, Baburao. *Maran Swasta Hot Ahe.* 1968. 2d ed. Pune: Continental Prakashan, 1980.

Bansode, Hira. *Phiryad.* Pune: Samaj Prabodhan Sanstha Prakashan, 1984.

Bhagat, Datta. *Dalit Sahitya: Disha Ani Dishantar.* Nanded: Abhay Prakashan, 1992.

Bhagwat, Shobha. *Dalit Purushanchya Atmacharitratil Stree Pratima.* Pune: Streevani Prakashan, 1987.

Dangle, Arjun, ed. *Poisoned Bread.* Bombay: Orient Longman, 1992.

Dhasal, Namdeo. *Tuhi Iyatta Kanchi, Tuhi Iyatta.* Bombay: Ambedkar Prabodhini, 1981.

Hovell, Laurie. "Namdeo Dhasal: Poet and Panther." Bulletin of Concerned Asian Scholars 23: 2 (1991): 77–83.

Kamble, Shantabai. *Majya Jalmachi Chittarkatha.* 2d ed. Pune: Sugava Prakashan, 1990.
Kulkarni, G. M., and Vidyadhar Pundalik. *Dalit Sahitya: Ek Samajik-Sanskritik Abhyas.* Pune: Sugava Prakashan, 1992.
Kulkarni, Roopa, trans. and commentary. *Bauddhacharya Aswaghoshanchi Vajrasuchi: Mul Sanskrit Pathya.* Bombay: Lokvangmaya Gruha, 1992.
Kusare-Kulkarni, Arati. *Dalit Swakathane: Sahityaroop.* Nagpur: Vijay Prakashan, 1991.
Mane, Lakshman. *Upara.* Bombay: Granthali, 1980.
Manohar, Yeshwant. *Utthangumpha.* 1977. 2d ed. Pune: Continental Prakashan, 1980.
Yeshwant, Loknath. "Teen Kavita." *Asmitadarsh* 25:3 (1992): 145 (Diwali issue).
Zelliot, Eleanor. "Buddhist Women of the Contemporary Maharashtrian Conversion Movement." In *Buddhism, Sexuality and Gender,* edited by Jose Ignacio Cabezon. Albany: State University of New York Press, 1992.

SELECTED BIBLIOGRAPHY

Achalkhamb, Rustum. *Gavaki.* Pune: Shree Vidya Prakashan, 1983.
Bagul, Baburao. *Suda,* 1970.
———. *Jehnva Mi Jat Chorli Hoti,* 1976.
———. *Maran Swasta Hot Ahe.* 2d ed. Pune: Continental Prakashan, 1980.
———. *Ambedkar Bharat.* Vol. 1. 1st ed. Pune: Rajahasa Prakashan, 1981. 4 vols.
Bagul, Charudatta. *Polis Havaldarachi Diary: Kadambari.* 1st ed. Pune: Menaka Prakashan, 1982.
Bansode, Hira. *Phiryad.* Pune: Samaj Prabodhan Sanstha, 1984.
Bhagat, Datta. *Dalit Sahitya: Disha Ani Dishantar.* Nanded: Abhay Prakashan, 1992.
Bhagwat, Shobha, ed. *Dalit Purushanchya Atmacharitratil Stree-Pratima.* Pune: Stree Vani Prakashan, 1987.
Bhagyavant, Tushar. *Kondala.* Kolhapur: Ajab Pustakalaya, 1986.
Bhave, Sumitra. *Pan On Fire: Eight Dalit Women Tell Their Story.* Translated by Gauri Deshpande. New Delhi: Indian Social Institute, 1988.
Bhoir, Bhagvan. *Unhatle Jhad.* Thane: Swapnil Prakashan, 1992.
Chendvankar, Pralhad. *Audit.* 1st ed. Bombay: Abhinav Prakashan, 1976.
Dahake, Vasant Abaji. *Pratibaddha.* Bombay: Mauj Prakashan Gruha, 1981.
Dangle, Arjun. *Chavni Halte Ahe.* 1st ed. Bombay: Karmveer Prakashan, 1977.
———. *Hi Bandhavarchi Manse.* Pune: Magova Prakashan, 1979.
———. *Dalit Vidroh.* Bombay: Granthdhar, 1991.
———, ed. *Poisoned Bread.* Bombay: Orient Longman, 1992.
Dethe, Bhimsen. *Horpal.* Bombay: Adoni Prakashan, 1977.
———. *Iskot.* Bombay: Sambodhi Prakashan, 1980.
Dhasal, Namdeo. *Golpitha.* Pune: Neelkantha Prakashan, 1975a.
———. *Murkha Mhataryane Dongar Halavila.* Pune: Magova Prakashan, 1975b.
———. *Amachya Itihasatil Ek Apariharya Patra, Priyadarshini,* 1976.
———. *Hadaki Hadval.* Pune: Asmita Prakashan, 1981a.
———. *Tuhi Iyatta Kanchi, Tuhi Iyatta.* Bombay: Ambedkar Prabodhini, 1981b.
———. *Khela.* Bombay: Praas, 1983.
———. *Gandu Bagicha.* Bombay: Ambedkar Prabodhini, 1986.
Gadekar, Vimal. *Rutubandh.* Chandrapur: Suprabha Prakashan, 1990.
Gaekwad, Lakshman. *Uchalya.* Pune: Shree Vidya Prakashan, 1987.

Gajvi, Premanand. *Devnavari.* 1st ed. Bombay: Abhinav Prakashan, 1981.
———. *Ghotbhar Pani.* 2d ed. Bombay: Majestic Prakashan, 1987.
Hivarale, Sukharam. *Sabdayan.* Aurangabad: Tara Mhatre, 1978.
Ingale, Ramchandra T. *Maharancha Sanskritik Itihas.* Nagpur: Abhijit Prakashan, 1987.
Jadhav, P. U. *Mharuda.* Vasari: Milind Prakashan, 1986.
Jagtap, Bapurao. *Neelya Pahadachya Kavita:* Kala Prakashan, 1982.
Jhodge, Nanasaheb. *Phanjar.* Bombay: Sindhu N. Jhodge, 1982.
Kamble, Anila. *Majhya Kavita.* Pune: Menaka Prakashan, 1983.
Kamble, Aruna. *Ramayanatil Sanskritisangharsha.* Bombay: Panther Prakashan, 1982.
Kamble, Baby. *Geena Amucha.* Pune: Rachana Prakashan, 1986.
Kamble, Balvant. *Nishedh.* 1st ed. Bombay: Abhinav Prakashan, 1981.
Kamble, Shantabai. *Majya Jalmachi Chittarkatha.* 2d ed. Pune: Sugava Prakashan, 1990.
Kamble, Uttam. *Kumbhamela Sadhuncha Ki Sandhisadhuncha.* Pune: Sugava Prakashan, 1991.
Kharat, Shankarrao. *Sangava.* 1st ed. Pune: Continental Prakashan, 1962.
———. *Titvicha Phera.* 1st ed. Pune: Sadhana Prakashan, 1963.
———. *Daundi.* 1st ed. Pune: Continental Prakashan, 1965.
———. *Gavshiv.* Pune: Venus Prakashan, 1970a.
———. *Hatbhatti.* 1st ed. Pune: Kulkarni Granthagar, 1970b.
———. *Gavacha Tinopal Guruji,* 1971.
———. *Jhopadapatti.* Pune: Inamdar Bandhu Prakashan, 1973.
———. *Mulakhat.* Pune: Indrayani Sahitya, 1978.
———. *Phutpath.* Pune: Inamdar Bandhu Prakashan, 1980.
———. *Taral Antaral: Atmakatha.* 1st ed. Pune: Continental, 1981.
———. *Aja Itha, Udya Titha.* Aurangabad: Anand Prakashan, 1983a.
———. *Mi Majhya Gavachya Shodhat.* 1st ed. Pune: Pratima Prakashan, 1983b.
Kiravle, Krishna. *Ambedkari Shahiri: Ek Shodh.* Pune: Nalanda Prakashan, 1992.
Kondvilkar, Madhav. *Mukkam Post: Devache Gothane.* Bombay: Majestic Book Stall, 1979.
———. *Kala Tyakalchya.* Devrukh: Gloria, 1990.
Kulkarni, G. M., and Vidyadhar Pundalik. *Dalit Sahitya: Ek Samajik Sanskritik Abhyas.* Pune: Sugava Prakashan, 1992.
Kulkarni, Roopa. *Bauddha Pandit Acharya Ashwaghoshkrut Vajrasuchi.* Translated by Roopa Kulkarni. Bombay: Lokvangmaya Griha, 1992.
Kumbhojkar, Lalita, ed. *Dalit Kavita: Ek Darshan.* Pune: Pratima Prakashan, 1984.
Kusare-Kulkarni, Arati. *Dalit Swakathane: Sahityaroop.* Nagpur: Vijay Prakashan, 1991.
Lanjewar, Jyoti. *Disha.* Nagpur: Nikhil Prakashan, 1982.
———. *Dalit Sahitya Samiksha.* Pune: Sugava Prakashan, 1992.
Limbale, Sharankumar. *Utpaat.* Ahmedpur: Parivartan, 1982.
———. *Akkarmashi.* Pune: Shree Vidya Prakashan, 1984.
———. *Baramashi.* Pune: Shree Vidya Prakashan, 1988.
Mane, Lakshman. *Upara.* Bombay: Granthali, 1980.
———. *Bund Darvaja.* Bombay: Granthali Prakashan, 1984.
Manohar, Yeshwant. *Utthangumpha.* 2d ed. Pune: Continental Prakashan, 1980.
Meshram, Bhujang. *Ulgulan.* Kalyan: Tathagat, 1990.
Meshram, Keshav. *Hakikat Ani Jatayu,* 1972.
———. *Chayaban,* 1973.

———. *Utkhanan.* 1st ed. Bombay: Popular Prakashan, 1977.
———. *Pokharan.* 1st ed. Bombay: Popular Prakashan, 1979a.
———. *Samanvay.* Bombay: Parchure Prakashan Mandir, 1979b.
———. *Kharvad.* 1st ed. Aurangabad: Dhara Prakashan, 1980a.
———. *Sabdangan.* Bombay: Dinapushapa Prakashan, 1980b.
———. *Patraval.* 1st ed. Bombay: Dinapushpa Prakashana, 1981a.
———. *Rutleli Manse.* Bombay: Dinapushpa Prakashana, 1981?
———. *Jugalbandi.* 1st ed. Aurangabad: Parimal Prakashan, 1982.
———. *Akasmat.* Pune: Suresh Agency, 1984.
———. *Bahumukhi.* 1st ed. Kolhapur: Prakara Prakashan, 1984.
———. *Gal Ani Abhal.* Pune: Suresh Agency, 1987.
———. *Maranmal.* 1st ed. Pune: Suresh Agency, 1988.
———. *Vidrohi Kavita.* 1st ed. Pune: Continental Prakashan, 1978.
———. *Vidrohi Kavita.* 2d ed. Pune: Continental Prakashan, 1987.
Meshram, Yogendra. *Jaganyacha Prashna.* 1st ed. Kolhapur: Prachara Prakashan, 1989.
More, Dadasaheb Malhari. *Gabal.* Pune: Shree Vidya Prakashan, 1983.
More, Damodar. *Namantar Kavita.* Panchasheel Prakashan, 1991.
Mun, Vasant. *Bauddhakalin Strijivan.* Pune: Sugava Prakashan, 1989.
Murugkar, Lata. *Dalit Panther Movement in Maharashtra: A Sociological Appraisal.* Bombay: Popular Prakashan, 1991.
Nimbalkar, Vaman. *Gavkusabaheril Kavita.* 2d ed. Nagpur: Prabodhan Prakashan, 1979.
———. *Mahayuddha.* Nagpur: Prabodhan Prakashan, 1987.
Pantavane, Gangadhar. *Mulyavedha,* 1974.
———. *Mukanayak,* 1976a.
———. *Vidrohache Pani Petale Ahe,* 1976b.
———. *Patrakar Dr. Ambedkar.* 1st ed. Nagpur: Abhijit Prakashan, 1987.
Pantawane, Gangadhar, and Chandrakar Nalge, eds. *Dalit Katha.* Kolhapur: Ajab Pustakalaya, 1981.
———. *Lokarang.* 1st ed. Pune: Suresh Agency, 1987.
Patil, Ramesh. *Nikharyatil Phule.* Nagpur: Sanghamitra Prakashan, 1988.
Pavade, Kumud. *Antahsphot.* Aurangabad: Anand Prakashan, 1981.
Pawar, Daya. *Kondvada.* Pune: Magova Prakashan, 1974.
———. *Baluta.* 1st ed. Bombay: Granthali, 1978.
———. *Chavadi.* Bombay: Dinapushpa Prakashan, 1983a.
———. *Vital.* Pune: Mehta, 1983b.
———. *Balut: Ek Vadal.* Bombay: Rohan Prakashan, 1987.
———. *Dhammapad.* Pune: Deshmukh Ani, 1991.
———, ed. *Kallapa Yeshvant Dhale Hyanchi Durmil Diary.* Bombay: Maharashtra Rajya Sahitya Sanskriti Mandal, 1985.
Pawar, Urmila. *Sahav Bot.* Bombay: Sambodhi Prakashan, 1988.
———. *Chauthi Bhint.* Bombay: Sambodhi Prakashan, 1990.
Phadake, Bhalchandra. *Dalit Sahityachi Prakashyatra.* Aurangabad: Anand Prakashan, 1980.
———, ed. *Dalit Rangabhumi: Ekankikancha Sangraha.* 1st ed. Pune: Suresh Agency, 1982.
Polke, Partha. *Abharan.* Bombay: Granthali Prakashan, 1984.
Rangarao, B. *Andharachya Kavita.* Amaravati: Abhijit Prakashan, 1986.
———. *Vedana-Samvedana:* Praas, 1992.

Sapakale, Tryambak. *Surung.* Aurangabad: Asmitadarsha Prakashan, 1976.
Sarvagod, Mukta. *Mitleli Kavade.* Amalner: Chetshree Prakashan, 1982.
Sathe, Annabhau. *Pharari.* Kolhapur: Chandrakant Sethye Prakashan Mandir, 1962.
———. *Mangala.* Kolhapur: Chandrakant Sethye Prakashan Mandir, 1963.
———. *Mayura.* Bombay: Raja, 1968.
———. *Agnidivya.* Pune: Vidyarthi Prakashan, 1969.
———. *Murti,* 1970.
———. *Varanecha Vagha.* 2d ed. Bombay: Majestic Book Stall, 1971.
———. *Barbadha Kanjari,* 1972.
———. *Phakira.* 7th ed. Pune: Navamaharashtra Prakashan, 1974.
———. *Abi.* 1st ed. Bombay: Bhagvandas Hiraji Prakashan, 1979.
———. *Ladi.* 2d ed. Bombay: Bhagvandas Hiraji Prakashan, 1979.
Shinde, Bhika Shiva. *Kalokhachya Garbhat.* 1st ed. Pune: Neelkantha Prakashan, 1981.
Shinde, N. M. *Jatila Jat Vairi.* Bombay: Popular Prakashan, 1991.
Sonkamble, P. E. *Athvaninche Pakshi.* Aurangabad: Chetana Prakahsan, 1979.
Surve, Narayan, ed. *Dalit Kavyadarshan.* Bombay: New Age Printing Press, 1992.
Talware, Shriranga. *Dhulpati.* Pune: Mansamman Prakashan, 1985.
Tupe, Uttam Bandu. *Katyavarchi Pota.* Pune: Mehta Publishing House, 1981.
———. *Khai.* 1st ed. Bombay: Majestic Prakashan, 1988.
Vatkar, Namdev. *Katha Majhya Janmachi.* Bombay: Majestic Book Stall, 1983.
Waghmare, Janardan. *Hak Ani Akrosh.* Pune: Shreevidya Prakashan, 1984.
Waghmare, Yogiraj. *Udrek.* Bombay: Abhinav Prakashan, 1978.
Wankhade, M. N. *Dalitanche Vidrohi Wangmaya.* Nagpur: Prabodhan Prakashan, 1981.
Yeshwant, Loknath. *Ata Houn Jau Dya!* Chandrapur: Muktachand Prakashan, 1989.

14

Parsi Literature in English

C. VIJAYASREE

INTRODUCTION: HISTORY AND CONTEXT

The Parsis are an ethnoreligious minority in India living mostly on the west coast of the subcontinent, largely in Bombay. As their name implies, Parsis are of Persian descent. The word "Parsi" means a native of "Pars" or "Fars," an ancient Persian province now in southern Iran. They are followers of Prophet Zoroaster, and their religion was founded around 2000 B.C. The Parsi religion came to be called Zoroastrianism in the West because its prophet, Zarathushtra, was known to the ancient Greeks as Zaroster. After the Arab conquest of Iran in the seventh century, they fled their homeland and came in large numbers to India, seeking peace and freedom to practice their religion. At the time of their entry into India, their old priest is reported to have promised the then-king of Gujarat, Jadhav Rana: "We shall try to be like this insignificant amount of sugar in the milk of your human kindness" (Nanavutty 1977, 40). They did, indeed, remain true to their promise: they blended with the Indian milieu even while retaining their distinct cultural identity and contributed richly to the socioeconomic life of modern India.

According to a recent census conducted by the government of India, the Parsis constitute only 0.016 percent of the total population of India. Although the Parsis are a minuscule community in the vast Indian population, their contribution to the emergence of modern India has been remarkable. They began as agriculturalists, and soon they entered various fields of economic activity, including industry, trade, commerce, social work, and technology. In every field, they set for themselves high standards of excellence and strove to live up to them. They have never been mere survivors; they have, all along, been supreme achievers. They did, indeed, secure a place for themselves in India on the grounds of merit and talent, making their community indispensable to the country.

Business and industry have undoubtedly been the forte of Parsis, but their contribution to literature, too, has been quite considerable. Their wide exposure to the intellectual movements in and outside India, their generally perceptive response to life, and their innate adaptability to the vicissitudes of cultural change—all these enabled Parsi writers to produce a significant body of literary writing, which now forms an important component in the Indian literature in English. Parsi writing falls into two phases: the early phase or "colonialism," which includes the pre-1950 writing, written largely in imitation of the British; and the second phase, comprising works written after 1947 or, for numerical neatness, 1950, which may be termed "postcolonialism," when Parsi writing settled into an established tradition acquiring a distinct form and identity of its own.

THE EARLY PHASE: UNTIL 1950

Parsis as an immigrant community have displayed a remarkable linguistic adaptability. When they arrived in India in the seventh century, they willingly made Gujarati, one of the Indian languages, their native tongue. But most Parsis are bilingual, and they retained their links with Persian, the language of their culture and tradition. Parsis were among the first communities in India to have acquired acquaintance with European languages. In the first phase of European colonialism—the phase of commercial ventures—many Parsis became mediators to transact the business of the French, Portuguese, and British traders. Parsi association with the British and the English language goes back to the seventeenth century and is reflected in some of the Parsi family names, such as Merchant, Doctor, Batliwala, Sodawaterwala, Readymoney, and Paymaster, derived from English words.

The process of Westernization, thus, began much earlier among the Parsis than among other sections of Indian society. They were among the earliest to have opted for English education because they realized they needed English for social and occupational mobility under the new dispensation. When the British started the Elphinstone College to impart higher education to Indians, Parsis represented the largest number of pupils. A new generation of Anglophile Parsi intellectuals, English in "spirit," "manners," and "morals," emerged by the turn of the century, and the first set of Parsi writers in English belongs to this class.

Poetry

In the early phase, Parsi writers showed a preference for poetic forms. English enthusiasm for poetry was fervently imitated by young Parsi intellectuals. These writers were brought upon the English literary tradition and were immensely influenced by the British romantic and Victorian poets. They wrote sonnets, lyrics, and odes imitating the English masters of verse such as Wordsworth, Shelley, and Tennyson. Most colonial peoples and their writers went through a phase of imitation in the initial stages of their colonial experience, but Parsi attempts at assimilation into the colonizers' culture appear to be unprecedented. As a minority group, they always believed that they could survive only by being loyal to the ruling authority. In addition, they were conscious that they owed their prosperity to the British raj. Their loyalty, therefore, sprang from conviction, and their prime objective was to follow the British as closely as possible in every aspect of life, including arts and literature.

Behramji Malabari (1853–1912), who played a vital role as a journalist, editor, and social reformer for nearly three decades and rendered yeoman service to Indian society through his intellectual and thought-provoking journals, *The Indian Patriot, The Voice of India,* and *East and West,* is one of the most important literary figures of this early phase. His long verse autobiography, *The Indian Muse in English Garb* (1876), was hailed as the first book of the first Parsi poet. It is a collection of poems dealing with everyday experience of life—both joyous and sorrowful, in easy and effortless language. The poem, written in rhyming couplets, offers delightfully satiric portraits of the poet's contemporaries and contains echoes from Dryden, Pope, and Goldsmith. Satire, which was to become the mainstay of Parsi writing later, was the singular strength of Malabari's work.

Even as Parsis sought affiliation with the British, they retained their steadfast faith in their religion. A great deal of Parsi poetry in the early phase is religious. Poets often expressed their prophet's teachings or their own religious experience and sentiment in measured poetic lines. Maneckji Bejani Pithawala's *Afternoons with Ahura Mazda* (1919) is a poetic celebration of the power of the Divine; his *Links with the Past* (1933) offers an authentic interpretation of the thought and ideals of the sacred books of Parsis. D. M. Gorwalla narrates the life of the prophet in his long devotional poem *The Light of Iran or the Coming of Zarathushtra* (1935). Khabardar Ardeshir Framji's *Zarathushtra, the First Prophet of the World* (1950) consists of 101 religious sonnets that touch upon the life and teaching of the Parsi prophet Zoroaster. It is interesting to see how these poets adapt the English poetic discourses, such as a sonnet, ode, and narrative poem, to communicate the message and essence of their own religion.

Parsi poetry often turned eulogistic as the writers paid poetic tributes to their colonial masters. Parsis generally believed that the British brought welfare, prosperity and progress to India. A number of Parsi writers published occasional verses celebrating some important event or other in the colonial history. Rustom Barjorji Paymaster was, for instance, one of the most accomplished poets of this phase. His early works declare his loyalty to the British and pay handsome tributes to the rulers. *The Nazrana or India's Offerings to Her King Emperor on His Coronation* (1902) and *Sunset and Sunrise: Being Odes on the Death of Queen Victoria* (1917) are a part of his imperialist writings.

There was also a small body of nationalist poetry. While the majority of Parsis kept off the nationalist movement, some influential Parsis, such as Dadabhai Naoroji, Pherozshah Mehta, and D. E. Wacha, played an active role in the movements launched by the Indian National Congress. A few Parsi writers, inspired by the triumvirate of Parsi congressmen, wrote nationalist poems with patriotic fervor. Paymaster himself wrote *Navroziana or the Dawn of the New Era* (1917), paying a handsome tribute to Naoroji, "the Grand Old Man of Indian Politics." F. J. Karaka's *The Fight for Freedom* (1940) celebrates the sacrifices rendered by freedom fighters. Since the Parsi involvement in the nationalist movement itself was marginal, nationalism did not have much impact on Parsi writing.

A large number of Parsi poets of this period drew their inspiration from the British romantic poets, mainly Wordsworth, Shelley, and Keats, and produced imitative verse of short-lived eminence. The thematic scope of Parsi romantic poetry included a wide range of human emotions, such as love and fulfillment, loss and loneliness, friendship and fellow feeling. While lyric was the most popular form, traditional metrical structures, such as ode and sonnet, were also used with deftness and felicity. However, the imagery and symbolism largely remained borrowed, and the verse lacked originality and authenticity. Fredoon Kabraji's *A Minor Georgian's Swan Song; Fifty One Poems* (1944); Homi Cowasji Dotiwalla's *My Ramblings on the Sacred Parnassus* (1939); Peshoton Sarobji Goolbai Dubash's *Romance of Souls: A Philosophic Romance in Verse* (1918) and *Spiritual and Other Poems* (1930); and Jehangir R. P. Mody's *Golden Harvest* (1932), *Golden Gleanings* (1933), and *Verses Grave and Gay* (1933) are some of the works belonging to this trend.

Drama and Theater

The Parsi contribution to the development of drama and theater in preindependence times is worth recording. As early as 1850, Elphinstone College, Bombay, had its Parsi Dramatic society for the performance of English plays. At this stage, no Indian had yet ventured into writing plays in English; this early theater staged several successful performances of Shakespeare's plays. Sometimes, the dramatists parodied Shakespeare's works, and such performances drew large audiences. Parsis were responsible for starting professional Gujarati theater as well. Around 1867–68, Victoria Natak Mandal began under the guidance of K. N. Kabraji. Plays dealing with Gujarati life and manners, as well as contemporary social and political issues, were performed. Fardoon Marzban and Jehangir Marzban were among the earliest to have given a boost to Parsi drama. Jehangir Marzban presented vignettes of Bombay life in his humorous plays and won the title "the Mark Twain of Parsis" for his satiric portrait of men and manners. In terms of technique, the Parsi theater blended Western theatrical traditions and local forms of dramatic representation for popular entertainment. It evolved no new forms but adapted the borrowed techniques for an effective dramatization of contemporary life.

While drama as performance was quite active, drama as literary form was almost nonexistent during this period. Historical accounts show that C. S. Nazir's *The First Parsi Baronet,* a verse play in English, appeared in 1866. But this obviously remained an isolated effort and did not develop into a trend or tradition. Barring some adaptations of classical plays, such as K. H. Dastur's *The Tragedy of Nero* (1905), Jehangir Mody's *Hector, Prince of Troy* (1932) and a lone social play, Meherjee Peroze's *Dolly Parsen* (1918), there were no published plays during this period.

Fiction

There was very little Parsi fiction in the preindependence times. Kaikhusrau Edalji Ghamat's *My Friend, the Barrister* (1908) is a hilarious account of a Parsi's going to England to study law. Ardeshir F. J. Chinoy and Dinbai A. J. Chinoy published a novel, *Pootli, A Story of Life in Bombay* (1915), about Parsi life at the turn of the century. It is a simple and straightforward chronicle of Parsi life. D. M. Gorwalla's *Saarda the Tale of a Rajput Maid* (1931) is a historical romance. D. F. Karaka is the most important novelist of this phase since he attempted serious political novels, running the risk of raising controversial issues at a politically sensitive time. A brilliant journalist and reputed biographer, Karaka published three novels between 1940 and 1944. *Just Flesh* (1940) deals with the English life in the early decades of the twentieth century. It presents ideological conflicts between two generations of Englishmen through the clash between a conservative father and his socialist son. *There Lay the City* (1942), set in Bombay, fictionalizes the impact of World War II on the lives of the city dwellers. *We Never Die* (1944) is a political novel focusing on the struggle for independence in a small north Indian village. Karaka's anxiety to make ideological statements mars the artistic quality of his work. Yet, his work is significant, as it marks the end of imitation and the beginning of self-assertion. However slight the Parsi writing in the early phase may be, it reveals two of the distinctive characteristics that are to form the Parsi literary sensibility in the later phases—social reform and satire.

THE SECOND PHASE: 1950–90

The end of British rule in India in 1947 brought great changes for Parsis, threatening the community's unity and kinship ties. Throughout the nationalist struggle, most Parsis largely maintained an attitude of aloofness, not only because they enjoyed a special status in the British government but also because they felt estranged from the ideology of Indian nationalism, which entailed a revival of cultural heritage of India, in general, and Hinduism, in particular. Parsis could not identify themselves with the process of formation of a new Indian historical consciousness, as they lacked a corresponding access and attachment to Indian history. Indian independence, hence, created a sense of insecurity, a crisis of identity, and a strong need for self-definition among Parsis.

The root of the identity crisis of Parsis lies in the consciousness of most of the Parsis of being, first of all, Parsis and only secondly Indian/Iranian citizens. Belonging to the Parsi community was not, however, in view of political social structures, dependencies, and relationships, adequate for them to form an autonomous identity. Parsis had to orient and reorient themselves to different systems and authorities—the Hindu kings of Gujarat, the Moghul rule, the British government, and the new India after independence—due to historical exigencies. The orientation of Parsis to various reference systems led to various identities, which sometimes endangered the community's unity. Indian independence, for instance, indirectly effected further fragmentation of Parsi community. The partition of India resulted in a violent division of the minority community into two nations; the departure of the British left them in a state of stasis until they regained their will to survive and seek realignments; a large number of Parsis who felt they had no future in independent India migrated to the U.K., the United States, and Canada in search of a better break. With all these rapid changes and further dispersal, Parsis in India felt their identity menaced. Postcolonial Parsi writing, hence, addresses the problems of identity and belonging and attempts redefinitions of self and society.

Poetry

The modernism of Joyce and Pound provided the suitable aesthetic for the poetic expression of postcolonial disillusionment of the Parsi poets. All the major poets of this phase—K. N. Daruwalla, Adil Jussawalla, Kersey Katrak, and Gieve Patel (popularly known as the Parsi Quartet)—began writing in the modernist mode, but, in the course of their writings, what may be called "Parsi modernism" takes shape. The first major characteristic of these modernists was setting out on a search for new values in the face of changing social and political structures. The years that followed independence were not those of fulfillment of promise. Independence did not usher in an era of the expected prosperity. The postindependence political chaos, the holocaust of world wars, the bloodbaths that followed the partition, widespread corruption, scarcity of essential commodities, unemployment, and poverty, along with a general moral and ethical decline, created a feeling of futility and frustration among people. Parsis, as a progressive minority, felt disillusioned by the decline in the general standard of living. The writers, hence, urge social change and reform.

Another significant feature all the Parsi writers seem to share is the need for self-definition. They often try to reexamine their own ethnic identity and analyze their own cultural situation: what it means to be a Parsi. Third, the poets turned to secular themes. They turned away from religion and sought meaning and order in everyday existence. They moved away from the idealism and romanticism of their predecessors. They were no longer lured by the "sacred Parnassus," "spring blossoms," and "spiritual romances;" instead, they described the dirt, squalor, and poverty of their environs in an unsentimental tone. Finally, poets employed irony and satire as their modes of representation, since these provided them with the advantages of a binocular vision.

Keki N. Daruwalla is the most prolific and accomplished of the Parsi poets of this phase. His work is particularly significant since it steers clear of religious and sectarian conflicts seeking anchorage in the land and landscape. Talking of his religious background, he is reported to have said, "I am neither a good Parsi—hardly ever having lived like one, nor a Hindu or Muslim." . . . A bit of everything which really means nothing" (Nabar 1977, 1). He does not melancholically brood over this aspect of his experience but roots himself deeply in the sociopolitical ethos in which he grew up. He is deeply involved with the predicament of his country and people, and, to him, poetry, above everything else, becomes "a social gesture."

Social satire, demystification of myth, and realistic rendering of contemporary sociopolitical situations are the significant features of his poetry. He elaborates the contradictions, paradoxes, ironies, hypocrisy, violence, and corruption that pervade contemporary India. He exposes and lashes with his satiric whip all sections of Indian society—academicians, bureaucrats, politicians, poets, priests, pseudo-Gandhians, police officers, and the masses. In *Under Orion* (1970), his first collection of poems, the dominant mood is anger, and these verses cover a wide range of subjects, including curfew, riots, crime, corruption, death, disease, and poverty. Being a police officer by profession, he was exposed to life in the raw, and he turns this experience into evocative poetic images. Satire is the strong point of his second collection, *Apparition in April* (1971). He retells the familiar legends of Karna and Carvak and resurrects the heroes of history, Martin Luther King and Gandhi, and dispels the aura that surrounds these legendary figures by positing them in the present, which has no respect for any values. Daruwalla's characteristic humor can best be seen in the poem addressed to Gandhi. He shows how Gandhism has become a much-bandied-about, little understood concept in contemporary Indian sociopolitical life. Gandhi is remembered once a year, says Daruwalla, on the Gandhi Jayanthi day as butchers shut up shop, and people go without mutton. In *Crossing of Rivers* (1976), a more serious and much better organized collection of poems, he projects the intriguing paradoxes with which the holy city of Varanasi bristles. There are filth and poverty here; there are also faith and devotion. Varanasi becomes the microcosm of India. *Winter Poems* (1980), as the title suggests, is a rather sad account of people's predicament as they are faced with the violence of hostile nature; greed and avarice of power mongers; the erosion of social and religious values; and the indifference of God.

In his more recent work, Daruwalla moves out of the modernist skepticism and frustration. He begins to feel that existence extends beyond the immediate phenomenal reality and that poetry in the last 10 years has become increasingly spiritual. He now turns to religion to seek meaning in the present. *The Keeper of the Dead* (1982), which won the poet the Sahitya Akademi Award for 1985, deals with the themes of love, desire, and death. The poet probes the mystery of death, deriving insights from Parsi eschatology and the Islamic view of life. Daruwalla has always been labeled "a landscape poet," and he calls his sixth collection by the same title, *Landscape* (1987). These poems are rooted in landscape both outer and inner and offer graphic verbal images. "The Round of the Seasons" in this collection is a powerful poetic evocation of Indian seasons: Vasantha, Grishma, Varsha, Sharad, Hemanth, and Sisir. To Daruwalla, the place is real, and the only identity one can find is with the soil where one is born.

In sharp contrast, Adil Jussawalla shows a persistent preoccupation with the theme of exile and alienation. In his own words, his writing is about the effect of living in lands he can neither leave nor love nor properly belong to (1973, 89–90). *Lands End; Poems* (1962), his first collection of poems, lacks a unifying focus and reads like a collection of disconnected musings, covering a wide range of themes, such as time, nature, love, man–woman relationship, autobiographical reminiscences, and contemporary social context. These early poems of Jussawalla show the influence of British poets like Donne and Eliot. His better work is contained in the second anthology, *The Missing Person* (1976). "The missing person" in this anthology largely appears to be the alter ego of the poet himself and typifies a middle-class intellectual educated abroad trying to relocate himself in his own, but no longer familiar, social milieu. In "The Exile's Story," Jussawalla tells the tale of a Parsi emigrant to England. When the Mahatma and his followers got what they wanted, the Parsi community was unsure about its future in independent India. The elders advised their youth "to pack" and leave; thus arrives the Parsi emigrant in England. His only urge is to prove and to succeed. Jussawalla deals with the theme of the return of an exile in poems such as "Approaching Santa Cruz Airport, Bombay," "Nine Poems on Arrival," and "Immigrant Song." Much of his writing revolves around the psychic fragmentation experienced by an exile or émigré.

Gieve Patel shares common concerns with Daruwalla and locates his poetry firmly within the social matrix. But what one finds in his work is an unvarnished tale of horror, pain, torture, and death. He is a doctor by profession, and, hence, human pain and agony are a part of his everyday experience, and he voices them in a direct, unemotional, yet forceful tone. Consequently, the reader is shocked out of his or her complacency into a sudden realization of violence and pain in all their grim reality. His first two collections, *Poems* (1966) and *How Do You Withstand, Body?* (1977), deal with the suffering of humans in a dehumanizing environment. His focus is on a tormented soul caught in a tormented body. The poet observes the ugliness and violence of the world around him with a dispassionate and ironic detachment, though occasionally involvement and emotion stage a sudden return. In a more recent collection, *Mirror, Mirroring* (1991), the poet moves into the postmodernist phase, calling into question the observing self in his poetry. "Postmodernism" as it appears in Parsi writing of the last decade or so is, in essence, adopted from the West and has not taken any indigenous form or shape.

Kersy D. Katrak is different from the other three of the Parsi Quartet: he avoids the serious and somber tone and chooses the comic vein, although the subject remains the social situation. His first two anthologies, *A Journal by the Way* (1968) and *Diversions by the Wayside* (1969), contain a number of personal poems addressed to his friends Keki Daruwalla and Nissim Ezekiel, to his wife, Usha, and to his newborn child. He blends gentle satire and genial mirth in these early poems. In his later work, *Underworld* (1979) and *Purgatory: Songs from the Holy Planet* (1984), Katrak shows preference for verbal effects and indulges in a great deal of wordplay. He uses a variety of new devices ushered in by postmodernism, such as parody, pastiche, collage, and intertextuality. He parodies earlier poets like Yeats and Eliot, re-creates the rhythms of nursery rhymes, and deals with the serious in a comic tone. His poems, written in mono/disyllabic lines with the brevity of telegraphic messages employing apparently unconnected images, read like jigsaw puzzles. The poet makes fun of everything and everyone: religion, God, Godmen, academe, and poets, including himself. He erases the margins between the sacred and the profane, the serious and the comic, the public and the private, dealing with all experience in playful mirth. He neither complains about, nor sulks over, his marginality but affirms it as an alternative tradition and celebrates it. Thus, Parsi poetry in English in the last 40 years, began in a rising wave of modernism; evolved an idiom and expression suitable for an effective expression of Parsi experience of change, transition, exile, and marginality; and entered a new phase of postmodernist self-reflexivity.

Drama and Theater

Unlike poetry and fiction, Parsi drama has not registered very notable gains in the postindependence period. Srinivasa Iyengar attributes the paucity of Indian drama in English to the "fact that the natural medium of conversation" among Indians "is the mother tongue rather than English" (1962, 236). The Parsi community, however, shows an instinctive preference for, and interest in, the dramatic mode. In the postindependence period, Bombay theater groups continued to play an important role in play production, and the Parsi contribution to this has been considerable. Gieve Patel, the Parsi poet, has been an important figure in the emergence of Indian experimental drama in English. His plays deal with social issues in a witty, satiric tone. *Princes* (1970) dramatizes a feud between two Parsi families over the possession of a male child; *Savaksa* (1982) is about the marriage between a 60-year-old man, Savaksa, and 20-year-old Perin; *Mr. Berham* (1981), his most successful play, allegorizes the colonial relationship, projecting a kind of Prospero–Caliban paradigm through the relationship between Mr. Berham and Naval, a tribal boy the former adopts.

Another important Parsi playwright of this period is Dina Mehta. She chooses real-life incidents and dramatizes them effectively. *The Myth Makers* (1969) is a three-act play dealing with a sudden spurt of communal violence in the city of Bombay. Her *Brides Are Not for Burning* (published 1993) is a powerful dramatization of the devastation wrought by the dowry system in Indian society. Despite antidowry legislation, dowry continues to be in vogue, often claiming a heavy toll of human lives. Dina Mehta's play won the BBC prize for radio plays in 1979. Farrukh Dhondy wrote a number of plays, all of which were produced in London. *Mama Dragon, Romance, Romance,* and *The Bride* were some of his well-known productions. *Romance, Romance,* a play based on the Asian experience in England, dramatizes the generation conflict in the context of an immigrant population. While a father tries to have an arranged marriage for his daughter, the university-educated girl asserts her freedom of choice, and the ensuing conflict is dramatized in a comic vein. Parsi drama in English, like the Indian English drama in general, has been slight and has not been able to revitalize the Indian dramatic tradition.

Fiction

The Parsi novel in English was the last to make its appearance but made quick progress in terms of both quantity and quality. Perin Bharucha's *The Fire Worshippers* (1968) is the first significant work of fiction in the postcolonial phase. It gives a comprehensive account of Parsi life and culture. This novel is of greater historical and sociological value than literary interest. *Minari* (1967) by Nargis Dalal also appeared in the 1960s but made little impact, since it reads more like a routine film story and shows little literary merit.

The last two decades, 1970–90, have been particularly fruitful in the field of Parsi fiction. Several young Parsi writers who settled abroad published their first novels during this period, creating ripples in the Indian and the world literary scene. The fiction written by Parsis in these 20 some years has added up to form a significant portion of Indo-English fiction and has acquired the distinction of a subgenre. A large number of these novelists—Saros Cowasjee, Rohinton Mistry, Farrukh Dhondy, Firdaus Kanga, and Boman Dasai—live abroad, and this body of writing may well be described as expatriate Parsi writing. These writers have arrived on the scene after the high tide of modernism almost subsided. Most of them, living as members of minority groups in Western countries—the U.K., the United States, or Canada—experience a double colonization and often address problems of postcoloniality in their work. It is, therefore, useful to look at their work primarily as "minority literature" engaged in the evolution of a counterhegemonic discourse.

The Parsi novel in English shows all the distinctive features of "minority discourse": (1) a persistent preoccupation with the problems of identity, (2) articulation of collective consciousness, (3) political involvement, and (4) an active assertion and even celebration of marginality. At the heart of the Parsi novel is the issue of identity. The responses here range from conflicting and even shattering feelings of unbelonging and alienation to a reconciliation of differences into a multicultural ideal.

Saros Cowasjee's writing exemplifies the first trend. His two novels *Goodbye to Elsa* (1974) and *Suffer Little Children* (1982) present the confessional autobiography of Tristan Elliott, an Anglo Indian settled in Britain. In the predicament of Elliott, Cowasjee portrays the sense of loss and rootlessness experienced by a minority community. *Goodbye to Elsa* narrates a series of sexual misadventures Elliott goes through in his search for love and companionship. He ends up in an asylum at the end of the novel. *Suffer Little Children* is more in the form of a farce and deals with Elliott's involvement in the feminist movement and his foiled efforts to find a female companion. These half-serious, half-comic tales of expatriate living unmistakably project the exile's pathetic urge for recognition and acceptance. Cowasjee's short stories in the two volumes *Stories and Sketches* (1970) and *Nude Therapy and Other Stories* (1978) also generally deal with the predicament of exile, but some stories in the second collection set in India of the 1940s and 1950s such as "My Father's Medals," focus on the sociopolitical situation of India of the times. While Cowasjee's handling of the theme of exile, in spite of its witty presentation, conjures up a predominantly pathetic view of emigrant life, Rohinton Mistry's short stories deal with the same theme in a genuinely comic tone. "Squatter" and "Swimming Lessons," both included in *Tales of Ferozshah Baag* (1987) and set in Canada, relate the tribulations of two immigrants—Sarosh (Sid) and Kersi, respectively. While Sarosh, who strives to become completely Canadian, abandons his obsession and returns to India, Kersi makes peace with his new home. In either case, Mistry rules out the need for pessimism.

Much of Parsi fiction, however, treats exile as a mere phase and seeks to root itself in the ethnic locale of the Parsi community. The writers, despite being expatriates, locate their work in Indian-Parsi life, more specifically in Bombay, which has always been the epicenter of Parsi culture. They write with a deep sense of admiration for their community, an intimate knowledge of its virtues and weaknesses, a warm affection for its eccentricities, and a loving consideration for the preservation of its cultural identity. They do not try to romanticize or apotheosize their community. Their preoccupation is with the commonplace emotions, habits, and rituals that define quotidian community life. The Parsi community in all its diversity comes alive in these works.

Bapsy Sidhwa's *The Crow Eaters* (1978) deals with the fluctuating fortunes of Junglewallas, a Parsi family under the raj, in the early twentieth century. Fredoon Junglewalla, Freddy for short, who starts from nothing, gradually rises to the level of being listed in "the Zarathusiti Calender of Great Men and Women." This meteoric rise, as Sidhwa ironically observes, is made possible by sycophancy, allegiance to the British, and Anglicization. Freddy, like several others of his community, views the nationalist movement with suspicion. He pointedly disapproves of the movement launched by Dadabhai Naoroji, "a misguided Parsi from Bombay," and is afraid that independence might simply mean sharing of the national cake by the majority communities—Muslims and Hindus. Bapsy Sidhwa's book met with initial resistance, since her frank and forthright portrayal of Parsi life was construed as an unfair representation of the community. In Sidhwa's own words, this saga of Parsi life springs from her enormous affection for the community and is a "labour of love" (1980).

Rohinton Mistry's *Tales of Ferozsha Baag* records the vibrations of Parsi life, Ferozsha Baag's choosing a residential apartment complex in Bombay as its focus. Mistry's focus is on the psychological problems associated with marginality. Firdaus Kanga's *Trying to Grow* (1990) is built around the painful experience of a physically handicapped boy—Daryus Kotwal—in trying to grow into adulthood. The flowering of the adolescent sensibility is unraveled against the background of the close-knit family of the Kotwals. The novel is at once a bildungsroman and a family saga.

Boman Desai's *The Memory of Elephants* (1992) has all the characteristics of a family chronicle, though presented in science fiction garb. Hormus Seervai, the central character of the novel, is a young Parsi scientist doing research in an American university. He makes a memory machine or mono scan to study how memories become encoded in the brain. The problem starts when Homi uses this gadget to relive the intensity of a sexual experience he has had with his girlfriend. As Homi repeats this replay experiment, the machine malfunctions, and he slips from his personal memory into the collective consciousness. Homi collapses into a coma physically, while his consciousness becomes a voyeur to the history of his family and race as well; and a marvelous panorama of Parsi life unfolds.

Farrukh Dhondy's work steers clear of the pangs of alienation and lacks the ethnic identity of typical Parsi writing. A new agenda of multiculturalism emerges clearly from his writing. As a writer working in the multiracial British society, Dhondy sees his own role as a catalyst in bringing about the assimilation of, and understanding between, varied and culturally divergent groups and traditions. Most of his short stories deal with multiethnic situations and view multiculturalism as the reality of our times. This major thrust of his work is most forcefully expressed in his novel *The Bombay Duck* (1990). Here the two central characters—Gerald Blossom and Xerxes Xavaxa (for short, Mr. XX)—are shown to be engaged in a struggle for survival. They resort to various means, including changing of names, religion, and identity in their quest for lucrative jobs. They try their hand at different trades ranging from playacting to baby trading, and their struggle is portrayed against multicultural settings, including India, Britain, and America. Dhondy attacks religious fundamentalism and parochialism and portrays the multiethnic reality of our times in all its complexity.

As in Parsi poetry, the sociopolitical issues figure prominently in fictional writing as well. Parsi novels turn explicitly political, picking on specific political events for elaborate treatment and analysis. This political nature of Parsi fiction is significant in view of the earlier evasion of political issues. This may be viewed as the writers' emancipation from the impact of colonization, which compelled them to remain outside the political and policy-making processes. Parsis show an accuracy in documentation and a deep involvement with the sociopolitical situation. The major political events of the last 50 years, including the partition, the emergency, Indo-Pakistan and Indochina Wars, and the Bangladesh war, find representation in Parsi accounts of contemporary life. Bapsy Sidhwa's *The Bride* (1983) unfolds the travails faced by a young girl, Zaitoon, married into the tribal community of Kohistan, as she tries to break the fetters and escape back into freedom. Zaitoon is portrayed as a child of partition, since all her woes begin in her being orphaned at the age of four on account of the communal violence that broke out following the partition. Sidhwa's next novel, *Ice-Candy Man* (1988), is yet another powerful account of partition. The novelist traces the impact of this important political event on human destinies.

Rohinton Mistry's *Such a Long Journey* (1991) re-creates the sociopolitical situation of the 1970s in India. It is the story of Gustad Noble, a little man who puts up a brave fight against a largely hostile society as he gets entangled in a series of complications and finds himself implicated in several crimes during the Bangladesh War of the 1970s. Mistry combines fact with fiction, the real with the imaginary, and tells a compelling tale of a common man's struggle to retain dignity in the face of crises. Gustap Irani's *Once upon a Raj* (1992) is a hilarious farce dealing with the conflicts between an Indian princely state and the British government. Dina Mehta's *And Some Take a Lover Too* (1993), set against the backdrop of the Quit India movement, authentically records the responses of a Parsi girl, Roshni Wadia, to Gandhism and the Indian national movement. Roshni has all the admiration for Gandhi and his way of life, but she feels like an outsider in the Gandhian scheme of things. Her response typifies the ambivalent attitude of Parsis to the Gandhian movement.

All these writers are engaged in an active exploration of marginality. Their protagonists are propelled by a desire to identify themselves by achieving some kind of centrality but they are often betrayed and remarginalized. The struggle will continue until they learn to celebrate their own marginality and define themselves through it. However, their struggle against the hegemonic systems is, in itself, a declaration of their autonomy and their refusal to be controlled by, or co-opted into, the dominant culture and is, in a way, a celebration of their own marginality.

The greatest strength of Parsi fiction lies in its successful evocation of the comic. It is fair to say that an important part of Parsi literary imagination is critical, ironic, and mockingly humorous. Parsis as a mature community have learned to laugh at themselves. All the Parsi novelists portray the oddities and eccentricities of their community more with a sense of indulgent affection than with one of chastisement. Whatever the theme they elaborate, whatever the general mood they portray, the comedy of life always breaks through, energizing their narratives and placing their works in a larger human perspective. They choose the satiric mode and view the world around them from an ironic point of view. Their satire is devoid of bitterness or didacticism. It is, in fact, accompanied by a bemused indulgence and an affectionate tolerance. The writers seem to hold that incongruity is a part of existence and is more a reason for a comic, rather than a tragic, response.

Parsi novelists, having been educated in the West and exposed to the modernist and postmodernist movements in fictional writing, show a preference for experimental constructs. They create counterdiscourses in reorienting the Western discursive strategies to the narrative needs of their own peculiar postcolonialist and marginal experiences. Saros Cowasjee's work uses confession and autobiography as the basic mode, shares the features of the "campus novel," and unmistakably belongs to the tradition of black humor writing. Firdaus Kanga's *Trying to Grow* is a commendable achievement in autobiographical fiction. Bapsy Sidhwa's *Ice-Candy Man* is historiography in the postmodernist sense. Boman Desai's achievement lies in adapting the science fiction mode to suit the requirements of a family saga. In some of his tales, Rohinton Mistry employs a writer-narrator and uses the self-reflexive techniques of metafictional narration. On the whole, all these writers show an intimate knowledge of the life they portray and a firm control over fictional form. Their work is a significant contribution to the emergence of the new Indo-English novel.

CONCLUSION

Parsi writing in English, thus, has come a long way, moving from initial imitation to innovation, from diffidence to self-confidence, from dependence to autonomy. Parsi poets and novelists in the postcolonial period continue to draw their forms from the West, but they successfully adapted, reoriented, and sometimes subverted these borrowed structures and developed counterdiscourses to dismantle the hegemonic assumptions contained in the canonical forms. They are alert to the political implications of all contemporary sociocultural developments and respond sensitively to all forms of domination, however subtle they may be. They made a significant contribution not only to postcolonial Indian writing in English but also to the tradition of minority writing.

WORKS CITED

Iyengar, K. R. Srinivasa. *Indian Writing in English.* 1962. New Delhi: Sterling Publishers, 1985.

Jussawalla, Adil. "The New Poetry." In *Readings in Commonwealth Literature,* edited by William Walsh. Oxford: Clarendon Press, 1973.

Nabar, Vrinda. "Keki N. Daruwalla: Poetry and a National Culture." In *Indian Poetry in English: Essays in Criticism,* edited by Vasant Shahane and M. Sivaramakrishna. Hyderabad: Osmania University Press, 1977.

Nanavutty, Piloo. *The Parsis.* New Delhi: National Book Trust, 1977.

Sidhwa, Bapsy. "Preface." In *The Crow Eaters.* New Delhi: Sangam Books, 1980.

SELECTED PRIMARY BIBLIOGRAPHY

Bharucha, Perin. *The Fire Worshippers.* Bombay: Strand Book Club, 1968.

Chinoy F. J. Arderhir, and A. T. Dinbai Chinoy. *Pootli: A Story of Life in Bombay.* London: T. Werner Laurie, 1915.

Cowasjee, Saros. *Stories and Sketches.* Calcutta: Writers Workshop, 1970.

———. *Goodbye to Elsa.* London: Bodley Head, 1974.

———. *Nude Therapy and Other Stories.* New Delhi: Orient Paperbacks, 1978.

———. *Suffer Little Children.* New Delhi: Allied, 1982.

Dalal, Nargis. *Minari.* Bombay: Pearl, 1967.

Daruwalla Keki. N. *Under Orion.* Calcutta: Writers Workshop, 1970.

———. *Apparition in April.* Calcutta: Writers Workshop, 1971.

———. *Crossing of Rivers.* New Delhi: Oxford, 1976.

———. *Winter Poems.* Delhi: Allied, 1980.

———. *The Keeper of the Dead.* Delhi: Oxford University Press, 1987a.

———. *Landscape.* Delhi: Oxford University Press, 1987b.

Dastoor, K. H. *The Tragedy of Nero.* London, 1905.

Desai, Boman. *The Memory of Elephants.* New Delhi: Penguin, 1992.

Dhondy, Farrukh. *Romance, Romance and the Bride.* London: Faber, 1985.

———. *Bombay Duck.* London: Cape, 1990.

Dotiwalla, Homi Cowasji. *My Ramblings on the Sacred Parnassus.* Bombay: Author, 1939.

Dubash, Peshoton Sarobji Goolbai. *Romance of Souls: A Philosophic Romance in Verse.* London: Luzac, 1918.

———. *Spiritual and Other Poems.* Karachi: Nusserwanji, 1930.

Ghamat Kaikhusrau, Edalji. *My Friend, the Barrister.* Bombay: n.p., 1908.

Gorwalla, D. M. Saarada. *The Tale of a Rajput Maid.* Bombay: n.p., 1931.

———. *The Light of Iran or the Coming of Zarathustra: A Narrative Poem.* Bombay: n.p., 1935.

Irani, Gustap. *Once upon a Raj.* Bombay: Orient Longman, 1992.

Jussawalla, Adil. *Lands End; Poems.* Calcutta: Writers Workshop, 1962.

———. *The Missing Person.* Bombay: Clearing House, 1976.

Kabraji, Fredoon. *A Minor Georgian's Swan Song: Fifty One Poems.* London: Fortune Press, 1944.

Kanga, Firdaus. *Trying to Grow.* Delhi: Ravi Dayal, 1990.

Karaka, D. F. *Just Flesh.* Bombay: Thacker, 1941.

———. *There Lay the City.* Bombay: Thacker, 1942.

———. *We Never Die.* Bombay: Thacker, 1944.

Karaka, F. J. *The Fight for Freedom.* Bombay: Thacker, 1940.

Katrak, Kersey. *A Journal by the Way.* Calcutta: Writers Workshop, 1968.

———. *Diversions by the Wayside.* Calcutta: Writers Workshop, 1969.

———. *Underworld.* Calcutta: Writers Workshop, 1979.

———. *Purgatory: Songs from the Holy Planet.* New Delhi: Arnold Heinemann, 1984.

Khabardoor Ardeshir, Framji. *Zarathustra, The First Prophet of the World; 101 Sonnets.* Bombay: Author, 1950.

Malabari, Merwanji Behramji. *The Indian Muse in English Garb.* Bombay: Merwanji Novroji Daboo, 1876.

Meherjee, Peroze. *Dolly Parsen.* Bombay: Daftur Akshar Press, 1918.
Mehta, Dina. *The Myth Makers.* Delhi: ENACT 35, 1969.
———. *And Some Take a Lover Too.* Bombay: Rupa, 1992.
———. *Brides Are Not for Burning.* New Delhi: Rupa Books, 1993.
Mistry, Rohinton. *Tales of Ferozshah Baag.* Canada: Penguin Books, 1987.
———. *Such a Long Journey.* London: Faber and Faber, 1991.
Mody Jehangir, R. P. *Golden Harvest.* Bombay: n.p., 1932a.
———. *Hector, Prince of Troy.* Bombay: Author, 1932b.
———. *Golden Gleanings.* Bombay: Author, 1933.
———. *Verses Grave and Gay.* Bombay: n.p., 1938.
Patel, Gieve. *Poems.* Bombay: Nissim Ezekiel, 1966.
———. *How Do You Withstand Body?* Bombay: Clearing House, 1976.
———. *Mirror, Mirroring.* Madras: Oxford University Press, 1991.
Paymaster, Rustom Barjorji. *The Nazrana or India's Offerings to Her King-Emperor on His Coronation.* Bombay: D. B. Taraporevala Sons, 1902.
———. *Sunset and Sunrise: Being Odes on the Death of Queen Victoria and the Accession of King Edward VIII.* Bombay: n.p., 1902.
———. *Navroziana or the Dawn of the New Era.* Bombay: n.p., 1917.
Pithawala, Maneckji Bejanji. *Afternoons with Ahura Mazda.* Poona: n.p., 1919.
———. *Links with the Past; Poems.* London Poetry League, 1933.
Sidhwa, Bapsy. *The Crow Eaters.* New Delhi: Sangam Books, 1980.
———. *The Bride.* London: Jonathan Cape, 1983.
———. *The Ice-Candy Man.* London: Heinemann, 1988.

REFERENCES

Cowasjee, Saros. *Studies in Indian and Anglo Indian Fiction.* New Delhi: Indus, 1993.
Doctor, Geetha. "The Parsi Quartet." *Parsiana* (April–May 1974): 14–22.
Iyengar, K. R. Srinivasa. *Indian Writing in English.* New Delhi: Sterling, 1962; rev. ed., 1985.
Karaka, Dosabhai Framji. *History of the Parsis.* 2 vols. Delhi: Discovery Publisher House, rep. 1986.
King, Bruce. *Modern Indian English Poetry.* Delhi: Oxford University Press, 1987.
Kulke, Eckehard. *The Parsees in India: A Minority as Agent of Social Change.* Delhi: Bell Books, 1978.
Naik, M. K. *A History of Indian English Literature.* New Delhi: Sahitya Akademi, 1982.
Nanavutty, Piloo. *The Parsis.* New Delhi: National Book Trust, 1977.
Nelson, S. Emmanuel. *Writers of the Indian Diaspora.* London: Greenwood Press, 1993.
Paranjape, Makarand. "The Novels of Bapsy Sidhwa." In *Commonwealth Fiction,* edited by R. K. Dhawan. New Delhi: Classical, 80–103.
Pathak, R. S., ed. *Recent Indian Fiction.* New Delhi: Prestige Books, 1994.
Shahane, Vasant, and M. Sivaramkrishna, eds. *Indian Poetry in English.* Delhi: Macmillan, 1980.

15

Sanskrit Poetics

ARASU BALAN

The origin of Sanskrit literary and critical traditions in India is as old as the history of Western literature. In spite of an increasing volume of writing on the Sanskrit literary heritage and the intersections between Sanskrit and Western aesthetic ideas, erroneous assumptions about the concerns and values of Sanskrit poetics persisted even among the committed Orientalists. For instance, Indians, according to Max Muller, "cared so little for history; no wonder that social and political virtues were little cultivated, and the ideas of the Useful and the Beautiful scarcely known to them" (Muller 1978, 18). William Knight, too, feels that "there is scarcely a trace of feeling for the Beautiful in the Brahmanical or Buddhist writings" (17). If such an underestimated role of the sensuous is an example of the falsified ideas in Sanskrit poetics, Thomas Munro claims that the misunderstanding of Sanskrit aesthetics springs from the Western "over-reliance on deduction from metaphysical assumptions about beauty or on highly specialized linguistic analysis" (7). Apart from the difference in intellectual and aesthetic concepts in Oriental and Occidental traditions, the reason for the erroneous views on Sanskrit aesthetics would well be an absence of helpful discussions. Even an introductory analysis of classical Indian poetry, most of its early texts written in Sanskrit, is too complex and broad for this chapter, but I restrict myself to a brief outline of its major trends. My focus is on the ways in which Sanskrit aesthetics evolved, and I conclude with a brief sketch on the aesthetic principles and concerns of modern poetry and drama in India.

VEDIC AND LATER HERMENEUTICS

The four Vedas—*Rg, Sama, Yajur,* and *Adharvana*—dated anywhere from 2500 B.C. to 600 B.C., not only are the earliest Sanskrit literary texts but have also defined compositional rules and aesthetic principles of the Sanskrit literary heritage. The Vedic hymns also show the origin of self-consciousness and rational questioning in the Sanskrit literary tradition characterizing any literary criticism. In the Vedas, celebration of supernatural power is reconciled with the realization of creative instincts in people, which are equated with the divine activity itself. Thus, God becomes a poet in *Rg Veda:* "He who is the supporter of the worlds of life, He, Poet, cherishes manifold forms by his poetic power" (XIII, 41.5). Poem is as spontaneous as a stream (X, 68.1), but it is, at once, an expression of divine afflatus and a verbal construct. As one Vedic poet sings, "As an expert artisan constructs a chariot, so have I composed this hymn for thee, O Agni!" Divinity itself is no less a human construct in the poetic form: "The Beautiful Winged, though He is one, the wise poets shape, with songs, in many figures" (X, 114.5).

As Rajasekhara's *Kavyamimamsa* in the late ninth century puts it, literary criticism is the fifth Veda. The early Sanskrit critics not only differentiated between poetic language (*kavya*) and intellective language (*sastra*)—similar to the distinction the modern British critic I. A. Richards would foreground in his *Principles of Literary Criticism*—but also defined rules for poetic composition. In anatomizing poetic methods, some Sanskrit writers reduced techniques to rigid rules, whereas some others distinguished between the technical and lexical aspects of poetry. Being the oldest Sanskrit text, the *Rg Veda* drew the attention of the earliest aestheticians. Panini in the fourth century B.C. laid down rules for various forms of expressions in the Vedas and other texts, and Yaska in the fifth century B.C. came up with a definition of similes in the Vedas. Many critics have felt that early critical analysis in India went too far in its formal analysis. For example, Sushil Kumar De remarks that the early Sanskrit aestheticians were too concerned with grammatical rules at the cost of aesthetic sensibility (De 1963, 27; see also Dwivedi 1969, 178–80). If the analysis of style rigidified from Aristotle and Isocrates to the Middle Ages in the West (Wimsatt and Brooks 1957, 142–43), in India, too, the technical study of rhetorical methods in poetry sometimes led to a focus on mere systematization and inane ornamentation.

MAJOR SCHOOLS AND CONCEPTS

The earliest literary debates in Sanskrit seem to have focused on the distinctions between aesthetic and merely ornamental aspects of poetry. The Riti school thus focused on "style," a concept similar to figures of speech in English tradition. Sweetness of words, forceful or smaller compounds, and alliterations were considered to mark the style of poetry (Dwivedi 1969, 14). As Roland Barthes informs us in his *The Semiotic Challenge,* the classical Western trivium did not differentiate among grammatica, dialectica, and rhetorica. For Sanskrit poeticians, too, grammatical rules were meant for rhetorical effects. For Patanjali (second century B.C.), Bhamaha, Rudrata, and Dandin (all three lived in the eighth to ninth centuries), language consisted of word (*sabda*) and sense (*artha*) but the ornamental aspect (*alamkara*) of poetry was more than a mere combination of word and sense. Thus emerged the Alamkara school, which claimed figures to be the most essential element of poetry. As Bhamaha insisted, "even the charming face of a damsel does not shine stripped of ornament" (Mukunda Sharma 1968, 9). The rhetorical tools are embellishments (*alamkara*) and characteristics (*laksana*), the former being external like jewels on a body, and the latter being intrinsic like the beauty of the body itself. Bharata (second century) distinguished in his *Natyasastra,* the earliest Sanskrit treatise on aesthetics, about 36 marks of *laksana,* and Bhamaha cited 43 kinds of *alamkara.* Dramaturgists like Bharata were more conscious of the difference between the intrinsically poetic and the merely ornamental aspects of language, and poeticians like Bhamaha ignored such distinctions. But the term *alamkara,* in general, meant more than mere figures of speech for Sanskrit aestheticians. Comparable would be the sometime confusions between tropes (metaphor, simile, synecdoche, personification, and so on) and figures of speech (alliteration, zeugma, and so on) in Western poetics. Bhamaha himself defined *alamkara* as "that which gives sufficiency to a composition to be classed as poetry." Later on, *alamkara* expanded its meaning to include characteristics and embellishments to such an extent that the sixteenth-century writer Appayya Diksita listed some 124 kinds of *alamkara* (Dwivedi 1969, 10–11).

The clearest connection between the technical and the aesthetic principles in Sanskrit poetics emerged in the grammatical concepts of Bhartrhari (seventh century) and the interpretation of these concepts by Anandhavardhana (ninth century). In Bhartrhari's *Vakyapadiya,* the meaning of a word or sentence was the indivisible unit of grammar. Such a grammatical unity (*sphota*) was a pure and suggestive energy (Coward 1976, 31–38). Anandavardhana created a link between grammar and poetics by using Bhartrhari's idea of the suggestive power of a word for the suggestiveness of poetry itself in general. For Bhartrhari, the spoken word offered the inner meaning and took the shape of *sphota.* Anandavardhana claimed that this implicitness of a word was the very poetic principle of suggestiveness. Thus, Sanskrit poetics, which always has assumed an active response in a reader and a creative process that presupposes such a subjective response (Munro 1965, 67–74), came to identify feeling (*rasa*) and suggestiveness (*dhvani*) as the distinguishing features of poetry. Even though *rasa* and *dhvani* were closely connected, as feeling is something that can only be suggested and not directly expressed, both these poetic principles have had their own history.

Traditionally, a discussion of *rasa* begins with an experience of Valmiki, who composed the well-known epic *Ramayana* in the third century B.C. The poet is said to have been inspired to write the epic after an emotional experience in a forest when a hunter killed a male Krauncha bird that was mating with a female bird. After condemning the hunter in his agony, the poet later claimed to his pupils that his spontaneous utterance, "kim idam vyahrtam maya?" [What is this that has been uttered by me?], was nothing but poetry. Anandavardhana saw in this story the germ not only of poetry but also of criticism because the poet consciously posited that only an intense realization of an external event was the germ of poetry (Sankaran 1929, 7–8). Thus, Valmiki's emotional experience and his later rationalization of such a moment embodied an intense feeling, which defines *rasa.* In the Western aesthetics, too, poets like William Wordsworth, John Keats, Oscar Wilde, and Charles Baudelaire and critics like John Stuart Mill and Walter Pater have stressed the emotional part of a literary experience. For example, Pater in his *Renaissance* spoke of "wisdom, the poetic passion, the desire of beauty, the love of art for its own sake." But the concept of *rasa* gave a unique role to emotion and joy in Sanskrit poetics.

Bharata's *Natyasastra* used the term *rasa* in the poetic sense for the first time, but the word had an earlier history with different senses. In the *Rg Veda,* it meant the taste of a drink, the ecstatic experience of taste, and then a unique taste that gave a sense of joy (Sankaran 1929, 2–3). For Bharata, *rasa* was "a realization of one's own consciousness as colored by emotions." As the French critic Rene Daumal elaborated it, *rasa* "is neither an object, nor an emotion, nor a concept; it is an immediate experience, a gustation of life, a pure joy, which relishes its own essence as it communes with the 'other'—the actor or poet" (41). *Rasa* was an emotional disturbance, like Valmiki's at the death of the Krauncha bird, which depended on, but could not be reduced to, its experiential constituents because of its pure immediacy and intensity. It was also distinguished by the dissolution of egoistic or appetitive side of emotions. Thus, it was at once subjective and transcendental. *Rasa* in Bharata's original description and Abhinavagupta's redefinition of it were a balance among various moods such as serenity, love, joy, compassion, violence, valor, awesomeness, loathsomeness, and wonder, somewhat like I. A. Richards's definition of poetry as an organization of various impulses. It was an emotion that orchestrated other feelings for an identity with what one saw or read, but, at the same time, it was beyond ordinary modes of experience (*bhava*) felt for its own sake without subjective affectations. The poetic presentation universalized the situation for an objective experience of an emotion for its own sake beyond personal conflicts or anxiety. In its purest form, *rasa* was also identified as a merger with the Absolute. Rhetoricians with devotional orientation usurped the theory of *rasa* for the celebration of the Supreme Brahman (Dwivedi 1969, 195–200).

Rasa was an emotional impact in a literary experience that was effected through suggestiveness (*dhvani*). For poeticians like Anandavardhana, *dhvani* was a literary value in itself. The passage Mukunda Sharma quotes is a good example of the metaphoric discourse that defines *dhvani:* "The sight of heroes does not so delight in their beloveds' breasts red [*sic*] with saffron anointment as in the temples of enemies' elephants, painted deep in vermillion" (60). The trope apparently praises valor at the cost of love. But the comparison implicitly suggests that the breasts of the women are as large as the temples of the elephants. For Anandhavardhana, what suggestiveness could do would not be possible for ordinary or direct speech. The Dhvani school revitalized some hackneyed ideas in Indian poetics and focused on the authentic role of poetic language (Mukunda Sharma 1968, 59–73). Anandavardhana included the total mood of a poem under the word *dhvani* and thereby removed any perceptible distinction between *rasa* and *dhvani* (Coward 1976, 85; Dwivedi 1969, 173).

If *dhvani* in Anandhavardhana's interpretation meant both the external element of the word's suggestive power and the internal element of aesthetic impact, Abhinavagupta in the tenth century used the term to talk about *atman,* the aesthetic experience. Abhinavagupta's theory of *rasadhvani* enumerated in his *Locana* only took Anandhavardhana's reconciliation between *rasa* and *dhvani* to its logical conclusions. If *rasa* took one to the transcendental levels, *rasadhvani,* which was beyond *rasa* and *dhvani,* could also accomplish a consummate merger with the Absolute (Coward 1976, 86–87). The combination of aesthetic and religious principles, too, was the hallmark of Sanskrit devotional lyrics. Sankaracarya's *The Saundaryalahari* (Flood of Beauty) is a good example of religious poetry in which the divine is neither completely above the human nor beyond sensuous attributes.

CLASSICAL DRAMA AND DRAMATURGY

It is impossible to separate the history of Sanskrit drama from that of Sanskrit poetry. The *Vedas* themselves have some dramatic scenes, and *Natyasastra,* the text on which Sanskrit poetics to a great extent relies, is basically on dramaturgy. The divine blessing that Bharata claimed for theater in the text was a supreme celebration of any creative activity. In Bharata's explanation of the origin of drama, God announced the role of theater when the devilish forces claimed representation in it: "Neither your nature nor that of the gods is exclusively represented by the theatre, for it describes the manifestations of the triple world in its entirety. Sometimes law, sometimes play, sometimes wealth, sometimes quiet, sometimes laughter, sometimes warfare, sometimes passion, sometimes violent death." If, as we have seen, poetic principles were sometimes appropriated for religious purposes, in *Natyasastra* God outlined the purposes of drama, which seem to be for both didactic and recreational goals: "It is a receptacle of activity, for superior, inferior, and average men; it engenders useful teachings, and, from moments of tension to those of relaxation, it renders all joys" (Daumal 1982, 49).

Like the imitative theories of Western drama, which have their origin in Aristotle's *Poetics,* Bharata's elaborations define dramaturgy as imitation of actions. Dhananjaya's *Dasarupaka* (tenth century) expanded this definition to an imitation of a state or condition (*avastha*). For Bharata, a play had five stages: beginning (*arambha*), effort (*prayatna*), possibility of attainment of the object (*praptyasa*), certainty of attainment (*niyatapti*), and fruition (*phalagama*). As opposed to Aristotle's stipulation on the unity of time for the whole play, Bharata wanted only an act to be within a day. A play consisted of the primary (*adhikarika*) and subsidiary (*prasangika*) plots. Spectacle for Bharata not only meant dresses and makeup, as it is for Aristotle, but also meant gestures and involuntary states like tears and tremor. Despite the divine order at the beginning of *Natyasastra* on the comprehensive representation of human beings in drama, most of the Sanskrit plays were about characters with royal or divine or mythic origins. Thus, if we should go by the Aristotelian definitions of a comedy, which is supposed to be about inferior characters, and of a tragedy, which is about distinctive characters, most of the Sanskrit plays should be considered tragedies, because most of the protagonists in Sanskrit dramas were ideal types who inspired the viewers to emulate them (Dwivedi 1969, 18–28; Coomaraswamy 1956, 44). Critics have argued that such typical characters in Sanskrit plays dramatized a well-defined and ordered reality that always moved toward a happy end. Such a tradition has been contrasted with the Western heritage, in which plays would often foreground the separation between the self and external forces (Dimock 42–50), either because of the protagonist's weakness, as in Aristotle's views on tragedy, or because of the tragic situation, as in Northrop Frye's interpretation of tragedy in *Anatomy of Criticism.* These observations do not mean that the common and the low characters were not represented in classical Sanskrit plays at all. Dramatic types like Prakasana, Prahasana, Bhana, and Vithi depicted social life of lower order with invented plots as opposed to the typical plots in legendary and heroic plays. Other genres like novels (*akhyayika*), too, portrayed common life, but most of such works have been lost beyond recovery (Chaitanya 1975, 287, 375).[1]

MODERN POETRY AND DRAMA

The new intellectual atmosphere that prevailed during the British rule in India brought with it an aesthetic thrust in journalistic activities (Dwivedi's *Sarasvati* is the best-known literary journal) and a political awareness in the literary world that worked as powerful forces in gaining political independence in 1947. Without weakening its basis in the traditional principles of Sanskrit aesthetics, literatures of modern India have taken different shapes and explored new possibilities. Poets in Hindhi, Bengali, and other regional languages have manipulated the classical models of religious (*bakhti*) and romantic poetry with a new temper. The mingling of sensuous and religious values and the celebration of different *rasas* continue to dominate poetry written in various languages of the country. In modern times, the classical poetics, on one hand, has defined regional prose and poetry in India, and, on the other, it has been adapted, expanded, and even radically reformulated for various aesthetic, social, and political agendas in contemporary literatures. Exposure to Western modes of thinking, too, has changed social and individual values, often creating a fine combination of Oriental and Occidental possibilities. The changing social hierarchies, too, have shifted the ideological undercurrents of the discursive practices. Adil Jussawalla's remark that modern writing "reflects the Indian petty bourgeoisie's present inability to find a dynamic role for itself in a society which is slowly transforming itself from the semifeudal to the capitalist'' (Jussawalla 1974, 34) only foregrounds the complexities that have emerged from such a problematic social situation.

The ideas of Rabindranath Tagore (1861–1941), the poet, novelist, and dramatist, at once recapitulate and reformulate some of the fundamental concepts of Sanskrit poetics. For example, his claim that the emotional energy that is not exhausted by the question of self-preservation finds its outlet in art (1945, 11) would remind one of the focus on the superabundance of emotions in *rasa* and a celebration of spiritual life in Sanskrit poetry. But the sense of alienation spurred by an acute awareness of the evils of existence, ''when thrones have lost their dignity and prophets have become an anachronism, when the sound that drowns all voices is the noise of the marketplace,'' brings to Tagore's poetry a modern temper that is not exactly congenial to Sanskrit poetry and an idealist resilience that is typically identified as Indian. Tagore has also projected unique characters in his plays who deviate from the traditional types and insisted on the problematic nature of language and life in his prose writings. As he expresses it in *Reminiscences,* clarity is not the important function of language, and an understanding of a consciousness is difficult (72). Sri Aurobindo (1872–1950), too, has been an influential literary figure, whose *The Future Poetry* encompasses most of his ideas on poetry and spiritual life. Poetry, for Aurobindo, is an expression of the highest level of self-realization. Poetic intensity springs from spiritual vision behind words (1953, 22). The spiritual significance of poetry does not mean a separation of aesthetics from physical life because, for Aurobindo, poetry mediates between ''the immaterial and the concrete, the spirit and the life'' (288). This transcendental role of poetry is not at the cost of what Sanskrit poetic tradition has considered to be aesthetically paramount: for Aurobindo, delight is the essence of existence, and, for a poet, beauty is more important than truth and even life itself (331). Ananda K. Coomaraswamy is another writer who has eloquently mediated between the East and the West on literary and religious matters by identifying common elements in both traditions and interpreting classical concepts in the light of Western formulations.

The nonconformist and dynamic spirit of modern literatures in India can be exemplified by the modern thinking that Tagore and other writers introduced to the country and the ways in which their own ideas were rejected by, for instance, the Bengali poets, such as Buddadeva Bose, Jibanananda Das, Nazrul Islam, and many others (Kripalani 1971, 87–95). Classical Hindi poetry, once confined to romantic descriptions of female figures and celebration of Krishna's dalliance with his countless lovers, now includes thematic and formal experiments. Instead of describing nature mostly as a background for the emotions of characters, modern Hindi poetry recognizes the beauty and the value of the physical world in its own right. Most important, poetry has come to be defined in terms of the subjectivity and the myriad voices of the poet rather than in terms of hidebound aesthetic conventions and social ideals (Schomer 1983, 19–43). Modern Indian literature—in various genres, such as short stories and drama—has increasingly become realistic in recognizing the demand for recording the experiences of the common and the underprivileged and, as Mulk Raj Anand notes, the many paradoxes that are characteristic of such a complex society (Anand and Rao 1986, 227–32). The infiltration of Western ideas through an exposure to other cultural modes and the increasing emigration of Indian writers to other countries have created an awareness of the complexity of the empirical and aesthetic issues. For some writers in India, such a foreign influence even seems imperative. Gopalakrishna Adiga, a Kannada poet, claims that Indian writers should go to T. S. Eliot and W. H. Auden to inject the native poetry "with the blood of reality" (Amur, 1979, 69). Many Indian poets have also used unconventional moods, such as a consciousness of emptiness and aimlessness.

Like poetry, modern Indian drama has derived its identity from Sanskrit plays and dramatic theories, but the thematic content and technical innovations in contemporary Indian plays show an assimilation of native and Western traditions. To a great extent, Western playwrights like William Shakespeare, Bernard Shaw, Eugene O'Neill, and Henrik Ibsen have shaped the contemporary theater in India. With the social awareness that led to the political freedom of the country, Indian drama transcended its early obsession with mythological themes to a sensitivity to social themes such as individual freedom, women's plight, and economic oppression; it also found new ways of adapting the classical themes to the sensibilities of the modern audience, which wants more realistic portrayals. Girish Chandra Ghosh (1844–1911), D. L. Roy (1863–1913), K. P. Khadilkar (1872–1948), R. G. Gadkari (1885–1919), and Agha Kashmiri (1879–1935) are some of the well-known names in contemporary drama. There is considerable interaction among playwrights and producers of various languages. Regional plays get translated and enacted in other Indian languages. For example, Rajinder Nath has been bringing dramas from other languages for the Hindi audience, and Narayan Panikkar has translated classical dramas in Sanskrit to Malayalam, a language spoken in the state of Kerala, with the folk elements of the state. Journals like *Enact, Sangeet Nataka* (both published from Delhi), *Quarterly Journal* (published from Bombay), and *Marathinatyasamiksha* have made professional and critical exchanges on theater possible. Local clubs and societies on drama have created a popular support for drama as both an art and an entertainment. The National Academy of Music, Dance, and Drama, with federal help, has been a tremendous support to drama since 1954.

Vijay Tendulkar, a Marathi playwright, has been one of the most successful and controversial since the 1950s. His plays, like *Shantala! Court Chalu Ahe (Silence! The Court Is in Session,* 1967), expose the frozen values with which social forces marginalize individuals with unhomogenized behaviors and assumptions. C. T. Khanolkar is another Marathi dramatist whose plays, such as *Ek Shoonya Bajirao* (Bajirao the Cipher, 1971), exhibit unconventional plots and an awareness of the problems of artists. Girish Karnad is known to the outside world for his plays, like *Tughlaq.* Tughlaq, the fourteenth-century Muslim ruler of India, has traditionally been considered a political failure. But Karnad's play sees in the character a modern symbol of a bold derelict fraught with conflicts in an unsympathetic world. Theater in Karnataka has found innovative dramatists like Adya Rangacharya, Kailasam, and Shriranga. Rangacharya has used symbols and humor in his numerous plays. His plays, like *Shokachakra* (1952), also demand a new social structure devoid of any hierarchization.

Thus, there has been a complex but unbroken aesthetic tradition in India. Sanskrit aesthetics is significant in encompassing diverse emotions and codifying them for artistic expressions; it is also quite sophisticated in enumerating poetic theories that show the unifying and stabilizing role of art. As Thomas Munro explains it, Indian aesthetics from its Sanskrit origin onward has created a connection between a metaphysical worldview and the empirical life (1965, 75). Compared with the ongoing debates on the relationship between literature and philosophy in the writings of Richard Rorty, Jacques Derrida, and others in the West, Indian poetics has never lost sight of the common ground among the aesthetic, religious, and intellectual levels of existence. Anticipating even the modern literary ideas with metaphysical orientations, like Heidegger's elaborations on art and Being, Sanskrit hermeneutics gives a poet complete liberty by systematizing all possible moods and themes in art within a cosmic awareness of existence. Indian poetics is also secular in elevating the poet as God (Prajapati), who subsumes the sensuous within the pious and the ethical within the artistic. All experiential distinctions disappear, and different systems, such as the poetic, religious, and moral, become one in the artistic world that Indian aesthetics celebrates.

NOTE

1. It is not clear how comprehensive and self-critical Sanskrit literature has been on portraying social life. The ways in which the caste of authors, most of whom belonged to the upper class, could have influenced the Sanskrit aesthetics and the presentation of castes and racial distinctions in its literature are yet to be documented. A social division that began with a labor stratification seems to have frozen into castes in the later part of the Vedic age; but several Vedic hymns celebrate equality. The caste system, which has often been identified as the distinctive feature of Indian society, has always coexisted with anticaste thinking. Comedies like *Mata Vilasa* from the seventh-century king Mahendra Varman criticize monks, and the eleventh-century satirist Kshemendra likewise decries a classification that relies on birth. For more general information, see, among others, Chaitanya (1975, 100–33, 352–59) and Christian (1987, 145–74).

WORKS CITED

Amur, G. S. *Images and Impressions: Essays Mainly on Contemporary Indian Literature.* Jaipur: Panchsheel Prakashan, 1979.

Anand, Mulk Raj, and S. Balu Rao. *Panorama: An Anthology of Modern Short Stories.* New Delhi: Sterling, 1986.

Aurobindo, Sri. *The Future Poetry.* Pondicherry: Sri Aurobindo Ashram, 1953.

Bahm, Archie J. "Buddhist Aesthetics." *The Journal of Aesthetics and Art Criticism* 16: 2 (December 1957): 249–52.

Chaitanya, Krishna. *A New History of Sanskrit Literature.* Westport, Conn.: Greenwood Press, 1975.

Chaudhury, Pravas Jivan. "Catharsis in the Light of Indian Aesthetics." *The Journal of Aesthetics and Art Criticism* 15 (1956–57): 215–26.

Christian, Imanuel. *Language as Social Behavior: Folk Tales as a Database for Developing a Beyond-the-Discourse Model.* Huntington Beach: Summer Institute of Linguistics, 1987.

Coomaraswamy, Ananda. *Christian and Oriental Philosophy of Art.* New York: Dover, 1956.

Coward, Harold G. *Bhartrhari.* Boston: Twayne Publishers, 1976.

Daumal, Rene. *Rasa, or Knowledge of Self: Essays on Indian Aesthetics and Selected Sanskrit Studies.* Translated by Louise Landes Levi. New York: New Directions, 1982.

De, Sushil Kumar. *Sanskrit Poetics as a Study of Aesthetic.* Berkeley and Los Angeles: University of California Press, 1963.

Dimock, Edward C., Edwin Gerow, and J. A. B. van Buitenen. *The Literature of India: An Introduction.* Chicago: Chicago University Press, 1974.

Dwivedi, R. C. *Principles of Literary Criticism in Sanskrit.* Delhi: Motilal Banarsidass, 1969.

Jussawalla, Adil. "Introduction." In *New Writing in India.* Penguin, 1974.

Knight, William. *The Philosophy of the Beautiful.* New York, 1891.

Kripalani, Krishna. *Modern Indian Literature: A Panoramic Glimpse.* Rutland, Vt.: Charles E. Tuttle, 1971.

Muller, Max. *A History of Ancient Sanskrit Literature So Far as It Illustrates the Primitive Religion of the Brahmans.* 1860. New York: AMS Press, 1978.

———. *Rig Veda, with Sayana's Commentary.* 4 vols. London, 1890–92.

Munro, Thomas. *Oriental Aesthetics.* Cleveland: Western Reserve University Press, 1965.

Sankaran, A. *Some Aspects of Literary Criticism in Sanskrit.* Madras: Madras University Press, 1929.

Schomer, Karine. *Mahadevi Varma and the Chhayavad Age of Modern Hindi Poetry.* Berkeley: University of California Press, 1983.

Sharma, Kaushal Kishore. *Rabindranath Tagore's Aesthetics.* New Delhi: Abhinav Publications, 1988.

Sharma, Mukunda Madhava. *The Dhvani Theory in Sanskrit Poetics.* Varanasi: Chowkhamba Sanskrit Series Office, 1968.

Tagore, Rabindranath. *Personality.* London: Macmillan, 1945.

———. *Reminiscences.* Delhi: Macmillan, 1983.

Wimsatt, William and Cleanth Brooks. *Literary Criticism: A Short History.* New York: Knopf, 1957.

SELECTED PRIMARY BIBLIOGRAPHY

Amur, G. S. *Images and Impressions: Essays Mainly on Contemporary Indian Literature.* Jaipur: Panchsheel Prakashan, 1979.

Anand, Mulk Raj, and S. Balu Rao. *Panorama: An Anthology of Modern Short Stories.* New Delhi: Sterling, 1986.

Anandhavardhana. *Dhvanyaloka with Locana.* Translated by Daniel H. H. Ingalls, Jeffrey Moussaieff Masson, and M. V. Patvardhan. Cambridge: Harvard University Press, 1990.

Aurobindo, Sri. *The Future Poetry.* Pondicherry: Sri Aurobindo Ashram, 1953.

Bahm, Archie J. "Buddhist Aesthetics." *Journal of Aesthetics and Art Criticism* 16:2 (December 1957): 249–52.

Barthes, Roland. *The Semiotic Challenge.* New York: Hill and Wang, 1988.

Baumer, Rachel Van, and James R. Brandon, eds. *Sanskrit Drama in Performance.* Honolulu: University Press of Hawaii, 1981.

Bharatha Muni. *Bharatiyanatyasastra: Selections.* New Delhi: Munshiram Manoharlal, 1971.

Bhatta, Somadeva. *Kathasaritsagara.* Translated by C. H. Tawney and edited by N. M. Penzer. Delhi: Motilal Banarsidasa, 1968.

Chaitanya, Krishna. *A New History of Sanskrit Literature.* Westport, CT: Greenwood Press, 1975.

Chaudhury, Pravas Jivan. "Catharsis in the Light of Indian Aesthetics." *Journal of Aesthetics and Art Criticism* 15 (1956–57): 215–26.

Christian, Imanuel. *Language as Social Behavior: Folk Tales as a Database for Developing a Beyond-the-Discourse Model.* Huntington Beach: Summer Institute of Linguistics, 1987.

Coomaraswamy, Ananda. *Christian and Oriental Philosophy of Art.* New York: Dover, 1956.

Coward, Harold G. *Bhartrhari.* Boston: Twayne, 1976.

Daumal, Rene. *Rasa, or Knowledge of Self: Essays on Indian Aesthetics and Selected Sanskrit Studies.* Translated by Louise Landes Levi. New York: New Directions, 1982.

De, Sushil Kumar. *Sanskrit Poetics as a Study of Aesthetic.* Berkeley: University of California Press, 1963.

Dimock, Edward C., Edwin Gerow, and J.A.B. van Buitenen. *The Literature of India: An Introduction.* Chicago: University of Chicago Press, 1974.

Dwivedi, R. C. *Principles of Literary Criticism in Sanskrit.* Delhi: Motilal Banarsidass, 1969.

Frye, Northrop. *Anatomy of Criticism: Four Essays.* Princeton, NJ: Princeton University Press, 1957.

Jussawalla, Adil. "Introduction." *New Writing in India.* Delhi: Penguin, 1974.

Knight, William. *The Philosophy of the Beautiful.* New York, 1891.

Kriplani, Krishna. *Modern Indian Literature: A Panoramic Glimpse.* Rutland, VT: Charles E. Tuttle, 1971.

Muller, Max. *Vedic Hymns.* Part I. Delhi: Motilal Banarsidass, 1973.

———. *A History of Ancient Sanskrit Literature So Far as It Illustrates the Primitive Religion of the Brahmans.* 1860. New York: AMS Press, 1978.

———. *Rig Veda, with Sayana's Commentary.* 4 vols. London, 1890–92.

Munro, Thomas. *Oriental Aesthetics.* Cleveland: Press of Western Reserve University, 1965.

Narayan, R. K. *Ramayana.* London: Chatto and Windus, 1973.

Oldenberg, Hermann. *Vedic Hymns.* Part II. Delhi: Motilal Banarsidass, 1967.

Prasad, Jaishankar. *Ansoo* (Tears). Jhansi: Sahitya Sadan, 1925.

Rajasekhara. *Kavyamimamsa.* Banaras: Caukhamba Samskrta Siriza Aphisa, 1931.

Richards, I. A. *Principles of Literary Criticism.* New York: Harcourt, 1938.
Sankaracarya. *The Saundaryalahari.* Edited and translated by W. Norman Brown. Cambridge: Harvard University Press, 1958.
Sankaran, A. *Some Aspects of Literary Criticism in Sanskrit.* Madras: Madras University Press, 1929.
Schomer, Karine. *Mahadevi Varma and the Chhayavad Age of Modern Hindi Poetry.* Berkeley: University of California Press, 1983.
Sharma, Kaushal Kishore. *Rabindranath Tagore's Aesthetics.* New Delhi: Abhinav, 1988.
Sharma, Mukunda Madhava. *The Dhvani Theory in Sanskrit Poetics.* Varanasi: Chowkhamba Sanskrit Series Office, 1968.
Tagore, Rabindranath. *Personality.* London: Macmillan, 1945.
———. *Reminiscences.* Delhi: Macmillan, 1983.
Wimsatt, William, and Cleanth Brooks. *Literary Criticism: A Short History.* New York: Knopf, 1957.

16

Perspectives on Bengali Film and Literature

MITALI PATI AND SURANJAN GANGULY

INTRODUCTION

A commonplace Bengali word for "film" is *boi,* which literally means "book." While most younger Bengalis frequently use the words "cinema" and "movie," among the older generation "book" remains a synonym for "film." This unusual usage of "film" and "book" as synonyms calls attention to the fact that the modern Bengali film has a major debt to the rich tradition of nineteenth-and twentieth-century Bengali fiction.

In the Bengali culture, film is popularly critiqued as "text." Modern film versions of Bengali classics often reinterpret fictional texts to comment upon certain major contemporary social issues of Bengali and Indian society. Because of the literate Bengali moviegoer's attachment to the notion of "text," it is not uncommon to hear the members of the audience leaving a movie theater lamenting that the screenplay has distorted the essence of the "book."

For the usually literate Bengali audience, literature commands greater respect than popular film. Overall, modern Bengali film may be categorized as popular/commercial films and art films, and the "great books" of Bengali fiction often provide materials for successful screenplays. Like all Indian-made films, Bengali film reveals a sharp contrast in the overall quality of popular films and art films, although both types of film use well-known literary texts quite freely. The main distinction between commercial Bengali films made in Calcutta and the enormous number of commercial Hindi films produced in Bombay has been in the depiction of gender roles and the Bengali film's overall avoidance of explicit displays of sex and violence. However, in the 1990s, the Bombay formulas have become more influential in all regional Indian films.

Both Bengali commercial films and art films have relied fairly often on the classics of Bengali fiction in different ways. For the commercial filmmakers, the classics provide plots of reliable quality and hence good possibilities of making money. To ensure box office success, the commercial films have tended to cast the popular matinee idols of Calcutta over and over again in the leading roles in their screenplays of well-known Bengali novels, wreaking havoc with character development, symbolism, and visual imagery.

BENGALI COMMERCIAL CINEMA

Upon reexamining the films of the past four decades, one observes that this tendency of relying heavily on superstars, such as the late Uttam Kumar and Suchitra Sen, with their all-too-familiar mannerisms, diminishes the effective reinterpretation of texts. The screenplays tend to endorse the traditional values of Indian society even when the literary text contains a social and political critique. Cultural clichés tend to prevail instead of creative commentaries upon contemporary issues. Seven successful commercial films of the 1950s, 1960s, 1970s, and 1980s—*Rajlakshmi and Srikanta, Haar Mana Haar, Bipasha, Ami Shey O Sakha, Shilpi, Stree,* and *Chowrangi*—are analyzed here to show how the individualistic perceptions of the original literary texts are blurred in their movie reinterpretations and that an evolving cultural mythology of idealized gender roles becomes obvious to the viewer. Although the films span 30 years, there is little change discernible in the never-never land of the Bengali commercial cinema. In many ways, Bengali commercial screenplays and films reassert the traditional gender roles of Hindu culture that the novelists so frequently attempt to question. The literary text remains more subversive in terms of traditional values than the cinematic interpretations.

Three stereotypical clusters can be formed from the seven films analyzed in this chapter based on formulaic sentimental themes. These themes are also lasting, money-spinning formulas in the world of Bengali commercial film because they have second- and third-generation imitators. Interestingly, these formulaic film plots are based on Bengali fiction and are perhaps rooted in traditional Bengali culture. Two of the films—*Shilpi* and *Haar Mana Haar*—dwell on artist figures and their romantic relationships. *Bipasha, Rajlakshmi and Srikanta,* and *Stree* have weak (almost infantile) heroes and have their unreasonably devoted women involved in romantic plots. The third cluster is represented by *Ami Shey O Shakha* and *Chowrangi,* and their thematic unity lies in their depiction of the corruption of moral values in postcolonial Indian society.

Bengali films tend to de-emphasize women's attractiveness as sexual objects, concentrating, instead, on the Hindu traditional view of women as conscience-keepers of homes and even society, as strong individuals responsible for upholding moral standards and human values amid a world of erring men.

Rajlakshmi and Srikanta (date unavailable on videotape) has the overall quality of an early 1960s black-and-white miniseries that takes us back into nineteenth-century British India. The screenplay is based on the set of novellas centered around the travels of Srikanta written by the nineteenth-century Bengali social problem novelist Sarat Chandra Chattopadhyay.

The film begins with a shot of a handwritten page, presumably the opening of the original manuscript. This visual image suggests that the director, Kanan Bhattacharya, opens the "book" and that she seeks to preserve the authenticity of the fictional narratives. The hero, Srikanta, appears to be a member of the anarchists in his village who break the taboos of Brahminical Hinduism. Srikanta and his friends are staunchly supported by the local physician, who has a Western education. The conflict between Western logic and moribund, nineteenth-century, rural Hindu taboos is clearly developed in the opening scenes, and this authentic critique comes from the writer himself.

Although well educated, Srikanta has no immediate family and hence does not belong in the social structure of a nineteenth-century Bengali village. The hero accepts an invitation from a rajah to join the traditional princely hunt (*shikar*). There is a swift transition in setting from the poverty of the village Brahmins to the wealthy living conditions of the prince. In this wealthy environment, he finds out that the beautiful singer Rajlakshmi is a girl from his village. An adolescent romance revives in an unusual setting.

The episodes in the crematorium illustrate the hero's disregard for superstitions and of the heroine's obvious affection and concern for what she considers self-destructive behavior. The meaning of the ghostly voices cannot be explained with relevance to plot and character. Perhaps they are only eerie special effects that made the film exciting to its original audiences over 30 years ago.

Rajlakshmi reclaims Srikanta as her own. Their love is obviously platonic, but it is intense, for he refuses the hand of an unseen bride chosen for him by his relatives. Most of the romantic scenes rely heavily on facial expression. Very little physical affection is displayed. He pledges faith to her, for he cannot marry her in the nineteenth-century social structure. He leaves for the colonial frontier in Burma. The film ends, but the novellas continue to describe the wanderings of Srikanta in Rangoon.

Rajlakshmi O Srikanta casts the late superstar Uttam Kumar in its leading role, and many of its flaws are traceable to this actor's style. Similar situations are present in the 1960s romantic tragedy *Shilpi,* based on the fiction of a less-known regional author, Nitai Bhattacharya. *Shilpi* is a critique of the caste-based social class system, which has been a chronic problem in Indian society for centuries. Dhiman, a working-class boy artist, comes to the house of a wealthy landlord, or zamindar, receives his patronage, becomes educated, and starts to flourish as an artist. The zamindar's only child, Anjana, falls in love with Dhiman. Her mother reprimands her on pursuing a childhood friendship. The heroine's family forces her to break up their friendship, which has turned to love. This formulaic plot of a weak hero but a strong heroine has often recurred in the romantic dramas of many Bengali films. The antihero of modern fiction is the origin of such character depiction. In such depictions of leading male roles, Bengali films are markedly different from Bombay films, which emphasize machismo to this day.

Defeated by the rigid class structure of Bengal in the early twentieth century, the rejected hero returns to his slum origins to die of tuberculosis. Single shots heighten the pathos of the end. Anjana becomes chronically depressed. The seductive heroine takes the lead in the courtship, while the naive hero is quite restrained in his showing of feelings. The focus on woman's ability to express her emotions freely indicates that the spirit of the 1960s had made its mark on Bengali films.

There are close parallels between *Shilpi* (1966) and *Haar Mana Haar* (1972), based on the novel *Mahasweta,* written by mid-twentieth-century novelist Tarashankar Bandopadhyay. *Haar Mana Haar* is the story of an artist and his muse. Mahasweta, the heroine, functions as a muselike figure inspiring the artist hero. The hero is a nationalist and a grassroots educator of orphan schoolboys. The romance is set in a village school run by the hero, where she becomes a teacher. His neurotic wife dies conveniently after several episodes of making trouble in the school. He secretly paints his feelings into his pictures. The use of canvases as a communication medium suggests that the director is beginning to move away from the limitations of film as "text" toward a greater use of symbolism. Again, there is a very strong heroine, but the casting of Suchitra Sen and Uttam Kumar with their typical mannerisms detracts from character development to its fullest extent.

Bipasha is a 1968 version of a novel by Tarashankar Bandopadhyay of the same name. The valley of the river Beas (Sanskrit "Bipasha") had been the scene of tragic Hindu–Muslim communal riots in the late 1940s. As a teenager, the heroine loses her family in the riots and comes to Delhi.

Bipasha depicts middle-class Bengali society in the first half of the century as being full of taboos. The plot focuses on the redemption of the hero by the heroine, who saves him from suicidal depression and helps him to find his parents. Once again, Uttam Kumar as a romantic hero plays the part of a boy who has not grown up. As in *Rajlakshmi O Srikanta,* the camera focuses on eyes, face, and bust in tense emotional scenes. In a traditional Hindu way, man is depicted as a confused sinner and the woman as a self-sacrificing redeemer.

Stree, a 1972 film version of Bimal Mitra's popular novel of the same title, is another critique of the emptiness and absence of values in the lives of the wealthy in colonial Bengal. The plot is the eternal triangle of the childhood sweetheart married to a rich, insensitive, debauched landlord. The wandering hero returns to find his lady gone forever. Madhab Dutta, the landlord, and Mrinmoyee have a loveless marriage. He returns drunk every night. Sitapati, Mrinmoyee's teenage sweetheart, is a photographer. He is the artist figure in this plot, and his vision is also the camera's vision. Hence, the camera emphasizes Mrinmoyee's loneliness and attractiveness, dwelling on her face and bust. Because this film is Sitapati's narrative, the plot of woman as pursuer and man as pursued reverses the traditional romantic schemes of the patriarchal Bengali culture. The plot turns on the heroine's sexuality in this romantic melodrama, focusing on her adultery as her revenge on her husband. Despite her middle-class values, she has a son by Sitapati whom her husband believes to be his child. The screenplay presents class differences sympathetically. Both men suffer in their friendship because they desire to be competent fathers to the boy. Tortured by his love for Mrinmoyee and the boy, which he cannot reveal, Sitapati leaves and joins the nationalist movement. He is jailed. The heroine dies. An old pendant she used to wear on a chain around her neck reveals the identity of her lover. The infantile Madhab Dutta goes to kill the dying Sitapati; then he kills himself. He has also gone bankrupt. The melodramatic ending of the screenplay is at variance with the novel and suggests that a wealthy life of leisure is, in itself, a form of madness in the eyes of the working middle class, the audience to whom the Bengali authors and directors address their works.

Chowrangi (1980) is based on well-known modern novelist Shankar's fiction with the same title. The text and the film provide the audience with the same kaleidoscopic view of life in downtown Calcutta through the eyes of Satta Bose, the manager of a large downtown hotel, the Shah Jehan. The fiction and film resemble Western films and novels that use hotel settings. The theme of the film is the corruption of Bengali urban society and the decline in values, a recurring topic in the literature and films of postcolonial India. The call girl Karabi commits suicide when she realizes that she can never marry her lover because she is a permanent social outcast from middle-class respectability. Satta's own girlfriend dies when her plane explodes in flames. He leaves the hotel. In the final scenes, he is at the seaside remembering her song. *Chowrangi* is one of Uttam Kumar's better films. The supportive relationships of an earlier period are absent, and women are destroyed in a vicious man's world. The influence of Bombay on regional Bengali films is evident in this transition.

In *Ami Shey O Sakha* (1975), a film based on the fiction of popular modern novelist Asutosh Mukhopadhyay, we have a screenplay written by the author himself. The heroine is a writer who opens her autobiography, her ''book'' by the seaside. The entire film is a flashback. A young history professor and her graduate students tour Mogul ruins. Monkeys attack the women's group. Two men rush to their rescue. A romance develops between two urban professionals. Scenes revolve on witty repartee. The men are physicians in a partnership. The writer heroine marries one of the physicians.

The focus of the film changes to a critique of the medical malpractices of the Third World. The hypocrisy of Indian society in sexual matters fosters these malpractices, such as illegal late abortions and hysterectomies. The physicians Prasanta and Sudhir are friends, colleagues, almost brothers, who separate on the Poddar malpractice case, as the greed of the medical profession is exposed in this film. The wife symbolizes conscience in an attempt to return to traditional Hindu norms in a changing and morally corrupt society.

Yet, even in commercial films that criticize society, there is no clear attempt to develop the social and political critique that compares with the art films of the same period directed by Satyajit Ray, Mrinal Sen, and Ritwik Ghatak. The most significant difference between art films and commercial films is in the art films' capacity to engage in sociopolitical controversy.

SATYAJIT RAY AND THE BENGALI ART CINEMA

While Bengali commercial cinema has continued to churn out tepid adaptations of well-known novels, skirting controversy and only hinting at change, the so-called art cinema of Satyajit Ray, Mrinal, Sen and Ritwik Ghatak (which now includes Gautam Ghosh, Buddhadeb Dasgupta, Aparna Sen, and Utpalendu Chakravarty) has been far more radical in framing a social and political critique. What is often overlooked is the fact that many of the films by these filmmakers are based on literary texts. Since Satyajit Ray (1921–92) is the most prominent name on this list and has consistently adapted short stories, novellas, and novels to the screen, his work serves as a prime example of the "other" Bengali trend in transforming text into film.

The product of a progressive, reform-minded family of poets, writers, and artists with strong links to the Bengali Renaissance, Ray spent his early years in a highly literate household, complete with printing press and a children's magazine edited by his father (which Ray would revive in 1961, the year that also saw his emergence as an extremely popular writer for young people). Thus, when Ray decided to make his first film, he turned to a classic of Bengali literature, *Pather Panchali* by Bibhuti Bhusan Bandopadhyay, and later made three more films based on his work. Another writer for whom Ray had an enormous veneration all his life was Rabindranath Tagore. *Charulata* (1964), *Teen Kanya* (Three Daughters, 1961), and *Ghare Baire* (The Home and the World, 1984) all have their source in Tagore. *Devi* (The Goddess, 1960) is also linked to Tagore since he provided the author, Prabhat Mukhopadhyay, with the germ of the story. Then, in the politically tense climate of the late 1960s and early 1970s, Ray chose to adapt two novels—*Aranyer Din Ratri* and *Pratidwandi*—by Sunil Ganguly, whose work differed radically from the liberal humanist tradition of Bandopadhyay and Tagore. His protagonists, who live in the urban jungle of Calcutta, are mostly young men caught in the rat race, struggling to hold onto their inherited values in the face of betrayal and compromise.

Since the work of these three writers constitutes the basis for important and diverse films by Ray, it would be appropriate to explore his cinematic manipulation of the written text through a study of *Pather Panchali* (The Song of the Little Road, 1955), *Charulata,* and *Pratidwandi* (The Adversary, 1970). But, first, it is necessary to examine Ray's own views about the relationship between text and film.

Ray has reiterated from time to time the importance of story in his films, going so far as to affirm that he prefers stories with a beginning, a middle, and an end *in that order.* Accordingly, one notices in his work the following: the classical unities of time, place, and action; linearity; cause–effect relationships; psychologically complex characters who serve as causal agents; and a preference for realism, all of which have been branded as "literary" traits influenced by the very conventions of the source material. What critics and detractors often overlook is the fact that Ray's conservative storytelling masks a highly idiosyncratic system. As Robin Wood has pointed out, the films tell stories, but they are "built on a complicated pattern of echoes and cross-references, both thematic and visual, with almost every incident finding an echo somewhere, down to details of camera-movement and set-up" (1971, 13). Wood is describing an intricate structuring process in which all things are placed in a variety of contexts and endlessly qualified and requalified until they acquire a multiplicity of meanings. In this musical balancing and counterpointing of elements, Ray subtly subverts the literary text he has inscribed on film. The viewer enters a dense, richly textured filmic text in which the most disparate elements are interrelated through repetition and variation. What emerges within the contours of a traditional plot is a cinematic "cellular" (Ray's own term) universe in which even the smallest details convey a sense of the larger, the whole (Issakson 1970, 120). With this formal sense of the written text radicalized, one must consider the radicalization of content.

Pather Panchali is said to have revolutionized Indian film in terms of language and subject matter. Shirking the crude melodrama of popular mainstream cinema, Ray chose Italian neorealism as a model for his deeply humanistic portrayal of village life from the perspective of a Brahmin family and their son, Apu. The film, thus, has little to do with the pastoral genre of Bengali cinema with its overblown romantic rhetoric and its reductive oppositions between the corrupt city and the redemptive rural world. Likewise, it has little to do with most of the conventions of mainstream Bengali pastoral literature, which nourished that genre and which Bandopadhyay himself rejected. Instead, in his portrayal of nature, which is a constant backdrop to the human drama in *Pather Panchali,* Ray subverts the popular stereotype of a benign and bountiful mother nursing her children. Nature is beautiful and life-sustaining, but it can also kill. Apu's older sister, Durga, revels in the first monsoon shower, but the soaking leads to a cold, and Durga dies a few days later during a severe storm when nature seems to unleash its fury on humans (the house in which the family lives collapses). Ray describes this duality inherent in nature through unobtrusive details as well, focusing on a litter of kittens that lives with the family and that steadily dwindles in number until only a few manage to survive. Thus, nature is shorn of its romantic aura and is given a realist basis in relation to human existence and experience.

The same unsentimental tone surfaces in Ray's handling of children and childhood. Much has been written about the scene in a field of flowery grasses where Apu and Durga glimpse their first train, but that moment endures (like other moments of discovery in the film) because we know how hard life really is for them. The conventional idyll of a pastoral childhood is dropped in favor of the "ring of truth"—what it is like to grow up in poverty, to be accused of theft, to watch a sister die and hear the mother's heartrending wail, and finally to be uprooted from home (Ray 1976, 33). Yet, within this tragic and precarious world, Ray captures all the magic of childhood without sacrificing his realist aesthetic.

Ray's commitment to realism is also apparent in the way he films *Pather Panchali.* The normal lens is used consistently to reproduce everyday human vision, and eye-level shots tend to dominate. Exteriors are shot in natural light; interiors, in "bounced lighting" to create a lifelike quality. Ray's preference for the long take and the moving camera reinforces our sense of a lived-in world, since time and space are rendered whole. Moreover, Ray's frame is a highly inclusive frame in which nothing is too trivial to be exempt. Thus, reality is captured in all its forms, and what is conventionally beautiful has no place in Ray's scheme of things unless it is relevant within a certain context. The roots of Ray's poetic realism lie here—in the many juxtapositions and interrelationships he fashions out of seemingly incompatible material. He knows how to exploit the cinema's ability to travel back and forth through space, to present multiple points of view, to create significant parallels, and to suggest, rather than proclaim. What makes *Pather Panchali* a great film is that, in the final analysis, it is a truly cinematic work, inspired by a book but never bookish. Thus, its most radical message in 1955 to Bengali cinema (and to Indian cinema) was that it, too, must stop being literary and simply be film.

Charulata, made nearly 10 years later, extends the visual language of *Pather Panchali* and is probably Ray's most perfect "cellular" film, with complicated cross-references and counterpointing of motifs that attest to the influence of Mozart's chamber music on its structure. In Tagore's novella, set in the 1870s, a young wife neglected by her husband falls in love with his cousin. Ray maintains the story line but embellishes it with many little nuances that give it texture and density of meaning.

The film is full of moments that have been described as "pure cinema," where nothing happens as such, and yet so much happens. In the opening sequence, with virtually no dialogue, Charulata wanders through the large empty rooms of her house, picks up a book to read, looks out of a window through a pair of opera glasses, and sits down at a piano. From these seemingly irrelevant details, we sense her loneliness and her boredom, her interest in the world outside, and her love of reading. The scene, of course, does not exist in Tagore's story; only the cinema can do justice to such a moment. Similarly, when seated alone on a swing in the garden, she feels the first stirrings of love for cousin-in-law Amal; the camera holds onto her face and captures each flicker of emotion. After peering at Amal through her opera glasses, when she trains them on a mother cradling her child in a neighboring house, a connection immediately springs up among her childlessness, her desire for Amal, and her loneliness. Thus, Ray's understated style achieves a new complexity and sophistication in *Charulata.*

This success in creating a cinematic equivalent of Tagore's text is matched by Ray's success in creating, perhaps for the first time in Bengali cinema, a female protagonist who is defined in her own terms and within her own space. In this respect, he goes even further than Tagore, describing Charulata's subtle move toward independence from a twentieth-century perspective.

Although confined to her inner sanctum, Charulata can sense that the world outside is changing. Her husband, a Western-educated liberal who runs a progressive newspaper, earnestly believes in reform, but his work keeps him so busy that he has no time for her. Ray frequently alternates scenes in which the two of them are together with scenes where she is alone but trapped, nevertheless, within her role of the dutiful housewife. Attracted to Amal who is of her age, shares her literary tastes, and gives her attention, she has a chance to be free, but the self-serving Amal is too weak to sustain her bid for freedom through forbidden love. In the end, despite the prospect of a reconciliation with her husband, she is doubly alone, but with a sense of her own self and her own space within a world of men.

Although *Charulata* never reads like a feminist manifesto, it is a film in which Ray clearly supports the emancipation of women from the strictures of a repressive society. By linking her inner change to change in the sociopolitical macrocosm, he emphasizes the need for women to participate in the moment of historical transformation. In his later films, Ray was even more forthright about women having to resist the cultural taboos of their time.

Pratidwandi was Ray's first film to grapple with the contemporary scene, the Calcutta of the late 1960s in the grip of "revolution." This was the time of the Naxalites, a Maoist guerrilla group that disrupted daily life in the city with bombs, pipe guns, and bullets. In Ray's film about a jobless young man, there is a new sense of urgency. To capture the intrusive reality of the streets, Ray chose to abandon his preferred classical model of continuity in favor of the subversive aesthetic of dislocation.

Pratidwandi opens in negative, with shots of a corpse being carried out of a house for cremation. This highly idiosyncratic beginning is a pointer to what is to come: more sequences in negative, disorienting jump cuts, freeze shots, flashbacks, and dream and fantasy scenes. There is virtually nothing here that could be called bookish. Ray marshals the resources of the cinema to give us a sense of the disjointed thinking process of his protagonist, Siddhartha, a medical student, forced into the rat race by his father's death. The Calcutta he experiences is likewise a city out of joint, given to political rallies, sudden bomb blasts, squalor and poverty, bureaucratic chaos, and indifference to the plight of the victims. In the end, Siddhartha has to dislocate himself from the city and from the woman he loves for life in a small town. In chronicling his frustrations, Ray makes an indictment of the social and political system in India that is new to his work. It is also new to Bengali cinema with its watered-down protest films and its refusal to adapt literary texts considered politically inflammatory.

At the same time, Ray does not openly endorse revolution. Siddhartha is not a gun-toting revolutionary, but a vulnerable and troubled man who does not find ready answers in the political tracts that his Naxalite brother reads. Ray shows him to be more responsive to the memory of a bird call he had heard as a child, rather than to the chant for revolution. Siddhartha, unlike his brother, has not committed himself to an ideology but can still think and feel on his own. Thus, when his anger explodes at the end during an interview scene, it stems from an inner rage and is not a calculated political gesture. While Ray condemns the moral anarchy he sees around him, he is not willing to dictate solutions as an ideologue. This does not weaken the film; in fact, Siddhartha and his problems become all the more real. *Pratidwandi,* then, is an important film that anticipates *Seemabaddha* (Company Limited, 1971) and *Jana Aranya* (The Middle Man, 1975), which together would constitute the Calcutta trilogy, Ray's bleak testament about contemporary India.

The film is also remarkable in the way Ray refuses to idealize the middle-class home as a small haven of Bengali values within the corrupt metropolis. After wandering the streets most of the day, Siddhartha returns every night to a dingy flat to hear his mother complain about his sister's moral turpitude and to endure his brother's talk of revolution that will never happen. Ray frequently uses chiaroscuro lighting to suggest the cell-like confines of this world within which each is a prisoner. It is no different when Siddhartha visits his girlfriend, Keya's flat where she lives with her father. The father complains all the time like Siddhartha's mother and blames the problems of the city on the young without any real understanding of their problems. Like Siddhartha, Keya will leave home and city and shift to Delhi.

Perhaps the most complex character in the film is Sutapa, Siddhartha's sister, who is the sole breadwinner of the family, a good-looking woman with material ambitions, bent on furthering her career even if it means reciprocating the sexual advances of her boss. Ray refuses to turn her story into one of guilt and redemption; instead, Sutapa remains a strong-willed, independent woman who, despite Siddhartha's demand that she resign, keeps her job and seems to have no regrets about her relationship with her boss. In her defiance of middle-class morality and the role created for her by her class, she introduces a brand of feminism that is also new to Ray's cinema.

Thus, the move away from the conservative, literary cinema begins with Ray, who remains a major source of inspiration for those committed to a cinema that is socially, politically, as well as stylistically progressive. Among them, Ritwik Ghatak and Mrinal Sen are Ray's contemporaries, who also made their first films in the 1950s but, unlike Ray, were firebrand Marxists with a specific political agenda in mind.

Ghatak (1925–76) grew up in East Bengal (now Bangladesh) and could never reconcile to the partition of India, which made him a stranger in his own country. His major films, *Meghe Dhaka Tara* (The Cloud-Capped Star, 1960), *Komal Gandhar* (E Flat, 1961), and *Subarnarekha* (1962), describe the personal and cultural dimensions of this tragedy in an epic style that fuses the mythic with the ordinary. Resisting the temptation to graft Western ideas onto his films, Ghatak created an original cinema that has roots in his native Bengal and draws on folklore, myth, memory, local traditions, and the collective experience of people displaced by history. While some of his films are based on short stories by contemporary Bengali writers, Ghatak's daring, expressionistic use of camera as well as sound constantly draws attention to the cinematic idiom he forged.

Mrinal Sen has made nearly 30 films, in which he examines the social and political injustices rampant in India and the plight of the common person, who is always the victim. In his complex analysis of the nature of oppression in films like *Calcutta 71* (1972), *Chorus* (1974), *Parasuram* (Man with the Axe, 1978), and *Akaler Sandhaney* (In Search of Famine, 1980), Sen has tried his hand at different genres and experimented with form in ways that point to the influence of Godard, Brecht, Rocha, and others. He remains India's most celebrated political filmmaker actively committed to changing society by loudly proclaiming its ills to the people.

Of the new generation of filmmakers, Aparna Sen, a popular star of Bengali commercial cinema, has directed three films, all centered around women. *36 Chowringhee Lane* (1981) is about an Anglo-Indian schoolteacher coming to terms with old age, loneliness, and rejection; *Paroma* (1983) focuses on a married woman who causes scandal in her middle-class home by having an affair with a young man; and in *Sati* (The Wife, 1989), a woman is married to a tree. Sen is the first woman filmmaker of the Bengali cinema to explore gender issues from a feminist angle.

Three other filmmakers of this "other" cinema deserve mention. Buddhadeb Dasgupta's films—*Neem Annapurna* (Bitter Morsel, 1974), *Dooratwa* (Distance, 1978), *Grihajuddha* (Crossroads, 1981), *Phera* (The Return, 1986), and *Tahader Katha* (Their Story, 1991)—trace the moral and spiritual decline of a society where commercial values are replacing human values. Utpalendu Chakravarty, a political activist turned filmmaker, has made films that describe the problems of specific groups like tribals (*Moyna Tadanta* [Post Mortem, 1981]) and workers (*Chokh* [Eye, 1982]). Finally, Gautam Ghosh has made wholly cinematic adaptations of work by Tagore and, recently, Manik Bandopadhyay (*Padma Nadir Majhi* [Boatmen of Padma, 1991]). But he is best known for his films dealing with the poor and the exploited (*Dakhal* [Occupation, 1982] and *Antarjali Jatra* [Voyage Beyond, 1988]), in which he especially emphasizes the oppression of women.

Despite the work of these filmmakers, lack of funds and poor distribution threaten the survival of this cinema. Moreover, like the Bengali commercial film industry, it has to reckon with its Goliath—the all-powerful Bombay cinema, which swamps its markets and lures away audiences. Yet, hope for the Bengali cinema lies in the making of such films, for if a meaningful cinema is to evolve, it must reformulate its political stance as well as its reliance on the text and aspire to be truly cinematic.

NOTE

We are very grateful to Kironmoy Raha for providing dates and English titles for a number of films.

WORKS CITED

Issakson, Folke. "Conversation with Satyajit Ray." *Sight and Sound* (Summer 1970): 114–20.

Ray, Satyajit. "A Long Time on the Little Road." In *Our Films Their Films.* Calcutta: Orient Longman, 1976.

Wood, Robin. *The Apu Trilogy.* New York: Praeger, 1971.

Selected General Critical Bibliography

This is a brief, general bibliography of critical works that are useful as introductions to the general subject of twentieth-century regional Indian literature. For specific titles and studies in the various literatures, see the bibliographies accompanying the survey chapters.

Ahmad, Aijaz. "Indian Literature—Notes towards a Definition of a Category." In *Theory: Classes, Nations, Literatures.* London: Verso, 1992.

Bailey, Greg. "On the Deconstruction of Culture in Indian Literature: A Tentative Response to Vijay Mishra's Article." *South Asia* 12:1 (1989): 85–102.

Bardhan, Kalpana. "Introduction." In *Of Women, Outcastes, Peasants and Rebels.* Berkeley: University of California Press, 1990.

Chatterjee, Partha. *The Nation and Its Fragments: Colonial and Postcolonial Histories.* Princeton, NJ: Princeton University Press, 1994.

Das, Sisir Kumar Das. "Prologue." In *A History of Indian Literature, 1800–1910: Western Impact, Indian Response.* Delhi: Sahitya Akademi, 1991.

Datta, Amaresh. *Sahitya Akademi Encyclopaedia A to Z.* Delhi: Sahitya Akademi, 1987.

Dev, Amiya, and Sisir Kumar Das. *Comparative Literature: Theory and Practice.* Calcutta: Allied, 1989.

Devy, G. N. *After Amnesia: Tradition and Change in Indian Literary Criticism.* Bombay: Orient Longmans, 1992.

George, K. M. *Modern Indian Literature: An Anthology: Surveys and Poems.* Delhi: Sahitya Akademi, 1992.

Guha, Ranajit, ed. *Subaltern Studies.* Vols. 1–8. Delhi: Oxford University Press.

Joshi, Umashankar. *Indian Literature: Personal Encounters.* Calcutta: Papyrus, 1988.

Mukherjee, Meenakshi. *The Twice-Born Fiction: Themes and Techniques of the Indian Novel in English.* London: Heinemann, 1971.

———. *Realism and Reality: The Novel and Society in India.* Delhi: Oxford University Press, 1988.

Niranjana, Tejaswini. *Siting Translation.* Berkeley: University of California Press, 1992.

Omvedt, Gail. *Dalits and the Democratic Revolution.* New Delhi: Sage, 1994.

Padikkal, Shivarama. ''Inventing Modernity: The Emergence of the Novel in India.'' In *Interrogating Modernity,* edited by Dhareshwar, Niranjana, and Sudhir. Calcutta: Seagull Press, 1993.

Spivak, Gayatri. *Imaginary Maps.* London & New York: Routledge, 1995.

Tharu, Susie, and K. Lalitha. *Women Writing in India.* 2 vols. New York: Feminist Press, 1993.

Index

Abbas, Ghulam, 343
Abol-Tabol (Gibber-Gabber), 60
Adalja, Varsha, 127
Adiga, Gopalakrishna, 161, 169–70, 171
Agarkar, Gopal Ganesh, 215
Agarwala, Anandachandra, 27
Agarwala, Chandrakumar, 26–27
Agarwala, Jyotiprasad, 27, 29–30, 35
Agha, Vazeer, 348, 350
Agnisakshi (Witness by Fire), 197
Agyeye (writer), 146
Ahluwalia, Jasbir Singh, 257
Ahmad, Aijaz, 1
Ahmad, Nazeer, 334
Āhmed, Ābul Mansur, 69–70
"Aj Akhan Waris Shah nun," 254
Akilan (writer), 296, 297–98, 296, 300
Alekar, Satish, 237
Āli, Syed Mujtabā, 60
Alibābā, 48
Ambedkar, Bheemrao Ramji, 363, 364–65, 374
Ami Shey O Sakka, 411, 414
Amjad, Majeed, 345
Amma, Balamani, 198
Amma, K. Saraswati, 198
Anand, Mulk Raj, 89, 92, 95 n.4
Ananda Bazār Patrika Group, 61–62, 64
Angare, 342
Annadurai, C. N., 300
Antherjanam, Lalithambika, 193, 197, 198
Anuththama (writer), 297
Anya Jivan, 39–40
Apte, Hari Narayan, 215–16
Arifi, Shad, 345
Asan, Kumaran, 182, 183–85
Ashk, Upendranath, 146
Assamese: Its Formation and Development, 29
Assamese language, 21, 24, 29; missionary influence on, 22, 23
Assamese literature, 21–42; ballads and pastorals in, 27; biography in, 25, 28; contemporary (1950s to present), 35–42; drama in, 28–30, 34–35, 41–42; essay in, 25, 28; farce and satire in, 28, 29; and film, 29–30; historical background of, 21–23; *Jayanti* era in, 32–35; Jonaki era in, 10, 21, 24, 25–27; and journals, 21, 22, 23, 24, 25, 26, 28, 32, 33; modernism in, 34; one-act play in, 41; *Orunodoi* era in, 23–25; poetry in, 26–27, 31, 33, 36–37; popular culture in, 30; prose in, 27–28, 33–34, 37–41; Romanticism in, 25–27; sociopolitical themes in, 24–25, 32–35, 37–40, 41; stream-of-consciousness narrative in, 38; surrealism in, 40; symbolism in, 36, 41; Western influ-

ence in, 39, 41; women writers in, 23, 30–32, 39–40; women's portrayal in, 25–31
Atre, P. K., 220, 224
Azad, Abul Kalam, 335
Azad, Muhammad Husain, 332, 333
Azmi, Khalilur Rahman, 349–50, 354

Baburav, Bolara, 166
Badarayan (poet), 115
Bagul, Baburao, 368–69, 370, 371
Bai, Meera, 124
Bakshi, Chandrakant, 120
Balachandar, K., 300
Balākā (Swans), 52
Balakumaran (writer), 296–97
Balan, Arasu, 398
Balashankar (poet), 104
Baliwala, Khurshadji Maherwanji, 109
Balwant, Bawa, 255
Bamsi (The Flute), 53–54
Bandyopādhyāya, Bibhūtibhūṣaṇ, 58, 415
Bandyopādhyāya, Māṇik, 59
Bandyopādhyāya, Tārāśaṅkar, 59
Banerjea, S. B., 89
Bangladeshi literature. *See* East Pakistan and Bangladesh, literature of
Bansode, Hira, 375–76
Bapat, Vasant, 227–28
Barua, Ajit, 37
Barua, Amulya, 33
Barua, Bhaben, 37
Barua, Birinchi Kumar (Bina Barua), 34
Barua, Durga Prasad Majindar, 29
Barua, Gunabhiram, 25
Barua, Hemchandra, 24–25, 33
Barua, Mahasveta, 21
Barua, Navakanta, 36, 39
Barua, Padmanath Gohain, 27
Barua, Satya Prasad, 35
Baruah, Swarnalata, 31
Baruani, Kabya Bharati Dharmeswari, 31
Baruva, Parvati Prasad, 27
Barve, Anil, 236–37
Basanti, 148–49
Basheer, Vaikom Muhammad, 193
Basu, Amrtalāl, 48
Basu, Buddhadeb, 56
Basu, Pūrabī, 78–79
Basu, Rajśekhar (Parasuram), 59
Basu, Samareś (Kālkūt), 60–61
Bedekar, Malatibai, 223
Bedi, Rajinder Singh, 343
Beisya (The Prostitute), 33
Bendre, D. R., 161, 164
Bengal Renaissance, 45, 80 n.1
Bengali culture, and Hindu-Muslim identity, 45, 66–67, 69
Bengali film, 58, 59, 60, 61, 410–20; art, 415–20; and classic fiction, 410–11; commercial, 411–14; Marxism in, 419–20. *See also* Rāy, Satyajit
Bengali language, 66, 69–70, 79–80
Bengali literature (preindependence Bengal and West Bengal), 45–66; colloquial speech in, 46, 50; drama in, 47–48, 50, 64–66; essay in, 48–49; humor in, 60; journals and little magazines in, 45, 50–51, 55–56, 64; Kallol generation in, 55–58, 59; modernism in, 54, 55; of Muslim community, 51; poetry in, 51–52, 56–57, 62–64; postmodernist, 64; prose in, 48–62; short story in, 49; sociopolitical themes in, 49–50, 55; women prose writers in, 50, 62; women's situation in, 49. *See also* East Pakistan and Bangladesh, literature of; Tagore, Abanindrañath
Betai, Sundarji, 115
Bezbarua, Lakshminath, 27–28
Bhagat, Niranjan, 118
Bhagwat, Durga, 235
Bhagyalakshmi, N. V., 174
Bhajian Bahin'' (The Fractured Arms), 284
Bhandari, Mannu, 152
Bharathi (periodical), 324
Bhárathi, Subramanya, 8, 290, 292
Bharucha, Perin, 391
Bhasi, Thoppil, 200
Bhaskara Pattelar and My Life, 196
Bhatia, Nandi, 134
Bhattacarya, Bijan, 64–65
Bhaṭṭācārya, Sanjay, 58
Bhattacharya, Birendra Kumar, 34, 38–39
Bhattacharya, Hiren, 37
Bhave, G. A., 229–30

Bhayani, Utpal, 122
Bhullar, Gurbachan, 283
Bhuyan, Surya Kumar, 28
Bidyābiṇod, Kṣirodprasād, 48
Bihari, Banke, 256
Bipasha, 411, 413
Borade, Raosaheb, 232
Borah, Lakshminandan, 40
Bordoloi, Nirmalprabha, 36–37
Bordoloi, Rajanikanta, 28
Borgohain, Homen, 39
Borgohain, Nirupama, 39–40
Borkar, B. B., 221
Borthakur, Himendrakumar, 41
Botadkar (poet), 108
British censorship, 153 n.6
British colonial influence, 22, 101–2, 103, 207–8, 212, 213, 383–84, 385
Broker, Gulabdas, 116–17
Buddhism, 185, 364–65

Cakrabartī, Amiya, 56
Cakrabartī, Nīrendranāth, 63
Cakrabartī, Śibrām, 60
Carey, William, 212
Caṭṭopadhyaya, Baṅkimcandra, 80 n.2
Caṭṭopādhyāya, Mohit, 65
Caṭṭopādhyāya, Śakti, 63
Caṭṭopadhyaya, Saracandra, 49–50
Caturaṅga (The Quartet), 52
Caudhurī, Munier, 70
Caudhurī, Pramatha, 50
Chakbast, Braj Narayan, 335
Chakravarty, Utpalendu, 420
Chalam, Gudipati Venkata, 321
Chandar, Krishan, 342–43
Changanpuzha (poet), 187
Chare Bāire (The Home and the World), 52–53
Charter Act, 84, 85
Charulata, 417–18
Chatrik, Dhani Ram, 252
Chatterjee, Bankim Chandra, 89
Chatterjee, Sudipto, 45
Chaudhari, Rahuvir, 120
Chauhan, Subhadra Kumari, 146
Chellappa, C. S., 292, 293
Chemmeen (The Prawn), 192
Chiplunkar, Vishnushastri, 213–14, 215, 239 n.8
Chitre, Dilip, 233–34
Cho (playwright), 300
Choodamani, R., 295
Chowrangi, 411, 414
Chughta'i, Ismat, 343
Collected Works of Mahatha Gandhi, 112
Coomaraswamy, Ananda K., 404
Cowasjee, Saros, 392, 395

Dagh (poet), 338
Dalal, Jayanti, 116
Dalal, Suresh, 119–20
Dalit literature, 175, 363–77; and American black civil rights struggle, 365–66, 368; Buddhist influence in, 364–65; influence of Phule and Ambedkar in, 363–65; language and representation issues in, 368–72, 373, 376; magazines/journals of, 367; Marxist influence in, 365; Panther movement in, 370–71; pre-Panther, 368–70; self-narrative in, 12, 372–73, 374; spoken dialects in, 371–72; use of term "Dalit," 365–66; women writers in, 374–76
Dalit Sahitya: Ek Samajik-Sanskritik Abhyas, 371, 377 n.3
Dalpatram (poet), 102–3
Dalvi, Jayawant, 230–31
Damle, K. K. (Keshavsut), 216–17
Damodaran, K., 202
Dandekar, G. N., 231
Dangle, Arjun, 370
Danish, Ihsan, 340
Darshak (writer), 116
Daruwalla, K. N., 387, 388–89
Das, Bholanath, 27
Dāś, Jibanānanda, 57
Das, Jogesh, 40
Das, Kamala, 91
Dasan, Bhárathi, 291–92
Dasan, Kanna, 292
Dasgupta, Buddhadeb, 420
Datta, Bhabananda, 34
Datta, Hiren, 37
Datta, Michael Madhusūdan, 80 n.2

Datta, Satyendraāth, 51
Datta, Sudhindranāth, 56
Dave, Harindra, 120
Dave, Jyotindra, 111
Dave, Randchodbhai Udayram, 110–11
Dayal, Prabh, 256
Dayaram (poet), 101
De, Bisñu, 57
Debī, Āśāpūrnā, 62
Debī, Mahāśwetā, 62
Debī, Nirupamā, 50
Debī, Priyambadā, 51
Deo, Shripad D., 207
Deo, Veena, 363
Deś (journal), 63
Desai, Anita, 90–91, 95 n.4
Desai, Boman, 393
Desai, Deepakba, 124
Desai, Mahadev, 112–13
Desai, Ramanlal, 109, 110
Desai, Ranjit, 232
Desai, Shantinath, 170
Desani, G. V., 90, 94
Deshmukh, Gopal Hari, 212
Deshpande, Atmaram R., 220
Deshpande, Gauri, 230
Deshpande, P. L., 234–35
Dev, Kesava, 193
Deva, Ramachandra, 160
Deval, G. B., 217
Devanagari script, 136, 137, 141, 212
Devanura Mahadeva, 175
Devi, Nalinibala, 31–32
Dhand, Raghbir, 284–85
Dharmapuranam (The Saga of Dharmapuri), 195
Dharmaraja, 190
Dhasal, Namdeo, 370–71
Dhir, Santokh Singh, 279, 280, 282–83
Dhondy, Farrukh, 391, 393
Dhoomketu (writer), 109, 110
Dhruv, Anandshankar, 105–6
Dhruv, Saroop, 125
"Diddubaatu," 324
Dighe, R. V., 231–32
Din, Joshua Fazal, 267
Divatia, Chaitanya, 124
Do Ladkiyan, 150–51
Duara, Jatindranath, 27
Duggal, Kartar Singh, 263, 271–72, 280–81, 282
Dumont, Louis, 15–16
Dutt, Toru, 85, 86, 92
Dutt, Utpa, 65
Dutta, Nilima, 40
Dwivedi, Nanilal Nabhubhai, 104

East Pakistan and Bangladesh, literature of: contemporary prose in, 76; drama in, 75; Hindi-Muslim unity in, 69; little magazines in, 76–77; poetry in, 73–75; and political/ideological upheavals, 70–71; quest for national identity in, 69–73; women writers in, 77–79
Ekuśe Februārī (February 21), 71, 77
Eliot, T. S., 94, 169, 226, 389, 390
Elkunchwar, Mahesh, 237
"Englandor Vivaran," 24
English Education Act, 84–85
English language usage: in literary study, 7–8, 17 n.8, 84; missionary influence on, 84–85. *See also* Indian literature in English; Parsi literature in English
English literary influences, 9–10
Ezhuthachan, Thunchath, 181

Faiz, Faiz Ahmad, 341–42
Ferdous, Hasan, 45
Film, Indian: influence on regional literature, 7; realist narrative in, 12–13, 17 n.11. *See also* Bengali film; Rāy, Satyajit
Forster, E. M., 53

Gadgil, Gangadhar, 228
Gadkari, R. G., 217
Gandhi, Mohandas: and caste system, 365; literary influence of, 10, 112–16, 124, 140, 185, 221; nationalist movement of, 107, 140–41, 197, 218–19, 388; writings of, 111–12
Gaṇgopādhyāya, Nārāyaṇ, 59
Gangopādhyāya, Sunīl (Nilalohit), 61, 63
Ganguly, Suranjan, 410
Gargi, Balwant, 270–71
Gargi, Paritosh, 273

Ghalib (poet), 338
Ghamat, Kaikhusrau Edalji, 386
Ghatak, Ritwik, 419–20
Ghose, Kasiprasad, 86
Ghose, Manmohun, 85, 87
Ghose, Sri Aurobindo, 86, 94, 404
Ghosh, Gautam, 420
Ghosh, Girish Chandra, 47–48
Ghosjāyā, Śailabālā, 50
Gitanjali (*Song-Offering*), 47, 86
Gītimālya (Song Garland), 52
Godghate, Manik, 234
Gokak, V. K., 161
Gokhale, Arvind, 228–29
Gorā (The Fair One), 47
Gorhe, C. S., 219–20
Goswami, Hemchandra, 27
Goswāmī, Jay, 64
Goswami, Mamoni Raisom, 40
Goswami, Prafulla Dutta, 34
Gracy (writer), 199
Gujarti language, 100, 102, 103, 107; British influence on, 101–2
Gujarati literature, 100–28; Age of Scholars (Pandit Yug) in, 105–7; critical writing in, 105–7, 113–14, 115–16, 121–22, 127; Dalit writing in, 123; drama in, 108, 109, 110–11, 127; Gandhian writers in, 112–16, 124; missionary influence on, 101; modernist movement in, 118–22, 125; nationalist and humanistic trends in, 107, 114–16; and newspapers and periodicals, 102, 104, 107; Parsi writing in, 109, 124; poetry, post-1850, 102–3, 104, 106, 108, 124–25; poets of middle phase, 100–101; postindependence, 117–22, 124–27; post-Pandit Yug prose, 109–10; post-Suresh Joshi period, 121–22; *prithvi* meter in, 106; prose development in, 103–4; rural settings and colloquialisms in, 117, 123; saint-poets of Bhakti movement, 100–101; social themes in, 105; socialist influence on, 107–8, 116–17; sociopolitical influences on, 107, 114–16, 117–18; Western influences in, 107–8, 118; wit and humor in, 111; women writers in, 123–27
Gupta, Jagadīś, 58–59
Gupta, Maithilisharan, 136
Guru, Kamta Prasad, 137

Haar Mana Haar, 411, 413
Haidur, Qurratul Ain, 351
Halbe, Lakshman, 213
Hali, Altaf Husain, 332–33, 335, 346
Hanfi, Ameeq, 350
Haq, Hāsān Azizul, 72–73
Haq, Syed Śāmsul, 75
Hariaudh, Ayodhya Singh, 138
Hasrat, Sukhpalvir Singh, 247
Hazarika, Bhupen, 37
Hindi language: Sanskrit vocabulary in, 137, 138; segregation/differentiation from Urdu, 136, 137–38
Hindi literature, 134–53; *Chhayavadi* phase in, 10, 143–44, 153 n.8; colonial censorship in, 153 n.6; evocation of India's past in, 138–39; Gandhi's nationalist movement, 140; and Hindi film, 410; and Hindi-Urdu divide, 136–40; and nationalism, 136–46; one-act plays in, 142–43; partition narratives in, 146–47; poetry, classical and modern, 404; portrayal of women in, 144–46; progressive, 141–43; Sita (fictional character) in, 149, 153–54 n.9, 376; and sociopolitical upheavals, 135, 136–46, 146–47; village life in, 147; women writers in, 149–52
Hindustani language: dialects of, 138, 143; Gandhi's support of, 140–41
Hosen, Mīr Maśārraf, 68
Hosen, Rokeyā Sākhāwāt, 77
Hosen, Selinā, 78
"Hum Sarar," 151–52
Husain, Abdullah, 351
Husain, Intizar, 348, 351

Idappally (poet), 187
Ikkavamma, Thottakkat, 200
Ilyās, Ākhthāruzzāmān, 73
Iman, Akhtarul, 345
Inamdar, N. S., 232–33

Indian academic discipline: regional literature in, 7–9; use of English language in, 7–8, 17 n.8, 84
Indian languages: British influence on development of, 22, 101, 102–3; 153 n.6, 207–8, 212, 383–85; Devanagari script in, 136, 137, 141, 212; hierarchy in, 6–7; missionary influence on, 5, 22, 23, 101, 161; and regional publishing, 5–7
Indian literature in English, 84–94; Anglo-European influences in, 86–87; appropriation of exoticized Other in, 92–93; drama in, 94–95; evolution of, 84–85; global awareness in, 93–94; Indo-Anglians versus regionalists in, 87–88; novels, 1935 to 1970, 88–91; poetry, early developments in, 85–87; poetry, 1950s, 1960s, and 1970s, 91, 92; Romanticism in, 86; underprivileged as subject matter in, 404–5; Western critics' role in, 91–92; women's writing in, 94. *See also* Parsi literature in English
Indian People's Theatre Association (IPTA), 64, 143
Indulekha, 189–90
Iqbad, Muhammad, 336–38, 346–47
Irani, Gustap, 394
Iyengar, Masti Venkatesha, 161, 166–67
Iyer, P. R. Rajam, 295
Iyer, Ullur S. Parameswara, 183, 185, 186
Iyer, V.V.S., 294

Jafri, Ada, 352–53
Jafri, Ali Sardar, 341, 342
Jagtar, Rampuri, 259
Jalandhari, Hafeez, 340
Jasimuddīn (poet), 71–72
Jasuja, Gurcharan Singh, 273
Jauhar, Muhammad Ali, 335
Jayanti (journal), 32, 33
Jayomohan (writer), 297
Jhaveri, Krishnala M., 106–7
Jhaveri, Mansukhlal, 115–16
Jivanor Batot, 34
Jnan Peeth Award, 254
"Jōgi," 164
Johnson, Samuel, 25
Jonaki (journal), 21, 26, 28
Joseph, Sarah, 199
Joshi, Ramanlal, 121
Joshi, Shivkumar, 118
Joshi, Suresh, 118–19
Joshi, Umashankar, 13, 114–15, 118
Joshi, V. M., 221
Joyce, James, 108, 387
Joymati (film), 30
Joymati Knowari, 30
Jussawalla, Adil, 387, 389

Kabraji, Kekhushru, 109
Kādir, Ābul, 68
Kahlor, Mohan, 265
Kailasam, T. P., 161, 172
Kākana Kōṭe, 167
Kakati, Banikanta, 29
Kalachandar, K., 300
Kalapi (poet), 104
Kalelkar, Saka Saheb, 112
Kalepani, Diwan Singh, 252–53
Kali for Women (feminist publisher), 94
Kalita, Dandiram, 35
Kalki. *See* Krishnamurthi, R.
Kallol (journal), 55
Kāmāl, Sufiā, 68, 77–78
Kamble, Arun, 374
Kanekar, Anant, 220–21, 224
Kanga, Firdaus, 395
Kannada language and culture, 162–63
Kannada literature, 160–76; Bandaya (Protest) movement in, 175; feminist writers in, 160; and little magazines, 162; major literary figures of, 166–68; missionary influence on, 161; modern language and new stanzaic patterns in, 163; Navōdaya Sāhitya (Renaissance), 161–62; Navya Sāhitya movement in, 170–71; Navya theater in, 171–73; novels in, 165–68; poetry and poetic drama in, 163–65; progressive, 168–70; Sanskrit and European translations in, 162, 163, 165, 166; untouchable caste writers in, 175; village life in, 165, 166; women's writing in, 173–75

Kant (poet), 104
Kanthan, Jaya, 294–95
Kanthapura, 87
Kanwal, Jaswant Singh, 262–63
Kanyasulkam, 315
Kapadia, Kundanika, 126
Karaka, D. F., 386
Karandikar, Govind V., 227
Karandikar, Vinayak J., 217
Karanth, Shivarama, 167–68
Karnad, Girish, 7, 15, 171–72, 405–6
Karnik, M. M., 231
"Katil," 141
Katrak, Kersey, 387, 390
Kaur, Ajit Kaur, 283–84
Kazmi, Nasir, 349, 354
Keeper of the Dead, The, 388–89
Kerala, 180–81, 191–92. *See also* Malayalam language; Malayalam literature
Ketkar, S. V., 221–22
Khabardar, Ardoshir Faramji, 109
Khadilkar, K. P., 217
Khairi, Rashidul, 334
Khandekar, V. S., 221, 222–23
Khanolkar, C. T., 234, 405
Khasakkinte Ithihasam (The Legends of Khasak), 195
Khatoniyar, Jamuneswari, 31
King, Martin Luther, 365, 368, 388
Knippling, Alpana Sharma, 84
Kolhatkar, Shripad K., 217
Kondvilkar, Madhav, 373
Kripabor Baruar Kakotor Topola (Kripabor Barua's Bundle of Papers), 28
Krishna, Rentala Gopala, 318
Krishnamacharyulu, Dharmavaram, 315
Krishnamurthi, M. G., 165
Krishnamurthi, R. (Kalki), 12, 294, 296, 297, 300
Krishnan, Rajam, 297
Kulkarni, G. A., 229–30
Kulkarni, Roopa, 376
Kumar, Shiv, 258
Kumari, Sugatha, 199
Kurup, G. Sankara, 187–88
Kuruskhetra, 188
Kuvempa (writer), 161, 164–65

Lāhiṛī, Tulsī, 64–65
Lakshmi (writer), 297
Lakshminarayana, Unnava, 321
Lāl Śālu, 71
Litikai (The Pages, or Lackeys), 28
Lobhita, 35
Lohia, Ram Manohar, 171

Madgulkar, Vyankatesh, 229
Madhali Stiti, 215
Madhavikutty (Kamala Das), 198
Madia, Chunilal, 117
Mahādēvi, Akka, 160
Mahanta, Keshav, 33
Maharashtra: history of, 207, 208–12; Marathi language of, 207–8, 238 n.6. *See also* Marathi literature
Māhmud, Āl, 72
Maitreya, Akṣaykumār, 49
Majaz, 341, 342
Majumdār, Līlā, 62
Majumdār, Mohitlāl, 56
Malabari, Beheramji, 109, 384
Malapalli, 321
Malayalam language, origins of, 180–81
Malayalam literature, 180–203; caste as suject matter in, 184–85, 187; criticism in, 191; drama in, 200–201; great poets in, 183–86; Marxism in, 191; modern poetry in, 182–83; novel development in, 181–82, 189–91; postmodernism in, 188–89, 194–99; progressive writers in, 191–93; rhyme dispute in, 182; Romanticism in, 183, 186–88; Sangam period in, 180, 181; and Text Book Committee of Travancore, 181; women writers in, 196–99
Malegaḷalli Madumagaḷu, 165
Malgonkar, Manohar, 90
Malihabadi, Josh, 340
Malik, Said Abdul, 33, 38
Mallabarman, Adwaita, 60
Māndiddunnō Mārāya, 166
Mane, Lakshman, 372, 373
Mani, Vettom, 202
Mankad, Mohammad, 120
Manohar, Yeshwant, 369–70
Manto, Sa'adat Hasan, 343

Maran Swasta Hot Ahe (Death is Getting Cheaper), 368–69
Marar, Kuttikrishna, 191, 201
Marathi language, 207–8, 238 n.6
Marathi literature, 207–30; and British colonialism, 207–8, 212; criticism in, 214; drama in, 217, 223–24, 235–37, 405; first grammar and dictionary in, 212; little magazines in, 233; Marxism in, 218–219; modernism in, 226–28, 33; nineteenth century, 211–13; novel, emergence of, 212–13; novel, historical, 232–33; poetry, contemporary, 226–27, 234; poetry, late nineteenth/early twentieth centuries, 216–17; poetry, Ravikiran Mandal group in, 220; postindependence, 224–37; *powadas* and *lavani* (romantic songs) in, 210; pre-nineteenth century, 208–10; prose, late nineteenth/early twentieth centuries, 213–16; realism in, 228; regional, 230–31; rural (gramina sahitya), 229, 231–32; sociopolitical themes in, 219–22, 224; *Vākari* movement in, 210; women writers in, 223, 230. *See also* Dalit literature
Mardhekar, B. S., 226
Markandaya, Kamala, 90–91
Marxist influence: in Bengali film, 419–20; in Dalit literature, 365; in Hindi literature, 141–43; in Kannada literature, 168, 175; in Malayalam literature, 191; in Marathi literature, 218–19; in Panjabi literature, 253, 257; in Telugu literature, 311, 313–14, 322
Marzban, Jehangir, 385
Masood, Nayyar, 348
"Master Carpenter, The," 188
Medh, Susmita, 127
Medhi, Kaliram, 34
Meena'i, Ameer, 338
Meerabai (princess and poet), 100
Meeraji (poet), 344
Meghani, Jhaverchand, 114
Mehta, Arab, 127
Mehta, Chandravadan, 111
Mehta, Dhansukhlal, 110
Mehta, Dina, 390–91
Mehta, Hansa, 126
Mehta, Jaya, 125
Mehta, Lajjaram, 144–45
Mehta, M., 293
Mehta, Nandshankar Tuljashankar, 103
Mehta, Narasingh, 100
Mehta, Sharda, 126
Mehta, Sumatiben, 124
Mehta, Tarulala, 127
Menon, Asha, 202
Menon, Chandu, 182, 189–90
Menon, Nalappat Narayana, 187
Menon, Vallathol Narayana, 182, 183, 185–86
Minhas, Miran Bakhsh, 267
Miri Jiyori, 28
Misha, S. S., 258–59
Missionary influence on language and literature, 5, 22, 23, 84–85, 101, 161
Mistry, Rohinton, 393, 394, 395
Mitra, Aruṇ, 63
Mitra, K. R., 216
Mitra, Manoj, 65
Mitra, Narendranāth, 59
Mitra, Premendra, 56–58
Mitra, Pyaricharan, 88
Mohan, Sarala Jag, 100
Mohani, Hasrat, 335
Monto, Sa'dat Hassan, 280
Mostāfā, Golām, 69
Mukhopādhyāya, Prabhāt Kumār, 49, 415
Mukhopādhyāya, Śailājananda, 58
Mukhopādhyāya, Subhas, 63
Muktibodh, Sharatchandra, 227
Mun, Meenakshi, 374
Munshi, K. M., 109–10
Munshi, Lilavati, 126
Murthy, U. R. Anantha, 161, 170–71
Musaddas-i Madd-o Jazr-i Islam, 333
Muslim identity: and Aligarh movement, 331–32, 334; effects of partition and independence on, 345–49; and emergence and spread of Urdu language, 330; and Hindu relations, 136–40, 346–49; and Khilafat movement, 335–37; and Pakistani nationalism, 347–48; and revolt of 1857, 330–31

Muththu, Vaira, 293
My Story, 198

Naheed, Kishvar, 353
Naidu, Sarojini, 86, 92
Nair, Guptan, 191
Nair, M. T. Vasudevan, 193–94
Nambiar, Kunchan, 181
Namboothiripad, E.M.S., 202
Nanalal, Kavi, 108
Nanautavi, Muhammad Qasim, 332
Nanda, Ishwar Chander, 268–69
Nandi, N. R., 318
Narasimhachar, P. T., 164
Narasimhachar, S. G., 161, 163
Narasinghrao (poet), 106
Narayan, R. K., 89–90, 92, 95 n.4
Narayanababu, Srirangam, 311, 312
Narayanan, K. Raja, 294, 297
Narmad (poet), 102
Narula, Surinder Singh, 262
Nāsrin, Taslimā, 78
Nath, Rajinder, 405
Nathalal, Diwaliben, 124
Nationalism, anticolonial: effect on regional literature, 5–6, 10, 107, 112–16, 124, 136–46, 185, 221, 255–56; and Gandhi, 107, 140–41, 197, 218–19, 388; and modernization, 218–19, 225–26; and Romanticism, 10
Nayak, Panna, 125
Nazir, C. S., 385–86
Nazrul Islām, Kāzī, 55, 67–69
Neki, Jaswant Singh, 258
Nemade, Bhalchandra, 233–35
Nigah, Zehra, 353
Nilkanth, Ramanbhai, 105
Nilkanth, Vidagauri, 125
Nirala, Suryakant Tripathi, 144
Niyazi, Muneer, 350
Nomani, Shibli, 334

"O Mor Aponar Desh" (My Dearest Country), 27
Orunodoi (journal), 21, 22, 23, 24
Osmān, Śaokat, 71

Padamanji, Baba, 213
Pai, M. Govinda, 161
Pakistan: creation of, 68–69; Panjabi drama in, 274–75; Panjabi fiction in, 267–68; Panjabi poetry in, 259–60; swomen poets of, 352–56. *See also* Urdu literature
Palakeel, Thomas, 180
Pandey, Mrinal, 151
Pandya, Navalram, 103–4
Pandya, Savitagauri, 124
Panicker, Ayyappa, 188
Panicker, V. C. Balakrishna, 183
Panikkar, Narayan, 405
Panikker, Sardar K. M., 202
Panjab, religious revivalism movements in, 249–50
Panjabi, socialist realism in, 278–79
Panjabi language, development of, 250
Panjabi literature, 249–85; drama, 268–77; drama, experimental, 272–73, 275, 277; drama, postindepence, 272–75; drama, progressive, 270–72; *ghazal* in, 260; historical, 263–64; Marxist influence in, 253, 257, 262, 263, 271, 279; and nationalist struggle, 255–56; novels of Gujjar and Machhiara tribes in, 265; poetry, 1935 to 47, 253–55; poetry, contemporary, 260; poetry, experimental, 257–59; poetry, postindependence, 256–60; poetry, progressive (*pragtivadi*), 256–57, 259; postindependence, 256–60; prose, 261–68; rural cultural ethos in, 264–65, 282–83; sex and pornography in, 280–81; short story in, 278–85; Sikh history in, 263, 267; Singh Sabha movement in, 250–53; socialist realism in, 261, 262–63; stream of consciousness in, 266–67; women's situation in, 254–55, 261
Pannikar, Rajini, 149–50, 150–51
Pannikker, Sardar K. M., 202
Parashmoni, 33–34
Parikh, Gita, 125
Parsi immigrant community: adaptation and Westernization of, 382–83; in Gujarti literature, 109, 124; identity crisis of, 386–87

Parsi literature in English, 382–95; British influence on, 383–84, 385; drama, postcolonial, 390–91; drama, preindependence, 385–86; fiction, postcolonial, 391–95; fiction, preindependence, 386; modernism in, 387–90; poetry, nationalist, 384–85; poetry, postcolonial, 387–90; religion in, 384; satire and humor in, 383, 385, 386, 390, 394–95; self-identity in, 387–88, 391–92; sociopolitical issues in, 393–94; women's situation in, 391
Patel, Dhiruben, 126
Patel, Gieve, 387, 389–90
Patel, Pannalal, 117
Pathak, Heeraben, 124
Pathak, Ramanayan, 113
Pathak, Saroj, 127
Pathakji, Jaimangauri, 124
Pather Pāṁcali, 58
Pather Panchali (The Song of the Little Road), 415, 416–17
Pati, Mitali, 410
Patlikar, Ishwar, 117
Pawar, Dava, 373
Pawar, Urmila, 374, 375
Paymaster, Barjorji, 384, 385
Pendse, S. N., 230
Persian language, 249
Phadke, N. S., 221, 222
Phookan, Anandaram Dhekiyal, 24
Phookan, Milamoni, 36
Phookanani, Padmavati Devi, 30–31
Phule, Mahatma Jyotiba, 212, 214, 363–54, 374
Pichamurthi (poet), 292, 293
Pillai, C. V. Raman, 182, 190, 200
Pillai, E. V. Krishna, 200, 202
Pillai, K. C. Kesava, 183
Pillai, Kavimani Désika, 291
Pillai, N. N., 200
Pillai, Thakazhi Sivasankara, 192
Pillai, V. Ramalingam (Namakkal Kavignar), 291
Pillai, Vayala Vasudevan, 201
Pillai, Véda Nayakam, 295
Pingal (Prosody), 103
Piththan, Putumai, 292, 294
Pound, Ezra, 226, 387
Prapanjan (writer), 298
Prasad, Jaishankar, 139, 143, 144
Pratidwandi, 418–19
Preetlari, Gurbakhsh, 278
Premanand (poet), 101
Premchand, 6, 136, 145, 342; Gandhi's influence on, 140, 141–42
Pritam, Amrita, 253, 254–55, 281
Priyamvada, Usha, 150
Progressive Writers' Association, 116–17, 141–42, 278, 338, 340–43
"Pryatamar Sithi" (My Beloved's Letter), 27

Qureshi, Omar, 329

Rabha, Bishnu, 30
Raghava, Ballari, 317
Rāhmān, Hāsān Hāfizur, 71
Rāhmān, Śāmsur, 73–74
Raichoudhuri, Ambikagiri, 27
Raichoudhuri, Susibrata, 35
Rajagopalan, K. P., 292
Rajalkshmi (writer), 197–98
Rajamannar, P. V., 317
Rajan, Balachandra, 90–91
Rajkhowa, Benudhar, 28–29
Rajlakshmi O Srikanta, 411–12
Rajpothe Ringiyai, 38
Raman, T. Janaki, 294
Ramanujan, A. K., 161, 171
Ramdas (poet-saint), 209, 238 n.3
Ram-Navami (play), 25
Randhawa, Afzal, 267
Rangaram, P. V., 317
Rao, A. N. Krishna, 168
Rao, Gollapudi Maruthi, 318
Rao, Gurajada Appa, 308–9, 315, 324
Rao, Hattiyangadi Narayana, 161, 163
Rao, Kodavatiganti Kutumba, 322
Rao, Raja, 87–88, 89, 90
Rao, Rajalakshmi N., 174
Rao, Rayaprolu Subba, 308
Rao, Sistla Umamaheswara, 311
Rashid, N. M., 344–45
Rashtriya Swayamsevak Sangh (RSS), 219

Ravi, Ravinder, 284
Ray, Dwijendralal, 48
Rāy, Maṇīndra, 58
Rāy, Satyajit, 58, 59, 60, 61, 415–20
Rāy, Sukumār, 60
Realism, regional: and film, 12–13; pan-Indian themes in, 11–12; and women's situation, 12
Reddy, C. Narayana, 314
Reddy, C. R., 308
Reddy, Pattabhirami, 311, 312
Rege, P. S., 226–27
Regional literatures: and academic discipline, 7–9; aesthetics and ideology interplay in, 13–15; "Indianness" paradigm in, 8; philosophical paradigms in, 15–16; Romanticism in, 10–11; and Western literary genres, 9–13
Regional publishing: and British rule, 5; local aspect of, 6; and religious instruction, 5–6; and unifying effects of print-capitalism, 7
Renu, Phanishwar, 147
Revolutionary Writers' Association, 313
Riyaz, Fehmeedah, 353
Romanticism, 10–11
Rushdie, Salman, 93
Rye, Madhu, 122

Safeer, Pritam Singh, 255
Sagar, Lala Kirpa, 252
Śahīdullāh, Mohammed, 69
Sahitya Acadamy, 3
Sahitya Academy Award, 279, 282, 283, 388
Sahitya Pravarthaka Sahakarana Sangham (SPCS), 203
Sahni, Bhisham, 147, 148
Saikia, Basanta, 41
Saikia, Bhabendranath, 41
Samsa (playwright), 172
Sandhu, Gulzar Singh, 283
Sandhu, Waryam, 284
Sanibarer Cithi (The Saturday Post), 55
Sanjayan (writer), 202
Śaṅkar (Maṇiśaṅkar Bandyopādhyāya), 61
Sankari, Siva, 297
Sanskrit, 398–406; classical drama and dramaturgy, 402–3; grammatical concepts and poetic principles in, 399–402; misunderstanding of concerns and values of, 398; in modern poetry and drama, 403–6; *rasa* (feeling) and *dhvani* (suggestiveness) in, 400–402; schools and concepts, 399–402; translations in Kannada, 162, 163, 165, 166; Vedas, 398–99
Saraiya, Anniben, 124
Saraswati (journal), 138
Saraswatichandra, 4
Sarathy, Indira Partha, 296
Sarathy, N. Partha, 296
Sarma, Puranam Subrahmanya, 325
Sarna, Mohindyer Singh, 281
Sarshar, Ratan Nath Dar, 334
Sastri, Madhunapanthula Satyanarayana, 312–13
Sastry, Chellapilla Venkata, 308
Sastry, Divakarla Tirupati, 308
Sastry, Korada Ramachandra, 314
Sathyanarayana, Viswanatha, 312–13, 321
Satyarthi, Devinder, 279
Sayyid, Ahmad Khan, 331–32
Sehrai, Harnam Dass, 267
Sekhon, Sant Singh, 262, 270, 279, 282
Sen, Aparna, 420
Sen, Atulprasād, 51–52
Sen, Mrinal, 419, 420
Sen, Rajanīkanta, 51–52
Sen, Samar, 56
Sengupta, Acintyakumār, 58
Sengupta, Jatīndranāth, 561–15
Setty, Narahari Gopalakrishnama, 319
Sevasadan, 145
Shah, Suman, 122
Shakir, Parveen, 353
Shamal (poet), 101
Shanteshwar, Vina, 174
Sharma, Arun, 41
Sharma, Bhagwati Kumar, 120–21
Sharma, Radheshyam, 122
Sharma, Ramachandra, 161, 164, 170
Sheth, Chandrakant, 121
Shilpi, 411, 412–13
Shirwadkar, V. V. (Kusumagraja), 221

Shivani (writer), 150, 151
Shriranga (playwright), 172–73
Shuguftah, Sara, 353–54
Shukla, Jyotsna, 124
Shukla, Ram Chandra, 137
Shukla, Srilal, 147
Siddhalingaiah (poet), 175
Sidhwa, Bapsy, 392–93, 395
Sikhs, 249, 250–52, 263, 267. *See also* Panjabi literature
Singh, Amrik, 272–73
Singh, Atamjit, 249
Singh, Bhai Vir, 250–51, 261
Singh, Giani Kesar, 265–66
Singh, Gurdial, 264
Singh, Gursharan, 277
Singh, Harasaran, 273
Singh, Haribhajan, 258
Singh, Khushwant, 90
Singh, Maheep, 284
Singh, Mohan, 253–55, 281
Singh, Nanak, 261, 278
Singh, Narinderpal, 263
Singh, Puran, 251–52
Singh, Sujan, 278–79
Sircar, Bādal, 65
Sita (fictional character), 149, 153–54 n.9, 376
Sitanshu (poet), 121–22
Sittal, Sohan Singh, 264–65
Sneharashmi (poet), 115
Sonkamble, P. E., 373
Sorabji (writer), 89
Spivak, Gayatri, 1, 3
Sreejan, V. C., 202
Sri, P. S., 289
Sri Rangaraju Charitra, 319
Srikanthayya, T. N., 162
Srikantia, B. M., 161, 163–64
Sriranga (writer), 161
Stree, 411, 413–14
Subbarayudu, G. K., 306
Subbu, Koththa Mangalam, 297
Sudharmar Upakhyan (Sudharma's Tale), 30
Sujatha (writer), 296
Sundaram (poet), 115
Swapnastha (poet), 116
Śyāmalī, 50

Tagore, Abanindrañath, 51, 52–56, 68, 69, 86; and film, 404, 415, 417, 420; final message of, 55; *gadya kabitā* (free prosaic verse) of, 56; humanist and political views of, 45, 46–47, 52, 53, 54; important works of, 46; influence of, 46; spiritualism of, 52
Taladanda, 15
Tamil literature, 289–301; ancient and classical roots of, 289–90; detective fiction in, 296; devotional (*bhakthi*) lyrics in, 290–91; drama in, 299–300, 300–301; and film, 7; idealist/romantic aesthetic in, 13; mythological and historical plays in, 298–99; New Wave poetry in, 293; novel in, 295–98; poetry, 10, 290–93; *puthuk Kavithai* (new poetry) in, 292–93; short story in, 294–95; social realism in, 296, 299–300; sociopolitical aspects of, 301 n.1; women writers in, 295, 297; women's roles in, 301 n.1
Telugu language, modernization of, 307–8
Telugu literature, 306–26; *bhava kavitvan* movement in, 309–10; colloquial idiom in, 307–8; contemporary novel in, 323–24; development of novel in, 319–22; drama in, 314–19; historical development of, 306; Marxism in, 311, 313–14, 322; modern and contemporary drama in, 317–19; modern poetry in, 308–14; nationalism in, 316; new experimental poetry in, 313–14; politics in, 316–17; progressive poetry (*Abhyudaya Kavitvam*) in, 311–12, 313; prose experimentalism in, 322–23; prose poetry (*vachana kavitvan*) in, 313; rise of modernism in, 306–7; sociopolitical aspects of, 320–21; verse dramas in, 316; women's writing in, 323
Tendulkar, Vijay, 235, 405
Terang, Rong Bong, 40
Thakore, Balawantrai, 106
Thampuran, Valiya Koyil, 181

Thampy, Velu, 189
Thanvi, Ashraf Ali, 332
Things Fall Apart, 267–68
Thomas, C. J., 200
Thottam, Mary John (Sister Benigna), 197
Thyagabhoomi, 12, 296
Tilak, B. G., 214, 215, 218
Tilak, Narayan W., 217
Tiwana, Dalip Kaur, 264, 283
T.K.S. brothers, 299, 300
Topivala, Chandrakant, 122
Tridedī, Rāmendrasundar, 48
Tripathi, Govardhanram N., 4, 6, 105
Trivedi, Vishnuprasad, 113–14
Trivedi, Yaswant, 122
Triveni (writer), 173–74

Uchaveyilum Ilam Nilavum (Midday Sun and Tender Moonlight), 197–98
Ugra, Pandey Bechan Sharma, 145
Umarawadia, Batubhai, 111
Untouchables. *See* Dalit literature
Upara, 372
Urdu language, 249, 329; origins of, 330, 332; and Pakistani nationalism, 346–48; and partition and independence, 345–49; publishing in, 138, 330; segregation/differentiation from Hindi, 136, 137–38
Urdu literature, 329–58; and Aligarh movement, 331–32, 334; *ghazal* in, 15, 333, 335, 338, 345, 349–50, 354–56; and Halqa-yi Arbab-i Zauq (Circle of Connoisseurs), 344–45, 354; Khilafat movement in, 335–38; new *ghazal* in, 354–56; poetry in, 335, 349–50; postindependence, 349–52; progressive, 338, 340–43; prose in, 334; reform movements in, 331–34; Romanticism in, 340; support of Hyderabad state for, 336; Western influence in, 339; women writers in, 352–54. *See also* Muslim identity
Usha, O. V., 199

Vaidehi (writer), 174
Vaidya, Vijayrai K., 113
Varma, A. R. Rajaraja, 181
Vartak, S. V., 223
Vatsala, P., 199
Veeresalingam, Kandukuri, 307, 319
Vijayalakshmi, C., 313
Vijayan, O. V., 194–95
Vijayasree, C., 306, 382
Virk, Kulwant Singh, 282
Viswambhara, 314

Wāliullāh, Syed, 71
Walsh, William, 92
Warerkar, B. V., 221, 222
Western literary genre, influence of, 9–13
Women Writing in India: 600 B.C. to the Present, 94
Women's situation: in Assamese literature, 25–31; in Bengali literature, 49; in Dalit literature, 374–75; and Gandhian movement, 197; in Hindi literature, 148–52; in Malayalam literature, 197–99; in Marathi literature, 222; nationalist movement's portrayal of, 12, 144–46; in Pakistani literature, 352; in Panjabi literature, 254–55, 261; in Parsi literature, 391; in Tamil literature, 301 n.1; in Telugu literature, 307; in twentieth-century realisms, 12; women writers portrayal of, 29–31

Yaganah, Mirza Yas, 338
Yajnik, Indulal, 113
Yakeshchandra, Sitanshu, 121
Yati, Nityachaitanya, 202
Yeats, W. B., 86, 390
Yeshwant, Loknath, 373

Zacharia (writer), 195–96
Zaman, Fakhar, 268

About the Contributors

ARASU BALAN has published several stories in Tamil, a collection of poems, and a novella in English.

MAHASVETA BARUA is currently working on a sociohistorical study of Baptist missionaries in Assam.

NANDI BHATIA is an instructor in Hindi at the University of Texas at Austin. She is writing a dissertation on postcolonial Indian drama.

SUDIPTO CHATTERJEE is a playwright, poet, and director/performer from Calcutta. He has written extensively in Bengali and English and translated several authors from Bengali to English. He specializes in nineteenth-century Bengali theater.

SHRIPAD D. DEO is a sociologist with an interest in Marathi literature. He teaches at Colorado State University.

VEENA DEO teaches at Hamline University in St. Paul, Minnesota. She is on the editorial boards of *Signs* and *Critique* and works in African-American and postcolonial literatures.

RAMACHANDRA DEVA has translated Shakespeare into the Kannada and a Sanskrit play, *Bhagavadajjukiyam,* into English. He has published short stories, plays, poems, and critical works.

HASAN FERDOUS has studied in Dhaka, Bangladesh, and Kiev, Ukraine. He has been involved in the editing of the *Daily Sanghad* and the weekly *Dhaka Courier* in Bangladesh and was editor of the *Voice of Bangladesh.* He works for an international organization in New York City.

SURANJAN GANGULY teaches at the University of Colorado, Boulder. He has published in many journals, including *The Toronto Review* and *The Michigan Quarterly Review.* He is currently writing a book on Satyajit Ray.

SARALA JAG MOHAN translates from and into Gujarati, Hindi, and English. She is a recipient of the Dwivageesh Award of the Bharatiya Anuvad Parishad and the Katha Award. Among her translations is the award-winning *Asooryalok.*

ALPANA SHARMA KNIPPLING teaches at the University of Nebraska, Lincoln. Her work has appeared in anthologies and journals, including *Modern Fiction Studies.* She is writing a book on Indo-Anglian writing.

NALINI NATARAJAN has taught at universities in Delhi, the United States, and Puerto Rico. She publishes on the Caribbean and postcolonial and women's studies and is currently Associate Professor at the University of Puerto Rico.

THOMAS PALAKEEL teaches creative writing at Bradley University in Peoria, Illinois. He writes in Malayalam and English and has published in *Yatra, Short Story International,* and other journals.

MITALI PATI specializes in Renaissance drama and postcolonial literature and film. She has publications on Christopher Marlowe, Robert Kroetsch, and Bharati Mukherjee.

OMAR QURESHI is working on the politics of ethnicity in Pakistan.

ATAMJIT SINGH teaches at the University of California, Berkeley. A former head of the School of Panjabi Studies, Guru Nanak Dev University, Amritsar, he has published many books on Panjabi literary criticism.

P. S. SRI is Professor of philosophy and literature at Royal Roads Military College, Victoria, B. C. He has published a book on T. S. Eliot, Vedanta, and Buddhism and has won a UNESCO First National Prize for his short story "The Vision." He publishes in the Tamil magazine *Ananda Vikatan.* He has also translated Tamil authors into English.

G. K. SUBBARAYUDU is a lecturer at the Department of English, Osmania University, Hyderabad.

C. VIJAYASREE is Reader of English at Osmania University and has published widely in India and the United States.

ISBN 0-313-28778-3
90000>
EAN
9 780313 287787
HARDCOVER BAR CODE